In 1926

In 1926

LIVING AT THE
EDGE OF TIME

Hans Ulrich Gumbrecht

HARVARD UNIVERSITY PRESS
Cambridge, Massachusetts
London, England
1997

Library of Congress Cataloging-in-Publication Data

Gumbrecht, Hans Ulrich.
In 1926: living at the edge of time / Hans Ulrich Gumbrecht.
p. cm.
Includes index.
ISBN 0-674-00055-2 (alk. paper). — ISBN 0-674-00056-0 (pbk.: alk. paper)
1. Civilization, Modern—20th century. 2. Popular culture—History—20th century.
3. Nineteen twenty-six, A.D. 4. Civilization, Western—20th century. I. Title.
CB427.G86 1997
909.82'2—dc21   97-30904

For Ricky

CONTENTS

....

Codes Collapsed

Frames

User's Manual

Where to Start

Do not try "to start from the beginning," for this book has no beginning in the sense that narratives or arguments have beginnings. Start with any of the fifty-one entries in any of the three sections entitled "Arrays," "Codes," and "Codes Collapsed" (the alphabetical order of the subheadings shows that there isn't any hierarchy among them). Simply start with an entry that particularly interests you. From each entry a web of cross-references will take you to other, related entries. Read as far as your interest carries you (and as long as your schedule allows). You'll thus establish your individual reading path. Just as there is no obligatory beginning, there also is no obligatory or definitive end to the reading process. Regardless of where you enter or exit, any reading sequence of some length should produce the effect to which the book's title alludes: you should feel "in 1926." The more immediate and sensual this illusion becomes, the more your reading will fulfill the book's chief aim. Note: you can, if you like, experience this effect *without* reading the last two chapters, "After Learning from History" and "Being-in-the-Worlds of 1926."

Mode(s)

In the sections "Arrays," "Codes," and "Codes Collapsed," the writing aims at being strictly descriptive. This discourse is meant to bring out dominant surface perceptions as they were offered by certain material phenomena, and dominant world views as they were produced by certain concepts during the year 1926. Each entry refrains as far as possible from "expressing" the author's individual "voice," from in-depth interpretations, and from diachronic contextualizations through the evocation of phenomena and world views that occurred "before" and "after" 1926. Each entry is thus supposed to reach maximum surface-focus and concreteness. If possible at all, the style and the structure of the entries would be determined by the individual phenomena that each of them thematizes. In their convergence and divergence, finally, the entries do not seek to produce any specific "mood" (or *Stimmung*). Should some readers discover, for example, a certain "Heideggerian temper" in this book, such an impression would have to be explained as a symptom of the impact that the year 1926 had on Heidegger, rather than as a symptom of the author's ambition to imitate Heidegger's style. In contrast to the fifty-one entries, "After Learning from History" and "Being-in-the-Worlds of 1926" are written in the author's current academic prose (which he did not take as a license for trying to frustrate nonspecialized readers).

Stakes

To make at least some readers forget, during the reading process, that they are *not* living in 1926. In other words: to conjure some of the worlds of 1926, to re-present them, in the sense of making them present again. To do this with the greatest possible immediacy achievable through a historiographic text (as opposed to, say, photographs, sound-documents, or material objects). Although the author had to invent a specific textual form for each entry, the success of this book as a whole depends on the claim that it was *not* "invented" (i.e., on the claim that its content is completely referential). The effect of conjuring the past is based on this more or less "ontological" implication. A historical novel (if the author were at all capable of writing fiction) would not have done the job—at least, it would not have done the same job. And what is *not* at stake? The author's tenure, he hopes; his financial situation, he fears; as well as any attempt at interpreting or understanding the worlds of 1926 (either intrinsically or from what preceded and followed it). Finally, the author would not be disappointed if he learned that the worlds of 1925 or 1927 (and so forth) were not much different from those worlds that he reconstructed for 1926. His book is not about producing an individual description of the year 1926; it is about making present a historical environment of which we know (nothing more than) that it existed in some places during the year 1926.

Question

This is not necessarily and "hermeneutically" the sole question that a reader needs in order to understand this book; rather, it is the question that the author thinks pushed him to write: What can we do with our knowledge about the past once we have given up the hope of "learning from history" regardless of means and cost? This—by now lost—didactic function of history (at least, a certain conception of this didactic function) seems to be closely related to the habit of thinking and representing history as a narrative. If this is true, then a postdidactic attitude vis-à-vis our knowledge about the past must imply the quest for nonnarrative forms of historiographic representation. But the argument that begins with these steps is already too "streamlined." The real question behind the question of what to do with our knowledge about the past is not only the—more or less technical—question of how to write or represent history. It is above all the question of what we imagine the past "to be" (the question about the past as "raw material"), before we even begin to think about possible forms of its representation.

Theses

Since we do not know what to do with our vast and rapidly accumulating knowledge about the past (history no longer having any obvious pragmatic function), we should examine the more or less preconscious impulses that may motivate our fascination with history. This book presupposes that a specific desire is at work here: a desire "to speak to the dead"—in other words, a desire for first-hand experience of worlds that existed before our birth. In catering to this desire, the book brings forth—more implicitly than explicitly—certain features of what "we" (educated people within the Western culture of 1997) imagine "history" to be. We all seem to agree that we no longer think history as a "unilinear" and "totalizing" dynamic of "development." Beyond this negation, however, there is no single dominant form of imagining and representing history. If we imagine and represent it synchronically, as this book does, we realize that the elements of such a synchrony do not converge into a coherent and homogeneous picture. Nevertheless, and perhaps paradoxically, this book suggests the existence of a "web" or "field" of (not only discursive) realities that strongly shaped the behavior and interactions of 1926. So strong indeed is this impression that, at least implicitly, this book makes a plea against any claims for subjective or collective agency. And how could a book concerned with historical simultaneity *not* arrive at this very conclusion? After all, there are no concepts of action and agency that do not require sequentiality as their frame of reference. Yet this is exactly the one form of thinking history with which the idea of historical simultaneity is incompatible.

Context

We cannot avoid the impression that the current intellectual situation in the humanities—at least when seen from the present—marks a comparatively weak moment. (Of course, such an impression may change in retrospect; it also may suffer from the usual problems of self-reflexive assessments.) At any rate, the present appears to be a moment of great sophistication when it comes to affirming that some certainties and assumptions "no longer work"—and of even greater reluctance when it comes to filling the gaps that the vanished certainties and assumptions have left. The present moment seems to correspond to the "end of metaphysics," as Derrida describes it in *Of Grammatology:* we are beyond metaphysics but will never really leave metaphysics behind us. We also lack strong alternatives to options that no longer seem viable. Marxism is but a nostalgic or embarrassing memory, especially in its more recent resurrections and reembodiments (good intentions will not fix an outdated epistemology!). Deconstruction has either turned sour and sectarian (there's an air of Latter-Day-Saintliness about some of today's deconstructors in their black apparel), or has been absorbed by the general interpretative and hermeneutic mood. The charm (and the punch) of New Historicism has withered all too rapidly. And so on. To make matters worse, the author feels that a great deal of pressure is being brought to bear upon his generation to come up with something new, something not exclusively skeptical; but he thinks that he is not particularly good at programmatic writing—i.e., at the genre of writing that, undoubtedly, is required here. Still, he feels that he and the scholars of his generation should become for the scholars of the next generation what Reinhart Koselleck, Niklas Luhmann, Jean-François Lyotard, Richard Rorty, Hayden White, and Paul Zumthor (a purely male kinship, he admits with contrition) have been for him. The possibility of failure notwithstanding, this book is, for the moment, the best he can offer as a reaction to this self-imposed expectation.

"Help"

"Help," in the sense offered by our computer screens, can be found in the chapters "After Learning from History" and "Being-in-the-

Worlds of 1926." Especially for readers with a professional interest, these chapters provide a double contextualization of the book as belonging to a specific intellectual and academic situation. "After Learning from History," on the one hand, describes contemporary concepts and contemporary uses of "history," and is meant to show how both the experiment that constitutes this book and the structure in which it is realized are reactions to the specific status of "history" in our present. The chapter also explains why the author chose a random year as the topic of his book—though he does not go so far as to claim, in the end, that this year has a particular (but hitherto hidden) importance. "Being-in-the-Worlds of 1926," on the other hand, suggests how this book can be used for things other than making present the worlds of 1926. The test cases are intensely historical readings of three texts—readings performed in the context of the "worlds of 1926" as they are presented in the fifty-one entries. The texts of reference are Martin Heidegger's *Sein und Zeit,* Hans Friedrich Blunck's *Kampf der Gestirne,* and Carl Van Vechten's *Nigger Heaven.*

Purpose

The author never intended this book to contain anything edifying, either morally or politically. But sometimes, as we all know, our best intentions fail to protect us against our most embarrassing urges. The author likewise had no strong investment in being original, being witty, producing stylistic beauty, and so on. The book's main intention is best captured in the phrase that was its original subtitle: "an essay on historical simultaneity." The book asks to what extent and at what cost it is possible to make present again, in a text, worlds that existed before its author was born—and the author is fully aware that such an undertaking is impossible. Although the book shares some of the leitmotifs of what can be called "postmodern philosophy" (the unwillingness to think History as a homogeneous, totalizing movement, the argument in favor of a "weak" conception of subjectivity, the fascination with material surfaces), there is, the author thinks, only one reason that it should be recognized as "post-modern," and this is a negative reason. The author believes that the academico-ideological battle for the preservation of "modern" and "modernist" (i.e., "nonpostmodern") values is a lost cause. But who's interested in the author's answer to a question that nobody asked him? If the book has no political or ethical message, should readers perhaps take its form as "the message"? This would imply that the author is hoping many scholars will pick up, imitate, and develop the discourse he "invented." The truth is, however, that he would feel almost guilty if his book ever created such a fashion (which does not seem to be a very serious threat anyway). For, needless to say, there is no dearth of academic trends or schools. Perhaps the problem is that, as things now stand, everything is doomed to remain an experiment.

ARRAYS

AIRPLANES

Airplanes look stout, rather than fragile or elegant. Some of them reach impressive dimensions, like the Dornier Superwal, a hydroplane with two 700-horsepower Rolls Royce engines and a wingspan of twenty-eight meters. Their wooden propellers are imposing, and are mostly connected to the nose rather than the wings. Many of them are biplanes. In monoplanes, the wings are located above the fuselage. These wings often cover the pilots, who sit either in narrow cabins of glass or behind low transparent windshields. In the latter case, the head and shoulders of the pilot become part of the airplane's silhouette; but even if the pilot's body is enclosed by the aircraft, it remains visible. The plane and the pilot together look like a centaur with a tiny head and an enormous body. This form can trigger two different chains of association. One might think of the human body as being reduced to a bust—a process in which some of its parts get lost and are replaced by the body of the aircraft. What remains of the pilot's body is integrated with the machine's body, and the pilot's life depends on the plane's ability to cohere as an assemblage of mechanical parts. Alternatively, one might think of the human body as having entirely vanished. But the human mind, symbolized by the pilot's head, has control over the much more powerful mechanical body of the aircraft.

In an interview for the *Berliner Tageblatt,* published on April 8, Lieutenant John A. Macready, who is identified as a professor of economics at "Leland Stanford University" and who claims to have recently

achieved the highest altitude in the history of aviation (39,588 feet),
describes the inability of the human body and the human mind to
perceive an aircraft's speed (which normally goes up to around a hundred
miles per hour) while looking out of the airplane: "You have no clear
picture of the speed at which you're moving in an airplane, unless you
take a look at one of the gauges. There are no indications by which you
can measure the speed, because you're passing through nothing but air."
The privileged experience of the pilot is not speed but the bird's-eye view
of land and sea: "One could eventually map the entire United States
through a series of high-altitude flights. Flying over Dayton at an altitude
of 3,000 feet or more, a pilot can look left and right: 100 miles to the
west is Indianapolis, 73 miles to the north is Columbus, and 57 miles to
the south is Cincinnati. At this distance, the cities become mere clouds
of smoke." [see **Roof Gardens, Center = Periphery (Infinitude)**] In passionately gendered words, the pilots, many of whom are flying aces from
the Great War, often interpret the altitude which they are able to reach
as a sign of their potential military superiority: "The man who occupies
the higher position and who forces his adversary down has the advantage."

   Airplanes intensify the effect of any kind of action or event, and they
therefore emerge as standard elements within many different genres of
narrative. On September 18 *Caras y Caretas* publishes a report, with
photographs, on the kidnapping of two boys from their school at Buenos
Aires. Allegedly, for a price of 4,000 pesos, they have been taken in a
Junkers plane to Rio Grande in Brazil, where their father is living. The
narrator's sympathy is with the technologically minded kidnapper, Federico Ernesto Meier, "the father who went straight to the root of his
lawsuit against his wife, pulling the two children out of the school where
they were studying, and moving them out of the country." For no obvious reason, the boxing gloves for the world heavyweight championship
fight between Jack Dempsey and Gene Tunney [see **Boxing**] are brought
to Philadelphia by airplane ("Gloves for Big Bout Arrive by Air Mail,"
New York Times, September 21). With even less practical necessity, Gene
Tunney, the challenger, travels by air from his training camp in
Stroudsburg, Pennsylvania, to Philadelphia, where the fight is to be held,
covering the distance in under ninety minutes (*New York Times,* September 23). This addition to the epic of a boxing match contains further
colorful details: "Gene traveled in a red Curtiss Oriole plane, piloted by

the expert hands of Casey Jones, noted for his feats of daring. The only other passenger was Wade Morton, driver of racing cars, who finished fourth in the last 500-mile classic at Indianapolis." [see **Automobiles**] Thus, not only does Tunney break a record even before the weighing-in ceremony ("For the first time in the history of heavyweight champion-ships, the challenger flew forth to the field of battle"); even more impres-sively, "not content with the prospect of facing Dempsey and destiny, [he] had to defy death, too." Since flying is associated with the risk of death, it imparts an aura of transcendence to those actions and events with which it becomes connected. Upon his arrival in Philadelphia, Tunney, the "Fighting Marine," gives one of his notorious "philosophi-cal explanations." "If I crash, it won't matter," declares the challenger to the crowd of journalists awaiting him at a Navy airfield. "After all, the longest life is very short. Of course, it's [promoter] Rickard's show, but it's my life, don't forget it." [see **Action = Impotence (Tragedy)**, **Immanence = Transcendence (Death)**] The stage directions for Jean Coc-teau's tragedy *Orphée* seem to invert this association between airplanes and dying. Since the myth of Orpheus deals with death, Cocteau wants the interior of Orpheus' house to remind the spectators of airplanes: "The decor will evoke the airplanes or ships in the trompe-l'oeil pictures taken by photographers at county fairs" (Cocteau, 17).

Every flight is a contest with death, and pilots may lose this contest even if they do not crash. According to the French magazine *Mon Ciné*, Rudolph Valentino dies of endocarditis and septicemia in a New York hospital on Monday, August 23, at 12:10 P.M. (exactly one month before the Dempsey-Tunney fight) because an airplane fails to arrive in time with life-saving medicine: bad weather forces it to land in Boston on its way from Detroit to New York. In Ernst Jünger's *Feuer und Blut,* air-planes are a recurrent element in the most extreme existential situations of the Great War. The first-person narrator sees, "on the summit of a small hill in the distance, the somber silhouette of a wrecked aircraft and a ruined house" (142), and his life is constantly being threatened by enemy planes that control the battlefield from above: "Aircraft hunt above us; one of them plummets to the ground, enveloped in flames. It is consumed by huge jets of fire" (156–157). Whenever the flying ma-chines are German, the ambiguous blend of danger and beauty turns into the more homogeneous impression of a dramatic landscape: "Night is falling. The sun has already disappeared in the west behind blood-red curtains. A German fighter squadron, which roars over the battlefield, sparkles in the last rays of the sun" (197).

Whereas, in such war scenes, men's lives depend on the smooth functioning of the aircraft of which the human body has become a subordinate part, flying as a sport stages the plane as a substitute body whose efficiency can be almost completely controlled (and, on the basis of such control, continually improved) by the human mind. Ultimately, the sporting competition is subsumed within the mass of technological testing and documentation—so much so, indeed, that it can take a long time to identify the winner of a contest: "The order in which the aircraft complete their routes is not necessarily decisive for the final ranking, since the technical performance still remains to be evaluated. The definitive result depends on a formula of six individual components, consisting of performance tests. These will probably be evaluated by the end of the week" (*Der Tag,* June 10). Such competitions and the record-breaking achievements that they yield herald a future in which daily life will be based on technology. The car-producer Renault donates a trophy, the "Coupe Renault," for nonstop long-distance flights. On October 28 and 29, it is won by the French pilots Costes and Rignot, who cover the 5,400 kilometers between Paris and Jask, on the Gulf of Oman, in thirty-two hours (*Années-mémoire,* 179). Flights composed of several legs, called "raids," are inaugurating new long-distance routes, such as Paris-Tehran, Paris-Peking, London-Sidney, London-Kapstadt, Berlin–Lake Baikal, and Spain-Argentina. In the context of this last "raid," the first transatlantic flight takes place: Ramón Franco, a brother of the youngest general in the Spanish army, along with two technicians, crosses the ocean in a hydroplane between Porto Praia and an island off the Brazilian coast. The style of Franco's diary, published several months after the completion of his enterprise, is remarkably unheroic. Ending with a brief summary of "the technical results of the raid," it is the narrative of an engineer [see **Engineers, Wireless Communication**] who presents his experience to a nonprofessional readership: "Within a very few years, what today can be accomplished only as a raid will become standard navigation, due to the great progress made by airplanes in a short period of time. In this raid, we have demonstrated that the airplane can successfully endure all types of weather, including tropical storms. Wireless communication has helped us to such an extent that in the future it will become indispensable for flights over water or desert"

(Franco, 286). Since Franco shuns all kinds of commercial publicity—he goes so far as to exclude the famous photographer Alonso from the crew after the first legs of his flight (108ff.)—he appears to be honestly surprised by his new celebrity status. [see **Stars**] In asking for an autograph, his admirers wish to acquire a trace of that body which has braved lethal danger: "There exists in this country [Brazil] a mania which we did not know about or foresee when we left. This mania certainly comes from England or the United States, because we Latins do not have it. It consists in the fact that everyone wants to collect and keep the autograph of any person who has distinguished himself in some way. We were the victims of this mania" (202).

Two different but complementary forms of economic exploitation accompany such pioneering enterprises. On a pragmatic level, the most recent technical insights find immediate application in the schedules of the fledgling commercial airlines. Germany's Lufthansa is founded on January 6; by December, it is scheduling flights to fifty-seven European cities, has inaugurated a regular night service between Berlin and Königsberg, and is selling tickets for as low as 20 marks. Such marketing makes airplane travel accessible for well-to-do professionals. The *Berliner Zeitung am Mittag* is partly distributed by air, and, during Whitsun week, Lufthansa for the first time offers round-trip packages on its Berlin-Dresden and Berlin-Copenhagen routes, including hotel and sightseeing fees, for 260 and 435 marks respectively (*Berliner Volks-Zeitung*, May 14). At the same time, sensational technical advances in aviation and their quick institutionalization generate more collective pride and enthusiasm than any other type of event. Flying thus becomes an arena of national competition. On May 9, U.S. naval officer Richard Evelyn Byrd, in a Fokker, makes the first flight over the North Pole, beating by three days a dirigible flown by an Italian-Norwegian team under the direction of Roald Amundsen and Umberto Nobile and sponsored by the Italian government (*Années-mémoire*, 116–117; *Chronik*, 95). [see **Polarities**] Ramón Franco seems determined to organize his flight as a purely Spanish enterprise. He carefully avoids entering into negotiations with an Italian team planning a transatlantic flight. The successful completion of his own independent Spanish raid triggers simultaneous national celebrations in Buenos Aires and Madrid, as well as a wave of fresh enthusiasm for the brotherly ties that supposedly link the world's Hispanic societies—despite the intense rivalry between Argentina, the rising star among non-European nations, and the resentful motherland (Gumbrecht, 171ff.). The firms of Buenos Aires compete in publishing high-spirited congratulatory addresses in the local newspapers and magazines: "Franco! . . . Messengers of peace from our beloved Spain. To all of you, golden eagles of the Hispanic race, the firm of M. Zabala renders the most fervent homage. Long live Argentina! Long live Spain!" (*Plus Ultra*, 118). The celebration of Franco's flight makes it seem like a resurgence and continuation of a glorious national tradition and thus leads, paradoxically, to a shift from symbols of progress to metaphors of frozen historical time. [see **Present = Past (Eternity)**] The name of Franco's plane, the *Plus Ultra* ("Ever Farther") points to ceaseless efforts to go beyond the boundaries of the known world, and also quotes the motto of the Spanish king Charles I, "on whose territory the sun would never set":

> It is Spain—she who one day,
> brandishing her sword,
> transcended all human limits,
> surpassed all human daring;
> and both in peace and in war
> captured the ocean in chains of servitude
> and encircled the earth with the manacles of slavery
> . . . She mastered time with her naked arm;
> nothing insurmountable checked her stride,
> so that the *Plus Ultra* engraved on her shield
> is the glorious motto of a sun that never sets!

With aviation now a core reference for manifestations of national pride and, subsequently, for feelings of national depression, the news that the Allies have lifted their postwar restrictions on the German aircraft industry is interpreted optimistically as marking a turning point in the destiny of the nation. Meanwhile, glider flying has become a compensatory ritual among the resentful German people (Fritzsche, 103ff.).

Motorized flying is an integral part of all collective and individual visions of the future. Silvio Astier, the teenaged hero of Roberto Arlt's novel *El juguete rabioso (The Furious Toy)*, dreams of a life as a flight engineer. But at the end of his first—and, as it turns out, only—day in the employ of the Argentinian military, he learns that there is no place for him because he is judged to be too gifted for mere auxiliary work: "Look, my friend, . . . Your place is in a technical school. We don't need intelligent people here—we need stupid brutes for this work" (178). In Bonamy Dobrée's essay "Timoteo o el teatro del porvenir," published in Ortega y Gasset's *Revista de Occidente,* theatergoers arrive in an air-taxi at the skyscraper which is the site of the futuristic national theater: "Our air-taxi left us on what seemed to be the nineteenth floor of a building, and we immediately entered an enormous funnel shaped like a hyperbola, whose walls consisted of rows of seats. It could hold about twenty thousand people and resembled a Roman amphitheater, although it differed in the unusual curve of the walls and in the fact that the seats continued right down to the bottom of the funnel" (171). This could easily be a set from Fritz Lang's film *Metropolis,* where "canyon-like walls of city blocks rise far above street level. Cars and trains speed along on overhead tracks; airplanes circle like moths" (Lang, 34). Indeed, the movement of the airplanes in *Metropolis* is as light and sometimes as jerky as that of moths. Hectically, they dart along corridors and schedules that are too complex for the viewer's gaze to comprehend.

But what filmmakers and writers envision as a highly automatized device of the future cannot completely escape the existential shadow of death. On February 5, the French pilot Ménard, his severely burned body grotesquely swathed in bandages, receives from his country's assistant secretary of state for aeronautics the cross of the Légion d'Honneur for having rescued numerous bags of mail from the wreckage of his plane (*Années-mémoire,* 29). On September 22, a three-engine Sikorsky aircraft with a French-American crew of four under the leadership of Capitaine Fonck fails to lift off from Roosevelt Airfield in New York for what is supposed to be the first transatlantic flight from west to east. The Sikorsky is destroyed in "a sheet of flame and a huge column of smoke." Two crew members die. In the press coverage of this accident, the language of high-tech normality turns into melodramatic existentialism. After saying their goodbyes "as nonchalantly as if [they] were seeing a friend off for a steamer trip," Capitaine Fonck's admirers "[watched] with anxious eyes as the machine gathered headway. Sikorsky stood with clenched hands, his strained face turned eagerly after his machine, as if he would lift it into the air by the sheer force of his hopes." After the crash, the two surviving participants in the enterprise struggle to stay calm. Lieutenant Curtin, the American second-in-command, tries "desperately to keep control of his nerves. He was outwardly calm, but it could be seen that he was fighting for self-control. Yet his spirit was just as strong as ever." The Frenchman is the first to regain his composure: "I have been through many more dangerous experiences," he says with a shrug (*New York Times,* September 22).

In a new children's book called *Winnie-the-Pooh,* a collection of tales about a teddy bear and his human friend Christopher Robin, the first story ironically mimics the double-edged feelings and words of heroic aviators. Like a pilot competing to set a world record for altitude, Pooh floats "gracefully up into the sky" holding on to Christopher Robin's big green balloon. Although he never manages to reach the honey in the beehive that he spies at the top of a tree, the bear proudly imagines how his friends must see him from the ground: "Isn't that fine?" shouts Pooh down to Christopher Robin. "What do I look like?" "You look like a bear holding on to a balloon," says Christopher Robin. "Not," says Pooh anxiously, "not like a small black cloud in a blue sky?" Once the bees discover Pooh, he naturally wishes to terminate his flight with all possible speed. Since he doesn't dare jump, Christopher Robin shoots the balloon with his toy gun—though he first hits Pooh by mistake. "The air came slowly out, and Winnie-the-Pooh floated down to the ground" (*World of Pooh,* 17ff.).

Related Entries

Automobiles, Boxing, Engineers, Polarities, Roof Gardens, Stars, Wireless Communication; Action = Impotence (Tragedy), Center = Periphery (Infinitude), Immanence = Transcendence (Death), Present = Past (Eternity)

References

Les Années-mémoire: 1926. Paris, 1988.
Roberto Arlt, *El juguete rabioso* (1926). Madrid, 1985.
Berliner Tageblatt.
Berliner Volks-Zeitung.
Caras y Caretas.
Jean Cocteau, *Orphée: Tragédie en un acte* (1926). Paris, 1927.
Chronik 1926: Tag für Tag in Wort und Bild. Dortmund, 1985.

Ramón Franco, *De Palos al Plata*. Madrid, 1926.

Peter Fritzsche, *A Nation of Flyers: German Aviation and the Popular Imagination*. Cambridge, Mass., 1992.

Hans Ulrich Gumbrecht, "Proyecciones argentino-hispanas, 1926." In *IIIo congreso argentino de hispanistas: España en América y América en España, Actas I*. Buenos Aires, 1993.

Ernst Jünger, *Feuer und Blut: Ein kleiner Ausschnitt aus einer grossen Schlacht* (1926). Hamburg, 1941.

Fritz Lang, *Metropolis* (1926). New York, 1973.

A. A. Milne, *The World of Pooh* (1926). New York, 1957.

Mon Ciné.

New York Times.

Plus Ultra (Buenos Aires).

Revista de Occidente.

Der Tag.

AMERICANS IN PARIS

"Six delightful days at sea . . . then Paris. The luxury of incomparable cuisine and service on the *Paris* and *France* adds six more days of Paris to your travels! These deluxe French liners sail to Plymouth, England, . . . then to Le Havre, where a special train is waiting to carry you to Paris in three hours. The one-class cabin liners go direct to Le Havre, the Port of Paris. Distances are short in France: the Riviera is just an overnight trip from Paris, . . . while North Africa is but a day's voyage across the Mediterranean. The New York–Bordeaux–Vigo Service will take you to the unusual beauty of southern France and Spain." As if to prove how much transatlantic traveling is in vogue [see **Ocean Liners**], the "Social Notes" in the September 21 issue of the *New York Times* echo this advertisement for the French Line with abundant references to members of high society departing for or coming back from Europe: "Mrs. S. Stanwood Menken and Arthur Menken are expected to arrive today after spending two months in Europe." "Mr. and Mrs. Harold Irving Pratt and Miss Eleanor Pratt of Welwyn, Glen Cove, L.I., will sail for Europe today." In an article of July 25, the Parisian correspondent for the *Berliner Morgenpost* is certainly right in interpreting this "flood" of Americans coming to the capital of France as "a consequence of inflation." Together with the continuing strength of the American economy, the crisis of the franc makes Europe accessible even for those whose names will never appear in the society column of any newspaper.

But why has it become an authentic social obligation, if not an obsession, to undertake such long and expensive voyages? [see **Center = Periphery (Infinitude)**] What do American travelers expect from being in Paris? Very few among them go to (or through) Paris for a specific purpose, as do several thousand American soldiers who in the early fall begin to withdraw from the occupied German Rhineland, along with French and English troops (*New York Times*, September 22). The sales strategies of the tourist industry suggest that, for the well-to-do majority of American travelers, France and Paris are the locus of ultimate refinement in lifestyle and culture. Now that technological progress has made transatlantic voyages relatively safe, first-hand experience of European culture is becoming a standard element in the education of adolescents from upper-middle-class families.

In *The Sun Also Rises*, Ernest Hemingway's first and already very successful novel, Jake, the narrator, and his friend Bill meet a family of American tourists on a railway trip from France to Spain [see **Railroads**]:

> In our compartment were a man and his wife and their young son. "I suppose you're Americans, aren't you?" the man asked. "Having a good trip?" "Wonderful," said Bill. "That's what you want to do. Travel while you're young. Mother and I always wanted to get over, but we had to wait a while." . . . "Say, there's plenty of Americans on this train," the husband said. "They've got seven cars of them from Dayton, Ohio. They've been on a pilgrimage to Rome, and now they're going down to Biarritz and Lourdes." "So, that's what they are. Goddamn Puritans." "What part of the States you boys from?" "Kansas City," I said. "He's from Chicago." "You both going to Biarritz?" "No. We're going fishing in Spain." (87ff.)

Having to share a compartment with these fellow Americans is an unwelcome interference in Jake and Bill's experience of Europe. Although the family from Dayton is on a cultural rather than religious pilgrimage, and although even Jake and Bill are merely following the instructions of the tourist industry to travel from Paris southward ("distances are short in France"), Hemingway's protagonists lump all other Americans together as "goddamn Puritans." For puritanism, Prohibition, and speechless admiration for European refinement are exactly what the characters in *The Sun Also Rises* and their real-life models (Hemingway's American friends in Paris) are trying to escape. Jake Barnes, the author's alter ego, is a journalist who has been left sexually impotent by a war injury and is seeking to restore meaning to his life. Brett, whose portrait is inspired by Hemingway's Paris acquaintance Lady Duff Twysden, can never overcome the trauma of her fiancé's death in the war. She seeks satisfaction (and of course finds frustration) in regular alcoholic and erotic excesses—after which she always returns to Jake, whose impotence makes such intermittent closeness part of a vicious circle. Robert Cohn, the character based on Harold Loeb, a wealthy Jewish émigré who once won the middleweight boxing championship at Princeton University [see **Boxing**], is in love with Brett—a passion that mirrors Loeb's affair with Lady Duff just as Brett and the narrator's scorn for Cohn mirrors the condescension that Lady Duff and Hemingway display toward Loeb. Jake's friend Bill, a writer from Chicago who has become successful in New York, is modeled on Bill Smith, Hemingway's companion from his youth in Oak Park, Illinois (Burgess, 48ff.). Rather than admiring the refinement of European culture, such representatives of the American "lost generation" are seeking in Paris what they miss at home: a more liberal attitude toward extramarital and homosexual relationships (Benstock, 99ff.; Prost and Vincent, 536ff.), a sympathetic milieu for their claims to artistic talent, and, above all, hard liquor. [see **Bars**] Their celebration of Gene Tunney's victory over Jack Dempsey in the world heavyweight boxing championship, as described by the *New York Times* on September 24, becomes a national orgy away from home: "The most typically American crowd gathered in a well-known American bar in the heart of Paris and over bottles of champagne and other cheering beverages; they were listening to the reading of bulletins brought every few minutes from an American newspaper's office."

Sometimes the immediate motive for an American's departure for Europe is an unhappy love affair or a divorce, as in the case of the highly acclaimed (and even more highly paid) designer Ralph Barton, who comes to Paris in March. If travelers from America have more than such purely negative motives, they are usually disappointed. For Parisian intellectuals indulge in feelings of crisis and rituals of self-flagellation that are liable to plunge lovesick foreigners like Barton into even deeper depressions: "Paris is a mess. I confess it who never felt this way about it before . . . Even the French are dismal about it and suicide is a regular subject. It is cold and wet every day. And I am impotent at last" (Kellner, 135; Willett, 168). Thus, ironically, the title of Hemingway's novel points precisely to what existentialist travelers can no longer find in Paris. It is taken from a passage in the Book of Solomon: "One generation passeth away, and another generation cometh; but the earth abideth forever . . . The sun also ariseth, and the sun goeth down, and hasteth to the place where he arose." The eternal rhythms of nature inspire American intellectuals to long for an elementary ground of life, for something resistant to their experience of the ever-changing and ever-frustrating superficiality of the world back home. [see **Authenticity vs. Artificiality**] Spain, Africa, and Latin America, even more than Paris, have become the spaces in which the intellectual imagination projects such desire. An often frenetic enthusiasm for the corrida and its rituals epitomizes the convergence between the concept of the body as the elementary ground of human existence and the traveler's longing for a sphere of transcendence. [see **Bullfighting**] This is why the characters of *The Sun Also Rises* follow Hemingway and his friends on a trip that they undertook in 1925 to the fiesta of Pamplona, whose local tradition allows spectators to join the toreadors in experiencing the presence of the animals' overwhelming physical strength as the presence of death. [see **Immanence = Transcendence (Death)**] This is why, instead of only imagining southern lands, it is important to be there.

Indeed, the advertising of the tourist industry no longer focuses exclusively on Paris. With wealthy customers also being invited to "Picturesque Spain, the Land of Romance and Beauty," it is difficult to draw any social distinction between middle-class tourists and intellectual tourists among the Americans in Europe. Referring to an upper-middle-class traveler with intellectual ambitions, D. H. Lawrence is probably being both serious and ironic when, in the opening chapter of *The Plumed Serpent* (20), he comments on his character's fascination with bullfighting in Mexico: "He was seeing LIFE, and what can an American do more!" [see **Authenticity = Artificiality (Life)**] Such seem to be the emotions with which Mrs. Walker—the wife of New York's mayor, making a goodwill tour of Berlin—reacts to her meeting with the recently appointed German president (and war hero) von Hindenburg, whose public image, at least among German intellectuals, is mainly that of a square-headed and increasingly senile military man. For Mrs. Walker, however, von Hindenburg is like Europe—he is old and he is life: "The greatest experience I had during my stay in Germany was yesterday's reception with *Reichspräsident* von Hindenburg. I thought I would meet a frail eighty-year-old, but, on the contrary, a grand old man stood before me who in no way seemed bowed under the burden of his years. I was greeted with youthful freshness, liveliness, and an astonishing elasticity. A heartwarming conversation followed" (8 *Uhr–Abendblatt,* October 19).

Americans from New York or the Midwest are not especially interesting; Europeans are far more impressed by the Latin Americans, who, either with their money or with their talent, conquer the Old World. While Carlos Gardel, a rising star among Argentinian tango singers in the incipient record industry [see **Gramophone**], is on his first triumphant concert tour in Spain early in the year (Collier, 85ff.), cattle ranchers and farmers from Rio de la Plata become notorious for picking up the entire tab at Parisian cabarets during long and often rowdy nights. Colonel Bigua, the hero of Jules Supervielle's novel *Le Voleur d'enfants (The Man Who Stole Children),* who lives in voluntary political exile in Paris, is perfectly capable of playing this role—yet he maintains a proud distance from French society, where "the voluntary sterility of so many French households" repels him (Supervielle, 61). Since his marriage is likewise sterile, Bigua creates his own "family" by abducting children on the crowded streets of Paris. In his sumptuous apartment, these children receive all the care and attention worthy of future heirs; their toys are designed to prepare them for the family's "return" to South America: "In an immense box is a South American farm, with a herd of cows wandering about the countryside. They breathe air from far away and find themselves in Paris as if by accident. These eucalyptus trees, if you set them up on the carpet—see how they make the space around them expand!" (14). Then, "with tragic . . . force" (155), fate intervenes. [see **Action = Impotence (Tragedy)**] Bigua falls in love with his latest acquisition, a teenaged girl whom, for a change, he has simply bought from her father. But Marcella instead yields to the impetuous sexual advances of Joseph, another of Bigua's "children," and becomes pregnant. Without hesitation, the jealous colonel expels this true father-to-be from the "family." Subsequently, he begins to lose his obsession with sterility: "This apartment, whose sterility I thought unalterable, is going to bring a living being into the world!" (186). Having broken the spell of his obsession, Bigua embarks on an ocean liner for South America with his wife and all of his "children"—only to discover that Joseph is following Marcella as a fellow passenger who no longer depends on his "father" to pay for his ticket. No other solution seems left to the colonel than to throw himself into the ocean—between a continent that he has never quite conquered and another to which those who have lost their hearts in Europe can never quite return.

Born in Latin America, Supervielle, who writes this strange narrative of transatlantic desire spanning "Paris, the Atlantic Ocean, and Uruguay" (222), is readily accepted as a French author by a broad reading public. North American citizens of Paris, in contrast, seem to make French friends only on the margins of society. Praising Barbette, an American cross-dresser who performs in the Parisian music halls, Jean Cocteau allows himself—hesitantly—to imagine New York as a space for his desire: "After years of Americanism during which the capital of the United States hypnotized us like a gun, leaving us with our hands up, Barbette's performance shows me at least the real New York, with the ostrich feathers of its sea, its factories, its highrise buildings made of tulle, its precision, its Siren voice, its jewelry, its plumes of light." Not without many implicit and explicit excuses, Walter Benjamin admits, in a review of the translation of an American novel, that what European intellectuals tend to ridicule as "American naiveté" has a charm and purity long vanished on their own continent: "The fact that this novel has been a bestseller for months puts the American public, which has been so harshly criticized, in a more favorable light. It demonstrates not only the childish affection the Yankees have for children . . . but actual naiveté, which finds joy in a love story that is beautiful only because the poet tells it with such unusual purity" (Benjamin, 43).

Other than as intellectuals who are perceived as different because of a lack or an excess of sophistication, North Americans are at best merely tolerated by Europeans as paying customers. Thus, while admitting that the example of American tourism has encouraged travel on the Continent, the head of the Hoteliers Association, in an article for the *Berliner Tageblatt* of July 25, maintains a strictly descriptive level of discourse: "Today's hotel guests get around quite a bit more than in the old days. Being cosmopolitan means being Americanized. It also means being influenced by sports and health concerns. These have revolutionized hotel cuisine. Who still eats thick soups nowadays?" In his concluding paragraph, however, he can no longer resist the temptation of ridiculing what is generally seen as Americans' lack of intellectual maturity: "Also, the hotel guest has become more political. In Germany, we cannot follow the American practice of providing each guest with a newspaper at breakfast. American guests may take a certain interest in whether they receive the *Chicago Tribune* or the *New York Herald* on their breakfast tray, but the German traveler would quickly vent his displeasure at the hotel if his newspaper did not precisely suit his political taste." For Europeans, the simplicity of American world views is proverbial. Like a contagious disease, it is seen as an immutable element in the character even of those emigrants who, after making a fortune in the New World, end up returning to their native country. Telling the saga of his respectable bourgeois family, the Alsatian novelist René Schickele refuses to take seriously such a repatriated ancestor: "In the course of the year, every peasant of Rheinweiler came to sit next to him at some gathering or other. Drinking in the village inn, he tried to explain to them what a cowboy or a farmer was like. It was his dream to transform them all into Americans, at least externally" (Schickele, 90). As a mass phenomenon, American tourists inspire feelings—and even acts—of hatred among Europeans. Especially in France, the money they spend evokes resentment rather than opportunism or even gratitude. The author of an article in the *Berliner Morgenpost* of July 25 clearly shares this view: "Around midnight those heavy 'See-Paris-by-Night' buses approach. Montmartre is their first destination. Up to the shining white church of Sacré Coeur, there is not much of a problem. But further uphill, where the painters and bohemians dwell as the last remnants of French culture, things become precarious. Several hundred Frenchmen surround the bus with threatening gestures: 'Stay home, you pork-dealers from Chicago! We hate you! We've had it with your ways! Go home and tell the tale of our sinful Babel, which you puritans are so scared of and which you don't even want to pay for!' After a fierce scuffle, the police succeeded in extricating the bus and restoring order."

Quite regularly, Europeans claim that nothing in North America appeals to them but money. The Parisian journalist Jacques Laval finds New York "a mass of banality, a city of abstinence and desolation, boresome without being noble, a city for which no one could possibly become homesick" (Heimer, 55). The voyages that Europeans undertake to Latin America are primarily business-related, like the visit of the former German chancellor Hans Luther to Argentina in November; but this part of the New World is regarded enthusiastically as the future: "I am convinced that no matter how brilliant the current situation of this country may be, a near future is awaiting it that will be many times more glorious" (*Caras y Caretas,* December). In contrast, when North America is the topic, only the poor see the world of capitalism as offering hope. This is the case with the main protagonist in Gerhart Hauptmann's drama *Dorothea Angermann.* Daughter of a Protestant pastor in a provincial German town, the pregnant Dorothea is forced by her father to marry the dissolute man who has corrupted her. The couple receive sufficient money for their passage across the Atlantic. But Dorothea's hopes are dramatically frustrated. She suffers a miscarriage, her marriage turns out the predictable failure, and all she finds in American society is humiliation: "They beat you, they abuse you. You have to go on the street to make money. One day they dress you in furs like a doll, the next day they let you stand naked in the cold. Oh, what eternal prostitution! . . . Your blood and your nerves change, something happens to you unconsciously—for if you were conscious, you would turn to stone with shame" (Hauptmann, 75). On August 8 the *Berliner Tageblatt* publishes an article on the fate of some German waitresses who have come to work at the U.S. Sesquicentennial Exposition in Philadelphia [see **Boxing**]—an article that seems like a malicious nonfictional version of Hauptmann's play:

> The bankruptcy of the Bavarian restaurant in Philadelphia has left 150 German waitresses (among them 75 from Bavaria) without any financial resources . . . The fate of the Bavarian waitresses is still uncertain because the owner did not leave any security deposits. Permission for their deportation to Germany is expected. But the girls refuse to leave the country because they have yet to receive their first payment. The waitresses who came despite the warnings of the German Embassy are now entirely dependent on public charity . . . It was a bizarre idea to open a Bavarian restaurant in the country of Prohibition. Probably Resl, Mirzl, and Fanny offered their guests a cool jug of—mineral water!

Without wanting to admit it, Europeans feel a tormenting blend of fascination and resentment. The only condition under which fascination and desire can be explicitly mentioned seems to be when they are categorized as pathological. In the *Almanach für das Jahr 1926,* published by the Internationaler Psychoanalytischer Verlag, Otto Rank presents materials from the talking cure of a deeply troubled young woman (diagnosed as "hysterical"). The key passage in her wishful vision of the future, which the analyst details for the almanac's readers, contains some striking parallels to the fate of Dorothea Angermann and the Bavarian waitresses in Philadelphia: "She begins her American life washing dishes . . ., but she ends up making a fortune and returns home crowned with success. Although this advanced version of the family romance stresses her identification with her successful father, she admits that in her original fantasy she started as a waitress in a small and dirty room— and then a wealthy American came: 'one of those who are already wealthy and no longer have to make money,' like her father" (*Almanach,* 183). The only problem for the analyst is the overabundance of possible interpretations for this Oedipal metanarrative, yet he never thinks to ask why America of all places is the scene of wish-fulfillment in this family romance, or why his patient's idealized father-equivalent has to be American.

At the end of his travel narrative *Rien que la terre,* the French novelist Paul Morand, a close friend of Ralph Barton, the New York designer who failed to find consolation in Paris for his broken marriage, muses on why Americans coming home to their country so enthusiastically greet the Statue of Liberty, whereas French travelers return to their shores weary and irritated: "Here, on this November evening, on this sad, unheated ship, tired and shivering colonials, low-class prostitutes perfumed with rotten luck, poorly paid and embittered functionaries, anxious family men afraid of risks, people who have seen their fortunes cut in half since they left France, opium smokers with bitter tongues—all are returning silent, their backs turned. . . Have we become the most acrid sons of this European race, the race that tigers refuse to eat because of its bitter flesh?" (Morand, 254–255). Might self-hatred be the reason Europeans hate Americans—and long for America?

Related Entries

Bars, Boxing, Bullfighting, Gramophones, Ocean Liners, Railroads, Authenticity vs. Artificiality, Action = Impotence (Tragedy), Center = Periphery (Infinitude), Immanence = Transcendence (Death)

References

8 Uhr–Abendblatt.

Walter Benjamin, "Review of Margaret Kennedy, *Die treue Nymphe.*" In *Gesammelte Schriften,* vol. 1. Frankfurt, 1972.

Shari Benstock, *Women of the Left Bank: Paris, 1900–1940.* Austin, 1986.

Berliner Morgenpost.

Berliner Tageblatt.

Anthony Burgess, *Ernest Hemingway.* Hamburg, 1980.

Caras y Caretas.

Jean Cocteau, "The Barbette Act." In Man Ray and Jean Cocteau, *Barbette.* Berlin, 1988.

Simon Collier, *Carlos Gardel: Su vida, su música, su época.* Buenos Aires, 1986.

Gerhart Hauptmann, *Dorothea Angermann: Schauspiel.* Munich, 1926.

Mel Heimer, *The Long Count.* New York, 1969.

Ernest Hemingway, *The Sun Also Rises.* New York, 1926.

Internationaler Psychoanalytischer Verlag, *Almanach für das Jahr 1926.* Vienna, 1926.

Bruce Kellner, *The Last Dandy: Ralph Barton—American Artist, 1891–1931.* Columbia, Mo., 1991.

Paul Morand, *Rien que la terre: Voyage.* Paris, 1926.

New York Times.

Antoine Prost and Gérard Vincent, eds., *Histoire de la vie privée,* vol. 5: *De la première Guerre Mondiale à nos jours.* Paris, 1987.

René Schickele, *Maria Capponi.* Munich, 1926.

Jules Supervielle, *Le voleur d'enfants.* Paris, 1926.

John Willett, *Art and Politics in the Weimar Period: The New Sobriety, 1917–1933.* New York, 1978.

ASSEMBLY LINES

Invented by Frederick Taylor and first used in the industrial production process by Henry Ford after 1914, assembly lines are no longer an exciting technological innovation. Everybody seems to be familiar with their structure and functioning—either by direct professional experience, or through the still-frequent use of the concept as a metonym for whatever is perceived as new (and even futuristic) in the world of labor. An assembly line consists of an endless chain which slowly moves through a factory building and on which large numbers of a single product are put together through the repeated and standardized operations of workers stationed along the chain. Assembly lines have revolutionized the involvement of the worker's body in the production process. They have inverted the traditional relation between the craftsman and his product: the worker has become stationary, while the product moves along the chain so that its progress toward completion is visible. Each worker's body performs, over and over, the same operation, and the pace of this repetition is determined by the movement of the chain. The worker's body thus enters a double structural coupling with the chain as a technical device. Not only does the speed of the body movements depend on the speed of the chain, but the complementarity among the individual operations performed by the bodies of different workers transforms these bodies, together with the chain, into one huge and complex production machine. The assembly line is an emblem of a double division of labor—among individual workers, and between the workers' bodies and a mechanical device. During the production process, however, this complex machine excludes the worker's mind. The worker is not supposed to speak to his colleagues (very often the noise in the factory and the distance between the workers make such communication even physically impossible). The less individualized (i.e., the more standardized) the workers' movements are, the better they fit into the overall production process and the more they contribute to its efficiency. No single worker— and not even the total group of workers on the line—can claim to be the creator of the product they manufacture.

Stereotypical depictions of industrial production make two recurrent associations between the assembly line and its environment. The bodies that are shown coupled to the assembly line are exclusively male, whereas women appear either sitting in front of individual production tables or performing assembly work at home (von Soden and Schmidt, 32ff.). Interestingly, however, women can be associated with the products that are serially manufactured on assembly lines. A German cartoon presents a kick-line of revue girls (the most famous group in Germany being the Tiller Girls) emerging from a factory building on an assembly line. The caption makes it clear that the role of the producer, which has been usurped from the workers, is now occupied by another male subject: "Ford takes over the production of Tiller Girls" (Jelavich, 182). [see **Revues**] More than in any other branch of production, assembly lines pervade the car industry—even in France where industrial technology is just beginning to catch up with American, English, and German standards (*Années-mémoire*, 174). This association of cars with the assembly line supports its discursive function as a metonym not only for the most advanced industrial technology but for a much-debated double paradox at the center of capitalism. As a rationalization of production [see **Sobriety vs. Exuberance**], the assembly line makes it possible to raise wages and, simultaneously, to lower the market prices of products. Seen from this first paradoxical angle—which is the frequently quoted angle of Henry Ford (Lethen, 20ff.)—the workers' alienation from the product, as it is imposed upon them by the new mode of production, seems to increase their chances of purchasing a car. [see **Automobiles**] An article in the *Berliner Tageblatt* of August 8 on "worktime in America" draws what appears to be the logical conclusion of such reasoning: the more efficiently the world of business and industry uses labor, the greater the chance that the working class and the lower middle class will be able to participate in the material blessings of capitalist production.

Rather than being divided (or at least ambivalent), opinions on such forms of "rationalized labor" are almost unanimously positive across the entire political and ideological spectrum. Socialists and industrialists mostly concur in their rhetorical efforts to minimize the alienating effects of the assembly line, such as the reduction of each worker to one and only one function within the production process, or the utilization of the worker's body for one and only one movement: "When the worker looks upstream and downstream from his point on the shore of the assembly line, he sees himself participate, through his meaningful limited role, in a colossal collective work" (Gottl-Ottlilienfeld, 17). As a politicized author with a proud revolutionary past and as an overly enthusiastic traveler in the Soviet Union, Ernst Toller is at first surprised to see similar methods pushed to their extreme by the self-declared Communist society. In an "experimental factory" in Moscow, the workers' bodies are literally attached to the machines—with the obvious goal of completely eliminating the mind as a potential obstacle to the standardization of their movements: "A machine teaches the correct position for hammering. The worker's arm is attached to a mechanical hammer which grasps his hand. The arm reproduces the hammer's movements for half an hour, until it becomes completely readapted to this mechanical rhythm" (Toller, 122). Though it is Toller's initial impulse to protest such "mechanization of man," such "stifling of all human creativity," he soon gratefully accepts an interpretation from the director of the experimental factory [see **Engineers**] according to which extreme rationalization of labor will be the necessary condition for higher productivity and, above all, for increased leisure time in the socialist future. [see **Present = Past (Eternity)**] "Through our research we hope to ensure that a particular job, which formerly took a worker eight hours to accomplish, will in the future require only two or three" (123).

Although similar opinions have been canonized in the Soviet Union since Lenin first formulated the project of integrating the assembly line into the emerging socialist system (*Die wilden Zwanziger*, 162–163), some observers remain skeptical. After less than a month in Moscow— and despite his desperate desire to be impressed by the new society (a desire which, if nothing else, he shares with Ernst Toller)—Walter Benjamin expresses astonishment over the prevailing uncritical attitude toward technology in the Soviet Union: "Everything technical is sacrosanct here; nothing is taken more seriously than technology" (Benjamin, 82). In the expressionist discourse of the Communist poet Johannes R. Becher, men coupled to machines belong to the scenery of a contemporary world of production that he constantly paints as a nightmare: "Machine-men I build, twelve per day. / Headless and with winged trunks; a thousand limbs: / Pliers, hammers; slit in the stomach to neigh" (Becher, 132). The name of the lyric "I" behind this fantasy, however, is "Director S. of Steel Ltd." It is an open question whether Becher would apply the same imagery to the bodies of Soviet workers coupled to Soviet machines. For the optimization of Taylorist modes of industrial production—within a Communist political order and for the sake of a socialist society—appears as a viable vision of future redemption from a class-based society.

Related Entries

Automobiles, Engineers, Revues, Sobriety vs. Exuberance, Present = Past (Eternity)

References

Les Années-mémoire: 1926. Paris, 1988.

Johannes R. Becher, *Maschinenrhythmen.* Berlin, 1926.

Walter Benjamin, *Moskauer Tagebuch* (9 December 1926–1 February 1927). Frankfurt, 1980.

Berliner Tageblatt.

Peter Jelavich, *Berlin Cabaret.* Cambridge, Mass., 1993.

Friedrich Gottl-Ottlilienfeld, *Fordismus: Über Industrie und technische Vernunft.* Jena, 1926.

Helmut Lethen, *Neue Sachlichkeit, 1924–1932: Studien zur Literatur des "Weissen Sozialismus."* Stuttgart, 1970.

Kristine von Soden and Maruta Schmidt, eds., *Neue Frauen: Die zwanziger Jahre.* Berlin, 1988.

Ernst Toller, *Russische Reisebilder* (1926). In *Quer durch: Reisebilder und Reden.* Heidelberg, 1978.

Die wilden Zwanziger: Weimar und die Welt, 1919–1933. Berlin, 1986.

AUTOMOBILES

Although fenders emerging from the runningboards are beginning to cover the high, slender tires, automobiles tend to display their anatomy as a technical construction. The axles are visible, the headlights project from the body, and many cars have a starting crank. Martin Heidegger chooses another isolated part of the automobile, the turn signal, as a paradigmatic reference in a discussion of sign usage and sign interpretation: "Motor cars are sometimes equipped with an adjustable red arrow, whose position indicates the direction the vehicle will take—at an intersection, for instance. The position of the arrow is controlled by the driver. This sign is a device which is ready-to-hand for the driver as he maneuvers the car, and not for him alone: those who are outside the car—and they in particular—also make use of it" (Heidegger, 78). As if to symbolize the separateness of their individual elements, most automobiles display majestic spare tires just ahead of the driver's door. Only some models, usually built by private firms, have a more compact form (*Années-mémoire,* 173; Römer, 24). As a general rule, the engine, passenger compartment, and trunk of the automobile are contiguous rectangular boxes of different sizes, rather than elements within a unifying shape.

With large cars—and when weather conditions allow—passengers customarily sit in the open, behind a chauffeur, whose uniform resembles that of a railway conductor. They often wear sporty leather caps. In this particular arrangement, the automobile may serve as a status symbol because it looks like a slightly modified version of a private horse-drawn carriage—that is, like a relic from less egalitarian days. It seems to be just such an aristocratic connotation that persuades Thomas Mann to purchase an automobile: "so I acquired an auto, a beautiful, six-seater Fiat sedan. Our dear Ludwig has already decked himself out as a chauffeur, so I sally forth at 33 horsepower, driving through the city, affably greeting people on all sides" (Kolbe, 377–378). For those members of international high society who cultivate avant-garde ambitions (among them the Spanish king, Alfonso XII), "motoring" and even racing have the status of a particularly modern hobby. A small but exclusive car-manufacturing plant figures among the multiple possessions of the narrator's family in René Schickele's novel *Maria Capponi* (427), and the father of his Italian lover Maria is constantly on the road inaugurating international Salons de l'Automobile (242; *Années-mémoire*, 175). Some of the brand names for luxury automobiles are redolent of such social distinction: Alfa Romeo, Austro-Daimler, Bentley, Bugatti, Chénard-Walker, Hispano Cease, Lorraine-Dietrich. Similar in this regard to flying, motoring as a sport takes organizational form mainly either as races consisting of several legs or as endurance tests for the automobiles' standard models. [see **Airplanes**] Since manufacturers are only beginning to discover the value of such competitions for their sales promotion (a forerunner in this regard is Mercedes-Benz A.G., which, in the *Berliner Tageblatt* of August 5, proudly advertises its "record-breaking victories in national and international competitions"), it is difficult to distinguish the exteriors of mass-produced automobiles [see **Assembly Lines**] from those of race cars.

Although traction remains a major practical problem (due to manufacturing methods, tire quality, and poor road surfaces), automobiles reach respectable levels of speed. The new six-cylinder 180-horsepower Mercedes has a maximum speed of about 100 mph (*Chronik*, 197), and the winner of the classic twenty-four-hour race at Le Mans sets a world record by covering 2,533.51 kilometers during the contest (*Années-mémoire*, 85, 172ff.). This disproportion between traction and engine performance makes automobiles dangerous for drivers and passengers. Magazines and newspapers are full of detailed accident reports, which are often accompanied by dramatic photographs of car wrecks and victims. In its November 6 issue, *Caras y Caretas* describes such an event that occurred in Buenos Aires: "An omnibus headed west on San

Eduardo Street was crossing Gualeguaychú when it was hit by an automobile bearing a license plate from Morón. The collision was so severe that the omnibus was split in two and the car sustained heavy damage. The public rescue service was called, and it was verified that the driver of the car and seven bus passengers had been injured. Witnesses claimed that the accident was the fault of Manuel Sánchez, the man who had been driving the automobile. The police detained him, putting him in the custody of the appropriate judge." It remains unclear on what grounds the witnesses can so clearly attribute the responsibility for this accident to the driver of the car. His immediate arrest by the police seems to suggest that driving a car is considered a potentially criminal act. For a Berlin taxi driver who kills two and injures three while passing a group of hikers on their way back to the city on the evening of Ascension, police arrest turns out to be a lifesaving intervention: "The guilty driver was pulled from the car by the agitated crowd and would certainly have been lynched on the spot if the police hadn't immediately taken him into custody. He was brought to the hospital, and there arrested by the police" (*Berliner Volks-Zeitung,* May 14). Unlike plane crashes, which journalists represent as episodes of heroism and tragedy [see **Airplanes**], the recurrent scenario in their coverage of car accidents involves aggressors and victims. For, at least in Europe, automobiles evoke strong feelings of social resentment. If Freder, the hero of Fritz Lang's film *Metropolis,* uses "a large white chauffeur-driven car" (Lang, 34) to ride to the office of his father, John Fredersen, the "Master of Metropolis," workers who later celebrate the proletarian revolt standing "on the roofs of the cars" (120) seem to be engaging in an act of compensation. In the eyes of Theodor Lessing, a Jewish philosopher scorned by his colleagues and persecuted by hordes of anti-Semitic students [see **Murder**], automobiles are metonymic for the dangers lurking in the modern world: "I hate the cries of the street merchants and newspaper vendors. I hate the ringing of the church bells, I hate the senseless noise of the factory sirens, but what I hate most is the stinking autos. Modern man has acted with total disregard and barefaced self-righteousness. We are defenseless against their all-powerful owners . . . In some cities—Cologne, for example, with its many old, narrow streets—the traffic is a constant public menace" (Lessing, 400ff.). Even those who can afford automobiles often refer to them as a negative metaphor that establishes a distance between their own respectable wealth and what they consider the demimonde.

Alluding to the present crisis of the French franc [see **Americans in Paris**], the *8 Uhr–Abendblatt* of May 19 presents a cartoon with racketeers traveling westward in a large chauffeur-driven automobile. In Thomas Mann's novella "Unordnung und frühes Leid," the only car owner is, predictably, a young stockbroker.

But such tensions between pride and resentment, between physical pleasure and the fear of death [see **Action = Impotence (Tragedy)**], occupy only part of the complex web of emotions that automobiles trigger. Before Bigua, a rich Argentinian landowner in exile, can lure the seven-year-old Antoine into his "magnificent limousine, so new that it still seems to be in the display window of a store on the Champs-Elysées" (Supervielle, 13), the child has lost all sense of direction amid the "cars and tires and horses passing by" on the busy streets of Paris (12). Contrasting with horse-drawn vehicles, cars have become the basic elements of a new everyday world and are now indispensable in numerous contexts. The *Berliner Morgenpost* impresses its readers by publishing, in the July 25 issue, a large map that explains in detail the way in which its papers are distributed daily by "air service" and "automobile express service." But if this map documents a proud claim to modern logistics, it is also true that the *Morgenpost* could not be competitive on a nation-wide basis without using airplanes and cars to reach its subscribers. In the United States, which accounts for 19 million of the world's 25 million automobiles (Germany, in contrast, has only 93,000), their integration into everyday life is far more advanced (*Chronik*, 100). As a consequence, the aristocratic aura of the automobile is vanishing, and the halo of an almost mythical fear surrounding the car is gradually transformed into a host of practical problems. With such pragmatic connotations, the automobile belongs to the normal technical environment of the young generation. Peugeot tries to accelerate this development by awarding twenty-one cars as prizes to the most brilliant French high school and university students (*Années-mémoire*, 31). Featuring numerous ads for gas-and-service stations in the neighboring city of Palo Alto, the student yearbook of Stanford University shows that the automobile has become a normal part of daily life, at least among students from well-to-do families (*1926 Quad*, 397, 405). Likewise, the *Handbook of Information* for Mount Holyoke College, which contains a long list of rules governing the lives of its female students, devotes much of the list to the particular problems of "motoring." These rules are a function of the school's isolated location in rural Massachusetts and of the (never explicitly mentioned) moral dangers that are associated with transportation by automobile: "(1) A student may always motor with a woman during the daytime. (2) In both daytime, and evening until 10:00 P.M., a student may motor with members of her immediate family or her guardian, close relatives (except those from M.A.C. and Amherst College), alumnae with their families, trustees, and members of the faculty and staff. Other students may be included. With the exception of this, all students must have permission and a chaperone for motoring in the evening" (*Handbook*, 31).

In Spain, the Ford Motor Company tries to conquer the emerging automobile market by appealing to the self-image of the "modern woman." "For the woman of today, who counts among her hobbies that of going for a ride and driving the car herself, we offer this Ford Torpedo two-seater model" (*Blanco y Negro*, back page). For male passengers, in contrast, automobile rides without any practical purpose are regarded as absurd. Such, at least, is what the behavior of a strictly business-oriented Madrid taxi driver indicates to one of his more leisured customers: "This fashion of making a return trip for no other reason than to enjoy the sun and air was incomprehensible to my driver; it increased the disgust and annoyance he undoubtedly already felt in response to my strange appearance" (*Blanco y Negro*, 49). Intellectuals—particularly intellectuals in technologically less advanced countries—admire emotional distance and technical competence regarding the everyday functions of the automobile even more than they admire record speeds and luxury cars. Traveling in Brazil, Filippo Marinetti pleases a young local journalist by describing his experience of the lively traffic in the streets of Rio de Janeiro: "Rio de Janeiro impresses me with a combination of phenomena that is unique in the world. Against the background of its tropical exuberance, it shows all the magnificent dynamism of contemporary life. For someone who adores movement and speed as much as I do, the loud and intense bustle of the traffic and of the teeming, restless masses is an incomparable joy" (Buarque de Holanda, 80). In similarly vibrant terms, Walter Benjamin dedicates his book *Einbahnstraße* to the Soviet woman he worships: "This street is called / Asja Lacis Street / after her who / as an engineer / bulldozed it through the author." [see **Engineers**] Under the heading "Tankstelle" ("Filling Station"), he then uses the functioning of engines as a metaphor for the role of opinions in everyday life: "Opinions are, for the huge apparatus of social life, what oil is for machines. One doesn't stand in front of a turbine and douse it with machine oil. One has to know how to put just a little of it on the hidden nuts and bolts" (Benjamin, 85).

Automobiles epitomize a new sensibility that appreciates the factual and the quotidian. [see **Uncertainty vs. Reality**] This symbolic function explains why, despite his antitechnological bias, Heidegger thematizes a new structural element of the car in his analysis of "durchschnittliche Alltäglichkeit" (Heidegger, 43; also Gumbrecht). But it is equally interesting that his reference to the turn signal as a paradigm for the usage of signs is directly followed by his reflection on the existential dimension of spatiality. For automobiles and the still unfamiliar speed with which they cover long distances contribute to the new collective experience of infinitude. [see **Center = Periphery [Infinitude]**] More precisely, the fear which their movement and even their sheer presence inspire becomes a metonym for the fear generated by a space whose structures and functions are no longer prescribed. The movement of automobiles is threatening because it is not regulated through generally acknowledged laws. By accusing drivers of arrogance, aggressiveness, and arbitrariness, and by criminalizing their actions, the public transforms this situation of contingency into an ethical problem. At the same time, the practical need for traffic regulations capable of structuring the space occupied by automobiles becomes a much-debated topic. Returning from the boxing match between Jack Dempsey and Gene Tunney [see **Boxing**], a *New York Times* journalist praises the flow of traffic in the city of Philadelphia: "Most Philadelphia streets are dedicated to one-way traffic. By a traffic rule which seems to be enforced pretty strictly, taxis are compelled to stop whenever a trolley car stops alongside them. Accordingly, taxis and trolleys move at pretty nearly the same speed, and the Philadelphia Rapid Transit deserves its name to a degree unusual with surface traffic" (September 24). In Berlin, traffic lights—initially criticized as an almost grotesque failure—are introduced on October 1. Only a few weeks earlier, on August 29, the *Berliner Tageblatt* tries to revise the firmly established discourse which accuses automobile drivers of immoral aggressiveness. With all due caution, it points to certain practices of the police, who, using the absence of clear structures in the traffic space as an excuse, set up speed traps: "It goes without saying that the drivers and chauffeurs who speed recklessly should not be protected. Those who do not observe the speed limits should, self-evidently, be punished. But there are those who would make a business out of such punishment, to the extent that public servants do nothing but sit with a stopwatch in their hand and wait for an automobile to commit an infraction. This borders on scandal."

Related Entries

Airplanes, Americans in Paris, Assembly Lines, Boxing, Engineers, Murder, Uncertainty vs. Reality, Action = Impotence (Tragedy), Center = Periphery (Infinitude)

References

Les Années-mémoire: 1926. Paris, 1988.
Antología de Blanco y Negro, 1891–1936, vol. 9. Madrid, 1986.
Associated Students of Stanford University, eds., *The 1926 Quad.* Stanford, 1926.
Walter Benjamin, *Einbahnstraße* (1926). In *Gesammelte Schriften,* vol. 4, part 1. Frankfurt, 1972.
Berliner Morgenpost.
Berliner Tageblatt.
Berliner Volks-Zeitung.
Sérgio Buarque de Holanda, "Marinetti novamente no Rio: As suas impressões do continente sul-americano relatadas durante uma visita a *O Jornal*" (1926). In Francisco de Assis Barbosa, ed., *Raízes de Sérgio Buarque de Holanda.* Rio de Janeiro, 1989.
Caras y Caretas.
Chronik 1926: Tag für Tag in Wort und Bild. Dortmund, 1985.
Hans Ulrich Gumbrecht, "'Everyday-World' and 'Life-World' as Philosophical Concepts: A Genealogical Approach." In *New Literary History* 24 (Autumn 1993): 745–761.
Martin Heidegger, *Sein und Zeit* (written 1926, published 1927). Tübingen, 1984.
Jürgen Kolbe, ed., *Heller Zauber: Thomas Mann in Munich, 1894–1933.* Berlin, 1987.
Fritz Lang, *Metropolis* (1926). New York, 1973.
Theodor Lessing, "Die blauschwarze Rose" (1926). In *"Ich warf eine Flaschenpost ins Eismeer der Geschichte": Essays und Feuilletons, 1923–1933.* Darmstadt, 1986.

Thomas Mann, "Unordnung und frühes Leid" (1926). In *Sämtliche Erzählungen*. Frankfurt, 1963.

Mount Holyoke College, *Students' Handbook of Information*. South Hadley, Mass., 1926.

New York Times.

Willy Römer, *Vom Pferd zum Auto: Verkehr in Berlin, 1903–1932*. Berlin, 1984.

René Schickele, *Maria Capponi*. Munich, 1926.

Jules Supervielle, *Le voleur d'enfants*. Paris, 1926.

BARS

More perhaps than his batting average of .372, his forty-seven home runs, and his one hundred forty-five RBIs, Babe Ruth's ostentatious enjoyment of the sensuous side of life impresses the fans. [see **Stars**] He is an exception to the rule that obliges great athletes to pay the price of asceticism for their outstanding performance. A stanza sung in the Babe's honor at a festive dinner of the New York Baseball Writers does not need to mention his records as a slugger [see **Boxing, Dancing**]:

> I wonder where my Babe Ruth is tonight?
> He grabbed his hat and coat and ducked from sight.
> I wonder where he'll be
> At half past two or three?
> He may be at a dance or in a fight.
> He may be at some cozy roadside inn.
> He may be drinking tea—or maybe gin.
> I know he's with a dame,
> I wonder: what's her name?
> I wonder where my Babe Ruth is tonight?
>
> (Ritter and Rucker, 135)

Everybody likes to see Babe Ruth breaking all the rules, especially the rules of Prohibition. Everybody also knows that he frequents "cozy roadside inns," and that he greatly prefers a glass of gin to a cup of tea.

But if Babe Ruth himself is a great exception—a celebrity whose drinking is an acceptable subject for journalists—his admirers follow a highly generalized pattern when they list bars and liquor along with the other pleasures in which he indulges, such as fist-fighting, dancing, and womanizing. For, in popular discourse, drinking and bars belong to a paradigmatic set of equivalent activities, and as such immediately become associated with a set of related situations.

In this sense, Bertolt Brecht's hyperactive insurance broker Kückelmann is a close cousin to the baseball writers' Babe Ruth: "He had stimulated his brain with strong American drinks, soothed himself with absolutely unsurpassable coffee, flogged his exhausted spirit with jazz, plunged into the cabarets of the comedians, and misused the revues of the Metropole as spiritual enrichment . . . He had landed in Aschinger's beer joint" (Brecht, 170). [see **Jazz, Revues**] Day after day, the back page of the *8 Uhr–Abendblatt* is filled with advertisements for the Berlin bars, beer joints, *(Bierquellen),* cabarets, dance halls, and revues to which Brecht refers. And the bars of Berlin are always linked with other forms of enjoyment: "The Parisienne: Berlin's largest nightclub. Come dance to the music of the Formiggini Band" (February 4). Or on October 2, in the same paper: "See the dance revue at the Rokoko Bar"; "Come to the Ballet des Plastiques at the Moulins [*sic*] Rouge Paris, where the most beautiful women dance."

It is one of the paradoxes in these years of Prohibition that, outside the United States, bars that serve hard liquor are frequently called "American Bars." The collective imagination constantly attributes hard drinking to one of the few nations where the public consumption of liquor has been officially banned. Bars and cocktails thus epitomize whatever European intellectuals denigrate—or dream of—as "Americanism." Drinking stands for lightness, speed, and superficiality, which are perceived as essential for the most modern lifestyles. [see **Authenticity vs. Artificiality**] Some of the metaphors that Americans themselves use for the world of illegal liquor-consumption are telling in this sense: "speakeasies," "bootleggers," "rumrunners." A satirical vision of the "theaters of the future" published by the *Revista de Occidente* elaborates on this association of bars and drinking with ways of life devoid of any "serious" function or meaning: "I came to have a great liking for these theaters. Certainly they came to be a vice for people inclined to emotion, because the vice of getting profound thrills with the same ease with which we order cocktails is a tonic which it is difficult to resist" (197). At the same time, bars are seen as appealing to human needs which are so basic that their satisfaction equals psychic regression. This may explain why the "roadside inn" in the poem about Babe Ruth is "cozy," and why the customers of the speakeasies are called "suckers." Finally—despite such associations with elementary desires—bars entice their patrons with sophisticated lighting and with the artificial colors of the cocktails. The virtuous and perverted hero of Marcel Jouhandeau's novel *Monsieur Godeau Intime* happily identifies the atmosphere of his favorite bar with the temptations of hell:

> In the middle of the night, he sat down in an atmosphere more brilliant than noon on a summer's day in Provence. Fruits and flowers hung from the ceiling, gleaming even on his short hair. His black gloves, which he never took off, made all the bare hands of the men and women around him stand out, holding their crème de menthe or blue absinthe in fine glasses . . . Sitting at a narrow table at the back of the room, between a steaming glass of punch and a scented candle, did Mr. Godeau read? Did he appear to read? Did he enter more profoundly into himself? Did he exalt, in this artificial light, his difference? Did he clasp God in his arms? (32–33)

Just as bars are typically mentioned along with a variety of other pleasure spaces, cocktails, by definition, consist of a variety of liquors. Even the inhabitants of the utterly corrupt South American republic that Ramón del Valle-Inclán invents in *Tirano Banderas* appreciate cocktails as a mark of sophistication: "The editor of *El Criterio Español,* at a nearby table, sipped the cool drink of pineapple, soda, and kir that had made the bar of the Metropol room famous" (54). This implicit complexity turns into individuality, since individual cocktails belong to a whole system of drinks. The waiters' trays are always full: "Above the brilliance of the pavement, the cries of street vendors. The zigzag of Nubian shoeshine boys. Clinking trays, which the waiters of American bars carry above their heads" (58). Likewise, the shelves of American bars are filled with bottles of different colors. It is the bartenders' art to generate a potentially infinite list of cocktails by combining the finite number of different liquors which those bottles contain. The world of pleasures in general and the world of American bars in particular function like grammars. As if bars and pleasures were languages, they are based on the principle of choosing from a finite number of basic elements. These elements are then transformed into a multiplicity of composite products—cocktails as well as long nights filled with different forms of sensual enjoyment. The series of composite products that can be generated according to this principle is open-ended, and the individuality of each of these products stands out against a background of infinite variation.

Describing the Shanghai Club as "the world's greatest bar," Paul Morand combines the grammar of cocktails with the grammar of pleasures: "the libertine cocktail, the 'Kiss-me-Quick'; the sentimental 'Love's Dream'; the poetic 'September Morn'; the 'Sensation'" (76). With even greater obsessiveness, Morand projects the grammar of cocktails onto the geographic map of the world:

> Cocktails of concentrated ingredients, which become even more concentrated when chilled—a sudden union of forces that had been lost when each was in its own bottle, a distillation of happiness received in one punch (where is the gentle caress of wines?), supreme balm of the tropics. Without speaking here of all our ordinary cocktails, observe merely the "Bamboo Cocktail" of the Anglo-Indians, the "Blenton" of the Royal Navy, the "Hula-Hula" of the Hawaiian Islands, the "Gin-Fizz" of the P. and O. steamliners. Sometimes, too, the sweet cocktails of southern lands: the "Sol y Sombra" of San Sebastián (like the "sun" and "shade" of arenas); the "chocolate cocktails" of the Brazilians—chartreuse, port, and fresh chocolate powder; and the "Gibson" of Yokohama, so unique with its white onion; not to mention the "H. P. W. Vanderbilt" and the "Bennett," baptized with the names of great billionaires by an obsequious bartender; finally the "min-nenoaba" or "laughing water" of the Indians. (74ff.)

Since cocktails connote lightness and lightness connotes traveling, bars and maps are frequently associated in people's minds. Walter Benjamin, in the entry "Stehbierhalle" ("Stand-Up Beer Hall") of his *Einbahnstraße*, highlights this very association between traveling and drinking as the most characteristic feature of the sailor: "The sailor hates the sea, and to him the subtlest nuances speak . . . He lives on the open sea in a city, where, on the Cannebière of Marseilles, a Port Said bar faces a Hamburg whorehouse and the Neapolitan Castell dell'Ovo stands on

Barcelona's Plaza Cataluña" (145). Like the shelves behind the bartenders and the minds of the sailors, the chest of a mysterious old man
standing at the door of a bar serves as surface for the inscription of a
similar map in *Monsieur Godeau Intime:* "By the door, an old man, a
giant Atlas, sat on a little stone bench, from morning till evening and
even into the night. The children who passed on their way to school
marveled at a panorama of the world—his chest, covered with flashing
signs which represented all the parts of the globe: Indochina, the Congo,
the Sahara, Tunisia, Mexico, Germany" (33).

The most paradoxical effect of Prohibition is that bars proliferate in
American cities during the dry years: "Two years after Corradini had
been able to find but 463 saloons [i.e., in 1924], Izzy Einstein, most
celebrated of Prohibition agents, estimated that there were a hundred
thousand speakeasies in [New York] . . . Dr. Charles Norris, chief medical examiner, said in his report to the mayor for 1925–26 that the
'speakeasies greatly outnumber the licensed saloons of former days'"
(Ashbury, 210). With strategies of repression failing, Prohibition agents
intensify their efforts—thus becoming part of a potentially endless
growth in illegal liquor traffic and illegal drinking: "The very fact that
the law is difficult to enforce . . . is the clearest proof of the need for its
existence" (Merz, 185). In B. Traven's novel *Das Totenschiff (The Death
Ship),* an American naval officer strongly admonishes the hero to abstain
from illicit pleasures, and the warning itself is enough to launch the sailor
on a tour of the harbor's bars and brothels—and subsequently on a
future of endless travel: "'Don't drink. This is a bad place,' said the
officer . . . 'No,' I responded, 'I never drink a drop of this poison. I know
what I owe my country even from far away. Yes, sir. I can be relied upon,
I swear to God, and I'm absolutely dry. You can rely on me.' I was out
and off the boat" (9–10). As the speakeasies constantly move to "yet
another place" in order to throw enforcement agents off the track, their
customers follow the principle of "yet another drink" (Kobler, 228).
Likewise, the metropolitan life of the protagonists in *The Sun Also Rises*
consists of a constant migration through the "wonderful gentility" (255)
of countless American bars, and even the rural atmosphere of a roadside
inn triggers the specific structure of the drinking ritual: "Two of our
Basques came in and insisted on buying a drink. So they bought a drink
and then we bought a drink, and then they slapped us on the back and
bought another drink. Then we bought, and then we all went back out

into the sunlight and the heat" (109). There is no geographic or cultural limit to this rule. In one of his sketches, the Munich humorist Karl Valentin sits in a local beergarden waiting for the fireworks to begin, while he is courting a nursery maid who drinks so rapidly that he and the waitress can hardly keep up: "Just a sip—drink a little, until the next one comes" (Valentin, 242).

Lightness is an attribute of drinking only so long as constant movement prevents the drinkers from becoming addicted. Consequently, addiction becomes associated with spaces that exclude movement. If a sentence such as "He always went up to the edge of the abyss to look" (Kessler, 447) stands as a metaphor for the addict's condition, traveling is the one mode of life which always helps a person cross the abyss without avoiding it. In jails (Valle-Inclán, 189), cellars (Becher, 61ff.), or neighborhoods that they never leave (Borges, 30), drinkers become addicted to alcohol—and even more frequently to "hard" drugs such as morphine or cocaine. [see **Immanence = Transcendence [Death]**] The opium smoker evoked in one of Brecht's sonnets "sleeps alone," forgets the world around her, and allows her body to waste away, transforming it into nothingness: "From one who smokes black smoke / one knows: she is now avid for nothing" (161). In contrast, the drinker whom Brecht describes in another sonnet prepares his body for a greater intensity of enjoyment by eliminating all volition: "As one pounds meat to tenderize it for eating, / So should one, in order to feast on one's own body, prepare one's self for consumption / (Drink schnapps, which gently caresses the palate) / . . . For lack of volition is what makes life worthwhile" (162).

One aspect of such "de-capitation," as Brecht calls it, is a form of forgetfulness resulting in relaxation. This is what the evil cook Mario in Gerhart Hauptmann's *Dorothea Angermann* seeks in a bar before he tries to blackmail his former employer's two sons: Hubert, himself a drinker whose failing health confines him to his shabby apartment, and Herbert, a morally correct university professor who wants to rescue Mario's wife, Dorothea, from a life on the streets. Not incidentally, the scene of the action is a town on the East Coast of the United States: "*Mario:* . . . Forgive my talkativeness—in order to kill time I had a whisky at the Union Bar. *Hubert:* This is the second time you've come. Would you please tell me as precisely as possible why you're here? *Mario:* It was in order to tell you why that I needed to fortify myself in the bar" (Hauptmann, 104). Relaxation through drink, however, is not exclusively a condition for crime. Lightness and speed can also bring out a spirit of reconciliation in even the most hardened criminals. On one occasion, drunkenness prevents Al Capone from getting involved in a potentially lethal fight: "I had a close immediate contact with Al Capone in about 1926. He urinated on my shoes. It happened in the men's room of the Croydon Hotel. He was drunk, and I was drunk. He didn't know who I was, but I knew him. I had the reputation of being the most vicious left-hook puncher in Chicago, that's the God's truth. We were on the verge of slugging it out when Al thought better of it. He didn't exactly apologize, but he admitted to a social error. I decided to overlook the indiscretion. We had a drink and whenever he saw me around town after that, it was 'Hello, kid, how you doing?'" (Kobler, 335).

Related Entries

Boxing, Dancing, Jazz, Ocean Liners, Revues, Stars, Authenticity vs. Artificiality, Immanence = Transcendence (Death)

References

8 Uhr–Abendblatt.

Herbert Asbury, *The Great Illusion: An Informal History of Prohibition.* New York, 1968.

Johannes R. Becher, *Maschinenrhythmen.* Berlin, 1926.

Walter Benjamin, *Einbahnstraße* (1926). In *Gesammelte Schriften,* vol. 4, part 1. Frankfurt, 1972.

Jorge Luis Borges, *El tamaño de mi esperanza* (1926). Buenos Aires, 1993.

Bertolt Brecht, "Die Opiumraucherin" (1926) and "Sonett für Trinker" (1926). In *Gesammelte Werke,* vol. 8. Frankfurt, 1967.

Bertolt Brecht, "Eine kleine Versicherungsgeschichte" (1926). In *Gesammelte Werke,* vol. 11. Frankfurt, 1967.

Gerhart Hauptmann, *Dorothea Angermann: Schauspiel.* Munich, 1926.

Ernest Hemingway, *The Sun Also Rises.* New York, 1926.

Marcel Jouhandeau, *Monsieur Godeau Intime.* Paris, 1926.

Harry Graf Kessler, *Tagebücher, 1918–1937.* Frankfurt, 1961.

John Kobler, *Ardent Spirits: The Rise and Fall of Prohibition.* New York, 1973.

Charles Merz, *The Dry Decade.* Garden City, N.Y., 1932.

Paul Morand, *Rien que la terre: Voyage.* Paris, 1926.

Revista de Occidente.

Lawrence S. Ritter and Mark Rucker, *The Babe: A Life in Pictures*. New York, 1988.

B. Traven, *Das Totenschiff* (1926). Hamburg, 1954.

Karl Valentin, "Das Brillantfeuerwerk oder ein Sonntag in der Rosenau" (1926). In Michael Schulte, ed., *Das Valentin-Buch: Von und über Karl Valentin in Texten und Bildern*. Munich, 1985.

Ramón del Valle-Inclán, *Tirano Banderas* (1926). Madrid, 1978.

BOXING

One of the literary figures dealt with in *El tamaño de mi esperanza (The Size of My Hope),* the first collection of critical essays by Jorge Luis Borges, a young author of growing renown in the literary circles of Buenos Aires, is George Bernard Shaw. Toward the end of the year, Shaw first rejects and then finally accepts the Nobel Prize for Literature (*Chronik*, 184, 194). Borges characterizes Shaw's work, with a paradoxical time-metaphor, both as a "reinvention of the Middle Ages" [see **Present = Past (Eternity)**] and as comparable in style to modern boxing: "Shaw, without stained-glass windows or relics and in an English that is contemporary with Dempsey, invents the Middle Ages" (95). How can Shaw's work be compared to boxing? It is indeed difficult to see what exactly motivates those countless intellectuals who, like Borges, use boxing as a metaphor. This tendency is all the more puzzling as there seems to be hardly any kind of experience or value which boxing may not occasionally represent. At first glance, the only relevant trait is the predominant (although certainly not exclusive) association of boxing with whatever and whoever appear invincibly strong. It is precisely in this sense that an Austrian journalist calls Robert Musil "champion of the spiritual boxers" (Fontana, 383). The Catalan painter Joan Miró must have a similar meaning in mind when he says in an interview, "I wouldn't enter the ring unless it was a championship bout. I don't want a friendly sparring match—now [is] the time to go for the title" *(New York Review of Books,* 16 December 1993, 45). In the Soviet Union, Victor Shklovsky uses yet another boxing metaphor to describe a necessary condition for such success: "Just as a boxer requires elbow room for his punch, so a writer requires the illusion of choice" (Shklovsky, 45).

It is above all the boxer's concentration, sobriety, and professionalism (nobody builds metaphors around amateur boxers) that make him an emblem of modernity. [see **Sobriety vs. Exuberance**] Thus, trying to stage the traditional allegory of Death via techniques of estrangement in his play *Orphée,* Jean Cocteau has Azrael, the "assistant" to Death, gesticulate like the referee of a boxing match: "Azrael counts with one hand in the air, like a boxing referee" (Cocteau, 62). For the philosopher Theodor Lessing, the boxer belongs to a set of modern figures whose smoking reveals a constant state of psychic tension: "When inner composure is required, one always lights up a cigarette. In plays and films, this well-known situation always recurs. A couple of politicians who can influence the rise and fall of their countries, a couple of bank executives conferring about investments worth millions—each of them reaches for a cigarette. The mountain climber who hovers over the abyss, the boxer setting out for the decisive bout—they always drag on a cigarette" (Lessing, 142). On the other hand, the intellectual's imagination also assumes that sobriety, tension, and concentration are states of mind which the boxer shares with his spectators. This is why boxing-match crowds have become a normative ideal for the modern theater audience (Mittenzwei, 219). It is an almost trivial provocation to say that sports events, especially boxing matches, will end up replacing the theater: "There are more and more voices announcing that the drama in its present form is in decline, . . . that the drama has outlived itself as an art form. Those who announce its death are burying it, in order to proclaim cinema, radio, operettas, revues, and boxing bouts as its heir" (*Vossische Zeitung,* April 4).

But even more important than any particular use of the boxing metaphor is the ubiquity of this field of imagination in all types of discourse. It appears, for example, in a best-selling introduction to contemporary astronomy, *The Internal Constitution of the Stars,* in which the author, A. S. Eddington, a physicist of international renown, compares the method of his analyses to the cinematic device of slow motion. Slow motion will transform the violence of certain movements into beauty and harmony: "The motions of the electrons are as harmonious as those of the stars but in a different scale of space and time, and the music of the spheres is being played on a keyboard fifty octaves higher. To discover this elegance we must slow down the action, or alternatively accelerate our own wits, just as the slow-motion film resolves the lusty blows of the prize-fighter into movements of extreme grace and insipidity" (Eddington, 20). [see **Uncertainty vs. Reality**] No intellectual seems able to escape the fascination of boxing. Those who feel obliged to despise this sport for reasons of taste, like Thomas Mann, still grudgingly admit that it is a key emblem of the present: "We live in an age in which uncompromising fidelity sometimes gets on our nerves, a real jazz-band age whose heroes are the prizefighter and the movie star, and which reveals all the details of their huge orgies. Amusing and spectacular orgies, I admit. It would certainly be philistine and petty bourgeois to complain loudly about the new age" (Kolbe, 378).

The power of boxing as a multifunctional symbol is apparent in myriad aspects of the everyday world. If these manifestations go beyond the reality of actual prizefighting, they reflect back on it, enhancing its social, economic, and legal status. As the *New York Times* laconically states on September 22, "The fight game is more respectable now, and also more prosperous." The German luxury liner *Hamburg,* departing for its maiden voyage to New York on April 8, features a boxing ring where the passengers can work out (*Chronik,* 73). [see **Ocean Liners**] Male celebrities, especially writers, artists, and actors, are eager to be photographed during their boxing practice—preferably nude from the waist up, wearing elegant pants and fashionable street shoes (*Die wilden Zwanziger,* 84; Burgess, 33). Two of the rare photo-reportages in *Caras y Caretas,* on October 12, focus on professional boxing, one being a summary of the world-championship bout between Gene Tunney and Jack Dempsey, and the other a preview of a forthcoming fight between the European champion Paulino Uzcudún and the Argentinian champion Angel Firpo, "the wild bull of the Pampa." Despite a "lack of experienced material" (*1926 Quad,* 223)—or in other (less boxing-adequate) words, despite a lack of collegiate tradition—the Athletics Department of Stanford University is trying to build a boxing team because, without such an opportunity, the range of extracurricular activities offered to its male students would lack a main attraction. Boxing is seen as one of the few activities capable of reaffirming male identity in an environment that is increasingly problematizing traditional gender distinctions. [see **Male = Female (Gender Trouble)**] When an anonymous article in the July 18

Chicago Tribune slanders movie star Rudolph Valentino as a "pink powder puff" and accuses him of fostering the "feminization of American males," the only "male" reaction he can imagine is to challenge the writer to a boxing match. When the challenge goes unanswered, his friend Jack Dempsey organizes a bout between Valentino and the New York sports journalist Buck O'Neill at the roof garden of the Ambassador Hotel. [see **Roof Gardens**] In the third round of this fight, Valentino floors his opponent—but the feat only partly restores his public image. This is why, according to Dempsey, his friend falls victim to yet another (and this time lethal) gender-obsessed act. Stricken with peritonitis less than a month later, Valentino hesitates too long before he finally consults a doctor (Morris, 181; Dempsey and Dempsey, 195ff.). [see **Airplanes**]

All across Europe and the Americas, nothing seems to matter more than boxing. On May 15, a boxing match—Paulino Uzcudún's European title bout—becomes the second live broadcast in the history of Spanish radio (the first was a bullfight; Díaz, 114). [see **Bullfighting**] But despite such enthusiasm, in which they indulge with ostentatious intensity, intellectuals find it difficult to explain their own and their entire society's fascination with boxing. It is symptomatic of this disproportion between enthusiasm and reflection that, early in the year, Bertolt Brecht begins publishing a series entitled *Lebenslauf des Boxers Samson Körner (Life of the Boxer Samson Körner)* in *Scherls Magazin* (Mittenzwei, 234–235)—and never finishes it. The fragment of this fictional biography contains many motifs that surface whenever boxing is treated in newspapers or in literary texts—motifs such as the modern metropolis, crime, ocean liners, drinking, treacherous black companions, and trouncings in early fights. But Brecht seems at a loss when it comes to finding a plot for his story (Brecht, 121ff.). He is more convincing in the parable "Der Kinnhaken" ("The Uppercut"), which describes the turning point in the hitherto promising career of the fighter Freddy Meinkes. Freddy is invincible so long as he never thinks about it, so long as he has the feeling "that he's not knocking into a man but breaking through him, that his hand cannot be stopped by something like a chin" (Brecht, 117). Then, a few hours before a title bout, Freddy's manager persuades him—seemingly with the best of intentions—to resist the sudden urge to have a beer. [see **Bars**] Freddy starts to think, and as he starts to think—and to control his body consciously—he can no longer be a good boxer. He gets k.o.'d in the second round. Following the generic rules of the parable,

Brecht's narrative ends with a broad conclusion: "A man should always do what he wants to do. In my opinion, you know, caution is the mother of the k.o." (120).

But while the spectacle of boxing makes all these strenuous psychological, sociological, and even philosophical reflections seem quite flat, it fosters the emergence of a refreshingly crisp journalistic style. This new discourse pretends to follow the quick moves and heavy blows of the fighters, and it revels in lengthy passages describing the colorful boxing world. It abounds in technical terms, and at the same time uses slang words which have never before appeared in print. Here is a passage from the coverage of a European welterweight-title fight in Milan by a special correspondent for the *Berliner Tageblatt*:

> The Velodrome was completely packed, as it always is when the event is organized by Carpegna. One has to give him the credit for the rise of boxing in Italy, for he brilliantly manages to handle the crowd and to put together an exciting program . . . As early as the second round, [Bosisio] took the lead by fending off his opponent's attacks and left hooks to the chin, racking up a huge advantage by the sixth round. In the next two rounds Romerio was repeatedly in serious danger; he spent time getting acquainted with the canvas, since he couldn't avoid three or four direct hits. From the tenth round on, the consequences of Bosisio's overtraining were apparent. He became tired, hit sloppily, and avoided surprise attacks only with great effort. His victory by decision was due entirely to his performance in the early rounds. (July 25)

If international media coverage may serve as an indicator, one of the highlights of the year is the contest for the world heavyweight championship between Jack Dempsey and his challenger Gene Tunney on September 23. Never before has such a large crowd come together to watch a boxing match; in fact, it is one of the most massive public gatherings ever assembled at a sports event. The bout takes place at the U.S. Sesquicentennial Exposition in Philadelphia, but the reasons for this choice have more to do with the internal politics and public image of boxing than with the schedule of events at this somewhat lackluster public fair. [see **Americans in Paris**] Given the unheard-of financial scope with which promoter Tex Rickard is planning the fight, New York appears to be the logical choice. But the New York State Athletic Commission considers

Harry Wills, the "Brown Panther," "a big, sharp-boxing but slow-moving Negro heavyweight," to be the leading contender and therefore refuses to allow Dempsey to appear in New York unless he agrees to fight Wills (Heimer, 11; André and Fleischer, 106ff.). Insisting, on the basis of his business experience, that "mixed fights don't draw well," Rickard opts for an all-white match and for the Sesquicentennial, although, ironically, the promotion of African-American culture is part of the exposition's official agenda (Rydell, 157ff.). Despite the surprisingly low level of prefight betting, which the *New York Times* describes as "the lightest in the history of heavyweight championship fights" (and assuming that the calculations which influence his decision are indeed financial), Rickard's move yields stupendous results. At a time when Babe Ruth is playing for the Yankees at an annual salary of slightly more than $50,000 (which many observers of baseball still find scandalously high (Ritter and Rucker, 135), the *New York Times* of September 24 publishes the following official numbers regarding the Philadelphia bout: "It was estimated the promoters would have a profit of about $500,000. The total paid admissions were 118,736. In addition, 25,732 were admitted on passes [for the Sesquicentennial], which makes the total attendance 144,468. The paid admissions were distributed as follows: $27.50 tickets, 28,903; $22, 12,805; $16.50, 23,014; $11, 19,589; $7.70, 15,747; $5.50, 18,678. It was also announced that Dempsey's end of the receipts would amount to approximately $700,000 and Tunney's to about $200,000." "Six governors and 2,000 millionaires" (*New York Times,* September 23) are in attendance, among them such celebrities as William Randolph Hearst, Joseph Pulitzer, Florenz Ziegfeld [see **Revues**], Charlie Chaplin, the Channel swimmer Gertrud Ederle [see **Endurance**], and the Roosevelt family (Heimer, 15).

The huge crowd puts transportation and traffic systems to a severe test [see **Airplanes, Automobiles**], which seems to interest the journalists no less than the actual fight: "The emphasis now is not on the fighters but on the customers." In special trains and private cars (for which only 1,500 parking spaces are available), about 50,000 people come from New York, and package deals for travel and admission have been sold in the Midwest (especially Chicago) and in California. Following the motto "Where there's a crowd there's bound to be an airplane circling overhead," promoters have provided the spectators, during the long hours spent waiting for the fight, with something to watch: "airplanes, spelling out advertising slogans with colored lights, diving and zooming near the crowd, but, by the luck which seems to attend aviators in the air above fight crowds, never landing" (*New York Times,* September 24). Journalists—in the general excitement that unites them with the crowd—announce a record number of records broken by their own media coverage. For the first time ever, the fighters will talk "directly from the ringside." The live radio broadcast, for which Rickard has sold the rights after an intense bidding war, is transcribed "in the *New York Times* office by three expert shorthand writers of the State Law Reporting Company, working in relays." An estimated 15 million listeners all across the United States follow the broadcast in their apartments or at dinner parties, as do fans in Argentina, Mexico, and Europe (including the Belgian crown prince, who is a declared supporter of Gene Tunney). Indeed, the "radio has replaced the [admission] ticket." This is true even for some of those whose disabilities prevent them from listening in: "the managing officer of the Illinois School for the Deaf has arranged with the Jacksonville Journal and the Associated Press to pass the details of each round to deaf-mutes standing in the streets outside the newspaper office" (*New York Times,* September 22). [see **Wireless Communication**]

Then the "lights [come] on and [flood] the horseshoe of the stadium with a soft radiance. The battery of loud speakers over the ring [begin] distilling dance music from Broadway successes, and set feet to tapping on the dusty ground of the ringside section in time to the latest song hits of Broadway." As Dempsey and Tunney make their entrance wearing "the most up-to-date covering in the bathrobe line that has ever been seen in the history of the prize ring," a heavy rain begins to fall on the open-air arena and on the crowd, and it continues throughout the fight. Their public images have shaped them into allegories of two different social groups, or, rather, of two different versions of the American dream. Jack Dempsey, the current champion, who bills himself as the "Manassa Mauler," comes from a large Colorado farming family, avoided military service in the Great War, and has made enormous amounts of money since he won the heavyweight title in 1919. In the intervening years, he has spent most of his time producing Hollywood movies and traveling the world with his wife, an ambitious actress. He is embroiled with his former manager in a nasty lawsuit, which has jeopardized the possibility of the Philadelphia bout. In contrast, Gene Tunney, the "Fighting Marine," possesses (and makes much of) an exemplary record as a soldier. His family background is Irish Catholic, he grew up in New York, and he stylishly incarnates the cultural ambitions that accompany social ascent. Sometimes, however, journalists lose patience with him: "I'm afraid Tunney will wake up to realize that he has been reading a poem by Shakespeare or Kipling, or one of those big writing fellows, and I'm thinking the title of the poem will be, 'A Fool There Was'" (*New York Times,* September 22).

These sharply different public personae translate into contrasting fighting styles. The adjective most frequently used for Tunney, even by his opponent, is "scientific" (Dempsey and Dempsey, 179ff.). He is "a cool, unruffled boxer" (*New York Times,* September 24); his eye and his mind always control his body. "Tunney is a good boxer in a boxing sense, while Dempsey never professed to be a boxer. Yet he is of the type of strictly fighting man who needs no boxing in any event" *(New York Times,* September 23). Dempsey's fans praise his "fighting fury" and his "tigerish, vicious rushes." His "chief second [has] laid out an elaborate program of instructions which [aims] for the champion to present an appearance of frightfulness, which it [is] hoped [may] scare Tunney into impotence." This image is staged to embody precisely that spontaneous, unselfconscious physical impetus that Brecht sees as the strongest protection against knockout.

The vast majority of the public seems to favor the sober Tunney. For the past seven years "the balance of popular feeling has always been against [Dempsey] in most of his big fights," even in his title bout against the French challenger Charpentier. "That nobody allowed his fears to sway his sentiment [is] proved by the demonstration in favor of Tunney, and against Dempsey, when the contestants [come] in" (*New York Times,* September 24). From the very first round, there is no doubt that Tunney will win. But despite the radio announcer's explicit bias for Tunney, it is impossible to avoid hearing the nostalgia in his voice when he remembers the performance of a younger and stronger Dempsey:

Tunney puts a right glancing blow to Jack's jaw, but it doesn't bother Jack at all. They are in the center of the ring. Jack backs away from Tunney's lead and takes a light right on the face. He backs away to the ropes. Jack does not show the speed he is accustomed to showing. It is not the Jack we are accustomed to at all . . . Everybody is howling, "Dempsey is groggy!" but he does not look so to me. This is not the

Jack Dempsey we were accustomed to see . . . Tunney hit him at least six times with rights and lefts to the face, and Jack gets another on the eye as the bell rings. The first round: Tunney's round by a mile.

Nine rounds later, when Tunney, tightly wrapped in white towels under the pouring rain (André and Fleischer, 108), is officially declared the winner on the basis of points, "there [is] a real burst of applause for the new champion"—yet nothing more than applause. Dempsey appears as "a sorry, pitiful subject . . . His mouth and nose [are spouting] blood, his left eye, bruised and battered, [is] closed tight and bleeding. There [is] a cut under his left eye an inch long." Meanwhile, something almost uncanny has happened. In the course of this humiliating defeat, Jack Dempsey has become the crowd's hero. "The crowd was mostly silent, and evidently pro-Dempsey, for there were few cheers and usually stony silence for the progress of Tunney as he poked Dempsey around the ring, and the only loud cheers were when Dempsey managed to land a few solid blows. It was a strangely silent and unenthusiastic crowd" (*New York Times,* September 24). [see **Silence vs. Noise**] Then "they started yelling. They seemed to forget their own discomfort and they shouted [Dempsey's] name" (Heimer, 23). Dempsey himself is no less astonished by this reaction than the journalists. As he recalls in his autobiography, "To my surprise, I was loudly cheered as I marched from the ring, more than I had ever been cheered before. People were screaming, 'Champ, Champ!' Could it be that the loss was really a victory?" (Dempsey and Dempsey, 201ff.).

Despite his civic virtues and his admirable boxing skills, Tunney is not a popular champion. But why has the defeat of September 23 transformed Dempsey into a popular hero? A possible answer to this question lies in a scene from Hemingway's novel *The Sun Also Rises.* During the fiesta in Pamplona, Brett, who is the central object of desire for all the male protagonists in the novel, enters into a passionate erotic relationship with a young bullfighter. Nobody is more jealous than Robert Cohn, the former "middleweight champion of Princeton" (Hemingway, 4). Although for him boxing has never been anything other, or anything more, than a chance to overcome his inferiority complex and his resentment as a Jew in a WASP-dominated social world, Cohn is a skillful boxer—and therefore finds it easy to beat up his rival in Brett's hotel room. Yet not only does this "victory" fail to help Cohn overcome his jealousy, but defeat makes the bullfighter even more attractive to Brett than his triumphs at the corrida:

> It seems the bullfighter fellow was sitting on the bed. He'd been knocked down about fifteen times, and he wanted to fight some more. Brett held him and wouldn't let him get up. He was weak, but Brett couldn't hold him, and he got up. Then Cohn said he wouldn't hit him again. Said he couldn't do it. Said it would be wicked. So the bullfighter chap sort of rather staggered over to him. Cohn went back against the wall. "So you won't hit me?" "No," said Cohn, "I'd be ashamed to." So the bullfighter fellow hit him just as hard as he could in the face, and then sat down on the floor. He couldn't get up, Brett said. Cohn wanted to pick him up and carry him to bed. He said if Cohn helped him he'd kill him, and he'd kill him anyway this morning if Cohn wasn't out of town. Cohn was crying, and Brett had told him off, and he wanted to shake hands. (Hemingway, 210)

In the ritual of bullfighting, victory and defeat do not exist. And although they do exist at the championship level of boxing, victory and defeat are not what the fascination with boxing is all about. Rather, boxing is about "Sein zum Tode" ("being-toward-death") and "Vorlaufen zum Tode" ("anticipation of death"; Heidegger, par. 7ff.). [see **Immanence = Transcendence (Death)**] Boxing has the potential to make death present to the spectators and, if Heidegger is right, it may thus help free them from multiple fears by which they unconsciously try to avoid the awareness of death in their everyday lives (par. 51, 53). Death is an integral part of man's physical life, since it brings that life to an end, and the anticipation of death therefore cannot be a function exclusively of the mind. This is an aspect of the existential analysis of death that Heidegger does not discuss. In order to imagine death, one must have the experience of exposing one's body to the threat of its destruction. Could this be why spectators are in awe of prizefighters, whose bodies bear the traces of almost lethal violence? Might this explain why journalists openly express their disappointment with a title bout that does not end in a knockout? "It was a disappointing transfer of a heavyweight title in one respect. The battle did not end in a knockout. Indeed, through its ten rounds the struggle held not even a knockdown. This was due to the fact that Tunney is not a finishing or destructive hitter" (*New York Times*, September 24). The spectators' sympathy never belongs to those whose skills and sobriety allow them to win a fight without facing death. On the twenty-third of September, 144,468 spectators in Philadelphia and 15 million radio listeners find the enlightened dream of controlling their bodies transformed into the utopian nightmare of consuming them.

Related Entries

Airplanes, Americans in Paris, Automobiles, Bars, Bullfighting, Endurance, Movie Palaces, Mountaineering, Ocean Liners, Revues, Roof Gardens, Wireless Communication, Silence vs. Noise, Sobriety vs. Exuberance, Uncertainty vs. Reality, Immanence = Transcendence (Death), Male = Female (Gender Trouble), Present = Past (Eternity)

References

Sam André and Nat Fleischer, *A Pictorial History of Boxing.* New York, 1981.
Associated Students of Stanford University, eds., *The 1926 Quad.* Stanford, 1926.
Berliner Tageblatt.
Jorge Luis Borges, *El tamaño de mi esperanza* (1926). Buenos Aires, 1993.
Bertolt Brecht, "Der Kinnhaken" and *Der Lebenslauf des Boxers Samson Körner* (1926). In *Gesammelte Werke,* vol 11. Frankfurt, 1967.
Anthony Burgess, *Ernest Hemingway.* Hamburg, 1980.
Caras y Caretas.
Chronik 1926: Tag für Tag in Wort und Bild. Dortmund, 1985.
Jean Cocteau, *Orphée: Tragédie en un acte* (1926). Paris, 1927.
Jack Dempsey and Barbara Piattelli Dempsey, *Dempsey.* New York, 1977.
Lorenzo Díaz, *La radio en España, 1923–1993.* Madrid, 1992.
A. S. Eddington, *The Internal Constitution of the Stars.* Cambridge, 1926.
Oskar Maurus Fontana, "Was arbeiten Sie? Gespräch mit Robert Musil" (1926). In Anton Kaes, ed., *Weimarer Republik: Manifeste und Dokumente zur deutschen Literatur, 1918–1933.* Stuttgart, 1983.
Martin Heidegger, *Sein und Zeit* (written 1926, published 1927). Tübingen, 1984.
Mel Heimer, *The Long Count.* New York, 1969.
Ernest Hemingway, *The Sun Also Rises.* New York, 1926.
Jürgen Kolbe, *Heller Zauber: Thomas Mann in Munich, 1894–1933.* Hamburg, 1987.
Theodor Lessing, "Psychologie des Rauchens" (1926). In *"Ich warf eine*

Flaschenpost ins Eismeer der Geschichte": Essays und Feuilletons, 1923–1933. Neuwied, 1986.

Werner Mittenzwei, *Das Leben des Bertolt Brecht oder: der Umgang mit den Weltraetseln,* vol. 1. Berlin, 1986.

Michael Morris, *Madam Valentino: The Many Lives of Natacha Rambova.* New York, 1991.

New York Review of Books.

New York Times.

Lawrence S. Ritter and Mark Rucker, *The Babe: A Life in Pictures.* New York, 1988.

Robert W. Rydell, *World of Fairs: The Century-of-Progress Expositions.* Chicago, 1993.

Victor Shklovsky, *Third Factory* (1926). Trans. Richard Sheldon. Ann Arbor, 1977.

Die wilden Zwanziger: Weimar und die Welt, 1919–1933. Berlin, 1986.

BULLFIGHTING

"Bullfight. Repulsive, deathly impression despite the varied wild, lively, and grandiose images. The slaughter of the decrepit, helpless old horses whose entrails are ripped from their bodies and sopped up with bloody rags is infuriating and vile. The beautiful, young, fiery bull enters, and after a half an hour is dragged out as a dead piece of meat. It evoked in me only anger and pity . . . I become more and more tired and exhausted. Finally, it was as if I'd been struck with an ax: inwardly, I was completely apathetic and filled to the brim with disgust. The whole night, it was as if I were continually being awakened by an intense, deafening noise." With such words of moral indignation, Harry Graf Kessler, whose mode of life connects the political world of Weimar Germany with high modern culture, reacts to a bullfight in Barcelona on Sunday, April 18. But Kessler's emotions cannot be quite as unequivocal as the words in his diary suggest. For only two weeks later, on May 2, he attends another corrida. This time, Kessler tries hard to separate the positive aspects of his impressions from the negative ones: "Yet again to the bullfight in the afternoon. A young, very deft matador with a sharply defined, almost Mongolian yellow-brown face: Agrabeno. Complete mastery, a dancer before the bull. It was beautiful and worth seeing, but the cowardly, cruel manner in which the horse was given to the bull as a prize remains appalling and horrifying. All in all, a display of shocking brutality, because the same people who turn this disgusting torture of animals into a show are the most graceful and serene dancers of Sardanas." Despite Kessler's best efforts, the distinction between the grace of the bullfighter's "dancing" movements and the concreteness of the killing does not quite eliminate his ambivalence. Kessler thus ends up doing what intellectuals (at least German intellectuals since the days of Hegel) so often do when they are bothered by ambiguities in their perception of the world. He switches from a tone of aesthetic and moral judgment to one of historico-philosophical speculation in which he tries to explain how cruelty and beauty can both be present in the bullfighting spectacle: "Harshness and grace, cruelty and beauty are tightly woven together here, as in ancient Greece. It seems to me that the Spanish soul is far more similar in structure to that of the Greeks than to that of any other European people, maybe because they have been formed by similar geographies and historical conditioning. Both the Greeks and the Spanish have, in decisive centuries, become *border peoples* protecting a very advanced culture whose existence is threatened by the Orient." [see **Center vs. Periphery**]

The "structure" of the "Spanish soul," as Kessler calls it, fascinates artists and their audiences all across the European-American world. Rudolph Valentino has become an international star with *The Four Horsemen of the Apocalypse,* a film based on a novel by the Spanish author Vicente Blasco Ibáñez, and a young actress from Sweden named Greta Garbo is inaugurating her Hollywood career with *The Torrent* and *The Temptress,* two movies likewise based on books by Blasco Ibáñez. Garbo receives enthusiastic reviews for her performance in *The Temptress,* where she enacts "the tragedy of a woman . . . who was being pursued by men who lusted for her body but did not love her spirit," but the "bursting desire for life" that she finds in John Gilbert, her costar in the following productions, inspires her to an even greater level of intensity in her subsequent work (Gronowicz, 205, 213). A touch of Spain is thus inevitable in the first real-life date of such a passionate couple: "I seated myself in Yackie's [i.e., Gilbert's] sports car, and we rode slowly through Hollywood. Yackie sang some Spanish melodies, and I gazed at the fields shining under the moon" (221). From Hollywood to Berlin, concepts such as "desire for life" and "tragedy" invariably become associated with Spain, and references to them often conclude with evocations of the bullfight. In a letter of May 13, mailed from Hendaye, France, where he is living in exile, the Spanish essayist and philosopher Miguel de Unamuno expresses his radical contempt for Miguel Primo de

Rivera's dictatorial government by calling the ongoing Spanish-Moroccan war "a bloody game, or a bullfight" (Unamuno, 193). Unamuno's bullfighting metaphor is immediately followed by a description of this political situation as tragic: "They can have the masculinity of males, of which they boast, but not the virility of the manly, or even the humanity of men. In a most solemn and tragic hour of Christian European civilization, they are guided by the mean motives of thieves and they sacrifice the most sacred material and moral interests of the fatherland to an undertaking worthy of brawling soldiers from the barracks." [see **Male vs. Female**]

What do this "solemn moment" in Christian European civilization and the title character of *The Temptress* have in common that makes them both seem "tragic"? And what does tragedy have to do with bullfighting? Both concepts refer to situations that imply a specific paradox. In tragedy, as in bullfighting, the confrontation with overwhelmingly strong opponents makes individuals aware of their own impotence—but they succeed, nevertheless, in displaying strength and dignity by maintaining a particularly intense presence. [see **Action vs. Impotence, Action = Impotence (Tragedy)**] Bullfighting becomes associated with tragedy because both the bull and the toreador are incarnations of potentially defeated strength. The bull and the bullfighter impose upon each other a direct confrontation with death, which is a part of life, life's inevitable fate. [see **Boxing, Immanence = Transcendence (Death)**] The bull is a symbol for the strength of life [see **Authenticity = Artificiality (Life)**], for the threat of death, and for lethal danger. In Ricardo Güiraldes' novel about the Argentinian Pampa, *Don Segundo Sombra*, these three connotations merge in a description of a herd of bulls: "Meanwhile, the herd raced closer in a silent throng. It was really a sight to see . . . It drew near like a single immense animal, carried by its own momentum in a fixed direction. We heard the dull thunder of the thousands and thousands of hoofbeats, the laborious breathing. The flesh itself seemed to produce a deep sound of exhaustion and pain" (Güiraldes, 219).

Whereas the "tragic" meaning of the bullfighting ritual emerges from the simultaneity of strength and impotence, it is the staging of an oscillation between seeking death and meting out death that imparts the structure of a tragedy to the corrida (Gumbrecht, 474ff.). Bullfighting shows, on the one hand, how nature, dominated by man, can become a lethal threat to man. In an interview with the magazine *Blanco y Negro*, the famous toreador Rafael, known as "El Gallo," insists that nobody will ever be able to control the bull completely and thus that sudden changes of fate are inevitable. All of his unique knowledge about bulls and bullfighting could not protect Rafael's brother Joselito, who is already canonized and remembered as the greatest toreador of all time, from receiving a fatal goring: "You don't know anything. It's all a question of luck. My brother knew more than anybody, and look at him now" (*Blanco y Negro,* 143). On the other hand, the final stage of the bullfight obliges the matador to provoke, for one last time, an outburst of the bull's potentially lethal force—and this very movement becomes lethal for the bull because it enables the bullfighter to plunge his sword into the animal's neck. Romero, the young bullfighter in Hemingway's novel *The Sun Also Rises,* masterfully enacts this oscillation between seeking death and imposing death: "He profiled directly in front of the bull, drew the sword out of the folds of the muleta and sighted along the blade. The bull watched him. Romero spoke to the bull and tapped one of his feet. The bull charged and Romero waited for the charge, the muleta held low, sighting along the blade, his feet firm" (Hemingway, 229). Emphasizing even more strongly the dual nature of the death element—a threat for the bullfighter which he turns into the animal's death—Henri de Montherlant describes how Alban, the hero of *Les Bestiaires,* exposes himself to lethal danger with a first, unsuccessful *estocada,* before he successfully deals the final blow to the bull's body:

> For a moment, he saw the ray of light, his sword, between his hand and the bull's back, glittering with golden blood, like the longer ray that, coming from the sun, struck the very body of Mithras. The shock knocked his body over onto the bull's left flank, and resonated in his wrist, making him think that he had broken it. He rolled over on the ground and stood up again, holding his wrist . . . The beast pushed the sword away. He picked it up without confusion, knowing that this was nothing but a slight hitch and that the next thrust would be decisive . . . He fell on the animal like a falcon, and then stood up, reeling, his hand on his heart, which was choking him. He stood before the beast and gasped for breath. The fight was over now." (Montherlant, 224)

Until the last gesture in a corrida, man's domination over nature must include the danger of becoming nature's victim. In an interesting analogy with boxing, illustrated by the frequent boxing metaphors in descriptions of bullfights (e.g., Montherlant, 206), a newspaper article on the championship bout between Gene Tunney and Jack Dempsey [see **Boxing**] compares Dempsey to a bull whose potentially lethal strength has to be controlled at every moment by his opponent's accomplished technique: "Tunney not only standing fearlessly before the bull-like rushes of Dempsey, the killer, but meeting this attack flat-footed and dealing out his blows with a marksman's accuracy . . ., or dancing away and pecking at the charging human in front of him (*New York Times,* September 24). Both boxing and bullfighting celebrate the presence of death, and from the presence of death comes the feeling that something irreducibly "real" is at stake in these rituals. [see **Authenticity vs. Artificiality, Uncertainty vs. Reality**]

The movements of the corrida become a continual oscillation between immobility and aggression. This is why bullfighting often looks like a dance or like a strictly choreographed ritual (Montherlant, 217; Kracauer, 9). [see **Dancing**] Whereas moments of immobility expose the body of the toreador and the body of the bull to the danger of death, their movement embodies their lethal threat. It is this contrast between death-defying immobility and death-bearing movement which Montherlant tries to capture in a series of drawings that depict the naked body of the bullfighter Juan Belmonte exposed to a bull's furious attack (Sipriot, 117ff.). Based on the same convergence of immobility and movement, the final moment of the corrida comes close to staging death as an experience of presence. The clean lethal blow of the bullfighter's sword creates a visible contrast between the last moment of the bull's life—and the following moment, in which the bull is already dead: "The beast staggered on its hind legs, tried to straighten itself, and at last fell back on its side, fulfilling its destiny. For a few seconds longer it blinked its eyes, and its breathing could be seen . . . It arrived ceremoniously at the height of its spasm, like a man at the height of his pleasure, and, like him, it stayed there, immobile" (Montherlant, 225). Trying to make death present by assigning death a place within life is a crucial matter in a world whose belief in the traditional religious conceptions of transcendence has largely vanished (Heidegger, 246ff.).

A final element in the complex chain of associations that characterizes the experience and the discourse of bullfighting is a longing for an impossible conflation of destruction and union. From the perspective of such longing, the relation between bull and bullfighter becomes one of erotic desire: "Then without taking a step forward, he became one with the bull" (Hemingway, 229). Standing next to the bull's dead body which, only a moment before, was a lethal threat to his own body, Montherlant's bullfighter hero experiences killing and sexual desire as indistinguishable: "He knew now that he had loved it, this monster, that all of his life had been focused on it from the moment when he had left the girl, that everything that troubles the consciousness is but a single trouble, that his terror and his hatred were nothing but forms of his love" (Montherlant, 225). [see **Mountaineering, Murder**] As a sexual combat, the corrida causes continual shifts in gender roles between the bull and the toreador. [see **Male = Female (Gender Trouble)**] In the initial stages of their "ritual dance," according to Siegfried Kracauer, the young bullfighter becomes the female object of the bull's male desire—a "little doll," a "tall heroine," an "orange female" (9). But in its analysis of the final moment of lethal destruction, Kracauer's "Bewegungsstudie" ("study of movement") abounds with symbols of maleness attributed to the toreador: "The boy unfurls a cape as red as a cock's comb. The blade which he hides behind this curtain is so long that he could use it to climb into the air . . . It is one single, gleaming, fleeting stab which pierces the wall" (10). [see **Male vs. Female**]

Bullfighting inspires the awe of a religious ritual because it promises to make present objects of transcendental experience. Death and desire are supposed to become visible. But ultimately bullfighting cannot keep this promise. The final stage of the corrida comes infinitesimally close to making death present, while the moment of death remains that of an imperceptible transition. Likewise, the desire floating between the bull and the toreador finds only an indirect articulation in the deconstruction of the culturally constructed gender binarism. Such multiple ambiguities and oscillations in bullfights elicit an endless interpretive discourse among the spectators, a discourse which never quite manages to overcome the resistance of its object to any stable conceptual constructions. On March 16, Henri de Montherlant organizes a public event in Paris, at the Vélodrome d'Hiver, which is announced under the title "Tauromachie . . . et Littérature." In front of five thousand spectators, Montherlant inaugurates his program by reading a text on "the cult of the bull through the ages." But eager for the presence of death rather than for a mediation through words, the crowd interrupts the poet in the rudest possible way: "Shut up! . . . The bulls! The bulls!" (Sipriot, 122f.). Since authors like Montherlant do not seem to understand that it is the impossibility of fulfillment which makes the desires underlying the bullfight so strong, they give in to the temptation to transform it into a religion. Thus, they return to the very dichotomy between immanence and transcendence whose blurring makes the bullfight so fascinating. [see **Immanence vs. Transcendence**] *Les Bestiaires* ends with the description of a utopian future in which an ancient "cult of the bull" dominates society. Montherlant even invents hymns in honor of the ancient and future bull deity: "I am the bull that, from Asia / to the forests of Liguria, / has ruled through Joy, Art, and Blood / over the peoples of the Mediterranean" (244).

In D. H. Lawrence's novel *The Plumed Serpent*, the initial experience of a Mexican bullfight ends in deep disillusionment for Kate, the female protagonist: "The last of Kate's illusions concerning bull-fights came down with a flop. These were the darlings of the mob? These were the gallant toreadors? Gallant? Just about as gallant as assistants in a butcher's shop. Lady-killers? Ugh!" (15). It is, however, this disappointment with bullfighting which disposes Kate to accept a brutal yet intensely fulfilling sexual subjection to her husband Cipriano, the founder of a bull religion which is supposed to become the revolutionary future of Mexico. Hemingway brings Brett's love affair with the young bullfighter Romero to a very different conclusion. The more strongly Romero's feelings correspond to the powerful sexual attraction that Brett experiences, the more she understands how impossible it will be for him to become part of her life, the life of a "lost generation" [see **Americans in Paris**], without losing the purity of his desire: "'You know I'd have lived with him if I hadn't seen it was bad for him. We got along damned well . . . I'm thirty-four, you know. I'm not going to be one of these bitches that ruins children" (254). Brett—and Hemingway—understand that bullfighting is neither immanence nor transcendence: it stages the impossibility of ever bringing the oscillation between the two to an end.

Related Entries

Americans in Paris, Boxing, Dancing, Mountaineering, Murder, Revues, Action vs. Impotence, Authenticity vs. Artificiality, Center vs. Periphery, Immanence vs. Transcendence, Male vs. Female, Uncertainty vs. Reality,

Action = Impotence (Tragedy), Authenticity = Artificiality (Life), Immanence = Transcendence (Death), Male = Female (Gender Trouble)

References

Antología de Blanco y Negro, 1891–1936. Vol. 9. Madrid, 1986.

Ricardo Güiraldes, *Don Segundo Sombra* (1926). Buenos Aires 1927.

Antoni Gronowicz, *Garbo*. New York, 1990.

Hans Ulrich Gumbrecht, "Inszenierte Zusammenbrueche, oder: Tragödie und Paradox." In Hans Ulrich Gumbrecht and K. Ludwig Pfeiffer, eds., *Paradoxien, Dissonanzen, Zusammenbrueche: Situationen offener Epistemologie*. Frankfurt, 1991.

Martin Heidegger, *Sein und Zeit* (written 1926, published 1927). Tübingen, 1984.

Ernest Hemingway, *The Sun Also Rises*. New York, 1926.

Harry Graf Kessler, *Tagebücher, 1918–1937*. Frankfurt, 1961.

Siegfried Kracauer, "Knabe und Stier: Bewegungsstudie" (1926). In *Das Ornament der Masse: Essays*. Frankfurt, 1977.

D. H. Lawrence, *The Plumed Serpent*. London, 1926.

Henri de Montherlant, *Les Bestiaires*. Paris, 1926.

New York Times.

Pierre Sipriot, ed., *Album Montherlant*. Paris, 1979.

Miguel de Unamuno, *Epistolario inédito* (1926). Madrid, 1991.

CREMATION

About one-fifth of the obituaries published in Berlin newspapers announce that the bodies of the deceased will be cremated. A large majority of these bodies are those of men [see **Male vs. Female**], most of whom have died in the prime of life. Although following no specific stylistic pattern, the wording of the obituaries tends to be sober: "Suddenly and unexpectedly, my dear husband departed, on Sunday afternoon. The devoted father of my child, the hotel manager Max John, just turned forty-seven. Next of kin: Anni John, born Hirning, and daughter Carola John. The cremation will take place Friday, June 11, 1926, at 8 P.M., in the Gerichtstraße Crematorium" (*Der Tag,* June 10). Only in a few of the obituaries that mention cremation are friends and former colleagues of the deceased asked to refrain from visits of condolence, a request which otherwise appears to be the general rule in Berlin. While the obituaries for some important people who will be cremated do include such a request for distance, most of the survivors seem to fear that the decision of their deceased relative in favor of cremation will have an alienating effect. This could be why they are eager to receive visits of condolence—expressions of continued friendship.

Obituaries published in the Berlin newspapers refer almost exclusively to members of the upper middle class and to high-ranking civil servants. If within these limits no specific social group or single profession stands out among those who opt for cremation, their death announcements create the impression that they have mostly lived in situations that emphasize individuality. There are the fifty-four-year-old "artistic painter" Max Fabian (*Berliner Tageblatt,* March 28), and the economist Dr. Ernst Lichtenstein, a single parent whose death is mourned by his colleagues from the "board of Hartwig Kantorowicz A.G.," and by his mother, "Julie Lichtenstein, born Zadek": "After a long period of suffering, my dearly beloved son, Dr. Ernst Lichtenstein, the devoted and selfless father of two boys, passed away quietly" (*Berliner Tageblatt,* October 8). One of the men who is cremated perished while actively seeking to confront death: "On August 19, 1926, at 2 P.M., my dear husband, our devoted father and grandfather, the engraver William Hartwig, age fifty, was killed in a mountain-climbing accident . . . The cremation will take place on August 30, 1926, at 4:30 P.M., in the Gerichtstraße Crematorium" (*Berliner Tageblatt,* August 29. [see **Boxing, Bullfighting, Endurance, Mountaineering, Immanence = Transcendence (Death)**)]

To have oneself cremated is an act of sobriety and worldliness. [see **Sobriety vs. Exuberance**] The most frequently cited reasons for such a decision are the considerably lower cost of this method in comparison with traditional burial, a concern for public hygiene, and, in tandem with the argument for hygiene, a demographically based fear that the expansion of cemeteries will end up reducing the space for the living. With a strong dose of sarcasm for those who wish to preserve their corpses, George Bernard Shaw brings all of these motives together: "Dead bodies can be cremated. All of them ought to be; for earth burial, a horrible practice, will some day be prohibited by law, not only because it is hideously unaesthetic, but because the dead would crowd the living off the earth if it could be carried out to its end of preserving our bodies for their resurrection on an imaginary day of judgment" (Mitford, 162–163). Shaw's reaction suggests that, among those who choose cremation, a motive even stronger than the wish to affirm one's rationality and sobriety maybe the desire to implicitly negate certain concepts of transcendence which have traditionally dominated in Western cultures. [see **Mummies, Immanence vs. Transcendence**]

Despite the truly passionate battles fought—and sometimes won—by pro-cremationists during the second half of the nineteenth century (Mitford, 162ff.), the Catholic Church and most Jewish communities continue to resist this practice. If Dr. Ernst Lichtenstein and his mother, Julie Lichtenstein, born Zadek, are Jews, as their names seem to indicate, cremation, for them, could be the ultimate logical conclusion of "emancipation" from their cultural roots and of integration into lay society. But as long as the renunciation of religion is a civil right which only a minority of citizens decide to exercise, the act of cremation connotes a claim to individuality on behalf of the deceased. [see **Individuality vs. Collectivity**] Whoever supports cremation seems an independent thinker and an ethically responsible person trying to live up to the demands of the Kantian categorical imperative. Opting for cremation also means making a distinction between the functions fulfilled by the body during one's lifetime and the ecological burden which the same body as a corpse will represent for the community of survivors. [see **Authenticity = Artificiality (Life)**] But such rationality regarding the material side of human life is not easy to distinguish from an aggressive spirit of asceticism played out on the body. Thus, paradoxically, the sobriety of the pro-cremationists bears strong religious connotations. [see **Hunger Artists**] It is in a religious sense—namely, as a holocaust implying the certainty of ultimate redemption—that the Communist poet Johannes Becher describes capitalism and war as a crematorium of proletarians: "The hell of fire swallows you. Meat coffin rugs / Rolled into one. Stomachs sliced. / Break, oh you bones! Already they bake into clumps. / As fine dust they trickle out of the chimneys" (Becher, 27–28).

Most important, perhaps, choosing cremation presupposes the courage to face the fact of one's own death before this death occurs. Nothing is more generally acknowledged, at least in Europe, than that such courage is a sign of composure (Heidegger, 235ff.)—and nothing represents more strongly an attitude of heroic subjectivity. But although in Europe (and especially in England) cremation becomes a way of confronting death as a part of human life, in the United States the funeral industry, since the beginning of the century, has successfully promoted embalming, the opposite way of coming close to a simultaneity between death and life. Whereas with cremation one chooses, during one's lifetime, to have one's dead body transformed into nothingness, embalming preserves the corpse of the deceased "in the semblance of normality, . . . unmarred by the ravages of illness, disease or mutilation" (Mitford, 71; Editors of Consumer Reports, 88ff.).

Related Entries

Boxing, Bullfighting, Endurance, Hunger Artists, Mountaineering, Mummies, Authenticity vs. Artificiality, Immanence vs. Transcendence,

Individuality vs. Collectivity, Male vs. Female, Authenticity = Artificiality (Life), Immanence = Transcendence (Death)

References

Johannes R. Becher, *Machinenrhythmen*. Berlin, 1926.

Berliner Tageblatt.

Editors of Consumer Reports, *Funerals: Consumers' Last Rights*. New York, 1977.

Martin Heidegger, *Sein und Zeit* (written 1926, published 1927). Tübingen, 1984.

Jessica Mitford, *The American Way of Death*. New York, 1978.

Der Tag.

DANCING

As the only artist of the American dance and music show *La Revue nègre,* the nineteen-year-old Josephine Baker, who within a few weeks has become the darling of the Parisian public, receives a contract to appear at the Folies Bergères. During the winter months, however, she gives two daily performances (at 8:30 P.M. and 11:15 P.M.) at Berlin's Nelson Theater. It is in Berlin that her dancing begins to fascinate the intellectuals of the Old World. Max Reinhardt, who dominates the German-speaking theater scene with his productions in Berlin, Vienna, and Salzburg, tries to persuade Baker to make a "serious" career on the stage: "The expressive control of the whole body, the spontaneity of motion, the rhythm, the bright emotional color: these are your treasures—no, not yours alone—these are American treasures. With such control of the body, such pantomime, I believe I could portray emotion as it has never before been portrayed" (Rose, 85).

There is a certain ambiguity in Reinhardt's reaction to Josephine Baker's dancing. On the one hand, he is impressed with its sheer form and its sensual presence ("the spontaneity of motion, the rhythm, the bright emotional color"). But on the other hand, he wants to see it as an "expression" or as a "portrait"—i.e., as a signifier for something "deep" (Reinhardt speaks of "emotions") that comes to the surface. [see **Authenticity vs. Artificiality**] Full of enthusiasm, Reinhardt phones his influential friend Harry Graf Kessler late in the evening on Saturday, February 13, and invites him to meet Baker at the apartment of the playwright

Karl Gustav Vollmüller. The entry in Kessler's diary referring to this occasion shows an oscillation similar to Reinhardt's: "Baker danced with extreme grotesqueness and purity of style, like an Egyptian or an archaic figure that performs acrobatics without ever losing its style. The dancers of Salamo and Tutankhamen must have danced this way. She does this for hours, apparently without getting tired, always finding new forms, as if in a game, like a playful child. Her body does not get warm; rather, her skin maintains its fresh, cool dryness. A charming creature, but almost completely unerotic" (Kessler, 455). [see **Mummies**] It remains unclear what exactly Kessler and Reinhardt see Baker expressing. The signified of which they "read" her body as a signifier is something vaguely archaic, something authentic, something more real perhaps than the reality of the contemporary world. At the same time, however, Kessler describes Baker's dancing as a pure surface phenomenon, consisting of endless varieties of form. This makes it into the movement of a body that has no more erotic appeal than the body of a child, a body whose skin remains cool and impenetrable. [see **Gomina**]

Or could this view simply be a reaction on the part of Kessler's offended masculinity? He is shocked to see the nude Baker tightly embracing a young woman in a tuxedo: "Between Reinhardt, Vollmüller, and myself lay Baker and Landshoff, wrapped around each other like a pair of beautiful young lovers" (Kessler, 456). [see **Male = Female (Gender Trouble)**] Since there is no easy way out of his confusion, Kessler goes to see Baker's show at the Nelson Theater the following week. But the only certainty he can find lies in the feeling that she stands for something that is stronger than his own culture. This something, he writes in his diary, is both "ultraprimitive and ultramodern": "Went again to the Negro revue at the Nelson in the evening (Josephine Baker). They are somewhere between the jungle and the skyscraper. The same is true of her music, jazz, in its color and rhythm. It is ultraprimitive and ultramodern. Their tension generates their forceful style; the same is true of the Russians. By comparison, our own culture is tame—without inner tension and therefore without style, like a limp bow string" (458, February 17). [see **Roof Gardens, Authenticity = Artificiality (Life)**]

At their very first meeting with Baker, Kessler, Reinhardt, and Vollmüller form the project of writing a ballet for her, "taken half from jazz, half from oriental music, perhaps from Richard Strauss" (Kessler, 456). [see **Jazz**] The script they end up writing is hopelessly trivial. Baker is supposed to play a dancer whose nude body awakens the young King Salomo's desire. But the more gifts she receives from the king, the less she is willing to yield to his advances. Then, in a final movement, her young lover appears—in a black tuxedo (460ff.). Baker still ignores this text, but she feels strongly inspired by an "expressionist" sculpture from Kessler's art collection: "Then she began to move, strongly and with grotesque expressions, in front of the grand Maillol sculpture. Clearly she entered into a dialogue with it. She looked long at it, imitating its position, unimpressed by the uncanny rigidity and force of its expression. A childlike priestess imparting movement to her body and her goddess. One could see Maillol was much more interesting and alive for her than men such as Max Reinhardt, Vollmüller, and myself" (461, February 24). For many weeks, Baker is undecided about whether to return to Paris and fulfill her contract with the Folies Bergères or to accept Reinhardt's offer and stay in Germany. What finally persuades her that the world of cabaret rather than the serious world of German theater offers the appropriate environment for her dancing is the news that the composer Irving Berlin has been hired for her show in Paris: "Herr Reinhardt hadn't mentioned Irving Berlin" (Rose, 89). The project of integrating Josephine Baker's body into the space of theatrical representation has failed.

Dancing is a synchronization of the rhythm of music with the rhythm of body movement. Rhythm is movement as form, form reconciled with the dimension of temporality, which is inherent in any kind of movement. At first glance, the temporality of movement seems to resist the stability of form (Gumbrecht, 717ff.). [see **Present vs. Past**] But movement can become form through the repetition of basic sequential patterns. Repetition makes the recurrence of such sequential patterns predictable, and it is thus that the form of certain sequential patterns becomes associated with the movement they are constituting. Their form makes this movement recognizable among movements that are based on different patterns, as well as among movements without form. Since rhythm creates form through recurrence, a given rhythm cannot produce anything new (although it may allow for variation within certain basic patterns). As soon as the sequential patterns underlying a rhythm begin to change, it ceases to exist. This is why rhythm inevitably exists in tension with the dual-level nature of signification and meaning, where different forms can stand for the same content (Gumbrecht, 720ff.).

Fascination with rhythm points to a fascination with the separation between the human body, which is capable of incarnating (that is, of becoming and being) a rhythm, and the human mind, which, as source of the dual-level relation between signifiers and signified, is never fully compatible with rhythm, because it cannot help associating becoming and being with meanings (Golston). Putting a body under the sway of musical rhythm therefore sets this body apart from the mind. In *A Vision*, William Butler Yeats has one of the participants in a conversation on poetry complain about a loss of "rhythmical speech," which (he believes) results from realism's fixation on representation: "You will remember that a few years before the Great War the realists drove the last remnants of rhythmical speech out of the theatre" (33). A conception of art that focuses exclusively on meaning-constitution and world-reference must neglect the sensual qualities of its material surfaces: "The realists turn our words into gravel, but the musicians and the singers turn them into honey and oil" (34). For Michael Robartes, another protagonist of Yeats's fictional colloquium, this very insight comes from a paradoxical love relationship with a ballet dancer: "I went to Rome and there fell violently in love with a ballet-dancer who had not an idea in her head. All might have been well had I been content to take what came; had I understood that her coldness and cruelty became in the transfiguration of the body an inhuman majesty; that I adored in her body what I hated in her will" (37).

"Transfiguration," not "expression," is the key concept in Yeats's reflections. The relation that he sees between the "body" and the "will" of the dancer is not a relation that follows the binary logic of the signifier and the signified. It is a transfiguration of one substance into a different substance. On the multiple social levels of Yeats's, Baker's, and Reinhardt's cultures, and in a wide variety of forms, dancing responds to this very distinction between a mode of convergence and a mode of divergence in thinking the mind/body relationship. This distinction also dominates the debate about *Ausdruckstanz,* or "expressive dancing," in Weimar Germany (von Soden and Schmidt, 152ff.). For a select intellectual public, Mary Wigman, who stands at the center of this movement, dances the "expression" of elementary emotions (such as passion, grief, mourning) and of elementary existential situations (such as idolatry, prayer, witchcraft). Often she combines her dancing with the recitation of classical texts—and there is a good chance that Max Reinhardt's insistence on "reading" the movements of Josephine Baker's body as "expressions" goes back to Wigman's widely admired style. In contrast, Valeska Gert, Wigman's main competitor on the Berlin dance scene, is a star of the cabaret stage. Instead of expressing meanings which are supposed to come from an "archaic depth," she strives to become a part of the contemporary world's "concrete reality" by portraying prostitutes, go-betweens, and circus girls. [see **Uncertainty vs. Reality**] It is thus no accident that the press associates Valeska Gert's dancing with Josephine Baker's (von Soden and Schmidt, 158).

The contrast between dancing as expression and dancing as body rhythm mirrors the central antinomy within the political world. The Italian novelist Mario Puccini sees the fox-trot, together with a number of other imported American dances (often called "jazz dances") as an obstacle to the development of Fascist art as an art of expression: "The coming of a Fascist art (that is, an art which improves the race and at the same time expresses it) is impossible so long as thousands and thousands of young people read short stories and novels—you know the ones I mean—that are set in nightclubs or theaters, and full of disreputable operettas and even more disreputable fox-trots" (Puccini, 258). At the opposite end of the political spectrum, the Communist poet Johannes R. Becher, while dutifully attacking the moral decadence of nightclubs and prostitution (Becher, 93, 99), consistently uses dancing as a metaphor for social and individual emancipation: "Oh, dance yourself out of / Your splintering thighs, / Tuschka!" (61ff.). The generations are distinguished by their preference for different styles of dancing, even more than by their preference for different political and social groups. [see **Present vs. Past**] In Thomas Mann's story "Unordnung und frühes Leid" ("Disorder and Early Sorrow"), Professor Cornelius fails to bridge the gap between his own taste and that of his teenaged children—and his reaction to a dance party which they organize at his house becomes even more negative when he sees what a strong emotional impact these modern rhythms have on his beloved four-year-old daughter [see **Gramophones**]:

> The young people dance eagerly—so far as one can it call dancing, this movement that they perform with such quiet devotion. Indeed, they move in strange embraces and in a new style, propelling their lower body by moving their shoulders and swaying their hips. They dance

slowly around the floor, obeying obscure rules, never growing tired, because one can't grow tired this way. No heaving breasts, no blushing. Here and there two girls dance together, sometimes even two boys; it's all the same to them. So they follow the exotic noises of the gramophone, which rotates under the sturdiest of needles to make the sound of the shimmies, fox-trots, and one-steps as loud as possible. The Double Fox, the African Shimmy, Java Dances, and Polka Creoles— wild, perfumed steps, now languid, now military style, with foreign rhythms, monotones with orchestral ornamentation, drums thumping and snapping, spewing out Negro amusement. (Mann, 514)

The younger generation is eager to assimilate the new rhythms of the fox-trot and the shimmy, the Charleston and the blackbottom. What many of them have learned in their professions comes out in their dancing: they let their bodies be coupled to rhythms imposed from outside. [see **Assembly Lines, Employees**] So tight is this coupling that the dancers relinquish all control over their bodies and continue moving until the point of total exhaustion. [see **Endurance**] So immediate is the connection of their individual bodies to the rhythm of the music that they need no longer be guided through coordination with a partner. Some contemporary observers hail this change as a new peak of gender emancipation. [see **Male = Female (Gender Trouble)**] Yet while the new dances certainly have a gender-neutralizing effect, they do not really foster individual freedom of choice; rather, they promote a shift from dependence on a partner to dependence on an external rhythm. Instead of a site of domination and surrender, the body of the dance partner becomes a site—or, rather, a point of reference—for association and coordination. This is the "deindividualizing" principle (Jelavich, 179ff.) of the kick-lines which conquer the revue stages, transforming the individual bodies of the "girls" into complex systems of well-coordinated limbs. [see **Revues**] This is also why the role of the gigolo does not turn into a role of surrender and therefore hardly ever humiliates male gender-pride. And, finally, this is why the new dancing bodies are so often perceived as pure, unerotic surface.

The erotic excitement of the interaction with a dance partner is replaced by the excitement of continually changing fashions in rhythm. Dance schools therefore emphasize the variety and novelty of the dances they teach: "To become an *exceptional* dancer—not merely a 'walk-around'—this is your opportunity to learn *all* of the latest Valencia, Fox Trot, Waltz, Tango, and Charleston steps for almost nothing! While becoming the very best dancer in your crowd, you will enjoy learning in a few private lessons and in a class of congenial people" (*New York Times,* September 22). Among the dances mentioned in this advertisement, the tango has a specific status, for two reasons. Together with the Valencia, and unlike the Charleston, it connotes, first, the "authenticity" of Spanish and Latin-American culture, which is the only current alternative to the "authenticity" generally attributed to the African and African-American worlds. [see **Bullfighting, Center vs. Periphery**] Second, among the dances performed by a couple, the tango is the only one that does not prescribe complementarity between the movements of the man and woman. Tango dancers look and act as if they did not see each other, and their bodies are supposed to follow the rhythm of the music independently from each other. Unlike the preestablished harmony of the traditional partner-dances, the harmony of the tango couple is staged either as emerging out of a free collaboration or as the—often violent—resolution of a potential conflict: "Not rounded, but broken, the rotation produces no center of gravity between the partners but oscillates from one to the other. If they stay at distance they lose each other, and will never come together" (Elsner and Müller, 318).

With its proliferation of old and new steps, dancing becomes assimilated to virtually every other form of entertainment. [see **Bars**] More than half the advertisements on the back page of the Berlin daily *8 Uhr–Abendblatt* invite the readers to dance events. With a slogan that seems inspired by the fashion for nonsense poetry, the Weidenhof, "Berlin's most spectacular dance palace," emphasizes the contrast between dull everydayness and the pleasure of moving one's body to the rhythm of the music: "When things become too lousy, come over to the Weidenhof" (October 19). Besides the "five-o'clock tea dance" with two orchestras, the Weidenhof offers, at 8 P.M. and for a public of spectators rather than dancers, a show by "Mme. Salome and her beautiful ballet. Twenty ladies of overwhelming grace and beauty." The Tanz-Cabaret Valencia features "five-o'clock tea dance, restaurant, bar, attractions," and a "lighted floor" which makes the dancers feel that they have found some other terrain than the stable ground of everyday reality. [see **Uncertainty vs. Reality**]

Such forms of light amusement, however, exist side-by-side with the seriousness of *Ausdruckstanz*. The premiere on Tuesday, December 14, of Arnold Fanck's film *Der Heilige Berg,* which marks Leni Riefenstahl's screen debut, is inaugurated by a young actress dancing to the music of Schubert's Unfinished Symphony (Riefenstahl, 59). [see **Mountaineering**] Next to the daily ad for the Nelson Theater, where Josephine Baker's German career has begun, the *8 Uhr–Abendblatt* announces, on October 19, a performance by Katjana Barbakoff, conjuring various ancient and exotic worlds: "Among the new dance styles: Majeftas Asiatika back to nature, a treasure preserved from the No Period" (October 19). The organizers of a ballroom event try to appeal to the older generation by launching, in Gothic letters, the "Senior Competition of the Berlin Blue-Orange Club, followed by a show under the auspices of the National Ballroom Dancing Association"; yet they also view children as potential customers of the dance palaces: "Parents who love their children take them to the world's first children's revue: 'All Puppets Dance.' A fairy-tale play in thirty scenes. Admiral Palace Theater" (October 22). The blurring of boundaries between the genders and among the various forms of participation in the dance world is epitomized by an advertise-ment for an establishment called Steinmeier am Bahnhof, Friedrichstraße 96, in the heart of Berlin's lesbian district (von Soden and Schmidt, 160). Under the heading "Täglich Tanz der schönen Frauen" ("Daily Dance of Beautiful Women"), it shows two women with haircuts *à la garçonne* dancing in a close embrace—with two smiling men gazing at them (October 2). [see **Male = Female (Gender Trouble)**]

Related Entries

Assembly Lines, Bars, Bullfighting, Employees, Endurance, Gomina, Gramophones, Jazz, Mountaineering, Mummies, Revues, Roof Gardens, Authenticity vs. Artificiality, Center vs. Periphery, Present vs. Past, Un-certainty vs. Reality, Authenticity = Artificiality (Life), Male = Female (Gender Trouble)

References

8 Uhr–Abendblatt.
Johannes R. Becher, *Maschinenrhythmen.* Berlin.
Monika Elsner and Thomas Müller, "Das Ich und sein Körper: Europa im

Tango-Fieber." In Manfred Pfister, ed., *Die Modernisierung des Ich*. Passau, 1989.

Michael Golston, "'Im Anfang war der Rhythmus': Rhythmic Incubations in Discourses of Mind, Body, and Race from 1850 to 1944." *Stanford Humanities Review 5*, supplement (1996): 1–24.

Hans Ulrich Gumbrecht, "Rhythmus und Sinn." In Hans Ulrich Gumbrecht and K. Ludwig Pfeiffer, eds., *Materialität der Kommunikation*. Frankfurt, 1988.

Peter Jelavich, *Berlin Cabaret*. Cambridge, Mass., 1993.

Harry Graf Kessler, *Tagebücher, 1918–1937*. Frankfurt, 1961.

Thomas Mann, "Unordnung und frühes Leid" (1926). In Mann, *Sämtliche Erzählungen*. Frankfurt, 1961.

New York Times.

Mario Puccini, "Text from *Critica Fascista*" (1926). In *Stanford Italian Review* (1990): 257–260.

Phyllis Rose, *Jazz Cleopatra: Josephine Baker in Her Time*. New York, 1989.

Leni Riefenstahl, *A Memoir*. New York, 1992.

Kristine von Soden and Maruta Schmidt, eds., *Neue Frauen: Die zwanziger Jahre*. Berlin, 1988.

W. B. Yeats, *A Vision* (1926). New York, 1961.

ELEVATORS

Three days before the championship fight between Jack Dempsey and Gene Tunney, and anticipating the arrival of "a host of pickpockets and other underworld characters" in Philadelphia [see **Boxing**], a detective bureau issues "a list of Don'ts in warning to the visiting fans." Some of these warnings are published in the *New York Times* on September 21. While it comes as no surprise that the bureau advises visitors not to "make friends with strangers," and not to leave valuables in automobiles or in hotel rooms, at least one of the rules raises a question: "Be particularly careful in elevators, as these are common places for persons to have pockets picked." Wouldn't an elevator, which prohibits escape immediately after a theft, offer a difficult strategic situation for a pickpocket? What possibilities for becoming invisible, if any, does a thief have in an elevator? In the collective imagination, elevators set the pace for the traffic within modern buildings, whose gigantic dimensions define them as complex, self-contained worlds. An oft-cited paradigm is the state-of-the-art hotel. Announcing its reopening after a complete renovation, Berlin's Hotel Excelsior, "the largest hotel on the Continent," proudly features a veritable system of elevators: "Six elevators regulate the traffic to the different floors day and night" (8 *Uhr–Abendblatt,* October 2). What would perhaps provide refuge for a thief fleeing one of these six elevators with a stolen purse is the anonymity and incessant rhythm of the hotel space. He could hope to be swallowed up by such complexity. Not only do the elevators circulate "day and night," but the pervasive spirit of rationality and systematization that governs the hotel [see **Sobriety vs. Exuberance**] has also made it an impersonal and anonymous place: "An implicit recommendation for my establishment is that it continues to be the only German hotel without porters, thus solving the tiresome problem of tips." As a building that contains its own intricate world, the hotel is fascinating—"One of Berlin's landmarks!"—because it pushes to the extreme the principle of autarky: "Its own electricity and power plant of 920 horsepower. Its own waterworks with a pumping capacity of 75,000 liters per hour. Complete self-sufficiency in all branches of operation. Its own daily hotel newspaper, published for five years . . . Its own 5,000-volume library." Complexity and autarky make the hotel as a system turn inward, and as an inward-turned system it does not seem to be much concerned with its environment. But since hotels and department stores are also emblems of the new sobriety, Adolf Hitler can point to them when he complains about the lack of monumental buildings in Berlin: "If Berlin were to meet the same fate as ancient Rome, our descendants would one day have nothing more to admire than a few Jewish-owned department stores and some hotels, as the most colossal works of our age and as characteristic expressions of our present culture" (Hitler, 291).

Instead of conveying a meaning to the outside world (as large buildings often do), hotels and skyscrapers enter into structural liaisons with even larger systems: "My valued guests enjoy the comfort and convenience of the underground tunnel that connects the Anhalter train station to the hotel." The systemic paradox of maximally closed systems achieving maximal openness toward their environments (Luhmann and De Giorgi, 30ff.) is one reason such large buildings can become dangerous environments themselves. The internal movement of hotels, which elevators set in motion and regulate, is as desubjectifying as the movement characteristic of modern dances and new systems of production. [see **Assembly Lines, Dancing, Employees**] This might finally explain why passengers in hotel elevators become easy victims for thieves and other criminals. Elevators are scarcely ever controlled by their passengers. They depend on operators (whose gestures, in turn, depend on the passengers' instructions) or, more frequently, on the continuous automatic movement of the cars, which are pulled by an engine along a quadrangular circuit consisting of two vertical shafts and two short horizontal rails. The name for such elevators in continuous movement—

"pater nosters"—has several connotations: the incessant rhythm of collective prayer; reliance on an invisible and independent (i.e., transcendental) source of movement [see **Immanence vs. Transcendence**]; and the fear caused by these elevators. With a pater noster, the passenger has only an instant to step into or out of the moving car. Between the departure of one car and the arrival of the next, the shaft is merely a black abyss.

The "Workmen's City" in the film *Metropolis* is an enormous sealed space beneath the open-air city. It is connected to the surface of the earth only by a pater noster running up and down the "New Tower of Babel, the machine center of Metropolis." At the beginning of the film, this elevator serves as a symbol of the workers' submission to a brutally anonymous system: "And they all had the same faces. And they all seemed a thousand years old . . . They moved their feet forward, yet they did not walk . . . The pater noster—the ceaseless elevator which, like a neverending series of well-buckets, transsected the New Tower of Babel—gathered men up and poured them out again" (Lang, 20). Desubjectification, however, not only reduces individuals to a mass of bodies; it also causes loss of agency, loss of control over one's fate. It thus becomes obvious that the continuous up-and-down movement of the elevator, in particular the circular up-and-down movement of the pater noster, mirrors that of the Wheel of Fortune, the most widespread traditional emblem of life's randomness. Transforming the elevator into a "decapitation machine," Johannes Becher also alludes to this metaphorical implication when he images a tour of the capitalist world as downward movement through a multistorey structure filled with scenes of misery:

> Electric, shining, oiled, and honking, the decapitation machine
> glides along.
> On the fifth floor: a woman in a bed, stoned and on her knees.
> On the fourth floor: glaring grimaces behind flying curtains.
> On the second floor: a toilet clearing its throat . . .
> First floor: an acrobat doing tricks.
> In the basement: they sleep on garbage. (Becher, 145)

When elevators move upward, in contrast, they become agents of redemption from the hardships of bodily existence. The six elevators of the Hotel Excelsior thus contain a promise: "The utmost perfection of modern hotel technology! . . . No staircases!" If rising above the ground is inevitably accompanied by the fear of losing the firm foundation under one's feet (see **Airplanes, Uncertainty vs. Reality**), this movement conquers, on the other hand, a spatial dimension that eliminates the claustrophobia—suffered by the workers in Metropolis—of living on an overcrowded surface. [see **Center = Periphery (Infinitude)**)] This is why roof gardens become the setting for an earthly paradise. [see **Roof Gardens**] If, however, rising above the ground in an elevator frees the passengers from the limitations of the human body as controlled by inertia and gravity, a price has to be paid for this redemption. Those who are redeemed must give up their claim to subjecthood—and in some cases they must even transfer it to another subject. The recipient of such transfers becomes a subject with a stronger agency, a subject in control of the entire system whose intrinsic movement the elevator embodies. This subject is personified in the profit-calculating owner and businessman. Predictably, therefore, the advertisement for the reopening of the Hotel Excelsior is written in the first person and signed "Curt Elschner, Owner."

While acknowledging the status of elevators as central emblems for the self-description of the contemporary world, the journalist Friedrich Sieburg, in an essay entitled "Adoration of Elevators," sheds an ironic light on the tendency of intellectuals to romanticize businessmen and to admire the concretizations of their power: "Meanwhile, European poets of all ages write about the American tempo, and about how it finds its expression above all in elevators. They pay exhilarated tribute to the American spirit—to its determination and to its straightforward dealmaking. They praise the efficiency of New York hotels (how promptly a guest can get his trousers ironed!), and speak with tears in their eyes about traffic regulations—while, cruising up and down the Hudson in their sleek boats, they toss the old German god overboard" (Sieburg, 274). [see **Action vs. Impotence, Immanence vs. Transcendence**]

Related Entries

Airplanes, Assembly Lines, Boxing, Dancing, Employees, Roof Gardens, Action vs. Impotence, Immanence vs. Transcendence, Sobriety vs. Exuberance, Uncertainty vs. Reality, Center vs. Periphery (Infinitude)

References

8 Uhr–Abendblatt.
Johannes R. Becher, *Maschinenrhythmen.* Berlin, 1926.
Adolf Hitler, *Mein Kampf* (1926). Munich, 1941.
Fritz Lang, *Metropolis* (1926). New York, 1973.
Niklas Luhmann and Raffaele De Giorgi, *Teoria della società.* Milan, 1992.
New York Times.
Friedrich Sieburg, "Anbetung von Fahrstuehlen" (1926). In Anton Kaes, ed., *Weimarer Republik: Manifeste und Dokumente zur deutschen Literatur, 1918–1933.* Stuttgart, 1983.

EMPLOYEES

Claus, the narrator in René Schickele's novel *Maria Capponi,* belongs to one of those bourgeois families of prewar Europe who have perfectly assimilated the mores of the feudal past. Venice has to be the place where Claus enjoys his first erotic adventures with Maria Capponi, the daughter of an industrial family from Milan. But the stormy romance of Claus and Maria does not end in marriage. Only a few days after his engagement to Doris, a serious young woman from Germany [see **Mountaineering**], Claus receives the announcement of Maria's wedding to "General X." Still, the atmosphere is charged with erotic tension when the two former lovers meet shortly thereafter during a vacation on the French Riviera. Maria has every reason to remind Claus of her new situation: "We must get used to the fact that I am now married . . . Or did you mean, Claus, that I would remain unmarried until my death, wandering through your dreams as an employee, so to speak?" (306ff.). A tone of resentment is apparent in Maria's image of walking through Claus's dreams like an "employee." But it is not immediately obvious why she uses this word. A hundred pages further into the novel, it comes up again when Claus's Alsatian relatives wonder whether their employees might quit and leave the family's possessions unprotected in the days following the end of the war: "I reassured them by claiming that no conscientious employee would desert if a fire were to break out in the back room of the store" (404).

Schickele's novel is just one example of a strong fascination—if not an obsession—with the concept of the employee. This fascination probably results from a number of ambiguities in the employee's role. On the one hand, employees are allowed to occupy a position of agency, since they are hired to perform certain tasks and can thus be held responsible (employees, according to feudal codes, are not supposed to quit their posts in burning buildings). On the other hand, employees are denied (or deny themselves) agency because they are not expected to take initiatives (employees are not supposed to change sides, even in a particularly opportune situation such as the end of the war in Alsace). The instructions that K. gives to his two "helpers" in Franz Kafka's *Schloss (The Castle)* epitomize the dynamics of this role. K. will ignore the difference between their names (and thus their respective individuality as "Artur" and "Jeremias") because such a conflation will make both of them responsible for any mistake one or the other might commit (and it will thus transform them into a single subject for any situation where "to have the agency of a subject" means "to be capable of being accused"): "I'll call you both Artur. If I tell Artur to go somewhere, you must both go; if I give Artur something to do, you must both do it. This has the great disadvantage of making it impossible for me to employ you on separate jobs, but it has the advantage of making you equally responsible for anything I tell you to do" (Kafka, 20). In view of the most widespread gender stereotypes, it is not surprising that the role of the employee carries a strong connotation of femininity, and that playing this role can make male characters seem androgynous. [see **Male = Female (Gender Trouble)**] Jeremias refers to Artur as "little darling," and invokes his "tender soul" (195). Barnabas—who, although not an employee of K., volunteers to support him whenever he can—really looks like a woman: "He reminded K. a little of the girl with the infant whom he had seen at the tanner's. He was clothed nearly all in white; not in silk, of course—he was in winter clothes like all the others—but the material he was wearing had the softness and dignity of silk. His face was clear and frank, his eyes larger than ordinary" (22).

Refusing to walk through Claus's dreams as an "employee," Maria Capponi protests a male attitude which, out of resentment against her marriage, makes her responsible for the existence of that marriage and at the same time contests her right to act as an independent subject. A similar asymmetry characterizes the role of secretary. Powerful men, such as John Fredersen, the Master of Metropolis, are surrounded by secretaries: "At a table near the big desk sit three secretaries. With a jerk, they come to life in unison and take down in large ledgers everything the Master says . . . Though they are as still as statues and move only the fingers of their right hand, each one, with sweat-covered brow and parted lips, seems the personification of breathlessness" (Lang, 36). The position of agency that is denied the secretaries is filled by a male voice giving dictation. Recording the Master's words makes the secretaries "breathless" and brings sweat to their brows because they can be held responsible for whatever goes wrong. So strongly and exclusively do the secretaries' bodies react to the pressures of their task that their interaction with the Master hardly ever displays an erotic dimension. Only in external business relations does a secretary's sex appeal shine through— but then it is used to further the interests of her employers: "The secretary enters. She is very attractive. And since her employer is either immune to this appeal or a purely platonic admirer, [the visitor] will glance at her more than once; and she knows how to turn this to her boss's advantage" (Benjamin, 133).

Besides these asymmetries of agency and gender, secretaries incarnate an ambivalence which is characteristic of the employee's role in general. Different in this respect from proletarian labor, secretaries' word-related labor can be regarded as a "mental" or "spiritual" activity. At the same time, however, the secretary's body, like the body of the proletarian [see Assembly Lines], is usually coupled to a machine—specifically, a typewriter. Although the typewriter itself does not set the rhythm for the secretary's movements (as industrial machines do for assembly-line workers), the rhythm of the dictation serves as the exterior determinant of her activity. Even the textual document she composes is the impersonal product of a typewriter. It is a text lacking in that very quality of subjective expression which makes handwriting an unavoidable object of interpretation (Kittler, 355ff.). Like the assembly-line worker, who is but a tiny part of a complex production process, the secretary has neither control nor ownership over her tools and her product. She does not even own her typewriter. Conversely, the secretary's body is often subsumed by the typewriter to such a degree that it is the dyadic unit—and not the technical device alone—which is considered to be the "writing machine." This is why an advertisement in *Caras y Caretas* (September 18) can depict a young woman embracing a typewriter, under the heading "This is the perfect typewriter!" Whenever male protagonists play secretarial roles, as is the case with "Tiny Nicomedes the Typist" (a cartoon in *Caras y Caretas,* November 6), these characters are given the most negative attributes currently associated with women. Opening his master's correspondence, Tiny Nicomedes steals a theater ticket. Predictably, the play that he sees is about the crime and punishment of a thief, and this plot makes Nicomedes lose all vestiges of his "masculine composure." He leaves the show and runs straight into his master who, without a ticket, stands waiting at the theater's entrance.

Germany alone now has 3.5 million nonindustrial employees, of whom more than 40 percent are women (fewer than 20 percent of German women work in industry). Concurrently, the typewriter and the calculator have become widespread in business administration, and there has been a shift from tailor-made to ready-made clothes. It thus follows that the positions most frequently occupied by women are those of secretary and saleswoman (*Chronik,* 36; von Soden and Schmidt, 25ff.). Certain status symbols that accompany these jobs lead the public to greatly overestimate the distance that separates industrial workers and nonindustrial employees. From this perspective, the situation of clerical and sales personnel in the United States emerges as a much-admired example. They are paid monthly (instead of weekly, as factory workers are); their workday is only eight hours; and, in their spare time, they can increasingly afford middle-class pursuits, which implies that they can pay for the services of other employees. Since they are devoted to pleasing, employees tend to adapt to the tastes of their employers and are strongly disposed to overlook the often flagrant forms of exploitation to which they are exposed. Female workers, instead of protesting salaries that lie 15 percent below those of their male counterparts (*Chronik,* 36), display that "will-to-happiness" which D. H. Lawrence finds characteristic of "most modern people"—but which he attributes especially to Kate, the protagonist of his novel *The Plumed Serpent* (Lawrence, 8). As a consequence of this commitment to happiness, secretaries and saleswomen wind up sending their modest income back to its source. They buy fashionable clothes or, at least, fashion magazines which help them dream of a change in their social status. The media, in exchange, furnish these women with an exuberantly positive self-image: "No one should think it strange that salesgirls are the most assiduous readers of fashion magazines and that they strive to find the most effective means to ward off their greatest enemy: age. They are the industrious worker bees of beauty; they are, more than anyone, worthy of our interest and esteem. We must salute them: they represent the best of our society" (*Caras y Caretas,* October 12).

This positive view of the young, industrious, well-dressed, and invariably female secretary or sales clerk contrasts starkly with the image of the factory worker, who—faceless, deprived of agency, and invariably male—becomes a metonym for what the middle class fears more than anything else: the anonymity of systems and institutions that absorb all individuality. [see **Individuality vs. Collectivity**] The characters in Kafka's *Schloss* illustrate this clearly. As soon as K.'s "helpers" Artur and Jeremias quit, K. realizes that his power over them was only relative, and he has reason to fear that they will carry negative reports of him to the powers in the castle, which dominate both master and servants: "Where is Artur?" asks K. '"The little darling, Artur?" replies Jeremias. "He quit. You were rather rough on us, you know, and the gentle soul couldn't take it. He's gone back to the castle to lodge a complaint" (195). If secretaries stand for the smiling side of the employee's role, the civil servant embodies its threatening aspects—for his employer, the State, is the largest and most anonymous system of all. What for some men makes female employees appealing—namely, their lack of individual agency—is viewed as a threat when it is associated with male workers. Men's facelessness evokes the unlimited power of the State.

Conversely, a representative of the State, like the Spanish dictator Miguel Primo de Rivera, can easily blame the effects of his own and his government's tyranny on the behavior of civil servants. He promises "not an absorbing, centralizing, bureaucratic, obstructive State, but a State that stimulates, supervises, and assists . . . State employees should cease their tyrannical behavior and instead learn how to be helpful" (Primo de Rivera, 149–150). Since everybody feels threatened by the State and its bureaucracy, no one gladly takes a government job—despite the financial security that comes with it. At the age of twenty-five, the physicist Werner Heisenberg is offered a full professorship at the University of Leipzig. Resisting both his family's urgings to accept this position and the temptations of all its academic privileges, Heisenberg opts for the less prestigious and less financially rewarding—but intellectually more challenging—alternative of working as Niels Bohr's research associate in Copenhagen (Cassidy, 216ff.). So long as dictators like Miguel Primo de Rivera continually stress the distance between themselves and their anonymous underlings, young men with high career hopes (and, therefore, strong assertions of agency) simply shy away from any role within the State's bureaucracy.

In *Mein Kampf,* Adolf Hitler claims to have rejected at an early age a career as a civil servant, which his father, a civil servant himself, had foreseen for him:

> For the first time in my life, scarcely eleven, I was forced into opposition. Firm and unwavering though my father was in carrying out long-planned goals and projects, his son was equally determined and obstinate in his refusal to follow those plans. I didn't want to become a civil servant. Neither encouragement nor "serious" discussions would alter my resistance in the slightest. I didn't want to become a civil servant, and said so over and over. All of my father's attempts to inspire me with a love or desire for this profession turned me in the opposite direction. To me it seemed boring and awful to be perpetually confined to an office, unable to do as one pleased and spending one's whole life filling out forms. (Hitler, 6)

Whoever wants to be a leader must resist being associated with the facelessness of the State and with that lack of agency which is characteristic of employees. Instead of embodying the threatening face of society, he must appear as society's natural savior. [see **Action vs. Impotence, Individuality = Collectivity (Leader)**]

Related Entries

Assembly Lines, Mountaineering, Action vs. Impotence, Individuality vs. Collectivity, Individuality = Collectivity (Leader), Male = Female (Gender Trouble)

References

Walter Benjamin, *Einbahnstraße.* In *Gesammelte Schriften,* vol. 4, part 1. Frankfurt, 1972.
Berliner Tageblatt.
Caras y Caretas.
David C. Cassidy, *Uncertainty: The Life and Science of Werner Heisenberg.* New York, 1992.

Chronik 1926: Tag für Tag in Wort und Bild. Dortmund, 1985.

Adolf Hitler, *Mein Kampf* (1926). Munich, 1941.

Franz Kafka, *Das Schloss* (1926). Frankfurt, 1968.

Friedrich Kittler, *Aufschreibesysteme: 1800/1900.* Munich, 1985.

Fritz Lang, *Metropolis* (1926). New York, 1973.

D. H. Lawrence, *The Plumed Serpent.* London, 1926.

Miguel Primo de Rivera, "Balance de tres años de Gobierno (5 septiembre 1926)." In María Carmen García Nieto, Javier M. Donézar, and Luis López Puerta, eds., *La dictadura, 1923–1930: Bases documentales de la España contemporánea,* vol. 7. Madrid, 1973.

René Schickele, *Maria Capponi.* Munich, 1926.

Kristine von Soden and Maruta Schmidt, eds., *Neue Frauen: Die zwanziger Jahre.* Berlin, 1988.

ENDURANCE

On Saturday, August 7, nineteen-year-old Gertrud Ederle of the United States swims the English Channel between Calais and Dover in fourteen hours thirty-two minutes. Winner of a gold medal at the 1924 Olympics and holder of the world record in the 400-meter freestyle, she first attempted the crossing a year ago, but gave up, exhausted, ten miles off the British coast. This time she has cut almost two hours from the previous record set by Enrico Tiraboschi of Argentina in 1923, thus becoming the only woman to beat all men among the record holders in an athletic competition (*Chronik,* 139). [see **Male vs. Female**] This achievement makes her an international celebrity. The city of Dover welcomes Ederle with a gala reception upon her arrival, and six weeks later the *New York Times* mentions her as being among the most famous spectators attending the championship bout between Jack Dempsey and Gene Tunney in Philadelphia, rounding out a list that includes Charlie Chaplin, William Randolph Hearst, and the Rockefeller family. [see **Boxing**]

Twenty-one days after Ederle's feat, another American, Clemington Cannon, becomes the second woman to cross the Channel. Though it takes her more than half an hour longer, Cannon, too, is welcomed in England with "tumultuous ovations." A special correspondent to the *Berliner Tageblatt* dedicates a full-length article to her achievement: "In the first two hours, Mrs. Cannon covered a distance of four English miles. During the morning she ate some chocolate. Later in the day she had to battle strong currents. Mrs. Cannon, a Danish-born American, is twenty-seven and a mother of two. After her arrival in Dover, she said to a representative of the press: 'I had decided either to succeed or to drown. I have to make money for my children.' Mrs. Cannon has been a professional swimmer since she was sixteen. She has already won a number of major competitions in America" (August 29; *Années-mémoire*, 46). On August 28, at 3:10 P.M., a few hours before Cannon's arrival on the British coast, three more swimmers, among them another American woman, set off independently to cross the Channel: "Three swimmers are taking advantage of favorable weather conditions to cross the Channel. The Egyptian Helmi started shortly before 11:00 last night, the Englishman Frank Perks around 11:20, and the American Carson shortly before midnight. Helmi gave up after only three hours and re-turned to Boulogne on the steamboat that was monitoring the crossing." Julian Carson, who takes seventeen minutes longer than Cannon and fifty-seven minutes longer than Ederle, is for a short time the third-fastest Channel-swimmer in history. Only two days later, however, the world record reverts to a man, when Ernst Vierkötter of Germany sets a new mark of twelve hours forty-two minutes. And this record will be broken in turn on September 11 by Georges Michel of France, with the almost incredible time of eleven hours six minutes.

The act of swimming the English Channel stages the human body in a struggle with the elements. Since an athlete's performance pushes the human body to the limits of its endurance, athletic feats can often be experienced as confrontations with death. "To succeed or drown" is the motto of all Channel swimmers. [see **Immanence = Transcendence (Death)**] Pointing to the need "to make money for my children," how-ever, Clemington Cannon's words also show that the dramatic alterna-tive between life (success) and death (drowning) is more than just an allegory for the hardships of human existence in general. Under such extreme physical and mental stress, the traditional hierarchy between male bodies and female bodies tends to vanish. [see **Dancing, Male = Female (Gender Trouble)**] On October 5, two months after the first successful crossing of the Channel by a female athlete, Violet Pierceu of France becomes the first woman to run a full marathon (twenty-six miles) against the clock (*Chronik*, 175). Those human bodies which successfully brave the elements and test their strength to the limit are often perceived as shining surfaces. Indeed, Channel swimmers protect themselves against the cold seawater by covering their skin with a layer of grease. [see **Gomina**] Although swimmers risk losing conscience during the crossing, those who succeed set an impressive example of the way in which human will can dominate the human body. At the same time, the mastering of the body is a form of instrumentalization, because Channel swimmers belong to an international avant-garde of athletes who receive considerable financial rewards for their performance. [see **Stars**]

While the public does not necessarily expect any practical results from acts that test the limits of the human body [see **Action vs. Impotence**], records are often broken in the effort to transcend spatial boundaries or surmount geographic obstacles. This is true for Channel swimmers, for pioneer long-distance aviators, for mountain climbers, and for winners of the Tour de France, who in several European countries enjoy the status of national heroes. [see **Mountaineering, Polarities**] Even before Lucien Buysse of Belgium wins the Tour in 248 hours forty-four minutes twenty-five seconds (*Années-mémoire*, 42), the organizers of this event begin to devise stringent new regulations, which, instituted in 1927, will increase the number of competitors who fall by the wayside in the Alps and the Pyrenees (Fassbender, 268ff.). The participants in the Tour de France must endure a composite competition that consists of more than twenty legs and a variety of different trials. Such bicycle races find their structural equivalent in popular relay races, which—instead of consisting of a series of legs—require a number of athletes to cover a large distance in sequence, often competing with members of opposing teams at various specialized tasks. Five weeks prior to setting a world record for a cross-Channel swim, Ernst Vierkötter wins a relay competition on Berlin's Spree River: "In the relay race, every swimmer is accompanied by a rowboat with relievers. Never was the Spree more alive than on this Saturday. Motorboats, paddleboats, and between them the heads of swimmers . . . Lining the riverbanks are improvised stands. By around 5:30, long before the arrival of the swimmers, all the tickets have been sold. Thousands still are standing on the shore by the parliament building. At 6:00 the first swimmers appear. 'Vierkötter! Vierkötter!' cries the crowd. He is the first. A tough race, and a battle to the finish with another swimmer. Vierkötter beats him by only two meters. Thunderous applause" (*Berliner Tageblatt*, July 25).

A so-called *Industriestaffel* ("industrial relay race") held in Berlin on

Sunday, August 29, is an even more complex example of this new fashion in the world of sports:

> The men have to cover a total distance of forty-four kilometers. Twelve runners, four bikers, three swimmers, and a rower make up a team. First, ten of the runners go into action, carrying the baton along Unter den Linden and Charlottenburger Chausseé up to the Tiergarten. From this point two bikers take over . . . A runner and a swimmer convey the baton to the rower, who has to maneuver his boat over the fifteen kilometers to Schildhorn. He passes the baton to a cross-country runner, who in turn gives it to two bikers. They speed by the Heerstraße train station . . . and head toward the Kronprinzenufer. The last two swimmers, who have to race against the current to the Reichstag, decide the outcome. (*Berliner Tageblatt*, August 29)

The *Industriestaffel,* as its name suggests, mimics the new style in industrial production [see **Assembly Lines**]: a complex system, based on the principle of complementarity, fulfills a specific function with a speed and an efficiency that go beyond the physical limits of even the strongest individual bodies.

Multiple forms of coupling between human bodies and high-performance engines bring an unprecedented expansion of physical experience and practical achievement. [see **Center = Periphery [Infinitude], Present = Past (Eternity)**] Their endurance and their resistance to the elements are tested in a new type of techno-sports competition that shares structural elements both with Channel swimming and with events like the Tour de France. The German Reichsverkehrsministerium (Ministry of Transportation) and the Reichspostministerium (Postal Ministry) donate the astounding prize of more than 250,000 marks for a multi-trial hydroplane race held at Warnemünde in July. A dauntingly complex series of individual tasks and evaluation procedures (see **Airplanes, Automobiles**), this *Seeflugtag* puts to an extreme test the endurance of both the airplanes and their pilots: "The results of the technical trials and the coastal flights can always be overturned by the so-called sea tests, in which each aircraft has to perform three takeoffs, three landings, and two loops against a strong wind" (*Berliner Tageblatt*, July 25). If, on the one hand, such events combine bodies and engines into a unit that is the functional equivalent of an athlete's body, they contribute, on the other hand, to the emergence of new forms of subjectivity that are different from the heroic subjectivity of traditional athletes. No other sport epitomizes this more traditional—and more "philosophical"—form of subjectivity as perfectly as long-distance running. [see **Individuality = Collectivity (Leader)**] For the upper-class adolescents in Fritz Lang's *Metropolis,* who meet "high above" the workmen's city in "Masterman Stadium, gift of John Masterman, the richest man in Metropolis," long-distance running is a sign of social distinction, and its representation in the film evokes stereotyped images of ancient Greek culture (Lang, 22ff.). In sports, the best traditional spirit of the discipline is embodied by the Finnish athlete Paavo Nurmi, who, until September 11, holds the world record for all events between 1,500 and 10,000 meters. Everyone knows that Nurmi runs with a stopwatch in his hand. [see **Timepieces**] His brand of competition is thus a battle of the will on two levels: first, against the pain in his body and, second, against the fleeting time that he measures. While his competitors normally have to slow down toward the end of a race, Nurmi tends to accelerate in the home stretch. This enclosure within a double loop of self-reference which makes him a heroic subject is Nurmi's unique strength—and his only weakness. On Saturday, September 11, in Berlin, this weakness causes Nurmi to lose a race, and his world record, in the 1,500-meter event to Otto Peltzer of Germany, who has recently broken the world record for 800 meters.

Instead of seeking, as Nurmi does, total control over his body through self-centered concentration, Peltzer observes both himself and his competitors from a distance, and then uses the opportunities that the moment may offer: "An hour before the race I did a warm-up lap, and to my surprise my legs felt quite light. From that moment on, I knew that Nurmi would not be able to escape so easily." Yet Peltzer gains advantage not only from his own bodily lightness, but also from Nurmi's inability to react to an opponent's challenge—an inability that is endemic to his character as an athlete. "I was still so fresh," said Peltzer, "that I could make continual small attacks on him, just to unnerve him, so that he would probably be unable to resist the next serious attack and would have to let himself be bypassed. At 1,300 meters he looked around to his left and did not see that I was just then passing him on his right. By the time he noticed me, he had already lost the race." Although Nurmi cannot counter the attack from Peltzer, the latter is willing to concede how much his performance depends on the mechanism of challenge and response: "If Nurmi had run a bit faster, I would certainly have run faster as well. This is why I was somewhat surprised that the finish time was still a world record. It's certainly a result of the fact that I always run well when led by a good runner. I could never do it alone" (*Chronik*, 161). Rather than engaging in a contest against himself, Otto Peltzer becomes a heroic subject in competition with other subjects, and it is perhaps for this reason that he wishes to triumph "with self-confidence and as a representative of the German cause."

Related Entries

Airplanes, Assembly Lines, Automobiles, Boxing, Dancing, Gomina, Mountaineering, Polarities, Stars, Timepieces, Action vs. Impotence, Male vs. Female, Center = Periphery (Infinitude), Immanence vs. Transcendence (Death), Individuality = Collectivity (Leader), Male = Female (Gender Trouble), Present = Past (Eternity)

References

Les Années-mémoire: 1926. Paris, 1988.
Berliner Tageblatt.
Chronik 1926: Tag für Tag in Wort und Bild. Dortmund, 1985.
Heribert Fassbender, ed., *Sporttagebuch des 20. Jahrhunderts.* Düsseldorf, 1984.
Fritz Lang, *Metropolis.* New York, 1973.
New York Times.

ENGINEERS

The first page of Walter Benjamin's book *Einbahnstraße (One-Way Street)* presents the reader with an enigmatic dedication: "This street is called / Asja Lacis Street / after her who / as an engineer / bulldozed it through the author." This is of course a variation on the classical statement "Dedicated to her/him who inspired the author," a variation specifically adapted to the nonmetaphorical meaning of Benjamin's metaphorical title. Asja Lacis appears as a street-laying engineer because Benjamin wants to thank her for having inspired the book which he entitles *Einbahnstraße*. Nevertheless, the violence inherent in the image of cutting the way for a street is a puzzling substitute for the rather ethereal influence of intellectual and artistic inspiration. The act of an engineer who manipulates an engine or a space does not seem commensurate with the free—and often loving—acceptance of such inspiration on the part of the artist. An implicit pun in Benjamin's wording, however, makes such a violent connotation plausible. Although the text says that Asja Lacis cut the street through the author ("im Autor"), the subtraction of just one letter ("im Auto") makes a car—emblem of the engineer's skill—the vehicle for the breakthrough. [see **Automobiles**] This reading also explains Benjamin's choice for the book title. He wishes to emphasize that, after initial resistance and hesitation (which made a certain amount of violence unavoidable), his commitment to the form of thinking which Asja Lacis has inspired in him is now unconditional. It has become an *Einbahnstraße*, a one-way street—a way with no possible return.

But can Asja Lacis, who inspired the great and unhappy love of Walter Benjamin's life, be pleased to be addressed as an "engineer"? Surprisingly, perhaps, the way in which she conceives of her job as the director of a "proletarian children's theater" in the Soviet Union (von Soden and Schmidt, 81ff.) allows for such associations between her profession and that of an engineer. Unlike what she would call the "bourgeois tradition" in education and art, her work with proletarian children is directed toward an explicit function and goal—the goal of active politicization. Professing the credo of materialism, "revolutionary" pedagogues, in addition, often base their work on a mechanistic conception of the human psyche. Such is the case with Ivan Petrovich Pavlov: "Pavlov's studies will, presumably, have decisive importance for philosophers. Likewise for teachers, politicians, judges, and artists . . . On the basis of the study of conditioned and unconditioned reflexes, a fundamentally new pedagogical technique will come into being" (Toller, 182). To treat a comrade with the technical competence and the violent "sobriety" of an engineer can therefore be an acceptable form of interaction among revolutionary Marxists [see **Sobriety vs. Exuberance**]—so long as this style is justified by a shared goal.

On Monday, December 6, Benjamin arrives in Moscow, where Asja Lacis is being treated at a sanatorium after suffering a nervous breakdown (Benjamin, *Tagebuch*, 177). During the two months he spends in the Soviet Union, the encounters with his beloved will be a long chain of frustrations culminating in a lonesome New Year's Eve: "More in the spirit of exploration than from genuine emotion, I asked her to come outside and give me one last kiss to mark the waning of the old year. But she wouldn't. I left, and spent New Year's Eve alone, but not sad" (86). Despite his desperate efforts, the exploration of Asja Lacis' mind is turning into an expression of Benjamin's unfulfilled love. This is why he wants to convince himself that Asja's refusal to kiss him is not a "sad" event, and this must also be why he tends to describe their relationship with those metaphors of revolutionary engineering which he feels will please her. His more spontaneous reactions to the popularity of this language in the Soviet Union, however, are of an almost aggressive skepticism: "Everything technical is sacrosanct here; nothing is taken more seriously than technology . . . It is known that the trivialization of love and sex is part of the Communist credo" (82, December 30). Despite Benjamin's anguished ambivalence, he writes *Einbahnstraße* in the stylistic and intellectual guise of an engineer. Headings like "Filling Station," "Standard Clock" [see **Timepieces**], "Construction Site," "Underground Works," "Interior Decoration," and "Fire Alarm" emphasize this intention, and Benjamin's very first reflection can even be read as a definition of the engineer's mind: "At the moment, the construction of life depends much more on facts than on convictions—on facts that never contribute to the shaping of convictions. Under these conditions, true literary activity cannot attempt to play itself out in a merely literary framework; such frameworks are more often the expression of sterility. Meaningful literary effectiveness can come only through an ongoing oscillation between actions and words; it must develop inconspicuous forms such as pamphlets, brochures, newspaper articles, and posters, rather than the ponderous universal gesture of the book. Only this language of immediacy is truly up to the tasks of the moment" (85). The engineer relies on "facts," not on vague "convictions." He wants to be efficient, rather than inspiring. Envisioning his goals within "active society," he carefully chooses specific instruments and "gestures." From the point of view of the engineer's social efficiency, both acts of analysis and acts of maintenance become functionally equivalent to acts of invention. He thus no longer does homage to the individualistic cult of creativity (Gumbrecht, "Fichier"). Whatever the engineer invents or analyzes—an engine or a modification in human behavior, a house or an entire society—presents itself as a technical system. Ultimately, the engineer conceives of himself as part of the technical systems which he builds and in which his work is coupled both to engines and to workers. [see **Assembly Lines, Elevators**]

The self-image of the American sailor in B. Traven's novel *Das Totenschiff (The Death Ship)* presupposes this very world view: "I was a simple deckhand. You see, sir, sailors hardly exist anymore—there's no longer any need for them. A modern freighter isn't a real ship. It's a waterborne machine. And you'd never believe that a machine needs sailors to care for it, even if you understood nothing of ships. This machine needs engineers" (Traven, 7). But while the engineer may shock conservative minds by defining himself as part of an engine and by thus claiming maximal distance from the heroic subject-roles of the genius and the creative artist, he embodies, at the same time, a variation within the tradition of individuality. *Homo faber* is the old name for a new type of identity that maintains the core element of an "inspired mind" but that, in place of the self-reflexive inspiration of the genius, substitutes inspiration that comes from contact with technical systems. In a program for the Bauhaus School, which inaugurates its new buildings at Dessau on Saturday, December 4 (*Chronik*, 198—199), the architect Walter Gropius explains this change: "Only by constant contact with advanced technology, with the diversity of new materials, and with new methods of construction is the creative individual able to bring objects into a vital relationship with the past, and to develop from that a new attitude to design—namely, 'Determined acceptance of the living environment of machines and vehicles'" (Galison, 717). Better than any other products of the engineer's work, large buildings concretize the complexity of his achievement, the social responsibility which it involves, and the para- doxical loop that ends up making the engineer an element of the "en- gine" which he constructs. This is why the architect emerges as the most paradigmatic incarnation of *homo faber*: "The architect? He was an artist and is becoming a specialist in organization . . . Building is only organization: social, technical, economic, mental organization" (Gal- ison, 717).

After resigning, on April 28, from his post as an elementary school teacher in the village of Ottertal, where he has used corporal punishment as an instrument in his role as a social engineer (Nedo and Ranchetti, 198ff.; Wuensche, 274ff.), Ludwig Wittgenstein decides to participate in the construction of a private house for his wealthy sister, Margarete Stonborough. What he seeks is a "legitimate challenge to his own indi- vidual clear-headedness and sense of function" (Janik and Toulmin, 207). Both the shape of this house and the manifestos of Adolf Loos, the architect with whom Wittgenstein collaborates, make it clear that such a "sense of function," for him, implies the same stern—and even aggres- sive—ideas about normative social behavior which have made Wittgen- stein a dramatic failure as a teacher. Loos writes: "Not every worker has the right to possess a house and a garden, but only those who have the yearning to develop a garden. Perhaps you would object that there is no reason for being so strict, and why should workers not possess a little luxury garden, with grassy lawns and roses? As I see it, I would sin against the modern spirit, were I not so strict" (Nedo and Ranchetti, 204). Despite the harsh economic restrictions under which government agencies continue to operate in Europe, city planning and complex housing projects are the fields in which the dreams of the architect as "social engineer" may become reality (*Chronik*, 127, 171). If "functionalism," as the governing principle of such projects, produces forms of a highly provocative "modernity," it also promotes sober techniques of optimization that avoid any extreme solutions. The theories of Wittgenstein's British friend, the economist John Maynard Keynes, follow the same guidelines. His publications articulate growing doubt as to whether capitalism, the "best piece of social machinery . . . on offer," can guarantee its own success (Skidelsky, 221). [see **Strikes**] At the same time, however, and despite his sympathy for the striking workers in England, Keynes is skeptical about the Communist belief in the need for revolutionary action: "No one has a gospel. The next move is with the head, and fists must wait" (233.).

Among politicians, the interpretation of their task as "social engineering" seems to generate the conviction that concrete tasks of engineering have to be high on the State's agenda. The Spanish government under Miguel Primo de Rivera gives priority to such problems as "disruptions in railway service and the deplorable condition of our highways" (García-Nieto, 147). The sixteen-year-old protagonist in Roberto Arlt's novel *El juguete rabioso (The Furious Toy)* ranks his dream professions accordingly: "More firmly than ever, I believed that a magnificent destiny lay before me. I could be an engineer like Edison, a general like Napoleon, a poet like Baudelaire" (Arlt, 171). The aura of the engineering profession shines so brightly that poets often associate it with the erotic appeal of a beloved (Benjamin's dedication of *Einbahnstraße* is by no means an exceptional case). The ode which Federico García Lorca writes on his friend Salvador Dalí, after months of unfulfilled desire spent close to him at the summer residence of Dalí's family in Cadaqués (Etherington-Smith, 72ff.), brings the description of "modern painters" together with mathematical connotations:

> Modern painters, in their white studios,
> Nip the aseptic flower from the square root.
> In the waters of the Seine, a marble iceberg
> Frosts the windows and withers the ivy.

Man treads boldly on streets paved with flagstones.
Crystals elude the magic of reflection.
The government has closed the perfume shops.
The machine immortalizes its musical compasses.

(García Lorca, 618)

What unites the lyrical "I" with his addressee is a "desire for forms and limits," which finds a response in the arrival of a "man who measures with a yellow meter" (619). Dalí's ultimate intellectual and artistic passion, however, is architecture: "You love a defined and precise matter, / Where the mushroom cannot set up camp. / You love architecture, which constructs in empty space" (620).

Thomas Mann is sensitive to the same erotic flavor—but his reaction remains far more ambiguous than García Lorca's. In his story "Unordnung und frühes Leid" ("Disorder and Early Sorrow") it is a student of engineering, Max Hergesell, whose dancing attracts the attention of Professor Cornelius and who becomes an object of envy for the professor's frustrated paternal ambitions. And it is again Hergesell whose coquetry in playing with the professor's little daughter causes the emotional "disorder" to which the title of the novella alludes. In its final scene, when the engineering student stands beside the girl's bed, calming her down with his soothing voice, Cornelius is torn between admiration and hatred: "Young Hergesell leans over the bars of the crib and rattles on, more for the father's ear than the child's, but Ellie does not know that—and the father's feelings toward him are a most singular mixture of gratitude, embarrassment, and hatred" (521).

The dark side in Professor Cornelius'—and Thomas Mann's—ambivalence toward the engineer goes back to the traditional prejudice against industrialization and its consequences—a prejudice which the German foreign secretary, Gustav Stresemann [see **League of Nations**], revives in a speech on July 6 to the Verein Deutscher Studenten (Association of German Students): "The age . . . of initial industrial development is considered a time of marked spiritual decline in literature and other intellectual areas. What German cities once had to offer in the architecture of their marketplaces has been swept away by powerful and impersonal forces" (Stresemann, 276). Whereas Stresemann's argument refers to the past, a different type of criticism views technology from the perspective of the future—a future in which the utopian dreams of "social engineering" may turn into a nightmare. This is apparent in an interview with Bertolt Brecht about the recent premiere of his drama *Mann ist Mann (Man Is Man)* specifically in the author's explication of the plot and its political significance. Brecht: "It's about a man being taken to pieces and rebuilt as someone else for a particular purpose." Interviewer: "And who does the rebuilding?" Brecht: "Three engineers of the feelings" (Willett, 153). [see **Individuality vs. Collectivity**] Nevertheless, the gestures and technique of Brecht's own "epic theater," which he demonstrates for the first time in *Mann ist Mann,* are themselves a type of "engineering of the feelings." Such manipulation of emotions from the stage assumes its most condensed, hyperbolic form in the role of the *modulador,* who is described in a satirical article on the "theater of the future" published in the *Revista de Occidente:* "Everything obeyed the control of one man, called the *modulador,* who prescribed the movements, the emotional processes, the voices, and everything else . . . The purpose of a drama . . . was to suggest a simple or complex existential state, and once the *modulador* had been informed of the required degree of intensity, it was incumbent on him to produce the necessary emotion" (*Revista de Occidente,* 172).

Similar criticisms of the futuristic claims generally attributed to the engineer (rather than propounded by actual engineers) often turn into a defense of the creative individual. The journalist Friedrich Sieburg is thus eager to describe the cult of the engineer as a—legitimate but not so innovative—contemporary version of the Romantic admiration for the genius: "What otherworldliness is apparent in this 'engineer romanticism,' which doesn't understand how a carburetor works, and is therefore unable to distinguish the breathing of our age from the rhythm of a six-cylinder engine. Those who used to dress in velvet and whimsical ties wear leather jackets today" (Sieburg, 275). [see **Gomina**] It is José Ortega y Gasset, the best journalist among the philosophers of his time, who finds a modernist form for such conservative feelings. The true intellectual adventure, according to him, lies not in the application of knowledge for specific purposes but in the unlimited production of knowledge. Seen from this perspective, the practice-oriented engineer is doomed to remain a secondary figure: "On the one hand, the analytical spirit is helpful for life; it creates practical resources; it is useful. On the other hand, it constructs the most abstract and superfluous edifices. So, of the enormous block of knowledge that constitutes modern science, only a tiny part yields anything useful. Applied science and technology are simply an appendix to the enormous volume represented by pure science, the science that believes itself to be without purpose or utilitarian goals" (*Revista de Occidente*, 122).

Related Entries

Assembly Lines, Automobiles, Elevators, Gomina, League of Nations, Strikes, Timepieces, Individuality vs. Collectivity, Sobriety vs. Exuberance

References

Roberto Arlt, *El juguete rabioso* (1926). Madrid, 1985.

Walter Benjamin, *Einbahnstraße* (1926). In *Gesammelte Schriften*, vol. 4, part 1. Frankfurt, 1972.

Walter Benjamin, *Moskauer Tagebuch* (1926). Frankfurt, 1980.

Chronik 1926: Tag für Tag in Wort und Bild. Dortmund, 1985.

Meredith Etherington-Smith, *The Persistence of Memory: A Biography of Dalí*. New York, 1993.

Peter Galison, "Aufbau/Bauhaus: Logical Positivism and Architectural Modernism." *Critical Inquiry* 16 (1990): 709–752.

Federico García Lorca, "Oda a Salvador Dalí" (1926). In García Lorca, *Obras completas*. Madrid, 1971.

María Carmen García-Nieto, Javier M. Donézar, and Luis López Puerta, *La dictadura, 1923–1920: Bases documentales de la España contemporánea*, vol. 7. Madrid, 1973.

Hans Ulrich Gumbrecht, "Fichier/Créativité." In *Théologiques* 2, no. 1 (1994): 61–80.

Allan Janik and Stephen Toulmin, *Wittgenstein's Vienna*. New York, 1973.

Thomas Mann, "Unordnung und frühes Leid" (1926). In Mann, *Sämtliche Erzählungen*. Frankfurt, 1963.

Michael Nedo and Michele Ranchetti, eds., *Wittgenstein: Sein Leben in Bildern und Texten*. Frankfurt, 1983.

Revista de Occidente.

Friedrich Sieburg, "Anbetung von Fahrstuehlen" (1926). In Anton Kaes, ed., *Weimarer Republik: Manifeste und Dokumente zur deutschen Literatur, 1918–1933*. Stuttgart, 1983.

Robert Skidelsky, *John Maynard Keynes, II: The Economist as Savior, 1920–1937*. New York, 1994.

Gustav Stresemann, "Student und Staat: Rede vor dem Verein Deutscher Studenten" (Berlin, 7 July 1926). In Stresemann, *Reden und Schriften: Politik, Geschichte, Literatur, 1897–1926,* vol. 2. Dresden, 1926.

Ernst Toller, "Russische Reisebilder" (1926). In Toller, *Quer durch.* Munich, 1978.

B. Traven, *Das Totenschiff* (1926). Hamburg, 1954.

Kristine von Soden and Maruta Schmidt, eds., *Neue Frauen: Die zwanziger Jahre.* Berlin, 1988.

John Willett, *Art and Politics in the Weimar Period: The New Sobriety, 1917–1933.* New York, 1978.

Konrad Wuensche, *Der Volksschullehrer Ludwig Wittgenstein: Mit neuen Dokumenten und Briefen aus den Jahren 1919–1926.* Frankfurt, 1985.

GOMINA

"Tiempos viejos," a tango recorded by Carlos Gardel, the rising star of Argentina's popular-music scene, takes as its subject the most characteristic feature of tango lyrics, an emotion that is both vague and definite. Evoking late nineteenth-century suburban Buenos Aires as a world of authenticity, this song inspires a feeling of nostalgic desire, and it does so by establishing a series of contrasts between a past that has disappeared and the artificial fashions of the present [see **Authenticity vs. Artificiality**]:

> Do you remember, brother? Those were the days!
> Ours were different men, more manly,
> No one knew about coke or morphine,
> Guys back then didn't use hair gel.
> Do you remember, brother, what times they were!"
>
> (Reichardt, 370)

Among the three substances which embody the present in this stanza—*coca* (cocaine), *morfina* (morphine), and *gomina* (hair gel), *gomina* has special significance. For "Tiempos viejos" was the musical finale of a play entitled *The Gomina Boys* before it was selected for the Gardel recording (Reichardt, 448). *Gomina* is the Spanish word for a substance made from rubber *(goma)* which men use to flatten their hair, to keep it straight, and to give it a particular sheen. Although, as a signifier, *gomina* never loses its strong association with Latin America, it becomes a loan-word in French, where it produces the verb form *se gominer* (Robert, 751). But Gardel's song about *gomina* is not the only evidence of such an emblem of up-to-date fashion. There are quite a number of other hairdos and headdresses that have an especially strong symbolic link to whatever appears to be "typically modern."

One of the first images in the film *Metropolis* presents the "Club of the Sons," in which a rich and elegant *jeunesse dorée* revels in mundane pleasures. The atmosphere of the "Eternal Gardens," the club's variety theater, is emblematized by the "nude back" of a revue girl "covered with exotic sequinned designs," and by another girl in "a long, flounced skirt, her nude breast swathed in a diaphanous shawl." Only the appear-ance of a third revue girl, who sports a sumptuous headdress, is high-lighted by the film script as representing the present: "Another girl, clothed in more contemporary garments and an elaborate headdress, curtseys toward the camera" (Lang, 24). The actress in the film is actu-ally wearing a turban similar to those that have become the trademark of Natasha Rambova, Rudolph Valentino's divorced wife (Morris, 174), and that embellish the public image of the French tennis star Susanne Lenglen. Charles Pelissier, a bicycle racer who causes a sensation in the world of sports by winning, at a very early age, the French cross-country championship [see **Endurance**], is dubbed "the Valentino of sports" because—thanks to *gomina*—he manages to keep his hair as smooth and glossy as the movie star's, even in the most grueling competitions (*An-nées-mémoire*, 178). By the end of Josephine Baker's first season at the Folies Bergères, it has become obligatory among the fashion-conscious women of Paris to imitate her slicked-down hair, and before the year is out, the new trend conquers the market with a product called "Bakerfix" (Rose, 100). Bakerfix, *gomina,* and a very popular Vaseline pomade whose label shows Valentino's face (Orbanz, 20) give hair that shining surface which fashionable people now wish to have over their entire body. White women put walnut oil on their skin because they envy the appearance of Josephine Baker's shining body under the spotlights of the revue theaters (Rose, 101). Rather than highlighting the natural tints of the skin, makeup is used for inscription on the body's surface—inscrip-tion that emphasizes its own artificiality. The shorts and bathrobes of professional boxers shimmer like the slicked-down hair of gigolos and movie stars. [see **Boxing**] The appeal of the Channel swimmers is heightened by the layer of grease that they smear on their skin, to protect their bodies from the cold. [see **Endurance**] Young intellectuals, such as the playwright Bertolt Brecht, show a preference for tight, black leather jackets (Lepp, "Ledermythen").

Displaying one's body under a shining surface and in tight clothes is a means of self-staging that relegates all who gaze to a role of mere spectatorship. One can be erotically attracted to such a staged body without necessarily wishing to penetrate it. For since it reflects light, the shining body offers resistance to the external gaze, and closes itself off to interpretations that seek deep meaning and the satisfaction of erotic desire. Not surprisingly, many men are confused by the fact that they are attracted to Josephine Baker yet feel no erotic desire. [see **Dancing**] Above all, giving a shape to one's hair and body—with Vaseline and *gomina,* as well as with all the other techniques that transform bodies into surfaces that lure the gaze—is an act that objectifies the body and thus sets a distance between the body and the mind. Surface bodies cannot be expressive bodies; they cannot be signifiers articulating whatever is going on in a person's mind. Rather, as artifacts, they appeal to judgments of taste and to artistic ambition, and they are not meant to escape the control of the mind which has created them. Not even a cross-country bicycle race will change the outline of the champion's slicked-down hair. Completely detached from the minds of their human creators and fully at their disposal, stylized bodies become the objects of either purely aesthetic or purely sensual pleasure.

Ever since Rudolph Valentino separated from his second wife, Natasha Rambova, he has been in a state of deep depression, and has engaged in countless sexual liaisons with actresses and admirers. For some, it is Rudy's hair which, more than any other part of his artifact-body, contains and radiates a magic appeal. Mont Westmore, Valentino's makeup artist, often overhears words of praise from the actor's *amours,* among them Nita Naldi. While standing on the bridge of Valentino's cabin cruiser, keeping his eyes peeled for the treacherous reefs off Catalina, "he could hear her melodious voice extolling Rudy's capabilities. Mont always was especially amused when she would comment on his soft, sweet-smelling hair" (Morris, 177). Such hair is frequently associated with drugs—as in Gardel's tango "Tiempos viejos"—and with other controlled substances. During the years of Prohibition in the United States, hair tonic serves as one of those liquids which the bootlegging industry transubstantiates into drinkable liquor: "Up to a point the Cosmo Hair Tonic Company was legitimate. They advertised widely. They even paid celebrities to endorse the product . . . The conversion to drinkable liquor took place in the basement of a flower shop under the direction of a chemist we all called Karl the Dutchman, who was formerly employed by a toothpaste manufacturer . . . To fake scotch, bourbon, rye or whatever, Karl would let the rectified alcohol stand for weeks in charred barrels in which authentic whiskey had been aged" (Kobler, 307). Those literary protagonists who wear highly stylized hairdos and elaborate headdresses tend to live at a pace and an intensity that help them avoid depression and despondency. [see **Bars**] No other scenario embodies this complex interaction between self-stylization, constant risk, and incessant speed more impressively than the world of the—always young and almost always successful—financial broker. He is continually pressed to make quick decisions, and he has all the latest communication techniques at his command [see **Employees, Telephones, Wireless Communication**]: "At that moment the manager arrived, all neat and polished, his hair shining, his face perfectly shaved . . . He was thirty-two years old and had hazel eyes. 'Get me Amsterdam,' he said, and a few minutes later he heard the sounds being made at the home of the manager of the Netherlands Bank, in Amsterdam" (*Revista de Occidente*, 2). [see **Center = Periphery (Infinitude)**]

In Thomas Mann's novella "Unordnung und frühes Leid" ("Disorder and Early Sorrow"), a young stockbroker dances at the party organized by the teenaged children of Professor Cornelius: "There is a tall, pale, spindly youth, a dentist's son, who lives by playing the market. From all the professor hears, he is a perfect Aladdin. He owns a car, treats his friends to champagne dinners, and thinks nothing of showering them with presents, expensive trifles in mother-of-pearl and gold" (Mann, 513). The author is equally fascinated by these shiny little gifts and by the pale complexion of the broker—as well as by that of yet another guest, the young actor Herzl, who plays character roles on the most renowned German stages. Cornelius is trying to cope with what seems a flagrant contradiction in Herzl's appearance. Although Herzl hides his natural expression behind a skillfully applied mask of makeup, the professor cannot help thinking that this makeup is meant to stand for a certain mood in the actor's mind: "Herzl the actor is small and slight, but he could grow a thick black beard, as you can tell by the heavy coat of powder on his cheeks. His eyes are larger than life, with a deep and melancholy glow. He has put on rouge in addition to the powder—those dull carmine highlights on his cheeks can be nothing but makeup. 'Odd,' muses the professor. 'You'd think a man would be one thing or the other—not both a melancholic *and* a user of cosmetics" (506). Only one of the guests at the Cornelius party, a fellow named Möller, departs from the prevailing code of extreme body-stylization. In contrast to the disciplined tautness of those who want their bodies to be pale or reflective surfaces, Möller's clothing is ostentatiously loose and his body is heavy and natural. At the same time, he is the only guest who prefers traditional German folk music to fashionable "jazz dances" [see **Dancing**], and who plays his own guitar instead of rendering up his body to the rhythms of the gramophone. Möller is described as "a typical *Wander-vogel*"—that is, a member of a proto-Fascist youth movement. "He has a wild tangle of hair, horn-rimmed spectacles, and a long neck, and wears kneesocks and a belted shirt. His regular occupation . . . is banking, but he is something of an amateur folklorist and collects folksongs from all localities and in all languages. He sings them, too, and at Ingrid's command has brought his guitar" (506). Möller's preference for shorts resonates with Hitler's views. Hitler has expressed concern that tight pants might be excessively confining for the bodies of young men—and might thus jeopardize Germany's future: "In particular, among our young people, clothing must be seen in the context of education. The boy who runs around in the summer wearing long pants . . . loses an important incentive for strengthening his body" (Hitler, 457).

Related Entries

Bars, Boxing, Dancing, Employees, Endurance, Stars, Telephones, Wireless Communication, Authenticity vs. Artificiality, Center = Periphery (Infinitude)

References

Les Années-mémoire: 1926. Paris, 1988.
Adolf Hitler, *Mein Kampf* (1926). Munich, 1941.
John Kobler, *Ardent Spirits: The Rise and Fall of Prohibition.* New York, 1973.
Fritz Lang, *Metropolis* (1926). New York, 1973.

Nicola Lepp, "Ledermythen: Materialien zu einer Ikonographie der schwarzen Lederjacke." *Österreichische Zeitschrift für Volkskunde 5*, no. 47 (1963).

Thomas Mann, "Unordnung und frühes Leid" (1926). In Mann, *Sämtliche Erzählungen*. Frankfurt, 1963.

Michael Morris, *Madame Valentino: The Many Lives of Natasha Rambova*. New York, 1991.

Eva Orbanz, ed., *Valentino: Biographie/Filmographie/Essays*. Berlin, 1979.

Dieter Reichardt, ed., *Tango: Verweigerung und Trauer, Kontexte und Texte*. Frankfurt, 1984.

Revista de Occidente.

Paul Robert, ed., *Dictionnaire alphabétique et analogique de la langue française*. Paris, 1967.

Phyllis Rose, *Jazz Cleopatra: Josephine Baker in Her Time*. New York, 1989.

GRAMOPHONES

As a "small fragment of a great battle," Ernst Jünger's war memoir *Feuer und Blut (Fire and Blood)* describes a German assault on trenches held by British soldiers. After a day of savage fighting, the narrator and some of his companions make a surprising discovery while they are exploring dugouts in recently conquered territory: "By the edge of the hollow we discover yet a second shelter built into the bank. It lies at ground level and even has windows. Before we enter it we call out a few times, holding grenades in our fists and threatening to throw them in the window. Nothing stirs; it appears to be abandoned. If the messengers were above, this is certainly where the officers live. Everything is comfortably furnished—even luxurious, in a way—and compared to our own standards seems almost unbelievable . . . But what is that, standing in the corner? A gramophone of all things. H. quickly sets it in motion, and a merry tune fills the air. No, such jokes go too far. We don't belong here, and are taking a grave risk—an Englishman could look in the window at any moment. I knock the machine onto the ground. A scratching sound, and it falls silent" (Jünger, 172ff.). The atmosphere of relaxed sociability evoked by this gramophone forms a grotesque contrast with the landscape of death surrounding the British dugout. But are the soldiers really taking a "risk" in playing that "merry tune"? Is the narrator right in fearing that the sounds may attract the enemy? Regardless of any questions about military appropriateness, his reaction points to a promise—and a threat—inherent in the gramophone itself: the gramophone makes present those who are absent or dead. [see **Imma-nence = Transcendence (Death)**] This is why it fits well in the landscape of death, and this is why the narrator, by destroying and thus silencing the gramophone, conjures the fear that the enemy will return—as revenants.

Since long before the days of the Great War's trenches, gramophones have served an important function for the international secret service. [see **Reporters**] In Egon Erwin Kisch's *Die Hetzjagd (The Hunt)*, the director of Austro-Hungarian intelligence, Colonel Umanitzky, proudly explains this state-of-the-art instrument to Archduke Viktor Salvator, who is inspecting the troops: "This device is a gramophone, which will be wound up before important conversations. Here is the mouthpiece . . . Whatever is said will be transmitted by a needle to the gramophone disk, and will be recorded" (Kisch, 48). To Colonel Umanitzky's disappointment, His Imperial Highness isn't the slightest bit impressed by the gramophone's practical advantages. Rather, Salvator sees it as an instrument for fulfilling his status-conscious desire to immortalize himself as a patron of the arts and sciences: "I will have such a machine installed at home and will record what I say in the course of the day. Every evening I will send this recording to the philosophy class at the Academy of Sciences. As you know . . ., I'm a patron of the Academy of Sciences" (48). Before reacting to Umanitzky's explanations with this proposal, the archduke indulges in an obsessive stream of erotic fantasies, and surmises that the closet in which the gramophone is hidden contains bottles of champagne. The association of recorded music with champagne, and with women invited in for the officers' pleasure, is both more absurd and more appropriate within the plot of Kisch's tragicomedy than the prince's idea of using the gramophone to address the Academy of Sciences. For the unspeakable scandal lurking behind these scenes is the private life of Colonel Redl, who was responsible for introducing contemporary technology—including the gramophone—to the imperial intelligence service, and who, as a homosexual, is now being blackmailed by foreign agents to sell top secrets of the Austrian army. [see **Male = Female (Gender Trouble)**] The play will end with Redl's suicide.

Eight years after the end of the war that Kisch takes as his setting, an important technical innovation strengthens the gramophone's link to sex and death. Microphones and loudspeakers are replacing the huge horn-shaped amplifiers that the early recording industry has been using to register and reproduce sounds. The first Argentinian artist to use the new technology is tango star Carlos Gardel: beginning on Tuesday, November 30, all his recordings will be produced with the microphone. At the same time, the Buenos Aires press comments on a change in Gardel's public presence: "It had been a long time since Señor Gardel had performed in public. He had been devoting his time exclusively to gramophone recording, which has made him the most widely known name among fans of popular music, not only here but also in Europe" (Collier, 86ff.). The introduction of the microphone is the only possible explanation for the fact that Jorge Luis Borges labels 1926 as the year of the "degeneration of the tango" (Borges, 96). But why would Borges view the most important technical advance in the history of sound recording as a catalyst for decline? What he misses in the most recent recordings must be the scratchy quality that is inevitable with traditional forms of sound reproduction. Perhaps to him this scratchiness is the concretization of a genre-specific perspective by which each tango performance stages itself at a nostalgia-filled distance from a more "authentic" past world. [see **Gomina**] Most artists who perform on radio and on recordings come to see that the microphone has revolutionized their profession. Only now do they become fully aware of the fact that their audience is not physically present while they are performing in the studio. Said one singer, "My first experience in front of the microphone would have been horrible, if I had not . . . brought my wife and kept her close by me on a little stool, where she replaced the audience in the most charming way. After the first few words I forgot that I was addressing an inanimate [yet uncannily living] apparatus, and I imagined that the audience was as friendly and warm as my wife always is" (Schrader and Schebera, 185).

Concomitantly, there is a change in the advertising strategies of the companies that make gramophones. In the September 18 issue of the Buenos Aires magazine *Caras y Caretas,* a number of manufacturers present their "talking boxes" without any variation in perspective or context. Gramophones appear in tandem with cameras and home film projectors, and, astonishingly, the descriptions of the record players regularly omit any mention of sound quality: "NIRONA is the ideal Gramophone / For its construction / For its reliability / For its size / For its price." Instead of technical data concerning the sound reproduction, names and faces of popular artists—such as "The celebrated national duet GARDEL-RAZZANO"—appear alongside drawings or photographs of the gramophones. But less than a week later, on September 23, the Columbia Phonograph Company publishes a huge ad in the *New York Times* which focuses exclusively on the "marvelous" sound quality provided by the new technique of electronic recording:

> ELECTRICAL recording is the one great advance in the recording art in twenty years. Columbia New Process Records, with Viva-tonal Recording, are absolutely the *same* as the voices and instruments that make them. All the beauty, brilliance, and clarity of the original rendition and all the volume, too. The human voice is human—undistorted, natural. The instruments are all *real*. The violin is actual. The guitar is a guitar and nothing else. Each of the different woodwinds is unmistakable, each of the brasses genuine. Even the difficult piano is the piano itself—no less. And besides all this is the marvelously smooth surface of the *record* made possible by the *Columbia New Process*—no sound of the needle, no scratching noise. You hear nothing but the music.

In the world of music, as in the worlds of fashion and dance, bodily gestures and their effects (that is, playing and singing) are associated with a smooth surface. [see **Dancing, Gomina**] Even more important, the advertisement for the Columbia Phonograph Company catches the reader's attention with multiple tautologies that try to deny any difference between the original sound and the technically advanced reproduction. Taken together, this praise of "electrical recording" and the performers' new awareness of their distance from their audience add up to a strange paradox: the more the artists become visually aware of their auditors' absence, the less these auditors realize that the performers' absence has acoustic consequences. In other words, the more the musicians' bodies are absent, the more their music is present. This is the very effect which the player-piano has been foreshadowing for years. Its mysteriously moving keys point to a body which is simultaneously absent and present.

Quite regularly, the gramophone becomes associated with death—and sometimes even with murder. This association can be made intuitively, as in the extreme images evoked by Johannes Becher's poetry [see **Mountaineering, Murder**]:

> Oh,
> Melting Love! . . . Gramophone-choirs
> Whimpering in the wind of chimes! Oh,
> Holy song once among them, which
> Trilled over the mountains through the shining snow . . .
> And the companions of the murder victim
> Rolled uphill now, with black hats from the pub,
> Over the grave dug at the midnight hour
> Like a drinking barrel . . .
>
> (Becher, 90, 63)

In contrast, for Thomas Mann, who worries about the amount of time he spends listening to classical music on the record player, the relation between death and the gramophone (which he calls "the little coffin made of violin wood") becomes an object of explicit reflection, in the early manuscripts for his novel *Der Zauberberg,* or *The Magic Mountain* (Kolbe, 379). And in his novella "Unordnung und frühes Leid," it is the sound—and the silence—of the gramophone that structures the young people's dance party at the home of Professor Cornelius. Their gramophone plays all kinds of music—with the explicit exception of Spanish folk melodies. [see **Bullfighting, Jazz, Authenticity vs. Artificiality**] It may thus be no accident that Luis Buñuel becomes a record collector only after moving from Madrid to Paris: "It was in Paris that I really learned how to dance correctly. I took dance lessons and learned everything . . . Above all, I played jazz, and continued to play my banjo. I owned at least sixty records, a considerable number at that time" (Buñuel, 75).

Setting the rhythm for styles of dancing and socializing that are no longer based on the expression of feelings and thoughts, the gramophone is an indispensable element of modern life. [see **Dancing**] But as an emblem of ecstatic modernity, it also provokes resistance which, in turn, defines the rifts between different generations and cultures. [see **Present vs. Past**] "We alone were still dancing, and we kept dancing until Herr Roux and the Anglo-Saxon Corsican . . . not only refused to wind up the gramophone but insisted that we had to stop disturbing the sleeping guests with our music" (Schickele, 331). For the philosopher Theodor

Lessing, who is committed to the most progressive political agendas and to the most conservative cultural values, nothing is worse than the noise of modern life. "I've decided to steal a pocketwatch at some point—with the hope of being arrested. In prison I will at least have peace from the rug beating, the piano playing, the car horns, the gramophones, and the telephones" (Lessing, 401). [see **Automobiles, Telephones, Silence vs. Noise**] Those who share Lessing's disgust at the cacophony of modern life are even more repelled at the way in which "electrically" reproduced music and mass-produced lyrics are superseding what they consider to be authentic forms of literature and culture.

> Every couple of weeks, someone takes a poll: "Who is the most popular poet of the year?" The answer to this question is always inadequate. The poets who are familiar to us shouldn't even be taken into consideration. Not Rilke or Cäsar Flaischlen, not Goethe or Gottfried Benn, but Fritz Grünbaum ("If You Can't Do It, Let Me Try!"), Schanzer and Welisch ("If You See My Aunt"), Beda ("Bananas, of All Things!"), Dr. Robert Katscher ("Madonna, You're Prettier Than the Sunshine")— and who else? Still quite a few, even before Flaischlen, Rilke, and Benn get on the list. *The 222 Latest Hits*—that's the most widely read lyric anthology. Every two months the contents are revised and updated. The whole thing costs just ten pfennigs. (Siemsen, 256; Kittler, 127)

Why doesn't anybody ever object to classical orchestras or folksongs? Why is it only the gramophone that provokes such strong emotions and such endless controversy? The enthusiasm and the irritation which it generates stem from one and the same cause. Producing human sounds in the absence of human bodies, the gramophone inspires both the fear of ghosts and the hope for eternal life.

Related Entries

Automobiles, Bullfighting, Dancing, Gomina, Jazz, Mountaineering, Murder, Reporters, Telephones, Authenticity vs. Artificiality, Present vs. Past, Silence vs. Noise, Male = Female (Gender Trouble), Immanence = Transcendence (Death)

....

References

Johannes R. Becher, *Maschinenrhythmen*. Berlin, 1926.

Jorge Luis Borges, "Historia del Tango." In Borges, *Prosa completa*, vol. 1. Madrid, 1985.

Luis Buñuel, *Mein letzter Seufzer*. Frankfurt, 1985.

Caras y Caretas.

Simon Collier, *Carlos Gardel: Su vida, su música, su época*. Buenos Aires, 1986.

Ernst Jünger, *Feuer und Blut: Ein kleiner Ausschnitt aus einer grossen Schlacht* (1926). Hamburg, 1941.

Egon Erwin Kisch, *Die Hetzjagd: Eine Tragikomödie in fünf Akten des K.u.K. Generalstabs*. In Kisch, *Hetzjagd durch die Zeit*. Berlin, 1926.

Friedrich Kittler, *Grammophon, Film, Typewriter*. Berlin, 1986.

Jürgen Kolbe, *Heller Zauber: Thomas Mann in München, 1894–1933*. Berlin, 1987.

Theodor Lessing, "Die blauschwarze Rose" (1926). In Lessing, *"Ich warf eine Flaschenpost ins Eismeer der Geschichte": Essays und Feuilletons, 1923–1933*. Neuwied, 1986.

Thomas Mann, "Unordnung und frühes Leid" (1926). In Mann, *Sämtliche Erzählungen*. Frankfurt, 1963.

New York Times.

René Schickele, *Maria Capponi*. Munich, 1926.

Bärbel Schrader and Jürgen Schebera, eds., *Kunstmetropole Berlin, 1918–1933: Die Kunststadt in der Novemberrevolution / Die "goldenen" Zwanziger / Die Kunststadt in der Krise*. Berlin, 1987.

Hans Siemsen, "Die Literatur der Nichtleser" (1926). In Anton Kaes, ed., *Weimarer Republik: Manifeste und Dokumente zur deutschen Literatur, 1918–1933*. Stuttgart, 1983.

HUNGER ARTISTS

In his poem "Der Hungerkünstler," the Communist writer Johannes Becher uses the profession of hunger artist as a metaphor for certain aspects of capitalist exploitation. Promising a health cure, an allegorical "usury dragon" lures "man" into one of those transparent boxes *(Hungerkästen)* where hunger artists display themselves before a crowd of paying spectators. Then the dragon stares fascinated into the "nothingness" of the cage: "I lock you up, man, in a hunger box: / There starve yourself healthy! With eyes crooked and crossed, / Glare into the nothingness. It's time to fast" (Becher, 147). The poem describes the way in which such "hunger people" are surrounded by billionaires who enjoy the sight of poverty and starvation in much the same way they appreciate artistic representations of Christ's crucifixion: "You, the hunger nation: in the billionaires' district / The stones sweat glittering gold; / The priest keeps watch over a newly bronzed Christ / hanging on the Cross. Stocks and bonds flutter around him like little angels" (136). Becher's metaphors are oblique—for hunger artists choose to stage their suffering as a publicly appealing (and therefore money-making) performance, whereas usually hunger is an involuntary condition of proletarian life. But the poet seems to accept this asymmetry—probably because it allows him to bring out an important sado-masochistic element in capitalist exploitation: proletarians accept their suffering all too willingly, and, for capitalists, displaying this torment to the public's gaze can bring financial returns.

A similar sado-masochistic dynamic attracts thousands of paying spectators to the hunger artists' cages—although it is often disguised under various philosophical and even theological discourses. The crowds in front of the cages admire the paradox of a human existence which, isolated from its earthly nourishment, acquires a quasi-transcendental aura: "We sip the wind, we taste the gases, / smoke fat with oil, coated in flaming red / we savor, and when it snows we graze the ground up. Mouth patched up" (Becher, 134). [see **Immanence vs. Transcendence**] With erotic pleasure, the spectators gaze at signs of putrefaction on the surface of bodies that seem close to the threshold between life and death: "For such a starving body grows budding ulcers / Look, they spring up around my throat in various colors" (135). Above all, hunger artists impress their audience because they seem to confront death with open eyes: "I still can feel it at the joints: / I am still flesh and bones. You, Light, / but slowly feed my death" (136). [see **Boxing, Bullfighting, Endurance, Mountaineering, Mummies, Six-Day Races, Immanence = Transcendence (Death)**] Like many professional athletes, hunger artists take their bodies to the limit between life and death—but unlike, say, boxers or bullfighters, they are free to choose the moment that ends the self-inflicted lethal threat. Like champion long-distance runners, the best hunger artists are striving to break records—but instead of pushing the limit as far as they can, they normally conclude their fast once they have beaten the previous mark. In late March, in Berlin, the hunger artist Jolly sets a new world record by going without food for forty-four days. On April 21, also in Berlin, the hunger team "Harry and Fastello" surpass this feat by just one day. Almost exactly a month later, on Saturday, May 22, Fred Ellern in Vienna concludes a public fast of forty-six days and six hours (*Chronik*, 98).

Since no one knows precisely where the boundary between emaciation and death lies for individual bodies, only death can prove that hunger artists have gone to the ultimate limit, and that, like the best boxers or mountain climbers, they have completely abandoned the principle of self-preservation. This problem of obtaining evidence of hunger artists' willingness to face lethal danger may account for the fact that the market for their performances has become unstable, although enthusiasm for professional sports in general is rapidly growing. While Jolly earns more than 100,000 marks from ticket sales, Harry and Fastello draw few people—not even enough to cover their expenses. To counter this decline, hunger artists begin to spice up their shows with attacks of frenzy and with ostentatiously aggressive behavior. This, however, seems only to create the impression that their control over the risk of starvation allows them to manipulate the spectators at will. The tone of a brief notice published by the *Berliner Volks-Zeitung* on May 14 reveals a general suspicion of deceit associated with the hunger artists: "Nelson, the hunger artist from Leipzig, who, as recently reported, was a swindler and was taken to the hospital, has not kept his promise to put himself at the disposal of the prosecuting attorney after his release from the hospital. According to the *Leipziger Tageszeitung,* Nelson, together with his manager, Schutzendübel, disappeared from Leipzig."

What the spectacle of starvation lacks is a degree of contingency that could relativize the hunger artists' professional self-control. Mountain climbers, Channel swimmers, and aviators expose themselves to the overwhelming powers of the elements, and runners and bicycle racers reach speeds that exceed the brain's reaction time. Speed, nature, and technology authenticate the seriousness of their confrontation with death, whereas the hunger artists' psychic breakdowns cannot help appearing artificial. [see **Authenticity vs. Artificiality**] Offering only minimal visual excitement within any span of time that a spectator can afford to spend in front of their boxes, the hunger artists perform feats that no longer correspond to the latest fashions in staging the drama of human existence. Their degree of personal agency remains too strong for starving to be perceived as a confrontation with death; their frail bodies underscore rather than question the strength of the human will. [see **Action vs. Impotence**]

Since 1924, four short prose texts by Franz Kafka under the title *Ein Hungerkünstler* have been on the market, in an edition by Die Schmiede, which also publishes the poems of Johannes Becher (Wagenbach, 189). The third of Kafka's pieces, which explores the psyche of a hunger artist, begins by affirming that the great age of this profession is coming to an end: "In the past few decades, interest in professional fasting has markedly declined" (175). The protagonist thinks nostalgically of the days when starving was an international sensation: "At any rate, one fine day the pampered hunger artist suddenly found himself deserted by the amusement seekers, who went streaming past him to other, more popular attractions. For the last time, his manager sent him on a rapid tour throughout half of Europe, to see whether the old interest mightn't still survive here and there. All in vain: everywhere, as if by secret agreement, people displayed a positive revulsion toward professional fasting" (181). Since he is only too aware of the reasons for this crisis, Kafka's hunger artist sinks into a depression that sometimes turns into fits of rage (which his manager tries to market as a psychologically interesting spectacle). The narrow, self-reflexive circle within which he monitors his own performance cannot help giving rise to suspicions of cheating: "No one could possibly watch the hunger artist every minute, day and night, and so no one could produce first-hand evidence that his fast really had been rigorous and continuous; only the artist himself could know that. Inevitably, then, he was the only spectator of his own fast who could be completely satisfied with the performance" (177). Even more important, Kafka's fictional hunger artist is frustrated by the fact that he never fasts for more than about forty days. He is aware that such a limit is arbitrary and undramatic:

> The longest period of fasting was fixed by his manager at forty days . . . Experience had shown that for about forty days the public's interest could be kept up by an increasingly vigorous advertising campaign, but that subsequently the townspeople would begin to lose interest, and support would begin to wane . . . So on the fortieth day the flower-bedecked cage was opened, enthusiastic spectators filled the hall, a military band played, two doctors entered the cage to declare the results of the fast through a megaphone . . . And at this point the artist always turned stubborn . . . Why stop fasting at this particular moment, after forty days? He had held out a long time, an immeasurably long time. Why stop now, when he was at the top of his form, or rather not yet quite at the top of his form?" (178ff.)

Systematically deprived of any dangerous proximity to death, the hunger artist enters a period of professional and emotional decline. He ends up in a circus, as part of the animal show. But even there nobody cares about him. When, days or perhaps weeks after his death, the circus attendants discover his corpse, he has finally managed to demonstrate his willingness to confront death—but he has crossed the boundary between life and death in the most unspectacular way.

The dead hunger artist is replaced by a panther. Unlike him, the animal is so full of life that, confined in the former hunger box, it offers an exciting spectacle for the paying crowd: "His noble body, filled almost to the bursting point with all that it needed, seemed to carry freedom around with it too. Somewhere in his jaws it seemed to lurk; and the joy of life streamed with such ardent passion from his throat that for the onlookers it was difficult to bear the shock of it. But they braced themselves, crowded around the cage, and were reluctant ever to move away" (185).

Related Entries

Boxing, Bullfighting, Endurance, Mountaineering, Mummies, Six-Day Races, Action vs. Impotence, Authenticity vs. Artificiality, Immanence vs. Transcendence, Individuality vs. Collectivity, Immanence = Transcendence (Death)

References

Johannes R. Becher, *Maschinenrhythmen*. Berlin, 1926.
Berliner Volks-Zeitung.
Chronik 1926.: Tag für Tag in Wort und Bild. Dortmund, 1985.
Franz Kafka, *Ein Hungerkünstler* (1924). In Kafka, *Die Erzählungen*. Frankfurt, 1961.
Klaus Wagenbach, *Franz Kafka: Bilder aus seinem Leben*. Berlin, 1983.

JAZZ

During the final press conference that Jack Dempsey holds at his training camp in Atlantic City, N.J., on Wednesday, September 22, twenty-four hours before his title fight with Gene Tunney [see **Boxing**], the heavyweight champion of the world is eager to show that he has the tastes of a gentleman of leisure:

> Dempsey was dressed in a gray suit, double-breasted coat, and white-bottomed trousers and wore a blue bow tie. While the interview was in progress, a moving van backed to the curbstone and two men entered the house to remove the articles which were not part of the furnished home the champion rented, for Dempsey is through with his West Atlantic City abode. The first thing the workmen tackled was a radio cabinet on which some Victoria records were lying. "Those records don't go out boys," the champion exclaimed as the moving men started to pick them up. "Put them on the table there for the time being." Dempsey explained that he was still as keen as ever for the jazz records, with now and then a waltz tune. "They're a great relief at times." (*New York Times,* September 23)

Of course, Dempsey's enthusiasm for jazz is part of a well-calculated media image. On the one hand, his image must fit the reputation of the "Manassa Mauler" as the incarnation of elementary physical strength. On the other, it strives to present the champion as an alternative to

Tunney, who is famous for bragging of his high-brow tastes: "After an evening meal . . . he retired to his room and his literature" (*New York Times,* September 23). Jazz is perhaps the only cultural form that combines the attributes of sophisticated taste and raw physical force. But can one really trust Dempsey's declaration of love for jazz if he admits, at the same time, that he occasionally replaces jazz with waltzes?

Whatever the truth may be, the white heavyweight champion of the world is not the only public figure to overstate his fondness for jazz, which is now generally perceived as an expression of African-American culture (Fordham, 20). Many writers—especially in Europe—would rather publicly state a preference for Jack Dempsey's taste than for Gene Tunney's. The hero of Bertolt Brecht's "Eine kleine Versicherungsgeschichte" ("A Little Insurance Story") finds that listening to jazz, together with consuming hard liquor and coffee and attending metropolitan revues, is a way of raising his energy level [see **Bars, Revues**]: "He had whipped up his flagging vitality with all kinds of jazz" (Brecht, 170). The poet Johannes Becher takes this motif of the connection between music and bodily energy one step further when, in a text on prostitutes ("Dirnen"), he describes gypsy music and jazz as setting different rhythms for sexual intercourse:

> Flesh
> kneading ourselves into meat: us,
> embracing, we were melting into each other,
> pasty . . . spraying
> sounds: gypsy violins! And hacking joints
> a bony whirlpool: the jazz-band.
>   (Becher, p. 75)

Physically fulfilling sex is sex that has been "whipped up" by the pace of other cultures, and while gypsy rhythms are associated with lubricity ("spraying sounds"), jazz suggests destruction ("hacking joints").

Although jazz as concept and metaphor invariably evokes scenes in which the human body is coupled to strong rhythms [see **Assembly Lines, Dancing, Employees**], it certainly does not belong to that series of cultural forms which regularly turn surface against depth, and sheer movement against expression. [see **Authenticity vs. Artificiality, Gomina, Movie Palaces**] White intellectuals wish to find in jazz the essence of an uncanny strength for which they have no appropriate words, but which confuses their value-hierarchies and enthrones black culture and black bodies as objects of desire:

> The negroes are here. All of Europe dances to the sound of their banjos. We can't help ourselves. Some say it's the rhythms of Sodom and Gomorrah . . . Why shouldn't it be those from Paradise? Here origin and decline are fused . . . and here we see the fusion of the "best" and the "worst" art. These negroes come from the darkest parts of New York. There they were despised and outlawed. These beautiful women may have been saved from a squalid ghetto, where they bathed their splendid limbs in dishwater. They're definitely not from the jungle—let's not kid ourselves. Nevertheless, they are a new, untouched race. Their dancing comes out of their blood, their life . . . The main thing is the negro blood. Drops of it are falling on Europe—a land, long dry, that has almost ceased to breathe. Is this the cloud that looks so black on the horizon? A shimmering stream of fertility? . . . Do the negroes need us, or do we not rather need them? (Goll, 257–258)

What provokes this reflection is the impossibility of attributing jazz—with all its connotations of authenticity—to the African continent, which, on the mental map of many European intellectuals, is a realm of authenticity and longing. [see **Center vs. Periphery**] Since jazz emerges from America's urban slums, it belongs to the very milieu in contrast to which white culture struggles to maintain its claim to superiority.

Those writers who accept the challenge of jazz are inspired to attempt redefinitions of culture as a whole. The culture of the present is seen as centered in a passionate "love" for authenticity and reality: "Music is today's most authentic art—a music for the unnamed, written for the masses. It's not important whether good jazz has lasting value, or whether it will be immediately replaced; either way, its time has come. Blaring and buzzing, playful and lightly sentimental, jazz has no beginning or end, with its merciless, rhythmic stamp" (von Wedderkop, 253). As part and condensation of contemporary reality, jazz relies on matter, on the primary physical qualities of sound, rather than on expression or form. It thus becomes the hope of a culture that is obsessed with having lost its stable ground. [see **Uncertainty vs. Reality**] "Ours is the age of matter and not of form, an age of quantity, an age for which nothing is so ridiculous and superfluous as the mere (sublime) form—art for art's sake. Our age seeks art not in expression, not in form, but in matter permeated with rhythm" (ibid.).

With flamboyant unpretentiousness and consistently heavy sexual connotations, the titles of many jazz recordings [see **Gramophones**] emphasize matter—especially food, which is to be relished: "Fat Meat and Greens," "Droppin' Shucks," "Mr. Jelly Lord," "Clarinet Marmalade," "Hot Mustard," "Cornet Chop Suey." These titles, as well as the name of one of the most famous jazz musicians, Jelly Roll Morton, indicate a preference for soft, only faintly structured types of food. This mirrors the prevailing perception of jazz as a music "without beginning or end," as a dynamic form that dissolves all traditional forms of culture. At the same time, these titles and names refer to the rich, spicy dishes of the American South, where jazz originates—though the most active performers and composers have moved north, mainly to Chicago (Fordham, 18ff.). In Chicago, jazz occupies center stage at some of the city's most popular entertainment palaces, such as Lincoln Gardens, and its sound is being lightened and polished by young white musicians, such as Benny Goodman, Bix Beiderbecke, and Gene Krupa. But above all, jazz has become the music of the speakeasies, where liquor is illegally sold and consumed during the years of Prohibition. [see **Bars**]

Fans and cultural critics mostly perceive jazz as the collective product of a band behind which individual musicians tend to disappear: "Jazz [is] largely an ensemble music, with improvisations being mostly a matter of texture and embroidery rather than the streams of spontaneous new melody" (Fordham, 21). A bold decision by the Chicago bandleader Joe "King" Oliver breaks the rules according to which such ensembles are constituted. He integrates young Louis Armstrong as a second cornet player into his Creole Band, and this move triggers a development that transforms jazz from a group product into a medium of unpredictable improvisation and individuality: "Armstrong was . . . doubling the number of notes he would squeeze into a bar, and sounding them at unequal lengths and with unpredictable emphasis. The music began to take on a tidal ebb and swell rather than the raglike rocking time that had gone before. He also seemed to build his improvisations over longer stretches, like miniature narratives." [see **Individuality vs. Collectivity, Individuality = Collectivity (Leader)**] Some musicians who work within the tradition of serious concert performance, such as Igor Stravinsky and Paul Hindemith, proudly admit that they integrate "elements of jazz" into their compositions (*Chronik*, 186). But many European intellectuals continue to resist jazz, as a predominantly African-American form. For Thomas Mann, jazz, boxing, and film mean nothing but "crudeness and flatness" (Kolbe, 378). The philosopher and journalist Theodor Lessing noisily complains about the noisiness of modern culture [see **Gramophone**]—yet not without a certain ambivalence: "Only recently our culture has adopted the custom of adding the strange effect of the human voice to the amazing panoply of sounds that include aggressive clinking against glass, abrupt crumpling of paper, clanging of steel, mournful tones of wood, stopped-up, clanging, clattering, clapping noises. We call the source of this nonsense and fun a jazz band. The Jays are such a jazz band" (Lessing, 232). Lessing's value judgments are situated between the poles of "nonsense and fun" throughout this text. It is as if he did not quite dare to come to an unequivocally negative conclusion. At the end of his essay, he praises both jazz and jays. But he denies them what by Western standards are the most heroic faculties of human existence—namely, the capacity of being creative and of being tragic: "Free flight is denied them. And when these show-offs and jesters enter the open space of the heavens, they become helpless and subdued. They are denied their own song. There is no song that they are forced to sing, but there is also none that they cannot simply imitate and echo. They are genuinely beautiful and barren. But this flight is without tragedy" (233). [see **Action = Impotence (Tragedy)**] Obviously, it is difficult to appreciate the strength of cultural forms before one has become familiar with them.

Related Entries

Assembly Lines, Bars, Boxing, Dancing, Employees, Gomina, Gramophone, Movie Palaces, Revues, Authenticity vs. Artificiality, Center vs. Periphery, Individuality vs. Collectivity, Uncertainty vs. Reality, Action = Impotence (Tragedy), Individuality = Collectivity (Leader)

References

Johannes R. Becher, *Maschinenrhythmen*. Berlin, 1926.
Bertolt Brecht, "Eine kleine Versicherungsgeschichte" (1926). In *Gesammelte Werke*, vol. 11. Frankfurt, 1967.
Chronik 1926: Tag für Tag in Wort und Bild. Dortmund, 1985.

John Fordham, *Jazz: History, Instruments, Musicians, Recordings*. London, 1993.

Yvan Goll, "Die Neger erobern Europa" (1926). In Anton Kaes, ed., *Weimarer Republik: Manifeste und Dokumente zur deutschen Literatur, 1918–1933*. Stuttgart, 1983.

Yasushi Ishii, "Recordings of 1926." Unpublished manuscript. San Francisco, 1994.

Jürgen Kolbe, *Heller Zauber: Thomas Mann in München, 1894–1933*. Berlin, 1987.

Theodor Lessing, "Die Häher" (1926). In *"Ich warf eine Flaschenpost ins Eismeer der Geschichte": Essays und Feuilletons, 1923–1933*. Neuwied, 1986.

New York Times.

Hermann von Wedderkop, "Wandlungen des Geschmacks" (1926). In Anton Kaes, ed., *Weimarer Republik: Manfeste und Dokumente zur deutschen Literatur, 1918–1933*. Stuttgart, 1983.

LEAGUE OF NATIONS

On Saturday, March 20, the philologist, philosopher, novelist, and former rector of the University of Salamanca, Miguel de Unamuno, writes a letter to his friend Jean Cassou from the Basque border-town of Hendaye, where he lives, having been exiled by the Spanish military government under Miguel Primo de Rivera. Unamuno is in a triumphant mood, although he expresses his feelings in words of sorrow and concern: "Ah, my dear Cassou, how the tragedy of my poor Spain and my poor heart deepens! I am beginning to lose hope that I shall live to see the sun of justice enlighten Spain. Geneva has taught us a good lesson, and the tyrannical government of Don Alfonso . . . must have understood that to gain a voice and a vote in a League of Nations it is necessary to be a nation" (Unamuno, 188–189). [see **Action = Impotence (Tragedy)**] The "good lesson" of Geneva which Unamuno mentions is a major defeat suffered by Spanish foreign politics, only three days earlier, at the League of Nations. During its annual plenary session in March, this international assembly was expected to approve the entry of Germany as a new member. The ideal of establishing a family of nations united by the shared goals of peace and territorial stability seemed finally to have prevailed over the economic interests and national resentments that had shaped the Treaty of Versailles in 1919. One of the prearranged conditions for Germany's return to the stage of international politics was its participation, as a permanent member, in the Council of Nations, the League's equivalent of a State's executive body. But Brazil, China, Poland, and Spain upset this scenario of harmony by making their approval of Germany's admittance contingent on their own permanent representation in the Council of Nations. Individually, none of these four countries was strong enough to impose its will. But a positive decision on Germany's entry could not be reached without them, because it required a unanimous vote. So the plenary assembly adjourned on March 17 (*Chronik*, 52ff.). This is the national humiliation to which Unamuno refers, and to which the Spanish government reacts by announcing its resignation from the League of Nations on June 10 (Langer, 992). For Unamuno, the dignity of a nation, which he believes Spain lacks, is embodied in the ethical values and public behavior of its representatives. Although by calling the members of Primo de Rivera's government "little tyrants for rent" he is explicitly pointing to their disregard for public opinion (Unamuno, 193), he presupposes, somewhat paradoxically, that the dignity of the nation and of every Spaniard—including the dignity of those who, like himself, are persecuted by their government—is compromised by the failures of Spain's politicians. From this perspective, belonging to a nation is indeed analogous to being a member of a family. [see **Collectivity vs. Individuality**]

In the context of the inadequate expectations arising from such a point of view and from the highly idealistic discourses that surround the League of Nations, Carl Schmitt, a professor of law at the University of Bonn, publishes a small book during the days of the debate over Germany's entry. Criticizing the current conflation of the semantics of individuality with the semantics of collectivity in the concept of nationhood [see **Collectivity = Individuality (Leader)**], as well as the reduction of conflicting political interests to the model of a family quarrel, Schmitt wishes to distinguish the State as a political system and from the people or nation: "In truth, the term *Völkerbund* refers to relationships between states and their governments, not between peoples or—despite the French appellation 'Société des Nations' or the English 'League of Nations'—between nations" (Schmitt, 4ff.). Consequently, the sphere of politics, where politicians negotiate relations of power, has to be separated from the world as a community of nations. On the basis of similar distinctions, Schmitt argues—counter to those who hail the League of Nations as the realization of a utopian ideal—that the acknowledgment of particular political interests, of their unavoidable conflict, and even of a hierarchy in the realm of political power is a necessary condition for the League's success: "We cannot solve the problem of the *Völkerbund* with calls for depoliticization. A *Völkerbund* can exist only so long as at least one major power has a political interest in it, or so long as the smaller powers united in it become a major power. A depoliticized *Völk-erbund* would neither be politically interesting nor make any contribution to world peace" (6ff.). In order for the necessary political conflict to exist, Schmitt believes, independent states must be defined by the borders of the territories over which they have jurisdiction. Thus, the programmatic idea of translating the boundlessness of humanity into a political reality without clear territorial borders [see **Center = Periphery (Infinitude)**] is, according to Schmitt, an immanent danger for the League of Nations: "Without borders there is no jurisdiction" (5).

Schmitt's analysis implies that international politics has reached an impasse because those who wish to open and develop this space do not understand that it can be occupied only by independent territorial states, whereas those who promote and protect particular national interests and territorial borders are unwilling to make the necessary distinction between nations and states. Since among the latter group the concept of the nation runs counter to the acknowledgment of shared international goals, the League of Nations comes under increasing attack from various national movements: "Geneva [has] so many enemies all over the world, from Chicherin to Mussolini and all the other nationalists. Scornful laughter from Hell would greet the failure of international democracy" (*8 Uhr–Abendblatt,* March 15). This explains why General Erich von Ludendorff, a veteran of the Great War who castigates Adolf Hitler's party for the mildness of its anti-Semitism, praises the "people's movement" for resisting an internationalist conspiracy that he blames on Jews, the Catholic Church, and the Freemasons: "Disarmament was meant to be the trump card of their politics, which corresponds completely to Jewish and Masonic ideology. The people are led into the web of Jewish politics or, they hope, into the Catholic State of God. Having already lost, the nations are now rendered spiritually defenseless. The nationalist movement alone offered serious resistance" (von Ludendorff, 54ff.).

Four days after the adjournment of the League's plenary assembly, the German president, Paul von Hindenburg, another World War general, arrives in Cologne to celebrate the withdrawal of French troops from the

Rhineland, which they have occupied since 1919 (*Chronik, 32, 55*). Hindenburg speaks both to nationalist assemblies and to their adversaries, who claim to represent internationalism in the name of a German democratic tradition. He is thus confronted with the impossible task of affirming both the position of those who see the liberation of the Rhineland as a victory over the League of Nations and the reaction of those who praise it as the glorious result of the League's peace policy: "In the evening, thousands of nationalist war veterans gathered on the Platz der Republik for a torchlight procession, which made a gorgeous and colorful image with its hundreds of flags. On the Neuer Markt, however, no imposing republican rally took place" (*Berliner Tageblatt*, March 21).

A different articulation of the tension between the German supporters and the German enemies of "Geneva" appears in their conflicting ways of structuring historical time. The nationalists claim that resisting and fighting the obligations arising from the Treaty of Versailles is a necessary precondition for Germany's future as a nation—and they are therefore eager to keep alive the humiliating memory of Versailles as a motivational resource. In contrast, Gustav Stresemann, who leads the German delegation in Geneva, has conceived of a foreign politics according to which the meticulous fulfillment of the Versailles treaty will ultimately enable everyone to forget it—and thus prepare the way for a future that is dissociated from the shameful past. [see **Present vs. Past**] On Friday, September 10, after months of hectic international and national negotiations (*Chronik*, 150ff.), Stresemann finally salutes Germany's entry into the League of Nations with a programmatic speech: "Far be it from me to speak of the problems the past. It is the task of the present generation to look toward the future. Let me emphasize that if long deliberation has preceded Germany's membership in the League of Nations, this may be a guarantee of stability and fruitfulness" (Stresemann, 303). Aristide Briand, the French prime minister and foreign secretary, expresses the same desire for a rupture with the past in his promise to fight any future urgings to make war: "No spirit of war here. If they rouse us against one another, if they push us, we will brush aside the temptation, because this would be the road to war, the road of blood, not our road" (*Années-mémoire*, 69).

On March 17, one week after Germany's entry into the League of

Nations, Briand and Stresemann meet for a lunch conversation at a small hotel in the French village of Thoiry, near the border with Switzerland. The postcards and the countless newspaper illustrations that commemorate their encounter follow the well-established pattern of showing deputies to the League of Nations united around a table. To see the representatives of former rival nations sitting together at a table for a long discussion without translators or any other witnesses seems to fulfill the dream of an international politics that will resemble the private relations of a family—even if the special menu for Briand and Stresemann's meeting obeys the nonprivate rules of the international diplomatic stage: "Selection of hors-d'oeuvres / Foie gras aspic / Trout au bleu / Chicken Henri IV / Duck with truffles and port / Peas fermière / Roast partridge canapé / Cheese plate / Fruit basket / Iced Vacherin" (*Années-mémoire*, 70). Less than three months later, on December 10, Gustav Stresemann and Aristide Briand jointly receive the Nobel peace prize. But despite such public recognition, Germany's integration into the League of Nations has probably impaired, rather than fostered, the reputation of this institution. While supporters of the League still hope that it will lead humankind to a future of supranational harmony, they begin to acknowledge that, so far, it has been more bureaucratically complicated than politically efficient: "One cannot underestimate the importance of the League of Nations. But it would not be difficult to show that the edicts of this highly respected assembly have existed much more on paper than in political reality. The League has been unsuccessful in extinguishing the fires of political crisis that have erupted all over the globe" (*8 Uhr–Abendblatt,* March 15). This incapacity of countries to negotiate a stable consensus and find collectively binding solutions to international problems has by now become almost proverbial—so much so, that a journalist can use it as a metaphor when chastising boxing champion Jack Dempsey for avoiding matches with his multiple challengers [see **Boxing**]: "It is harder to make a match with Mr. Dempsey than to ratify a treaty between nations" (Dempsey and Dempsey, 180).

Related Entries

Boxing, Individuality vs. Collectivity, Present vs. Past, Action = Impotence (Tragedy), Center = Periphery (Infinitude), Individuality = Collectivity (Leader)

References

8 Uhr–Abendblatt.

Les Années-mémoire: 1926. Paris, 1988.

Berliner Tageblatt.

Chronik 1926: Tag für Tag in Wort und Bild. Dortmund, 1985.

Jack Dempsey and Barbara Piattelli Dempsey, *Dempsey.* New York 1977.

William L. Langer, *An Encyclopedia of World History.* Boston, 1980.

General Ludendorff, *Vom Feldherrn zum Weltrevolutionär und Wegbereiter Deutscher Volksschöpfung, II: Meine Lebenserinnerungen von 1926 bis 1933.* Stuttgart, 1951.

Carl Schmitt, *Die Kernfrage des Völkerbundes.* Berlin, 1926.

Gustav Stresemann, "Deutschlands Eintritt in den Völkerbund: Rede in der Völkerbundsversammlung in Genf, 10.9.1926." In Stresemann, *Reden und Schriften: Politik/Geschichte/Literatur, 1897–1926.* Dresden, 1926.

Miguel de Unamuno, *Epistolario inédito* (1926). Madrid, 1991.

MOUNTAINEERING

Silence and eternity: these are the qualities that Hart Crane associates with the sublime landscape he evokes in his poem "North Labrador": "A land of leaning ice / Hugged by plaster-grey arches of sky, / Flings itself silently / Into eternity" (Crane, 21). [see **Silence vs. Noise, Present = Past (Eternity)**] Nordic nature, though awe-inspiringly cold and indifferent, is presented as an object of potential erotic desire—"potential" because no human being has ever been exposed to its temptations and because, therefore, no human gaze has ever awakened its sexuality: "Has no one come here to win you, / Or left you with the faintest blush / Upon your glittering breasts? / Have you no memories, O Darkly Bride?" The questions remain unanswered. For although ice and silence are subject to the "shifting of moments" as elementary temporal structures, they host no life that could transform this unchanging rhythm into the form of a history to be remembered. [see **Present vs. Past**] The sexuality that Crane associates with the icy mountains of North Labrador can be attributed only to the mountains themselves: "Cold-hushed, there is only the shifting of moments / That journey toward no Spring— / No birth, no death, no time nor sun / In answer."

In its November 6 issue, the Buenos Aires magazine *Caras y Caretas* publishes a poem entitled "Desde los Andes" ("From the Andes") which is likewise a lyrical evocation of an icy, mountainous South American landscape. But this poem differs from Crane's in that it explicitly stages and narrates man's confrontation with nature. This confrontation takes the form of a tension between a subject that bears all the conventional traits of the Romantic poet and the overwhelming closeness of the mountains, in which the Romantic subject senses the presence of death. [see **Immanence = Transcendence (Death)**] In its proud solitude and its "satanic" cynicism, the lyrical "I" at first rivals the coldness of the surrounding nature:

> My immoderate satanic pride
> finally trod, beneath its triumphant feet,
> the apex of the mountain heights, never before tracked,
> Not even by golden eagles . . .
> The sky laments my pain . . . and everything
> Is obliterated by darkness and undone by mire,
> And above the ice of the summit, standing tall,
>
> My soul is so frozen that it does not notice,
> Snarling over the cadaver of my life,
> That gigantic black bear—death!

Whereas Crane's poem involves no explicit subjectivity whose imagination could transform the mountains of North Labrador into an erotic body, the lethal threat of the mountains in "Desde los Andes" finally— and paradoxically—warms the icy spaces of the observer's soul. The menacing presence of nature imbues the poet-observer's view of his own existence with a pervasive anxiety that heightens and intensifies his feeling of life:

> The darkness spread and became denser,
> Almost palpable, like something alive;
> And a convulsive anguish shook
> The frozen peace of the immense mountain . . .
>
> And there was a silence of thoughtful pain
> That, thinking, increases its pain . . .
> Life became more sensitive,
> And emotion, deeper and more intense!

Ice and snow, the mountains and the cold, seem regularly and invariably to trigger such associations with death and sexuality. Even a modest sonnet on the month of January published in the Madrid weekly *Blanco y Negro* imparts this dual connotation to a description of frost-flowers, a canonical symbol of the domestication of sublime nature: "White archway of frost-flowers, / . . . / Are you a bridal veil? Are you a shroud? / A white sepulcher? A pearly tabernacle? / Lightning of death or glow of the moon?"

But icy mountains, lethal danger, and erotic desire are not exclusively a poetic pattern. With the same regularity as in lyrical texts, mountains appear as a landscape of death in the daily news: "The two students from Munich who, as we reported, have been missing since they hiked into the mountains from Innsbruck were discovered dead on the east face of the 'Wilder Kaiser'" (*Berliner Morgenpost*, July 25). [see **Cremation**] The *New York Times* features a "grim tragedy of the North" on its front page of September 25, under a headline that, once again, plays on the motif of ice and violent death: "Eskimo Killed Prof. Marvin . . .; Confesses Arctic Crime of Seventeen Years Ago; Victim, Reported Drowned, Was Shot." What follows are complicated but inconclusive conjectures about why "two Eskimo boys" murdered the young Cornell professor Ross G. Marvin on a North Pole expedition in 1909. [see **Murder, Polarities**] But the display of factual details tends to disappear behind the powerful images of the "Arctic crime" reiterated in many papers: "Kudlooktoo Says Explorer Went Mad and Left Other Eskimo to Die . . . They Declare They Invented the Tale of the Drowning in Fear of White Man's Wrath." Neither in newspaper stories nor in poems does the association of icy mountains with death require any explanation. The philosopher Theodor Lessing cannot imagine mountain climbers other than as "hovering over the abyss" (Lessing, 142), and the Communist poet Johannes Becher evokes the Alpine landscape of Davos as a natural place for rich people to die: "For years, however, quite a few had to lie / On deck chairs in Davos, spitting lungs; thus / We care for ourselves: guzzling rot" (Becher, 103). Only Egon Erwin Kisch, a journalist, seems to discuss the tension between the classic image of mountains as an idyllic environment and their scenic function as a theater of death and crime. Kisch begins his essay "Verbrechen in den Hochalpen" ("Crime in the Upper Alps") with an evocation of all the traditionally positive commonplaces and expectations related to Alpine landscapes: "Up in the highland pastures, there is no sin, let alone crime, that would not seem inconceivable: gently grazes the little lamb, softly the American woman says "How lovely," good-natured cows stare at the tourists, and the dairy farmer yodels"

(106). This ironic opening is followed by a long list of "scenes and memories of violence and homicide," embellished with countless gruesome details: poachers murdering gendarmes, guides killing cottagers, lovers shooting their rivals, and numerous perfectly preserved bodies discovered years after their death in deserts of snow and ice. Kisch examines various rational explanations for this frequent use of mountain landscapes as a stage for death and violence—only to reject them all. He concludes by simply affirming his awareness of the way in which mountains can be transformed into an uncannily idyllic world: "I can go out again to see the forests, mountains, and cabins where peace and civility are at home. The sun sets, and everything is lit by a glow of happiness. But I delude myself no longer" (109).

Kisch is equally familiar with the complementary association by which mountainous scenery becomes a place for dramatic sexual adventures. In his historical drama about Colonel Redl, the head of the Austrian intelligence service who sells government secrets to blackmailers when they threaten to reveal his homosexuality [see **Gramophones**], Kisch has Redl invite his lover on a mountain tour with the aim of distancing him from heterosexual temptation: "I want to tear you away from the fangs of this woman. She's a witch, I'm telling you. Come along with me— we'll have a splendid trip to the mountains . . . We'll go by car. In a sports car—I'll buy you a sports car" (40ff.). With strong Freudian inspiration, Arthur Schnitzler, in his *Traumnovelle (Dream Story)*, portrays the confusions of a married couple as they strive to recover the erotic tension and harmony of the early days of their relationship. The memory of their original sexual attraction leads back to a vacation they once spent in the southeastern Alps: "It was a beautiful summer evening on Lake Wörther, just before our engagement, and a very handsome young man stood before my window, which overlooked a large and spacious meadow. As we talked, I thought to myself—just listen to this: 'What a charming young man that is! He'd only have to say the word— the right one, of course—and I'd go out with him into the meadow or the woods . . . and tonight I'd grant him anything he might desire'" (Schnitzler, 13–14). If Schnitzler projects erotic desire and mountainous landscapes onto the past, G. W. Pabst, an Austrian film director whom Freud himself deeply admires, projects them onto the future. His film *Geheimnisse einer Seele (Secrets of a Soul)* tells the story of a chemist named Dr. Martin Fellmann. Pursued by traumatic childhood memories and guilt-ridden over a marriage that has remained childless for many years, he has become impotent and is obsessed with hallucinations about killing his wife. A Freudian cure offers Dr. Fellmann redemption from his sufferings and renews his sexual vitality. The final scenes of the film show the reconciled couple and their new baby happily enjoying a vacation—in an Alpine setting.

But how can a constellation that looks so much like a literary motif—mountainous landscapes, death, and sexuality—be part of the publicly shared stock of knowledge? And how is it possible that, as a complex element of social knowledge, this constellation even becomes a social reality? Numerous narratives of mountaineering develop and illustrate the tacit assumptions that frequently link icy mountains to erotic desire and violent death. In the third chapter of René Schickele's novel *Maria Capponi,* Claus, the narrator-protagonist, and his wife, Doris, set out for a trek across a glacier. Their relationship suffers from symptoms similar to those of the couples in Schnitzler's *Traumnovelle* and in Pabst's *Geheimnisse einer Seele.* This is why Doris and Claus not only rely on the psychic healing power of the Alpine environment, but find it important to undertake their tour without a guide. It is thus due to their own temerity that, after some hours of hiking and climbing, they fall into a crevasse. Or rather, they slowly glide into the abyss as the soft snow sinks beneath the weight of their bodies. The slowness of their fall into the subterranean spaces of the mountain plateau seems to announce that the hours of agony which follow will bring to Doris and Claus an ultimate experience of deep and genuine meaning. [see **Authenticity vs. Artificiality**] At first, they do not realize the danger of their situation. But when it finally occurs to them that no one will come to their rescue for quite a long time—because nobody knows where they were going—a strange euphoria comes over Doris. This confrontation with mortality intensifies her life spirit [see **Boxing, Bullfighting, Mummies**] and restores her ability to rouse Claus into an ecstasy of desire: "'No, we only wish to see how a person feels when crossing that smooth rainbow bridge! My dearest, you're a poet, though you've served in the infantry. Do you know now what you're experiencing? Your wife freezing to death!' . . . I took her in my arms. On the floor of the crevasse it was too narrow for us to lie side by side, but that didn't bother us. We sank into caresses—our blood, our ears roared with desire. 'Never have you loved me this way!' Doris exclaimed suddenly, and cried out again, her heart beating triumphantly'" (19). Between this peak of sexual fulfillment and the moment the couple finally drop off to sleep (a sleep that will bring death to Doris), they pass the hours reminiscing about the opportunities they missed to be united in such overwhelming love. Too often their best intentions of "giving themselves to each other" dissipated amid the distractions of everyday life. But now, in the presence of death, Claus and Doris intuitively understand that the essence of existence lies in the unconditional determination to experience life to the utmost. Losing one's life matters much less than the opportunity of realizing this potential: "Uprooted and ripped apart, reeling through time and space, she took possession of me, and I was afraid. She, however, was no longer afraid. She had forgotten fear and everything else—everything but her victory. 'You are mine at last, mine. No one can take you from me any more. Oh, Claus, how I love you!'" (20). Not only does Schickele try to convince his readers that imminent death enhances erotic intensity, but he strives to show that sexual fulfillment as complete openness to and possession of the other leads to thoughts of the ultimate limit: the death of oneself and the beloved. Death as a challenge makes possible the most heroic degree of subjective agency, which consists of possession of the self and the other. But at the same time, it is also the most radical limit of self-determination. [see **Action = Impotence (Tragedy)**]

Martin Heidegger, in his correspondence with a young teacher named Elisabeth Blochmann, a friend of his wife's, uses the word *Existenzfreudigkeit* ("existence-affirmation") to describe the willingness and capacity to focus on what he views as the authentic experiences of human life. On Wednesday, November 10, at the start of the winter schoolterm, he expresses his confidence that Elisabeth's new working environment in Berlin will not distract her from such intensity: "How are things going for you? The welter and strangeness will depress you only temporarily—in the end, they will make your mind freer. The big city . . . will not alter your *Existenzfreudigkeit*" (Heidegger and Blochmann, 18). These words of philosophico-existential encouragement are preceded by Heidegger's memories of a shared summer vacation when the mountainous landscape of the Black Forest, far away from the everyday life of the university and the big city, provided precious moments of inner concentration: "Your dear letter that greeted me upon my return to Marburg was like a bouquet of autumn flowers on my writing table. I thank you for it. It was still glowing with the beautiful days we shared in the Black Forest: our first walk to the cabin, in the twilight; the pleasure of being together; the view from the meadow to the peaceful contours of the dark mountains; playing with a ball in the glade; the descent through the meadow to the narrow path" (17). Concluding with a quotation from Rilke's *Stundenbuch (Book of Hours)*, Heidegger's passage on the concept *Existenzfreudigkeit* converges with Doris and Claus's central experience in Schickele's novel. The presence of death in the crevasse and the majesty of the Black Forest's mountainous landscape provide the certainty that human existence is all about possessing oneself: "Whoever is not rich, now that the summer is fading / will always have to wait and never possess himself."

Self-possession and erotic possession are important themes in the film *Der Heilige Berg (The Sacred Mountain)*, which premieres in Berlin on December 17. It tells of a mountain ascent by two friends who at first do not realize that they are in love with the same woman. As they become aware of this conflict, tensions arise, and their rivalry quite naturally leads to an accident in which they both die. This fictional drama is paralleled by a real one behind the scenes: the beautiful young Leni Riefenstahl, who plays the lead, fondly observes how the director, Arnold Fanck, and her colleague Luis Trenker vie for her sexual favors: "I grew closer and closer to Dr. Fanck, but although I greatly respected and admired him as a brilliant film pioneer and intellectual, as a potential lover he had no effect on me. I was unsettled, therefore, by the fact that Fanck grew more deeply in love with me day by day" (Riefenstahl, 47). One night, after filming some scenes in the Lower Alps, the director finds Riefenstahl lying in Trenker's arms. Fanck is "thunderstruck." He throws himself into a nearby river, but is rescued. The evening reaches its peak with a fight between the rivals. Riefenstahl manages to end this potentially lethal battle by pretending that she, too, is about to kill herself: "A brutal fistfight began, growing more and more violent. I tried to pull them apart but it was no use. I ran to the window, opened it, and climbed out on the sill as if I were going to jump. My plot worked. The men stopped fighting" (49). But instead of subsiding, the turmoil of desire and confusion grows ever more involved. When it comes time to shoot the final skiing scenes amid the majestic scenery of the Swiss Alps, a new drama develops: Fanck, Riefenstahl, and Trenker have problems figuring out the sleeping arrangements in a small cabin. This psychological (rather than physical) conflict also involves the cameraman, Schneeberger: "How would Fanck determine the sleeping arrangements? Normally two people would have slept on each bed, but since Fanck insisted on taking the upper bunk for himself, Trenker, Schneeberger, and I had to share the lower mattress. As a result, the room was filled with nervous tension and I couldn't fall asleep, nor could Trenker. Now and then, when Fanck fitfully rolled about overhead, I could hear the creaking of the wooden boards. The first person to doze off was Schneeberger, but, lying between him and Trenker, I didn't dare to move. After remaining awake for hours on end, however, I must have been overwhelmed at last by fatigue" (52ff.). The troubles and tensions, accidents and catastrophes continue until the crew and cast arrive in Berlin for the premiere of their film. The atmosphere of the big city has a healing, unifying effect on the male rivals and their female object of desire. But there is a price attached to this new solidarity. Berlin's world of fast-moving surfaces [see **Dancing, Movie Palaces**] lacks the existential intensity that so naturally comes from encounters with crevasses, deadly cold, and mountain peaks.

Related Entries

Boxing, Bullfighting, Cremation, Dancing, Gramophones, Movie Palaces, Mummies, Murder, Polarities, Authenticity vs. Artificiality, Present vs. Past, Silence vs. Noise, Action = Impotence (Tragedy), Immanence = Transcendence (Eternity), Present = Past (Eternity)

References

Antología de Blanco y Negro, 1891–1936, vol. 9. Madrid, 1986.
Johannes R. Becher, *Maschinenrhythmen*. Berlin, 1926.
Berliner Morgenpost.
Caras y Caretas.
Hart Crane, *White Buildings*. New York, 1926.
Martin Heidegger and Elisabeth Blochmann, *Briefwechsel, 1918–1969*. Marbach, 1989.
Egon Erwin Kisch, *Die Hetzjagd: Eine Tragikomödie in fünf Akten des K.u.K. Generalstabs*. In *Hetzjagd durch die Zeit*. Berlin, 1926.
Egon Erwin Kisch, "Verbrechen in den Hochalpen." In Kisch, *Hetzjagd durch die Zeit*. Berlin, 1926.
Theodor Lessing, "Psychologie des Rauchens" (1926). In *"Ich warf eine*

Flaschenpost ins Eismeer der Geschichte": *Essays und Feuilletons, 1923–1933.* Neuwied, 1986.

New York Times.

Leni Riefenstahl, *A Memoir.* New York, 1992.

René Schickele, *Maria Capponi.* Munich, 1926.

Arthur Schnitzler, *Traumnovelle.* Berlin, 1926.

MOVIE PALACES

In downtown Buenos Aires, right across the street from the bookstore where Silvio Astier, the hero of Roberto Arlt's novel *El juguete rabioso (The Furious Toy)*, works as a clerk, people are flocking to a movie theater: "As if in a beehive, people were moving through the courtyard of a cinema, whose little bell was pealing incessantly" (Arlt, 131). The word *cinematógrafo* (which Arlt uses for "cinema" and which emphasizes the act of film projection), as well as the "incessantly pealing" bell that summons people to the show, indicates the sharp contrast between this cinema in Argentina's capital and the movie houses on Berlin's fashionable Kurfürstendamm. The Gloria-Filmpalast is inaugurated on Monday, January 25, with a film version of Molière's *Tartuffe* starring Emil Jannings. Both the Gloria-Filmpalast and the Capitol-Filmpalast, which opens on Nollendorfplatz on January 6, can accommodate more than fifteen hundred moviegoers for each of their two or three daily shows, in a sumptuously decorated space (*Chronik*, 24). This space constitutes a world of its own [see **Elevators**]—a world that exists under artificial light and that comes alive solely to nourish the daydreams of moviegoing crowds. The doors to the projection hall are hung with velvet curtains. The graceful curve of its huge balcony and the rich fixtures make the spectators feel that they are entering a—modern—baroque palace. An orchestra pit and a broad stage separate the screen from the seating area. Many movie palaces have elegant boxes along the side walls, high vaulted ceilings, and sophisticated controlled lighting. As the lights begin to dim, the action on the screen engages the spectators' minds in a play of images which is always different from that of their everyday lives. But while the moviegoers' imaginations may roam far from the quotidian, their bodies remain enveloped in a sphere that fills the gap between the quotidian and the film plots. The concretization of this in-between sphere is the gorgeous artificiality of the movie palace.

Film itself has become part of "a glittering, revue-like entity . . . : the total artwork [*Gesamtkunstwerk*] of effects" (Kracauer, "Kult," 312). [see **Revues**] Symphonies from the classical repertoire—and sometimes even orchestral pieces composed for individual films—accompany the action on the screen. But what really transforms the movie palaces' shows into a *Gesamtkunstwerk* are the stage performances that precede the feature films: "The total artwork of effects assaults every one of the senses using every possible means. Spotlights shower their beams into the auditorium, playing over festive drapes or rippling through colorful growth-like glass fixtures. The orchestra asserts itself as an independent power, its acoustic production enhanced by the coordinated lighting. Every emotion is given its own acoustic expression, its color value in the spectrum—an optical and acoustic kaleidoscope which provides the setting for the physical activity on stage, pantomime and ballet. Until finally the white screen is lowered and the events of the three-dimensional stage blend imperceptibly into two-dimensional illusions" (Kracauer, "Kult," 312).

The need to reduce the cost involved in providing such musical accompaniment (which moviegoers have come to expect), as well as the desire to make it available even to small cinemas, leads to the final step in the technical development of the sound film. In April, Warner Brothers, with the financial assistance of the Wall Street banking group Goldman Sachs, establishes the Vitaphone Corporation, formally leases a new sound system from Western Electric, and for $800,000 secures the exclusive right to lease it out in turn to other studios. There is at first no question of making "talking pictures" but only the goal of replacing the orchestra with a technical device (Cook, 257ff.). The world premiere of this device takes place in the "Refrigerated Warner Theater" at Broadway and Fifty-second Street in New York City on Thursday, August 6: John Barrymore's costume drama *Don Juan* is shown with a recorded orchestral score performed by the New York Philharmonic. The feature is introduced by an hour-long, one-million-dollar program of sound-shorts, which is itself preceded by a brief filmed speech by Will Hays, president of the Motion Picture Producers and Distributors of America. He announces "the beginning of a new era in music and motion pictures" (258). When the Vitaphone production comes to Hollywood, it is enthusiastically greeted by an special issue of *Variety:*

> Vitaphone made its initial bow to the Pacific Coast tonight in the most brilliant premiere ever staged at Grauman's Egyptian theatre . . . Crowds began to pour into the incourt of the Egyptian as early as 7:45, and one by one as the celebrities arrived they were introduced over the loudspeaker. Powerful arc lamps played across the sky in gorgeous arcs and illuminated the outdoor foyer . . . True, it was a slightly incredulous audience that passed through the doors at 8:15. So much has been talked and written about sound and pictures that some were openly skeptical. But it was those who came doubtingly that passed out later warmest in their enthusiastic praise of a new art. (Cook, 259)

Rather than constituting an "alternative world," the actions on the screens of the movie palaces add up to a highlighted rerun of the main fascinations and concerns that prevail in everyday life: heroic individual and collective deeds from the remote or recent past, as in *Ben Hur* or Eisenstein's *Battleship Potemkin* [see **Action vs. Impotence, Individuality vs. Collectivity**]; the struggle between nature and technology, as in *The Lost World,* which depicts the invasion of London by a horde of dinosaurs [see **Authenticity vs. Artificiality**]; the complexities of human existence and the confrontation with death, as in the mountaineering drama *Der Heilige Berg (The Sacred Mountain)* or in F. W. Murnau's *Faust* [see **Mountaineering, Immanence = Transcendence (Death)**]; psychoanalytic treatment, as staged in the film *Geheimnisse einer Seele (Secrets of a Soul);* the tragedies of daily existence, as in Charlie Chaplin's *Gold Rush,* which comes to Berlin on February 23, or in Berthold Viertel's *K. 13513,* which portrays "the adventures of a ten-mark note" (*Chronik,* 220). [see **Sobriety vs. Exuberance, Action = Impotence (Tragedy)**] These last two films, in particular, give an impression of life as continuous movement and suggest that traveling can help the individual avoid falling prey to vices and addictions. [see **Bars**] Siegfried Kracauer's formulation for this effect of movies is elegant and apt: "The attention of the spectators is riveted to the peripheral, so that they will not sink into the abyss"

("Kult," 314). In *K. 13513,* which as a programmatic manifestation of the "New Sobriety" inaugurates the genre of the *Querschnittsfilm* ("cross-section film"), the main protagonist is a banknote that travels through a random sequence of transactions and existential situations.

In spite of—or perhaps because of—such ambitious projects, the German film industry is entering a period of extreme economic pressure. In return for an urgently needed loan of $4 million, the Ufa Company has incurred the contractual obligation of featuring twenty Paramount and Metro-Goldwyn productions per year: it must reserve 75 percent of the screen time in its own theaters for these American movies (Jacobsen, 526). Astonishingly, European actors and directors seem to seek such dependency on the American film world—even when it is not imposed on them by the market. Some of German cinema's most outstanding artists, among them Fritz Lang and F. W. Murnau, accept offers from Hollywood [see **Americans in Paris**], and the Fascist critic Anton Giulio Bragaglia recommends solving the current artistic crisis in the Italian movie industry by sending aspiring filmmakers to work as apprentices in Hollywood: "There's a lot of shouting back and forth. But where are the Italian directors who know how to make films like the Americans? . . . It's clear that a handful of people representing the various branches of this complex art should be sent off to America to study new film techniques, photographic media, and chemical processing. Only after two years of schooling should they be allowed to venture out" (Bragaglia, 253ff.). Through reflections of this kind, the film world becomes a prominent medium for the self-reference of contemporary society. In Siegfried Kracauer's view, moviegoers epitomize "the *homogeneous cosmopolitan audience,* in which everyone has the same responses, from the bank director to the sales clerk, from the diva to the stenographer" ("Kult," 313). [see **Employees**] The everyday life of this urban population, according to Kracauer, is a life of tension and disjunction. [see **Present vs. Past**] Film, instead of offering compensation, only heightens this feeling of strain. The medium cannot help producing such effects, explains Kracauer, because its very technique relies on the principle of reconfiguring a disjointed world: "Instead of leaving the world in its fragmented state, one is pulled back into it. With film, these pieces are newly reassembled, their isolation eradicated and their grimace smoothed away. From out of the tomb, they awaken to a semblance of life" ("Kaliko-Welt," 277ff.). As "mosaics" (277), both the two-dimensional world of film and, by contiguity, the interiors of the movie palaces cultivate a specific type of surface glamour (311, 315). [see **Dancing, Gomina, Stars**] Since Kracauer believes that the rhythm of this continuously moving surface world helps spectators to avoid the pitfalls of modern existence, he tends to deplore any signs of a return to more traditional forms of staging, including the live shows that have become customary in the programs of the movie palaces: "The integration of film into a homogeneous program deprives it of its potential effect. It no longer stands on its own, but becomes the crowning event of a type of revue which does not take into account film's unique characteristics. The *two-dimensionality* of film creates an illusion of the physical world without any need for supplementation. But if real bodies appear alongside the movie, the latter recedes into the flat surface and the deception is exposed. This destroys the specific space of the film" (316).

With films becoming a condensation of the contemporary everyday world, both spheres begin to establish a relation of remarkable permeability. On the one hand, the reality of political life invades the movie palaces. Weekly newsreels are produced by specialized crews, among which the French company Pathé-Journal holds a privileged place (*Années-mémoire*, 58ff.). Festive film events offer important opportunities for protagonists from the political and economic stage to cultivate their public image. The premiere of Murnau's *Faust* at the Ufa-Palast am Zoo on October 14 is attended by German chancellor Wilhelm Marx, foreign secretary Gustav Stresemann, and Hjalmar Schacht, the president of the National Bank (Jacobsen, 526). On the other hand, the film world frequently exerts an intensifying influence on the political scene. Throughout the spring and far into the summer, the censoring of Eisenstein's *Battleship Potemkin* by the German government sparks a fiery debate whose various positions become almost immediately identified with the different political parties and their programs (Schrader and Schebera, 199ff.; Willet, 48, 143). As a result, the movie palaces no longer publish advertisements focusing exclusively on story lines and actors but begin to tout their own financial success and technical achievements. In the *8 Uhr–Abendblatt* of August 28, the Ufa-Theater on Nollendorfplatz informs readers that "preparations for the European premiere of *Ben Hur*" will keep the house closed until September 6. Under the heading "Die ganze Kolonne zum *Ritt in die Sonne*" ("The whole gang out to *Ride into the Sun*"), the Primus Palast on Potsdamerstraße (known as "PPP") shows a drawing of a huge crowd pressing at its entrance and barely controlled by mounted police (8 *Uhr–Abendblatt,* February 4).

Going to the movies heightens and intensifies the spectators' experience of their own lives. In an early sequence, the film *Metropolis* presents "picture palaces," together with theaters, lecture rooms, a library, and a stadium [see **Endurance**], as the main attraction of the "Club of the Sons" where rich adolescents enjoy a life of exuberant luxury (Lang, 22). In "Unordnung und frühes Leid" ("Disorder and Early Sorrow"), Thomas Mann presents an example from the opposite end of the social hierarchy. Xaver Kleinsgütl, a good-looking peasant boy who works as servant to an impoverished bourgeois family, is fond of daydreaming about the movie world, much like the scions of Metropolis. The films that Xaver sees evoke a mood of joyful melancholy, and his hopes are firmly set on a career as a movie star: "With his whole soul he loves the cinema; after an evening spent there, he is often filled with melancholy and yearning, and tends to talk to himself. Vague hopes stir in him that someday he may make his fortune in that splendid world and belong to it by rights—hopes based on his shock of hair and on his physical agility and daring. He likes to climb the ash tree in the front garden . . . keeping a lookout for a film director who might chance to come along and hire him" (Mann, 513).

Some serious-minded intellectuals decry the conflation of cinema reality with what they call "real" reality. They take the opportunity to construct an image of high moral responsibility on the ontological distinction between the two. Miguel de Unamuno thus accuses Spanish government officials of confusing historical reality with film reality: "The judgment of history—which is for them a film—matters but little to them: the conceited tragedian without a moral or historical sense, the film actor obeying his destiny, seeks fame even though he is infamous" (Unamuno, 193, May 13). If Xaver Kleinsgütl, the dreamy Bavarian lad invented by Thomas Mann, were a real-life person, he could become the beneficiary of an obsessive rescue program for his generation designed by the Bavarian politician Adolf Hitler [see **Murder**]:

> Our entire public life today resembles a hothouse of sexual images and stimuli. One has only to look at the programs of our movie houses, music halls, and theaters; and one can hardly deny that this is not the

right kind of nourishment for people, especially the young. Shop windows and billboards use the basest means in order to attract the attention of the masses . . . This sultry, sensual atmosphere leads to ideas and stimulation at a time when a boy ought not yet to have an understanding of such things . . . Who will be surprised, then, that even among young people syphilis is beginning to find victims? And isn't it distressing to see how many physically weak and mentally corrupt young men receive their sexual initiation from a big-city whore? No—he who wishes to attack prostitution must first of all strive to abolish the mental predisposition toward it. He must clear away the filth of the moral contamination that emanates from the "culture" of our big cities, and must do so ruthlessly and unhesitatingly. (Hitler, 278–279)

Related Entries

Americans in Paris, Bars, Dancing, Elevators, Employees, Endurance, Gomina, Mountaineering, Murder, Revue, Stars, Action vs. Impotence, Authenticity vs. Artificiality, Individuality vs. Collectivity, Present vs. Past, Sobriety vs. Exuberance, Action = Impotence (Tragedy), Immanence = Transcendence (Death)

References

8 Uhr–Abendblatt.

Les Années-mémoire: 1926. Paris, 1988.

Roberto Arlt, El juguete rabioso (1926). Madrid, 1985.

Anton Giulio Bragaglia, "Text from Critica Fascista" (1926). Stanford Italian Review (1990): 251–254.

Chronik 1926: Tag für Tag in Wort und Bild. Dortmund, 1985.

David A. Cook, A History of Narrative Film. New York, 1990.

Adolf Hitler, Mein Kampf (1926). Munich, 1941.

Wolfgang Jacobsen, Anton Kaes, and Hans Helmut Prinzler, eds., Geschichte des deutschen Films. Stuttgart, 1993.

Siegfried Kracauer, "Kaliko-Welt: Die Ufa-Stadt zu Neubabelsberg" (1926). In Kracauer, Das Ornament der Masse: Essays. Frankfurt, 1977.

Siegfried Kracauer, "Kult der Zerstreuung: Über die Berliner Lichtspielhäuser." In Kracauer, Das Ornament der Masse: Essays. Frankfurt, 1977.

Fritz Lang, Metropolis (1926). New York, 1973.

Thomas Mann, "Unordnung und frühes Leid" (1926). In Mann, Sämtliche Erzählungen. Frankfurt, 1963.

Bärbel Schrader and Jürgen Schebera, eds., *Kunstmetropole Berlin, 1918–1933: Die Kunststadt in der Novemberrevolution / Die "goldenen" Zwanziger / Die Kunststadt in der Krise.* Berlin, 1987.

Miguel de Unamuno, *Epistolario inédito* (1926). Madrid, 1991.

Die wilden Zwanziger: Weimar und die Welt, 1919–1933. Berlin, 1986.

John Willet, *Art and Politics in the Weimar Period: The New Sobriety, 1917–1933.* New York, 1978.

MUMMIES

Early in the year, the small international community of Egyptologists, millions of newspaper readers, the Egyptian government, and even King George of England become involved in a long debate about the remains of the pharaoh Tutankhamen, who died around 1337 B.C. at the age of about eighteen (El Mallakh and Brackmann, 166ff.). His tomb, almost untouched by thieves, was discovered in 1922. The British archaeologist Howard Carter patiently explored a number of its chambers, classified myriad artifacts, and, in October 1925, finally penetrated the small room containing Tutankhamen's sarcophagus. After successively opening four coffins enclosed one inside the other, Carter found the young pharaoh's embalmed body and removed its linen wrappings. These actions have already generated heated discussion about the moral legitimacy of disturbing the dead without obtaining their consent during their lifetime [see **Cremation**], and now another question arises: Should Tutankhamen's body be returned to its sarcophagus and its original resting place, or should it be put on permanent display in a museum in Cairo, London, or New York? Carter counts "over 12,300 visitors to the tomb and some 270 parties to the laboratory" between January and March (Carter, xx; El Mallakh and Brackmann, 144ff.), but the Egyptian government expects that Tutankhamen's funerary splendor will attract even more tourists if it becomes easily accessible to the public. This attitude on the part of the Egyptians is strengthened by their desire to make a nationalist statement by resisting world opinion, which favors restoring the pharaoh's body to the place where it was found.

How can the tomb of a boy king become the focus of such worldwide concern? The objects it contains are no more beautiful than those found at most of the other royal burial sites in Egypt; and historians have little to say about Tutankhamen, other than the fact that he was a politically and culturally unimportant figure during his brief reign. In November, as Howard Carter writes the preface to the second volume of his study on the tomb, he struggles to understand the intensity of this fascination. Certainly he does not believe in the magic powers and otherworldly spirits that the European imagination has long associated with such sites: "It is not my intention to repeat the ridiculous stories which have been invented about the dangers lurking in ambush, as it were, in this tomb, to destroy the intruder. Similar tales have been a common feature of fiction for many years; they are mostly variants of the ordinary ghost story, and may be accepted as a legitimate form of literary amusement" (xxv). Carter comes closer to the source of his "awe" and his "bewildering, almost overwhelming" emotion (vii) when he remembers that the precious objects discovered in the tomb's antechamber, rather than impressing him with their value or with their possible historical significance, evoke the atmosphere of a long-lost form of privacy: "An almost incongruous miscellany of objects and furniture, caskets and beds, chairs, footstools, chariots and statues, filled the antechamber. These were heterogeneous enough, yet exhibiting, in not a few instances, a kindly art full of domestic affection, such as made us wonder whether, in seeking the tomb of a pharaoh, we had not found the tomb of a boy" (ix). But the mediation of a remote world through its artifacts turns into uncanny immediacy, as the archaeologist finally looks into the face of Tutankhamen and sees the past become present:

> The thrilling experiences . . . were many, but it seems now, as I look back, that it was when the last of the decayed bandages had been removed, and the young king's features were first revealed, that the summit of these moving impressions was reached. The youthful pharaoh was before us at last: an obscure and ephemeral ruler, ceasing to be the mere shadow of a name, had re-entered, after more than three thousand years, the world of reality and history! Here was the climax of our long researches! The tomb had yielded its secret; the message of

the past had reached the present in spite of the weight of time and the erosion of so many years. (xxiii)

Carter's emotion is not about beauty or historical knowledge. What drives his research is a desire parallel and complementary to the aspirations of those who actively seek lethal danger in order to make death a part of their lives. [see **Airplanes, Boxing, Bullfighting, Endurance, Hunger Artists, Mountaineering, Immanence = Transcendence (Death)**] Whereas athletes and aviators push their bodies to the point where life encounters death, the archaeologist—bearing an odd resemblance to the gramophone in this respect—makes it possible, through his slow and meticulous work, for the life of the past to cross the boundary of death and "re-enter the world of reality and history . . . in spite of the weight of time and the erosion of so many years." The face of the pharaoh Tutankhamen is the face of the past come alive and, at the same time, the face of an individual's death made present. [see **Individuality vs. Collectivity**] Carter thus titles two important sections of his book—the king's biography and the photographs of his skull—with a single word: the pharaoh's name (11, 112). For it is Carter's ultimate aim to provide an encounter with "Tutankhamen" himself.

The unwrapping of Tutankhamen's body is but the peak of a broad wave of contemporary "Egyptomania." What fascinates Howard Carter's readers more than anything else—the capacity of a person to anticipate and confront his or her own death [see **Cremation**]—is now being identified, with increasing clarity, as the constitutive element of ancient Egyptian culture. But this insight cannot fully explain why Egyptomania is turning into "Tutmania" (El Mallakh and Brackmann, 120ff.). The fashion industry adopts the styles, colors, and ornaments of the clothes found in Tutankhamen's tomb. Tutankhamen umbrellas and Tutankhamen walking sticks are sold everywhere. The Hotel Pennsylvania in New York City advertises the sound of Vincente López's popular band as "Tut-music," and hundreds of new products bearing "Tutankhamen" brand names are submitted to the U.S. Patent Office. Though the face of the pharaoh makes present the otherness of an individual death, such products and brand names rely on the appeal of ancient Egypt's cultural otherness amid modern everyday life (Clifford, 1–17). [see **Center vs. Periphery**] This is why a review article by Walter Benjamin condemns, with uncharacteristically strong irony, a tourist guide that views ancient

Egyptian myths from the standpoint of twentieth-century rationality: "'Whoever wishes to avenge himself on the dead and expel someone from the bliss of paradise need only chisel away the name of the deceased, and the poor fellow will lose everlasting life. These were the very childlike thoughts associated with the idea of immortality.' No, Mister Author! These are the very childlike presuppositions for a trip to Egypt" (Benjamin, 34). The tension between Benjamin's position and the position of the book he is reviewing epitomizes the distance that separates those who emphasize the otherness of remote cultures brought to life and those who try to integrate such cultures into the historical genealogy of their own Judeo-Christian tradition. In this spirit an article published on October 2 in the Argentinian magazine *Caras y Caretas,* under the title "A King of Ancient Chaldea, Five Thousand Years Ago, Amassed Riches Greater Than Those of Tutankhamen," sets up a strange competition between the artifacts excavated at the site of the biblical town of Ur and Howard Carter's discovery: "The details of dress and headgear are of a surprising realism. The facial features seem vibrant with life . . . Many jewels have been found, and, without fear of exaggeration, it can be affirmed that the treasures of King Ur-Engur surpass those of the already famous and much publicized Tutankhamen." [see **Center = Periphery [Infinitude], Present = Past (Eternity)**]

The Sunday edition of the *Berliner Tageblatt* on March 25 contains a long essay recounting an excursion to the Spree Forest, two hours by train east of Berlin. At first ironically referring to the trip as an "expedition," the author winds up launching into a solemn discourse that, in its pathos, rivals Howard Carter's description of the unwrapping of Tutankhamen's body. He has decided to visit the forest because he is intrigued by the unusual appearance and behavior of a peasant woman who regularly comes to Berlin to sell eggs, butter, and poultry: "Her black bonnet, which looks nothing like bobbed or Gretchen-style hair, swims like a strange waterbird through the crowd of fashionable hats; her full, stiff skirt whips around with a rhythm that is strange to us. Despite her nordic coolness, she appears somehow exotic. She has not yet been affected by the modern world's tendency to level everything. One senses it somehow: in contrast to you and me, who have 'only just arrived,' she is a native, one who possesses something steadfast, a clear and innate distinctness." The first layer of otherness which the Berlin journalist discovers in the near-but-remote Spree Forest is the banality that pervades the street life of Kottbus, its administrative center. Soon, however, he notices more archaic cultural forms and a strange linguistic accent, both of which are characteristic of a Slavic tribe known as the Wends. At the point where the impossibly present past engages in an improbable encounter with cultural otherness, the author comes upon some mummies—deep in the crypt of a local church. Although these mummies are only two hundred years old and have nothing to do with Slavic culture, they inspire in the beholder the same awe that Carter feels in the tomb of Tutankhamen. Compressing historical distance and straddling the border of death, they bring the past to life:

> Tutankhamen in the Spree Forest! The church has a crypt, with a dozen unsealed wooden coffins. Opening them, one finds authentic and surprisingly well-preserved mummies. They are not as old as the Egyptian mummies, but, skillfully embalmed, they have survived the air and humidity of two hundred years. There is an officer from the time of Friedrich Wilhelm I, with a dried-out skull resembling that of the late Ramses II in the Cairo Museum. The silks that surround him and the leather of his high riding-boots are remarkably well preserved. After two hundred years, his three-cornered hat is still tucked under his withered arm. Next to him lies a young woman with her newborn; and then some more male mummies. It is no different from the Sakkara.

Interpretation and its inherent desire for depth lead to such encounters. [see **Authenticity vs. Artificiality**] Tutankhamen's body lies in the innermost chamber of a tomb, in the innermost of four coffins. The process of discovering and unwrapping it requires enormous historical knowledge and technical expertise, and culminates in an experience that is overwhelming—and somehow definitive. But while this is an experience of authenticity, because it enables concrete relics of the past to enter the physical immediacy of the present, it is also an experience doomed to remain unfulfilled. Like Tutankhamen's body, from which the embalmers have extracted the brain and the inner organs, his face neither "contains" nor "yields" the essence of his life. Howard Carter gives a good historical explanation for the way in which ancient Egyptian artifacts resist interpretation and reconstruction: "Much must remain dark and obscure in the life of the ancient Egyptians . . . because the main idea behind the cults by which they are revealed to us, was to make clear to the living that which followed after death" (Carter, xxiv). Egyptian mummies, instead of pointing to a meaning, stand only for themselves—while they confer a faint halo of presence on the dead subjectivities to which they point. If the fragile body of Tutankhamen is a veil behind which nothing can be discovered—its "condition rendered the use of X-rays impossible" (xxii)—his golden outer sarcophagus is a shining surface which reflects (and rejects) the archaeologist's gaze. [see **Dancing, Gomina**] Highlighting the cultural distance which separates modern observers from the world of their historical imagination, this shining surface also intensifies the fascination which generates "Tutmania." Ultimately, it can stay alive only if the dead pharaoh's body is restored to its original distance from the present. On Sunday, October 31, Howard Carter rewraps Tutankhamen's corpse. It "will remain in his tomb, enclosed in his sarcophagus" (xxiii).

Related Entries

Airplanes, Boxing, Bullfighting, Cremation, Dancing, Endurance, Gomina, Gramophones, Hunger Artists, Mountaineering, Authenticity vs. Artificiality, Center vs. Periphery, Individuality vs. Collectivity, Center = Periphery (Infinitude), Immanence = Transcendence (Death), Present = Past (Eternity)

References

Walter Benjamin, "Rezension von Hans Bethge, *Ägyptische Reise: Ein Tagebuch*" (1926). In Benjamin, *Gesammelte Schriften,* vol. 3. Frankfurt, 1972.
Berliner Tageblatt.
Caras y Caretas.
Howard Carter, *The Tomb of Tut-ankh-Amen, Discovered by the Late Earl of Carnarvon and Howard Carter,* vol. 2. London, 1927.
James Clifford, "The Pure Products Go Crazy." In Clifford, *The Predicament of Culture.* Cambridge, Mass., 1988.
Kamal El Mallakh and Arnold C. Brackmann, *The Gold of Tutankhamen.* New York, 1978.

MURDER

On Sunday, August 8, the *Berliner Tageblatt* publishes a detailed report on a criminal trial that has concluded in Frankfurt. What makes this case so fascinating is, paradoxically, the absolute clarity of the facts. The defendant is a certain Fräulein Flessa. Her first name, age, and situation in life are not mentioned by the newspaper, but readers learn that she is "neither young nor pretty." Flessa has never denied committing the act she is accused of: with three shots from a revolver, she has murdered Dr. Seitz, a man of about forty whom the article describes as "an average, good-natured, easygoing, corpulent gentleman." The trial has failed to produce any definitive evidence concerning the relationship between Flessa and Seitz. The defendant claims that Seitz deflowered her, but the court seems to assume that she is still a virgin, and there has been no medical investigation on this point. For although the fact of Flessa's action is incontrovertible and the death penalty would thus be legally justifiable, the judges feel that a morally responsible evaluation of the case must be grounded on a different kind of evidence. This evidence, which they make strenuous efforts to produce, is the answer to the question: "What was going on in her soul . . . prior to and during the murder?" Such a question has the potential for transforming a legal issue into one of psychological interpretation, and for changing the status of the defendant from that of a deliberate malefactor to that of a mentally unbalanced individual. The less access the defendant gives to "what was going on in her soul," the more she has a right to be treated as a clinical case: "What can we learn about the roots of the crime if the culprit herself does not know? And she is certainly the least qualified to know . . . It was enough that her thoughts and desires were centered on [Dr. Seitz], that her sexuality had fixated upon him. He may have given little cause for this, but whatever he did cost him his life. Twenty years from now, the defense claims, such a trial will probably be unthinkable— there will likely be sanatoriums for such people."

Countless reports of similar homicides and murder trials fill the front pages of regional and international newspapers. But though they all deal with the topic of death, they say little if anything about the widespread debates on death as an aspect of the human condition. [see **Airplanes, Boxing, Bullfighting, Cremation, Gramophones, Mountaineering, Mummies**] The discussions of the existential dimension of death regularly underscore the need to "confront one's own death" as a specific form of self-reflection. But it is precisely the absence of such self-reflection that becomes decisive in the Flessa case (and in many other murder trials). The victim could by no means anticipate—let alone "confront"— his fate, and the defendant almost passionately refuses to become engaged in any form of self-analysis: "That she so violently resists speaking of the crime and her motives makes it clear that she doesn't want to face it." Whereas "confronting one's own death" is a mode of heroic (or tragic) agency, the legal system never succeeds in attributing a role of agency to Flessa. [see **Action = Impotence (Tragedy)**] Therefore, through a strange metonymic shift, the place of agency is taken over by the defendant's sexuality: "her sexuality had fixated upon him." But since the defendant's sexuality is not a possible subject for agency in the legal sense of the word, and since the defendant's mind renounces that very reflexivity which alone would constitute her as an agent, it is impossible to say that Flessa is responsible for "her" crime.

Whenever such problems of attribution arise in murder cases, the related public discussions become part and symptom of a profound change in the relation between individual and society. [see **Individuality vs. Collectivity**] For if, by renouncing a position of agency, individuals make themselves inaccessible to the law, then agency, responsibility, and guilt lose their point of reference and become free-floating categories. A possible solution to this dilemma, a solution that many intellectuals strongly advocate, lies in assigning responsibility to society as a collective subject. Once this approach is accepted, however, it becomes the right of the criminal, now redefined as someone with a pathological condition, to accuse society for the crime he or she has committed and to request clinical therapy. But providing therapy instead of punishment is only one of many options that emerge out of a more general crisis in the relation between individuality and collectivity. In the Flessa case, the Frankfurt court settles on a compromise. The defendant is neither acquitted nor given the death penalty. She is sentenced to seven years in prison *(Zucht-haus),* and her deed is defined as "attempted homicide in conjunction with involuntary manslaughter." No lower degree of agency can be attributed to someone who admits that she has taken another person's life.

A wide range of models for renegotiating the relation of individual to society emerges from the newspaper coverage of such cases. Society looks particularly bad whenever the legal system fails to identify the perpetrator of a crime. With three full pages of photographs, the September 18 issue of *Caras y Caretas* offers its readers the illusion of participating in the prosecution of the "mysterious murder of Dr. Carlos A. Ray in his villa in Vicente López." A physician, city councillor, and member of Buenos Aires high society, Carlos A. Ray has been found murdered in the bedroom of his beautiful home, where he was living with his lover, the widow María Poey de Canelo, attended by an impressive number of servants. *Caras y Caretas* presents detailed exterior and interior views of the house, as well as profiles of all the suspects, strongly orienting readers' speculations toward the figure of Ray's mistress and toward the possibility of a crime of passion. Two weeks later, the style of the coverage has changed considerably. It now features photographs of fourteen judges, public prosecutors, and specialists in forensic medicine, and describes the approach that each one would take toward solving the "sensational murder of Dr. Carlos A. Ray."

Rarely is decisive evidence unearthed after such a long period of uncertainty. In August, the French press reports on the belated solution to another "mysterious" case of murder. The body of Marie-Louise Beulagnet is exhumed and—at the grave site—is subjected to a second autopsy, which reveals that she was strangled. This triggers a confession by her lover, Charles Guyot *(Années-Mémoire,* 47). Much more frequently, however, the weakness of the legal system is implicitly—sometimes even explicitly and provocatively—highlighted by criminals who confess without being under any kind of pressure. After converting to

Christianity, two "Eskimo boys" who, more than seventeen years ago, killed the American explorer Ross G. Marvin in the icy wastes of Greenland, come forth with the truth, although the public had been entirely persuaded by their made-up story of Marvin's drowning (*New York Times*, September 25). [see **Polarities**] Johannes Spruch, who has stolen a million dollars' worth of precious stones from a Berlin jeweler, turns himself in to the police with an almost frivolous air—only to regret his decision and call himself "a blockhead and an idiot" the very next morning (*8 Uhr–Abendblatt,* October 2). Such blatant contempt on the part of thieves and murderers undermines the authority of the police and the legal system—doubly so if the situation turns out to be a setup: "A young man who admitted his guilt yesterday in a bar, and who repeated his 'confession' before the authorities, had to be released because it was revealed that, under the influence of alcohol, the 'murderer' had 'confessed' simply in an effort to make himself interesting" (*Berliner Volks-Zeitung,* May 14).

Cases like this evoke widespread existential fear that any stable ground for cognitive certainty has been lost. [see **Uncertainty vs. Reality**] In his first successful film, *The Lodger,* Alfred Hitchcock leads the audience to believe that his main protagonist must be a new Jack the Ripper. As a mob is about to lynch him, the information spreads that the true murderer has been found—and the lodger's life is thus spared at the very last moment. Using a similar narrative strategy, Agatha Christie, in *The Murder of Roger Ackroyd,* lets the detective Hercule Poirot solve a crime on the basis of evidence that is unavailable to the reader—for the murderer turns out to be the first-person narrator. One conclusion from such fictional and nonfictional examples is obvious: if the existence of ultimate truth can no longer be taken for granted, the law and the State risk losing their authority over the individual—because their authority is based on a truth-claim.

This crisis of truth converges with the shift toward a clinical view of criminal behavior: both problematize legal and governmental authority. Early in the year, the attention of everyone in France becomes focused on a trial in which the question of agency has never been subject to any doubt. In Bombon, a small village near Melun, members of a sect known as "Our Lady of the Tears" flog—and almost kill—the parish priest. For three years they've been convinced that the priest has bewitched Marie Mesmin, the founder of their community. As a legal case, the incident offers no ambiguities. The sect's accusation is absurd—not least because it is based on a single visit of the priest to Marie Mesmin's house in Bordeaux, during which he offered her some gifts from his parishioners. But what no doubt intrigues readers are hints that the victim sympathizes with the heterodoxy of his enemies (after all, he has collected and offered gifts to Marie Mesmin), a strange intensity in the gazes of the priest and the accused, pictures of the whips that were used, and, finally, a photograph in which the accused, all in black clothes, try to shield their faces from the lens of the reporter's camera (*Années-Mémoire*, 184–185). The gothic quality of these images calls into question the claim that French society is based on rational principles.

Meanwhile, an even more bizarre case occupies the public's attention in Germany. On January 19, a jury in Hannover sentences Hans Grans, the lover and accomplice of Friedrich Haarmann, to twelve years in prison (Lessing, 304). Grans has sold the clothes of more than fifty boys and young men, many of them male prostitutes, whom Haarmann murdered while having sex with them, and then dismembered. Haarmann himself "estimates" that he killed "about thirty" people (Lessing, 278). What most attracts the popular imagination is Haarmann's obsession with biting his victims at the climax of his sexual excitement and letting them bleed to death. Since it is impossible to attribute legal responsibility to defendants whose pathologies are so evident, the public turns its attention from the perpetrator either to the social environment in which the crime has occurred or to the horrifying morphology of the victims' dismembered bodies. Probably inspired by the Haarmann case, Johannes Becher's poem "Der Würger" ("The Strangler") derives its impact from its gruesome details and images:

> Parade of the murdered in
> the morgue. The first procession: headless
> torsos and skulls speared through with knives
> between the thighs, one
> jack-o'-lantern like an unearthly fireball. The second
> procession: the hanged generations. Twisted-up, bruised
> bodies, spiraling; their chewed-through tongues,
> torn like rags, between their teeth. Third
> procession: buckets full of rotting fruit. Gleaming
> earlets, noses, sharpening each other, diapered
> in newspaper: printed linen.
>
> (Becher, 35)

Theodor Lessing, a philosopher at the Technical University of Hannover and a part-time journalist who covers the Haarmann case for several newspapers and magazines, has been repeatedly excluded from the courtroom for criticizing the tribunal's procedures. With explicit reference to the work of Sigmund Freud, Lessing urges that Haarmann's crimes be analyzed on a psychoanalytic basis. He thus joins a growing number of writers and political activists who draw attention to the judicial system's loss of authority. *Vorwärts,* the daily newspaper of the German Social-Democratic Party, goes so far as to question the moral legitimacy of the prosecutor's investigations: "Even when the prosecutor is a man of honor, his whole attitude must be directed against the accused, and he thus instinctively and automatically turns away from any possibility of exonerating them" (*Vorwärts,* July 25). Lessing certainly has more specific reasons to protest. He is incensed that the Hannover court, in the trial against Grans, refuses to acknowledge evidence of Haarmann's psychological subjection to his lover: Haarmann was eager to please Grans by offering him the clothes of his victims, but the murders were not instigated by Grans, as the prosecutor seems to assume (Lessing, 304ff.). Furthermore, Lessing reveals that, until the time the crimes were discovered, the police used Haarmann as a spy in Hannover's red-light district. Such relentless criticism and protest make the police, the court, and the State of Lower Saxony appear, paradoxically, as agents in the ongoing confusion between crime and the law, individual and society. But the State takes its revenge on Lessing. After a boycott of his courses by Fascist student organizations at the University of Hannover, a boycott triggered by another series of newspaper articles in which Lessing, a Jew, has dared to lampoon the nation's president, Paul von Hindenburg, Lessing is relieved of his professorship (Chronik, 111).

The Haarmann case epitomizes the public's fascination with murder as a phenomenon in which various crises of Western culture are converging. This is why the Haarmann trial generates such diverse images, incidents, and stories. And it has additional ramifications for the weakening of the State's authority: the agitation by Fascist students is part of a broader tension between the judicial system and far-right groups over the issue of the so-called vehmic murders (*Chronik,* 17, 33). Since the end of the war, the German government has failed to demobilize and disband the paramilitary Freikorps (volunteer corps), although they repeatedly infringe on constitutional rights and although their very existence violates the Treaty of Versailles, which has reduced the German army to 100,000 men. Even more dangerous than such infractions of national law and international contract are the Freikorps' internal (vehmic) executions of former members who are believed to be traitors or dissenters. It is widely suspected that the agents of these crimes escape prosecution because they enjoy the secret protection of judges and government officials. In fact, however, the vehmic murderers cannot be identified within their own organizations because they mirror—and push to an extreme—the internal confusion of public institutions. On Thursday, February 4, the *8 Uhr–Abendblatt* publishes excerpts from the trial of Sergeant Göbel, a member of the Schwarze Reichswehr (Black National Army). Göbel's testimony makes it evident that even those Freikorps groups that think they are in control of their members can be continually surprised and intimidated by other subgroups, which interfere with their actions and thus expose individual members to the danger of being held responsible for crimes committed in the name of the organization. No other writer describes more perceptively than Franz Kafka the bureaucratic forms that emerge from this chaos in the interactions between individual, society, and State. The brief letter which K. receives from the Castle oscillates among various structural patterns and presuppositions regarding the relation between the authorities and the addressee: "My dear Sir: As you know, you have been engaged in the count's service. Your immediate superior is the mayor of the village, who will give you all the particulars concerning your job and the terms of your employment, and who will oversee your work. I myself, however, will try not to lose sight of you. Barnabas, the bearer of this letter, will report to you from time to time to learn your wishes and communicate them to me. You will find me always willing to oblige you, insofar as that is possible. I would like my workers to be contented" (Kafka, 23). K. suffers from this confusion of hierarchical levels. As if stricken with a sudden disease, he hastily goes to bed after reading the letter. And although it does not contain any threat, K. begins to develop strong symptoms of paranoia:

> K. . . . began to read the letter again by the light of a candle. It was not a consistent letter. In part it dealt with him as with a free man whose independence was recognized—in the mode of address, for example,

and the reference to his wishes. But there were other places in which he was directly or indirectly treated as a minor employee, hardly visible to the heads of departments; the writer would try to make an effort "not to lose sight" of him; his superior was only the mayor, to whom he was actually responsible; probably his sole colleague would be the village policeman. These were inconsistencies, no doubt about it. They were so obvious that they had to be faced. It scarcely occurred to K. that they might be due to indecision. (23–24)

With similar perspicacity, Adolf Hitler analyzes the crisis in the relations between the State, the judicial system, and the individual. His main interest lies in identifying strategies through which the State, in its weakness, can be overturned. From this angle, Hitler sharply criticizes the vehmic trials and the execution of "traitors" because this practice endangers, for the sake of relatively minor political goals, faithful supporters of the extreme right by exposing them to prosecution by the State. Distancing his own party as much as possible from all hierarchical confusion, he chooses to make it visibly distinct from military and paramilitary units. For Hitler, the public arena is where the collective agency and strength of his party must be displayed:

> In order to prevent the movement from assuming a secret character at the outset, the very breadth of its membership—in addition to the uniforms, which had to be immediately recognizable to everyone—would be a factor in its effectiveness and would make it known to the public at large . . . [It had to] be trained so completely to embody this idea that from the beginning its horizon would expand, and the individual would see that his mission was not to eliminate some lesser or greater scoundrel but to devote himself to establishing a new National Socialist People's State. By this means, however, the fight against the current government was removed from the sphere of petty revenge and plotting and was elevated to a great war of destruction, born of a determined enmity against Marxism and its creatures. (Hitler, 612)

To announce and to lead "a war of extermination" in the public sphere, to commit murder in the name of the nation—these options that emerge from the breakdown of the relation between individual and society. If the fascination with murder is the most obvious symptom of the disintegration of order, the role of the charismatic political leader as a synthesis of individuality and collectivity becomes the most widely accepted solution to this crisis. [see **Individuality = Collectivity (Leader)**] Such leaders have the power to declare murder legitimate.

Related Entries

Airplanes, Boxing, Bullfighting, Cremation, Gramophones, Mountaineering, Mummies, Polarities, Individuality vs. Collectivity, Uncertainty vs. Reality, Action = Impotence (Tragedy), Individuality = Collectivity (Leader)

References

8 Uhr–Abendblatt.
Les Années-mémoire: 1926. Paris, 1988.
Johannes R. Becher, *Maschinenrhythmen.* Berlin, 1926.
Berliner Tageszeitung.
Berliner Volks-Zeitung.
Caras y Caretas.
Agatha Christie, *The Murder of Roger Ackroyd.* London, 1926.
Chronik 1926: Tag für Tag in Wort und Bild. Dortmund, 1985.
Adolf Hitler, *Mein Kampf* (1926). Munich, 1941.
Franz Kafka, *Das Schloss* (1926). Frankfurt, 1968.
Theodor Lessing, "Der Fall Grans" (1926). In *Wortmeldungen eines Unerschrockenen: Publizistik aus drei Jahrzehnten.* Leipzig, 1987.
New York Times.
Vorwärts: Berliner Volksblatt—Zentralorgan der Sozialdemokratischen Partei Deutschlands.

OCEAN LINERS

....

In Agatha Christie's novel *The Murder of Roger Ackroyd*, Dr. James Sheppard not only commits the central crime, serves as first-person narrator, and plays the genre-specific role of admiring companion and assistant to the detective, Hercule Poirot; as a physician, he also is officially in charge of his victim's health. A truly sophisticated criminal, Sheppard profits from this relationship in order to build an alibi. Following a dinner at Ackroyd's home, he stabs his patient and returns to his own house, which he shares with his sister Caroline. There he receives a phone call and tells Caroline that Ackroyd's butler is on the line: "Parker telephoning . . . They've just found Roger Ackroyd murdered" (49). At this point, however (as will later become clear), Ackroyd's servants have not yet found their master's corpse. The telephone call thus gives the murderer a strategic advantage: he can be the first to arrive at the scene of the crime. So important is this detail in his master plan that when the detective at last confronts him with the carefully reconstructed facts, Sheppard speaks of it, with pretended irony, as his ultimate defensive position: "'And the telephone call?' I asked, trying to rally. 'You have a plausible explanation for that also, I suppose?'" (306). Not without a certain degree of professional appreciation for the complexity of Sheppard's plot [see **Murder**]—and with even greater pride in his own intellectual achievement in unraveling it—Poirot indeed comes up with an answer:

I will confess to you that it was my greatest stumbling block, when I found that a call had actually been put through from King's Abbot station. I at first believed that you had simply invented the story. It was a very clever touch, that . . . I had a very vague notion of how it was worked when I came to see your sister that first day and inquired as to what patients you had seen on Friday morning . . . Among your patients that morning was the steward of an American liner. Who more suitable than he to be leaving for Liverpool by the train that evening? And afterwards he would be on the high seas, well out of the way. I noted that the *Orion* sailed on Saturday, and having obtained the name of the steward I sent him a wireless message asking a certain question. This is his reply you saw me receive just now.

Of course the content of the telephone call, which, under some pretext, Sheppard asks his American patient to put through to him, has nothing to do with the crime. But its function in Christie's novel reveals the ambiguities and liminalities of traveling on ocean liners. Passengers on ocean liners are indeed "well out of the way," beyond the reach of the law and of many other everyday constraints. The world of ocean liners— a world without stable ground—is an unreal world. [see **Uncertainty vs. Reality**] This is why Sheppard can legitimately hope that the steward who sails on the *Orion* will never testify against him. But passengers on ocean liners are out of the everyday world only for a limited time, and, given the latest developments in communications technology [see **Wireless Communication**], they are never totally unreachable. Poirot's exchange of wireless messages with the steward, who has unwittingly come to play such an important part in Sheppard's plot, leads to the conviction of the murderer.

The specific forms of experience associated with this ambiguous situation of being simultaneously out of and in the world depend to a great extent on whether a passenger's cabin is located on an upper deck or a lower deck—so much so, indeed, that life on an ocean liner has become an allegory for social injustice. In his poem "Seefahrer" ("Seafarer"), Johannes Becher plays out multiple aspects of the contrast between these two groups of passengers:

> The giant ship—quietly humming turbines;
> the ocean thunders as it spurts.

A tennis court on board. Luxury cabins.
Whispering telephone lines. Seventy tons.
A ship such as this is like an animal: it has
joints, and stomach, and lungs, eyes, and eyes.
Man strolling high above, your limbs swinging happily—
Don't forget us! We are buried deep in the bowels.
. . . How wonderful this world is for the man above:
he takes his leisure in an easy chair, and a gong
calls him to dinner.
. . . We, a pack of slaves down in the hold—
What can we do? Wrap your fist
in a rag! . . . Covet
not your neighbor's possessions!

                                   (Becher, 124–125; also 102)

The contrast between rich and poor passengers becomes even more apparent upon their transition back to the everyday world, which tends to reject those who, in traveling across the ocean, try to escape poverty or persecution: when the ship arrives at its destination, they are often arrested or sent back to the country from which they came. The same everyday world, however, eagerly absorbs first-class passengers, who own, govern, or charm the real world. Jack Gales, the hero of B. Traven's novel *Das Totenschiff (The Death Ship),* an American sailor who has been stranded in a European coastal town without his passport, learns how hopelessly naive it is to expect that the law will ignore the difference between rich and poor. The American consul in Paris politely but firmly refuses to issue Gales a new passport, yet the same functionary openly displays his eagerness to perform this very service for an opulently dressed woman with a foreign accent—who happens to be the wife of a famous banker. The consul is not the slightest bit disconcerted by Gales's indignation: "'How could you tell she was an American citizen? She can't even speak English properly . . .' 'In her case, I don't need any evidence. Her husband, Mr. Reuben Marcus, is one of the most prominent bankers in New York. Mrs. Marcus came over on the *Majestic,* and occupied the most expensive stateroom—I saw her name on the passenger list.' 'Yes, I understand. You said it, Mr. Consul. I came over on a freighter, as a lowly deckhand. That, I see, makes all the difference . . . A big banking firm is the only evidence needed to prove a man a citizen.'" (Traven, 49).

From the perspective of Becher and Traven, individuality is a privilege of the rich, and it means that one is exempt from the constraints of the law. [see **Individuality vs. Collectivity**] The poor, in contrast, are treated as individuals only in private conversation: "I've told you that, under the circumstances, I've no power whatsoever to do anything for you . . . I'd like to be able to give you the document you need, but I can't . . . Frankly, I believe your story. It sounds true . . . But I'll tell you just as frankly: if the French police ever brought you here and asked me to identify you, I would vehemently deny your claim to American citizenship" (Traven, 49).

If the reintegration of upper-deck and lower-deck passengers into the everyday world produces such dramatic divergence, the contrast between the spheres of nonreality they inhabit during the voyage is by no means less impressive. Mere survival on board is a daunting challenge for the poor and the marginal. Indeed, Bertolt Brecht tries to show, in his fragmentary novel *Lebenslauf des Boxers Samson-Körner (Life of the Boxer Samson Körner),* that transatlantic crossings offer the best possible preparation for a career as a prizefighter. [see **Boxing**] In some episodes, Körner is a starving stowaway hiding from the crew. [see **Hunger Artists**] In others, he appears on deck and must then buy the sailors' complicity by doing their work and submitting to their sexual advances. [see **Male = Female (Gender Trouble)**] The black cook Jeremiah Brown even insists on making public his erotic relationship with Körner: "He organized boxing matches on deck, supposedly to demonstrate my strength, which had so impressed him . . . Brown would sit there on a small stool, looking at me with a fascinated grin and continually drawing the spectators' attention to some trick of mine, or other things of that sort. He also liked to feel my muscles, and would praise them like a connoisseur" (138). Another protagonist, an American black man named Kongo, is a professional boxer who takes vacations from the rigors of his job (and from the constraints of Prohibition) by traveling across the ocean in a state of complete inebriation. [see **Bars**] What makes the unreal world of ocean liners appealing to stowaways (like Körner) and dropouts (like Kongo) is a tradeoff between the two aspects of their situation that relate to the absence of the law on board: stowaways and dropouts are at the mercy of the crew, but they are also beyond the reach of any State authority. Their legal punishment (for traveling without paying the fare and for crimes committed before departure) must be deferred, and this postponement affords precious time in which they can try to win allies before reentering the everyday world.

For upper-deck passengers, in contrast, the unreal world of ocean liners is a realm of play. While the rich and beautiful are impatiently awaited on both sides of the ocean, as indicated by the society columns in papers like the *New York Times* [see **Americans in Paris**], they indulge in high-class sports such as tennis and golf—but also in soccer games and boxing matches, which they would hardly consider appropriate pastimes in their real-world lives (*Chronik*, 73). On his frequent voyages between Argentina and Europe, the Argentinian tango singer Carlos Gardel delightedly observes all the carnivalesque rituals that mark the crossing of the Equator. He concludes long nights of dancing and music with sumptuous meals, and he gives lavish tips to the stewards and waiters (Collier, 74ff.). But even the upper-deck passengers face a tradeoff—the inverse of the one that confronts stowaways and dropouts. The wealthy have long been used to a transcontinental lifestyle. Since ocean liners are the only means of transportation available between the continents, the rich and beautiful cannot avoid losing a week between their various spheres of action. This situation causes serious conflicts for Rudolph Valentino, who early in the year finds himself traveling back and forth between Paris, where he is being divorced from Natasha Rambova, and the West Coast of the United States, where he has to fulfill studio obligations (Orbanz, 136; Morris, 176ff.). To make things worse, there are just two passages per week between France and the United States. According to a timetable published in *Le Figaro* on Thursday, March 18, the *Orléans* departs from Cherbourg on March 19, the *France* from Le Havre on March 24, the *Deutschland* from Boulogne on March 27, and the *Paris* from Le Havre on March 31.

Trying to describe a possible scenic effect for his play *Orphée,* Jean Cocteau alludes to "the airplanes or ships used in trompe-l'oeil photographs at county fairs" (17). This brief instruction stages the temporal rift between the imposed unreality of a long ocean voyage and the unreality of a transatlantic flight. [see **Present = Past (Eternity)**] Meanwhile, the *New York Times* announces, on September 22, that the Goodyear Rubber Company and the U.S. government have begun negotiations to establish a "New York–London line of dirigibles . . . A dirigible of 6 million cubic feet should be able to fly the Atlantic Ocean in two and one-half days or not more than three, and should prove a successful commercial venture in oceanic travel." As a result of growing demand for transatlantic conveyance, as well as growing impatience on the part of passengers, the market for ocean liners has become unstable (*Chronik,* 73). Companies such as the Panama Pacific Line and the Munson Steamship Lines react, in their advertisements, by presenting the tradeoff involved in steamship travel—loss of time versus enjoyment of dreamlike luxury—as an advantage: "Finest Ships—Fastest Time," or "Largest and Fastest Ships in the Service." But against the background of fast-paced modern life [see **Present vs. Past**], ocean liners are widely perceived as stubborn relics of the past. Even a traveler as unhurried as the Berlin celebrity Harry Graf Kessler cannot help being slightly disappointed by his voyage from Genoa to Barcelona on the *Principessa Mafalda,* one of the ships that Carlos Gardel prefers for his travels between Argentina and Spain: "In the morning, went to the Navigazione Generale, Spanish Consulate, etc., in a mad rush. Midday, beginning at twelve o'clock, on the South American ocean liner . . . the *Principessa Mafalda.* A lovely ten-thousand-ton ship, really pleasant and even luxurious (though the luxury is somewhat faded), furnished in sober Louis XVI style. Spacious, airy white sleeping cabins. Excellent food. Only a few passengers in the first-class salon" (470). Much more outspoken than Graf Kessler is the French novelist Paul Morand, who, after a voyage around the world, is obsessed with the idea that the earth's finite surface has no more secrets to be discovered [see **Polarities, Center = Periphery (Infinitude)**]: "To the long list of things that make existence unbearable, I add the fact that we are forced to live crowded together on a globe of which three-quarters is occupied, alas, by water (which could just as well have been found in the air or under the ground). We will succumb in the end; we will waste our lives in this locked compartment, sealed up in the economy class of this little sphere lost in space. For the earth is astonishingly small; only boats permit us to doubt this smallness, because they still move so slowly. Someday soon, we will realize that the steamship companies have deceived us" (11).

Not even a passage across the Pacific seems exciting to Morand: "Twelve days in a white fog, which becomes lilac toward evening—impenetrable, with no stars to mark our position . . . A few meters of sea on either side, and one horizontal abyss after another. Never saw another ship" (27). What impresses him, however, is the vertical dimension, the depth of the sea, which he experiences as a constant threat—as if only by touching the seabottom can the unreal world of the ocean liner acquire an existentially stable ground: "Below me, the Kuril Trench. No fear of running aground tonight: the sea is nine kilometers deep" (29). Any movement along this vertical axis is lethal. Writing a feature on deep-sea fishing, the journalist Egon Erwin Kisch is moved to metaphysical reflection upon seeing a shark that has been brought to the surface in the nets of a trawler: "We slit the animal open. Its liver filled the largest bucket. In its stomach was a jumble of flounder, cod, sole, and fish from distant places, some half-digested and some completely intact. A mass of eggs, the largest ones the size of chicken eggs, the smallest ones barely visible, filled the ovaries. In two bags lay unborn young, around fourteen days before their birth. Had we come here to prevent them from living?" (Kisch, 12). This question concerning the rights and obligations of man as master over a fully explored—and fully exploited—planet is crucial for a culture that is struggling to integrate its vanishing horizon of transcendence with the sphere of immanence. If there is no God, one of the many questions to be renegotiated is the extent to which humankind can allow itself to dominate nature.

The depths of the ocean connote death and eternity, and thus offer a contrast to the rapid flow of time in everyday life, with which ships can no longer keep up. It may be this link that makes the American painter Edward Hopper use deep-sea trawlers as a central motif in his pictures (Levin, 176ff.). [see **Immanence = Transcendence (Death)**] And the association is central to Traven's *Totenschiff*. In the concluding scene of the novel, Jack Gales and his companion Stanislaw are adrift in the ocean clinging to the last remaining plank of their freighter, whose owners have scuttled it to collect the insurance. When Stanislaw drowns himself, the exhausted, hallucinating Gales sees this "voyage into the depths" as a voyage into eternity, and thus as a voyage toward the redemption which they cannot find on the surface of the earth:

> He jumped. He did it. He jumped. There was no riverbank. There was no port. There was no ship. No shore. Only the sea. Only the waves rolling from horizon to horizon . . . He made a few splashing strokes in no particular direction. Then he raised his arms. He went down. In deep silence. I looked at the hole through which he had slipped away. I could see the hole for a long time. I saw it as if from a great distance . . . He'd signed on for a long voyage. For a very great voyage. I

couldn't understand this. How could he have signed on? He had no sailors' card. No papers whatsoever. They'd kick him off right away. Yet he didn't come to the surface. The Great Skipper had signed him on. He'd taken him without papers. And the Great Skipper said to him: "Come, Stanislaw Koslowski, give me your hand. Shake! Welcome aboard, sailor! I'll sign you on, to crew for a fine ship. An honest and decent ship. The finest we have. Never mind the papers. You won't need any here. It's an honest ship. Go to your cabin, Stanislaw. Can you read what's written above the crew's quarters? . . . 'He who enters here shall be forever free of pain!'" (216)

Related Entries

Americans in Paris, Bars, Boxing, Hunger Artists, Murder, Polarities, Wireless Communication, Individuality vs. Collectivity, Present vs. Past, Uncertainty vs. Reality, Center = Periphery (Infinitude), Immanence = Transcendence (Death), Present = Past (Eternity)

References

Johannes R. Becher, *Maschinenrhythmen*. Berlin, 1926.

Bertolt Brecht, *Der Lebenslauf des Boxers Samson-Körner* (1926). In Brecht, *Gesammelte Werke*, vol. 2. Frankfurt, 1967.

Agatha Christie, *The Murder of Roger Ackroyd*. London, 1926.

Chronik 1926: Tag für Tag in Wort und Bild. Dortmund, 1985.

Jean Cocteau, *Orphée: Tragédie en un acte et un intervalle* (1926). Paris, 1927.

Simon Collier, *Carlos Gardel: Su vida, su música, su época*. Buenos Aires, 1988.

Le Figaro.

Harry Graf Kessler, *Tagebücher, 1918–1937*. Frankfurt, 1961.

Egon Erwin Kisch, *Hetzjagd durch die Zeit*. Berlin, 1926.

Gail Levin, *Edward Hopper: The Art and the Artist*. New York, 1980.

Paul Morand, *Rien que la terre: Voyage*. Paris, 1926.

Michael Morris, *Madame Valentino: The Many Lives of Natasha Rambova*. New York, 1991.

New York Times.

B. Orbanz, ed., *There's a New Star in Heaven—Valentino: Biographie, Filmographie, Essays*. Berlin, 1979.

B. Traven, *Das Totenschiff* (1926). Hamburg, 1954.

POLARITIES

In the presence of Benito Mussolini, the Italian-built dirigible *Norge* is solemnly handed over to the Norwegian explorer Roald Amundsen at a Rome airport, on Saturday, April 10. The *Norge* is eighty-two meters long, has a volume of 19,200 cubic meters, and is propelled by three German Maybach engines of 260 horsepower each. It was designed and constructed by Umberto Nobile [see **Engineers**], and is about to undertake the first flight over the North Pole, for which Amundsen has won generous sponsorship in the United States (*Années-mémoire*, 116–117; *Chronik*, 95). On April 6, 1909, Robert E. Peary of the United States became the first to reach the North Pole by an overland route—and barely two and a half years later Amundsen led an expedition to the South Pole. Eleven months before the departure of the *Norge* from Rome, he made an unsuccessful attempt to reach the North Pole in a hydroplane (*Die wilden Zwanziger*, 153ff.). [see **Airplanes**]

Flying by way of Pulham, Oslo, and Leningrad, the *Norge* arrives at a specially constructed hangar on Kings Bay in Spitzbergen, on Friday, May 7. But a few days later Amundsen and Nobile, who is the commander of the dirigible, receive word that Richard Evelyn Byrd and Floyd Bennet, two U.S. Navy pilots, have already reached the Pole—on May 9 at 9:04 A.M., aboard a three-engine Fokker. Their round trip from Kings Bay lasted sixteen hours. Similar record-breaking races, which evoke worldwide interest because they confirm the idea of man's complete domination of the planet [see **Endurance, Ocean Liners, Center =**

Periphery (Infinitude)], leave the losers with the challenge of setting new goals to be reached and new thresholds to be crossed. Thus, after flying over the North Pole on May 12 at 1:25 P.M., Amundsen and Nobile continue their voyage and undertake the first crossing of the Arctic Cap. They land at Teller, Alaska, near the town of Nome, on May 14, around 8:00 A.M.

The newspaper coverage of the *Norge* enterprise shows how multiple interests and fascinations converge in such record flights. By dropping American, Italian, and Norwegian flags over the spot in the icy landscape that is believed to be the North Pole (navigation devices do not provide ultimate certainty), Byrd and Bennet, Amundsen and Nobile not only intend to give evidence of their achievements to posterity; they also—willingly or unwillingly—inscribe both expeditions in the final stage of Western imperialism's quest for territorial possessions. Moreover, these adventures are surrounded with an aura of lethal risk [see **Immanence = Transcendence (Death)**]: the weather conditions are extreme (the *Norge* loses its way in dense fog, and is coated with a ton of ice by the time it lands) and communication with the aircraft during their flights is limited. [see **Wireless Communication**] After two days during which the *Norge* has been out of contact range, a transmission from the dirigible is eagerly awaited all over the world. On its front page of Friday, May 14, the *Berliner Volks-Zeitung* offers good news—but it spices its report of the *Norge's* landing with gestures of uncertainty that keep alive the public's suspense: "According to an Associated Press report from Seattle, the airship *Norge* was expected at 11:00 A.M. local time in Nome. Rumors in circulation here have the airship passing Point Barrow in Alaska at 1:00 A.M." Two days later the *Berliner Lokal-Anzeiger* definitely confirms the arrival of the dirigible in Alaska, but the article is written in a tenuous style that refers to unsubstantiated foreign sources: "According to a radio report from Bremerton at 6:25 A.M., the radio station at Saint Paul heard the *Norge* speak with the radio station at Nome." The same newspaper publishes Umberto Nobile's telegram to his wife, thus inviting its readers to participate in this enterprise from an intimate angle: "Arrived happily in Teller, Alaska. The trip seems like a dream. Kisses, warmest regards. Nobile."

Part of the coverage in the *Berliner Lokal-Anzeiger* is a commentary by Professor Albrecht Penck, who takes a somewhat more jaundiced view of the expedition. Referring to the dangers that Arctic weather poses for human life, the author draws attention—evidently with both jealousy and admiration—to Amundsen's mastery in staging and marketing his enterprises:

> For days the position of the airship was a real cause for worry in New York and Oslo. People were discussing in detail what would happen to it with the bad weather setting in. It is, of course, easy to imagine such a scenario. But all such speculations are pointless. Concern about the weather was mistaken—it was simply a result of Amundsen's cunning. As he prepared for a trip to the South Pole, he told the whole world that he wanted to go to the North Pole, and he beat Scott by a nose. Last year, when he tried to fly to the North Pole, he didn't return for twenty-five days; when a friend asked me whether I was worried about Amundsen's fate, I replied dryly, "Wait another three weeks and Amundsen will let himself be rescued"—and I was right.

Such criticism is turned into lively parody by A. A. Milne in *Winnie-the-Pooh*, Chapter 8, "In Which Christopher Robin Leads an Expoitition to the North Pole." When Pooh, the teddy bear, asks his friend, the boy Christopher Robin, why he proposes to go on an "expoitition" to the North Pole (Pooh means "expedition"), Christopher Robin answers with a definition of the North Pole that converges with Professor Penck's ironic remarks about the goals of Amundsen's voyage: "'It's just a thing to discover,' said Christopher Robin carelessly, not being quite sure himself" (105). The "expoitition" which finally gets under way consists of a "long line of everybody" (106); it is motivated both by the food-loving Pooh's desire to consume all the "Provisions" and by Christopher Robin's ambition to reach "Dangerous Places." Then Roo (the baby kangaroo) falls into a pool, thus providing the "expoitition" with an exciting opportunity to carry out a rescue and, incidentally, to discover a Pole:

> "Get something across the stream lower down, some of you fellows," called Rabbit. But Pooh was getting something. Two pools below Roo he was standing with a long pole in his paws, and Kanga [Roo's mother] came up and took one end of it, and between them they held it across the lower part of the pool; and Roo, still bubbling proudly, "Look at me swimming," drifted up against it, and climbed out . . . But Christopher Robin . . . was looking at Pooh. "Pooh," he said, "where

did you find that pole?" Pooh looked at the pole in his hands. "I just found it," he said. "I thought it ought to be useful. I just picked it up." "Pooh," said Christopher Robin solemnly, "the Expedition is over. You have found the North Pole!" "Oh!" said Pooh. (116–117)

For the international public, the North Pole and the South Pole are not merely "things to be discovered." Despite the considerable talents of Amundsen and others in self-promotion and sales technique, the poles are much more than marks that motivate intense competitions and then disappear from the collective mind. Those who follow the voyages of self-declared "explorers" in the daily papers are encouraged to imagine the polar regions as zones where human life becomes the object of strange and uncontrollable forces. When the *New York Times,* on September 25, publishes an article entitled "Arctic Crime of Seventeen Years Ago," concerning the murder of Ross Marvin by two Eskimos during Peary's North Pole expedition of 1909, it strongly emphasizes the "unnatural behavior" underlying this crime: "The brown native of the Far North has certain childlike qualities. Under pressure of hardship and anxiety he becomes panicky . . . the Eskimo will under such circumstances behave in an altogether unnatural way. He will steal, mutiny, or desert. Yet theft, defiance, or rebellion may be furthest from his usual character." Such influences are associated with the specific geophysical conditions of the polar regions. After their flight over the North Pole, Byrd and Bennet describe at length how they succeeded in navigating without magnetic compasses, which are unusable in that zone of the planet (*Années-mémoire,* 117). Paul Morand uses anthropomorphic terms to describe the simple fact that the earth can be circumnavigated more quickly at its poles than at the Equator: "If one wants to go around the world several times in an hour, one should go to the Pole and make tight turns around it. If one prefers indolent tourism and the illusion of space, one should go toward the Equator. There, the globe with its frozen extremities hides its burning loins in a thick cloth of vegetation. Its stomach roasts in the sun" (9). [see **Ocean Liners**]

In similar reflections, and in the enterprises and experiments that trigger them, the fact of the earth's roundness—hitherto known only theoretically—is being transformed into a dimension of everyday experience. While Byrd, Bennet, and Morand challenge, in different ways, the premise that the world is a physically homogeneous space [see **Uncer-**

tainty vs. Reality], the voyage of the *Norge* from Europe across the North Pole to Alaska and down the West Coast of North America confuses the relation between center and periphery in the mental mapping of the world. [see Center vs. Periphery, Center = Periphery (Infinitude)] With the form and motion of the earth becoming factors relevant to practical daily activities, the movements of human beings emerge as something more complex than those of bodies going from point to point within an intrinsically stable space. With the disappearance of the transcendental realm once inhabited by God, movement can assume a new status as one of the transcendental conditions for human life [see Immanence vs. Transcendence]. "I realize here, at the moment of landing, that I do not like traveling—I like only movement. It is the sole truth, the sole beauty. I will not be ashamed of my life so long as it is mobile. The only fixed point: the idea of change. My imperfect art is nothing but the measurement taken between two changing points" (Morand, 31–32).

Related Entries

Airplanes, Endurance, Engineers, Ocean Liners, Wireless Communication, Center vs. Periphery, Uncertainty vs. Reality, Center = Periphery (Infinitude), Immanence = Transcendence (Death)

References

Les Années-mémoire: 1926. Paris, 1988.
Berliner Lokal-Anzeiger.
Berliner Volks-Zeitung.
Chronik 1926: Tag für Tag in Wort und Bild. Dortmund, 1985.
A. A. Milne, *Winnie-the-Pooh* (1926). New York, 1957.
Paul Morand, *Rien que la terre: Voyage.* Paris, 1926.
New York Times.
Die wilden Zwanziger: Weimar und die Welt, 1919–1933. Berlin, 1986.

RAILROADS

....

⊸⊷

The world of railroads is a world of random encounters. This is the premise of a story written by Azorín, one of the most popular Spanish authors, and published in the Madrid magazine *Blanco y Negro*. During a ten-minute stop on a train ride, a man named Adolfo leaves his compartment to buy some refreshments at the station restaurant. The service is slow, he begins to run out of time, and then he gets caught up in an argument with the waiter. A young woman, the daughter of the restaurateur, intervenes; her appearance becomes a turning point in Adolfo's life. Attracted by her beauty, he ignores the voices of his friends urging him to hurry back to the platform—and the train leaves the station with all of his luggage. But Adolfo soon celebrates his wedding, and he will be the owner of the restaurant until his wife dies, twenty years later.

In the second part of Azorín's narrative, readers learn that the story they have followed thus far is being told by Adolfo to Antonio and Pepe, two young fellow travelers, while they are approaching the very same station that he left on the spur of the moment as a widower only a short time ago: "When my wife died, everything was over for me. Even the restaurant in the train station was unbearable . . . One day, as the express train was stopping, I boarded a car to greet a friend . . . And I didn't get off . . . The train started up and I stayed on board" (*Blanco y Negro*, 131). There is a moment of profoundly reflective silence, and then Adolfo puts the story into perspective with an even more profound philosophical observation: "As Heraclitus said, 'Time is a little boy who is playing with dice.' What can we do! That's life: accidents, coincidences . . ." Surprisingly, this is not the end of Azorín's story. In the third and final scene, Adolfo and Antonio are calling Pepe back to the train—he's gotten off at the station to buy some refreshments. He misses the train and becomes the husband of the new restaurateur's pretty daughter. Although the text ends with a reiteration of the Heraclitean aphorism, the plot undermines rather than confirms any interpretation of the events as a case of sheer randomness. Can it be random that a random event and its circumstances repeat themselves at an interval of more than twenty years? [see **Uncertainty vs. Reality**]

Another railroad story by Azorín, published in the same issue of *Blanco y Negro*, likewise draws readers' attention to patterns of recurrence beneath the apparent randomness of the railroad world. In the narrow corridor of a sleeping car, Manolo literally runs into Clarita, a friend from his adolescence. The last time he saw her was many years ago, at a tumultuous party; they quarreled, and he left in the wee hours. Still unmarried, Manolo makes every possible effort to revive the erotic attraction that once existed between him and Clarita. Clarita, in contrast, consistently diverts their conversation to the beauties of the Castilian landscape as it passes before their eyes in the dawn light. Finally Clarita explains to Manolo that she is on her honeymoon: just yesterday she married one of his former rivals. Without another word, she disappears into a compartment of the sleeping car. When Manolo subsequently meets up with Rafael, Clarita's husband, the reunion is scarcely a surprise for him; yet he plays his part perfectly in this "random" encounter. While Rafael extols the erotic charms of his young wife, Manolo takes over Clarita's role from the earlier conversation and praises the purely aesthetic charms of the Castilian countryside. Thus, exactly as in the story about Adolfo, Pepe, and the pretty daughters of the station's restaurateurs, one notes a repetitive pattern in the chiastic relation between Manolo and the honeymooners. In the final scene, all three protagonists have adopted forms of behavior that help them overcome feelings of jealousy and frustration. Rafael introduces his bride to Manolo, and both Clarita and Manolo act as if they have never seen each other before: "Here comes my wife. I'll introduce you to her . . . Clarita, my friend Manolo Bazán." "Pleased to meet you, sir." "Madam, the pleasure is mine" (*Blanco y Negro*, 119).

How can the railroad system, with its intricate synchronization, serve as an emblem of randomness? Trains, tracks, schedules, stations, station restaurants, and restaurateurs' families constitute a world of contingency with respect to individual needs and expectations because the railway system's internal complexity cannot be adapted to them. [see **Elevators**] No individual traveler will ever be able to anticipate the encounters in a railway car or a station restaurant, and trains will never wait for passengers who wish to bring their randomly begun conversations to a happy conclusion. This independence of the railway system from the world of chance interactions is also illustrated in Thomas Mann's "Unordnung und frühes Leid" ("Disorder and Early Sorrow"), where the nanny of Professor Cornelius' children teaches them a simple little poem:

Train, train,
Locomotive proud,
Goes away, or maybe stays,
Toots its whistle loud.
(Mann, 500)

Reports of deadly railway accidents always present trains as agents of fate and ascribe to the victims full responsibility for their deaths: "The management of the Altona Railroad reports that at 6:10 A.M. four workers were killed and two were severely injured by a freight train arriving at the Berkenthin station from Hamburg. Apparently the victims thought that the alert which had sounded referred to train 70122 coming from the opposite direction and therefore failed to notice the approach of train 7599, which came along their track" (*Berliner Volks-Zeitung*, November 6). In Jules Supervielle's novel *Le voleur d'enfants (The Man Who Stole Children)*, the portrait photo of a rich bourgeois who has died in a train accident reminds his family of man's impotence in the face of destiny, and, as readers soon come to understand, it thus foreshadows the imminent kidnapping of his son: "Wherever the widow goes in the room, the dead man follows her with his cold, paper gaze. That energetic chin could not have been separated from life without some difficulty. He's the father of the child, framed in his role of ineffectual observer . . . He died in perfect health in a train accident and seems to object night and day that it is unjust, that he has not had his fill of life, that not long ago he was authoritarian and jealous" (Supervielle, 44–45). [see **Action = Impotence (Tragedy)**]

Often, merciless conductors incarnate the arbitrariness of the railroad system. [see **Employees**] In Ernest Hemingway's novel *The Sun Also Rises,* the first-person narrator and his friend Bill, traveling on a train from Paris to Spain, give a generous tip to the conductor in hopes of obtaining a table in an already booked-up dining car. But although the employee pockets the money, he is by no means ready to change the order of the reservations—and he remains politely unimpressed by the passengers' furious reactions: "'Give him ten francs.' 'Here,' I said. 'We want to eat in the first service.' 'Thank you,' [the conductor] said. 'I would advise you gentlemen to get some sandwiches. All the places for the first four services were reserved at the office of the company.' 'You'll go a long way, brother,' Bill said to him in English. 'I suppose if I'd given you five francs you would have advised us to jump off the train.' '*Comment?*' 'Go to hell!' said Bill" (Hemingway, 87). For the American sailor who travels through Europe without a passport in B. Traven's novel *Das Totenschiff (The Death Ship),* a disconnected exchange with the conductor during a train ride from Paris to Limoges adumbrates his dealings with a bureaucracy that will never even begin to acknowledge the specific circumstances of his precarious situation:

> All of a sudden the conductor walked through the corridor and opened the door to the compartment in which I was sitting. I had no time to attend to my urgent private business. So I sat there and looked him straight in the face . . . He opened the door, glanced at me doubtfully, made a gesture as though to close the door again, and then said, "Excuse me, sir, where did you say you wanted to get off or change trains?" He said this in French. I could grasp the meaning, but not the exact words. So I had no answer ready . . . The conductor gave me no time to explain. "Would you please let me have your ticket again?" he asked. (Traven, 50)

All these aspects of the railroad as an autonomous, inflexible, threatening system are summed up by a horrible nightmare in G. W. Pabst's "psychoanalytic" film *Geheimnisse einer Seele (Secrets of a Soul).* A telegram in which the main protagonist's good-looking cousin, a traveler in exotic lands [see **Wireless Communication, Center vs. Periphery**], announces his intention to spend some days visiting him and his wife turns the host's self-reproaches and frustrations over a childless marriage into the impulse to murder his beloved—and gorgeous—spouse. Over and over, the cousin appears in his dreams as a huge figure sitting on the cars of an express train which the poor husband cannot stop because he stands behind a railway barrier, and can only gesticulate helplessly. Psychoanalytic treatment brings an understanding of and redemption from this torture. The husband's impotence and the fears resulting from it go back to a Christmas eve during his childhood when he received an electric train set, and when the little girl who was to become his wife offered her Christmas present, a baby doll, to the cousin.

Train schedules and the railroad system in general are associated with unalterable fate, but whoever is willing (and patient enough) to explore their internal structure will be able to use it to great personal profit. In this spirit, the New Year's edition of the "Reise- und Bäder-Beilage" ("Travel and Spa Supplement") to the Berliner Börsen-Zeitung (January 3) offers its readers detailed information concerning the official rules for occupying and keeping seats in a railway car: "Many travelers are mistaken about the seating vouchers in railroad compartments. Our inquiries addressed to the main transportation authority provided the following information: According to official regulations, a seat is regarded as occupied by a passenger only when it is covered with a handbag or an article of clothing. The small numbered cards which are located near the compartment doors hold seats only until the train leaves the station." An article in the same "Reise- und Bäder-Beilage" seems to promise a description of the famous American Pullman cars that will be integrated into the service of the French National Railway Company on Friday, September 10 (Années-mémoire, 48), but it turns into a detailed systemic account of the Twentieth Century Express that links New York and Chicago: "This train is so heavily used that it must always run in two segments. Each of the two trains has thirty-two employees. On the trip from New York to Chicago, the engine is switched in Harmon (thirty-three miles outside New York) and then in Buffalo, Niagara, and Toledo. The longest stretch without a change of engine is the approximately 300 miles between Buffalo and Toledo. For the entire trip, thirty-eight tons of coal are required." [see **Present vs. Past**]

Such immense (albeit transparent) complexity is the result of a long process of technological innovation whose most recent additions, on-board telephones and automatic coupling devices between cars, are introduced in January (Chronik, 17; Années-mémoire, 139). [see **Tele-**

phones] The simultaneity of these two innovations epitomizes the paradoxical rule according to which the increasing internal autonomy of a
system (automatic coupling) occurs in tandem with a greater degree of
openness toward its environment (on-board telephones). Meanwhile, the
railway system has reached a point of such internal complexity that it
has become a metonym for the entire civilized world. The German poet
Johannes Becher sees urban environments as already dominated by
trains: "Trains soar above you; / dig yourself into invisible slices of track.
/ Zigzag!" (90). The painter Edward Hopper, in contrast, is fascinated
by the smooth integration of railroad tracks into the rural landscape
(Levin, 265–266). Having become independent from and almost coextensive with the social world, the railway system even fosters the emergence of specialized criminal gangs on its margins. A group of thieves
organized by a Hockenheim cigar-producer has filled an entire ware-
house with merchandise stolen from the Berlin–Babel freight train (*Berliner Volks-Zeitung*, November 6). At the other end of the social spectrum, owners of expensive suburban houses desperately seek ways to
protect their neighborhoods from what they see as a rapidly spreading
blight: the use of decommissioned railway cars as family homes (Kisch,
264). Regardless of social or legal status, whoever lacks contact with the
railway system seems doomed to the life of an outcast—or blessed with
a life that is not controlled by the State bureaucracy. The hero of Bertolt
Brecht's unfinished novel *Der Lebenslauf des Boxers Samson-Körner*
invents for himself a birthplace "far from the railroad tracks," because
this allows him to maintain the fiction that he is an American citizen.
Nobody would travel all the way to a small village in the State of Utah
to prove him wrong: "So let me say right off that I was born in Beaver,
Utah, USA, in the Mormon area close to the Great Salt Lake. I can also
suggest why I was born there: because Beaver, Utah, isn't on the railroad.
It's a place where you can have twelve wives. But if you want to see the
house where I was born, you can't get there except on foot. That's one
side of the matter. It's very important, because that's the only reason I
came to be a proper Yankee . . . To look at the other side: I was born in
Zwickau, Saxony, because that's where I first saw daylight" (Brecht,
121).

The internal structures and laws of railroads cannot be negotiated by
individuals—and they are therefore seen as an emblem of imposed existential randomness. But they also have grown into systems which, being

coextensive with the world, exclude the possibility of outside observation. This is why railroads emerge as a favorite metaphor in discourses that strive to explain to nonspecialist readers the most revolutionary insights in modern philosophy and science. In such texts, trains stand for certain frame conditions of human existence which are so general that they tend to be overlooked. Theodor Lessing, for example, uses the Orient Express to illustrate his conception of human consciousness:

> On the Orient Express, which constantly moves around the earth, a thinking being was born. This thinking being knew nothing of the fact that it was born on the Orient Express. Riding on the train became this person's way of experiencing the world. As a thinking being in later years, the person began to philosophize. This philosophy asserts the following: "Here I stand, the natural center of the universe. The single fact of which I can be certain is my consciousness. The earth, in contrast, moves. The trees, streets, people, telegraph poles—everything passes by tirelessly. Everything changes, everything flows" . . . I sit on a stone, off in a remote place, and speak to my heart: "What a poor fool this thinking being is. It doesn't even suspect that everything remains perpetually the same. It is born on the Orient Express. This express train which constantly moves around everything in a circle is called 'consciousness.'" (Lessing, 348–349)

Lessing's parable is by no means original. It has long been familiar through Albert Einstein's publications on relativity: "I stand at the window of a railway carriage which is traveling at a uniform speed, and drop a stone on the embankment, without throwing it. Disregarding the effect of air resistance, I see the stone fall in a straight line. A pedestrian who observes the event from the footpath notices that the stone falls to earth in a parabolic curve. I now ask: Do the 'points' traversed by the stone 'in reality' form a straight line or a parabola?" (Einstein, 9). So frequent is Einstein's use of this image that, only a few pages further on, he can invite his readers to return with him "to our old friend the railway carriage . . . traveling along the tracks" (16).

Related Entries

Elevators, Employees, Telephones, Wireless Communication, Center vs. Periphery, Present vs. Past, Action = Impotence (Tragedy)

··

References

Les Années-mémoire: 1926. Paris, 1988.

Antología de Blanco y Negro, 1891–1936, vol. 9. Madrid, 1986.

Johannes R. Becher, *Maschinenrhythmen.* Berlin, 1926.

Berliner Börsen-Zeitung.

Berliner Volks-Zeitung.

Bertolt Brecht, *Der Lebenslauf des Boxers Samson-Körner.* In Brecht, *Gesammelte Werke,* vol. 11. Frankfurt, 1967.

Chronik 1926: Tag für Tag in Wort und Bild. Dortmund, 1985.

Albert Einstein, *Relativity: The Special and General Theory* (1916). New York, 1961.

Ernest Hemingway, *The Sun Also Rises.* New York, 1926.

Egon Erwin Kisch, "Der Herr der Waggonvilla." In *Hetzjagd durch die Zeit.* Berlin, 1926.

Theodor Lessing, "Es ist nur ein Übergang" (1926). In Lessing, *"Ich warf eine Flaschenpost ins Eismeer der Geschichte": Essays und Feuilletons, 1923–1933.* Neuwied, 1986.

Gail Levin, *Edward Hopper: The Art and the Artist.* New York, 1980.

Thomas Mann, "Unordnung und frühes Leid" (1926). In Mann, *Sämtliche Erzählungen.* Frankfurt, 1963.

Wolfgang Schivelbusch, *Geschichte der Eisenbahnreise: Zur Industrialisierung von Raum und Zeit im 19. Jahrhundert.* Frankfurt, 1979.

Jules Supervielle, *Le voleur d'enfants.* Paris, 1926.

B. Traven, *Das Totenschiff* (1926). Frankfurt, 1954.

REPORTERS

In its June 26 issue, the magazine *Die literarische Welt* presents a debate on "news reporting and literature." Together with a number of nationally prominent authors, such as Max Brod, Alfred Döblin, Leonhard Frank, and Heinrich Mann, the journalist Leo Lania analyzes the impact of news reporting on contemporary literary styles and genres. Lania focuses on the relation between what he calls "the penetrating voice of the present" and a particular style of thought: "The penetrating voice of the present cannot be ignored. It pushes the most romantic dreamers from their remote corners into the merciless light of day. There, all things acquire new shapes and colors, and their meaning and existence disclose themselves only to those who have the courage to measure its contours without presumption. To look at them, to listen to them, to experience them anew turns them further into lived experience" (Lania, 322). Coming at the end of a sequence of verbs—"measure," "look," "listen"—that are meant to characterize the reporter's relation to the world, the concept *Erleben* receives specific emphasis in Lania's text. It returns in the highly unusual substantive form *der Erleber* ("the experiencer") in a series of quotations from recent review articles with which the Berlin publisher Erich Reiss Verlag advertises the fifteenth edition of Egon Erwin Kisch's book *Der rasende Reporter (The Raging Reporter)*. In the two years since its original publication, this volume of about thirty essays, most of which were previously published in newspapers, has consolidated Kisch's

national reputation as an outstanding representative of "literary sobriety" [see **Sobriety vs. Exuberance**]: "Kisch is a pleasant sort of nonlitter-
ateur, experiencer, observer, seeker of facts. His book *Der rasende Reporter* outweighs volumes of novellas with its sensational materials, the
rhythm and tempo of its style, the plasticity of its form, its tragedy and
humor, its incisiveness and wit" (Kisch, 361).

What explains the insistence on *Erleben* in all this enthusiasm about
Kisch's prose? Normally translated as "lived experience," the word *Erleben* is emerging as a key concept in phenomenological philosophy,
where it is defined as distinct from *Erfahrung* ("experience") and also
from *Wahrnehmung* ("perception"). Whereas "perception" refers to the
mere apprehension of the world by the senses, "experience" includes
both the act and the result of interpreting the perceived world on the
basis of previously acquired knowledge. *Erleben* is situated between
"perception" and "experience." It adds to perception the focusing on
what is being perceived, but it does not include interpretation. *Erleben*
is more than just sensory contact with the environment—but less than
the transformation of the closely regarded environment into concepts. Its
philosophical definition explains why *Erleben* is considered so important
for the reporter. No substitutes for *Erleben* can be found through concepts or through the transmission of knowledge: it requires that the
observer be physically near the object observed. The reporter must be a
participant-observer. [see **Uncertainty vs. Reality**] This condition makes
plausible the general assumption that the reporter's role is linked to the
high level of social mobility in American society: "In America, students
work during the holidays as farmers, waiters, telegraph employees; doc-
tors work as farmers. Almost everyone works at a dozen professions, and
people acquire a clear understanding of their social existence—an existence to which, from childhood on, they are connected by a hundred
threads" (Lania, 323). A good reporter is actively familiar with certain
sectors of everyday life—as is, for example, the famous French athlete
Géo André, who has become a journalist for the magazines *La Vie au
grand air* and *Le Miroir des sports* (*Années-mémoire,* 119).

Whereas traditional truth-claims depend on a distance between the
observer and the world—a mode of living which Lania despises as "sec-
ond-hand" (322)—the fact that reporters are concerned with lived experience means that there is an emphasis on physicality in their public
image. Reporters are constantly stimulating their senses with cigarettes

(Kittler, 317), and a famous painting of Kisch depicts his upper body as being covered with tattoos—inscribed with the world he so acutely observes (Zimmermann, 143; Willet, 108). In order to withstand the immediacy of multiple impressions and (as the etymology of the word "reporter" suggests) "carry back" these impressions to the reading public, reporters need "strength," "energy," and "courage" (Kisch, 361). For them, surface contact with phenomena is not a lack of depth but a cognitive advantage: "A precondition for 'prying the seed from its shell' is the knowledge that things and institutions are superficial" (Lania, 323). Like so many other ways of moving across surfaces [see **Bars, Dancing, Gomina**], the life of the "raging reporter" is a "steeplechase through time" (a phrase that serves as the title of Kisch's second book). Only speed can prevent the reporter from getting caught in the depths of interpretation and experience. The process of writing down his impressions in longhand may become too time-consuming for the reporter, and his work therefore often depends on the interface between typist and typewriter (Kittler, 317). [see **Employees**]

Admirers of the reporter are divided between those who appreciate his style as extremely subjective and those who see it as the epitome of objective "sobriety" (Zimmermann, 149). Both views are grounded in the inherent ambiguity of lived experience. Insofar as the reporter refrains from all interpretations and judgments, simply "carrying back" impressions from his direct contact with the world, he is "objective." But these impressions are always contingent upon the random circumstances in which they are formed, and therefore cannot be associated with objectivity-claims based on the belief that randomness does not exist—a belief that derives from reflection and interpretation. [see **Authenticity vs. Artificiality**] This lack of conceptual penetration in the reporter's cognitive style results from the time-pressures of a world that seems to be moving into the future with ever-increasing speed. [see **Timepieces, Present = Past (Eternity)**] Such a world no longer functions on the basis of ideas and values: "Those who succeed in clinging to reality manage to survive the disappearance of ideas and values" (Kisch, 371). Since the reporter can live only in the present, he has no time to select objects of particular relevance for his work, and he therefore lets intuition lead him to the (seemingly insignificant) items of interest in everyday life. Kisch writes about deep-sea fishing, eating ham in Prague, an airplane flight from Prague to Paris, the room where Lenin lived in Zurich, crimes in

the Upper Alps, historical monuments at Salzburg. But even in essays
with such narrowly circumscribed topics, Kisch provides running heads
that change throughout each text and that signal the topics discussed on
individual pages. He thus emphasizes the rapid pace of his observations.

The restless life of the reporter and his surface view of the world are
linked with the collective—and often repressed—fear that ultimate truths
are no longer available. By exploiting the most advanced communications technologies [see **Telephones, Wireless Communication**], the reporter is often able to address the need for specialized information in
societies that are rapidly growing more and more diverse. There are so
many European reporters touring the United States and the Soviet Union
[see **Center = Periphery (Infinitude)**] that some standard, genre-specific
routes begin to emerge. These itineraries regularly include, in the American case, visits to the Ford manufacturing plants in Detroit, the stock-
yards of Chicago, and the studios of Hollywood (Zimmermann, 150).
Visitors to Russia, such as Benjamin, Kisch, and Toller, never miss an
opportunity to observe conditions in the newly organized factories and
report about workers' reactions to socialist modes of production. In the
library of an automobile factory in Moscow, Ernst Toller discovers,
among the Russian classics, books by Johannes Becher and Egon Erwin
Kisch, and he is so impressed with Soviet proletarians' thirst for information that he casts this impression in slightly moralizing terms for his
German readers: "The thirst for knowledge among the workers persists.
I notice a bulletin board which is covered with queries. Workers who
need clarification about something write their questions on a card. Whoever knows the answer posts a card with a response. I read the following
questions: 'What does *polar* mean?' 'What does *contradictory* mean?'
'What's a hypothesis?' 'Who knows something about Sinclair?' 'Who
knows something about Einstein?' 'Who knows something about Mexico?' Every factory, every prison, every school, every house has its bulletin board" (Toller, 114). In a world where the need for rapid production
and circulation of knowledge becomes itself a central element of knowledge, the market for periodical publications cannot help expanding.
There are 3,812 newspapers in Germany, of which 112 appear daily in
Berlin (*Chronik*, 61). In many Western countries, the information industry has become an important part of the national economy, and its
impact on the political process can be decisive.

Although this development is particularly marked in England, France,

Germany, and the United States, a comparable advance is evident in the metropolitan centers of Latin America. On May 15, *O Jornal do Brasil,* a daily paper in Rio de Janeiro, publishes a long interview with the Italian poet Filippo Marinetti. Despite his obvious reservations about Marinetti's Fascist politics, the interviewer, a young journalist named Sérgio Buarque de Holanda, presents the visitor's views without any critical comments: "We prefer to hear the political Marinetti, because for him politics is a pure form of poetry. In his politics and in his poetry, we find the same contradictions, incoherences, and lightning-flashes of beauty. These qualities make him an intriguing and exceptional person in the general confusion of the twentieth century" (Buarque de Holanda, 76). It is less Marinetti's opinions than his contradictions that render him an interesting topic for the newspapers, and being interesting is a good enough reason for *O Jornal do Brasil* to invite him for a second interview after he has visited São Paulo, Montevideo, and Buenos Aires. This time, Buarque de Holanda presents Marinetti as if his famous guest were himself a reporter. Marinetti appears as a traveler whose perceptions have been sharpened by the countries he visits: "I return to Brazil full of enthusiasm. Rio de Janeiro in particular has offered me many lively and extremely pleasant impressions. This city has stimulated my physical and intellectual sensibility in the most beautiful and festive way" (79).

The interventions of censorship, which are a big concern (and a big opportunity for self-stylization) among intellectuals and artists [see **Movie Palaces**], may occasionally interest reporters as a topic but do not particularly hinder their journalistic activities. After all, the reporter strives to fascinate readers with lived experience, rather than to persuade them of the rightness of his own opinions. In Ramón del Valle-Inclán's novel *Tirano Banderas,* there is a scene in which an editor-in-chief explains to a young journalist that his report on a rally held by the political opposition is too favorable to be published. The editor suggests replacing the discursive mode of political commentary with the tonality of lived experience. According to him, the government will benefit if the opposition's rally is depicted as a circus show: "Here's an idea which, if successfully developed, would assure you professional success: write the article as if you were describing a circus act, with trained parrots. Emphasize their harangues. Begin with the most courteous congratulations to the Harris Brothers Company" (Valle-Inclán, 57). Far from protesting this strategy of political manipulation, the young reporter responds with a mixture of flattery and enthusiasm: "What a first-rate journalist you are!"

Related Entries

Bars, Dancing, Employees, Gomina, Movie Palaces, Telephones, Timepieces, Wireless Communication, Authenticity vs. Artificiality, Sobriety vs. Exuberance, Uncertainty vs. Reality, Center = Periphery (Infinitude), Present = Past (Eternity)

References

Les Années-mémoire: 1926. Paris, 1988.

Sérgio Buarque de Holanda, "Marinetti, homen político" (1926). In Francisco de Assis Barbosa, ed., *Raízes de Sérgio Buarque de Holanda.* Rio de Janeiro, 1989.

Chronik 1926: Tag für Tag in Wort und Bild. Dortmund, 1985.

Egon Erwin Kisch, *Hetzjagd durch die Zeit.* Berlin, 1926.

Friedrich Kittler, *Grammophon, Film, Typewriter.* Berlin, 1986.

Leo Lania, *Reportage als soziale Funktion* (1926). In Anton Kaes, ed., *Weimarer Republik: Manifeste und Dokumente zur deutschen Literatur, 1918–1933.* Stuttgart, 1983.

Ernst Toller, "Russische Reisebilder" (1926). In *Quer Durch: Reisebilder und Reden.* Munich, 1978.

Ramón del Valle-Inclán, *Tirano Banderas* (1926). Madrid, 1978.

John Willet, *Art and Politics in the Weimar Period: The New Sobriety, 1917–1933.* New York, 1978.

Peter Zimmermann, "Die Reportage." In Thomas Köbner, ed., *Zwischen den Weltkriegen: Neues Handbuch der Literaturwissenschaft,* vol. 20. Wiesbaden, 1983.

REVUES

....

Wherever the French writer Paul Morand goes in his voyages around the world, he seeks the exciting atmosphere of high-rise buildings: "Spasmodic conflagrations of publicity. The burning skyscrapers, the hanging gardens of the Plaza, the Majestic, and the Carlton, the greatest hotels and brothels of Shanghai belong to the Spanish Fathers. In those luxurious rooftop clubs dance the wives of English officers . . ., judges of the Joint Commission, and Russian refugees" (Morand, 67). But a dance show that he sees at the roof garden of a skyscraper in downtown Shanghai provokes in Morand an abrupt negative reaction—and even feelings of cultural self-hatred: "Tragic entrance of a music-hall act: six women, three costumed as yellow jockeys and three as pink horses. What are Asian epidemics next to these Western poisons?" (67–68). [see **Roof Gardens**] Why does Morand describe this spectacle as "tragic" and "poisonous" when, at the same time, he admires Shanghai's advertisements, traffic, architecture, and bars, which are also the products of Western colonization? [see **Action = Impotence (Tragedy)**] Accustomed to the spectacles offered on the stages of North American and European cities, he sees this show in Shanghai as an inferior imitation—a paltry entertainment with only six dancers, who moreover are quite unglamorously got up as jockeys and horses. Revue directors in Paris, Berlin, and New York may easily spend a quarter of a million dollars on costumes and sets for a single production (Klooss and Reuter, 53). They employ hundreds of stagehands and use ultramodern technical equipment—such as powerful loudspeakers, colored lighting, telephones, even huge movable swimming pools (Schäfer, 3). [see **Telephones**] It is thus no wonder that their advertisements emphasize sheer quantity above all else: "Fifty enormous pictures, one hundred delightful models, two hundred enchanting women, one thousand innovative ideas, two thousand fantastic costumes" (Carlé and Martens, 66). Since numbers matter, money matters; and since money matters, revue spectacles are a feature of affluent cities where theaters can fill their expensive seats once or even twice every day (Jelavich, 165). Some of Berlin's largest traditional theaters, such as the Komische Oper and the Grosses Schauspielhaus, which can hold up to three thousand people, are now hosting revues, while others are being transformed into huge movie palaces. As the young journalist Siegfried Kracauer laconically states, "It cannot be overlooked that there are *four million people* in Berlin" (313). [see **Movie Palaces**]

A dramatic economic gap separates this flourishing industry from the popular forms of entertainment in colonial cities and provincial towns. Wherever the revue culture finds sufficient interest and financial support, it develops into veritable systems of competing companies and shows. Nine revues are inaugurated in Berlin alone during the fall and winter season. Among them, James Klein's program at the Komische Oper has a reputation for being the most licentious; Erik Charell's show at the Grosses Schauspielhaus presents the widest international range of performers; and Hermann Haller's spectacle at the Admiralspalast boasts the most sophisticated sets (see Carlé and Martens, 66; Jelavich, 165ff.). The advertisements on the back page of the *8 Uhr–Abendblatt* indicate the extent to which successful revues depend on balancing the immense size of their productions with sufficiently large audiences: "The only true theater sensation in Berlin! Grand revue, 200 performers, low prices" (Komische Oper, August 29). "150 girls, 400 performers! Sunday afternoon, 3:00. Entire show at much reduced prices" (Grosses Schauspielhaus, October 19). "Often imitated—never matched! Two Sunday performances, 3:00 and 8:15. Afternoon show half-price" (Admiralspalast, October 22). The September 22 issue of the *New York Times* runs announcements both for Florenz Ziegfeld's *Follies,* with the show "Glorifying the American Girl" (in two "popular priced" matinees on Wednesdays and Saturdays), and for Earl Caroll's *Vanities,* "The Greatest of All" (with matinees on Thursdays and Sundays). In Paris, *Le Figaro* of March 17 advertises the program of the recently reopened

Moulin Rouge, featuring the dancer Mistinguett and "the eighteen Hoff-man Girls." The competition includes "La Folie du Jour" (a vehicle for Josephine Baker) at the Folies Bergères; Jacquy Fragsy at the Concert Mayol; and the current show at the new, particularly elegant Champs-Elysées Music Hall (*Années-mémoire*, 86ff.). As a system of entertain-ment, the revues concentrate in certain neighborhoods. In Paris, the Champs-Elysées boulevard is becoming an alternative to Montmartre as the classic entertainment district, and while Berlin's Friedrichstraße, near the river Spree, has long been notorious for its nightlife (Carlé and Martens, 177), a new center is emerging in the western part of the city, around Kurfürstendamm. All these revue companies in France, Germany, and the United States compete for the most popular stars and the trendi-est groups in an international market. England seems to participate only on the producer side. Hermann Haller hires the London-based Tiller Girls away from Ziegfeld's *Follies* (Jelavich, 175). Berlin's Nelson Thea-ter loses to the Folies-Bergères in an intense bidding war for Josephine Baker. [see **Dancing**] Despite the often eccentric contents of their pro-grams, revues have become a normal element in the everyday life of big cities. The proletarian uprising in Fritz Lang's film *Metropolis* is directed against Yoshiwara, the city's "pleasure center," where "great curtains hang from the ceiling" and "the gilded youth of Metropolis dance wildly" (117). And in Jules Supervielle's novel *Le voleur d'enfants (The Man Who Stole Children)*, theaters—along with railway stations and crowded streets—are among the scenes that trigger the criminal imagi-nation of the main character, Colonel Bigua, who acquires a family by abducting children: "At the music hall, when a family of trapeze artists was announced, Bigua thought, 'It may be my daughter who's about to come on stage'" (72).

What are the elements that distinguish revues from other spectacles, such as cabaret acts, operettas, and more traditional forms of theater? How does this type of entertainment attract the large crowds of wealthy spectators that are essential for its survival? Its most important ele-ment—which also figures largely in the fantasies and appetites of its audience—is the display of half-nude female bodies. In Germany and France, complicated legal battles have produced a compromise which, while acknowledging "artistic value" in the nudity of "living pictures" that reproduce classical paintings and historical scenes, prohibits female dancers from baring their breasts: "Women dancers must cover completely their posterior, private parts, and navel with opaque fabrics, so that during the dance movements these body parts are not revealed. Furthermore, the breasts must be covered at least to the extent that the nipples cannot be seen during dance movements" (Jelavich, 163; Klooss and Reuter, 47). The constant threat of police intervention aimed at enforcing such rules adds to the genre-specific fascination, which is further intensified by openly pornographic program brochures (Jelavich, 179; Klooss and Reuter, 51) and by the revues' racy titles: "Houses of Love," "On and Off," "Berlin Unbuttoned." From a strictly quantitative point of view, however, sex is only a minor ingredient of such acts. Their internal rhythm is set by kicklines consisting of ten or more female bodies that dance with precise synchronization to the sound of fast-paced music. Kicklines are often interpreted by spectators and critics as the epitome of the deindividualizing and desubjectivizing mid-level jobs that have recently become open to women; and like those jobs, they have a desexualizing effect (Jelavich, 175–176). [see **Assembly Lines, Employees, Male vs. Female, Male = Female (Gender Trouble)**] The sex appeal of the dancing girls is as reduced as that of the diligent secretaries. On the one hand, kicklines thus contrast sharply with the nudity of "living pictures," but on the other they reveal a further—intrinsic—dichotomy between the drill of their coordinated movements, as an element of sobriety, and the lavish ornamentation that surrounds their choreography. Whether connected as "living curtains" (Klooss and Reuter, 60; Schäfer, 43) [see **Sobriety vs. Exuberance**] or arranged in tableaux of historical scenes, the ornamentalized bodies participate in the deindividualizing dynamic of the kicklines. But ornamentalization can also produce a contrast between the multiple anonymous bodies of the "girls" in the chorus and the central bodies of revue stars whose importance is marked by flamboyant costumes. The feather boa which has become the trademark of the Moulin Rouge star Mistinguett can metamorphose into gigantic butterfly wings (Schäfer, 52; Années-mémoire, 86). Like a shining pearl [see **Gomina**], Josephine Baker lies in an enormous artificial shell which descends slowly from the ceiling to the stage; when it opens, its mirrored inner surfaces display multiple reflections of her brown body (Schäfer, 49).

Once Josephine Baker begins to dance, she incarnates yet another aspect of the revue's fascination—namely, a projection of authenticity onto African and African-American forms of culture: "She is the real thing [*das Echteste*]. She is blackness at its purest . . . She imparts rhythm, which comes from her blood, from the jungle. She takes us back to our childhood, when, visiting black neighborhoods, we were whipped up by the beating of the kettle drums, with blacks crying out strange prayers and moving their limbs. This is what the revue is all about!" (*Berliner Börsen-Zeitung,* January 3; see Schrader and Schebera, 114–115). [see **Authenticity vs. Artificiality**] Several loops of strange associations underlie whites' enthusiasm for black bodies. The otherness of these bodies opens a path back to an imagined source of white cultural (or racial?) identity, and when spectators concentrate on the surface perceptions offered by black dancers, they have the illusion that they are attaining some deep level of authenticity. Jazz is the appropriate music for such images, and its rhythms add to the speed which characterizes the staging of the revue. [see **Present vs. Past**] This speed, in turn, is part of a general effort at condensation. Since most revue theaters do not offer sufficient space for the hundreds of fast-moving bodies—the stage of the Folies-Bergères, for example, is only 9.3 meters wide and 7.2 meters deep (Schäfer, 38; Klooss and Reuter, 33)—stairways become a necessary component of the sets. In addition to accommodating a greater number of actors and dancers, stairways dramatize the appearance of the star as a gigantic, colorful event that brings a resplendent body and its aura close to the spectators. [see **Jazz, Stars, Center = Periphery (Infinitude)**] Speed and condensation, however, merely counterbalance the revues' essential heterogeneity; they never neutralize it. As the various numbers are performed, the visual and acoustic effects accumulate but do not complement one another in any overarching plot structure. Though revues are frequently organized as a series of historical tableaux or exotic landscapes (Jelavich, 3, 168; Schäfer, 34), neither the shared element of temporal and spatial alterity nor the thread of the emcees' words and jokes can provide a definitive impression of unity. For Siegfried Kracauer, "the surface glamour of stars, films, revues, and production values" lies in their capacity to present "in a precise and undisguised manner to thousands of eyes and ears the *disorder* of society. This is precisely what enables such shows to evoke and maintain that tension which must precede inevitable and radical change. In the streets of Berlin, one is often struck by the momentary insight that someday all this will suddenly burst apart. The entertainment to which the general public throngs ought to produce the same effect" (315). Revues reflect a world that is constantly on the verge of explosion; at the same time, they prevent this explosion from occurring.

Nevertheless, the revue as a genre occupies only a marginal place in Kracauer's analysis, whose main reference point is the movie theater. As a live show, the revue cannot compete financially with the film industry, which yields a much higher return on investment; and despite the admirable achievements of revues' producers, stage directors, actors, and dancers, the new technical medium of motion pictures has far greater potential for pushing the surface impressions of speed and condensation to new limits. While revues may succeed briefly in "intercepting . . . the departing audience, which is streaming from the stage to the cinema" (Jelavich, 168), the transitional status of the genre is apparent in the fact that many of the former theaters which revues have occupied for several years are now being transformed into movie palaces. Toward the end of the year, James Klein loses ownership of the Komische Oper through bankruptcy, and Erik Charell begins to plan a new type of show, which he calls the "revue-operetta" (Jelavich, 186).

Related Entries

Assembly Lines, Bars, Dancing, Employees, Gomina, Jazz, Movie Palaces, Roof Gardens, Stars, Telephones, Authenticity vs. Artificiality, Male vs. Female, Present vs. Past, Sobriety vs. Exuberance, Action = Impotence (Tragedy), Center = Periphery (Infinitude), Male = Female (Gender Trouble)

References

8 Uhr–Abendblatt.

Les Années-mémoire: 1926. Paris, 1988.

Günter Berghaus, "Girlkultur: Feminism, Americanism, and Popular Entertainment in Weimar Germany." *Journal of Design History* 1 (1988): 193–219.

Berliner Börsen-Zeitung.

Claude Berton, "Réflexions sur le Music-Hall." *La Revue de Paris* 6 (1929): 653–675.

Wolfgang Carlé and Heinrich Martens, *Kinder, wie die Zeit vergeht: Eine Historie des Friedrichstadt-Palastes Berlin.* Berlin, 1987.

Marcel Denise, "Les merveilles du Music-Hall vues de coulisses." *Lectures pour tous* 8 (1926): 46–56.

Le Figaro.

Fritz Giese, *Girlkultur: Vergleiche zwischen amerikanischem und europäischem Rhythmus und Lebensgefühl.* Munich, 1925.

Atina Grossmann, "Girlkultur, or Thoroughly Rationalized Female: A New Woman in Weimar Germany?" In Judith Friedlander et al., eds., *Women in Culture and Politics: A Century of Change.* Bloomington, 1986.

Wolfgang Jansen, *Glanzrevuen der Zwanziger Jahre.* Berlin, 1987.

Peter Jelavich, *Berlin Cabaret.* Cambridge, Mass., 1993.

Reinhard Klooss and Thomas Reuter, *Körperbilder: Menschenornamente in Revuetheater und Revuefilm.* Frankfurt, 1980.

Franz-Peter Kothes, *Die theatralische Revue in Berlin und Wien, 1900–1938: Typen, Inhalte, Funktionen.* Wilhelmshaven, 1977.

Siegfried Kracauer, "Kult der Zerstreuung: Über die Berliner Lichtspielhäuser" (1926). In *Das Ornament der Masse.* Frankfurt, 1977.

Fritz Lang, *Metropolis* (1926). New York, 1973.

Paul Morand, *Rien que la terre: Voyage.* Paris, 1926.

New York Times.

Edgar Schäfer, "Körper und Inszenierung: Spektakel im Paris der zwanziger Jahre." Unpublished manuscript, Siegen, 1987.

Bärbel Schrader and Jürgen Schebera, *Kunstmetropole Berlin 1918–1933: Die Kunststadt in der Novemberrevolution / Die "goldenen" Zwanziger / Die Kunststadt in der Krise.* Berlin, 1987.

Jules Supervielle, *Le voleur d'enfants.* Paris, 1926.

ROOF GARDENS

There are only a few French intellectuals who, like Paul Morand, admit they are interested in the cultural phenomena associated with American capitalism. Among the many things that fascinate Morand in the United States and Canada are high-rise buildings, which feature prominently in his travel account *Rien que la terre*. Struggling to find a language that resonates with their status as emblems of modern life's glamorous New Sobriety, he describes the skyscrapers of downtown Manhattan as "erect[ing] their fifty magical stories, like Chaldean astrological towers, to follow more closely the star of the dollar" (Morand, 16). [see **Sobriety vs. Exuberance**] This comparison between New York's skyscrapers and ancient Mesopotamian structures built for astrological observations may be technically inappropriate, but it is consistent with a widely popular pattern of dual-level experience. Morand attributes modern economic functions to these architectural marvels and to their enormous internal complexity [see **Elevators**], but he draws the model for his analogy from his knowledge of the ancient world. [see **Authenticity vs. Artificiality**]

After crossing North America in an express train [see **Railroads**], Morand arrives in Vancouver, where he performs the first gesture that has become obligatory for tourists from Europe: "I go up to the sixteenth floor and come out on the roof of the Vancouver Hotel. There is a terrace with a strip of soot where, in front, are growing those silly flowers which find their way to the English heart more quickly than words can. The blue amphitheater of the Rockies always presents the same show, which is the city. The circle is broken only by a crooked bottleneck, which gives access to the Pacific" (21). For a number of reasons, Morand experiences the rooftop of his Vancouver hotel as an ambiguous space. It belongs to a skyscraper and is therefore part of the admirable achievements of *homo faber*. [see **Engineers**] But it also offers a view of nature in the surrounding area. This "nature" is itself ambiguous because, although it is the sublime nature of the Pacific Coast, it also serves as a stage for the cityscape of Vancouver. And such double ambiguity is overdetermined by yet a third ambiguity stemming from the town's geographic location on the border of Western civilization, between the North American continent and the Pacific: "This is the 'Land's End' of the West" (23). Bringing together such multiple contrasts between civilization and nature in a space of simultaneity, the rooftops of skyscrapers are an ideal site for a paradox. They are frequently transformed into roof gardens, and as roof gardens they ostentatiously display nature as artifice. [see **Center = Periphery (Infinitude)**]

Although the city in Fritz Lang's film *Metropolis* does not feature a roof garden, its vertical space is structured according to the same organizational principles that Morand invokes. From the upper stories of the skyscrapers in Metropolis, the industrial work and the production of capital are constantly monitored. Here resides John Fredersen, the Master of Metropolis, himself a functioning element within the overwhelming internal complexity of the building and of the city as its environment [see **Employees**]: "Again we look through the canyon-like streets. Far above everything else, storey upon storey, rises the building known as the 'New Tower of Babel.' In the cognitive center of this New Tower of Babel lives the man who is himself the brain of Metropolis . . . The scene shifts to an immense office. A great window looks out over the city in the background, while in the foreground is a vast semicircular desk with clocks and writing materials on it and a couple of thickly upholstered armchairs at a table beyond. A thin, gaunt-looking man . . . walks across the room, wagging a finger as he dictates to his secretaries off-screen" (Lang, 35). Even higher than this office, indeed high above the entire city, loom two gigantic structures: Masterman Stadium, built by the rich fathers of Metropolis for their sons, and Eternal Gardens, the club where the sons seek amusement. Consisting of stalactites and ferns, the artificially produced nature of Eternal Gardens carries the same connotation of archaicism as the skyscrapers in Morand's text ("Chaldean astrological towers") and as the building that contains Fredersen's office ("New Tower of Babel"). The intrinsic ambiguity of Eternal Gardens as a border-space between nature and the city's technological civilization is underscored by a ceiling which, although it covers the elegant club, is as transparent as a shining membrane: "The milk-colored glass ceiling above the Eternal Gardens was an opal in the light which bathed it . . . Strange convoluted stalactites rise to the ceiling; there are ferns and greenery on every side" (23–24).

While roof gardens constitute a sphere of luxury, and while the upper stories of skyscrapers are reserved for the systems' self-observation, rooftops without artificial nature are the place where culture meets the sky as its infinite environment. This is why rooftops have a magnetic attraction for architects. Architects belong to the environment of buildings because they construct them, but they also assign themselves specific tasks within the buildings' internal functioning. [see **Engineers**] During a visit to New York, Le Corbusier frequently climbs "to the roof of a friend's apartment house at night and let[s] the Manhattan of vehement silhouettes sweep over him" (Hawes, 219). The daylight version of this New York panorama appears in two watercolors by Edward Hopper in which the random configurations of railings, chimneys, billboards, and huge water tanks join in a cityscape that seems to mimic nature. The convergence and tensions between technology and nature are a common element in Hopper's work, which brings together rooftops, railroad tracks running through the countryside, and steamers fighting the waves of the ocean (Levin, 239–240, 265–266, 176ff.). Meanwhile, German newspapers report on the first skyscrapers rising in historic town centers. Among them, the seventeen-storey Wilhelm-Marx-Haus in Düsseldorf dramatically emphasizes its rooftop by surrounding this space with a two-storey semitransparent gallery (*Chronik*, 56).

As a general rule, however, the outside of such new high-rises is "unassertive." When Rosario Canela, a star among New York architects, designs 101 East 72nd Street as a sober "thirteen-story limestone-and-brick palazzo," it is his ambition to fill the interior of this building with combinations of "simplexes, duplexes, maisonette apartments with private street entrances, penthouses, and roof garden apartments (including a triplex with fifteen rooms and an elevator direct to its door)" (Hawes, 225ff.). The architectural development of such enormous buildings has reached the stage where they contain apartments the size and shape of free-standing houses. Skyscrapers thus turn into an environment for other buildings, and as such they occupy a sphere and fulfill a function traditionally attributed to nature. This is yet another perspective which makes plausible the flowers, ferns, and trees growing on the skyscrapers' roofs. So fancy are the multistorey apartments, the houses-within-houses, that "the apartment architect [is] the man of the hour." In its second year of publication, the *New Yorker* magazine features "a regular column, signed either 'Duplex' or 'Penthouse,' which [reports] in depth on the best new buildings in town" (Hawes, 221). The advertising of leading real estate firms attests to the status of this fashion as a concrete everyday reality. In the *New York Times* of September 21, the firm of Pease and Elliman offers "Duplex Roof Garden Apartments" at 210 Madison Avenue, with "unusually large rooms and high ceilings" and including "full housekeeping." Slawson and Hobbs presents a "9-Room Duplex on 15th floor" and an "11-Room Roof Bungalow with 4 Baths" at 277 West End Avenue, "overlooking Schwab Mansion." This display of space—within the circumscribed space of a large apartment building and in the border-zone of its encounter with nature—merits the term "exceptionally distinctive."

No other space condenses the tensions between nature and civilization, between outside and inside, between authenticity and artificiality to such a degree as the roof garden. Thus, when Jack Dempsey organizes a boxing match in July between his friend Rudolph Valentino and a sports journalist [see **Boxing, Reporters**], in order to quash reports of Valentino's alleged "homosexual inclinations," this public act of negotiation between a sexuality viewed as "unnatural" and a virility desired as "natural" [see **Male = Female (Gender Trouble)**] can be staged only at a roof garden. The one chosen is the roof garden of New York's Ambassador Hotel (Orbanz, 128).

Related Entries

Americans in Paris, Boxing, Elevators, Employees, Engineers, Railways, Reporters, Authenticity vs. Artificiality, Sobriety vs. Exuberance, Male = Female (Gender Trouble)

References

Chronik 1926: Tag für Tag in Wort und Bild. Dortmund, 1985.

Elizabeth Hawes, *New York, New York: How the Apartment House Transformed the Life of the City, 1869–1930.* New York, 1993.

Fritz Lang, *Metropolis* (1926). New York, 1973.

Gail Levin, *Edward Hopper: The Art and the Artist.* New York, 1980.

Paul Morand, *Rien que la terre: Voyage.* Paris, 1926.

New York Times.

Eva Orbanz, ed., *There Is a New Star in Heaven—Valentino: Biographie, Filmographie, Essays.* Berlin, 1979.

SIX-DAY RACES

In the *Berliner Volks-Zeitung* of Saturday, November 6, the coverage of the six-day bicycle race being run at the Sportpalast describes a particularly dramatic incident. Though some participants have already been eliminated after only thirty-six hours of competition ("the six-day field is thinning out"), it is the performance of the American athlete Horder that first excites intense interest: "The American, lagging behind the other competitors, suddenly collapsed and lay motionless on the track. The doctor ordered an hour-long break. Then Horder reappeared, much to the general enthusiasm of the crowd, his arm and head bandaged. He rode a lap but fell down again with glazed eyes, as if dead. The situation was clear: he was too doped up. Yet not even now did Horder quit. Instead he got better and better, won several prizes in grand style, and proved himself a true six-day man." For a moment, the spectators have seen death in Horder's eyes, and this extreme circumstance, together with his ability to face and overcome it, earns him the honorary title of "true six-day man." [see **Boxing, Dancing, Mountaineering, Mummies, Immanence = Transcendence (Death)**] Six-day bicycle races, like dance marathons, were invented in the United States (*Chronik*, 26), and just as in the ongoing competition for cross-Channel swim records [see **Endurance**], Americans excel in pushing their bodies to the absolute limit—the moment when spectators can watch the competitors face death. The use of performance-enhancing drugs, which increases both physical energy and the risk of death, is generally accepted as an element that adds to the thrill of the show.

More, perhaps, than any other form of competition based on physical endurance, six-day bicycle races appeal to the fascination with pure movement—movement that can no longer be seen or functionalized as bridging the distance between two places. [see **Polarities**] Even though, during the 144 hours of the competition, the best six-day racers end up covering around 3,000 miles, they remain in the same building, circling around a wooden track with dangerously steep curved sides. In addition to being confined in this space, six-day bicycle races, like the popular relay races [see **Endurance**], are deindividualizing. They typically involve thirteen teams, each consisting of two athletes who regularly take turns. Rather than the movement of individual bodies, the continuous movement of a six-day race is therefore the movement of small systems. A third level of denaturalization, besides those of the racetrack and of deindividualization, lies in the arbitrariness of the rules that set the pace for the competition. Although the reporter Egon Erwin Kisch, half ironically, associates the six days of the bicycle race with the six days in which God created the world (Kisch, 229), the contrast between the seven days of the week as a "natural" time frame and the six days of racing underscores such arbitrariness. [see **Uncertainty vs. Reality**] The morning hours of each race, when very few spectators come to the arenas, are discounted as "neutralization time." The teams must continue their movement around the track, but they can neither gain advantage over nor fall behind their competitors. From early afternoon until the wee hours, in contrast, the race is frequently accelerated by "chases." [see **Present vs. Past**] Individual spectators or companies offer cash prizes or samples of their products to the winners in many different mini-races, for which the sponsors are free to set the rules. Such prizes may go to the team that wins "the next five laps," posts the fastest lap of the night, or covers the greatest distance in a given amount of time. This procedure enables spectators to buy influence over the speed of the competition, and since each prize is announced publicly, they can also compete for the attention of the crowd.

In the sports arenas of Chicago, New York, Paris, Brussels, and Berlin (*Années-mémoire*, 100ff.), six-day races turn the structures of the external world upside down. They absorb energy and attention so completely that athletes and spectators alike become blind to events in their everyday environment (Kisch, 228–229). [see **Elevators, Roof Gardens**] According to its intrinsic rules, the world of six-day racing is most animated in the late evening and the wee hours, whereas "neutralization time" coincides with that part of the day during which labor in offices and production plants is most intense. Conversely, the distribution of seats in the arenas, which, except for the morning hours, are regularly sold out, repeats and dramatizes the social structures of the everyday world. The bleachers, far away from the racetrack, are occupied by a proletarian crowd which is mainly interested in the competition as an athletic performance. The ringside seats, however, are a favorite meeting place for the demimonde. In addition to this elementary hierarchization, a bridge above the cyclists connects the seating area to the enclosure at the center of the track—but it is accessible only to those who are willing to pay a sizable additional fee. On this interior "stage," surrounded by the speeding racers, a show much like a revue is taking place. Popular bands play loud music, chorus girls swing their legs, bartenders offer alcoholic drinks with exotic names, and high-class prostitutes approach customers before thousands of spectators. [see **Bars, Revues**] In the middle of this performance by professionals and wealthy parvenus, a man with a megaphone orchestrates the rhythm of the six-day world. He keeps the crowd informed about the progress of the competition, announces the sponsors and prizes for individual chases, and introduces bands, singers, and celebrities. In his role, the fascination with movement and rhythm, the interest in the limits of physical performance, and a voyeuristic participation in the sex market converge. Through the announcer's voice, the diverse crowd of the six-day races becomes intoxicated with the echo of its own excitement.

Squeezed in between the racetrack and the central space reserved for bands, bars, and the demimonde is a row of thirteen boxes which, for six days, are the residences of the competing athletes. Here they sleep and eat, take warm baths, and are massaged by their trainers. All their activities can be observed from the seats, and the privileged spectators in the center can even talk and shake hands with them. Fascinated by such proximity, the French writer Edgar Morand registers every detail in the life of the six-day racing heroes: "The racers' area had been pushed toward the end of the track, near the bend. Each man had a little wooden house with a cot closed off by curtains. Stenciled letters read: 'Velox Station,' 'Petitmathieu Team,' 'Van den Hoven.' A spotlight lit up the booths, allowing the crowd to see every gesture of its favorites, even when they were at rest. The trainers came and went in white hospital coats, with a clinking of plates, among the oil and grease stains, preparing mixtures of egg and camphor on garden chairs" (*Années-mémoire*, 103). Concerns and actions that, outside the arena, belong to the space of privacy become part of a public performance within the artificial daily life of the six-day race. No other event fulfills more perfectly that desire which makes actors and athletes into stars: the audience's desire to follow their private life as closely as their performance. This becomes possible for the spectators because they share with their heroes a space in which the boundary between private and public is erased. Little wonder that some fans stay in this world, close to the stars, for 144 hours—until, on the seventh day, they return to their jobs and families.

Related Entries

Bars, Boxing, Dancing, Elevators, Endurance, Mountaineering, Mummies, Polarities, Revues, Roof Gardens, Stars, Present vs. Past, Uncertainty vs. Reality, Immanence = Transcendence (Death)

References

Les Années-mémoire: 1926. Paris, 1988.
Berliner Volks-Zeitung.
Chronik 1926: Tag für Tag in Wort und Bild. Dortmund, 1985.
Egon Erwin Kisch, "Elliptische Tretmühle" (1926). In Kisch, *Der rasende Reporter; Hetzjagd durch die Zeit; Kriminalistisches Reisebuch*. Berlin, 1983.
Leo Lania, "Reportage als soziale Funktion" (1926). In Anton Kaes, ed., *Weimarer Republik: Manifeste und Dokumente zur deutschen Literatur, 1918–1933*. Stuttgart, 1983.
Sling, "Sechstagerennen." In Sling, *Die Nase der Sphinx, oder Wie wir Berliner so sind: Feuilletons aus den Jahren 1921–1925*. Berlin, 1987.
John Willet, *Art and Politics in the Weimar Period: The New Sobriety, 1917–1933*. New York, 1978.

STARS

·····················

⊲⊳

The promotional flier of Christy Walsh, Babe Ruth's manager, features the names of twelve nationally famous athletes, among them Lou Gehrig, Babe Ruth himself, and Pop Warner, the coach of Stanford's successful football team. Arranged in a semicircle, the names are each printed within the outline of a star, and Walsh's text explicitly refers to this design: "Stars available for Personal Appearance, Merchandise Endorsements, Exhibition Baseball Games, Vaudeville, Moving Pictures, Radio, and All Forms of Commercial Contracts, under Christy Walsh Management, 570 Seventh Avenue, New York City" (Ritter and Rucker, 158). Stars are marketable, and not only because they have specific skills that large crowds of spectators are eager to admire—for example, in "Exhibition Baseball Games." Stars also gratify the more diffuse desire to enjoy their "Personal Appearance" and to imitate them.

Weeks before the end of the cabaret and revue season in Paris, where Josephine Baker has risen to new heights of stardom, "Josephine Baker dolls, costumes, perfumes, [and] pomades" fill the shopwindows, together with a product called "Bakerfix," which helps women smooth down their hair into a glossy cap so they can look more like the much-admired black dancer (Rose, 100). [see **Gomina**] The movie actor Rudolph Valentino sports a hairstyle that has "caused a worldwide boom in the sale of Vaseline." He has also launched the fashion of wearing a goatee, and, breaking traditional gender taboos, has made wristwatches and "slave bracelets" widely popular among men (Orbanz,

20ff.). Consumers buy such products because they cannot resist the desire to imitate the body stylizations of the stars they worship. Among manufacturers, such mimetic behavior on the part of the consumer triggers a two-pronged strategy: they strive to associate their merchandise with famous names, and they thus build brand loyalty instead of product appreciation. Especially in the film industry, this strategy ends up generating "loyalty to a name, whether it be that of an actor, a studio, or a theatre" (Valentine, 37). But although mimetic desire relating to stars' bodies can be transferred to names (of, say, film studios or movie palaces), it is unclear whether the suicide of some of Valentino's fans when they learn of his death on Monday, August 23, is an emotional reaction of despair or a completely automated form of imitation: "At the news of Valentino's death, two women attempted suicide in front of Polyclinic Hospital; in London a girl took poison before Rudy's inscribed photograph; an elevator boy at the Ritz in Paris was found dead on a bed covered with Valentino's photos" (Orbanz, 107). In any event, stars inspire followings, and since followers are successfully persuaded that they can fashion their own bodies according to the model of their heroes, stars become icons of individuality as well as incarnations of collective identity. [see **Individuality = Collectivity (Leader)**] But although the status of the stars thus oscillates, during their lifetime, between extreme closeness and extreme remoteness in relation to the fans' quotidian, their death makes them part of a heavenly sphere that contains the primary referent of the word "star." [see **Immanence vs. Transcendence**] Only a few weeks after Valentino's death, a recording with the title "There's a New Star in Heaven Tonight" comes on the market (Orbanz, 137). [see **Gramophone**] Some of the people who took their own lives in his wake may have done so in the hope of joining him in this strangely secular sphere of eternity. [see **Immanence = Transcendence (Death)**]

Who can become a star? Certainly not the typical intellectual, as Heinrich Mann notes with more frustration than irony, in analyzing the current situation of the literary writer. Such an author "has no readers who are sophisticated intellectuals and who thus would consider writing as an endeavor far worthier than boxing. Certainly none of them would think him a great figure. Does he wish to go his own way alone, or with only a few followers? Often, he can't afford to do this, for purely financial reasons" (320). In even stronger tones of protest, Heinrich's brother Thomas points to a hierarchy of public roles which he identifies as a symptom of cultural decay: "We live in . . . a real jazz-band age whose heroes are the prizefighter and the movie star, and which reveals all the details of their huge orgies" (Kolbe, 378). However intensely Thomas Mann may resent this scenario, he is certainly right in singling out athletes, movie stars, and popular musicians as the true stars of the moment (Willet, 102). For stardom depends on performance. Only a body in performance can be a presence that enhances the spectator's desire for emulation and spatial closeness. Only a body in performance can be seen by a collective as the incarnation of a specific type of individuality. [see **Individuality = Collectivity (Leader)**]

But not every body in performance becomes the body of a star. Exceptional physical achievements are only one criterion for stardom. Babe Ruth's *noms de guerre* show that, even in his case, when it comes to constituting a halo of stardom, athletic prowess and a particular physical appearance unite with certain collective fantasies and something as incidental as the sheer sensual pleasure of alliteration. He is known as "the Behemoth of Bust, the Colossus of Clout, the Caliph of Clout, the Maharajah of Mash, the Rajah of Rap, the Sultan of Swat, the Wazir of Wham, the Bambino" (Ritter and Rucker, 101). Earlier than other sectors of the entertainment world, the film industry has understood that in order to manufacture true stars, one must manufacture their private lives as part of their public personae. Stars may explicitly claim the right to keep their private lives private, but the very nature of their profession cannot help blurring the distinction between private and public. For only a private body made public (or a public body staged as a private body) will stimulate a collective desire for individual closeness. From the earliest days of her Hollywood career, Greta Garbo observes how eagerly her male screen partners try to transform their fictional love stories into real love stories—and she is furious to see that they do so with strong encouragement and support from the studios (Gronowicz, 189ff.). Soon, however, she takes an important step in her career by succumbing to the charms of leading man Jack Gilbert. Her previous lover, the Swedish film director Mauritz Stiller, offers a caustic analysis of the situation: "In the opinion of most critics, Gilbert is emotionally shallow and his interests lie not in film but in women. Escapades with them are touched up in the publicity department and sent to the press. His adventures have caused him to become an idol of the lonely American woman, and his poor acting is covered up by his so-called good looks" (212).

This amalgamation of movie stars' fictional lives and private lives has a functional equivalent among star athletes, who often act out fictional lives that more or less parallel their private biographies as represented in plays or in films. Unlike competitions in ballparks or arenas, such art forms are capable of staging motifs of privacy (Ritter and Rucker, 84–85). Jack Dempsey combines the two aspects of this promotional strategy in a Broadway production entitled *The Big Fight: A Drama of New York Life*. Playing "a champion who [is] tempted by a betting syndicate to throw the big fight for a cool million bucks" (and who of course stays clean), the heavyweight champion of the world is joined on stage by his wife, Estelle Taylor, a modestly popular Hollywood actress. In this particular case, however, the public manufacture of private identity ends up working against the star. The live performance reveals a grotesque discrepancy between the champion's impressive body and his high-pitched, almost feminine voice (Dempsey and Dempsey, 182ff.).

Although it is impossible to identify outstanding achievements or talents as the sole criterion for all the varieties of stardom, there is hardly any star whose biography does not follow the narrative pattern of a meteoric rise from unhappy childhood to national or international celebrity. Babe Ruth "never had a real childhood in the usual sense of the word," because his parents sent him to a reformatory before he was seven (Ritter and Rucker, 8). Brought up with numerous siblings in an impoverished Utah family, Jack Dempsey began his career as a prizefighter at fifteen, out of sheer financial necessity. Like Ruth and Dempsey, Valentino was born in 1895; he lost his father at the age of ten, emigrated to the United States at eighteen, worked as a gardener and a gigolo, and tried for a long time without success to be cast in a Hollywood movie—before his big break came around 1920. The greatest of all stars, Charlie Chaplin, had perhaps the most wretched childhood: his mother, an actress, was mentally ill, and they lived in poverty in the London slums. Through the roles they play as actors or as athletes, the bodies of the stars often keep alive, like open scars, the memories of their traumatic past. While such scars can underscore the star's ultimate triumph as a miraculous event, they also encourage fans to dream of a similarly glorious personal destiny—however depressing their own life-situations may be.

But even after the stars have crossed the role-specific threshold between penury and glory, the private aspects of their public personae often remain clouded by unhappiness. Babe Ruth, who enjoys the admiration of millions of American boys (Ritter and Rucker, 162–163), will never be a father. Rudolph Valentino, "who desperately wants a child," is blamed by his wife "for a miscarriage caused by reckless driving" (Morris, 178). Valentino falls into a depression after his divorce from Natasha Rambova in January, and the Babe's wife suffers from nervous breakdowns which the press eagerly interprets as reactions to her spouse's notorious womanizing (Ritter and Rucker, 128–129). Charlie Chaplin's wife, Lita Grey, leaves him on November 30 and takes their little boys, Charles and Sidney (Robinson, 662–663). A brief reconciliation between Jack Dempsey and his wife after his loss of the world championship is merely a prelude to their final separation. Such emotional emptiness and family woe in the life of the star only intensify the fans' desire to occupy a role by the side of the admired body. In Chaplin's case, the socially marginal life which he evokes repeatedly in his films makes these fantasies particularly concrete:

> One night, . . . coming out of Grauman's Egyptian [movie theater], I was striding the short distance between the theater and our favorite restaurant when I recognized, a few steps ahead of me, the familiar outline of Charlie. Instinctively, I slowed down, and I cannot express what melancholy overwhelmed me when I realized the total solitude of the most popular man in the world . . . At the corner of Cherokee Street an important event occurred—important for Charlie at least . . . He met a dog. A fat, common mongrel who was sitting waiting for who knew what. And Charlie stopped, abruptly. He had found someone to talk to. And he started to question the dog, who probably recognized in him a comrade, because it offered him its paw." (Robinson, 372)

Stars never appear completely blameless in their publicized private unhappiness. But although, at least in the case of male actors and athletes, such responsibility does not detract from their popular appeal, reckless behavior and family crises may well affect the quality of their professional performance—to the point of jeopardizing their entire careers. Following his divorce, Valentino is involved in a number of serious car accidents (Orbanz, 136). Since Babe Ruth scored only twenty-five home runs in the previous season, the press begins to ask "whether he eats, drinks, or screws himself out of baseball," and he is "almost universally believed [to be] a has-been" (Ritter and Rucker, 135)—until the Sultan of Swat gears up for what will become his best season with the Yankees so far. Anticipating outrageous financial claims from his wife's lawyers and facing a federal tax bill of more than $1.1 million, Chaplin temporarily suspends work on his film *The Circus* on Sunday, December 5 (Robinson, 371). Three days before his title fight against Gene Tunney, Dempsey is served "with a summons which commands him to appear [in court] to defend the suit for an accounting brought by ex-judge James Mercer Davis of Camden on behalf of Jack Kearns, deposed manager of the champion." Dempsey's immediate reaction in a press interview exemplifies how stars manage to make the best of such challenges by transforming them into evidence of their courage and strength: "These lawsuits, injunctions, restraining orders, and attachments are annoying when they come at you from all sides, but if the people back of all this expect that they can cause me to worry myself out of the title, they will wake up to find themselves badly mistaken" (*New York Times*, September 21).

On an individual level, it is the need for public love and support which often helps champions and leading actors to become even greater stars. Attending a boxing match less than a month after his humiliating defeat at Tunney's hands, Dempsey receives an impressive ovation from the crowd, "an uproar of several minutes, with feet-stamping and paper being showered from the second balcony, while for Gene there were mingled cheers and boos" (Heimer, 60). [see **Boxing, Action = Impotence (Tragedy)**] Suzanne Lenglen, who almost single-handedly attracts so many spectators to women's tennis that she can embark on a professional career, has long been perceived as aloof and arrogant. Only a downturn in her career as an athlete will warm the public's feelings for her. Unhappy over the playing schedule that she is assigned at the Wimbledon meet in June, Lenglen declines to appear at the Royal Family's reception for outstanding players. She is so vehemently attacked by the British press that she will never again compete in this key tournament (*Années-mémoire*, 161). Had the incident not occurred, however, an intellectual like Heinrich Mann would probably not have deigned to see Suzanne Lenglen as a model for moral behavior: "In the world in which we suffer, she is an example of human unwavering—and thereby is beautiful" (Heinrich Mann, 304).

An almost boundless power over millions of fans and an equally striking inability to live a life of happiness with their partners and relatives come together in the stars' public personae. This is why Charlie Chaplin, alluding to the private frustrations that may have contributed to Valentino's death at the height of his career, speaks of this event as "one of the greatest tragedies that has occurred in the history of the motion picture industry" (Robinson, 369). [see **Action = Impotence (Tragedy)**] Most stars are acutely aware of the dual-level nature of their existence, and, somewhat astonishingly, it does not seem to work against them if they publicly speak about its implicit problems. Dempsey describes his "pal" Valentino as "an intelligent, oversensitive individual who allowed himself to be packaged by Hollywood and didn't like the result" (Dempsey and Dempsey, 195). Beginning with her very first Hollywood movie, Greta Garbo insists on the distinction between her own artistic appreciation of her films and the simultaneous awareness that "as a commodity [she] was quite precious to MGM" (Gronowicz, 187). It thus no longer make a difference for the status of the established stars whether they decide to actively join the sphere of artificial glamour or stay at a distance from it. [see **Authenticity vs. Artificiality**] In either case, they cannot avoid having their private lives exposed on the public stage. Instead of resisting this exposure, stars might as well give in to the demands of their fans—and shake hands with Albert Einstein and Mahatma Gandhi, as Chaplin does (Chaplin, 320ff., 340ff.); pose for the press in bathrobes at the breakfast table, like Babe Ruth and Jack Dempsey (Ritter and Rucker, 118); or appear at the fabulous parties organized by the media magnate William Randolph Hearst and his mistress Marion Davies, where the short-circuit between the private sphere and the public sphere is symbolically closed (Chaplin, 308ff.; Dempsey and Dempsey, 191).

Meanwhile, highly skilled managers exploit every opportunity on the market for the stars to attract the world's gaze. Hollywood actors regularly attend the premieres of their films on the East Coast (Orbanz, 136). Appearing on the stages of vaudeville theaters and in daily exhibition games during the off-season, Babe Ruth tours numerous cities between Minneapolis and California that have no major league teams—and the baseball commissioner has long given his blessing to such "barnstorming" (Ritter and Rucker, 148). [see **Center = Periphery (Infinitude)**] Even the highly conservative organization that regulates tennis is willing to temporarily suspend the formal demarcation between amateur and professional sports when serious business interests are at stake: "According to a report from New York, the American Tennis Association has decided that Suzanne Lenglen, despite her status as professional, may continue to play against American amateurs. Based on this report, it is possible that a new match between Suzanne Lenglen and Helen Willis is on the horizon" (*Berliner Tageblatt,* August 5; *Années-mémoire,* 160–161). Finally, "with improvements in artificial ice making and the building of rinks capable of holding large crowds," the summer months are full of activity in preparation for the next season of the fledgling National Hockey League. While hockey officials establish detailed rules for selling, optioning, and exchanging players and devise a system for documenting attendance records, no less than four new franchises are established: the Chicago Blackhawks, the Detroit Falcons, the New York Rangers, and the Toronto Maple Leafs (Diamond, 31ff.).

Bringing more athletic events and more Hollywood films to a greater number of towns, stadiums, and movie palaces, the entertainment industry steadily improves its services for a public that wants to be close to its stars. But the more this desire for closeness is gratified, the more it reaches new levels of intensity: ultimately, fans dream of seeing their own bodies transfigured into the individual, admired, unique bodies of stars. This fills their existence with eternal longing for an eternally postponed moment of recognition. Xaver Kleinsgütl, the good-looking young servant of Professor Cornelius' family in Thomas Mann's story "Unordnung und frühes Leid" ("Disorder and Early Sorrow") spends much of his time waiting for this moment: "He loves the cinema with his entire soul. After an evening at the movies, he tends to feel melancholy—filled with yearning and apt to talk to himself. He harbors vague hopes that someday he will make his fortune in that splendid world and become an accepted member of it—basing his hopes on his thick head of hair, his nimbleness, and his daring. He's fond of climbing the ash tree in the front garden, rising from branch to branch up to the very top, and then scaring the wits out of anyone who spots him. In this perch, he lights up a cigarette and puffs away at it as he sways back and forth, keeping a lookout for any film director who might pass by and hire him" (513).

Of course, the film director for whom young Kleinsgütl is waiting in the treetop will never show up—at least not before the end of Mann's story. Should he indeed appear, it would be better if he were from

Hollywood than from Berlin. For only through promotion on the American market can talented, good-looking young women and men become international stars. The American market dominates the various national entertainment industries because it systematically subordinates the intrinsic qualities of theatrical, musical, and athletic performance to the public's collective desire to be in the presence of adored individual bodies. Stars are created by this desire.

Related Entries

Boxing, Gomina, Gramophone, Movie Palaces, Authenticity vs. Artificiality, Immanence vs. Transcendence, Silence vs. Noise, Action = Impotence (Tragedy), Center = Periphery (Infinitude), Immanence = Transcendence (Death), Individuality = Collectivity (Leader)

References

Les Années-mémoire: 1926. Paris, 1988.

Charles Chaplin, My Autobiography. New York, 1964.

Jack Dempsey and Barbara Piattelli Dempsey, Dempsey. New York, 1977.

Dan Diamond, ed., The Official National Hockey League 75th Anniversary Commemorative Book. Toronto, 1991.

Antoni Gronowicz, Garbo: Her Story. New York, 1990.

Mel Heimer, The Long Count. New York, 1969.

Jürgen Kolbe, Heller Zauber: Thomas Mann in München, 1894–1933. Berlin, 1987.

Heinrich Mann, Sieben Jahre: Chronik der Gedanken und Vorgänge. Berlin, 1929.

Thomas Mann, "Unordnung und frühes Leid" (1926). In Mann, Sämtliche Erzählungen. Frankfurt, 1963.

Michael Morris, Madam Valentino: The Many Lives of Natacha Rambova. New York, 1991.

New York Times.

Eva Orbanz, ed., There's a New Star in Heaven—Valentino: Biographie, Filmographie, Essays. Berlin, 1979.

Lawrence S. Ritter and Mark Rucker, The Babe: A Life in Pictures. New York, 1988.

David Robinson, Chaplin: His Life and Art. London, 1985.

Phyllis Rose, *Jazz Cleopatra: Josephine Baker in Her Time*. New York, 1989.
Maggie Valentine, *The Show Starts on the Sidewalk: An Architectural History of the Movie Theatre*. New Haven, 1994.
John Willet, *Art and Politics in the Weimar Period: The New Sobriety, 1917–1933*. New York, 1978.

STRIKES

....

✏️

British Trade Union Congress announces that at midnight the workers of the printing, iron, steel, chemical, gas, electric, construction, railway, and transportation industries will join the coal miners in their strike, which began on May 1. As a "general strike" with more than two million participants, it seems to be the realization of an old dream for the theorists of the Left: the dream of paralyzing society by withdrawing the support of those labor groups who are the least appreciated and the most poorly paid.

For several months the political scene in Great Britain has been dominated by the threat of this event. During the previous year, the owners of the coal mines announced their intention to increase the length of the workday (currently seven and a half hours) and simultaneously to lower wages. [see **Timepieces**] The miners' unions have not only declared their unwillingness to even discuss these proposals; they have also replaced regional agreements, which were keeping wages low, with a nationally unified tariff treaty. In this situation of irreconcilable conflict, the government has intervened as arbiter. It has provided subsidies to maintain the income level of miners, and it has appointed a commission of experts to conduct an in-depth study of the British coal industry. On March 10, this commission comes up with a recommendation which, not surprisingly, has the character of a compromise. It suggests, as an obligation to be imposed upon the owners, a radical reorganization of production sites, and it argues against lengthening the workday. On the other side, the commission regards wage cuts as inevitable and does not acknowledge the need for a nationally unified tariff agreement. Since neither of the opposing parties is willing to move toward an agreement within the range of these options, and since the report also persuades the government to cancel subsidies as of May 1, the workers end up being shut out and therefore begin their strike. Representing the coal miners, the Trade Union Congress now takes up the negotiations with the government—threatening to join with all its various subsections in a general strike. On May 3 the government cancels the negotiations: some workers at the *Daily Mail* have refused to print an article containing remarks critical of the unions, and British officials interpret this as the beginning of a general strike. Only hours later, Prime Minister Stanley Baldwin declares in a parliamentary speech that, since the Glorious Revolution, England has never been closer to civil war (*Chronik,* 90; Parker, 121ff.).

Despite such solemnly threatening words, none of the three parties involved seems to believe that the latest dramatization of their conflict will yield any new results. For several months the government has been accumulating reserves of food and coal. As Chancellor of the Exchequer, Winston Churchill has prepared a detailed emergency plan which includes the formation of a strike-breaking committee, the maintenance of most transportation services, and the production and nationwide distribution by airplane of a news circular entitled the *British Gazette* (Gilbert, 474ff.). The tone of the *British Gazette* is so conciliatory and its reports on the workers' inclination to return to the negotiating table are so optimistic, that public opinion soon begins to shift from the government to the miners. On May 12 the Trade Union Congress calls off the general strike. This, however, only complicates the situation: "Today, after the breakdown of the general strike, the difficulties are probably even greater than on the day the strike broke out. The owners, or at least certain circles of owners, have turned the failure of the general strike into a counterattack. They take the position that the general strike is a violation of the law, since the workers have broken their wage contracts. Now the industrialists claim to have the law on their side, when it comes to making new wage contracts and locking out whomever they want to . . . This tactic has created a state of tremendous agitation among the workers" (*Berliner Volks-Zeitung,* May 14).

The struggle between miners and owners continues for another six months; and from September on, both parties reject any mediation by the government, whose disappointment is expressed by Churchill in unusually blunt terms: "These people think themselves stronger than the State. But that is a mistake" (Gilbert, 479). On November 19 the coal miners' union ends up accepting a settlement which verges on capitulation. While the miners succeed in keeping the workday to seven and a half hours, they agree to a wage cut of about 10 percent and give up demands for a nationally unified tariff treaty (*Chronik*, 181). But although the owners have won the battle, they may well have lost the war. The labor struggle in Great Britain, which has lasted half a year, has weakened the British coal industry vis-à-vis its competitors on the Continent, and the experience of the general strike has persuaded even some of the most conservative politicians that they cannot lend their unconditional support to the side of capital (Parker, 121–122).

The events in Britain, which are perceived as a test case for the sociopolitical future, attract international attention. Leon Trotsky, whose loss of influence and power culminates in his exclusion from the Soviet Politburo in October (*Chronik*, 166), interprets the general strike in Great Britain as the ultimate confirmation of his concept of continuous revolution and his belief that the Soviet Party should support such developments wherever they occur. But instead of trying to understand the failure of the workers and their unions to win this battle, instead of making an intellectual effort that would probably oblige him to revise his political and theoretical position, Trotsky yields to the temptation to blame the outcome of the general strike on his rival Stalin. He criticizes him for having supported the wrong representatives within the British Communist movement: "If the general strike proved the rightness of the Marxist forecast, as opposed to the homemade estimates of the British reformists, the behavior of the General Council during the general strike signified the collapse of Stalin's hopes" (Trotsky, 525–526). This is shortsighted: it reveals how much Trotsky's personal resentment prevails over his political views; moreover, he omits the obvious key question— namely, whether the socioeconomic frame-conditions that gave rise to the Marxist theory of class struggle can still be taken for granted.

For more than five years, the unemployment rate in Great Britain has oscillated between a minimum of 11 and a maximum of 16 percent. Exports of raw materials and of products from literally every industrial sector have fallen dramatically, especially in comparison to those of the United States and the major continental nations. Particularly in the coal industry, the number of workers is constantly decreasing. This complex negative picture is due mainly to the Great War's long-lasting effects on the international market and, some economists suggest, to the way the Treaty of Versailles has hampered the world economy. The crisis is especially severe in Britain because the nation's industrial plants are technologically outdated and because British owners typically offer unusually stiff resistance to major innovations (Parker, 111ff.). [see **Assembly Lines**] Lacking legally acceptable ways to intervene in the national economy, the British government tries to help revitalize the world market by returning to the gold standard and to the prewar exchange rate between the pound and the dollar. But while this measure diverts a growing flow of capital to British banks, it further diminishes exports, which suffer as a result of the overvalued British currency.

Under these circumstances, it seems preferable for owners to cope with the complete standstill of an entire industrial sector, rather than constantly regulate and downscale the level of productivity without being able to lower wages. Workers, unless they attempt a proletarian revolution, have to rely more on appeals to the social and ethical responsibility of their governments [see **Murder**] than on the threatening power of strikes—which no longer really threaten. On both sides of the political conflict, certain concepts of class-struggle ideology begin to look like relics of a remote past. [see **League of Nations**] In an address to the Verein Deutscher Studenten (Association of German Students) on July 6, Foreign Secretary Gustav Stresemann declares that taking an arrogant, superior attitude toward the working class is a dangerous legacy from prewar times: "And there is another phenomenon, one that I consider largely responsible for the alienation between the socialist worker and the bourgeois—namely, the completely erroneous attitude of the so-called elevated classes, who distanced themselves from everything connected with the workers' movement, which is rooted in class resentment rather than dogma. [One recalls scenes in which] a student, still with lofty notions from academia and school songs in his ears, goes off to war and meets a worker there. He feels: You and I are strangers; we don't belong together" (Stresemann, 277–278). Although Stresemann of course knows of the ongoing struggle between workers and owners in the coal industry, he seems to be envious of Britain, where, in contrast to Germany, political mediation between the antagonistic groups is possible "because, despite the oppositions and the conflicts of opinion, between Baldwin and Chamberlain on one side and MacDonald on the other, the rift between the dominant class and the subordinate class is much less dramatic than it was in prewar Germany" (278–279).

The higher value in whose name Stresemann argues for a new spirit of reconciliation—and through which British politicians justify their interventions during the days of the general strike—is that of the entire nation's well-being. It is from exactly the same angle that Adolf Hitler suggests a radical redefinition of the concept "strike." He no longer sees strikes as a proletarian weapon for class struggle, but considers them a device for optimizing the national economy: "For the National Socialist labor union, . . . the strike is not a means of smashing and destroying national production, but rather a strategy of making money by fighting against bad conditions which, because of their antisocial character, reduce the performance of the economy and thus jeopardize the existence of the entire community . . . The National Socialist employee must realize that a flourishing national economy leads to his own material happiness . . . The National Socialist employee and the National Socialist employer are both representatives of and spokesmen for the same national unity" (Hitler, 676). [see **Employees, Individuality vs. Collectivity**] Although Hitler takes care to announce that strikes will be unnecessary—and therefore illegitimate—in the future National Socialist state, and although he openly admits that his sympathetic view of the workers' plight is motivated by his desire to win their support for the National Socialist Party, his reactions to the new labor situation are far more analytic than those of Stresemann, who seems exclusively interested in minimizing any kind of conflict, and does not realize the potentially revitalizing impact of such confrontations for the national economy. Hitler, in contrast, is not only capable of identifying the positive aspects of strikes, but also proposes a distinction between the "material value" and the "ideal value" of labor. On the basis of this dichotomy, he tries to combine the enhancement of individual motivation through a hierarchy of income levels with the creation of a collective spirit of solidarity: "Material compensation will be allotted to those whose labor is productive for the community; spiritual compensation, however, must lie in the high regard that each person earns by devoting his individual talents to the collectivity of the nation. It is no disgrace to be a workman, but it is certainly one to be a civil servant who steals his labor from God and his daily bread from the people" (484).

Stresemann, Hitler, and the British government all react to the profound transformations that are taking place in the economic and social
systems. But in doing so, they continue relying on the classic pattern of
a "natural" antagonism between labor and capital. The British economist John Maynard Keynes, in contrast, publishes a short book entitled
The End of Laissez-Faire which outlines a very different and more
complex distribution of roles and functions within national economies
(Skidelsky, 225ff.). Keynes starts with the thesis that capitalism's belief
in individual motivation and in self-regulatory market forces, as well as
socialism's reliance on the political efficiency of strikes and the ultimate
possibility of the proletarian revolution, emerged out of a particular
situation in the world economy—a situation that was characterized by
three different forms of equilibrium: a balance between capital and labor,
a balance between saving and consumption, and a balance in trade
between the United States and Europe. With the vanishing of this scenario, he sees the "semi-autonomous bodies" of large companies shaping
up as decisive agents between the all-embracing collective body of the
State on the one side and individual workers and owners on the other
(227). Since Keynes is convinced that the economists in charge of these
semi-autonomous bodies are becoming more distant from participation
in the political process and more knowledgeable about science and technology, he argues that they deserve to assume the leadership of society.
While his proposal seems, in part, just another variation of the familiar
idea that leadership is associated with the point at which individuality
and collectivity converge [see **Engineers, Stars, Individuality = Collectivity (Leader)**], Keynes's model is actually quite different from the traditional one: rather than identifying this place of convergence with the
State or with an individual politician, he believes that political parties
and the State should refrain from intervening in the economy. "With
technical questions removed from party warfare, political debate would
. . . largely revolve around the nature of the ideal society of the future"
(228). [see **League of Nations**]

Since Keynes's analysis leaves behind the still generally accepted model
of class struggle, it is highly confusing for his readers. A review article
on the German translation of his book published by the Social Democratic daily *Vorwärts* on August 1 begins by assuming, on the basis of
Keynes's critique of socialism, that he must be a partisan of capitalism.

As if this were contrary to Keynes's intentions, the essay then goes on to argue that his concept of capitalism, rather than following the nineteenth-century model, comes close to a new type of socialism which is already practiced by the German Social Democratic Party: "Coming up with many varieties of capitalism, Keynes, like Molière's bourgeois gentleman, apparently does not know that he speaks almost socialist prose, or else he pretends to be ignorant in order to avoid criticism." In the end, *Vorwärts* feels so strongly obliged to discover a difference between Social Democratic politics and Keynes's new style of economic thought, that it reverts to the most traditional discourse of class struggle: "In reality, Keynes's tame capitalism is nothing other than socialism without any great ideals or perspectives—in other words, without the essence of proletarian socialism . . . Socialism is not merely an economic question, an issue of 'more equitable material distribution.' It is likewise a question of the rise of the masses toward self-determination and freedom of choice, even in the economic sector. The masses yearn not only for greater satisfaction of their material needs but also for a new social order whose harmony will consist in the lack of class distinctions. The authentic goal of socialism is the abolition of classes, the classless society." Meanwhile, the British coal miners are learning that economic reality has no place for such utopian hopes.

Related Entries

Airplanes, Assembly Lines, Employees, Engineers, League of Nations, Murder, Stars, Timepieces, Individuality vs. Collectivity, Individuality = Collectivity (Leader)

References

Berliner Volks-Zeitung.
Chronik 1926: Tag für Tag in Wort und Bild. Dortmund, 1985.
Martin Gilbert, *Churchill: A Life.* New York, 1991.
Adolf Hitler, *Mein Kampf* (1926). Munich, 1941.
R. A. C. Parker, *Das zwanzigste Jahrhundert, I: 1918–1945.* Frankfurt, 1967.
Robert Skidelsky, *John Maynard Keynes: The Economist as Savior, 1920–1937.*
    New York, 1994.

Gustav Stresemann, "Student und Staat: Rede vor dem Verein Deutscher Studenten" (Berlin, 7 July 1926). In Stresemann, *Reden und Schriften: Politik,
Geschichte, Literatur, 1897–1926,* vol. 2. Dresden, 1926.

Leon Trotsky, *My Life: An Attempt at an Autobiography.* New York, 1970.

*Vorwärts: Berliner Volksblatt—Zentralorgan der Sozialdemokratischen Partei
Deutschlands.*

TELEPHONES

······································

The student yearbook of Stanford University features a full-page advertisement for the Pacific Telephone and Telegraph Company. Not surprisingly, it presents the telephone as a medium which, by making travel almost superfluous, partly fulfills humankind's dream of becoming omnipresent: "Take a weekly trip home—over the telephone" (*1926 Quad*, 429). [see **Airplanes, Polarities, Center = Periphery (Infinitude)**] A drawing below this slogan shows two elegantly dressed young men, apparently college students, sitting in front of a window that affords a view of the university's main buildings. Both wear neckties. The student on the right is dressed in a suit and holds a pipe; his companion wears an athletic sweater and is speaking into the mouthpiece of a telephone, while pressing the receiver against his ear. The caption reads: "I passed my finals, Mother!"

Telephone technology makes it possible for this student to celebrate graduation in a novel state of dispersion: his emotions at home, his body at Stanford, and his voice in both places. Establishing a "thrilling" contiguity between two individuals (Kittler, 1985, 81ff.), the telephone connection in this particular case is the functional equivalent of an umbilical cord: "Pleasant news for your mother to hear. More pleasant (almost exultant, one might say) for you to tell! And the thrill in telling is to be found in really *saying* it to Mother." The father is mentioned only in the context of everyday college life—and even there, he remains in the background (symbolized by a much smaller typeface): "Find out

how much pleasure and encouragement you can get from weekly telephone talks with Mother and Dad." Clearly, the implied readers of this
text are college students from wealthy families for whom long-distance
calls are no longer a sensational innovation but not yet a normal habit.
The mother's ear is the object of desire through which the Pacific Telephone and Telegraph Company tries to attract students' attention. And
even less exciting telephone routines, such as finding out the rates for
long-distance calls, will put them in contact with the ear and voice of a
woman, who embodies the role of operator: "If your hometown is not
listed, the Long-Distance Operator will be glad to give you the rates."
Such conversations with the operator are about to become a privilege of
long-distance customers. In Berlin, a direct-dial system is inaugurated on
August 15—and the *Vossische Zeitung* offers its readers meticulous instructions for using it: "How do you get connected? The 'face' of the
new apparatus has points like a clock, going from 1 to 0. The dial
rotates, and each number is associated with a hole. You put your finger
into the appropriate hole and pull the dial around until your finger is
stopped by a bar" (*Chronik,* 141).

In Thomas Mann's story "Unordnung und frühes Leid" ("Disorder
and Early Sorrow"), though it takes place in the days prior to direct
dialing, Professor Cornelius' children enjoy the telephone as a favorite
toy. Not only do they find it natural to invite friends to a dance party by
telephone, but they also use this technology in order to play practical
jokes. The telephone allows them to be present and absent at the same
time, by making their bodies invisible and their voices infinitely trans-
portable: "They place calls to every corner of the world. Claiming to be
shopgirls or the Duke and Duchess of Mannsteufel, they ring up opera
singers, state officials, and church lords, and are persuaded only with
difficulty that they have dialed the wrong number" (495). As pleasant as
such tricks may be for the Cornelius children, their parents would not
pay the considerable base fees for telephone service if it were simply for
such amusements. The expense can be justified only because the telephone is used for more serious things and, above all, because it is a status
symbol: "Many people had to give up their telephones the last time the
fees were raised, but so far the Corneliuses have been able to keep theirs,
just as they have kept their large house, which was built before the war,
by dint of the salary Cornelius draws as professor of history—a million
marks."

Although in the United States, and among European teenagers who adore whatever they imagine is the American way of life, the telephone may be used for fun and games, elsewhere it is primarily a professional tool for business and for the government. [see **Employees**] In a short narrative by "Pedro" (Pierre) Girard entitled "Curiosa metamorfosis de John" ("The Curious Metamorphosis of John"), translated from French into Spanish for the *Revista de Occidente*, the telephone figures as a metonym for closed systems [see **Elevators**]—systems that never establish contact with their natural environment, though their intrinsic structure does not exclude this possibility: "In the oak-and-leather appointed office of John S. S., the head of the bank John S. S. and Company, one would never guess that it was autumn outside. Not a single elm leaf lay on the carpet. No more was known of the season than what the newspapers said. Doubtless it would have been possible to telephone someone out in the country, to ask if the willows had turned yellow . . . , but the frosted windows prevented him from seeing the sky" (*Revista de Occidente*, 1). When John arrives at his Paris office early in the morning, he immediately picks up the telephone in order to gather information about recent developments on the international stock market from a number of colleagues at foreign banks. His conversations take place in a world lacking all trace of geographic distance, except perhaps for some strange noises in the receiver which regularly accompany long-distance calls (Kittler, 1986, 89): "'Get me Amsterdam,' he said, and a few minutes later he heard the sounds being made in the home of the manager of the Netherlands Bank, in Amsterdam. Inexplicable noises, the banging of a Dutch oven, the rattle of a coffee mill" (2). Later the same day the cold-hearted banker falls in love, and his emotions and behavior undergo that remarkable metamorphosis to which the title of the story alludes: he becomes just another young man full of romantic dreams, and he finally learns to enjoy the beauty of Paris in the fall. Only in the final scene does John revert to his old mind-set, when he begins to think of his beloved Juliet in purely economic terms. His return to the closed world of business and bureaucracy is marked by a telephone call: "A wife! He was going to have a wife! A thousand duties imposed themselves on him: . . . to get together a sum as a wedding gift for her; to invest it in shares of Crédit Lyonnais. What was the current price of Crédit Lyonnais' stock? John ran to the telephone. 'Hello! It's me—yes, me, the manager. Fine. And you? . . . What's Crédit Lyonnais trading at?

Holding steady? Please make a note: buy one hundred shares tomorrow. No—no premium. Cash, if possible. How's the market? Steady? Thanks—I'm fine now. Yes, tomorrow in my office" (39–40).

Outside the world of bureaucracy and business, telephones assure the presence and accessibility of power, and in doing so they invariably establish hierarchical relations. In Franz Kafka's *Das Schloss (The Castle)*, K. has just arrived at the inn below the castle and is about to get some rest after a long walk through the snow, when a young man comes to him wishing to request formal permission to spend the night in the village. K. firmly refuses to let the young man proceed with this request— until he realizes that a telephone is hanging right above his head: "So there was a telephone in this village inn? Evidently they maintained the highest standards. This particular instance surprised K., but on the whole he had expected it. The telephone seemed to be placed almost directly over his head, and in his drowsy state he had overlooked it. If the young man must telephone, he could not, even with the best intentions, avoid disturbing K." (8). "On the whole," K. is not surprised by the presence of a telephone, because he finds it natural for the castle to have power over the village. Within this hierarchical relation, the world at the "upper" end of the telephone line is itself hierarchically structured: "The castellan was asleep, but an under-castellan, one of the under-castellans, . . . was available." Once the question regarding the legitimacy of K.'s presence in the village is passed on to the "central chancellery," the young man hangs up the telephone. With growing apprehension and with the admiration of a typical subaltern, K. waits for an answer: "Nor was [the castle] lacking in industriousness: the central office had a night service." The first call to come back from the castle confirms K.'s worst fears: no one has been expecting him to arrive. "But the telephone rang again—with special insistence, it seemed to K. Slowly he raised his head [from the bed]. Although it was unlikely that this message also concerned K., they all stopped short and [the young man] took up the receiver once more. He listened for a fairly long time, and then said in a low voice: 'A mistake, is it? I'm sorry to hear that. The head of the department himself said so? Very odd, very odd. How am I to explain it all to the land surveyor?'" (9). [see **Silence vs. Noise**] All of a sudden, K. is in a position of superiority vis-à-vis the young man who has made a formal request to him—but K.'s role is by no means (and will never be) a role of agency.

Having wasted the first workday after his arrival, K. plans finally to go to the castle with his assistants. Since it has by now become obvious to him that this will require permission, he has the assistants call the castle once again: "The 'no' of the answer was audible even to K. at his table. But the answer went on and was still more explicit. It ran as follows: 'Neither tomorrow nor at any other time'" (20–21). To the astonishment of the guests at the inn, K. decides that he will call the castle himself. But his daring attempt ends in humiliation. The loud static in the connection makes it clear how far away he is from the castle, and the voice at the other end of the line betrays the violence inherent in the power relation between the castle and the village: "The receiver emitted a buzz of a kind that K. had never before heard on a telephone. It was like the hum of countless children's voices—yet not a hum. Rather, the echo of voices singing at an infinite distance, blended by sheer impossibility into one high but resonant sound that vibrated in the ear as if trying to penetrate beyond mere hearing" (21). As a last effort, and as an act of instinctive self-protection, K. pretends to be one of his own assistants. But he can neither deceive the castle's bureaucracy nor escape the violence of the voice on the other side: "K. was listening to the new note and almost missed the question: 'What is it you want?' He felt like laying down the receiver. He had ceased to expect anything from this conversation. But being pressed, he replied quickly, 'When can my master come to the castle?' 'Never,' was the answer. 'Very well,' said K., and hung up" (22).

From his work as a legal agent for the Arbeiter-Unfall-Versicherungs-Anstalt (Workers' Accident Insurance Agency) in Prague, Kafka must know first-hand what it is like to deal with an authority figure at the other end of a telephone connection (Wagenbach, 104). This figure is of course always a man, who, regardless of the sex of the person at the other end, assigns to this person a role of passivity and resignation. [see **Employees, Male vs. Female, Action = Impotence (Tragedy)**] In Jules Supervielle's novel *Le voleur d'enfants (The Man Who Stole Children)*, a well-to-do widow and mother receives a pneumatic express-letter saying that her only son has been abducted: "The next morning, at eight o'clock, Hélène was brought a typewritten letter which had been sent by pneumatic tube: 'No need for concern. I've got Antoine. He's perfectly happy and surrounded by all sorts of comforts. If he ever shows a desire to return to his mother, I'll bring him back *myself*'" (55). These words, like the language of the castle administration in *Das Schloss,* preclude resistance, all the more so since the medium of tube mail emphasizes the current technology of most telephone conversations: the people at opposite ends of the line are physically connected by a wire or tube. Although a wireless telephone service from New York to London begins in January (Heimer, 100), Denmark joins the European telephone network ten months later with a cable running through the North Sea to the German town of Warnemünde (*8 Uhr–Abendblatt,* October 19). [see **Wireless Communication**] Between tube mail and wireless communication, the classic telephone network thus remains the primary technical device by which the State makes its power felt. Once Antoine's mother and Colonel Bigua, the "man who steals children" in Supervielle's novel, have reached a surprising agreement, Hélène asks her servant Rose to call the police and say that any further investigations are unnecessary, since the child has been found. "'Where?' a deep voice at the other end of the line asked with severity. But, suddenly trembling, Rose hung up, without really knowing why. And her mistress approved" (118).

Despite their already overwhelming authority, the State and its bureaucracy seem to aspire to an even greater degree of surveillance—and a greater degree of power presence without bodily presence. In Fritz Lang's film *Metropolis,* this vision is a reality for Fredersen, the "Master of Metropolis." At the height of the workers' revolt, he receives a tickertape message from Grot, the engineer in charge of the "central power plant." The technical circumstances of Fredersen's return call evidently take it through three different levels of yet another hierarchical power relation: "In the office of the Master of Metropolis, we see a large tickertape machine on the wall by the door. Fredersen comes in, inspects the tape, then turns a dial on the apparatus. Seen from behind, he turns another dial. The characters 'HM2' appear on an illuminated screen in front of him. Then a series of images from the central power plant appear beneath. Fredersen adjusts the picture to 'hold' as the image of Grot, the chief engineer, appears by a control panel, rushing nervously to and fro. Fredersen picks up the receiver of a telephone next to him and presses a button" (Lang, 102). Confronted with the workers' threat to destroy the central power plant, the engineer panics. But the picture phone makes it impossible for him to hide his nervousness from the Master's view. [see **Employees**] Finally, Grot receives a definitive order from Fredersen's end of the line, an order meant to eternally establish the Master's control over the workers: "Title: 'If they destroy the power plant, we will flood the workers' city.' Fredersen's eyes bulge as he suddenly shouts, shaking his fist. Title: 'Open the floodgates!'" [see **Action vs. Impotence**]

The telephone ranks high among the emblems of the way in which anonymous powers are intruding ever more brutally into the spheres of nature and privacy. [see **Automobiles, Gramophones**] As a State employee, the philosopher Theodor Lessing feels no less victimized by electronically transmitted violence than all those protagonists of novels and films who find themselves at the subordinate end of a telephone connection: "Banish the 'symbols of culture' from the thoroughly wired landscape, filled with advertisements and smokestacks; perhaps one site will remain holy and unspoiled. I've decided to steal a pocketwatch at some point—with the hope of being arrested. In prison I will at least have peace from the rug beating, the piano playing, the car horns, the gramophones, and the telephones" (Lessing, 401).

But nobody would seriously wish to renounce the telephone and its technical benefits. In Ernst Jünger's war diaries, the description of a bomb and gas attack culminates in the destruction of a telephone line: "Clouds of bombers have visited the towns in the hinterlands. For hours, powerful fires have battered the farthest camps. Every street under fire. The artillery positions are blanketed with mustard gas, the telephone lines are destroyed" (Jünger, 106). Not unlike the connection between a son and his mother, the power relation mediated by the telephone produces situations that are both a vital necessity—and a source of fear. Everyone suffers from the surveillance and dependency which the telephone represents and imposes. At the same time, however, people have the impression that life would be impossible without the structuring interventions of power. [see **Individuality = Collectivity (Leader)**] It is better to be connected to a violently authoritarian voice than to no voice at all.

Related Entries

Airplanes, Automobiles, Elevators, Employees, Gramophones, Polarities, Wireless Communication, Action vs. Impotence, Individuality vs. Collectivity, Male vs. Female, Silence vs. Noise, Action = Impotence (Tragedy), Center = Periphery (Infinitude), Individuality = Collectivity (Leader)

References

8 Uhr–Abendblatt.

Associated Students of Stanford University, eds., The 1926 Quad.

Chronik 1926: Tag für Tag in Wort und Bild. Dortmund, 1985.

Mel Heimer, The Long Count. New York, 1969.

Ernst Jünger, Feuer und Blut: Ein kleiner Ausschnitt aus einer grossen Schlacht (1926). Hamburg, 1941.

Franz Kafka, Das Schloss (1926). Frankfurt, 1968.

Friedrich Kittler, Aufschreibesysteme, 1800–1900. Munich, 1985.

Friedrich Kittler, Grammophon, Film, Typewriter. Berlin, 1986.

Fritz Lang, Metropolis (1926). New York, 1973.

Theodor Lessing, "Die blauschwarze Rose" (1926). In, "Ich warf eine Flaschenpost ins Eismeer der Geschichte": Essays und Feuilletons. Neuwied, 1986.

Thomas Mann, "Unordnung und frühes Leid" (1926). In Mann, Sämtliche Erzählungen. Frankfurt, 1963, pp. 491–522.

Revista de Occidente.

Jules Supervielle, Le voleur d'enfants. Paris, 1926.

Klaus Wagenbach, Kafka: Bilder aus seinem Leben. Berlin, 1983.

TIMEPIECES

All kinds of timepieces are invading the world of fiction. In the opening sequence of Hemingway's novel *The Sun Also Rises,* a young French-woman with a "wonderful smile" (and bad teeth) gets invited out for a drink—and later to dinner—by Jake Barnes, the first-person narrator. [see **Americans in Paris**] Between the drink and the dinner, Jake and Georgette drive through the streets of Paris in a horse-drawn cab: "Settled back in the slow, smoothly rolling *fiacre* we moved up the Avenue de l'Opéra, passed the locked doors of the shops, their windows lighted, the Avenue broad and shiny and almost deserted. The cab passed the *New York Herald* bureau with the window full of clocks. 'What are all the clocks for?' she asked. 'They show the hour all over America.' 'Don't kid me'" (Hemingway, 15). It is unclear whether Georgette understands Jake's explanation about the clocks in the window of the *New York Herald.* Does she know that the globe is divided into twenty-four time zones? Is she aware that, at the moment she is talking to Jake, the time of day in Paris is different from the time in each of the other twenty-three zones? [see **Polarities**] At any event, temporal simultaneity is not a form of experience that matters to Georgette. Her life depends on random encounters in the streets and cafés of Paris, and needs no horizon beyond this limited world.

There are few literary protagonists who ever think about time zones or the relativity of time, and even fewer who can return from the sphere of relativity into closed individual chronotopes. The banker John S. S., in a short story published by the *Revista de Occidente* under the title "Curiosa metamorfosis de John" ("The Curious Metamorphosis of John"), is one of these cosmopolitan heroes: "After eating, John went out bareheaded . . . to stroll through the Luxembourg Gardens. It was the time of day when . . . clerks usually made the cylinders of the calculating machines turn like lottery drums and when the exchange rate of the Swiss franc in Constantinople rose. John began to laugh, thinking about it. Because this time of day, when the mail was delivered and the New York Stock Exchange closed, was also the time for kids' afternoon snacks, the time for cupcakes" (*Revista de Occidente*, 10–11). Most likely from a lack of pertinent everyday experience, the author of this story confuses the relation between Eastern Standard Time and Central European Time. Early evening in New York corresponds to around midnight in Paris, and not to early afternoon. Within the narrative, however, it doesn't matter whether Paris or New York is six hours ahead. Even as John must take into account the plurality and relativity of time zones when making decisions for his bank, so he must forget about them—banish them from his reality—if he wants to enjoy the beauty of a Paris afternoon. [see **Uncertainty vs. Reality**]

The analysis of labor provides a different view of time-relativity. Rising rates of productivity are often described as an extension of conventional time (*Chronik*, 22). Capitalists and socialists share this fascination because, at least theoretically, such "extensions of time" could yield profits on both sides of the class struggle. [see **Strikes**] An official Soviet slogan recommends achieving this goal by incessantly producing "like a chronometer" in which the "impetus of the October Revolution" and "the pulse of American life" should ideally converge (Lethen, 22). [see **Present vs. Past**] In Jean Cocteau's play *Orphée*, even the allegory of death is associated with hectic activity and a shortage of time. Before Eurydice is taken to Hades, Madame Death enters the space of human life [see **Immanence = Transcendence (Death)**] by means of a complicated machine that produces different levels of speed and intensity: "*Death: . . .* We have a wave seven and a zone seven-twelve. Set everything to four. If I raise, you can go up to five. Don't go past five under any circumstances" (Cocteau, 58). Just before Madame Death is catapulted into the world of the living, her assistants realize that, among their numerous instruments, they have forgotten a watch, which they now have to borrow from the spectators: "Ladies and gentlemen, Madame

Death has instructed me to ask: Would someone in the audience be so kind as to lend her a watch?" (62). While in the real world industrial workers must either speed up their movements or adjust their rhythm to the pace of machines if they want to "extend" the duration and efficiency of their labor [see **Assembly Lines**], Death's assistants in *Orphée* have the imaginary privilege of slowing down the rhythm of time itself: "*Death: This is Azrael's job. He's changing our speeds. An hour for me should be a minute for* [Orpheus]" (60).

Workers who have to meet higher standards of productivity—but also capitalists and politicians who pay interest on capital loans—always feel that time is passing too quickly. From this perspective, on July 27 Prime Minister Poincaré of France draws a dramatic picture of his government's finances: "If the measures we are requesting from you are not approved, we will lose 11,000 francs per minute, 660,000 francs per hour, 16 million francs per day" (*Années-mémoire,* 72). By showing a clock whose dial is divided into ten hours instead of twelve and whose second hand proceeds with unusual speed, Fritz Lang, in the first scene of his film *Metropolis,* doubly symbolizes this constant feeling of time shortage as an essential component in proletarian life: "On the enormous face of the clock in the New Tower of Babel—the machine center of Metropolis—the seconds tick away, as regular in their coming as in their going. The clock is divided into only ten segments; the two main hands are almost vertical, while the second hand sweeps jerkily around" (19). Freder, the savior of the proletarians, tries to slow the pace of the second hand. Invoking the Master of Metropolis (his father, John Fredersen) and quoting the *New Testament,* he embodies the workers' collective desire for liberation from the ever-accelerating rhythm of labor: "His mouth opens and he shouts in agony . . . His arms are outstretched, holding the gigantic clock-hands as if he were suspended from them, crucified. Again he shouts in agony: '. . . Father! I did not know that ten hours could be such torture!'" (52).

Frequently, visions of the earthly paradise are related to such metaphors of salvation from the tyrannical rhythms of time. They even surface in Jack Dempsey's description of the fabulous parties organized by his friend Billy Seeman, the son of the White Rose Tea king: "Seeman's apartment over the Village's Pepper Pot was a popular gathering place (and watering hole) for Broadway mugs, bootleggers, gangsters, Follies girls, models, and the usual assortment of newspapermen, politicians, and drifters. They came and went as though the clock had no hands" (Dempsey and Dempsey, 180–181). [see **Bars, Reporters, Revues**] Walter Benjamin is so eager to see Moscow and Soviet society liberated from the pressures of time, that he actively ignores the Communist Party's exhortations to accelerate the pace of labor: "I believe there are more watchmakers in Moscow than in any other city. This is all the more strange because people here make very little fuss about the time . . . If you observe the way they move about in the streets, you seldom see anyone in a hurry, except when it is very cold. Always casual in their attitude, they walk in a zigzag. Thus, it is interesting that posted in an assembly hall there is a sign with the inscription: 'Lenin said that time is money.' In order to proclaim this banality, they need to invoke highest authority" (Benjamin, 1980, 70–71).

Yet the notion of "having time" is much more ambiguous than Benjamin seems willing to admit. If increased productivity means yielding greater profits for owners but intensified suffering for workers, liberation from time's despotic rhythms has its obverse—namely, marginalization from everyday life. In Johannes Becher's poem "Die Rumpf-Ruderer" ("The Torso-Rowers"), legless war veterans are depicted as cast out of life's mainstream because they are unable to follow the pace of time with their bodies: "They put me upright in a corner, against the wall. / A blanket over me. The clock drips the hours. / It would be nice to limp forward, one-legged" (Becher, 9–10) But while surrendering one's body to a collective rhythm is a nightmare for Becher, he repeatedly associates fast-moving clocks with the awakening and redemptive power of revolutions, as in the following poem about revolutionary utopias:

> The dying
> Bodies snatched away at midnight
> Rattling out of the floating beds
> Clocks whirring, blowing faces
> Haunt the crumbling space.
> (Becher, 12; also 109)

As much as Becher longs for a revolt, he seems to admit that the pace of revolutionary transformations inevitably entails chaos and new suffering. The presence of timepieces amid such turmoil—even the presence of timepieces whose movement is accelerated—guarantees at least some structure, continuity, and control. Thus, in Ramón del Valle-Inclán's novel *Tirano Banderas,* cathedral bells ring twelve times before the outbreak of a revolution that will end a bloody dictatorship: "The cathedral clock fell silent. The twelve peals still hung in the air . . . Stampedes of gunpowder. Military bugle calls. A crowd of nuns, bareheaded and in their shirtsleeves, came to the profaned door of the convent shouting and praying" (Valle-Inclán, 266). In a poem by Federico García Lorca, when the paramilitary *guardia civil* attacks a town of gypsies, all clocks come to a standstill:

> The town, free of fear,
> multiplied its gates.
> Forty members of the civil guard
> came through them to plunder.
> The clocks stopped,
> and the cognac in its bottles
> disguised itself as November.

> (García Lorca, 456)

Feeling victimized by the chaos that results when all structured forms of historical time vanish, Professor Cornelius in Thomas Mann's story "Unordnung und frühes Leid" ("Disorder and Early Sorrow") becomes an unlikely ally of García Lorca's gypsies. He "hates the newfangled ways because they are lawless, incoherent, and aggressive" (498), and he therefore overreacts whenever his young servant Xaver Kleinsgütl mistakenly tears off more than one sheet from the calendar on his desk: "Every morning, while the professor is having his breakfast, he tears a leaf from the calendar in the study—but doesn't make the slightest effort to dust the room. Dr. Cornelius has often told him to leave the calendar alone, for he tends to tear off two leaves at a time and thus to add to the general confusion" (Mann, 512–513).

More and more, it seems as if keeping time is keeping the world from falling apart. [see **Present = Past (Eternity)**] During the apocalyptic frenzy of a World War battle, Ernst Jünger views his wristwatch as "the only reality": "Only the little circle that the watch makes on my wrist is still real. Ghosts may appear or the world may come to an end; nothing can surprise me at this point. I don't hear the shooting anymore—I'm beyond the point of noticing it. And my perception no longer registers individual appearance. In the roar of excess, feelings have far outdistanced the bounds of human values. Courage, pity, fear—none of these exist any more. There remains only a whirling system of power in which landscapes and people are included as if it were a different zone, subject to different laws. At 9:40 it will be in place" (Jünger, 110–111). The artillery attack begins at 5:05 A.M., and will be followed by a ground assault at 9:40 A.M. The sheer presence of timepieces provides a certain amount of structure amid the chaos of war. For individual soldiers, they offer an existential "direction" toward the immediate future, a direction that gives shape and vitality to their actions: "We're in that wilderness where one laughs while one's teeth are chattering, the senses keyed up to an incredible acuteness, as before a great, decisive deed. Early in the morning I speak with the battalion commander for the last time, and we synchronize our watches to the second. We part with a firm handshake. From now on we're completely focused, each of us following the steady movement of the luminous hand on his watch. Every five minutes the time is called out. An ever shorter distance separates us from the moment, 5:05, at which the artillery assault is supposed to begin" (98–99). [see **Action vs. Impotence**] Such an attack, in modern warfare, is the model for the existential situation which Martin Heidegger metaphorically describes as "running ahead into death" (Heidegger, 262ff.)—and which, without time measurement, can never adopt a form (252ff.).

Keeping time requires keeping numerous watches and clocks in parallel, so that their mutual confirmation can substitute for the lack of a natural ground. This is the insight that the journalist Egon Erwin Kisch takes away from a visit to the Hydrographic Institute of the Austrian navy: "Every clock has its moment of adjustment: at the same time every day, each one is wound up in a predetermined order . . . The question 'Excuse me, do you have the time?' is easily asked, but is not easily answered by the expert" (Kisch, 198). Time that is kept in the form of a constant rhythm needs to be publicly visible. Perhaps the seven-year-old Antoine in Jules Supervielle's novel *Le voleur d'enfants (The Man Who Stole Children)* would not get lost in the bustling streets of Paris if he could only read the huge clock standing next to him: "For a good five minutes he has been alone with a kind of shame or dread, he could not say which. Night falls. Paris begins to close in on Antoine. To his right there is a pneumatic clock. If only he could tell the time, he would feel less alone. This white face with its two hands stubbornly remains unrecognizable to him and pursues an idea to which the child must remain a stranger" (Supervielle, 11). On Potsdamer Platz in the heart of Berlin, where the traffic is denser than anywhere else in Europe [see **Automobiles**], a policeman stands on the platform of a tower with traffic lights above him and a clock below (Boberg, Fichter, and Gillen, 142; Schuette, 21). The most popular meeting place in Germany's capital is the so-called Normaluhr ("standard clock") at the Zoo railway station, a round clock with two concentric dials, the first numbered from one to twelve and the second from thirteen to twenty-four (Boberg, Fichter, and Gillen, 192). Its name serves as the title for one of the reflections in Walter Benjamin's *Einbahnstraße (One-Way Street)*. Benjamin undermines the feeling of security that comes from constructing, keeping, and publicly displaying time in visible form. Truly great insights and inventions, according to him, will never be associated with measuring time: "Only the weaker and more distracted people derive incomparable joy from completing something and feel that life has thus been restored to them. For the genius, each caesura, each stroke of fate, adapts itself peacefully to the labor performed in his workshop" (Benjamin, 1972, 88).

Related Entries

Americans in Paris, Assembly Lines, Automobiles, Bars, Polarities, Reporters, Revues, Strikes, Action vs. Impotence, Present vs. Past, Uncertainty vs. Reality, Immanence = Transcendence (Death), Present = Past (Eternity)

References

Les Années-mémoire: 1926. Paris, 1988.

Johannes R. Becher, *Maschinenrhythmen.* Berlin, 1926.

Walter Benjamin, *Einbahnstraße* (1926). In Benjamin, *Gesammelte Schriften,* vol. 4, part 1. Frankfurt, 1972.

Walter Benjamin, *Moskauer Tagebuch, 1926–1927.* Frankfurt, 1980.

Jochen Boberg, Tilman Fichter, and Eckhart Gillen, eds., *Die Metropole: Industriekultur in Berlin im 20. Jahrhundert.* Munich, 1986.

Chronik 1926: Tag für Tag in Wort und Bild. Dortmund, 1985.

Jean Cocteau, *Orphée: Tragédie en un acte et un intervalle* (1926). Paris, 1927.

Jack Dempsey and Barbara Piattelli Dempsey, *Dempsey.* New York, 1977.

Federico García Lorca, *Romance de la Guardia Civil Española* (1926). In García Lorca, *Obras completas*. Madrid, 1971.

Martin Heidegger, *Sein und Zeit* (written 1926, published 1927). Tübingen, 1984.

Ernest Hemingway, *The Sun Also Rises*. New York, 1926.

Ernst Jünger, *Feuer und Blut: Ein kleiner Ausschnitt aus einer grossen Schlacht* (1926). Hamburg, 1941.

Egon Erwin Kisch, "Mysterien des Hydrographischen Instituts." In Kisch, *Hetzjagd durch die Zeit*. Berlin, 1926.

Fritz Lang, *Metropolis*. New York, 1973.

Helmut Lethen, *Neue Sachlichkeit, 1924–1932: Studien zur Literatur des "Weissen Sozialismus."* Stuttgart, 1970.

Thomas Mann, "Unordnung und frühes Leid" (1926). In Mann, *Sämtliche Erzählungen*. Frankfurt, 1963.

Revista de Occidente.

Wolfgang U. Schuette, *"Mit Stacheln und Stichen": Beiträge zur Geschichte der Berliner Brettl-Truppe "Die Wespen," 1929–1933*. Leipzig, 1987.

Jules Supervielle, *Le voleur d'enfants*. Paris, 1926.

Ramón del Valle-Inclán, *Tirano Banderas* (1926). Madrid, 1978.

Michael Young, *The Metronomic Society: Natural Rhythms and Human Timetables*. Cambridge, Mass., 1988.

WIRELESS COMMUNICATION

An illustration in a German book on "image transmitting" *(Fern-bildtechnik und Elektrisches Fernsehen)* features the technical utopia of television in a military context (Lertes, 7). The lower half of the picture shows a man in uniform (not a German uniform) sitting at a control panel in front of a state-of-the-art radio receiver and a huge screen, which re-presents what the upper part of the picture shows as "reality": an unmanned military airplane crossing a mountainous region near the sea, with a town in the center of the landscape. Following four other aircraft of the same type, the unmanned plane in the foreground seems to be part of a squadron which is under attack from a biplane flying above them. What attracts the reader's attention to the unmanned aircraft are six "electric eyes" in the form of lenses that are pointing right and left, below and above, ahead and behind. The objects registered by these electric eyes appear on the six segments of the screen in front of the officer. While he looks at them intently, manipulating a handle with his right hand, three other servicemen who stand behind him are following the transmission of the air combat with obvious excitement.

The entire picture seems to suggest that the officer at the control panel is steering the unmanned aircraft (and perhaps the entire squadron). But even if this is not part of the intended meaning, the image clearly shows that "electric television" is not exclusively (and perhaps not even primarily) an extension of the human senses or human perception. In this particular utopia, television makes it possible to intervene in a war without physical risk. [see **Timepieces**] What matters is the presence of an officer at the scene of battle—presence as an agent yet not necessarily as a body. Although no such technical or military device yet exists, something similar to it is expected to evolve. On Wednesday, January 27, the British engineer John Logie Baird introduces to the public his "televisor," which makes possible (on a very rudimentary level) the wireless transmission of moving pictures (*Chronik*, 21). Baird emphasizes that such "seeing by telephone" is nothing but the logical consequence of "hearing by telephone," a feat which has become commonplace in government and business over the past fifty years (Elsner, Müller, and Spangenberg, 195). Meanwhile, the wireless transmission of still pictures is being integrated into the speed-oriented technical repertoire of the press in France (*Années-mémoire*, 121) [see **Reporters**], in Germany (*Chronik*, 75), and in the United States, where the *New York Times* publishes telephotographic coverage of the September 23 boxing match between Dempsey and Tunney on the morning following the fight. [see **Boxing**] A wireless telephone service that operates fifteen hours a day is established between Long Island (U.S.) and Rugby (U.K.) in February, at a minimum cost of seventy-five dollars for three minutes of conversation (*Chronik*, 39).

All these rapidly spreading innovations in communications technology and the new forms of experience that they provide generate an atmosphere of fascination and almost boundless optimism. Appealing to such attitudes, the title of a rather dry essay on the elementary physics of wireless communication published by the Buenos Aires magazine *Caras y Caretas* on October 2 deliberately ignores all the problems of practical realization that engineers confront. It offers the ultimate utopia: "Wireless telephony connects the stars to the earth." The text itself gives a much more prosaic view of this exciting promise. Instead of describing phenomena of intergalactic communication, as some readers must have expected, it explains the new scientific practice of identifying the physical properties of celestial bodies through the analysis of the light waves they emit. As if the author felt an obligation to apologize for misleading the imagination of the public, he then switches to contrasting this highly specialized research agenda with more popular versions of utopian thinking: "It is true that the man in the moon will not use the telephone, because the sun does not speak and the telephone is not absolutely necessary for radio transmissions. Spectroscopy now permits us to affirm

that the sun contains all the elements known to exist on our planet."
Although the possible impact of such technological innovations on
everyday life is unclear, their multiplicity and the speed with which they
develop suggest that the present moment marks a particularly important
transition in history—the moment at which the systematic exploitation
of the human senses and human perception has finally begun: "Our eyes
are delicate receptive instruments that can register data at 4,000 to 8,000
angstroms."

A similar tone of self-congratulation pervades a report in the July 25
issue of the *Vossische Zeitung*—"Zwiesprache mit Südamerika" ("Dialogue with Latin America")—concerning a radio-receiving station that
establishes long-wave connections between Germany and Argentina.
This text not only goes into the scientific facts but, even more, emphasizes the aesthetic side of technology, and it thus becomes an illustration
of concepts such as "the New Sobriety" and "functionalism." While the
buildings of the radio station (the Trans-Radio-Gesellschaft) look surprisingly shabby from the outside, their interior corresponds to the new
norm of soberly functional beauty: "Amid the flat, limitless meadows of
the Frisian island of Sylt, surrounded by grazing sheep and horses and
completely lost beneath the infinite jubilation of the lark, lies a row of
boarded-up barracks. An apparently ordinary, dark brown, tar-covered
building, topped by loose wires that sway between two tilted weather
vanes . . . But as one enters through the small anteroom . . . , one's
impression immediately changes. A long line of doors extends down a
narrow corridor—room after room, systematically done up in the bright,
clean decor of modern office space." [see **Sobriety vs. Exuberance**] This
space is permeated by a very specific sound which, even on the telephone,
always precedes long-distance communication: "Throughout the building wafts a curious noise—a high-pitched sound which always hovers at
the same frequency, broken into short segments, repeatedly stopping and
starting." [see **Telephones**] Finally, the journalist enters the transmission
room and is overwhelmed by the sublime appearance of this technological sanctuary: "The eye of even the most unsophisticated layman would
be impressed by these illuminated dials of porcelain and metal, by this
machinery. The same apparatus has been exported to Buenos Aires, and
it has greatly improved the reputation of German technology through its
unheard-of precision and quality."

The future utility of this impressive device is unclear, and no one knows how long it will take before wireless communication between Argentina and Germany will become more than just a technological marvel. For the time being, the "dialogue with Buenos Aires" is frequently interrupted by long silences, especially during the daytime. [see **Silence vs. Noise**] Such asymmetry between boundless admiration for new technologies and vague ideas about their possible uses can provoke ironic reactions. Focusing on phototelegraphy, the advertising section of Stanford's student yearbook pushes to a level of absurdity the journalistic ambition of minimizing the temporal gap between newsworthy event and published report: "The march of science has given to the editors of this section an opportunity to show for the first time the marvels of phototelegraphy. The above picture, showing one of the editors looking with pride at his section in the *Quad* on the *very day it came out,* was taken on the campus here this morning, when the yearbook was distributed. Proofs of the photograph were sent . . . to the engraver in San Francisco, who telegraphed a half-tone engraving back in time to get into the last section of this book. Thus does new invention allow us, so to speak, to get ahead of ourselves. Ain't Science wonderful!" (*1926 Quad,* 423).

Although the transmission of telegrams was partly integrated into the new technology of wireless communication at an early date, the telegram as a medium invariably bears connotations of the past. If wireless communication often seems a future vision that is hailed prematurely, the telegram has become history even before it has achieved broad institutionalization. [see **Present = Past (Eternity)**] Only in the preindustrial South American republic whose backwardness Ramón del Valle-Inclán depicts in his novel *Tirano Banderas*—and only for a representative of the outmoded bureaucratic style prevailing in the Spanish diplomatic service—can the telegram look like a gesture of modernity. But even in the novel, it is unclear whether the Spanish ambassador isn't speaking with a certain degree of irony when he urges an ambitious colonist to send a telegram to the government in Madrid: "Much-honored Don Celestino, you are one of the most remarkable financial, intellectual, and social figures in the colony . . . Your opinions are highly respected . . . But you are not yet Spain's ambassador. A real disgrace! Yet there is a way you can become ambassador: send a telegram requesting my transfer to Europe. I will support your petition" (Valle-Inclán, 33).

More than a time-saving device, the telegram has become a rhetorical strategy. Simply by virtue of its cost, and the condensed language it suggests (Kittler, 358–370), the telegram underscores the urgency and irreversibility of certain decisions and actions. Gerhart Hauptmann makes use of this effect in his play *Dorothea Angermann*. When Herbert Pfannschmidt, a young university professor with particularly high moral standards, wants to leave a family reunion without giving the impression that he dislikes his relatives, he has his wife send him a telegram: "Unfortunately I have to take the night train to Breslau tonight, since my wife telegraphed that there is a meeting at the university president's office tomorrow afternoon" (Hauptmann, 139). The telegram-specific, personal form of delivery adds an element of privacy. In Marcel Jouhandeau's novel *Monsieur Godeau Intime,* Véronique invites the hero— whom she adores—to her home by telegram: "Véronique telegraphed M. Godeau, asking him to come that very evening to the rue du Sentier" (Jouhandeau, 45–46). Paradoxically, this blend of urgency and privacy often causes the recipients of telegrams to hesitate before they read them. As a child, the narrator of René Schickele's *Maria Capponi* spends a vacation in Venice with his eccentric, good-looking, unmarried Aunt Sidonia. Whenever a telegram is handed to her at the hotel's reception desk, Sidonia comes up with an infinite number of reasons to make her nephew, instead of herself, open the envelope: "The doorman handed Aunt Sidonia a telegram. Alas! The red strip bespoke urgency . . . 'You open it!' she commanded . . . I opened it as my father would open telegrams: slowly, fold by fold, with a sullen face, looking for the sender's address" (Schickele, 100). Hours later, the opened telegram still lies unread on a table, and each time her nephew wants to read it to her, Sidonia makes desperate efforts to prevent him from doing so: "'Claus, it is certainly a very, very bad message. Why don't you read it first—then it won't hurt me. Claus, you have to read it,' she begged. But when I extended my hand to pick up the telegram, she threw herself over the table with arms outstretched and buried it underneath her" (101).

Frequently, the privacy, urgency, and fear that surround telegrams are projected onto the radio. The West German Broadcasting Company (WDR) cannot establish a studio in Cologne until the end of the Rhineland occupation, because the French military authorities are persuaded that the radio encourages espionage (*Chronik,* 182). As soon as economic and political circumstances allow the radio to develop its potential, however, it takes over those functions of immediacy which

other forms of wireless communication have failed to assume. [see **Individuality vs. Collectivity, Center = Periphery (Infinitude)**] Broadcasting
becomes a point of convergence and condensation between innovative
research, industrial production, and consumer participation. By January,
the number of regular radio listeners in Germany has grown from 1,500
(in 1924) to over a million. In February, nine originally independent
radio stations with an average daily airtime of nine hours merge into the
Reichs-Rundfunk-Gesellschaft (National Radio Association) under the
control—and with the support—of the Postal Ministry (*Chronik,* 20). In
Latin America the impact of the new medium is even stronger. The
number of radio stations in Buenos Aires has already reached a level of
saturation (Gallo, 9). The pages of *Caras y Caretas* are full of advertisements for radio sets and radio tubes—ads that often devote more enthusiasm to technical details than to the products' usefulness: "*Get the
perfect vacuum!* A few years ago, an incandescent lamp containing a
vacuum of one-millionth the density of air was considered something
extraordinary. But that wasn't good enough for our Radiotrons. In the
laboratories that do innovative work for RCA, scientists use a process
of rarefaction to produce electronic tubes with an internal pressure one
ten-millionth of that of an electric lamp. To ensure that you get depend-
able service and constant satisfaction from your receiver, you should buy
tubes with the best possible vacuum" (September 15).

In Berlin, the 138-meter-high steel Funkturm (Broadcasting Tower) is
inaugurated at the opening ceremony for the third annual German
Broadcasting Exhibition on Friday, September 3. With its restaurant and
panorama platform [see **Roof Gardens**], the Funkturm attracts vast numbers of visitors and brings them close to the popular new medium. But
the structure is above all hailed as a monumental expression of contemporary achievements in technology and culture: "Every age has its serious matters, but also its joys, and if one only tries hard enough, the
technical expression of a new age can also be given beautiful form"
(Schrader and Schebera, 182). If news, literary readings, language
courses, and all kinds of music have so far dominated the radio pro-
grams, engineers are now working hard to facilitate the live broadcasting
of outdoor events. Spanish radio stations offer transmissions from a Red
Cross gala bullfight in Madrid on March 16, from a boxing match
featuring the European champion Paulino Uzcudún in Barcelona on May
15, and from the opening Mass of the Third Eucharistic Congress in

Toledo on October 20 (Lorenzo, 114–115). French broadcasters specialize in live shows "from the streets of Paris," and cover part of the
popular Tour de France (*Années-mémoire*, 156ff.). [see **Endurance**] No
other impresario uses the new medium more successfully than Tex
Rickard, Jack Dempsey's promoter. An estimated fifteen million radio
listeners all across the United States, Latin America, and Europe follow
the title fight between Dempsey and Gene Tunney on the evening of
September 23, while heavy rainfall seriously impairs the quality of the
journalistic accounts transmitted by telegraph. Not without
astonishment, the *New York Times* reports one day later that, although
this fight has drawn the largest number of spectators in the history of
boxing, "the crowd that hung outside the stadium [was] probably the
smallest" ever. The technologically produced immediacy of the live radio
broadcast has become largely accepted as a substitute for physical presence at or near the place of action: "But the radio was the biggest
counter-attraction. As soon as the unfortunates without tickets or the
means to buy them realized that gate-crashing was out of the question
and that they would hardly be near enough to hear the shouts of those
within the stadium, many of them returned to their homes or paid their
way into the exposition grounds to hear the fight returns by radio."

As the "radio revolution" visibly changes many everyday habits, it
ends up generating concerns about possible effects on human perception
and emotions (*Chronik*, 20). Amid the general enthusiasm over wireless
communication, a debate is reviving about the possibility of transferring
thoughts from one mind to another without any external signs or manifestations. This discussion provokes a reaction by Sigmund Freud regarding the relationship between telepathy and psychoanalysis. Of course,
Freud cannot fully subscribe to what others have presented (and claim
to master) as the techniques of telepathy, because this would weaken the
reputation of psychoanalysis as the most powerful method of detecting
and manipulating hidden mechanisms in the human mind. On the other
hand, psychoanalysis would fail to live up to its growing stature if its
inventor had no rejoinder at all to the challenge offered by telepathy.
Predictably, Freud adopts an attitude of skeptical affirmation: "Even if
the reports of telepathic occurrences (inaccurately called thought-trans-
ference) are submitted to the same critique with which we have fended
off other occult assertions, there remains a considerable amount of material that one cannot so easily neglect. Some observations and experi-

ments lead us to a sympathetic view of telepathy, although they do not yet provide ultimate certainty" (Freud, 29). Having gone this far, Freud focuses on a number of clinical cases where, he postulates, psychoanalytic theory can identify the convergence of certain preconscious predispositions between two persons as a key condition for the occurrence of telepathy: "On behalf of some experiments undertaken in a private circle, I have repeatedly had the impression that the transference of emotionally charged memories can be achieved without difficulty. One may venture to say that the ideas, which are supposed to be transferred during the course of analytic treatment, may come into harmony with the ideas of another person in whom they would have otherwise remained unrecognizable. Based on a number of such observations, I am willing to conclude that such transferences come almost easily at the moment that an idea emerges from the unconscious, when it crosses over from 'primary process' to 'secondary process'" (31).

Freud's comment belongs to a larger tendency to redefine, as parts of the empirical world, phenomena that have traditionally been categorized as transcendental. [see **Immanence vs. Transcendence**] While telepathy transforms the divine privilege of seeing the human soul from inside into a psychological method, technical devices based on wireless communication begin to transform the erstwhile divine privilege of omnipresence into everyday reality. Both developments seem informed by a desire for unrestrained immediacy in the sphere of human interactions. But despite the idea underlying the military's utopian view of television, this is not just a desire to be present as an agent, yet corporeally absent. It is also a desire for closeness and company. A poster for a French radio called the Radiola shows a clown standing behind a radio listener who sits in a comfortable chair (*Années-mémoire,* 159). It is unclear whether the clown's bodily presence can be perceived: he holds his hand over the listener's head, without touching it. The immediacy of the electronic media can go no further.

Related Entries

Airplanes, Boxing, Endurance, Reporters, Roof Gardens, Telephones, Timepieces, Immanence vs. Transcendence, Individuality vs. Collectivity, Silence vs. Noise, Sobriety vs. Exuberance, Center = Periphery (Infinitude), Present = Past (Eternity)

References

Les Années-mémoire: 1926. Paris, 1988.

Associated Students of Stanford University, eds., *The 1926 Quad*.

Caras y Caretas.

Chronik 1926: Tag für Tag in Wort und Bild. Dortmund, 1985.

Lorenzo Díaz, *La radio en España, 1923–1993*. Madrid, 1993.

Monika Elsner, Thomas Müller, and Peter M. Spangenberg, "The Early History of German Television: The Slow Development of a Fast Medium." In *Historical Journal of Film, Radio, and Television* 10 (1990): 193–218.

Sigmund Freud, "Die okkulte Bedeutung des Traumes." In Internationaler Psychoanalytischer Verlag, *Almanach für das Jahr 1926*. Vienna, 1926.

Ricardo Gallo, *La radio: Ese mundo tan sonoro*. Vol. 1: *Los años olvidados*. Buenos Aires, 1991.

Gerhart Hauptmann, *Dorothea Angermann*. Berlin, 1926.

Mel Heimer, *The Long Count*. New York, 1969.

Marcel Jouhandeau, *Monsieur Godeau Intime*. Paris, 1926.

Friedrich Kittler, "Im Telegrammstil." In Hans Ulrich Gumbrecht and K. Ludwig Pfeiffer, eds., *Stil: Geschichten und Funktionen eines kulturwissenschaftlichen Diskurselements*. Frankfurt, 1986.

P. Lertes, *Fernbildtechnik und elektrisches Fernsehen*. Frankfurt, 1926.

New York Times.

René Schickele, *Maria Capponi*. Munich, 1926.

Bärbel Schrader and Jürgen Schebera, eds., *Kunstmetropole Berlin, 1918–1933: Die Kunststadt in der Novemberrevolution / Die "goldenen" Zwanziger / Die Kunststadt in der Krise*. Berlin, 1987.

Ramón del Valle-Inclán, *Tirano Banderas* (1926). Madrid, 1978.

Vossische Zeitung.

CODES

ACTION VS. IMPOTENCE

In Hemingway's novel *The Sun Also Rises,* Jake Barnes, the first-person narrator, and his friend Bill Gorton, a rising star in the literary circles of New York, go trout fishing on the Spanish side of the Basque Pyrenees. It's cold in the little hotel where they spend the night, and since Bill is convinced that wine and liquor alone won't "keep us warm permanently," they order a hot rum punch: "I went out and told the woman what a hot rum punch was and how to make it. In a few minutes a girl brought a stone pitcher, steaming, into the room. Bill came over from the piano and we drank the hot punch and listened to the wind. 'There isn't too much rum in that.' I went over to the cupboard and brought the rum bottle and poured a half-tumblerful into the pitcher. 'Direct action,' said Bill. 'It beats legislation'" (114). What exactly is the point of Bill's joke? Why is it "direct action" to increase the alcohol content of a rum punch? And why does it "beat legislation"? The answer lies in the various contexts of this gesture. Jake hasn't even asked Bill whether he wants a stronger drink—his own certainty is sufficient for him to make the change, wordlessly. During the hours to come, this Action will give the two friends a feeling of warmth in a chilly environment where people do not even know how to mix a rum punch. Pouring "a half-tumblerful [of rum] into the pitcher" far exceeds what guests in a little hotel in the Spanish Pyrenees can normally expect.

A direct Action, then, is an Action that does not necessarily follow from the circumstances in which it occurs. It is an Action that attracts attention through the tension it establishes with its environment. Who-ever performs a direct Action seems to claim implicitly that it is abso-lutely the right thing to do, apart from generally accepted reasons, ex-pectations, or legislation. Once such an Action has been performed, its mere facticity as a transgressive event appears to sanction the subjective grounds out of which it emerged, thus encouraging repetition or continu-ation. Many German authors use the word *Tat* for "direct Action," and they thereby distinguish it from *Handeln* and *Handlung*—forms of Ac-tion which, as part of what Heidegger calls "average everydayness," are expectable and do not require particularly strong subjective decisions. It is thus not surprising that *Tat* becomes a key concept in Ernst Jünger's *Feuer and Blut (Fire and Blood)*, an account of trench warfare during the Great War: "There is a lot of smoking, despite the bad air, and the jokes and cheers of encouragement create an atmosphere of joviality. The candidates of the great world-historical examination are feverishly tense, but quite optimistic. The quiet chattering of teeth, the incredible alert-ness of the senses, which precede the great and decisive *Tat*, sound through each laugh" (98). Here again, an Action—more precisely, the waiting for an imminent Action—generates an atmosphere of intensity. It stands in sharp contrast to the chaotic environment of trench warfare. Intensity and alertness come from the future. They produce a specific anxiety, which results from the vague proximity of death and victory in the future. [see **Boxing, Bullfighting, Mountaineering, Immanence = Transcendence (Death)**]

There is no direct Action, no *Tat*, without this tension coming from and pointing toward the future. It is no accident that the German peri-odical *Die Tat* is subtitled *Monatsschrift für die Zukunft deutscher Kul-tur (Monthly Journal for the Future of German Culture)*. Once an Action has occurred and has thus been transformed into an experience on which one can look back, it immediately becomes an incitement toward further Actions. It is this motivational component which surrounds the Action with the halo of an aesthetic object: "Yes, if it were not for the golden shine that goes with the hardness of extraordinary deeds and which Fate perhaps produces only in order to make us willing to carry out its plans by giving us the illusion of harboring great individual happiness, we would have given up a long time ago. Let the city dwellers call us mercenaries and adventurers; we know that man fulfills his greatest and most natural duty with the highest degree of satisfaction" (Jünger, 46).

Direct Actions are "hard" because they disregard the feelings of those whom they may hit—and sometimes even the expectations of those on whose support they rely. *Taten* do not emanate from principles of legitimacy or from generally acceptable reasons. [see **Uncertainty vs. Reality**] The individual strength of those who act lies not in rationality, but in their determination to do whatever they intuitively encounter and identify as an absolute, fated obligation. Once they make such eminently subjective decisions, the agents' subjecthood, paradoxically, is absorbed in an overwhelming flow of vitality: "Every individual stands secretly governed and directed before the deed *(Tat)*—drawn into an irresistible, powerful current with all the fever of his life" (Jünger, 116). [see **Authenticity = Artificiality (Life)**] Narrating events from a different battlefield of the Great War, T. E. Lawrence has a more somber view of the same existential situation. What Jünger describes as a vitalizing flow of physical strength appears to Lawrence as the "enslaving" state of being possessed: "As time went by, our need to fight for the ideal increased to an unquestioning possession, riding with spur and rein over our doubts. Willy-nilly it became a faith. We had sold ourselves into its slavery, manacled ourselves together in its chain-gang, bowed ourselves to serve its holiness with all our good and ill content . . . By our own act we were drained of morality, of volition, of responsibility, like dead leaves in the wind" (Lawrence, 29).

If direct Action enhances physical and sensual tension to the highest pitch, its counterpart is a slackness that often connotes sexual Impotence. Evoking a world of prostitutes, criminals, and their victims, the lyrics of Argentinian tangos oscillate between these extremes, between direct Actions that "break legislation" and states of exhaustion that lack all physical strength and emotional warmth:

> Accordion from the slums,
> old and flat,
> I found you like a child
> abandoned by its mother
> in the door of the convent
> with unplastered walls,
> in the lantern light
> that lit your way in the night.
> . . . I took you up to my room,

I rocked you to sleep in my cold bosom.
I, abandoned too,
found myself in this brothel.
You wanted to console me
with your hoarse voice
and your painful notes,
increasing my obsession.

                                        (Reichardt, 210)

Not without considerable difficulty, the philosopher Theodor Lessing
tries to make spiders and flies into symbols representing a similar contrast. While he praises spiders as passionate lovers, he accuses flies of a
"promiscuity" that yields blindly to the opportunities of random encounters: "Whereas spiders fight for their females and try to lure them
with their beauty, flies live in blind promiscuity, incessantly changing
their partners in broad daylight" (Lessing, 253). Those who are absorbed
and defeated by the rhythms of the everyday world often appear as
masses of numbed, deindividualized bodies—like the proletarians in
Fritz Lang's film *Metropolis:* "Men, men, men. And they all had the same
faces. And they all seemed a thousand years old. They walked with
hanging fists, they walked with hanging heads. No—they moved their
feet forward, but they did not walk" (Lang, 21–22). If extreme states of
depression sometimes turn into outbursts of revolt, such sudden attacks
usually have no lasting effect. They are mere expressions of despair.

In Roberto Arlt's novel *El juguete rabioso (The Furious Toy)*, Don
Gaetano and Doña María, Jewish bookdealers in whose store Silvio
Astier (the protagonist) earns a miserable living, are an allegory of Impotence and the impotent reaction against it. Doña María regularly
humiliates her husband with outbursts of uncontrollable temper in front
of customers and employees. Soon, however, Silvio Astier learns that
these attacks stem from the frustration caused by Don Gaetano's Impotence: "'But what's the point of these arguments?' 'I don't know . . . they
don't have kids . . . he's not a man'" (56). Over and over, it is thus Doña
María (and not Don Gaetano) who ends up doubly embarrassed—embarrassed by her husband's Impotence and by her own behavior. She
compensates for this with gestures of special generosity toward her
employees: "Wrapping her arms in the folds of the kerchief, she recovered her usual proud bearing. On her pale cheeks, two white tears

trickled down slowly toward the corner of her mouth. Moved, I mur-mured, 'Madam . . .' She looked at me, and without changing her ex-pression, smiling a strange smile, she said: 'Go, and come back at five.'"

All these connotations and counter-connotations, which give the idea of direct Action the complexity of an everyday myth, converge in Adolf Hitler's *Mein Kampf.* Hitler believes that the "aristocratic principle in nature" and "the privilege of force and strength" stand in opposition to the movement of the masses and the "Jewish doctrine" of Marxism: "The Jewish doctrine of Marxism rejects the aristocratic principle in nature; instead of the eternal privilege of force and strength, it values the mass of numbers and their dead weight. Thus, it denies the value of the individual in man" (Hitler, 69). Making explicit the potential gender polarity of this discourse, Hitler derives from it a boundless legitimacy for the physical violence of a male leader: "The psyche of the masses is not receptive to half measures or weakness. Like a woman—whose psychic state is influenced less by abstract reasoning than by an indefin-able, sentimental longing for complementary strength, and who will submit to a strong man rather than dominate a weakling—the masses love the ruler rather than the suppliant, and inwardly are more satisfied by a doctrine which tolerates no rival than by the grant of liberal free-dom" (44). [see **Male vs. Female, Individuality = Collectivity (Leader)**] Consequently, Hitler defines leadership as a "social responsibility" so deeply convinced of its own superiority that it can treat the masses with "ruthless resolution"; he refers to "a deep feeling of social responsibility toward the establishment of better foundations for our development, combined with the ruthless resolution to destroy incurable social tu-mors" (29). Indeed, it is only by breaking the rules of political legitimacy that the leader can give his Actions the status of *Taten*—and that he himself can emerge as a genius. Hitler disguises this precarious claim in a series of rhetorical questions: "Is the inability of a leader proved by the fact that he fails to win over the majority of a crowd to a certain idea—a mass of people who have been brought together more or less by acci-dent? Has this crowd ever been able to grasp an idea before its greatness was proclaimed by its success? Is not every ingenious *Tat* in this world the visible protest of genius against the inertia of the masses?" (Hitler, 86).

While the political philosophies that advocate direct Action cover a spectrum as wide as that between fascism and anarchism, its proponents all share the triple conviction that the world of today [see **Present vs. Past**] is permeated by fearful confusion, that it therefore urgently needs to return to a state of order, and that such order can emerge only from the certainty specific to individual intuitions. Within this emotionally charged world view, the fear of losing control is even stronger than the desire for clarity. If Henri de Montherlant praises the art of the bullfighter as "mastery over events, in the war of everyday life" (Montherlant, 115), he is concerned less with the specific form of this mastery than with the ability to find and maintain a form at all—a form that conjures the threat of entropy represented, for Montherlant, by the bull's physical force. Any Action that displays an identifiable shape must be preferred over hesitation and irresoluteness. It is less the effect of the Action that matters than its status as a perceptible form. This explains why the cult of the *Tat* always underscores its visibility, and often even its radiance. The underlying impression of being confronted with a dramatic alternative between imminent chaos and a decisive opting for form produces a tension between, on the one hand, reflection, thought, and language, and, on the other, Action as an implicit affirmation of what already exists. Quoting from his novella "Tod in Venedig" ("Death in Venice"), Thomas Mann makes the ability "to leave things where they are" into an aesthetic principle, and turns it against psychoanalysts' claim that they provide people with existential orientation in a dizzyingly complex world: "'But it seems that a noble and active mind blunts itself against nothing so quickly as the sharp and bitter irritant of knowledge. And it is certain that the youth's constancy of purpose, no matter how painfully conscientious, was shallow beside the mature resolution of the master of his craft, who made an about-face, turned his back on the realm of knowledge, and passed it by with averted eyes, lest it lame his will or power of action [*die Tat*], paralyze his feelings or his passions, or deprive any of these of their conviction or utility.' This was written with a strong anti-analytic bias, and was misinterpreted as an example of suppression; but the unscientific capacity to leave things where they are is actually the source of that insolence without which the artist cannot exist" (33). Writing about the problematic relation between direct Action and thoughts or words, Heinrich Mann agrees with his brother's skepticism about all intellectual attitudes: "Naturally, the world with its *Taten* has no interest whatsoever in the words that a young poet secretly creates for himself. Would it set itself in motion according to the will of such words?" (279). [see **Silence vs. Noise**] After three more pages of pessimism comes a modest consolation: if an incompatibility separates words from Actions, words may perhaps have an impact on future Actions. "Even when the writer himself does not act, he serves as the conscience for those who do. But in that case, shouldn't he act? Maybe in the name of future agents? Books of today are *Taten* of tomorrow, because the writer carries with him an image of future generations" (282). Literature and philosophy are thus caught in a paradoxical position regarding the myth of direct Action. With a considerable investment of words and thoughts, many authors commit themselves to the world of *Taten*—and thereby contribute to the increasing devaluation of their own intellectual world.

Because of—rather than in spite of—the anxiety and fear it implies, actionism becomes a way of life for some people. Antonin Artaud, in the prospectus for his Théâtre Alfred Jarry, promises spectators emotional stress that is every bit as real as that found in the world outside the theater: "Such is the human anguish which the spectator will feel as a result of the performance. He will be shaken and unsettled by the internal dynamism of the show taking place before his eyes. And this dynamism will be in direct relation to the anguish and preoccupations of his whole life . . . The spectator who comes to us will know that he is coming to subject himself to a real operation in which not only his spirit but his senses and flesh are at stake. If we weren't sure we would wound him as seriously as possible, we would feel inadequate to our most essential task. He must be entirely certain that we are capable of making him cry out" (Artaud, 19). Such actionism makes possible the enjoyment of one's own pain no less than the pain inflicted on others. This explains why *Taten* often appear as painful obligations that fate imposes on those who act. They often give individuals the proud—and masochistic—feeling that they bear an excess load of responsibility for the sake of mankind or, at least, for the sake of their own nation. [see **Individuality vs. Collectivity**] The journal *Die Tat* seems to specialize in assigning such existential burdens: "This is German guilt, which can be atoned for only through German Tat . . . Today fate is summoning the German man, not the German people or the German state, to act decisively" (Bittner, 517–518). Whoever uses the discourse, the mythology, and the emotional tone of direct Action—Hemingway and Hitler, Artaud and Thomas Mann, Heinrich Mann and Montherlant—helps transform the dream of a new aristocracy into a reality that is at once threatening and appealing. This reality claims sadistic cruelty as a right, which it derives from an indulgence in masochistic pleasures. Hans Grimm's geopolitical novel *Volk ohne Raum (Nation without Space)* brings together all these features in a reading experience that is ultimately confusing. [see **Center vs. Periphery**] As one critic writes, "It must be said that this is a manly book. Not in the sense that women could not read it or could not be captivated by it. For being manly is not a question of sex but a question of character. Being manly is *Tat* instead of idle talking, self-control instead of complaining. It is manly to shamefully hide one's innermost feelings—for a woman or for one's fatherland—instead of making them public. In this sense, Grimm's book is a manly book. And in this sense there are still more than enough women in our confused times and in our troubled nation—particularly, women who accept without complaint a life that has become so difficult and harsh—who will read, cherish, and respond deeply to this book . . . *Volk ohne Raum* is not literature in the sense of verbal art—it is *Tat*" (Strauss und Torney, 555).

Related Entries

Boxing, Bullfighting, Mountaineering, Center vs. Periphery, Individuality vs. Collectivity, Male vs. Female, Present vs. Past, Silence vs. Noise, Uncertainty vs. Reality, Authenticity = Artificiality (Life), Immanence = Transcendence (Death), Individuality = Collectivity (Leader), Male = Female (Gender Trouble)

References

Roberto Arlt, *El juguete rabioso* (1926). Buenos Aires, 1980.
Antonin Artaud, "Théâtre Alfred Jarry: Première année—Saison 1926–1927." In Artaud, *Oeuvres complètes*, vol. 2. Paris, 1961.
Karl Gustav Bittner, "Werdet deutsche Menschen!" *Die Tat: Monatsschrift für die Zukunft deutscher Kultur* 18 (1926): 502–518.
Ernest Hemingway, *The Sun Also Rises*. New York, 1926.
Adolf Hitler, *Mein Kampf* (1926). Munich, 1941.
Ernst Jünger, *Feuer und Blut: Ein kleiner Ausschnitt aus einer grossen Schlacht* (1926). Hamburg, 1941.
Fritz Lang, *Metropolis* (1926). New York, 1973.

T. E. Lawrence, *The Seven Pillars of Wisdom*. (1926). Garden City, 1936.

Theodor Lessing, "Spinne und Fliege" (1926). In *"Ich warf eine Flaschenpost ins Eismeer der Geschichte": Essays und Feuilletons, 1923–1933*. Neuwied, 1926.

André Malraux, *La tentation de l'Occident*. Paris, 1926.

Heinrich Mann, *Sieben Jahre: Chronik der Gedanken und Vorgänge*. Berlin, 1929.

Thomas Mann, "Mein Verhältnis zur Psychoanalyse." In Internationaler Psychoanalytischer Verlag, *Almanach für das Jahr 1926*. Vienna, 1926.

Henri de Montherlant, *Album Montherlant*, ed. Pierre Sipriot. Paris, 1979.

Dieter Reichardt, ed., *Tango: Verweigerung und Trauer, Kontexte und Texte*. Frankfurt, 1984.

Lula von Strauss und Torney, *"Volk ohne Raum." Die Tat: Monatsschrift für die Zukunft deutscher Kultur* 18 (1926): 554–555.

AUTHENTICITY VS. ARTIFICIALITY

People are obsessed with seeing things as either authentic or artificial. This absolute distinction seems to stem from a widespread insecurity concerning the status of nature—not only nature as environment but also nature as a norm for different modes of human life. Even a book as academic as I. A. Richards' *Science and Poetry* evokes the problems arising from this insecurity: "Day by day, in recent years, man is getting more out of place in Nature—in the Nature which his ancient habitus of thought formed for him. Where he is going to he does not yet know, he has not yet decided. As a consequence he finds life more and more bewildering, more and more difficult to live coherently" (Richards, 18). For Siegfried Kracauer, this experience is symbolized by film studios—by their clutter of random objects and the welter of scenes they produce. Disorder then becomes an emblem for the prevailing state of contemporary reality. Artificiality, however, is not disorder itself but the reconfiguration of its elements into stories and plots that are not perceived as unnatural: "There are many scenes, stuck next to one another like the tiles of a mosaic. Instead of leaving the world in its fragmented state, one is pulled back into it. With film, these pieces are newly reassembled, their isolation eradicated and their grimace smoothed away. From out of the tomb, they awaken to a semblance of life" (Kracauer, 277–278). A more conventional way of describing the same impression is the motif of mankind's growing isolation within nature—the main theme of Maurice Maeterlinck's scientific-philosophical novel *La vie des termites*. The evolution of intelligence has condemned humans to a position of eccentricity: "Almost certainly, we used to be much more tightly linked than we are now to that universal soul with which our subconscious still communicates. Our intelligence has separated us from it, separates us from it more and more. Is our progress, then, isolation?" (Maeterlinck, 206). Richards, Kracauer, and Maeterlinck share not only the belief that human life has lost its correspondence with nature, but also the conviction that, despite this loss, a natural order of things must still exist somewhere. This is why the French novelist Georges Bernanos can postulate "the need to give back to souls the taste for the authentic" (Bernanos, 240). Explicitly or implicitly, opting for Authenticity presupposes a belief in nature as cosmology and, consequently, a quasi-religious respect for any traditional forms or structures that one can identify.

Such veneration of the given contrasts sharply with the urge to find a new rapport between humanity and its environment, a rapport that is not based on any natural law and that sometimes must even actively avoid perspectives and views produced by nature or mediated by tradition. This position acquires an element of Artificiality through the gesture of going against the grain of tradition or nature. But Artificiality does not deny the existence of those objects which everyday language identifies as "nature," nor does it suggest a specific distance from them—it merely suspends the idea of their normative status. Artificiality thus encourages the invention of new—rigorous, crazy, surrealist—orders under which things and humans can come together. It does not acknowledge any limits, even for the most extreme forms of body fashioning [see **Gomina, Male = Female (Gender Trouble)**] or the most unheard-of levels of athletic achievement. [see **Endurance**] Since Artificiality rejects any assumption of natural coherence, it tends to make things and bodies seem disconnected, isolated, fragmented, and exclusively self-referential. Pushed to its extreme, it can encourage the project of artificially constituting what is seen as quintessentially natural—for example, a family (Supervielle, 158, 211).

On the other hand, the world view of Authenticity presupposes an already given distinction between the substantiality of a depth and the lightness of a surface—a binarism that parallels the distinction between a meaning (depth) and the forms of its expression (surface). This similarity becomes as obvious in philosophical speculations as in astrology and astrophysics: "We may think of the star as two bodies superposed, a material body (atoms and electrons) and an aetherial body (radiation). The material body is in dynamical equilibrium, but the aetherial body is not; gravitation takes care that there is no outside flow of matter, but there is an outside flow of radiation" (Eddington, 20). Whatever man perceives as belonging to the surface level—the signifiers of human language, as well as the radiation of a star—needs to be deciphered as the expression of a meaning that is located at a certain depth. The cosmological world is a world to be interpreted, read, and understood—and this obligation and urge to read the world as the articulation of an underlying order converges with an obsessive need to experience it as ontologically structured. In other words, the complementarity of expression and interpretation serves as an antidote to randomness and entropy. Expression and interpretation are facilitated by the expectation of an increase in order and clarity: "Expression puts an end to the opacity and chaos of things in a disconnected state. The meaning of the spiritual creation which we build out of the elements of our life . . . consists in its ability to make the world within us transparent, and to make us transparent to the world that surrounds us—so that life and self may penetrate each other, and a flow of meaningful life may unite whatever is separated" (Hartmann, 238). The great debate about fascism and culture in the Italian journal *Critica Fascista* elevates this relation between expression, interpretation, and order to the level of an official program. If Massimo Bontempelli defines fascism as "a whole orientation of life, public and private—a total and perfected order that is at once practical and theoretical, intellectual and moral, application and spirit," then art in Fascist society is expected to both identify and express this "total and perfect order": "For *art* is the sensitive instrument that must at once demarcate and foster, express and bring to maturation, the fecundity of the third epoch of civilization: the Fascist Era" (Bontempelli, 248–249).

Whereas Authenticity invariably suggests and postulates an order that conveys meaning to all of its elements, Artificiality rejects the idea of such an all-pervading meaning. Opting for the nonauthentic, Ernst Jünger ironically characterizes humans by their need to ask "the pointless question concerning authentic meaning" (Jünger, 5). For the first-person narrator in Luigi Pirandello's *Uno, nessuno e centomila (One, No One, and One Hundred Thousand)*, true peace of mind comes from the psychic strength of those who do not give in to the neurotic urge to interpret the world. A precondition for this strength lies in suppressing the habit-ual tendency toward reflexivity: "Let us say, then, that inside us there is what we call peace. Don't you think so? And do you know what it comes from? From the simple fact that we have just left the city—that is, left a *constructed* world: houses, streets, churches, squares. Yet *constructed* not only in this sense, but also in the sense that no one lives there anymore just for the sake of living, like these plants, without knowing what living is. In fact, they live for something that doesn't exist and that we ourselves put into life—for something that gives meaning and value to life: a meaning, a value, that here, at least in part, you manage to lose, or at least whose worrisome vanity you recognize" (Pirandello, 49). In contrast, Artificiality—a sphere that no longer counts on an underlying meaning—makes the distinction and the complementary relation between surface and depth obsolete. Surface no longer equals the materiality of expression, and depth no longer equals the spirituality of meaning. Artificiality opens up the possibility of perceiving things—and even persons—as either purely spiritual or purely material. Thus, the hero of Marcel Jouhandeau's *Monsieur Godeau Intime* divides his time between Véronique, a woman who is pure intellect and will, and Rose, who "had the freshness, the health, and at the same time the fragility of a wild rose, of eglantine. She was only a delicious body, without a soul perhaps, a woman of Mohammed" (22). In the end, Véronique's formidable spirituality succeeds in dominating matter, and also Godeau. It is her existential triumph to assume care of Godeau who, stricken by a terrible disease, indeed decays into sheer—repulsive—matter: "Véronique saw M. Godeau crumble away little by little before her eyes, but she did not turn pale with disgust . . . She herself was still dressed in an ivory antiseptic shield, her hair hidden under a turban. Clean and shining, a diamond statue, she touched the pus as if it were water . . . Soon, there was nothing left of M. Godeau but his torso, and the stumps of his legs and arms. A sort of head without eyes, nose, or lips topped this torso, broken by a wild, toothless mouth which, with its tongue barely attached by a thread of blood, stammered at the twilight, lying exposed on the knees of Véronique" (424–425). Such views of the human body as pure—and in this case stinking—matter inspire and legitimize popular initiatives in favor of cremation. On the other hand, since bodies that are only matter no longer require interpretation or spiritual penetration, they can be joined and experienced on a level of pure sensual perception. [see **Dancing, Reporters, Revues**] But such sensual perception is often strangely unerotic. Bodies without depth get caught, and catch others, in rapid movements and rhythms; they inspire mimetic desire; they intoxicate their spectators. Yet they do not seduce other bodies or drag them into the abyss of addiction or perversion. [see **Bars**] Above all, artificial worlds are worlds of barren sexuality. [see **Stars**]

Genealogy, prophecy, and historical time, possession and loss, reflexivity, emancipation, and addiction are allied with Authenticity. It is the dimension of agency and subjectivity which, by interpreting, produces the belief in that cosmological order whose existence the subject's thoughts and actions always presuppose. Even failed actions can matter in the world of Authenticity because they express an agent's project, courage, or capacity to resist adversity. [see **Action vs. Impotence, Action = Impotence (Tragedy)**] Reason and logic are concepts which articulate the expectation that such subjectivity and such agency proceed in accordance with an ultimately transcendental—that is, cosmological—order of things. [see **Immanence vs. Transcendence**] On the side of Artificiality, however, the laws and rhythms of whatever happens appear as the laws and rhythms of particular systems without any normative status. [see **Railroads, Timepieces**] Each system's structures and procedures seem inevitably contingent from the perspective of every other system. The functionalization of bodies within individual systems presupposes and causes their fragmentation [see **Assembly Lines, Employees**]—a fragmentation that ends up producing gender neutrality. Sobriety is the appreciation of this functioning of parts within a system and of their submission to its laws. But even those forces or agents that keep alive, drive, and inspire a system are never independent of it and can never completely observe or manipulate it from outside. [see **Engineers**] In Bertolt Brecht's drama *Mann ist Mann (Man Is Man),* the innocent Chinese packer Galy Gay, whom the colonial army transforms into a "human fighting machine," is a product of the military system and obeys that system's laws to the letter. On the other hand, the colonial army as a system could not exist without being constantly ignited by such internally produced fighting machines. With his first victory barely won, Galy Gay whips up himself and his companions for the next battle:

> And already I feel inside me
> The wish to sink my teeth
> Into the enemy's neck,

An instinct to slaughter
Families and providers,
To fulfill the task
Of the conqueror.
　　　　　(Brecht, 376)

Both Authenticity and Artificiality bear clear, frequently recurring marks of particular times and spaces. Opting for Authenticity means opting for tradition and the past (often with nostalgic enthusiasm), whereas opting for Artificiality means opting for the future (often with the impression of yielding to an inevitable fate). Artificiality's future and Authenticity's past are generally perceived as moving in opposite directions. The future seems always to be increasingly ahead of the present, whereas the past appears more and more remote. Past and future no longer meet in a chronotope of continuity, but offer themselves as diametrically opposed polarities. North America—and sometimes the big cities of Europe—symbolize the world of Artificiality and, for better or worse, anticipation of the future. Authenticity is seen as surviving in Latin America and in the geographic periphery of Europe, mainly in Spain and here and there on the African continent. This mapping explains why Europe constitutes a horizon of desire for so many American intellectuals of the Lost Generation and why, having arrived in Europe, many of them discover that the big European cities do not (or no longer?) offer the longed-for Authenticity. [see **Americans in Paris**] Therefore, many of them move on from Paris or Berlin to Spain, which they experience as a nation, as a country determined by its history, as a country that ultimately acts and reacts emotionally—like a person. In the same way Ernest Hemingway tries to escape the Artificiality of the United States, Jorge Luis Borges rejects the complex connotation of Authenticity attributed to Argentina. But unlike Hemingway, Borges avoids the binary logic that would lead an Argentinian intellectual to embrace Artificiality: "I do not want either progressivism or creolism, in the current understanding of these words. The first is a way of subjecting us to being almost North American or almost European, a persistent almost-being-others; the second, once a term of action (the cavalryman's taunt to the South American—he who went mainly on horseback mocking him who went mainly on foot), is today a term of nostalgia (timid craving for the countryside)" (Borges, 14).

By engendering multiple distinctions, the contrast between Authenticity and Artificiality produces social order. If Gene Tunney controls his fists and his boxing strategy like an intellectual by relying on reflexivity (it's no coincidence that he claims to read Shakespeare), the public persona of jazz fan Jack Dempsey—that of a fighting machine—converges with Brecht's artificially produced character Galy Gay. [see **Boxing**] Similarly, Heinrich Mann observes that the classical understanding of stage acting as an incarnation of abstract character concepts has now been replaced by a much more body-oriented style of performance: "The body of the diva has to represent pride of the spirit. The diva is now fading away, even as others are emerging who are different, if not opposite, to her. What do the few remaining great character actresses of Europe think about the younger generation, whose appearance on stage is more motor-driven than character-driven?" (Mann, 276). The distinction between Authenticity and Artificiality cuts right through the world of dance, setting apart Mary Wigman's *Ausdruckstanz* from Valeska Gert's grotesque Variété performance, from Josephine Baker, and from the popular kicklines. [see **Dancing**] At the opposite pole of the same binary logic, Heinrich Mann sees the latest dance fashions of Berlin as a liberation from depth or expression, and he associates them with the collapse of the social hierarchy: "Skillful couples execute well-calculated steps as if they were playing chess. There is nothing behind these steps . . . What really matters is to unburden oneself of thoughts and to be in great physical shape. This disposition improves the relations between the sexes and even between the social classes. Thanks to their physical achievements, sons of the people now rise to become socially important—even in the eyes of the capitalists" (306–307).

Jorge Luis Borges sets the tangos of the past apart from those of the present, because the latter try too hard to reproduce what came naturally in the old days: "The current tango, performed with picturesque detail and laborious underworld jargon, is one thing; the old tango, performed with pure bravado, shamelessness, and flamboyant pride, is quite another" (Borges, 29–30). But instead of remaining on the level of desperate Artificiality, which Borges finds distasteful, many new tangos base their self-staging on the acknowledgment of the qualitative difference between present and past, thus generating temporal depth through self-denunciation:

Where are the boys of those days?
Yesterday's pals, where are they?
Only you and I remember . . .
Remember those women,
Faithful, big-hearted girls,
Who used to scuffle at Laura's dances,
Each one defending her love.
                                        (Reichardt, 370)

Such attempts at grasping the past's Authenticity stem from a paradoxical motivation. For example, the desire of the archaeologist Howard Carter to speak with Tutankhamen is a function of the way in which Tutankhamen's mask seems to resist Carter's efforts to extract from it the secrets of the ancient Egyptian world. [see **Mummies**] The more difficult it is to discover a content behind or beneath what is identified as an expression, the stronger is the conviction that such a hidden content really exists. This is why the "expressionless eyes" of an African dignitary lead the American zoologist F. G. Carnochan "to the revelation of ancient tribal secrets, . . . some of which [will] eventually be of great value to medical science. It took two separate expeditions to Africa and the better part of four years to make the journey, from the Africa everyone can see, to that which few have seen. But it was worth the trouble" (Carnochan and Adamson, 18, 23).

Ultimately, the difference between Authenticity and Artificiality is a question of perspective rather than an ontological contrast. Max Reinhardt's interpretation of Josephine Baker's dancing as the expression of an archaic cultural force is not necessarily wrong just because it diverges from Baker's self-perception. Such oscillations between alternative perspectives of identical phenomena, however, mark the point at which distinctions and social constructions of reality may collapse. Trying to distinguish body-machine couplings in Soviet factories from those in U.S. factories, Ernst Toller introduces the (more than) precarious notion of a collective proletarian subjectivity on the Soviet side which controls—in its own interest—the use of individual proletarian bodies. In contrast, the battlefield experiences of the Great War lead Ernst Jünger to believe that matter has come to dominate mankind: "A battle is nothing but a terrible way of assessing production on both sides, and the victory goes to the competitor who produces faster and more recklessly. This is the obverse of our historical moment, in which the dominance of machine over mankind, of servant over master, finally becomes evident" (Jünger, 23–24). Only a few pages further, however, he describes how a young soldier, absolutely certain of his impending death in action, laughingly throws away a half-filled bottle of wine. Jünger is so deeply moved by this gesture that his feelings go to the opposite extreme: "Man is superior to matter as long as he can face it with a proper attitude, as long as he is unable to imagine an aspect of those external powers that could break the resistance of a courageous heart" (26). As if in accordance with an underlying logic, Jünger's book ends with the fusion of matter and man: "Ahead of us is our strongest weapon and symbol, the towering wall of fire and steel. At this moment it is our likeness: a unity, but a unity consisting of gleaming atoms. Its hot, shouting breath longs for us, seduces us into the marriage of weapon and body" (138).

Related Entries

Airplanes, Americans in Paris, Assembly Lines, Bars, Boxing, Cremation, Dancing, Employees, Endurance, Engineers, Gomina, Railroads, Reporters, Revues, Stars, Timepieces, Action vs. Impotence, Immanence vs. Transcendence, Sobriety vs. Exuberance, Action = Impotence (Tragedy), Male = Female (Gender Trouble)

References

Georges Bernanos, *Sous le soleil de Satan* (1926). Paris, 1973.

Massimo Bontempelli, "Contributions to the Great Debate on Fascism and Culture in *Critica Fascista*" (1926). *Stanford Italian Review* 8 (1990): 248–250.

Jorge Luis Borges, *El tamaño de mi esperanza* (1926). Buenos Aires, 1993.

Bertolt Brecht, *Mann ist Mann* (1926). In Brecht, *Gesammelte Werke,* vol 1. Frankfurt, 1967.

F. G. Carnochan and Hans Christian Adamson, *The Empire of the Snakes.* London, 1935.

A. S. Eddington, *The Internal Constitution of the Stars.* Cambridge, 1926.

Otto Hartmann, "Zur Metaphysik des künstlerischen Tanzes." *Die Tat* 18, no. 1 (April–September 1926): 237–238.

Marcel Jouhandeau, *Monsieur Godeau Intime.* Paris, 1926.

Ernst Jünger, *Feuer und Blut: Ein kleiner Ausschnitt aus einer grossen Schlacht* (1926). Hamburg, 1941.

Siegfried Kracauer, "Kaliko-Welt: Die Ufa-Stadt zu Neubabelsburg" (1926). In Kracauer, *Das Ornament der Masse: Essays*. Frankfurt, 1977.

Maurice Maeterlinck, *La vie des termites*. Paris, 1926.

Heinrich Mann, *Sieben Jahre: Chronik der Gedanken und Vorgänge*. Berlin, 1929.

Luigi Pirandello, *Uno, nessuno e centomila*. Milan, 1926.

Dieter Reichardt, ed. *Tango: Verweigerung und Trauer, Kontexte und Texte*. Frankfurt, 1984.

I. A. Richards, *Science and Poetry* (1926). New York, 1970.

Jules Supervielle, *Le voleur d'enfants*. Paris, 1926.

CENTER VS. PERIPHERY

··

Hardly anybody ever discusses what is generally acknowledged to be the Center of the world map. Whoever speaks or writes about the world as a spatial object refers explicitly—and almost exclusively—to the Periphery. It is as if only the various continents and countries of the Periphery represented specific concepts and qualities. [see **Authenticity vs. Artificiality**] Perhaps this contrast between Periphery and Center results simply from the impression that all possible phenomena, opinions, and perspectives are constantly present at the Center, whereas the various spaces on the Periphery are—at least temporarily—deprived of some among them. Wherever it may come from, the contrast between the unmentioned Center and the much-discussed Periphery is a stable assumption, stable enough indeed to stand for the geographic distance between the two zones. It constitutes a two-dimensional mapping—a mapping without perspectival illusions, deceptions, or ambiguities.

The western Periphery and the eastern Periphery of this map are occupied, respectively, by the United States and the Soviet Union. For obviously different reasons, both Soviet society and American society are usually seen as representing the future—a view that makes them a threat to some people and a hope to others. The desire to look into the future must be the reason so many reporters, intellectuals, and poets find it exciting and important to visit and write about these two countries. Whatever the United States may embody as a potential future, it is overwhelmingly loud, aggressive, and surface-oriented. This is the future of artificiality. Without necessarily representing the opposite of artificiality, the future associated with the Soviet Union is a dream of collectivity, a dream (or nightmare) of individual goals and hopes merging in consensus and harmony. [see **Individuality vs. Collectivity**] Contrasting more sharply with the United States than with the Soviet Union, the spaces lying on the southern Periphery of the map are worlds of authenticity where an elementary and archaic order is supposed to have survived—an order guaranteeing that all phenomena preserve their original cosmological meanings. From this perspective, Latin America and Africa become objects of nostalgia. But while it seems to be the symbolic function of Africa to keep present something very remote, archaic, and vague [see **Mummies**], Latin America's authenticity becomes associated with a particular vitality. One often gets the impression that Latin America will play a leading role in the future. [see **Americans in Paris, Authenticity = Artificiality (Life)**] In contrast, the main connotation of Asia is that of a culture in irreversible decay. Always associated with radical forms of individuality—which establish a potential contrast between Asia and the Soviet Union—Asia's artistic and intellectual achievements are widely admired. But even André Malraux, whose book *The Temptation of the West* makes a passionate effort to draw intellectual attention to the Asian world (and who seems to hope that Asian culture will overcome its tendency toward decadence) introduces W. Y. Ling, one of his heroes, in a strangely decadent light: "Mr. Ling is Chinese and, as such, displays a Chinese sensibility and way of thinking, which are not sufficient to destroy the books of Europe" (Malraux, 11–12).

The unmarked Center of the map is occupied by Europe and Great Britain. It excludes the Soviet Union and Spain. The worldwide enthusiasm which Spanish life is evoking may well come from this exclusion. Since Spain is not associated with the Artificiality of contemporary culture (Edschmid, passim), it becomes the European enclave of an Authenticity which, though it lacks the future-oriented potential of Latin America, is saturated with references to a common European history. For many travelers, crossing the Spanish border means returning to an unalienated world of traditional values. The praise of Spain that Hemingway's protagonist Jake Barnes implies in an ironic remark about French waiters is typical of this feeling: "I overtipped [the French waiter]. That made him happy. It felt comfortable to be in a country where it is so simple to make people happy. You can never tell whether a Spanish waiter will thank you. Everything is on such a clear financial basis in France. It is the simplest country to live in. No one makes things complicated [as in Spain] by becoming your friend for any obscure reason" (Hemingway, 243). During a Mediterranean cruise in late April and early May, Harry Graf Kessler, a wealthy and sophisticated advocate for German culture, fills his diary with lengthy descriptions of Spanish coastal cities (Kessler, 476), whereas French and Italian towns are mentioned only briefly, because they belong to that cultural realm of the Center with which Kessler is already familiar. As a reaction to Spain's status of eccentricity, Kessler's diary helps one understand why Miguel de Unamuno's notion of the "Europeanization of Spain" and the "Hispanization of Europe" receives such enormous international interest and approval (Curtius, 226–227).

In contrast to the Periphery of the map, France, England, Germany, Italy, northern Europe, and most of eastern Europe are neither symbols of the future nor remnants of the past. They are Authenticity and Artificiality, individualism and collectivism. They are the present and the Center; their politics constantly receive worldwide attention; and their cultures have become a norm for thousands of American tourists. But if the Center is everything, then nothing specific can be said or written about it. It is neutral. For many Germans, such neutrality is becoming an authentic ideal. It generates a concern with the impression German tourists may give while traveling abroad: "If excessive laughter and unnecessary noise are already an embarrassment at home, they come across as an imposition or even as a provocation abroad. The German traveler cannot be cautious enough. Nothing has contributed more to the negative image of Germans abroad than their inclination either to constantly disparage the charms of the foreign country in comparison to the advantages of Germany, or to uncritically praise the virtues of the host country" (Thierfelder, 523).

Center and Periphery merge with and complement each other when they confirm the distance that separates them. French and Spanish politicians are probably serious when, on the occasion of a bilateral treaty signed in July, they refer to their military rule in Morocco as "splendid civilizing labor" (García-Nieto, 146). Ramón Franco bases his pioneering airplane flight from Spain to Buenos Aires on very similar premises, thus indirectly perpetuating Spain's colonial role vis-à-vis Argentina—an attitude that he does not seem to perceive as contradicting Spain's eccentric position in the European context. He explores "the possibility of accomplishing a raid [a long-distance flight] that would make the greatness of Spanish aviation known beyond our borders and that [would confirm] the indisputable glory won on the fields of Africa. Looking at a map of the world and examining the possible routes for such a raid—which would reveal not only the merit of the pilot but the achievements of scientific research, and which would establish norms for future aerial navigation from one continent to another across seas and deserts—I understood that the flight to the Plata combined all this with the dangers of the ocean and of the equatorial region, a great incentive for any aviator. The enterprise would thus tighten the union between Spain and the young Castilian-speaking nations on the continent discovered by Columbus" (Franco, 5–6). [see **Airplanes**] Just as Franco conceives his project within a completely Eurocentric mapping, so the French travel writer Paul Morand has no doubt that America's Pacific Coast is the end of the Western world, "the Western Land's End" (Morand, 23). At the other extreme of the map, Morand describes a review theater in China but sees in it only a "tragically bad imitation" of the European model (67ff.). [see **Revues, Roof Gardens**]. Perpetuating age-old traditions of intellectual arrogance, these authors feel no ambivalence about the project of fighting "always and definitively the American despiritualization" (Heinrich Mann, 309). In even more aggressive tones, the Fascist novelist Mario Puccini defends the "simple, homey, provincial" elements of Italian culture against any influence of American Artificiality (259).

Very few voices from the Periphery ever challenge such views of Europe as the implied Center. Somewhat surprisingly, the inhabitants of Buenos Aires and Argentinian politicians enthusiastically play along with the staging of Franco's flight to South America as the revival of a distant colonial past (Gumbrecht, 179ff.). For the Uruguayan-French novelist Jules Supervielle and for his Uruguayan-born hero Colonel Bigua, who seems to live in political exile in Paris, even the most gloriously romanticized image of the Periphery is still the image of a colonial space: "The colonial house with its old habits awaited him there beneath the sky, so blue, without a crack. Ah! To hear at Las Delicias . . . , passing by his room three times a week, the live chickens that the shopkeeper held too tightly under his arm while taking them to the kitchen" (Supervielle, 211). Ramón del Valle-Inclán certainly comes close to political reality when he has the fictional Latin American dictator Banderas justify his government's repressive policies with imperialist slogans about the indigenous population, adopted from the Spanish colonial tradition: "So humble in appearance, yet they are ungovernable! The scientists are not wrong when they tell us that the original communal organization of the native has been defeated by Spanish individualism, the source of our leadership" (Valle-Inclán, 211).

If the Periphery is ever capable of aggression, it turns against the United States and not against the European Center. Valle-Inclán's dictator blames "Yankee industrialism" for the revolution that will bring his rule to an end. And going beyond merely an ironic similarity between this invented military dictator and a real Japanese Communist, Nakano Shigeharu's poem "Imperial Hotel" identifies colonialism primarily with American capitalism:

> This is the West
> The dogs use English
>
> This is the proper West
> The dogs invite me to the Russian Opera
>
> This is the West: A Western Exposition
> The Japanese marketplace for kimonos and shopworn curios
>
> And this is a prison
> The guard jangles his keys
> . . . . .
> And then this is a cheap dive
> The old fat guy is roaring drunk
>
> And also this is a cheap whorehouse
> The women walk naked
>
> And this is a hole
> Black and fetid.
>
> (Silverberg, 119ff.)

American intellectuals at home seem little concerned with such accusations. The Special Lectures program of Mount Holyoke College, one of the more conservative academic institutions, subsumes Europe under a perspective of nationalism: "William Fletcher Russell, Ph.D., New York, N.Y.: 'Education and Nationalism with Special Reference to Recent

Educational Reforms in Europe.'" A large majority of the program's topics, however, refer to non-European cultures, and are contextualized by the even more future-oriented theme of the internationalization of politics: "Dr. James B. Pratt, Williamstown: 'The Nature of Present-Day Buddhism.' Mr. Rabrindra C. Nag, Calcutta, India: 'The Social and Political Philosophy of Gandhi.' William R. Shepherd, Ph.D., New York, N.Y.: 'Friendship between the Americas.' Rev. Leyton Richards, Birmingham, England: 'The Heavy Price of World Peace'" (Mount Holyoke, 20–21).

As long as the distinction between Center and Periphery is generally accepted on both sides, it establishes stable relations of geographic distance on the map and, as a premise for everyday life, gives people the impression that they inhabit a homogeneous world space. [see **Center = Periphery (Infinitude)**] Such a homogeneous, geometric space is a space that neither undergoes quantitative changes nor ever interferes with human actions and behavior. It is under the assumption that people live in a homogeneous space that the burgeoning of the world's population generates feelings—partly justified and partly phobic—of collective claustrophobia and imminent chaos. For example, the mayor of Berlin, who is politically responsible for one of the most rapidly growing towns in the world, is obsessed with establishing a normative spatial order by attributing discrete functions to each of the city's different neighborhoods: "Vitally important problems call for a solution . . . What matters is a new division between residential, industrial, and commercial sectors of the city. The present chaos makes it necessary to overcome such disorder with a new mapping" (Schrader and Schebera, 140). Immense urbanization projects that become every architect's dream, high-rise buildings that develop into virtually independent systems, new traffic regulations, increasingly complex railway schedules—these are only a few of the numerous practical responses stimulated by future-oriented fears of population growth and designed to prevent the ultimate demographic catastrophe. [see **Automobiles, Elevators, Engineers, Railroads**]

Geopolitics is the ideologico-political answer to the same set of concerns and questions. It lies at the point where a Euclidean conception of world space comes together with a largely mythological notion of history [see **Authenticity vs. Artificiality**] and with the realization that the imperialist process of conquest and distribution has come to an end. Explicitly acknowledging these three frame-conditions, the Italian government begins draining of the Pontine Marshes as a means of enlarging the nation's territory (*Conquista della Terra,* 51). Adolf Hitler emphasizes an interest in both history and geography in the description of his high school years: "My best efforts were in geography, and perhaps even more so in history. These were my two favorite subjects, in which I was the best in the class" (Hitler, 8). Instead of trying to play down the tension between his efforts to assume leadership of the German nation and his birth in Braunau, on the Austrian-German border, Hitler presents this relation as a providential sign of his own historical vocation. Geopoliticians know only the contrast between inside and outside, and therefore neutralize the ambivalences typically found in border spaces and transitions: "Today I consider it my good fortune that fate designated Braunau as the place of my birth. For this small town is situated on the border between those two German states whose reunification seems, at least to us of the younger generation, a task to be furthered through every possible means every day of our lives . . . Common blood belongs in a common Reich" (Hitler, 1). The ideal of "living inside" goes along with a moralization of space. Whoever lacks space, according to Hitler, is condemned to physical and mental disease: "Now let us imagine the following: In a basement apartment consisting of two stuffy rooms lives a worker's family of seven people . . . In such circumstances, people live not with one another but on top of one another . . . The poor little boy, at the age of six, senses things which would make even a grown-up shudder. Morally infected, undernourished, his poor little head covered with lice, the young 'citizen' wanders off to elementary school . . . The three-year-old has now become a youth of fifteen who despises all authority. Familiar with only dirt and filth, the young fellow knows nothing that could rouse his enthusiasm for higher things" (32–33). If claustrophobia and the obsessive desire to occupy a spacious Center are among the key motifs in Hitler's *Mein Kampf,* they constitute the exclusive topic of Hans Grimm's 1,300-page novel *Volk ohne Raum (Nation without Space).* Grimm shares Hitler's belief that a lack of individual and collective space is associated with disease. His protagonists hate "the unbearable German confinement, within which the members of the community become necessarily quarrelsome, servile, base, and malformed" (671). Yet Grimm emphasizes that acquiring colonies would not solve the problem of national space. The only conclusion that his hero Cornelius Friebott can draw after many years in Southwest Africa is that he must return to

Germany and commit himself to a solution that is rather casually mentioned in *Mein Kampf*: "For Germany, therefore, the only possibility of fulfilling a sound territorial policy was to be found in the acquisition of new soil in Europe proper. Colonies cannot serve this purpose, since they do not appear suitable for settlement by Europeans on a large scale" (Hitler, 153). The Periphery is not good enough to solve the geopolitical problems of the Center.

Although nationalist geopoliticians emerge as the most passionate opponents of the League of Nations, both sides share two certainly pre-ideological feelings—namely, a phobia about borderlands as ambiguous spaces and a desire to inhabit a homogeneous world. But if geopoliticians aim at making the borders of national Centers invisible by pushing them as far as possible toward the Periphery, the ultimate—and opposite—task of the League of Nations is to transform the world map into a homogeneous living space for humankind by eliminating all existing borders. Delivering a public address on Saturday, January 16, Albert Einstein observes a surprising division between the supporters of national geopolitics and those of internationalization: "It must be admitted that scientists and artists, at least in the countries with which I am familiar, are guided by narrow nationalism to a much greater extent than are public men" (Clark, 438). As a general assessment, Einstein's optimism regarding politicians and his pessimism regarding intellectuals may be adequate—especially for Germany. Hans Grimm's *Volk ohne Raum,* for example, is reviewed with much respect—and often with open enthusiasm—even by some in the left-wing press: "[It is] not literature, in the sense of verbal art. It is an action and a spiritual event. It is a wake-up call" (von Strauss und Torney, 555). [see **Action vs. Impotence**] At the same time, those well-intentioned politicians who support the League of Nations become increasingly unpopular because practicing politics without territorial borders is impossible. [see **League of Nations**] Their weakness is the potential strength of the nationalist geopoliticians.

Related Entries

Airplanes, Americans in Paris, Automobiles, Bullfighting, Elevators, Engineers, League of Nations, Mummies, Railroads, Reporters, Revues, Roof Gardens, Action vs. Impotence, Authenticity vs. Artificiality, Individuality vs. Collectivity, Authenticity = Artificiality (Life), Center = Periphery (Infinitude)

References

Ronald W. Clark, *Einstein: The Life and Times.* New York, 1971.

La Conquista della Terra: Rassegna Nazionale dell'Opera per i Combattenti— Fascicolo Speciale. Rome, 1932.

Ernst Robert Curtius, "Unamuno" (1926). In Curtius, *Kritische Essays zur europäischen Literatur.* Bern, 1950.

Kasimir Edschmid, *Basken, Stiere, Araber: Ein Buch über Spanien und Marokko* (1926). Berlin, 1927.

Ramón Franco, *De Palos al Plata.* Madrid, 1926.

María Carmen García-Nieto, Javier M. Donézar, and Luis López Puerta, eds., *La dictadura, 1923–1930: Bases documentales de la España contemporánea,* vol. 7. Madrid, 1973.

Hans Grimm, *Volk ohne Raum.* Munich, 1926.

Hans Ulrich Gumbrecht, "Proyecciones argentino-hispanas, 1926." In *III Congreso Argentino de Hispanistas: España en América y América an España,* vol. 1. Buenos Aires, 1993.

Ernest Hemingway, *The Sun Also Rises.* New York, 1926.

Adolf Hitler, *Mein Kampf* (1926). Munich, 1941.

Harry Graf Kessler, *Tagebücher, 1918–1937.* Frankfurt, 1961.

André Malraux, *La tentation de l'Occident.* Paris, 1926.

Heinrich Mann, *Sieben Jahre: Chronik der Gedanken und Vorgänge.* Berlin, 1929.

Paul Morand, *Rien que la terre: Voyage.* Paris, 1926.

Mount Holyoke College, *Catalogue, 1925–1926.* South Hadley, Mass., 1926.

Mario Puccini, "Contribution to the Great Debate on Fascism and Culture in *Critica Fascista*" (1926). *Stanford Italian Review* 8 (1990): 257–260.

Bärbel Schrader and Jürgen Schebera, *Kunstmetropole Berlin, 1918–1933: Die Kunststadt in der Novemberrevolution / Die "goldenen" Zwanziger / Die Kunststadt in der Krise.* Berlin, 1987.

Miriam Silverberg, *Changing Song: The Marxist Manifestos of Nakano Shigeharu.* Princeton, 1990.

Jules Supervielle, *Le voleur d'enfants.* Paris, 1926.

Fritz Thierfelder, "Der deutsche Reisende im Auslande." *Die Tat* 18, no. 1 (April—September 1926): 518–526.

Ramón del Valle-Inclán, *Tirano Banderas* (1926). Madrid, 1978.

Lulu von Strauss und Torney, "*Volk ohne Raum.*" *Die Tat* 18, no. 1 (April—September, 1926): 554–555.

IMMANENCE VS. TRANSCENDENCE

Often, a writer will use concepts and metaphors of a traditionally religious nature just to show that humans can do without them. One of the key intellectual concerns of the moment is to transform elements of Transcendence into elements of Immanence. Notions and images of Transcendence frequently seem to be evoked only so that they can be immediately rejected, almost contemptuously. The distinction between everyday worlds and transcendent worlds scarcely ever goes unchallenged. Discourses of political ideology are the most obvious exceptions to this tendency, but it is not always clear whether the transcendent spaces that they denote are meant to be taken seriously or seen as purely ornamental. The Italian playwright Ernesto Forzano, for example, opens his drama *Rapsodia Fascista* with a conventional conversation in the allegorical mode between the "Genius of Rome" and "Italicus, the moving spirit of fascism." At first glance, it seems unlikely that Forzano believes in the potentially transcendent content of this scene, because the sacrificial mechanism to which he alludes remains completely invisible. The death of hundreds of thousands of young Italians is presented as the price paid for the (Fascist) resurgence of the nation: "(Italicus appears. His cloak falls off, and he appears in a black shirt. He holds the almighty torch in his right hand and throws back his head. He walks with slow steps, as if attracted by the flame.) *Italicus:* . . . Exult, Italy! . . . Spirits, exult / in the hundreds of thousands of dead / who gave their youth in the holocaust! / Your sacrifice was not in vain! . . . / Rome, rise up! . . .

For us, brothers! . . . For us!" (16). Forzano's drama takes place during the years between the end of the Great War and the Fascist seizure of power in the fall of 1922. Its three acts—entitled "First Sacrifice," "Second Sacrifice," and "Holocaust"—correspond to episodes in the life of the hero, Orazio Romanis. Orazio must renounce his Communist father (first sacrifice), give up his relationship with his lover, Anna, who is likewise the child of a Communist (second sacrifice), and witness the death of his uncle Antonio, a veteran of Garibaldi's wars of liberation, due to a stray Fascist bullet (holocaust). But since none of Orazio's multiple sacrifices has any direct impact on the Fascist revolution, Forzano's plot makes transcendent sense only if one assumes the existence of a divine power to whom these sacrifices are directed and who may be favorably influenced by them.

Typically, the religious implications of political discourse remain on this strange intermediate level. The distinction between an immanent sphere and a transcendent sphere is so vague that readers can, if they wish, discount it as merely a rhetorical effect. But they can also fill these faintly contoured Immanence/Transcendence dichotomies with their own religious or ideological beliefs. The myth of redemption is as important for Johannes Becher's Communist poems as it is for Forzano's Fascist drama. Becher's "Proletarisches Schlaflied" ("Proletarian Lullaby") is indeed constructed around a dream of redemption: "Sleep, my dear child. / Let the colorful little rocking horses sway you! / Dancing children surround you in jubilation, and you speak / Words of redemption, revealed to you by the Creator of Light" (Becher, 26; also 33, 43, 88, 96). The understanding of this stanza largely hinges upon the discursive status that the reader wishes to attribute to the "Creator of Light," who is revealing "words of redemption" to the child. A discursive relative of Hegel's *Weltgeist,* Becher's "Creator of Light" can either be understood as a deity (which would give this text a clear religious dimension) or remain without any personalized reference. A similar alternative exists with respect to the mythic national past. [see **Present vs. Past**] It has become popular all over Europe to speak of "unredeemed lands" (often actually using the Italian phrase *terre irredente*)—a phrase that can either imply a prehistory in which divine punishment stripped a nation of part of its territory, or be just a conventional metaphor for the political situation of national minorities (Hinkepott, 772–775). [see **Center vs. Periphery**] Hans Grimm's geopolitical novel *Volk ohne Raum*

(Nation without Space) is one of those texts which explicitly exclude the possibility of toning down the myth of redemption to a purely meta-phorical status. Grimm offers no alternative to a religiously grounded world view. His protagonists therefore reject all forms of pragmatism as the greatest danger to the national interest: "He has identified two enemies. The first is the sort of property which is interested only in its own preservation and which alternatively appears in the guise of Econ-omy or of *Realpolitik.* The second is the Social Democratic Party" (Grimm, 662).

Adolf Hitler's relation to the dimension of Transcendence is far more complex. On the one hand, in the autobiographical passages of *Mein Kampf* he occasionally uses words that are traditionally religious; on the other, he never fully eliminates the possibility of reading them as merely ornamental elements. Concepts like "fate" or "providence" can thus be either metonyms for a divine being or metaphors for randomness: "For this other world is thoughtless. Thoughtlessly, it allows things to go on as they will; lacking intuition, they do not foresee that sooner or later fate will take revenge if it is not placated in time. How grateful I am today to providence, which bade me go to this school. There I could not sabotage what I disliked. It educated me quickly and thoroughly" (Hitler, 28–29). One of Hitler's rhetorical strategies consists of support-ing his racist theories by means of two other discourses: he presents racism both as fulfilling God's will and as corresponding to the laws of nature. "Eternal Nature inexorably avenges transgressions against her laws. Therefore, I believe today that I am acting in accordance with the wishes of the Almighty Creator: by warding off the Jews, I am accom-plishing the Lord's work" (Hitler, 70). Theology and science exist in a complementary relation here. The natural sciences have contributed more than any other institutionalized field of knowledge to redefining traditional concepts of Transcendence under the premise of Immanence, as well as to producing new concepts of this type. Hitler's racism can therefore appeal simultaneously to readers who believe in a biologically grounded world view and to those who are traditionally religious.

Nature and science are the dominant contexts for transforming clas-sical concepts of Transcendence into concepts of Immanence. Thus, Maurice Maeterlinck's novel *La vie des termites* strives to reduce the problems of individual existence, society, and religion to a purely bio-logical dimension. Toward the end of the book, Maeterlinck defines the limit of this experiment by identifying total knowledge of the laws of nature with the status of divinity. But even such divine wisdom could not guarantee perfect happiness among living beings: "Such a man came close to being God; and if God himself was unable to make his creatures happy, there is reason to believe that this was impossible" (185). Although Maeterlinck coins the particularly appropriate expression "absorption in God" (185) for the constitution of transcendental concepts from the observation of nature, he himself practices the absorption of God into popular science—a practice that now pervades the intellectual scene. Henri de Montherlant pursues a similar strategy of oscillation between Immanence and Transcendence: "The more intimate our relations with nature become, the closer we get to the supernatural" (*Album Montherlant,* 107). Starting out quite conventionally by comparing bees and wasps to different types of human social life, the philosopher Theodor Lessing ends up discovering in nature what used to be defined as Transcendence: "But when autumn comes, with the cold wind sweeping over the fields and food becoming scarcer and scarcer, at last something mystical happens, so strange that it truly touches on ultimate mysteries of redemption. A whole population is extinguished. Only a single fertile wasp creeps around the roots and dwelling places of the earth, preserving for the new year the memory of a vanished world of forms. Might Buddha have discovered the secret of Nirvana in the solitary life of these wild wasps?" (Lessing, 256–257). Lessing is not the only intellectual who tries to connect theology and the observation of nature with Asian thought. In its fourth year, the influential *Deutsche Vierteljahrsschrift für Literaturwissenschaft und Geistesgeschichte (German Quarterly for Literary Studies and Intellectual History)* publishes an essay that tries to legitimize the growing affiliation between transcendental speculation and empirical science in the West by likening it to a similar relationship in the Indian intellectual tradition: "In this sense, the character of the spiritual world of India is determined by the close relationship between yoga and empirical science . . . The sciences mediate practical knowledge about the types and effects of the various metamorphoses, in which the divine presents itself in the world of appearances. Yoga, however, is the only means by which one may grasp the absolute essence of this 'being' beyond the veil of its metamorphoses" (Zimmer, 56–57). [see **Uncertainty vs. Reality**]

The most rhetorically complex way of absorbing Transcendence into

Immanence lies in the paradoxical projection of metaphysical effects onto everyday reality. Some sections in Louis Aragon's novel *Le paysan de Paris (The Peasant of Paris)* read like a manifesto for this aggressive blurring of the border between Immanence and Transcendence: "New myths are born under each of our footsteps. Where man has lived, where he lives, legend begins . . . It is a science of life that belongs only to those who have had no experience of it. It is a living science that engenders and kills itself. Is it still possible for me (I am already twenty-six) to participate in this miracle? Will I be able to sustain this sense of the marvelousness of the everyday?" (Aragon, 14). The narrator's wanderings through "his village" (Paris) and the estranging attention that he devotes to every material detail yield a revised concept—and a new program—of metaphysics: "The notion or knowledge of the concrete is, then, the object of metaphysics. The movement of the spirit tends to make itself perceived concretely" (240). The young librarian and amateur philologist Erich Auerbach shares Aragon's enthusiasm for the concreteness and paradoxical spirituality of everyday life. Astonishingly for someone outside academia, he thus dares to criticize the lack of concrete detail in Racine's dramas of passion: "This hyperbole of sensual individuality is all the more difficult to grasp as [Racine's] characters . . . lack a concrete worldly existence. They remain at an unworldly and unreal distance. They are allegories, empty vessels of their autonomous passions and instincts" (Auerbach, 379–380).

The ability of the sphere of Immanence to absorb transcendental concepts and motifs is apparently limitless. When Jules Supervielle invents a hero for his novel *Le voleur d'enfants (The Man Who Stole Children)* who wishes to "control destinies as God does" (60), when Gerhart Hauptmann has the protagonists of his play *Dorothea Angermann* define fate as "ordinary everydayness" (73) and providence as "randomness" (121), and when Sigmund Freud announces in his entry "Psychoanalysis" in the *Encyclopedia Britannica* that the discipline which he founded will increasingly become a "science of the unconscious" (265), it is obvious that man, everydayness, and the unconscious serve as substitutes for God, fate, and Transcendence. On the other hand, there seems to be a threshold across which the absorbed Transcendence returns like a revenant. One reason for this return of Transcendence is the impossibility of celebrating the disappearance of Transcendence before its former presence (or the previously existing belief in its presence) has been mentioned. Jean Cocteau uses this mechanism—and falls prey to it—in his rewriting of the Orpheus myth. Although there is scarcely any other myth whose archaic versions are more centered on the threshold between Immanence and Transcendence, Cocteau multiplies the occasions for his protagonists to cross this boundary. In addition to Eurydice's death and Orpheus' descent into the underworld, Cocteau stages two complex appearances of Madame Death on earth [see **Timepieces**], has Orpheus join Eurydice in the underworld after her second death, and even lets the couple return to their home at the end of the play. This happy ending coincides with the general tendency toward the absorption of Transcendence into Immanence—for Orpheus and Eurydice realize that their earthly home is their true paradise, and that the glazier who used to fix the windows which they broke during their matrimonial fights has been acting as their guardian angel: "*Orpheus:* . . . Lord, we thank you for having assigned us our dwelling place and our household as our only paradise and for having opened to us your paradise. We thank you for having sent the glazier to us, and we blame ourselves for not having recognized your guardian angel" (118–119).

On Tuesday, June 15, the German millionaire and arts patron Harry Graf Kessler attends the premiere of *Orphée* in Paris—and leaves the theater deeply disappointed by the intricate scenic display with which Cocteau makes his simple philosophical point:

> The tickets cost a hundred francs (as much as those for the Ballet Russe). The usual elegant, international audience. Many Americans, English, even Japanese. The piece, which many have praised as extraordinary, disappointed me. It doesn't come to terms with the topic—no real tragedy, no real comedy. And then there's that impossible, embarrassingly funny angel in the middle (flattering the trendy taste for Catholicism), embodied by a repulsively sweet, eccentric young man who seemed to come from a low-life hairdresser's. This sweet young man ended up ruining the evening for me. But I also found it difficult to bear Madame Pitoeff, who was once again appearing onstage eight months pregnant—which is especially grotesque for a Eurydice. I was so mad at Cocteau . . . that I left hurriedly after the performance, without greeting him." (Kessler, 486–487)

Angels are much in demand these days, since they both deny and accentuate the threshold between Immanence and Transcendence [see **Imma-**

nence = Transcendence (Death)]—so much so that, according to Graf
Kessler, the angel in Cocteau's *tragédie* comes straight out of the playwright's life: after a religious conversion earlier in the year, Cocteau
believes that he himself has become an angelic being (Kessler, 447).
There are angels almost everywhere. "You kill like an angel" (Montherlant, *Les Bestiaires,* 230) is just about the highest compliment that an
experienced bullfighter can pay a young colleague. In "Reyerta," one of
the poems in Federico García Lorca's *Romancero gitano (Gypsy Romance)* black angels with long, dagger-shaped wings mourn the victims
of a fight:

> A harsh playing-card light
> cuts out, with acid green,
> maddened horses
> and silhouettes of riders.
> Into the olive-tree cup
> two old women are crying.
> The bull of the fight
> goes up the wall.
> Black angels carry
> handkerchiefs and snow water.
> Angels with great wings
> like jackknives from Albacete.
>
> (García Lorca, 428–429)

One does not always need topics with such obviously religious connotations in order to bring back the concepts and metaphors of Transcendence. Whatever seems dangerous, exciting, or simply new can activate
a halo of quasi-religious words and attitudes. Bars and drinks become a
means of access either to hell or to heaven. The "adoration of elevators"
emerges as a standard phrase among those who criticize Europeans'
enthusiasm for the American way of life. Admiration for some recently
introduced wireless communication devices appears to trigger a revival
of interest in telepathy. Gramophones are increasingly associated with
the desire to speak with the dead. The film industry invents a new heaven
of stars. [see **Bars, Elevators, Wireless Communication, Gramophones,
Movie Palaces, Stars**] Even where such discourses no longer explicitly
refer to worlds beyond—or below—the sphere of everyday life, as is the

case with the *crónicas* of the Brazilian journalist António de Alcântara Machado, there is always a note of myth and eccentricity in the description of technological innovations: "The obsession of today is the radio. Not long ago, people were passionate about the gramophone. It actually became one of the tortures of mankind. The radio replaced it. Nobody can resist the temptation to listen at least once to a sound coming from unknown, exotic countries" (Alcântara Machado, 140). It is no wonder that Fritz Lang's hyperallegorical film *Metropolis* portrays machines acting as deities: "Then, from their glittering thrones, Baal and Moloch, Huitzilopochtli and Durgha, arose. All the god-machines got up, stretching their limbs in fearful liberty. Hungry fires flared up from the bellies of Baal and Moloch, flicking out of their maws" (Lang, 106; also 38).

If the prevailing intellectual ambition of the moment is to absorb Transcendence into Immanence, and if this aim—paradoxically and for a number of different reasons—ends up multiplying the references to transcendent worlds, an equally marked reaction to the absorption of Transcendence consists in the belief that the time is ripe for inventing new mythologies or for reviving traditional forms of religious discourse. A particularly extreme example of such a new mythology is found in D. H. Lawrence's novel *The Plumed Serpent*. Lawrence shares Fritz Lang's fondness for Aztec deities. But whereas in *Metropolis* the transcendent aspects of the plot develop out of problems caused by social injustice, Lawrence's fictional religion is based on aggressively phallocentric sex. "The sacredness of sex," to use the phrase of a female character, is by no means a metaphor: "How wonderful sex can be, when men keep it powerful and sacred, and it fills the world! Like sunshine through and through one" (Lawrence, 467). Likewise, the metaphysical discourse in which Lawrence solemnly describes erotic experience, as well as his reference to a male lover as a "god-demon," are to be taken seriously: "She could conceive now her marriage with Cipriano; the supreme passivity, like the earth below the twilight, consummate in living lifelessness, the sheer solid mystery of an abandon . . . She had only known his face, the face of the supreme god-demon; with the arching brows and slightly slanting eyes, and the loose, light tuft of a goat-beard. The Master. The everlasting Pan" (467). Henri de Montherlant is, if possible, equally solemn about the religion he extracts from the death-mystique of bullfighting. His novel *Les Bestiaires* ends with a strangely utopian epilogue that celebrates a return to the rituals of a pre-Christian bull religion: "They shared the supper, serving themselves, as in a mystical communion of bull-worshippers. They broke a mint branch on the threshold to flavor their tea . . . They saw, through the open door, night slowly descending. They heard, through the open door, the eternal sound of the tide" (235). The extent to which Montherlant feels religiously and politically committed to the ritual of the bullfight becomes apparent in his public letter to Gaston Doumergue, the president of the French Republic—a letter printed at the beginning of *Les Bestiaires*. After thanking Doumergue for allowing bullfights to be reestablished in France and after complimenting him on his birth in the southern provinces, "in the midst of the bull religion," Montherlant, surprisingly, refrains from dedicating his book to the president. He fears that such homage might endanger Doumergue's life (7–8). Outside his own world view, of course, Montherlant's gesture only shows how grotesquely he overestimates the importance of the current French debate on the moral and spiritual legitimacy of bullfighting. There are certainly greater threats to the president's life than those coming from Montherlant's opponents. On the other hand, his passionate commitment is a telling symptom of the emotional intensity that characterizes the search for religion, mythology, and Transcendence among French intellectuals.

In France, the *renouveau catholique* ("Catholic renewal"), the longing for a new immediacy in Catholic theology and religious practice, far outweighs the desire to invent new mythologies. An essay on the state of French Catholicism in the German magazine *Die Tat* describes this movement with unabashed admiration: "Without a doubt, Catholicism is advancing; it is . . . in the position of conqueror . . . Its known followers amount to at most 10 million, but these zealously spread the propaganda and believe themselves to be fulfilling a mission. More and more, Catholicism is becoming a movement with its own art, economic beliefs, and responsibility for the world" (Hartmann, 886). Even a novel that breaks as many moral taboos as Jouhandeau's *Monsieur Godeau Intime* cannot do without at least one protagonist who wishes to sanctify the everyday world through acts of Christian charity: "Eliane devoted herself entirely to God and to the sick. The community and the hospice saw her as a saint that the Church would one day beatify: she loved God not as 'a being' that one has heard about and whose existence one is supposed to believe in, but as a being that one has met on earth, whose face one has seen and whose voice one has heard in youth, with whom one has played on a mountainside as a child, and in whose intimacy one has never ceased to live in the depths of one's heart" (Jouhandeau, 13). As a reactivation of traditional concepts of Transcendence, the *renouveau catholique* pays specific attention to this motif of the world's sanctification. It promotes the (re)transformation of Immanence into Transcendence. Such a form of religiosity explains why French intellectuals are becoming ever more interested in Christianity's mystical tradition, in which the experience of God is brought to the highest—and most uncanny—degree of subjective closeness and intensity. French theologians initiate an effort to promote the Spanish mystic and poet Saint John of the Cross to the status of a Doctor Ecclesiae Universalis (*Catholicisme*, 446), and the Vatican document in which Pope Pius XI confirms the Church's favorable decision on Saint John's behalf indeed emphasizes the theme of the world's sanctification: "Some of his works and epistles, despite the complexity of their arguments . . ., are so adapted to the reader's understanding that they can serve as an orientation and school for those faithful souls who wish to attain a more perfect life" ("Sanctus Ioannes," 380). In the context of the *renouveau catholique,* the first novel by Georges Bernanos, an insurance agent with more religious ardor than stylistic subtlety, marks an important event. It tells the story of an intellectually naive, ethically heroic village priest named Donissan, whose many efforts to rescue souls and bodies in the name of the Lord, and whose multiple acts aimed at sanctifying the everyday world, fail dismally. But Donissan's life gains significance and meaning from his— theologically problematic—insight that human existence, without knowing it, is part of an eternal battle between God and the Devil: "The world is not a well-organized machine. God throws us between Satan and himself, as his last rampart. It is through us that, for centuries and centuries, the same hatred has striven to reach him; it is in poor human flesh that the ineffable murder is consummated. Ah! As high and as far as prayer and love can lift us, we take Satan with us, attached to our flanks—a horrible companion, erupting in peals of laughter!" (Bernanos, 190). None of Donissan's attempts to sanctify the world is noticeably successful. The *renouveau catholique*—like all the other neoreligious movements of the day—has no real interest in the possibility that God, angels, or saints might intervene and actively change the course of worldly events. [see **Action = Impotence (Tragedy)**] Individual existence is supposed to be significantly affected by religion, whereas the social and the political worlds remain out of its reach. For if the absorption of Transcendence into Immanence means ultimately giving back to Transcendence some of its former importance, this occurs within the frame-condition of an "incommensurability of earthly and religious actions"—as Max Brod, Kafka's editor, describes it (Brod, 305). As if seeking to become an emblem of this very incommensurability, the Twenty-Seventh International Eucharistic Congress takes place in Chicago, the new capital of organized crime. [see **Center = Periphery (Infinitude)**] Is Al Capone's city being sanctified when, on Monday, June 21, John Cardinal Bonzano, the archbishop of Chicago, celebrates Mass in Soldiers Field Stadium, accompanied by a choir of 60,000 parochial-school children?

Related Entries

Bars, Bullfighting, Elevators, Gramophones, Movie Palaces, Stars, Timepieces, Wireless Communication, Center vs. Periphery, Present vs. Past, Uncertainty vs. Reality, Action = Impotence (Tragedy), Center = Periphery (Infinitude), Immanence = Transcendence (Death)

References

António de Alcântara Machado, "Ano 1926." In Alcântara Machado, *Obras,* vol. 1: *Prosa preparatória; Cavaquinho e Saxofone.* Rio de Janeiro, 1983.

Louis Aragon, *Le paysan de Paris.* Paris, 1926.

Erich Auerbach, "Racine und die Leidenschaften." *Germanisch-romanische Monatsschrift* 14 (1926): 371–380.

Johannes R. Becher, *Maschinenrhythmen.* Berlin, 1926.

Georges Bernanos, *Sous le soleil de Satan* (1926). Paris, 1973.

Max Brod, "Nachwort zur ersten Ausgabe" (1926). In Franz Kafka, *Das Schloss.* Frankfurt, 1968.

Catholicisme hier, aujourd'hui, demain, vol. 6. Paris, 1967.

Jean Cocteau, *Orphée: Tragédie en un acte et un intervalle* (1926). Paris, 1927.

Ernesto Forzano, *Rapsodia Fascista.* Genoa, 1926.

Sigmund Freud, "Psycho-Analysis" (1926). In *The Standard Edition of the Complete Psychological Works,* vol. 20. London, 1959.

Federico García Lorca, "Reyerta" (1926). In García Lorca, *Obras completas.* Madrid, 1971.

Hans Grimm, *Volk ohne Raum,* vol. 2. Munich, 1926.

Hans Ulrich Gumbrecht, "'I redentori della vittoria': Über den Ort Fiumes in der Genealogie des Faschismus." In Hans Ulrich Gumbrecht, Friedrich Kittler, and Bernhard Siegert, eds., *Der Dichter als Kommandant: D'Annunzio erobert Fiume*. Munich, 1996.

Hans Hartmann, "Vom französischen Katholizismus." *Die Tat: Monatsschrift für die Zukunft deutscher Kultur* 17, no. 12 (March 1926): 881–890.

Gerhart Hauptmann, *Dorothea Angermann*. Berlin, 1926.

Hinkepott, "Die deutsche Irredenta." *Die Tat: Monatsschrift für die Zukunft deutscher Kultur* 17, no. 10 (January 1926): 772–775.

Adolf Hitler, *Mein Kampf* (1926). Munich, 1941.

Marcel Jouhandeau, *Monsieur Godeau Intime*. Paris, 1926.

Harry Graf Kessler, *Tagebücher, 1918–1937*. Frankfurt, 1961.

Fritz Lang, *Metropolis* (1926). New York, 1973.

D. H. Lawrence, *The Plumed Serpent* (1926). London, 1933.

Theodor Lessing, "Biene und Wespe oder Bürgerlich und Romantisch" (1926). In Lessing, *"Ich warf eine Flaschenpost ins Eismeer der Geschichte": Essays und Feuilletons, 1923–1933*. Neuwied, 1986.

Maurice Maeterlinck, *La vie des termites*. Paris, 1926.

Henri de Montherlant, *Les Bestiaires* (1926). Paris, 1929.

Henri de Montherlant, *Album Montherlant*, ed. Pierre Sipriot. Paris, 1979.

"Sanctus Ioannes a Cruce confessor ex ordine Carmelitarum excalceatorum, Doctor Ecclesiae Universalis renuntiatur" (1926). *Acta Apostolicae Sedis, Annus XVIII*, vol. 18.

Jules Supervielle, *Le voleur d'enfants*. Paris, 1926.

Heinrich Zimmer, "Zur Rolle des Yoga in der geistigen Welt Indiens." *Deutsche Vierteljahrsschrift für Literaturwissenschaft und Geistesgeschichte* 4 (1926): 21–57.

INDIVIDUALITY VS. COLLECTIVITY

Individuality, according to a frequently expressed opinion, is not strong enough to maintain its independence against a hostile and overwhelmingly powerful society. Seemingly unaware of how widespread this impression is among intellectuals in the political and cultural centers of the West [see **Center vs. Periphery**], the journalist António de Alcântara Machado views the individual's inability to cultivate a personal sphere of thought and emotion as a symptom of a specifically Brazilian form of provincialism: "We still suffer from a very narrow and old-fashioned social environment, in which everybody knows and fears everybody else. It is a provincial world that confuses truth with boldness and tactlessness with honesty. The individual sphere is not allowed to have secrets. The whole community sees every movement and overhears every word" (196). Robert Musil makes the opposite association. For him, it is the almost hyperbolic ability to play all the roles offered by modern society that gives Ulrich, the hero of his novel in progress, the flair of a particularly urban character—but it is this same worldliness that makes it impossible for Ulrich to develop an individual identity. Ulrich "discovers that his existence is contingent, that he can see—but never reach—its essence. Existence is not and will never be complete. It can adopt all possible forms without ever losing the impression of being contingent" (Fontana, 382). The plot of Bertolt Brecht's drama *Mann ist Mann* is an extreme version of the same idea. Some colonial soldiers transform a modest worker and family man into a fighting machine that combines

the aggressive drive of an archaic animal with the technical perfection of
a guided missile:

> And already I feel inside me
> The wish to sink my teeth
> Into the enemy's neck,
> An instinct to slaughter
> Families and providers,
> To fulfill the task
> Of the conqueror.
> Hand me your soldier's pass.
>
> (Brecht, *Mann ist Mann*, 376)

To deprive the conquered of their soldier's passes means to withdraw
even the minimal identity that society normally leaves at every individual's disposition. Identity cards of every type have thus become symbols
for the strained relation between Collectivity and Individuality. The
individual's liberty is sometimes reduced to the exclusive (yet limited)
right to move in space, and even this slight independence must be confirmed by a bureaucratic document. A person's presence can never substitute for an identity card: "'No sailor's card?' He opened his eyes wide in
sheer astonishment, as if he had seen a ghost. The tone of his voice
carried the same strange amazement as if he had said, 'What? You don't
believe there's such a thing as seawater?' Apparently, it was incomprehensible to him that there could be a human being with neither a passport nor a sailor's card" (Traven, 14). [see **Ocean Liners**]

Hopes for a better future are based on the invention of new social
structures or on the emergence of collective movements, rather than on
individual action. Even great individual achievements of the past, like
Bismarck's forging of a new German state, are expected to find their
continuation in collective activities: "Germany is alive. The aristocrats
have abandoned the nation when guidance was most needed; but the
people, whose character Bismarck did not understand until it was too
late, have endured and thus have rescued his work" (Ludwig, 683).
Those few forms of Individuality which provide relative independence
with respect to society hardly ever contribute to changes in the sphere of
Collectivity. One such form—silence—achieves independence at the price
of isolation. None of the multiple and widely admired rituals through

which individuals achieve self-affirmation by confronting death fulfills a pragmatic function within society. Pilots, for example, master their planes or end up yielding to them, but this struggle never offers any concrete service to a third party. Most of the idolized and imitated stars are incapable of sustaining even an average family life. [see **Airplanes, Stars, Silence vs. Noise, Immanence = Transcendence (Death)**] Only those public protagonists who are not only unreachable but impenetrable seem to be protected against society's manipulations. Stars with this particular quality contemptuously pay society back for all the slings and arrows that normal individuals have to endure. This is why Heinrich Mann—among many other authors—considers Suzanne Lenglen to be much more than just a tennis champion: "One could find Suzanne Lenglen ugly, but her courage is so fresh that nobody ever perceives her as plain . . . Her eye is infallible, and her body has the lightness of a gaze. It is as if she had wings that carry her everywhere, everywhere on the tennis court and everywhere in the world. She is untroubled by the world from which we suffer—and this is what makes her so beautiful" (Mann, 304). Like Heinrich Mann, António de Alcântara Machado reveres Suzanne Lenglen as a symbol of absolute liberty—though he doesn't even know how to spell her name: "Victorious in every single championship, Susanne Senglen, the queen of tennis, shares the fate of her noble sisters. Often the newspapers write about potential husbands, and they even announce precise wedding dates . . . In reality, Susanne Senglen remains unmarried. But she doesn't even bother to deny those ever-circulating rumors about a change in her civil status. And this is the right thing to do. Instead of being married to a duke or to a prince, she maintains her own absolute freedom" (Alcântara Machado, 138).

In André Malraux's *La tentation de l'Occident (The Temptation of the West),* a Chinese traveler argues that in Europe the relation between art and society is filled with tension, whereas in Asia the two spheres interact harmoniously. The reason for this difference, according to him, lies in the European obsession with imagining society as a sphere of action: "With you, . . . admiration results from an action. For us, it is only the consciousness of existing in accordance with the most beautiful mode. Through the artforms that you once called sublime, you express an action and not a state. This state, which we know only by virtue of what it grants to those who possess it, this purity, this disintegration of the soul in the bosom of eternal light—Westerners have never pursued it or sought to express it" (Malraux, 35). [see **Action vs. Impotence**] From an American perspective, a distant and unresolved relation between individual and society can become an object of awe—in the sense of both admiration and disapproval. This ambiguity permeates a description of Parisian academic life by the students of Stanford University: "As for college life at the University of Paris, there is none in the American sense of the term. There is no campus . . . There is no college spirit, no athletic teams, no intercollegiate debating, not even a college newspaper . . . The University of Paris is not 'collegiate.' It has no paternalistic restrictions or campus traditions. Only for the individual student of real ability and ambition is it a place of study" *(1926 Quad)*. Once the fear of solitude is overcome, however, extreme individual isolation can turn into an unambiguous object of desire. The idea of "being detached from all human relationships" makes Fridolin, the protagonist of Arthur Schnitzler's *Traumnovelle (Dream Story)* feel both uneasy and liberated: "Although this idea made him shudder a bit, it also reassured him, for it seemed to free him from all responsibility, and to loosen all bonds of human relationship" (Schnitzler, 31). Luigi Pirandello's novel *Uno, nessuno e centomila (One, No One, and One Hundred Thousand)* is a highly sophisticated—and radical—exercise in this type of reflection. Disillusionment with society launches the protagonist into a career of willful alienation. He has discovered that, instead of consisting of a single public persona, his identity is different for each of his friends and relatives (hence the title of the book). Thus, he wants not only to distance himself from society, but also to repress the self-observation that gives him an agonizing feeling of fragmentation. He wants to shed his familiar self. "So I wanted to be alone. Without myself. I mean without that me that I already knew, or thought I knew. Alone with a certain stranger, whom I already obscurely felt I would be unable to get rid of and who was myself: the stranger inseparable from myself" (Pirandello, 15). The ultimate alienation from society—and the most subtle form of revenge against it—is achieved toward the end of Pirandello's novel, when the hero can claim that he has methodically given up and destroyed all the structures and habits (including property and language) that normally make an individual a member of a community: "Not only completely alienated from myself and from everything I call mine, but with a horror of remaining anyone at all, possessing anything at all. No longer wanting anything, I knew that I could not speak" (225).

However far such cultivation of Individuality may go, the social roles it produces are hopelessly heroic forms of resistance—nothing but relics of a distant past. [see **Present vs. Past**] The future, in contrast, is invariably associated with ideas and ideals of Collectivity. Collectivity thus becomes a site of experimentation, because those who favor it over Individuality are not sure which principles could—or should—serve as the foundation for a new society. When Adolf Hitler postulates that "the instinct of preserving the species is the first cause of the formation of human communities; this makes the State a folk organism, and not an economic organization" (Hitler, 165), "folk" and "State" are synonymous and refer to a biologically constituted group. For Carl Schmitt, in contrast, a clear distinction between State and people is an elementary precondition for any legal situation. He thus reserves the sphere of politics for the State alone (Schmitt, 4–5). Likewise, Ernst Jünger's war memoirs evoke the State—and not the people or the nation—as a quasi-transcendent point of reference for the military actions he describes: "The frightful thunder of battle is still increasing. It is as if it wanted to exploit its ultimate, insane potential. Within our limited space, the State that we represent erects a likeness of its unlimited violence before our senses, filling our bodies with its right to power and expansion" (Jünger, 107). Friedrich Panzer, a historian of language and rector of the University of Heidelberg, rejects both the formal definition of "Collectivity" as State and the association of Collectivity with a biologically grounded concept of "people." After denying, in unusually strong terms, that the notion of "race" has any intellectual legitimacy, he proposes that each individual language be seen as embodying the unity of people, nation, and culture: "This is the decisive fact. At all times—and especially in our modern, highly intellectualized times—a nation derives its essential ground from its language" (Panzer, 6). Only on the political Left does the question regarding the unifying principle for social groups find a unanimous response: solidarity will come from economic equality. This is the program and the justification for the Soviet Union's dramatic social changes, which intellectuals find so fascinating. During his visit to Moscow, Ernst Toller is happy to see that people wear cheap clothes, that everybody is earning small salaries (although Toller is astonished to see that some disparities persist), and that teachers and students are supposed to have the same rights in the classroom (Toller, 92, 113, 127, 185). Opinions diverge, however, when it comes to the rights which a socialist Collectivity is supposed to have over Individuality. Toller cannot quite approve of a legal system that sentences a young woman to ten years of prison because she does not denounce her husband for being a spy in the service of the Polish government: "'And why didn't you report your husband? Why didn't you?' asked the supervisor who accompanied me. 'I will not betray my own husband,' she replied. The supervisor, a Communist, shook his head. For him the collective stands higher than the individual. He would not hesitate, he told me, to shoot his best friend, if this friend had betrayed the goals of the collective" (Toller, 142).

A literary example of this considerable instability in the relation between Collectivity and Individuality is the heterogeneous style of the letter which K. in Franz Kafka's *Schloss* receives from the castle's administration: "It was not a consistent letter. In part it dealt with [K.] as with a free man whose independence was recognized . . . But there were other places in which he was directly or indirectly treated as a minor employee, hardly visible to the heads of departments" (23–24). In his book *La vie des termites,* Nobel Prize winner Maurice Maeterlinck works to develop a scientific discourse which so eagerly stages itself as an allegory of sociological problems and their different political interpretations that the reader risks overlooking the primary biological content. This is Maeterlinck's general characterization of the termites' social life: "A new sort of destiny—perhaps the cruelest social destiny—has been added to those which we already know and which hitherto sufficed for us. No rest except in the final sleep; illness itself is not permitted; and every weakness amounts to a death sentence. Communism has become cannibalism and then coprophagy, for under Communism one feeds, so to speak, on excrement. It is hell such as the winged hosts of a beehive could imagine it" (Maeterlinck, 155–156). Nobody describes more clearly the situation from which all these problems and discourses emerge than the literary critic I. A. Richards. Like most intellectuals, he starts out by claiming a hierarchical relation between Collectivity and Individuality: "We must recognize that man is a social being, that only by a dehumanizing fiction we do regard him as an individual." What makes Richards' statement unusual, however, is his willingness to admit that a convincing model of a new social order is not apparent in the current situation: "Tradition is weakening. Moral authorities are not as well backed by beliefs as they were; their sanctions are declining in force. We are in need of something to take the place of the old order" (Richards, 40–41).

Since there are no generally accepted collective ideals or goals, private interests easily dominate the scene. But because the breakdown of the collective sphere is a much-feared possibility, aggressive mass instincts brutally target those who dare to activate such fear. This is the mechanism behind the case of Theodor Lessing, a fifty-four-year-old associate professor of philosophy at the Technical University of Hannover. In May and June, hundreds of nationalist students armed with oak maces occupy the classroom where Lessing is scheduled to teach; they persecute and physically threaten him on his way home from the university; and finally, thousands of students announce that they will transfer to the Technical University in nearby Braunschweig if Lessing is not fired (Marwedel, 289ff.). During the previous year, Lessing twice provoked the unstable collective psyche. He published a newspaper article on the newly elected *Reichspräsident*, Paul von Hindenburg, in which he ironically praised this war hero as the epitome of a specifically German style of thickheadedness. And in his press coverage of the trial against the mass murderer Haarmann, Lessing not only discussed the relation between crime and society, but also revealed a disturbing collaboration between Haarmann and the Hannover legal authorities, who had hired him as a police spy. [see **Murder**] The point of convergence between Lessing's interventions is apparent: focusing on two very different social situations, they both underscore how strained the relations are between Individuality and Collectivity. But only in conjunction with his Jewishness do Lessing's publications incite the national Right and its press organs. As in so many other persecutions of individuals, this act of aggression against an outsider substitutes for the nonexistent "national" unity. In mid-June, the Ministry of Culture in Berlin decides that Lessing's professorship should be downgraded to a paid research contract.

The only social roles that fit easily into the collective sphere are those devoid of any agency. This is why the status of the employee is among the most successful formulas of the day; this is why assembly lines have become an object of pride and a topic of intellectual conversation; and it is the relinquishing of independence that makes "intoxicating" new forms of dance so popular. In contrast, asserting the importance of individual instruments and musicians makes the ensemble work of jazz orchestras precarious. [see **Assembly Lines, Dancing, Employees, Jazz**] Rather than this difficult balance, most people want to experience how it feels to "irresistibly" become "part of a greater force" (Jünger, 102–103). But nobody knows how such irresistible incorporation can avoid being potentially dangerous. The manipulation of the masses by individuals thus becomes a topic of public concern. While Spanish intellectuals generally admire Miguel de Unamuno in his role as "excitator Hispaniae" (Curtius 245–246), they seem quite relieved that Unamuno voices his exhortations in exile, beyond the French border. The *Revista de Occidente* publishes a satirical article about the theater of the future, in which so-called *moduladores* engineer every single reaction of the audience: "The purpose of a drama . . . was to suggest a simple or complex existential state, and once the *modulador* had been informed of the required degree of intensity, it was incumbent on him to produce the necessary emotion" (172). [see **Engineers**]

Siegfried Kracauer, who suspects even architecture of illegitimately manipulating the population ("Zwei Flächen," 12), has no problem in hailing Martin Buber as a "leader of Jewish, especially of Zionist, youth" ("Die Bibel auf Deutsch," 173). [see **Individuality = Collectivity (Leader)**] What seems like a self-contradiction is just a symptom for the convergence of two tensions that haunt intellectuals. Much hope is invested in a morally justifiable Collectivity of the future, but there is little evidence that society will ever manage to devise such a structure. There is a vague desire for a leader who, emerging from Collectivity, will provide guidance and orientation, but this desire is contained by an almost phobic reaction against whoever dares to take an individual initiative that may have consequences for others. Mild irony is the attitude that the aristocratic characters of René Schickele's novel *Maria Capponi* display in response to this problem: "'Indeed,' said the duke, 'all we can hope for is a revolution. From below or from above or, if necessary, both at the same time. We're stuck. Nothing is working. Something has to happen soon, for the sake of humanity . . . Here they come,' he said, pointing to a group of fishermen who had just entered the room. 'They will be our new masters . . . The Lord be with you, fellows—we all had to begin somewhere'" (Schickele, 250). Bertolt Brecht, who is about to find his political identity as a Communist, likewise chooses an ironic tone to speak about his own longing for a leader: "The one bad thing about great men (because great men are indeed a bad thing) is that there are never enough of them" (Brecht, "Aus Notizbüchern," 16). In contrast, Karl Holl, the head of Berlin's Humboldt University, quotes Hegel, Prussia's state-philosopher, when he speaks—without irony but with obvious tautology—about great individuals: "The great protagonists of world history are those who, instead of focusing on subjective imaginings and opinions, have willed and achieved what was appropriate and necessary—those who know what is timely and necessary because they have seen it with their inner eye" (Holl, 19).

Related Entries

Airplanes, Assembly Lines, Dancing, Employees, Engineers, Ocean Liners, Murder, Stars, Action vs. Impotence, Center vs. Periphery, Present vs. Past, Silence vs. Noise, Individuality = Collectivity (Leader), Immanence = Transcendence (Death)

References

António de Alcântara Machado, "Ano de 1926." In Alcântara Machado, *Obras*, vol. 1: *Prosa preparatória; Cavaquinho e Saxofone*. Rio de Janeiro, 1983.

Associated Students of Stanford University, eds., *The 1926 Quad*.

Bertolt Brecht, *Mann ist Mann* (1926). In Brecht, *Gesammelte Werke*, vol. 1. Frankfurt, 1967.

Bertolt Brecht, "Aus Notizbüchern, 1919–1926." In Brecht, *Gesammelte Werke*, vol. 20. Frankfurt, 1967.

Ernst Robert Curtius, "Unamuno" (1926). In Curtius, *Kritische Essays zur europäischen Literatur*. Bern, 1950.

Oskar Maurus Fontana, "Was arbeiten Sie? Gespräch mit Robert Musil" (1926). In Anton Kaes, ed., *Weimarer Republik: Manifeste und Dokumente zur deutschen Literatur, 1918–1933*. Stuttgart, 1983.

Adolf Hitler, *Mein Kampf* (1926). Munich, 1941.

Karl Holl, "Über Begriff und Bedeutung der 'dämonischen Persönlichkeit'" (Lecture delivered in Berlin on August 3, 1925). *Deutsche Vierteljahrsschrift für Literaturwissenschaft und Geistesgeschichte* 4 (1926): 1–19.

Ernst Jünger, *Feuer und Blut: Ein kleiner Ausschnitt aus einer grossen Schlacht* (1926). Hamburg, 1941.

Franz Kafka, *Das Schloss* (1926). Hamburg, 1968.

Siegfried Kracauer, "Die Bibel auf Deutsch" (1926). In Kracauer, *Das Ornament der Masse: Essays*. Frankfurt, 1977.

Siegfried Kracauer, "Zwei Flächen" (1926). In Kracauer, *Das Ornament der Masse: Essays*. Frankfurt, 1977.

Emil Ludwig, *Bismarck: Geschichte eines Kämpfers*. Berlin, 1926.

Maurice Maeterlinck, *La vie des termites*. Paris, 1929.

André Malraux, *La tentation de l'Occident*. Paris, 1929.

Heinrich Mann, *Sieben Jahre: Chronik der Gedanken und Vorgänge*. Berlin, 1929.

Rainer Marwedel, *Theodor Lessing, 1872–1933: Eine Biographie*. Neuwied, 1987.

Friedrich Panzer, *Volkstum und Sprache*. Lecture delivered at the University of Heidelberg, November 22. Frankfurt, 1926.

Luigi Pirandello, *Uno, nessuno e centomila* (1926). Milan, 1936.

Revista de Occidente.

I. A. Richards, *Science and Poetry* (1926). New York, 1970.

René Schickele, *Maria Capponi*. Munich, 1926.

Carl Schmitt, *Die Kernfrage des Völkerbundes*. Berlin, 1926.

Arthur Schnitzler, *Traumnovelle*. Berlin, 1926.

Ernst Toller, "Russische Reisebilder" (1926). In Toller, *Quer durch: Reisebilder und Reden*. Munich, 1978.

MALE VS. FEMALE

Heinrich Mann rather likes the fashion of bobbed hair: "Everyone knows that bobbed hair is not only attractive, but also practical" (Mann, 300). If only it hadn't been invented in America! [see **Center vs. Periphery, Americans in Paris**] The association between bobbed hair and the image of the "American girl" triggers fears of cultural decay which European intellectuals fight with brave attempts at self-persuasion: "It is not yet completely clear whether we Europeans are doomed to head toward the American kind of derailment. We have old habits that can be revived. The younger generation, however, not only has a right to emphasize the physical aspects of life, but fulfills, in doing so, the higher mission of our time—and this is true above all for women. By playing tennis, they help reinvigorate—as they ought to—a formerly dominant continent. The women's task is an essentially romantic one, perfectly worthy of them" (Mann, 309). Fashion-conscious women wear short hair and short skirts because—at least according to the current interpretation—they have come to share with men the burden of physical labor and the joy of physical exercise. [see **Present vs. Past**] Girls look almost like boys—and this hardly ever creates difficulties in making distinctions. For better or for worse, the new closeness of the sexes reduces rather than increases the tensions between them. In such an atmosphere, sexual attraction can no longer be taken for granted, and it is indeed often replaced by friendship. "These girls dress much the way boys do; their hair is just as short. Since they also move and think alike, both sexes will soon have the same faces, and their bodies will eventually differ only in the most elementary aspects. What will happen if, in addition, they fall in love with each other? They won't do it out of any wish to be troublesome; they'll do it because they have no other friends left on earth. Young as they are, they already have to comfort each other. They confuse friendship with camaraderie" (309–310). [see **Dancing**] In Mann's view, the one positive aspect of the convergence between the sexes—and the obverse of the decrease in erotic tension—is the vanishing of mutual aggression: "We expect the battle between men and women to intensify in an era that is no longer familiar with humanism—an era which has just realized that protecting humanism is once again a painful necessity. Strangely enough, however, the sexes get along better today than in many other periods in history" (305).

Even more astonishingly, this shift toward a friendly tone between the sexes occurs when women and men are engaging for the first time in serious competition—for certain types of employment and for athletic records. [see **Endurance**] The classified section in the *Berliner Tageblatt* shows that women are about to conquer considerable territory at middle and upper management levels. Although Gebrüder Knopf, Karlsruhe, will accept only male applicants for the position of manager in their financial department, the North German Rubber-Coat Factory, which is seeking to fill a comparable position, will consider both men and women. The descriptions of secretarial jobs, now typically occupied by women [see **Employees**], often prescribe a level of competence that goes far beyond the tasks of typewriting and receiving visitors: "Starting ASAP, our company will hire an experienced and well-trained stenotypist for a position as secretary. Only female applicants with experience in the commercial sector and a wide-ranging general education will be considered." In Argentina, an ongoing parliamentary debate regarding civil rights and the female sex inspires the magazine *Caras y Caretas* to publish a photo feature about women in unusual professions: they appear as representatives in government, bricklayers, police agents, taxi drivers, railway conductors, sailors, and jockeys. In a more or less subtle way, however, the readers learn that this diversity by no means reflects social reality. An introductory note expresses the thanks of *Caras y Caretas* to three actresses for their collaboration, and the comments accompanying the photographs of their beautiful bodies—in professional disguises—betray the most old-fashioned type of male condescension: "Those who do not wish to be buried in bureaucracy will pursue manual professions which, like that of bricklayer, can still be edifying." Certain professions that adopt a new image of femininity do so because they rigorously eliminate agency from nonphysical work—and because roles without agency or physical work are invariably taken to be female. The language and behavior of K.'s assistants in Kafka's *Schloss,* for example, illustrate this fact. Likewise, the air of moral depravity which surrounds the figure of the gigolo (von Soden and Schmidt, 13) shows that gender equality remains a purely utopian claim.

Predictably, the few authentic innovations in the relation between the sexes encounter multiple forms of resistance within a set of unchanged basic values and social structures. This inertia is mainly represented by the institution of the family, for which gender equality is seen as a source of instability. It is no accident that it has become a literary convention to present marriage as the result of random encounters [see **Railroads**]: a high degree of insecurity, which is manifest in ever-increasing divorce rates, and disillusionment with concepts such as *Kameradschaftsehe,* or "marriage out of camaraderie" (*Die wilden Zwanziger,* 112, 124), seem to be the unavoidable price of gender equality. The spouses in Schnitzler's *Traumnovelle (Dream Story)* are both willing to consider extramarital adventures as nothing but dreams, in order to achieve a precarious reconciliation. Especially in Germany, a passionate public debate concerning the legalization of abortion emerges as a metonym for this crisis. Opinions, books, and films representing a broad range of political opinions (von Soden and Schmidt, 105) agree that sharing a life as a couple no longer implies parenthood as a "natural" consequence and obligation. For others, it is the experience of the Great War—rather than intrinsic problems between partners—that accounts for such a basic change in childbearing patterns. Those who are in favor of making abortion a legally protected option argue that the status of a single parent (with its social marginalization) creates an intolerably asymmetrical situation for women: "When people assert that abortion is a crime, one might object that in most cases it is motivated by shame, fear, weakness, moral conflict, and often the prejudice against 'fallen' women. The negative attitude toward life that has emerged from the war has weakened the desire to have children. Shall we procreate new victims for the mania of extermination?" (Gerloff, 795).

In the media, the feeling prevails that women and men should have the same rights and should be entitled to choose their social and professional situations independently of their sex. It is not ideologically motivated objections but procedural problems and institutional inertia that prevent this ideal from becoming a reality. For example, the constitution of Mount Holyoke, a women's college in Massachusetts, defines the school's "purpose" without any gender-specific restrictions: "The object of the Mount Holyoke College Community shall be to provide an all-inclusive organization through which . . . to furnish those conditions which shall best contribute to the spiritual, intellectual, and physical welfare of its members; to foster an intelligent interest in all phases of college citizenship; and by maintaining a government as nearly as possible like that in the world outside, to prepare its members for assuming the duties of active citizenship in their respective political communities" (*Handbook*, 7). No other achievements of Mount Holyoke alumnae are cited as proudly as their activities in the—predominantly male—world of the sciences. "Anti-toxin, which stopped the spread of tetanus in our army overseas, was prepared at the Mulford Laboratory by thirteen Mount Holyoke–trained scientists. That was one time when thirteen was a lucky number for the army . . . A Mount Holyoke woman was a bacteriologist with the Near East relief expedition . . . Mount Holyoke–trained scientists serve in the research laboratories of the country's basic industries" (*Catalogue*, passim). Despite this commitment to gender equality, student life is regulated with a severity that would be ridiculous at any men's college. There are complex rules regarding the conditions under which the young women are allowed to ride in a car [see **Automobiles**], or to walk and hike even in the vicinity of the school ("Students shall not walk in the evening around Upper Lake in groups of less than six, nor with men unless there are at least two couples"; *Handbook*, 28). Even the students' fathers are subject to the gender-based rigor of these rules: "A student wishing to take her father to her room may do so by securing the permission of the superintendent of the house" (40). The institutional ambivalence that is apparent in the way Mount Holyoke organizes its student's lives (a regime that is partly based on religious principles) is not so different from the individual ambivalence with which the German journalist and ex-revolutionary Ernst Toller reacts to women's new lifestyles in the Soviet Union. When it comes to general ideological statements, Toller is of course eager to appear as an enthusiastic advocate of equal rights between the sexes. Whenever he discusses specific situations, however, a male voice, disguised as the voice of reason, comes through. He finds the new Soviet laws against rape excessively harsh (Toller, 135). As a guest at a political rally of revolutionary women, he admires above all the "natural charm" of the speakers (109). And he observes with obvious satisfaction that a tendency toward sexual promiscuity in the years following the October Revolution has recently been countered by a return to more conventional forms of courtship: "During the initial years, the reaction against the constraints of bourgeois hypocrisy was extremely strong. People were searching for the 'full experience of life.' They despised all tenderness as an unnecessary complication, and romantic declarations as merely a veneer over biomechanical processes . . . But the sexes have now returned to a greater degree of mutual respect; they treat each other with more tenderness; they are less promiscuous. They are even writing love letters again . . . Marriages between very young people are frequent, and the number of divorces is decreasing" (146–147).

Gerhart Hauptmann's play *Dorothea Angermann* contains a heavy dose of straightforwardly chauvinistic comments regarding women, but they are all attributed to the least admirable male characters. When Pastor Angermann—who continually invokes the repressive norms of Protestant morality, though he never manages to control his own sexual appetites—learns from his young second wife that Dorothea (her stepdaughter and his daughter) has become pregnant, he reacts with the most archaic claim of male authority: "I have failed to maintain domestic discipline—not only with Dorothea, but also with you, and with all the womenfolk" (Hauptmann, 47). The young academic Herbert Pfannschmidt nobly insists on proposing marriage to Dorothea, but fails to dissuade her from a union with the brutal Mario, the father of her child. And Mario has nothing but scorn for Herbert: "I won—and I couldn't care less about your irony. You just got to know about women" (114). Of course, one cannot blame Hauptmann for the views of his most objectionable protagonists. On the other hand, however, the plot proves them right. Dorothea yields to Mario's advances, and becomes the agent of her own destruction by staying with him—in spite of (or perhaps because of) the humiliations he inflicts on her. The play thus seems to suggest that women are instinctually incapable of accepting that very equality which is owed them in the name of moral law.

In a letter to the poet Kurt Schwitters, the Bauhaus designer Marcel

Breuer makes fun of this situation in which the ideal—or the threat—of a new female identity begins to transform traditional gender stereotypes into an object of intense nostalgic desire. Breuer's parody describes, in strangely broken German, the outsize dimensions of a woman [see **Sobriety vs. Exuberance**] who offers the kind of protection to her male partner which a relationship between two independent persons must exclude. Breuer's nightmarish ideal of the female partner (which, he suggests teasingly, the new demand for gender equality seems to imply) is meant to converge with the archaic dream of an earth mother: "And now I'm looking for a woman. Must be heavy and big, no less than six foot. Trace of a mustache, good at cooking and sewing. No bobbed hair. Preferably in red polka-dot dress, face to match, and above all healthy. Hair black with gray streaks, breasts large. Hands especially must be fat and greasy . . . Name can only be Maria. Above all must have fine soul, feeling for what is tender, understanding for everything, such that I can weep out my pain on her bosom . . . Must enjoy backpacking and always bring a backpack on walks" (*Wechselwirkungen,* 331). Breuer's intuition is correct: none of the mother figures whose images are associated with the new institution of Mother's Day (von Soden and Schmidt, 97) has bobbed hair. If ideal mothers ever did, Adolf Hitler would not recall the days between the death of his "respected" father and that of his "beloved" mother with such intense longing: "Those were the happiest days of my life; they seemed like a dream to me, and so they were. Two years later, my mother's death put a sudden end to all those delightful plans. It came at the end of a long and painful illness that had seemed fatal from the very beginning. Nevertheless, it was a terrible shock to me. I respected my father, but I loved my mother" (Hitler, 16).

Hitler is certainly not the only male writer who worships his mother and thus grants women only one other role—that of prostitute. Prostitutes, for him, are "girls" who are unable to become mothers because they have had contact with Jews. "In no other city of western Europe could the relationship between Jewry and prostitution, and even now the white slave traffic, be studied better than in Vienna, with the possible exception of the seaports of southern France. When walking at night through the streets and alleys of Leopoldsstadt, one could witness at every step things that were unknown to the greater part of the German nation" (Hitler, 63). The plot of Fritz Lang's film *Metropolis* depends on the same binary distinction. On one side is Maria, the motherly protector of the workers' children, surrounded by symbols that emphasize her likeness to the Virgin Mary: "The leader was a girl with the austere countenance of the Virgin, the sweet countenance of a mother. She held two skinny children by the hand" (Lang, 27). Female evil is represented not only by the half-naked dancing girls in the "Club of the Sons" [see **Gomina**] but above all by Maria's double and antagonist, a robot which is programmed to incite the proletarian masses to revolution—and to self-destruction. A true prostitute of the machine age, the mechanical Maria is completely at the disposition of the masters of Metropolis, who financed her manufacture, and she casts an evil spell on all who listen to her. A similar structure defines the status of the female protagonists in Kafka's *Schloss*. As Max Brod's interpretation highlights, "women have (in the language of this novel) 'relations with the castle'—and women's importance derives from these relations, although they cause great confusion for individuals of both sexes" (Kafka, 303). Frieda has been the lover of one of the castle's administrators, and thus, for K., an erotic relationship with her—not unlike an erotic relationship with one's own mother—implies both a promise of protection and a threat of revenge. Woman's dual image as mother and prostitute is not only a literary conceit. In December, Italy's Fascist government imposes new standards of hygiene on the State-run brothels, as well as "a punitive tax on male celibacy" (de Grazia, 43–44). Such institutional measures are no doubt partly inspired by fear stemming from the spread of gender equality, and the government strives to encourage heterosexual relationships by extending as far as possible the traditional asymmetry between the male and the female partners. Virility becomes a general norm for Fascist life and art. The bifurcation of female identity—either mother or prostitute—is officially reduced to its positive pole and unofficially confirmed: "The model of masculinity and seriousness has great power over youths, and when they are summoned by the phantasm of art, they will neither embroider songs and lyrics with feminine intonations nor chatter about the same old love affairs with call girls and maids, nor fiddle around with words to come up with the same old descriptive trifles" (Puccini, 259). [see **Silence vs. Noise**] A decree of May 21 states that women should regard family matters and acts of charity as their natural fields of action, and excludes women from the Italian political world by prohibiting them from wearing the black shirt of the Fascist Party (*Chronik,* 94). No wonder then that Anna, the only female character in Ernesto Forzano's play *Rapsodia Fascista (Fascist Rhapsody),* is hoping that her lover, the young Fascist Orazio, will readily trade his ideological convictions for her hand and for the seat in parliament which her socialist father is able to offer him: "*Anna:* My Orazio a member of parliament! . . . How beautiful! . . . Wife of a deputy! . . . How happy I am! . . . *Orazio:* Don't torture me, Anna! Enough! Enough! . . . You're digging into my soul with your words . . . digging a hole . . . deeper . . . and more searing . . . than the one . . . that the enemy machine-gun dug . . . into my flesh!" (Forzano, 67–68).

In D. H. Lawrence's novel *The Plumed Serpent,* such asymmetry between the overwhelmingly strong General Cipriano and his wife, Kate, who maintains a permanent state of unconditional surrender, is hailed as the most perfect form of marriage. Not even the momentary bliss of an orgasm is conceded to Kate: "As she sat in silence, casting the old, twilit Pan-power over her, she felt herself submitting, succumbing. He was once more the old dominant male, shadowy, intangible, looming suddenly tall, and covering the sky, making a darkness that was himself and nothing but himself, the Pan male. And she was swooned prone beneath, perfect in her proneness. It was the ancient phallic mystery, the ancient god-devil of the male Pan . . . Ah! and what a mystery of prone submission, on her part, this huge erection would imply! Submission absolute, like the earth under the sky. Beneath an over-arching absolute. Ah! what a marriage! How terrible! and how complete!" (Lawrence, 332–333). The literary General Cipriano becomes the model according to which Lawrence's wife, Frieda, chooses her lover, Angelo Ravagli, a lieutenant in the Italian army (Maddox, 388–389). If Frieda, a woman of imposing weight and stature, has long played the role of protective mother for the sickly novelist, she now gives him the opportunity both to despise and to desire her in the role of prostitute.

Related Entries

Americans in Paris, Automobiles, Dancing, Employees, Gomina, Railroads, Center vs. Periphery, Present vs. Past, Sobriety vs. Exuberance, *Silence vs. Noise,* Male = Female (Gender Trouble)

References

Berliner Tageblatt.

Max Brod, "Nachwort zur ersten Ausgabe." In Franz Kafka, *Das Schloss* (1926). Frankfurt, 1968.

Caras y Caretas.

Chronik 1926: Tag für Tag in Wort und Bild. Dortmund, 1985.

Victoria de Grazia, *How Fascism Ruled Women: Italy, 1922–1945.* Berkeley, 1992.

Ernesto Forzano, *Rapsodia Fascista.* Genoa, 1926.

Meta Gerloff, "Der Frauenwille in der sozial-hygienischen und Kulturgesetzgebung." *Die Tat* 17, no. 10 (January 1926): 793–797.

Gerhart Hauptmann, *Dorothea Angermann.* Berlin, 1926.

Adolf Hitler, *Mein Kampf* (1926). Munich, 1941.

Franz Kafka, *Das Schloss* (1926). Frankfurt, 1968.

Fritz Lang, *Metropolis* (1926). New York, 1973.

D. H. Lawrence, *The Plumed Serpent* (1926). London, 1933.

Brenda Maddox, *D. H. Lawrence: The Story of a Marriage.* New York, 1994.

Heinrich Mann, *1926.* In Mann, *Sieben Jahre: Chronik der Gedanken und Vorgänge.* Berlin, 1929.

Mount Holyoke College, *Catalogue, 1925–1926.* South Hadley, Mass., 1926.

Mount Holyoke College, *Students' Handbook of Information.* South Hadley, Mass., 1926.

Mario Puccini, "From the Great Debate on Fascism and Culture: *Critica Fascista*" (1926). *Stanford Italian Review* 7 (1990): 257–260.

Arthur Schnitzler, *Die Traumnovelle.* Berlin, 1926.

Ernst Toller, "Russische Reisebilder" (1926). In Toller, *Quer durch.* Vienna, 1978.

Kristine von Soden and Maruta Schmidt, eds., *Neue Frauen: Die zwanziger Jahre.* Berlin, 1988.

Wechselwirkungen: Ungarische Avantgarde in der Weimarer Republik. Marburg, 1986.

Die Wilden Zwanziger: Weimar und die Welt, 1919–1933. Berlin, 1986.

PRESENT VS. PAST

The future occupies a subordinate position with respect to the past and the present. There is little practical (and even less philosophical) optimism left concerning the possibility of predicting the future. In the opinion of some people, change is occurring so rapidly that any kind of prognostication is impossible: "During the past five years, film has developed at a pace that makes predictions dangerous, for it will probably exceed even our wildest imaginations. Film never stands still. What was invented yesterday looks old-fashioned today" (Lang, 222). In these circumstances, the classical style of historico-philosophical speculation and its Marxist applications rapidly lose their appeal. Traveling in the Soviet Union, for example, the German Communist Ernst Toller encounters a general frustration among his hosts because the long-awaited German revolution has not yet arrived—and because Toller himself is no longer optimistic enough to argue that such an expectation is still warranted (Toller, 115). He feels that certain political concessions made by the Soviet government—among them, sanctioning the official cult around Lenin's embalmed corpse—jeopardize the possibility of transforming the Communist utopia into a reality: "There are calculations that just do not work in the long run. For a short while, they produce a good yield—but one day it becomes clear that they have not accomplished enough. One should not sacrifice the future to present concerns" (107). Teleological arguments coming from the political Right and predicting dramatic decay instead of society-wide contentment look no more convincing than the overly bright prophecies of the Communists. Robert Musil—comparing his own novel in progress, *Der Mann ohne Eigenschaften (The Man without Qualities)*, to Oswald Spengler's *Untergang des Abendlandes (Decline of the West)*—ironically admits: "I laugh . . . at all these declines of the West and their prophets!" (Musil, 382–383).

From Europe, the traditional center of the Western world, the United States and the Soviet Union may look like two different versions of the future [see **Center vs. Periphery**]. But chronologically speaking, these versions of the future are realities of the Present. Since it appears so surprising and complex, this Present attracts unusual amounts of intellectual and emotional energy. Especially in Germany, the Present is an object of intense philosophical reflection. Many intellectuals believe that conditions of life in the Present are such that devoting attention to any other time period is meaningless. "Our era does not count on a remote posterity. Its spiritual products are meant to be consumed, just like the products of any other kind of work. Even the people with the largest incomes do not accumulate capital—and nobody can pass it on to the next generation. With a certain amount of composure, we can focus on meeting the requirements of our own era and on living in it, as long as we manage to understand it" (Heinrich Mann, 272). There are even allegorical descriptions of this feeling: "It is impossible to ignore the penetrating voice of this present; it pushes the most romantic dream into the merciless light of day, where all objects adopt new forms and new colors. Their essence and meaning become accessible to those who dare touch their contours, visualize them, listen to them—transform them into lived experience" (Lania, 322). [see **Reporters**]

In an interview with Thomas Mann that treats the Present as a tension between the generations (Mann's and his children's), a young journalist suggests that what is considered human and must therefore simply be accepted overlaps with what is demonstrably legitimate according to explicit ethical criteria: "For every now and then—indeed, quite often— we are simply unable to look at certain things that were clearly evil for the older generation and find them 'bad' or 'illicit.' In other words, we are more relaxed and open-minded when it comes to distinguishing what is human from what is morally responsible" (W.E.S., 192). Compared to the Present, even the not-so-remote Past seems a world in which people were often carried away by their emotions and opinions, whereas now people have a more functionally oriented, sober attitude toward life. [see **Sobriety vs. Exuberance**] In *The Plumed Serpent* D. H. Lawrence depicts the same contrast, through the disparate reactions of a forty-year-old and a twenty-year-old to the atmosphere of a bullfight: "'Isn't it thrilling,' cried Owen, whose will-to-happiness was almost a mania. 'Don't you think so Bud?' 'Why, yes, I think it may be,' said Villiers, non-committal. But then Villiers was young, he was only over twenty, while Owen was over forty. The younger generation calculated its 'happiness' in a more business-like fashion. Villiers was out after a thrill, but he wasn't going to say he'd got one till he'd got it" (Lawrence, 9). [see **Bullfighting**] The most popular emblems of the new generation's sober hedonism are fit bodies and athletic rituals. Not surprisingly, Thomas Mann interprets such "sportification of our youth" as a return to certain ideals of classical Antiquity and, consequently, as a symptom for the impending demise of the Christian era (W.E.S., 193). Far from making such far-reaching associations, Ulrich Wilamowitz-Möllendorf, a celebrated professor of classical philology at the University of Berlin, sees the fashion for sports as nothing but a symptom of severe pedagogical crisis: "The danger does not lie in a lack of ability or intention—but there is indeed a danger. Above all, this has to do with a lack of general culture. No pedagogical program—much less sports—can take its place" ("Deutsche Zukunft," 219). But for Wilhelm Wien, an experimental physicist at the University of Munich, sports are a mark of the younger generation's enviable vitality: "Having recovered from the postwar chaos, the younger generation in Germany is fully dedicated to its task. I have certainly not observed any crisis or decline in quality. A particularly welcome development is the new emphasis on physical education" ("Deutsche Zukunft," 218).

The identity of the Present is normally not derived from a comparison with historically remote worlds. If the culture of ancient Egypt and the pre-Christian Mediterranean civilizations are frequently evoked, they stand for cosmological order and for an authenticity whose re-presentations shed a pessimistic—rather than a clarifying—light on the Present. [see **Authenticity vs. Artificiality**] The understanding of the Past, the description of the Present, and the periodization of time in general thus tend to involve identifying structures and patterns specific to the passage of time [see **Timepieces**], and not in comparing different historical periods: "In the flow of time, in this perpetual becoming that surrounds us, there are moments in which we rest—only to suddenly discover that something has materialized. Then we begin to understand how insignificant our effect on the world is, how things grow out of the depths and enter the realm of being, where they stay for a short while—only to disappear again" (Jünger, 5). But how can "time-objects proper" (Husserl, 3–93)—whatever is by definition in continuous flux—acquire shape or form? The general, and historically specific, answer to this question lies in the concept of rhythm. "Rhythm" here means the way in which time-objects achieve form: by passing repeatedly through recurrent patterns, in a process of continual change (Gumbrecht, 170–182). Thus, the intense efforts to describe and analyze the phenomenon of rhythm—efforts manifest in books like Charles Diserens' *The Influence of Music on Behavior* (Golston, 9), or André Coeuroy and André Schäffner's *Le Jazz*, which discusses topics such as "rhythm and percussion" and "rhythm among the blacks"—are the obverse of a general reluctance to describe and analyze the Present through large philosophico-historical comparisons. Once a rhythmic pattern has been identified, it can serve to characterize specific moments in the flow of time. It is thus that the fascination with rhythm becomes a part of the Present's self-reference. Jazz music and modern forms of dance, but also the labor of office and factory workers, are performed "to a frenzied rhythm" (Lang, *Metropolis*, 30). [see **Assembly Lines, Dancing, Employees, Gramophones, Jazz**] Rhythm is not only Authenticity and Artificiality; it also makes possible the coupling of systems to systems and of people to systems. [see **Elevators, Authenticity = Artificiality (Life)**] William Butler Yeats uses the contrast between rhythm and content to distinguish the cultures of different generations: "The realists turn our words into gravel, but the musicians and the singers turn them into honey and oil . . . You at any rate cannot sympathise with a horrible generation that in childhood sucked Ibsen from [William] Archer's hygienic bottle . . . 'I find my parents detestable,' said the young woman, 'but I like my grandparents'" (Yeats, 34–35).

In connecting the concept of "rhythm" to the notion of "generation," Yeats brings together two dominant responses to the crisis in the philosophy of history. The process of defining the Present as a generation inevitably involves comparisons with an immediately preceding Past; but it also overlaps with the idea of rhythm in at least three ways. First, it hardly ever extends back to a very remote Past; second, it allows for repetition and recurrence; and third, it normally does not develop long-

term models with teleological implications. Using the generation-concept
to distinguish the Present from the Past is a form of historico-philosophical minimalism. It is not surprising, then, that scholars frequently explain
their preference for this concept with negative arguments. For the art
historian Wilhelm Pinder, who declares he does not believe in "rigid
intellectual systems," the generation as a temporal form recommends
itself through its mere "practicability" (Pinder, xvii). In setting apart the
generation-concept from the concept of society, the literary critic Julius
Petersen hopes to minimize the level of abstraction in his description of
the German Romantics—as a generation (Petersen, 132, 140). Walter
Benjamin sees the current interest in the generation-concept as the outcome of a theological style of thinking (Benjamin, 281). And the Russian
Formalists Boris Eikhenbaum and Jurij Tynjanov use the concept to
mediate between a linguistically based analysis and a historical interpretation of literary texts (Eisen, 9).

One of the liveliest intellectual debates in Germany revolves around
generational conflict. It starts with an essay by Klaus Mann entitled "Die
neuen Eltern" ("The New Parents"); it continues with an interview in
which his father, Thomas Mann, defines "die neuen Kinder" ("the new
children") in response to questions from a journalist (W.E.S., 190–193);
and it ends with a furious rejoinder to both father and son by the
playwright Bertolt Brecht, a rising star among the young writers in
Germany (Brecht, 40ff.). Although the discussion inevitably focuses on
the contrast between the son's generation and the father's generation,
both Klaus Mann and Thomas Mann insist that one of the most salient
features of the Present is young people's indifference when it comes to
defining themselves in opposition to their parents. This means that even
the one, rather minimal, historico-philosophical element inherent in the
generation-concept—that is, the self-definition of each new generation
through a gesture of negation vis-à-vis the previous generation—has
been abandoned. The less the younger generations care about being
different, the more difficult it becomes to define them—and to perceive
the identity of the Present: "We consider it important not to destroy the
bridges between the generations, not to heap irony on all traditions
arrogantly and triumphantly, not to despise all forms" (W.E.S., 190).
Klaus Mann's father, of course, fully agrees: "Rather than discussing the
'new parents,' we should perhaps focus on the 'new children,' who have
become older and more understanding, and who, simply because they

have become grown-ups, are now able to see their parents with more justice" (W.E.S., 191). Bertolt Brecht, who is just now developing his public role as a Marxist *enfant terrible,* strongly protests such a lack of revolutionary energy: "Statistically, it may be true that the number of fathers murdered recently has slightly decreased. And these murders may be due solely to the fact that they help keep the wrist flexible. Still, such a decrease should not encourage the older generation to feel safe . . . Mr. Thomas Mann suggests that children have become older (meaning more understanding). In this formulation, children are of course as uninteresting as understanding children normally are. 'More interesting means new, and new means older'—that would be precisely to Thomas Mann's taste!" (Brecht, 41).

At the same time, the generation-concept brings the historian's distanced view of Past and Present closer to more subjective (if not more personal) ways of experiencing the passage of time. *Geistesgeschichte,* the flourishing German version of intellectual history, is eager to mediate between the subjective dimension and less personal records of the Past: "It is in this indissolubly mutual relationship, in this interdependence between the subjective (psychological) and the objective (phenomenological) appearance of the vital problems of the spirit, that *Geistesgeschichte* finds its meaning and its essence" (Unger, 191). Such emphasis on the existential dimension of time stems from the impression that it is increasingly difficult to grasp time as a social phenomenon. A painting by Edward Hopper entitled *Eleven a.m.* shows a naked woman with long brown hair sitting in an easy chair and looking through the large window of a well-furnished apartment (Levin, 274). From the perspective of the everyday social world, eleven *a.m.* is just the wrong time of day to be in a state of undress. Is this woman waiting for a lover, who may or may not show up? Whatever Hopper has in mind, this woman's time-state is not coordinated with "objective," social time. He paints her existing in subjective time—a time that cannot be represented by any clock, a time in relation to which "eleven A.M." is nothing but a random number. [see **Timepieces**]

The multiple difficulties that emerge in delineating the shape of the Present underscore both the fragility of objective time structures and the need to rely on time as a dimension of subjective experience. Martin Heidegger's *Sein und Zeit* is part of this philosophical situation. His chapter "Der existenziale Ursprung der Historie aus der Geschichtlichkeit des Daseins" ("The Existential Source of Historiology in the Historicality of *Dasein*") argues that what used to be regarded as the objective level of history is actually based on the—in a certain sense—subjective (419–420) level of the time of existence: "Whether the historiological disclosure of history is in fact accomplished or not, its ontological structure is such that in itself this disclosure has its roots in the historicality of *Dasein*. This is the connection we have in mind when we talk of *Dasein*'s historicality as the existential source of historiology" (392–393). But if human existence is thus described as "essentially oriented toward the future," this future holds nothing more than the individual's death. [see **Individuality vs. Collectivity, Immanence = Transcendence (Death)**] The Past, in contrast, is fate, materialized in the—collective—history of a nation, or *Volk* (384ff.). By defining history from an existential point of view, Heidegger moves the future back into the picture. But this only confirms the unavailability of any future that would not be merely subjective.

Related Entries

Assembly Lines, Bullfighting, Dancing, Elevators, Employees, Gramophones, Jazz, Reporters, Timepieces, Authenticity vs. Artificiality, Center vs. Periphery, Individuality vs. Collectivity, Sobriety vs. Exuberance, Authenticity = Artificiality (Life), Immanence = Transcendence (Death)

References

Walter Benjamin, "J. P. Hebel: Ein Bilderrätsel zum 100. Todestage des Dichters" (1926). In Benjamin, *Gesammelte Schriften*, vol. 2, part 1. Frankfurt, 1977.

Bertolt Brecht, "Wenn der Vater mit dem Sohne mit dem Uhu . . ." (1926). In Brecht, *Gesammelte Werke*, vol. 18. Frankfurt, 1967.

André Coeuroy and André Schäffner, *Le Jazz*. Paris, 1926.

"Deutsche Zukunft." *Süddeutsche Monatshefte* 24 (1926): 215–219.

Charles Diserens, *The Influence of Music on Behavior*. Princeton, 1926.

Sam Eisen, "Politics, Poetics, and Profession: Viktor Shklovsky, Boris Eikhenbaum, and the Understanding of Literature, 1919–1936." Dissertation, Stanford University, 1994.

Oskar Maurus Fontana, "Was arbeiten Sie? Gespräch mit Robert Musil"

(1926). In Anton Kaes, ed., *Weimarer Republik: Manifeste und Dokumente zur deutschen Literatur, 1918–1933*. Stuttgart, 1983.

Michael Golston, "'Im Anfang war der Rhythmus': Rhythmic Incubations in Discourses of Mind, Body, and Race, 1850–1944." *Stanford Humanities Review* 5, suppl. (1996): 1–24.

Hans Ulrich Gumbrecht, "Rhythm and Meaning." In Hans Ulrich Gumbrecht and K. Ludwig Pfeiffer, eds., *Materialities of Communication*. Stanford, 1994.

Martin Heidegger, *Sein und Zeit* (written 1926, published 1927). Tübingen, 1984.

Edmund Husserl, "Die Vorlesungen über das innere Zeitbewusstsein aus dem Jahre 1905." In Husserl, *Zur Phänomenologie des inneren Zeitbewusstseins, 1893–1917*. The Hague, 1977.

Ernst Jünger, *Feuer und Blut: Ein kleiner Ausschnitt aus einer grossen Schlacht* (1926). Hamburg, 1941.

Fritz Lang, *Metropolis*. New York, 1973.

Fritz Lang, "Wege des grossen Spielfilms in Deutschland" (1926). In Anton Kaes, ed., *Weimarer Republik: Manifeste und Dokumente zur deutschen Literatur, 1918–1933*. Stuttgart, 1983.

Leo Lania, "Reportage als soziale Funktion" (1926). In Anton Kaes, ed., *Weimarer Republik: Manifeste und Dokumente zur deutschen Literatur, 1918–1933*. Stuttgart, 1983.

D. H. Lawrence, *The Plumed Serpent*. London, 1926.

Gail Levin, *Edward Hopper: The Art and The Artist*. New York, 1980.

Heinrich Mann, *Sieben Jahre: Chronik der Gedanken und Vorgänge* (1926). Berlin, 1929.

Julius Petersen, *Die Wesensbestimmung der deutschen Romantik* (1926). Heidelberg, 1968.

Wilhelm Pinder, *Das Problem der Generation in der Kunstgeschichte Europas* (1926). Berlin, 1928.

Ernst Toller, "Russische Reisebilder" (1926). In Toller, *Quer durch: Reisebilder und Reden*. Heidelberg, 1978.

Rudolf Unger, "Literaturgeschichte und Geistesgeschichte." *Deutsche Vierteljahrsschrift für Literaturwissenschaft und Geistesgeschichte* 4 (1926): 177–193.

W.E.S., "Die neuen Kinder: Ein Gespräch mit Thomas Mann." *Uhu: Das Monats-Magazin* (August 1926): 190–193.

William Butler Yeats, *A Vision* (1926). New York, 1961.

SILENCE VS. NOISE

....

>❮❯<

There is an enthusiasm about Silence that often reaches the passionate one-dimensionality of an obsession. Noise becomes a frequently evoked but mostly vague background reference. In view of the tradition of defining the human species through its capacity to speak, it is astonishing that this obsession with Silence yields multiple suggestions concerning the formation and functions of subjecthood. They emerge from an intellectual and political environment where individual independence and self-determination are neither seen as generally available options nor unanimously hailed as positive values. If, in this context, Silence defines subjecthood, "de-fining" (from Latin *finis,* "boundary" or "end"), indeed means "setting limits" to subjecthood. There are two main perspectives from which the subject is thus defined. Silence can express the awe with which individuals are obliged (or even forced) to approach—often in an attitude of self-abnegation—whatever is considered to be categorically stronger than their own subjectivity. [see **Immanence vs. Transcendence**] But Silence can also bespeak self-control and self- containment, through which subjecthood gives itself a form in permanently distracting environments.

D. H. Lawrence's novel *The Plumed Serpent* explores Silence as a compo- nent of subjecthood that—paradoxically—presupposes subject-erasure. The heroine, Kate, becomes sexually involved with a man named Cipriano, a Mexican revolutionary and (the narrator strongly suggests) a demigod. Through this relationship, Kate acquires the belief that true sexual fulfillment comes not from sharing physical satisfaction with her male counterpart but, on the contrary, from being systematically denied the culminating moment of her own sexual pleasure. Lawrence associates the willing and "good" acceptance of this subject-erasing denial on the woman's side with "the silence of the men" (Lawrence, 349). [see **Male vs Female**] The insistence (construed as "bad") on female desire and on the female orgasm is marked by women's crying out in ecstasy: "When, in their love, it came back on her, the seething, electric, female ecstasy, which knows such spasms of delirium, [Cipriano] recoiled from her. It was what she used to call her 'satisfaction.' She had loved [her former husband] for this, that again, and again, and again he could give her this orgiastic 'satisfaction,' in spasms that made her cry aloud . . . [Cipriano], in his dark, hot silence would bring her back to the new, soft, heavy, hot flow, when she was like a fountain gushing noiseless and with urgent softness from the volcanic deeps. Then she was open to him soft and hot, yet gushing with a noiseless soft power" (451–452).

What appears here idealized as a hyperbolic mode of subjecthood and dignified with an aura of Silence is nothing less than a complicity with physical violence which does not even begin to address the victim as a subject. If, in a sexual relationship, a partner's consent to this erasure of subjecthood may sometimes produce a peculiar form of subjectivity, military procedure uses the same refusal to acknowledge others' subjecthood as a means of facilitating their extinction. In one of the few episodes where the first-person narrator of Ernst Jünger's *Feuer und Blut* is critical of himself, he measures his own behavior against exactly this standard. He has talked to an enemy instead of silently shooting him down. He has failed to confront himself and the enemy with what is stronger than subjecthood—namely, with death: "Cautiously I draw my pistol and aim at the English soldier who stands below me. Then I shout: 'Come here, hands up!' He jumps up, gazes at me as if I were an apparition, and disappears with a leap into the dark mouth of the tunnel. I am irritated with myself. I should have simply shot him instead of talking idly" (Jünger, 149) [see **Immanence = Transcendence (Death)**] On the side of the aggressor, Silence becomes the condition for unconditional use of violence. On the side of the victim, in contrast, speech is repressed by fright. In Federico García Lorca's *Romance de la Guardia Civil española (Ballad of the Spanish Civil Guard)*, the aggressors' Silence converges with the victims' Silence in the moments preceding a bloody assault by the police on a gypsy town—and these Silences form a "tunnel of Silence" when the police leave the scene of the massacre:

> Hunchbacked creatures of the night,
> Whenever they appear they impose
> A silence like dark rubber
> And a fear like fine sand.
> They enter wherever they wish,
> Concealing in their heads a vague astronomy
> Of insubstantial pistols.
> . . . Oh, town of the gypsies!
> The Civil Guard leaves
> Through a tunnel of silence
> While the flames flare up around you."
>
> (453, 457)

Only bodies that survive in a mutilated state break the spell of Silence. But in breaking this spell, they do not speak—they sigh. For when words are not addressed to a subject, one cannot respond to them as a subject (Lyotard, 130ff.).

> Rosa of the Camborios
> sits before her house sighing—
> Her two breasts cut off
> and lying on a platter.
>
> (456–457)

In contrast, whenever Silence is a refusal of speech on the part of a subject who was addressed as a subject, it becomes a weapon and a sign of strength. This type of Silence is the opposite of the unrestraint with which, giving up its boundary with the environment, a subject surrenders itself. As Greta Garbo recalls, Silence as a subject-constituting device can be obtained only at a high price: "Whatever I achieved came from my talent and hard work. To the last day of my life, I will defend this achievement against those who try to minimize my efforts and destroy me. To defend my achievement, I choose as a weapon complete silence. You can use this weapon very successfully if you have enough money to maintain absolute privacy. I use money and silence to shelter myself from those who try to belittle or destroy me. It is not easy, for I must always be on my own" (Gronowicz, 209). Garbo's behavior corresponds to an ideal that Adolf Hitler finds lacking in the present German system of education. Although he tries to explain his appreciation of Silence as a "male virtue" through its specific military functions, it appears that what Hitler really admires is the more general gesture of Silence as self-containment and as a willed distance from the environment: "How often one complained, during the war, that our people knew so little about being silent! How difficult this made it to keep even important secrets from the enemy! But one should ask oneself: Before the war, what did German education do to train the individual for secrecy? Even in school, unfortunately, wasn't the little tattle-tale preferred to his discreet comrade? Wasn't, and isn't, tale-telling looked upon as honorable 'frankness,' and discretion as shameful obstinacy? Did one endeavor at all to present discretion as a valuable manly virtue? . . . But in the case of war, this inclination to talk can even lead to the loss of battles and thus contribute substantially to the unfavorable outcome of a conflict" (Hitler, 460–461). While reticence thus has unquestioned positive value, verbosity is often perceived as a lack of tact—and sometimes even as a social pathology. Alcoholics tend to talk too much [see Bars]. American tourists on their rapid trips through Europe annoy their philosophically minded countrymen who are searching silently for authenticity. [see Americans in Paris] Even sophisticated criminals, like the narrator in *The Murder of Roger Ackroyd,* hate talkative people because they represent a potential security risk: "'I know,' said my sister. 'How did you know?' 'Annie told me.' Annie is the house parlourmaid. A nice girl, but an inveterate talker" (Christie, 3).

Beyond the level of purely correct—and therefore expectable—social behavior, noiselessness can become a sign of elegance. In Fritz Lang's metropolis, the sons of the Masters of Metropolis compete at sports wearing not only silk uniforms also "soft, supple shoes, with noiseless soles" (Lang, 22). Expensive cars have noiseless engines. The "entirely new Nash models," which are three to six times more expensive than the average car (which sells for $360), are "powered with the Nash 7-bearing motor—the world's smoothest type" *(Pages of Time).* [see Automobiles] But for all their value as status symbols, noiselessness and Silence remain primarily social virtues. They indicate a willingness to respect others' privacy—a willingness that may help others develop their subjectivity. This is why the philosopher Theodor Lessing complains bitterly about street Noise and automobiles, telephones and gramophones, factory whistles and even church bells (Lessing 398ff.). [see **Gramophones**] His colleague Martin Heidegger feels compelled to apologize for being able to think and write in any place other than his cabin in the Black Forest, which is surrounded by the Silence of nature: "It would be appropriate for this letter to come from the cabin; it should be written when the beech-logs are crackling on the fire and a thick cap of snow lies on the roof. Instead, here I sit [in Marburg] working on the transitional chapter" (Heidegger, 18–19). Seeking and maintaining Silence are signs that one is concentrating to the fullest on a given task. This rule applies as much to Lessing's and Heidegger's philosophical work as to the transatlantic flight of Ramón Franco and his companions. [see **Airplanes**] During the decisive leg of their voyage, the aviators do not talk to one another. They forget the Noise of the engines, and for two hours they are too far away from either the European or the American coast to receive any radio signals: "Alda and Rada made frequent visits to the smoking compartment, while Franco remained motionless, perhaps thinking about the hours that lay ahead. None of us spoke, and the flight seemed to go on in silence, since the Noise of the plane becomes imperceptible after a few hours and you hear only variations in sound, such as when an engine slows—a very disagreeable thing, and one that fortunately we did not hear at all on this voyage. From ten till twelve, the most complete silence reigned, even on the radio. Alda couldn't get anything on any station" (Franco, 143). Although the pilots' Silence is primarily a gesture of closure vis-à-vis their environment, it can also be interpreted—and is certainly meant to be interpreted—by that environment as a sign of complete intellectual and physical alertness. Even more "eloquent" is the Silence with which the pilots "answer," out of modesty and embarrassment, the overwhelming reception that greets them in the streets of Buenos Aires: "The grandeur of the celebration in Argentina, the huge reception, and the triumphant parade through the streets of the capital made us tremble with emotion. The silence that overcame us was more eloquent than anything we could have said with words" (246).

Silence tends to become eloquent, and words tend to become superfluous, whenever the world is seen from a perspective of Authenticity—that is, whenever it is taken for granted that phenomena, gestures, and persons have their inherent meanings within a cosmological order. [see **Authenticity vs. Artificiality**] Spanish pilots on a mission for their homeland belong to this world of authenticity as much as the *gaúchos* of the Argentinian Pampa who communicate in silence even the order to be silent: "We greeted each other as always. Together we rode about a mile in the usual manner. We didn't speak. Why not? Beneath the touch of his rough hand, I received a command of silence. Sadness made us reticent. We turned around to wish each other, smilingly, the best of luck. Don Segundo's horse rubbed haunches with mine, and I realized, in that turning away, everything that would separate our fates" (Güiraldes, 360). In a world where the slightest body movements are immediately interpreted as expressions, undeserved misery needs no words to attract the attention and generate the compassion it deserves. In Lang's film *Metropolis,* the workers' children appear noiselessly at the "Club of the Sons" with their protector, Maria: "Through the door came a procession of children. They were all holding hands. They had dwarfs' faces, gray and ancient. They were little ghostlike skeletons, clad in faded rags and smocks. They had colorless hair and colorless eyes. They walked on emaciated bare feet. Noiselessly they followed their leader" (Lang, 26; also 60). Despite all ideological divergence, Maria's silent appearances in *Metropolis* are similar to the appearances of a young widow in Hans Grimm's nationalist novel *Volk ohne Raum (Nation without Space):* "Grimm stood up. If he and the young woman remained silent for a while, it may have been because they were both remembering the man who was no longer physically near her but who nevertheless was by her side . . . She did not even mention the man. Nor did she wear the black apparel of a widow. But there was a double reference in her eyes" (Grimm, II, 666–667). The claim to be eloquently silent is not limited to those who are ideologically and philosophically conservative. Walter Benjamin, too, cherishes the idea of honoring an admired individual through—respectful—Silence: "Karl Kraus. Nobody more embarrassing than those who imitate him; nobody more hopeless than his enemies. No name more appropriate than his to be honored through silence" (Benjamin, 121).

Within the world of Authenticity, where meaning is always already given and therefore does not require language in order to become acces-

sible, eloquent Silence—and Martin Heidegger's "silence as an essential
possibility of speech" (Heidegger, 164; also Wohlfart and Kreuzer)—are
no longer paradoxes. Subjecthood is constituted here by identifying a
meaningful order of things and by suppressing any words that exceed it.
In contrast, only sounds and words brought forth in the name of a
collective cause are permitted to be loud—sometimes egregiously loud—
without being considered illegitimate. [see **Individuality vs. Collectivity**]
Describing his first days as a soldier in the Great War, Adolf Hitler
contrasts the quietness of the Rhine—whose national symbolic importance needs no words—with the sound of a collectively sung hymn which
is almost too moving for any individual soldier's breast: "Finally the day
came when we left Munich in order to start fulfilling our duty. Now for
the first time I saw the Rhine—the German river of rivers—as we were
riding west along its quiet waters, in order to protect it from the greed
of our old enemy. When through the delicate veil of the dawn's mist the
gentle rays of the early sun set the Niederwald Monument shimmering
before our eyes, 'The Watch on the Rhine' roared up into the morning
sky from the interminably long transport train, and I felt as though my
chest would burst" (Hitler, 180). Hans Grimm wants all the bells in
Germany to ring for the geopolitical cause he advocates in *Volk ohne
Raum.* More effective than Hitler in maintaining an impression of
Authenticity, Grimm manages, through the metaphor of the bells, to
present the German people as keeping an eloquent Silence: "Bells would
have to ring at the beginning of this book. The ringing should begin at
the tower of the monastery chapel in Lippolsberg, where I am writing . . .
But this would be only the beginning—all German bells are invited to
ring . . . And once all those metal voices between the river Maas and the
river Memel, between Königsau and Etsch and Southern Africa, are
sounding and tolling, . . . then all Germans shall raise their arms. They
shall advance demanding and silent, so that the silence of the millions
silences the music of heaven, so that God will be forced to look upon
their souls. And God shall acknowledge the outrageousness of their
fate—which they themselves are as yet unable to conceive, to articulate,
and to shout out loud" (Grimm, I, 9–10). In Jünger's description of a
Great War assault, individual soldiers kill silently, but the rhythmic
sound of engines and weapons marks the importance of this moment for
the history and fate of mankind: "And now it is 5:05 A.M.! A flickering

light enters the mouth of the tunnel, followed by a unanimous, unheard-of shouting, which immediately grows to extreme intensity, like a giant engine whose individual vibrations can no longer be distinguished . . . Every new second wants to swallow the previous second in its burning throat, although an increase of tension seems impossible. Compared to this raging outburst, all previous battles are fading away like children's play . . . Here, the only way of surviving is to let go and allow oneself be molded by the hand of the world spirit itself. Here, we experience history at a focal point" (Jünger, 101ff.). Jünger's formula of "letting oneself be molded by the hand of the world spirit" is just another example of subject-definition by setting limits to subjecthood. No individual voice can ever be heard over the din of modern warfare. Likewise, no individual voice can usually be identified among the noisy spectators of a boxing match. This is why the Silence of the huge crowd that accompanies the Dempsey-Tunney fight for the world heavyweight title is so eloquent. It announces that something important is about to happen—something beyond the individual victory or the individual defeat. [see **Boxing**] When the fight is over, and the more than 144,000 spectators begin yelling the name of Jack Dempsey, the defeated ex-champion, they honor a fighter who, because he has taken a severe beating from his opponent, has looked into the face of death. [see **Immanence = Transcendence (Death)**] Eloquent Silence and powerful collective voices always come from a perspective of Authenticity; they always confirm the belief in an existing cosmological order.

As antitheses to expressive Silence, one might cite the victims' sighs in Lorca's *Romance de la Guardia Civil española;* the sound of jazz; a gramophone playing in a Great War trench; the always expected, yet always disturbing ringing of the telephone in Kafka's *Schloss;* the strange sounds from the receiver that precede each telephone conversation and each radio transmission; the "strong needles" that amplify the recorded music played at dance parties. [see **Dancing, Jazz, Telephone, Wireless Communication**] All Noise that occurs for no particular reason stands opposite to Silence and expression. It is provocative without being eloquent. For while Silence may easily coincide with meaning, Silence and Noise do not go together—with perhaps one exception. Most of the many pictures that Joan Miró completes during the summer have no titles. But among the very few pictures that have titles are *The Cry* and *Dog Barking at the Moon* (Dupin, 498–499).

Related Entries

Airplanes, Americans in Paris, Automobiles, Bars, Boxing, Dancing, Gramophones, Jazz, Telephone, Wireless Communication, Authenticity vs. Artificiality, Immanence vs. Transcendence, Individuality vs. Collectivity, Male vs. Female, Immanence = Transcendence (Death)

References

Walter Benjamin, *Einbahnstraße* (1926). In Benjamin, *Gesammelte Schriften,* vol. 4, part 1. Frankfurt, 1972.

Agatha Christie, *The Murder of Roger Ackroyd.* London, 1926. :

Jacques Dupin, *Joan Miró: Leben und Werk.* Cologne, 1961.

Ramón Franco, *De Palos al Plata.* Madrid, 1926.

Federico García Lorca, *Romance de la Guardia Civil española* (1926). In García Lorca, *Obras completas.* Madrid, 1971.

Hans Grimm, *Volk ohne Raum,* 2 vols. Munich, 1926.

Antoni Gronowicz, *Garbo: Her Story.* New York, 1990.

Ricardo Güiraldes, *Don Segundo Sombra* (1926). Buenos Aires, 1927.

Martin Heidegger, *Sein und Zeit* (written 1926, published 1927). Tübingen, 1984.

Martin Heidegger and Elisabeth Blochmann, *Briefwechsel, 1918–1969.* Marbach, 1989.

Adolf Hitler, *Mein Kampf* (1926). Munich, 1941.

Ernst Jünger, *Feuer und Blut: Ein kleiner Ausschnitt aus einer grossen Schlacht* (1926). Hamburg, 1941.

Fritz Lang, *Metropolis* (1926). New York, 1973.

D. H. Lawrence, *The Plumed Serpent* (1926). London, 1933.

Theodor Lessing, "Die blauschwarze Rose" (1926). In Lessing, *"Ich warf eine Flaschenpost ins Eismeer der Geschichte": Essays und Feuilletons, 1923–1933.* Neuwied, 1986.

Jean-François Lyotard, *Le Différend.* Paris, 1983.

Pages of Time: 1926. Goodlettsville, Tenn., n.d.

G. Wohlfart and J. Kreuzer, "Schweigen, Stille." In Joachim Ritter and Karlfried Gründer, eds., *Historisches Wörterbuch der Philosophie,* vol. 8. Basel, 1992.

SOBRIETY VS. EXUBERANCE

Philosophical certainties and agreements based on broad consensus seem to be out of reach. Intellectuals, politicians, and business leaders concentrate on the pragmatic realities of everydayness, instead of trying to ground their actions in ultimate truths. [see **Uncertainty vs. Reality**] This everydayness has no context of religious transcendence from which stable meanings or goal-oriented visions could emerge. [see **Transcendence = Immanence (Death)**] A constant search for norms and models that would make it possible to assess and shape reality has replaced the old cosmologies. This search is conducted in the spirit of Sobriety, an attitude adopted by those who have abandoned the hope of achieving any kind of revealed knowledge or ultimate wisdom. In the dramatic words of the painter Oskar Schlemmer, who teaches at the Bauhaus [see **Engineers**], the longing for world-immanent norms is a way of resisting the threat of impending chaos: "If today's arts love the machine, technology, and organization, if they aspire to precision and reject anything vague and dreamy, this implies an instinctive repudiation of chaos and a longing to find the form appropriate to our times" (Willet, 117).

Neue Sachlichkeit ("New Sobriety"), the German name for this movement, underscores its tendency to focus on "things"—more precisely, on the calculable things of the quotidian. World-immanent things are expected to provide orientation and norms. The realm of industry is important to this new attitude, because it measures efficiency in money and units of labor and because industrial planning constantly invents new systems of organization and new professional roles. It is a common point of reference for artists, philosophers, and even Germany's Social Democratic Party. [see **Assembly Lines, Employees, Elevators, Railroads, Strikes**] This explains why the Social Democratic city administration of Dessau, a center for chemical manufacture and aircraft production south of Berlin with barely 89,000 inhabitants, offers a home to the Bauhaus after the school's negotiations with the German government concerning the expansion of its activities in Weimar have failed (Galison, 715). On a campus of soberly elegant buildings (most of them designed by Bauhaus teachers), the faculty inaugurates a program of study that tries to channel artistic imagination toward practical tasks. Looking to the needs of industrial production, this curriculum consists of cabinetmaking, metalworking, weaving, sculpture, theater, wall painting, advertising, typography, as well as a "basic course," taught by the Hungarian designer László Moholy-Nagy, in which contemporary mathematics is linked to philosophy (Willet, 120; *Wechselwirkungen*, 275–276).

Traditionally leftist intellectuals do not always find it easy to come to terms with their own growing admiration for the industrial methods. Eugen Diesel, whose father developed the diesel engine, publishes a book entitled *Der Weg durch das Wirrsal (The Road through Confusion)*, in which he interprets this fascination as a misguided reaction to an overly complex cultural and political situation. Despite his intentions, however, Diesel's descriptions often end up aggrandizing the leaders of business and industry. For example, nothing could be more flattering to the steel magnate Hugo Stinnes than a comparison with Alexander the Great: "Alexander conquers the Orient, placing its women, gods, wines, and festivals at his feet. Stinnes does likewise with manufacturing plants, cigarette factories, Carlton hotels, and stocks and bonds . . . One is blond, sensual, and full of life, and would like to be the son of Jupiter Ammon. The other is dark-haired, hates the arts, and has long declined all honorary titles" (Diesel, 135). An essay entitled "Die neue Sachlichkeit in der Schule" ("The New Sobriety in Education"), published by the influential magazine *Die Tat,* uses the current definition of Sobriety (a struggle against chaos) in order to legitimize the most recent curricular changes in secondary education. Sobriety comes to stand for collectivity-oriented instruction, and seems to distance itself from capitalism: "Our age is characterized by its lack of norms, and our culture is probably just beginning to come into existence, even as the new society has begun to emerge. The new direction in education has thus given up all specific content and tries to achieve the goal of sobriety merely through its methods and work techniques . . . The result is a turning away from instructor-centered teaching and the inauguration of cooperative and practice-oriented work habits. Both aspects mark the adoption of a new sobriety in teaching." (Ehrentreich, 235). [see **Individuality vs. Collectivity**]

In the opinion of both its partisans and its opponents, Sobriety is a major element in the definition of the present. [see **Present vs. Past**] This is why the concept hardly ever appears without the epithet "new." Ornamentation thus becomes an object of aesthetic nostalgia, but is not vigorously rejected as inimical to Sobriety. Walter Benjamin's description of the Alcázar palace in Seville exemplifies this perspective: "A type of architecture that follows the first impulse of fantasy. It is untroubled by any practical considerations. Its spacious rooms are open only for dreams and celebrations—that is, for the realization of dreams. Here, dance and silence become the leitmotif because all human movement is absorbed by the quiet unrest of the ornamentation" (Benjamin, 123). [see **Silence vs. Noise**] Wherever one can afford to set aside practical concerns, as is the case with music and dance, ornamentation no longer seems antithetical to function and its purity may even converge with the value of Sobriety: "For what strikes us in the 'pure' music of a Stravinsky, a Prokofiev, a Poulenc, or an Auric, as much as in that of Mozart, is that the tonal sequences, whose suggestive power elsewhere serves other ends, are here emptied of their original meaning, as if deconcretized and presented as simple ornamental formulas" (Coeuroy and Schäffner, 11–12). If this reflection on musical ornament leads to the praise of jazz as a form-oriented genre and thus to the recuperation of the ornament for contemporary art, Federico García Lorca's "Oda a Salvador Dalí" describes the way in which Surrealist painting secretly longs to discover natural proportions:

> A desire for forms and limits defeats us.
> Here comes the man who sees with the yellow straightedge.
> Venus is a white still-life
> And the butterfly collectors flee . . .
> Hygienic soul, you live on new marble.

You flee the dark woods of incredible forms.
Your reach extends no further than your grasp.

                              (García Lorca, 619)

Rather than ornaments and nonfunctional forms, the counterprinciples of Sobriety are Exuberance, proliferation, and eclecticism. Almost logically, therefore, the artistic historicism of the late nineteenth century is emerging as the epitome of bad taste: "São Paulo is an architectural salad. All possible and impossible styles are represented there. And all of them are in tension with the natural environment. The public and private buildings both clash with the context in which they are constructed. The city thus has the flavor of a world's fair" (Alcântara Machado, 171). Sobriety has become so internationally accepted that it forms a common thread between the polemical discourse of the Brazilian journalist António Alcântara Machado and an academic lecture by the German art historian Karl Holl. But Holl goes one step further than Alcântara Machado: he sees the economic and aesthetic Exuberance of the previous generation as a main reason for the present crisis. "Their leather-bound volumes of intimate poetry mark the low point of a boring period that was mired in content and that tried to hide its intellectual and moral emptiness under the colored garments of the past. We are confronted with the very moment in German history that was blown up like a bubble by its military victories and by the subsequent streams of capital—until the bubble finally burst with a tremendous noise" (Holl, 549).

Outside the realm of aesthetic experience, the forms and functions of everyday objects become frames of reference for the taming of unstructured plenitude. Bureaucrats and intellectuals alike are intent on avoiding empty discourses and tautologies—on establishing and maintaining a referential relation between discourses, ideas, and the world of things. This concern is as central for the Spanish government, which prides itself on rejecting "convoluted traditions of philosophy" (García-Nieto, 149), as for the philosophers of the Vienna Circle, who are reaching out for intellectual exchange with the Bauhaus (Galison, 715ff.). Ludwig Wittgenstein amiably agrees that the villa he has designed for his sister is *hausgewordene Logik, or* "logic-become-house" (Galison, 727). Fashion designers claim to follow the functional necessities of the new professional roles open to women, while geometrically designed clothes and bobbed hair *(Bubikopf)* contribute to the blurring of binary gender distinctions (von Soden and Schmidt, 18ff.). [see **Employees, Male = Female (Gender Trouble)**] The fear of ideas and forms that have no reference or function becomes a veritable *horror vacui*. Journalistic discourses become a model for literature, since they are supposed to resist the transformation of primary experience into interpretation. [see **Reporters**] On the other hand, the evaluation of abstract forms of reflection depends on their interpenetration with everydayness. This at least is the central premise of an article commemorating the eightieth birthday of the philosopher Rudolf Eucken: "We must resist being absorbed into a 'pragmatic culture,' as well as getting stuck in a romantic 'cult of the soul.' What is at stake is an intellectual penetration and structuring of the pragmatic world" *(Berliner Börsen-Zeitung,* January 3).

But while intellectuals are fascinated with such concepts as formalism and functionalism, the deceptive aspects of their implicit programs begin to appear. Trying to construct a spherical theater, the Bauhaus designer Andor Weininger learns that the most elementary forms are not necessarily the most functional *(Wechselwirkungen,* 438ff.). A discussion of the latest architectural experiments in Amsterdam, in an article published by the *Berliner Tageblatt* on August 5, cites the inhabitants' desire for nonfunctional ornamentation—a desire that can certainly not be satisfied by a purely geometric style: "This is why the leveling straightedges of urban developers should begin to take account of tenants' wishes. But if it is economically necessary to squeeze people into huge housing projects, one should at least, for god's sake, leave them their little ornaments above doors and windows. Fortunately, the Durch architects have realized that human dwellings cannot be built according to strict dogmas, and that the modern culture of sobriety contradicts the playful impulses of human nature. 'The architect as pedagogue' is a wonderful concept—but, like any other educator, he also needs to be a psychologist." Likewise, despite its irrefutable environmental rationale, cremation fails to satisfy the desire for a corpse beside which one can mourn the death of a loved one. [see **Cremation**] Finally, by renouncing all visionary elements in favor of *Realpolitik,* Germany's Social Democrats seem to encourage a longing for ideologies among their opponents: "We have to break the Social Democratic Party—so that hunger can know what it is longing for, so that the German people can finally learn to will their own will" (Grimm, 662). In the end, the search for normative forms and functions threatens to generate what it most fears: chaos, stemming from the desire for Exuberance and proliferation.

If the aspect of Sobriety that is represented by the German concept of *Sachlichkeit* (the focus on things and functions) entails its opposite (an urge for Exuberance and intoxication), another aspect of Sobriety—its intense alertness—often succeeds in containing such consequences. Alertness is the state of mind in which great athletes compete: their senses are wide open to the world, but they do not fuse with the world. [see **Boxing**] It is what Theodor Lessing has in mind when he speaks of a principle that avoids "the complete dispersion of the divine Eros, the functionalization and trivialization of sexuality" (Lessing, 245). It is also the drive and speed that helps individuals overcome drunkenness and loss of identity. [see **Bars**] For the young painter Joan Miró, focusing on the motif of the glaring sunlight becomes a way of resisting dispersion and loss of focus (Dupin, 160). Ernst Jünger sees such intense alertness as a reward for overcoming intoxication: "Man . . . was first formed in the fire of battle; now he gives a new and terrifying face to combat and its instruments. Today's troops no longer consist of those enthusiastic youths whose intoxicating dreams were sacrificed to the power of machines. Hardened by the searing flame, they stand firmly and soberly in a merciless world" (Jünger, 36). Jünger's attitude suggests self-sacrifice, as well as the willingness to destroy others. Like Sobriety, bleakness can be the opposite of Exuberance. And even Sobriety need not always be constructive.

Related Entries

Assembly Lines, Bars, Boxing, Cremation, Employees, Elevators, Engineers, Railroads, Reporters, Strikes, Individuality vs. Collectivity, Present vs. Past, Silence vs. Noise, Uncertainty vs. Reality, Male = Female (Gender Trouble), Transcendence = Immanence (Death)

References

António de Alcântara Machado, *Ano de 1926.* In Alcântara Machado, *Obras*, vol. 1: *Prosa preparatória; Cavaquinho e Saxofone*. Rio de Janeiro, 1983.

Walter Benjamin, *Einbahnstraße* (1926). In Benjamin, *Gesammelte Schriften,* vol. 4, part 1. Frankfurt, 1972.

Berliner Börsen-Zeitung.

Berliner Tageblatt.

André Coeuroy and André Schäffner, *Le Jazz.* Paris, 1926.

Eugen Diesel, *Der Weg durch das Wirrsal.* Stuttgart, 1926.

Jacques Dupin, *Joan Miró: Leben und Werk.* Cologne, 1961.

Alfred Ehrentreich, "Die neue Sachlichkeit in der Schule." *Die Tat* 18 (June 1926): 234–235.

Peter Galison, "Aufbau / Bauhaus: Logical Positivism and Architectural Modernism." *Critical Inquiry* 16 (1990): 709–752.

Federico García Lorca, "Oda a Salvador Dalí" (1926). In García Lorca, *Obras completas.* Madrid, 1971.

María Carmen García-Nieto, Javier M. Donézar, and Luiz López Puértola, eds., *La dictadura, 1923–1930: Bases documentales de la España contemporánea,* vol. 7. Madrid, 1973.

Hans Grimm, *Volk ohne Raum,* vol. 2. Munich, 1926.

Karl Holl, "Der Wandel des deutschen Lebensgefühls im Spiegel der deutschen Kunst seit der Reichsgründung." *Deutsche Vierteljahrsschrift für Literaturwissenschaft und Geistesgeschichte* 4 (1926): 548–563.

Ernst Jünger, *Feuer und Blut: Ein kleiner Ausschnitt aus einer grossen Schlacht* (1926). Hamburg, 1941.

Theodor Lessing, "Der Hühnerhof" (1926). In Lessing, *"Ich warf eine Flaschenpost ins Eismeer der Geschichte": Essays und Feuilletons, 1923–1933.* Neuwied, 1986.

Helmut Lethen, *Neue Sachlichkeit, 1924–1932: Studien zur Literatur des "Weissen Sozialismus."* Stuttgart, 1970.

Kristine von Soden and Maruta Schmidt, eds., *Neue Frauen: Die zwanziger Jahre.* Berlin, 1988.

Wechselwirkungen: Ungarische Avantgarde in der Weimarer Republik. Marburg, 1986.

John Willet, *Art and Politics in the Weimar Period: The New Sobriety, 1917–1933.* New York, 1978.

UNCERTAINTY VS. REALITY

....

⋈

There is a fear that truth may not be (and may never have been) available. As a venerable ideal, truth is firmly present. But beyond that, people long to perceive the world and its phenomena "such as they are"—that is, without any perspectival distortions. They do not want such insight and understanding to be subject to revision and historical change. They still hope that the possession of truth will improve the conditions of human existence. But the stronger such longing, desire, and hope grow, the less realistic they appear. This situation directly affects the work of most intellectuals, and it seems to have an impact on the behavior even of those who do not care about philosophical arguments. In response to this vanishing of truth as the ultimate criterion for knowledge, two different attitudes are emerging. On the one hand, some intellectuals complain that a world without truth is a chaotic world. They search for the causes of this crisis and for ways to resolve it. On the other hand, some thinkers, without repressing the knowledge of inevitable Uncertainty, try to come to terms with it. They have set aside, postponed, or deliberately neglected the question of how human cognition can reach the ultimate level of truth, and they try to assess the value of any item of knowledge exclusively according to the functions that it can fulfill for human life and interaction. Rather than the classic binarism "true versus false" (Luhmann, 167ff.), it is the distinction between "Uncertainty" and "Reality" that shapes people's disparate responses to the vanishing of the truth-criterion. If they do not complain about the consequences of this loss ("Uncertainty"), they insist on the practical necessity of using knowledge to orient human life, however provisional this knowledge may be ("Reality").

The perception of the present world as chaotic has become such a widely—indeed internationally—accepted commonplace that it can be invoked as a premise for more complex arguments without further comment. [see **Present vs. Past, Center vs. Periphery**] What the young Brazilian journalist Sérgio Buarque de Holanda describes as "the general confusion characterizing the first quarter of our century" (Buarque de Holanda, 76), and refers to as a contrasting background for the "exceptional personality" of Filippo Marinetti, becomes "a moment of chaos from which life in the world is suffering on all possible levels" for the Spanish art critic Antonio Méndez Casal, who tries to identify the place of Catalan painting in an international context (*Blanco y Negro*, 53). The same motif returns as "the confusion, absence, deformation of all human values—this harrowing uncertainty into which we are plunged," in Antonin Artaud's prospectus for his Théâtre Alfred Jarry (Artaud, 15). These authors all attribute confusion and chaos to the contemporary world itself (and not to the perspectives that they adopt as observers of this world). And they all experience such disorder as a particularly pressing problem of modern existence. In the first sentence of his presidential address, delivered at the University of Berlin on Tuesday, August 3, Karl Holl contrasts "the glorious decade of a hundred years ago" with the "urgent situation of our contemporary moment" (Holl, 1). On Tuesday, November 2, during a public rally in support of Munich's role as a "cultural center," Thomas Mann calls the present "a particularly demanding time" (*Kampf*, 7).

Images of chaos show a kinship with the metaphors—especially popular among German intellectuals—that depict the world as an unstable ground. Although the difference in meaning between the chaos metaphor and the instability metaphor is minimal, they facilitate associations that go in opposite directions. Whereas in images of chaos and confusion the loss of order is supposed to affect only the object world, one cannot imagine an unstable ground—let alone a shaking ground—that would not also have an impact on the observer's view. In Thomas Mann's story "Unordnung und frühes Leid," Professor Cornelius' wife refers to "the rocking of the ground under my feet, the topsy-turvy nature of all things" (494), as a way of describing the impact of postwar inflation on her world perception. A lead article, written outside Germany and published in the *8 Uhr–Abendblatt* on February 4, identifies a similar feeling of existential insecurity in connection with the German political situation, and it explicitly questions the value of its own analysis, which depends on such unstable ground: "There is a prize attached to walking under palm trees. The further one is from Germany (as it is my privilege to be these days), the more one begins to perceive, on every possible level, the volatility of the German situation. What will happen within the next two or three days? What will have happened before these lines appear before readers' eyes?" Not surprisingly—yet without any obvious reasons—the Fascist novelist Mario Puccini sees a male virtue manifesting itself in situations of stability: "For just as, politically and morally speaking, few European nations are today on par with us, so we could soon . . . give the world a remarkable example of health, of moral, civil, and intellectual strength. But only if we want to. Other peoples have, at least for the most part, lost that sense of virile stability and that contact with reality" (Puccini, 257). [see **Male vs. Female**] It is in the context of an obsession with instability that many Argentinian tango lyrics not only revive the topos of female fickleness but explicitly insist on the contrast between female inconstancy and the reliability and unselfishness that the lyric male "I" claims for himself:

> Don't let yourself be tricked, my heart,
> by her desire, by her lies;
> don't go and forget
> that she is a woman and that since the day she was born
> deceit has been one of her intimate qualities.
> Don't believe that it is envy or spite
> for all the evil she's done to me
> that makes me speak to you this way . . .
> You know well that there is no envy in my breast,
> that I am as I have always been.
>
> (Reichardt, 322ff.)

There are a number of typical everyday experiences—partly new and partly remembered from times past—that explain why unstable ground has become such a powerful metaphor. Key among them is the power *with* which modern weaponry can transform nature and landscape: "In no time, we see a number of hand grenades smash down, creating a straight line of explosions . . . We begin to feel that vague shaking of the earth under our feet. The enemy tries to smoke out those soldiers of our group that have fled into the tunnel" (Jünger, 134). In such scenes, the loss of a stable ground under the soldiers' feet literally coincides with the complete loss of existential security: "We rise, and we feel how the last secure plank is sliding away" (95). On a less dramatic level, this is a feeling with which sailors—and a growing number of transatlantic passengers—have long been familiar: "In the end I felt a craving to feel solid ground under my feet. I wanted to see people hustling about. I wanted to make sure that the world was still going on in the usual way" (Traven, 9). [see **Americans in Paris, Ocean Liners**] Rapidly developing transport technologies are transforming people's perception of the relation between the human body and the surface of the earth [see **Airplanes, Automobiles, Elevators, Railroads**], and the reactions to this transformation are not exclusively negative. As the now popular "illuminated dance floors" indicate, losing the ground under one's feet can also bring ecstatic happiness, a euphoria caused by an illusory departure from the hardships of earthly existence. [see **Dancing, Immanence vs. Transcendence**]

No other single event, however, has had a greater impact on both scholarly and popular attitudes toward the production of knowledge than Einstein's publication of his theory of relativity. While it is difficult to assess how much of this theory has become accessible to the nonspecialist public in the two decades since it initiated a revolution in theoretical physics, and while Einstein himself has been insisting that the physical principle of relativity has nothing whatsoever to do with philosophical relativism and even less with the relativism of everyday values (Graham, 109), there is no doubt that the connotations of the word "relativity" are rapidly generating a collective trauma: "The theory of relativity was seen by many laypeople as the denial of absolute standards and values. Coming at a time when the global political and economic environment was exceedingly unstable, and at a moment when the successful Russian Revolution had thrown into question the entire range of assumptions and values upon which European order was based, the new physics seemed to be one more threat to reliable standards. That Einstein was a political radical and a Jew did not help allay the misgivings of those who felt that the old order—political and scientific—was under attack from similar quarters" (Graham, 119). At least on a preconscious level, Einstein's own thought seems to have been influenced by the metaphorical proximity of physical relativity to existential instability. This is revealed by the fact that trains, which serve as a metaphor for people's changing relation to the—increasingly unstable—ground under their feet, are also the standard metaphor that Einstein and his students use to explain relativity (Salmon, 69ff.). [see **Railroads**] The train metaphor is such an obvious common denominator for scientific research and for a new experience of the human condition because it can symbolize, on different levels, the impression that the production of knowledge depends on the motion of the individual who is in the process of observing the world. In the context of physics, relativity thus leads to the conclusion that, as a surface (or rather as a ground) on which knowledge is produced, the earth is not homogeneous. If Einstein redefines space as "motion relative to a practically rigid body of reference," and if he points to a train and an embankment as examples of such bodies of reference, then it is clear that his world—at least his world of special relativity— will break up into a variety of individual spaces (Einstein, 10–11). A passenger riding on a train drops a stone from the train window; the stone's trajectory as observed by the passenger appears quite different from the trajectory as observed by a person standing on the embankment.

The relativity principle generates such a broad reaction because its basic outlines offer some striking similarities to certain collective obsessions of the moment. Among the observers of the current epistemological and practical instability, Walter Benjamin is one of the very few who manages to maintain an analytical attitude instead of indulging in dramatic hyperbole: "A stable situation is not necessarily a comfortable situation, and even before the war there were social groups for whom stability meant the stabilization of misery. Social decline is by no means less stable or more miraculous than social rise" (Benjamin, 94–95). Benjamin's reflection epitomizes two of the main practical insights stemming from the epistemological crisis. Knowledge is always contingent upon—and true or false in relation to—the position of the observer. This means that economic and social instability will seem a nightmare only to those who have a great deal to lose. But it also means that a situation which different observers agree to see as unstable when they look at it from a certain perspective can turn into the stability of change when it is seen from the next higher level. Intellectuals and writers, however, are still obsessed with finding the one and only appropriate distance between themselves and the objects of their gaze. In the first scene of Jules Super-vielle's *Le voleur d'enfants (The Man Who Stole Children)*, a little boy gets kidnapped in the crowded streets of Paris because he is too small to see the adults' faces: "Antoine . . . is short and can see before him only men's legs and hurrying skirts. On the pavement are hundreds of wheels that turn, or that stop at the feet of a policeman as grim as a rock" (9).

The impossibility of observing oneself has become another central topic of the moment. In *Uno, nessuno e centomila (One, No One, and One Hundred Thousand)*, Luigi Pirandello shows that a mirror, instead of validating an individual's reflection, can aggravate this problem. "Whenever I stood before a mirror," says the narrator, "a sort of arrest took place in me. All spontaneity was gone; every gesture of mine seemed fictitious or imitative. I could not see myself as a living being" (16). In Brecht's drama *Mann ist Mann (Man Is Man)*, the former packer Galy Gay, having been transformed into a perfect and terrible "fighting ma-chine," lacks the distance from his new role that would allow him to integrate it with his earlier life [see **Individuality vs. Collectivity**]:

> How does Galy Gay know, that it is he
> Who is Galy Gay?
> If his arm were hacked off
> And he found it in a hole in the wall,
> Would Galy Gay's eye recognize his arm?
> . . . . .
> And if Galy Gay were not Galy Gay,
> He would be the drinking son of a mother who
> Would be the mother of another, if she were
> Not his, and that son would drink as well.
>
> (Brecht, 360–361)

Transforming such lack of distance from one's own body and actions into something potentially heroic, Lawrence of Arabia insists that he will never claim the role of objective observer: "Since I was [the Arabs'] fellow, I will not be their apologist or advocate. To-day, in my old garments, I could play the bystander, obedient to the sensibilities of our theater . . . but it is more honest to record that these ideas and actions then passed naturally. What now looks wanton or sadic seemed in the field inevitable, or just unimportant routine" (Lawrence, 30–31). Yet another variation of the same problem emerges in Allen Tate's introduction to Hart Crane's collection of poems, *White Buildings*. Tate starts out with the premise that a core element in the identity of the modern poet is the poet's inability—perhaps even unwillingness—to "[apprehend] his world as a Whole." According to Tate, two reactions to this situation are possible. Poets can either register isolated, mostly sensual world-perceptions and transform them into isolated poems, or—and this is the case with Crane—they can conceive of their texts as fragments of a single world-vision that they have no hope of ever seeing as a totality but can never allow themselves to abandon: "A series of Imagistic poems is a series of worlds. [But] the poems of Hart Crane are facets of a single vision; they refer to a central imagination, a single evaluating power, which is at once the motive of the poetry and the form of its realization" (Crane, xii). Walter Benjamin again comes through with a particularly distanced comment on the question of cognitive distance. It is unclear whether his tone is ironic or nostalgic; but Benjamin leaves no doubt that cognitive distance, which was once a condition for the Authenticity and depth of understanding, is no longer achievable. At the same time, however, he finds a positive excitement in this loss of distance [see **Movie Palaces, Authenticity vs. Artificiality**]:

> Those who lament the decline of criticism are fools. Its hour has passed. For criticism depends on appropriate distance. It belongs to a world that consisted of perspectives and prospects, a world in which it was still possible to occupy a viewpoint. Meanwhile, things have come threateningly close to the body of human society. Today, to speak of an 'unbiased,' independent view is either a lie or an expression of intellectual incompetence. The most essentialist—and the most mercantile—view into the heart of all matters is the view of advertising. It makes the play with the observer's distance collapse and brings things dangerously close to our face—like a car which, growing to gigantic proportions, seems to emerge from the movie screen. And just as the cinema never presents furniture or façades as objects of critical reflection, because it aims exclusively at the sensational effect of their sudden closeness, so good advertising brings things close to us with the speed of the modern film. (Benjamin, 131–132)

Those who try to defend the classic concept and value of truth often have recourse to traditions of thought and meditation outside their own Western culture. The essay "Zur Rolle des Yoga in der geistigen Welt Indiens" ("On the Role of Yoga in the Spiritual World of India"), by the German philosopher Heinrich Zimmer, is a perfect example of this tendency: "Yoga is the only path that permits man to grasp the absolute essence of 'being' behind the veil of its metamorphoses—that being which is in all things but which man can experience directly only when it is presented to him beneath this veil, in his own innermost sphere" (Zimmer, 57). More appropriate than Zimmer's philosophical utopia is Siegfried Kracauer's grim allegory of the epistemological present: "A jury sits on invisible chairs along the sides of a quadrangular space. This is the moment of judgment—but the verdict will never be pronounced" (Kracauer, 13). What the epistemological moment seems to require, despite its desperate sophistication, is the courage for simple solutions. A man like Dr. Wilhelm Dieck, teacher of mathematics at the high school in the provincial north German town of Sterkrade, publishes a book (in Sterkrade!) with the imposing title *Der Widerspruch im Richtigen: Gemeinverständliche mathematische Kritik der geltenden Logik (The Contradiction in the Appropriate: A Generally Comprehensible Mathematical Critique of Contemporary Logic)*, in which he offers the insight that all the problems of world perception and knowledge production arise from simple contradictions intrinsic to the human mind—contradictions that humans will never be able to overcome. Dieck's final message is a naively arrogant call for epistemological modesty: "I must not forget to emphasize that my book definitely undermines the belief in the absolute power of ideas" (Dieck, 149). For all his pretentiousness, Dieck would not be a German high school teacher if he did not conclude his argument with a call to intellectual diligence and patience—and with a poem: "The past suffered from an overappreciation of the intellect. We will not really correct this mistake if we turn overappreciation into underestimation. It remains our task to work with perseverance and patience for the perfection of human knowledge . . . If a dreamer, full of sorrow, / will mourn the fading light of sunset, / open eyes and open minds will always greet / the first light of dawn in the east" (151).

Among those who believe that they have left the intellectual past behind, a boundless enthusiasm for Reality takes hold: "Our truly frantic love for Reality is unprecedented. Never has Reality appeared so appealing. This fact in itself proves what immense progress our era has made. More and more, humankind appears divided into two groups. But those who do not participate will disappear in gray anonymity" (von Wedderkop, 253). [see **Present vs. Past**] The world of the new Reality is breaking apart into an infinite number of everyday worlds, each of which has to be discovered, occupied, and cultivated. Such worlds are worlds constituted by different forms of praxis; they are modes of life, as is the world of Judaism in Siegfried Kracauer's description: "What we are talking about is a form of *practical life* . . . neither a theoretical state of consciousness nor an exclusively religious activity. Like the liturgical movement, for example" (Kracauer, 174). Even isolated occasions of celebration and joy are now seen as independent worlds, which exist through their isolation from, rather than their integration with, everydayness: "The things that happened could only have happened during a fiesta. Everything became quite unreal finally and it seemed as though nothing could have any consequences. It seemed out of place to think of consequences during the fiesta. All during the fiesta you had the feeling, even when it was quiet, that you had to shout any remark to make it heard. It was the same feeling about any action. It was a fiesta and it went on for seven days" (Hemingway, 159). The strangest and most striking new experience, however, is that of particular Realities being created with specific intentions and conscious strategies. In B. Traven's novel *Das Totenschiff (The Death Ship)*, the hero and narrator ends up on a ship that is deliberately sunk—and he thus becomes the victim of a plot that, he discovers, is the conventional Reality of insurance fraud. Yet despite all the lies and fictions on which this fraud is based, it is as real—and lethal—as any institutional or natural Reality could possibly be: "Hundreds of death ships [sail] the seven seas . . . All nations have their death ships. Never have there been so many dead, since the time the Great War was won in the name of true freedom and actual democracy" (Traven, 138). Initially, people seem to underestimate those Realities that reveal themselves to be based on conventions or strategies. But long before professional philosophers get used to an epistemological situation in which the truth-criterion is disintegrating, a tacit acknowledgment of the multiple nature of everyday reality has become part of daily life. This is the topic of Arthur Schnitzler's *Traumnovelle (Dream Story)*. A wealthy young doctor and his beautiful wife are vexed by the—correct—impression that the daily obligations of his medical profession and of her domestic concerns are stifling the passionate moments of their marriage: "Fridolin's profession summoned him to his patients at an early hour, while Albertine would not stay in bed longer because of her duties as a housewife and mother. So the ensuing hours passed, soberly and predetermined, in daily routine and work" (Schnitzler, 5). In this situation of disillusionment, Albertine gets entangled in fantasies about what her amorous past could have ideally been, whereas Fridolin enters a highly eroticized world that Schnitzler constructs as ambiguous—it may be either a daydream or a licentious Reality. At the end, when Fridolin is about to make a confession about this erotic life, which has turned into a nightmare for him, he finds Albertine full of understanding. From her own personal experience, she is familiar with the character of his dreams, and she can thus persuade him to stop worrying about how real they are. She can sense that there is no single, ultimate truth that would invalidate all the particular—sometimes passionate and sometimes boring—worlds and forms of their shared experience: "I'm sure that the reality of one night, let alone that of a whole lifetime, is not the whole truth" (Schnitzler, 135). With this philosophical insight, Albertine and Fridolin once again learn to appreciate the modest joys of everydayness: "So they lay silently, dozing a little, dreamlessly, close to each other—until there was a knock on the door, as there was every morning at seven. And—with the usual noises from the street, a victorious ray of light through the curtains, and the clear laughter of a child through the door—a new day began" (136). Schnitzler, however, is much too fond of Sigmund Freud's ideas to insinuate, as Louis Aragon does in his novel *Le paysan de Paris,* that all higher spheres of human existence and transcendence, and all mythology, ultimately emerge from everydayness: "New myths are born under each of our footsteps. Where man has lived, where he lives, legend begins" (Aragon, 14). [see **Immanence vs. Transcendence**] Schnitzler and Aragon display two different tonalities in their ways of coming to terms with a new experience of Reality.

Coming to terms with, or even opting for, this experience of Reality means acknowledging the same feeling of Uncertainty that pushes other people to the opposite reaction—namely, to refuse to embrace Reality with intellectual Sobriety. [see **Sobriety vs. Exuberance**] Far from excluding Uncertainty, Reality always presupposes and contains it. If there is any possibility of problematizing the contrast between Uncertainty and Reality, it comes from individual voices that, while they acknowledge the necessity of adapting to Reality, have not completely given up the dream of achieving truth. One of these voices is Adolf Hitler's. He is driven by the double desire to claim for himself the role of truth-bearing genius and prophet, and also to make sure that, if he fails to be accepted as a genius and prophet, he can still assume that nothing beats the pragmatic attitude of a successful politician: "Amid the monotony of everyday life, even important people often seem unimportant and hardly stand out against the average elements in their surroundings. But as soon as they face a situation in which others would despair or go wrong, out of the plain average child the ingenious nature grows visibly. Not infrequently, this occurs to the astonishment of all those who have had the opportunity to observe the child as he has grown up in the narrow confines of bourgeois life. As a result of this process, the prophet is rarely honored in his own country" (Hitler, 321). Others reserve the pursuit of truth for science. But if science, as José Ortega y Gasset suggests, is allowed to concern itself only with truth, then it becomes an institution that risks becoming detached from aspects of practical usefulness: "From the enormous block of knowledge that constitutes modern science, only a tiny part yields something useful. Applied science—technology—is simply an appendix to the enormous volume represented by pure science, the science that believes itself to be without purposes or utilitarian results. Intelligence, then, is a mainly useless function, a marvelous luxury of the organism, an inexplicable superfluity . . . It appears to us . . . as an activity that is primarily a pastime and only secondarily utilitarian" (Ortega y Gasset, 122—123).

The Brazilian journalist António de Alcântara Machado associates such scientific research, free of any practical value or application, with the United States, since both seem futuristic to him. [see **Present vs. Past, Center vs. Periphery**] He engages in a familiar psychological tradeoff: seeing the United States as ridiculous because then one can repress one's admiration for it. "The European newspapers are still worried about a telegram that they received from California. It was a truly horrifying telegram, revealing that an American astronomer has discovered a new universe. It's true: a new universe, with stars, planets, galaxies—everything a respectable universe needs. Discovering planets has become trivial for American scientists. They now go further than that . . . Amazing! You'll agree that their discovery is sensational. Compared to it, everything that the American imagination has invented so far seems small. The only bad thing is that this new discovery has no practical use whatsoever" (Alcântara Machado, 138–139). While a Brazilian journalist thus accuses the United States, and especially California, of promoting pure science as yet another excess of the present, Ray Lyman Wilbur, the president of Stanford University, insists on the extent to which an emphasis on practical usefulness—on Reality—has always characterized academic life on the West Coast: "Education for direct usefulness in life has always been an aim of this institution. To give men and women training without destroying personality or initiative, to keep a sense of personal freedom and responsibility, to consider the student a colleague of the teacher, and to stand for contributing helpfulness to the world outside have been its outstanding ideals" (*1926 Quad*, 246).

Related Entries

Airplanes, Americans in Paris, Automobiles, Dancing, Elevators, Movie Palaces, Railroads, Authenticity vs. Artificiality, Center vs. Periphery, Immanence vs. Transcendence, Individuality vs. Collectivity, Male vs. Female, Present vs. Past, Sobriety vs. Exuberance

References

8 Uhr–Abendblatt.
Antología de Blanco y Negro, 1891–1926, vol. 9. Madrid, 1986.
António de Alcântara Machado, "Ano de 1926." In Alcântara Machado, *Obras,* vol. 1: *Prosa preparatória; Cavaquinho e saxofone.* Rio de Janeiro, 1983.
Louis Aragon, *Le paysan de Paris.* Paris, 1926.
Antonin Artaud, "Le Théâtre Alfred Jarry" (1926). In Artaud, *Oeuvres complètes,* vol. 2. Paris, 1961.
Associated Students of Stanford University, eds., *The 1926 Quad.*
Walter Benjamin, *Einbahnstraße* (1926). In Benjamin, *Gesammelte Schriften,* vol. 4, part 1. Frankfurt, 1972.
Bertolt Brecht, *Mann ist Mann* (1926). In Brecht, *Gesammelte Werke,* vol. 1. Frankfurt, 1967.
Sérgio Buarque de Holanda, "Marinetti, homen político" (1926). In Francisco de Assis Barbosa, ed., *Raízes de Sérgio Buarque de Holanda.* Rio de Janeiro, 1989.
Agatha Christie, *The Murder of Roger Ackroyd.* London, 1926.

Hart Crane, *White Buildings*. New York, 1926.

Wilhelm Dieck, *Der Widerspruch im Richtigen: Gemeinverständliche mathematische Kritik der geltenden Logik*. Sterkrade, 1926.

Albert Einstein, *Relativity—The Special and General Theory: A Popular Exposition* (1917). New York, 1961.

Loren R. Graham, "The Reception of Einstein's Ideas: Two Examples from Contrasting Political Cultures." In Gerald Holton and Yehuda Elkana, eds., *Albert Einstein: Historical and Cultural Perspectives*. Princeton, 1982.

Ernest Hemingway, *The Sun Also Rises*. New York, 1926.

Adolf Hitler, *Mein Kampf* (1926). Munich, 1941.

Karl Holl, "Über Begriff und Bedeutung der "dämonischen Persönlichkeit." Address delivered in Berlin, August 3, 1925. *Deutsche Vierteljahrsschrift für Literaturwissenschaft und Geistesgeschichte* 4 (1926): 1–19.

Kampf um München als Kulturzentrum: Sechs Vorträge. Munich, 1927.

Siegfried Kracauer, "Zwei Flächen" (1926). In Kracauer, *Das Ornament der Masse: Essays*. Frankfurt, 1977.

T. E. Lawrence, *The Seven Pillars of Wisdom: A Triumph* (1926). New York, 1935.

Niklas Luhmann, *Die Wissenschaft der Gesellschaft*. Frankfurt, 1990.

Thomas Mann, "Unordnung und frühes Leid" (1926). In Mann, *Sämtliche Erzählungen*. Frankfurt, 1963.

José Ortega y Gasset, "Parerga: Reforma de la inteligencia." *Revista de Occidente* 4 (1926): 119–129.

Luigi Pirandello, *Uno, nessuno e centomila* (1926). Milan, 1936.

Mario Puccini, "Contribution to the Great Debate on Fascism and Culture in *Critica Fascista*" (1926). *Stanford Italian Review* (1990): 257–260.

Dieter Reichardt, ed., *Tango: Verweigerung und Trauer, Kontexte und Texte*. Frankfurt, 1984.

Wesley C. Salmon, *Space, Time, and Motion: A Philosophical Introduction*. Encino, Calif., 1975.

Arthur Schnitzler, *Traumnovelle*. Berlin, 1926.

Jules Supervielle, *Le voleur d'enfants*. Paris, 1926.

Hermann von Wedderkop, "Wandlungen des Geschmacks" (1926). In Anton Kaes, ed., *Weimarer Republik: Manifeste und Dokumente zur deutschen Literatur, 1918–1933*. Stuttgart, 1983.

Heinrich Zimmer, "Zur Rolle des Yoga in der geistigen Welt Indiens." *Deutsche Vierteljahrsschrift für Literaturwissenschaft und Geistesgeschichte* 4 (1926): 21–57.

CODES COLLAPSED

ACTION = IMPOTENCE (TRAGEDY)

For the young journalist Siegfried Kracauer, "Tragedy" belongs to a set of concepts whose connotations of depth compromise intellectual honesty in an age that believes in exteriority and surfaces. [see **Gomina, Movie Palaces, Stars**] "Truth is threatened only by the naive affirmation of cultural values that have become unreal and by the careless misuse of concepts such as 'personality,' 'inwardness,' 'tragedy,' and so on—terms which in themselves certainly refer to lofty ideas but which have lost much of their scope, along with their supporting foundations, due to social changes. Furthermore, many of these concepts have acquired a bad aftertaste because they unjustifiably deflect an inordinate amount of attention from the external damages caused by society onto the private individual" (Kracauer, 314). Kracauer subscribes to an ethical position which, on the assumption that individuals are widely determined by their social environment, denies that they can be held responsible for their Actions. [see **Murder, Individuality vs. Collectivity**] As he seems to suggest, this perspective is indeed incompatible with the classical concept of Tragedy, which deals with individuals entangled in the conflicting demands of different value systems. Tragic agents may choose one value system, but they will always be guilty vis-à-vis the other—and it is precisely this state of individual (often inescapable) guilt which Kracauer is no longer willing to accept.

Even those intellectuals whom Ernst Robert Curtius refers to as "eagerly breathing the air of tragedy" (Curtius, 231) would probably agree with Kracauer's view that the term's canonical meaning has become unacceptable. For among the key premises of contemporary intellectual life is that the grounds for ethical norms and cognitive certainties have vanished [see **Present vs. Past, Uncertainty vs. Reality**], whereas Tragedy generally involves conflicts between intrinsically stable normative systems. In situations of generalized uncertainty, however, when all norms have disappeared and when people cannot be held responsible for the consequences of their Actions, the one gesture that counts is to place Action, as a form that resists chaos, in opposition to the threat of disorder. [see **Action vs. Impotence**] Once the concept of Action is thus defined from both an aesthetic and a pragmatic perspective, Actions that fail can still be as valuable and beautiful—at least from the point of view of the agents—as Actions that turn out to be pragmatically successful. Nevertheless, Actions that fail have a far higher risk of fading into oblivion, and this is why failure ultimately jeopardizes even their existence as forms. It is through this paradoxical convergence of the beauty of Actions with the threat of their annihilation that a new, nonclassical notion of Tragedy comes into use. Calling an Action "tragic" means to protect its presence as a beautiful form.

But why would the Berlin press describe as tragic the case of a nineteen-year-old delinquent who has enjoyed all the privileges of an upper-class education? If the young man went too far in his endeavor to gain independence from the austere mode of life imposed on him by his family, he now exaggerates his good will as a defendant by confessing to more crimes than he can possibly have committed. Both reactions win him the sympathy of the public because they both almost touchingly exceed what would be necessary for him to acquire an individual profile:

> Yesterday a grand jury in Berlin had to deal with the tragedy of a young life. The accused was a nineteen-year-old man whose face clearly showed a superior intelligence and whose entire behavior could only be the product of an excellent education. Indeed, it became clear that he is from a well-respected, thoroughly religious family. Up until the war, his development was quite normal, but then he began to be confused. When his father came back from the war, he was probably too strict with the boy—which the father now greatly regrets, because this may have been the origin of his son's misfortune . . . In his very first interview with the police, the young man confessed to fourteen cases of

robbery. In five of these cases, however, the police have been unable to produce any substantiating evidence. (*Berliner Tageblatt,* August 8)

According to conventional ethical and even legal standards, this case makes the attribution of responsibility and guilt particularly easy because the delinquent has grown up under circumstances that should have prepared him to lead an orderly life. Calling his existence "tragic," therefore, seems to express nothing but an elementary unwillingness to discuss guilt or responsibility at all. In a grotesquely similar sense, the philosopher Theodor Lessing describes as "tragic" the efforts of an ostrich to fly, since its failure can certainly not be interpreted as an individual shortcoming (Lessing, 233). When the murder of a young American scientist by two Eskimos during a polar expedition is discovered seventeen years after the fact, the *New York Times* (September 25) presents the case as a Tragedy because forgoing the attribution of guilt gives the story a more enigmatic flavor [see **Polarities**] and helps discourage legally problematic prejudgments. When Greta Garbo calls the discontinuation of John Gilbert's contract with MGM studios a Tragedy, the word frees her from having to ask the uncomfortable question whether she could have used her own rapidly growing influence to help her former lover (Gronowicz, 201). Among those who are addicted to the concept of Tragedy, Adolf Hitler goes particularly far in underscoring the extent to which he denies any attribution of guilt or responsibility. Describing the miserable conditions in which the proletarians of Vienna lived around the turn of the century, he couples the word "tragic" to his interpretation of their status as victims: "I witnessed this personally in hundreds of scenes, initially with disgust and indignation; but later I began to grasp the tragic side and to understand the deeper reasons for their misery. Unfortunate victims of poor social conditions" (Hitler, 28). Hitler fears that if people see themselves as guilty, this will paralyze their capacity to act politically in their own interest: "This uncertainty is only too deeply rooted in one's own feeling of being guilty of such tragedies of demoralization. It paralyzes every sincere and firm decision, thus adding to the wavering and half-heartedness with which even the most urgent measures of self-preservation are taken. Only when a race is no longer burdened by the consciousness of its own guilt will it find the internal peace and external strength to cut down purposefully and brutally the wild shoots and pull up the weeds" (30).

It must be the ubiquitous use of the word "Tragedy" that encourages proto-philosophical efforts to redefine it. The larger discursive field in which these definitions take place associates the goal-orientedness of Action with the spiritual side of human life, whereas the materiality of life (that is, its biological basis) is supposed to explain the limitations and possible failures of Action. In his poetico-scientific treatise on termites, Maurice Maeterlinck transforms this conceptual configuration into a picture of what he calls the "tragic situation" of human existence: "The situation of man is tragic. His principal and perhaps his only enemy (all religions realize this and here are in agreement, for they have always dealt with it, under the name of "evil" or "sin") is matter. On the other hand, in himself all is matter, beginning with the part of himself that disdains, condemns, and would like at all costs to evade matter" (Maeterlinck, 209–210). For thirteen years, the countless readers of Miguel de Unamuno's philosophical bestseller *Del sentimiento trágico de la vida (The Tragic Sense of Life)* have been impressed with a similar contrast between spiritual and physical life. Referring to the recently published German translation of Unamuno's book, Ernst Robert Curtius presents this very polarity as its decisive component: "Unamuno's most important philosophical work is his book about the tragic sense of life. But it is somewhat problematic to call the book philosophical. For by "philosophy" Unamuno means not working with concepts but, rather, developing a world view out of a feeling of life. Life and reason are opposites for him. Whatever is vital is antirational; whatever is rational is antivital" (Curtius, 236). No other nation becomes as closely associated as Spain with the tragic side of human life that has to do with its biological basis [see **Bullfighting, Authenticity vs. Artificiality**]—a fact that may, at least among intellectuals, be partly due to Unamuno's international popularity. In Kasimir Edschmid's analysis of Spanish culture, this association is emblematized by cockfights because they stage a ferocious ritual of killing which is free from any abstract idea: "These movements of the battle between animals whose only feeling is that of annihilation make the most horrible impression which any battle under the shadow of death can make. These gestures remind us of the tragedy of Oedipus, who, blindfolded, turns toward the face of the gods. But the tragedy of these birds is even more intense because it does not imply any ideas. It just shows how monstrous killing is in its most maddening form" (Edschmid, 12). [see **Immanence = Transcendence (Death)**] Once a cockfight gets under way, it is impossible to stop it before one of the two animals has died. Thus, cockfights are seen as incarnating a new experience of war, and it is this new experience of war which shows that the biological component in the contemporary concept of Tragedy stands for facticity, and for whatever concrete conditions of Action exceed the control of the human will. For this reason, the young literary critic Erich Auerbach accuses Jean Racine's Tragedies of failing to represent the "sphere of everyday life" as it existed in their historical moment (Auerbach, 386), whereas he praises the relatively obscure French author Jean-Paul Courier, an eyewitness to the Napoleonic Wars, for the "tragic meaning" in the historical details and circumstances he so meticulously evokes (520). In Courier's books, "the world of facts, the overwhelming accumulation of pragmatic events, strangles all possible theory" (Auerbach, 514; also Gumbrecht, 104ff.).

The concept of Tragedy has become popular enough to revive the old question of how readers and theatergoers can take pleasure in unpleasant, "tragic" things. The historically specific answer to this question is obvious. On the one hand, the concept of "Tragedy" emphasizes those conditions of human existence which exceed the control of human Actions; but on the other, Tragedy offers a perspective from which human Actions can be praised even if they fail to accomplish their explicit goals. This type of aestheticization, however, which is a depragmatization of Actions that extends to their everyday contexts, is different from the traditional association between aestheticization and fictionality, which is more strictly confined to literature and its reception. Since literary texts and theatrical representations are expected to be nonreferential, readers and spectators can set aside any unpleasant aspect of their content. This is how scholars still analyze the problem: "Where the truly great work of art begins, one no longer thinks about real-world plots and persons, and on this absolute level of concentration, where artist and audience must meet, we quite naturally enjoy the tragic" (Wolff, 397). The new concept of Tragedy, in contrast, brings Action and its potential ineffectiveness together, along with a basic ambiguity in the emotional reaction to the success or failure of Actions: "We are incapable of structuring our affects in any meaningful way on the basis of simple binarisms such as 'joy/pain'" (Dieck, 148). Thus, the modality of aesthetic experience that corresponds to the new concept of Tragedy depends on acknowledging the limitations that facticity and fate impose on the human will. Only by taking into account these limits is it possible to appreciate the beauty and existential value of Actions regardless of their effectiveness.

Such sophisticated discussions notwithstanding, frequent use of the words "Tragedy" and "tragic" is indeed attended by the trivialization that Siegfried Kracauer mentions. Often these terms are nothing but high-sounding formulas with which authors try to protect collective and individual subjects against allegations of guilt. When Unamuno evokes "the tragedy that is intensifying over my poor Spain" (Unamuno, 188), he just wants to make sure that nobody but the members of the present government will be held responsible for the political crisis in his country. When the critics of Jules Romains' play *Le Dictateur* praise it as "the tragedy of the leader in modern democracy" (Romains, 31), they have understood that the author wishes to present dictatorship as a viable political solution and to set aside its negative aspects. So common is the apologetic use of the concept "Tragedy" that some literary texts employ it with obvious irony. Early in Agatha Christie's *Murder of Roger Ackroyd*, the first-person narrator describes as a "tragedy" the very case in which he will eventually emerge as the culprit (Christie, 10). Even the brutal dictator in Ramón del Valle-Inclán's novel *Tirano Banderas* does not hesitate to mention his own "politician's tragedy" (Valle-Inclán, 245). Adolf Hitler, however, is completely unironic when he refers to the "tragedy" of the Hapsburg monarchy (Hitler, 79, 175). For the word helps him ignore the impossibility of reconciling his own political program with a nostalgic view of history.

Related Entries

Bullfighting, Gomina, Movie Palaces, Murder, Polarities, Stars, Action vs. Impotence, Authenticity vs. Artificiality, Present vs. Past, Uncertainty vs. Reality, Authenticity = Artificiality (Life), Immanence = Transcendence (Death)

References

Erich Auerbach, "Paul-Louis Courier." *Deutsche Vierteljahrsschrift für Literaturwissenschaft und Geistesgeschichte* 4 (1926): 514–547.

Erich Auerbach, "Racine und die Leidenschaften." *Germanisch-Romanische Monatsschrift* 14 (1926): 371–380.

Berliner Tageblatt.

Agatha Christie, *The Murder of Roger Ackroyd.* London, 1926.

Ernst Robert Curtius, "Unamuno" (1926). In Curtius, *Kritische Essays zur europäischen Literatur.* Bern, 1950.

Wilhelm Dieck, *Der Widerspruch im Richtigen: Gemeinverständliche mathematische Kritik der geltenden Logik.* Sterkrade, 1926.

Kasimir Edschmid, *Basken, Stiere, Araber: Ein Buch über Spanien und Marokko.* Berlin, 1926.

Antoni Gronowicz, *Garbo: Her Story.* New York, 1990.

Hans Ulrich Gumbrecht, "'Pathos of the Earthly Progress': Erich Auerbach's Everydays." In Seth Lerer, ed., *Literary History and the Challenge of Philology: The Legacy of Erich Auerbach.* Stanford, 1996.

Adolf Hitler, *Mein Kampf* (1926). Munich, 1941.

Siegfried Kracauer, "Kult der Zerstreuung: Über die Berliner Lichtspielhäuser" (1926). In Kracauer, *Das Ornament der Masse: Essays.* Frankfurt, 1977.

Theodor Lessing, "Die Häher" (1926). In Lessing, *"Ich warf eine Flaschenpost ins Eismeer der Geschichte": Essays und Feuilletons, 1923–1933.* Neuwied, 1986.

Maurice Maeterlinck, *La vie des termites.* Paris, 1926.

New York Times.

Jules Romains, *Le Dictateur: Pièce en quatre actes.* In *La petite illustration: Revue hebdomadaire,* 23 October 1926.

Miguel de Unamuno, *Epistolario inédito.* Madrid, 1991.

Ramón del Valle-Inclán, *Tirano Banderas* (1926). Madrid, 1978.

Max J. Wolff, "Die Freude am Tragischen." *Germanisch-Romanische Monatsschrift* 14 (1926): 390–397.

AUTHENTICITY = ARTIFICIALITY
(LIFE)

··

In Thomas Mann's story "Unordnung und frühes Leid," Professor Cornelius is fascinated by one of the guests at a dance party organized by his teenaged children. [see **Gomina**] The appearance of this young man, an actor named Herzl, oscillates between the world of Authenticity and the world of Artificiality. Cornelius has heard that Herzl specializes in "character roles"—roles that embody certain aspects of the human psyche. At the same time, Herzl's behavior is clearly intended to convey an impression of profound melancholy. But while melancholy and character roles ally Herzl with Authenticity, Cornelius notices that this young fellow with his "huge, passionate, and deeply melancholic eyes" has applied cosmetics to his face: "those dull carmine highlights on his cheeks can be nothing but makeup" (Mann, 506). Potentially hiding—instead of expressing—his authentic feelings, the rouge on Herzl's skin turns him into an icon of Artificiality: "Odd," muses the professor. "You'd think a man would be one thing or the other—not both a melancholic *and* a user of cosmetics."

Such blurring of the boundary between Authenticity and Artificiality often provides aesthetic pleasure. Filippo Marinetti, in an interview with the newspaper *Jornal do Brasil,* explains his preference for Rio de Janeiro over São Paulo (which he describes as "an artificial metropolis, erected with ceaseless titanic effort") by repeatedly emphasizing the conjunction of exuberant nature and modern technology: "Rio de Janeiro impresses me with a combination of phenomena that is unique in the world.

Against the background of its tropical exuberance, it shows all the magnificent dynamism of contemporary life. For someone who adores movement and speed as much as I do, the loud and intense bustle of the traffic and of the teeming, restless masses is an incomparable joy. Especially so when I can appreciate this spectacle in a city like Rio, which consists of a multitude of small neighborhoods, separated by delightful gardens—in brief, a world that seems to suggest calm philosophical meditation rather than the suffocating labor of modern life" (Buarque de Holanda, 80–81). Analogous, in this respect, to a city like Rio de Janeiro, the architectural fashion for roof gardens satisfies the desire for a blend of Authenticity and Artificiality. Roof gardens are, so to speak, the place where skyscrapers—the most ambitious constructions of the human mind—come together with the nature that surrounds them. And within their precincts, plants flourish on artificial ground.

The same ambivalence is often seen by whites as passion when it is incarnated by African-American culture. Coming from the United States, black music and dance are generally perceived as Artificiality. But their African roots give them an equally strong connotation of Authenticity. [see **Authenticity vs. Artificiality**] For many of their white admirers, black dancers and musicians are representatives of prehistory: "Comes from [the] blood, from the jungle. [It] takes us back to our childhood" (*Berliner Börsen-Zeitung*, January 3). For others, however, they are America's present and Europe's future, sometimes even a future with the promise of a redemption from decadence: "They're definitely not from the jungle—let's not kid ourselves. Nevertheless, they are a new, untouched race. Their dancing comes out of their blood, their life . . . The main thing is the negro blood. Drops of it are falling on Europe—a land, long dry, which has almost ceased to breathe. Is this the cloud that looks so black on the horizon? A shimmering stream of fertility?" (Goll, 257–258). Ultimately, black music and dance become emblems of a simultaneity between an uncanny but appealing future and an archaic past: "Here origin and decline are conjoined . . . Here we see the amalgamation of 'the latest' and 'the earliest' art" (Goll, 257–258). But if African-American culture's ambiguous status between Authenticity and Artificiality explains why it is so fascinating to the European public, the same ambiguity makes this culture particularly difficult to describe. In their analysis of contemporary jazz, the French musicologists André Coeuroy and André Schäffner start out by taking issue with the idea of "pure music" and by claiming that jazz has a unique expressive capacity. While this would seem to position jazz on the side of Authenticity, the authors emphasize that the objects of reference for its "musical expressions" are limited to emotions—in all their vagueness—and that, compared to language, music is always characterized by a specific distance from and looseness in the relation between signifier and signified: "Like words, but to an infinitely greater degree, [musical expressions] are able to escape their primitive meaning, to assume another meaning, to have no meaning at all, or to wait until their context, whether sound or text, has specified the exact sense in which they should be taken in a particular case. Between them and their *meaning*, there is sufficient room for them to translate, with equal indifference, a particular state and then another, precisely opposite state . . . We will always observe this lack of feeling on the part of sound-terms for the meanings they take on" (Coeuroy and Schäffner, 10–11). Unable to solve the conceptual contradiction inherent in their argument (music is expression, but at the same time is not really expression), the authors simply end up defining jazz through its connotational relation with black ethnicity: "There the idea of *expression* aims no longer at the character of the thing expressed, but at the more generally ethnic tone in which two quite dissimilar things may be said" (108). But as intellectually stimulating as such problems may be, they show that the distinction between Authenticity and Artificiality is limited in its applications. Instead of arriving at a clarifying description, Coeuroy and Schäffner conclude by claiming that jazz is coextensive with Life: "In vain will we close our ears to jazz. It is life. It is art. It is the intoxication of sounds and noises. It is the animal joy of supple movements. It is the melancholy of passions. It is ourselves today" (145). [see **Silence vs. Noise**] If "being Life" means being everything, this final statement is not an attempt at a definition but an indirect admission that the phenomenon of jazz escapes all conceptualization.

Life has the strength of whatever is authentic—without being deep and without being, on the basis of such depth, an expression of anything. But Life also has the one-dimensionality, the intoxicating surface quality, of Artificiality—without, of course, being artificial. Nothing is as concrete and real as Life, yet Life eludes all subjective planning and order. [see **Immanence vs. Transcendence**] Life thus becomes a value that is almost obsessively attributed to whatever appears overwhelming and sublime, to whatever lies beyond the reach of concepts and conceptual distinctions (Fellmann, 142ff.): "Spanish dances can be compared only to the most elementary and eminent symbols of life, because they look simple, like everything that is truly sublime" (Edschmid, 79). No other cultural phenomenon is so closely and so frequently associated with the notion of Life—and with the facticity of death—as bullfighting. Bullfighting stages the oscillation between culture's triumph over nature and the neverending threat that nature poses to culture. It is a ritual based on a surface of colors and movements but also on the activation of deep, often strangely existentialist meanings. D. H. Lawrence makes fun of this proverbial association when he describes an American tourist watching a bullfight in Mexico: "He was seeing LIFE, and what can an American do more!" (Lawrence, 20).

Life exceeds the rationalities of all the different everyday worlds, and therefore acquires a transcendental status. This is why, in asserting that religion is superior to reason, Georges Bernanos can say: "Catholicism is not simply a rule imposed from outside. It is the rule of life—it is life itself" (Bernanos, 240). This is why Antonin Artaud, by claiming that his form of theater is closer to Life than any other, merely reinforces the old topos of art's divine vocation: "With this theater, we reestablish our bond with life instead of separating ourselves from it" (Artaud, 18). This, too, is why Silvio Astier, the young hero of Roberto Arlt's novel *El juguete rabioso (The Furious Toy)* lyrically praises Life after trying to set fire to the bookstore where he is leading a most frustrating existence: "A warmth as fresh as a little glass of wine made me feel friendly toward the whole world during those watchful hours. I said . . . Life, life, how pretty you are, life . . . Life, how pretty you are. Life . . . how pretty . . . My God, how pretty you are" (Arlt, 68). And toward the end of Pirandello's *Uno, nessuno, centomila (One, No One, One Hundred Thousand),* the hero finds that Life—the union with things and with nature— has freed him from all the constraints imposed by human time, language, and society: "I'm alive, and I don't conclude. Life doesn't conclude. And life doesn't know about names. This tree, a trembling breath of new leaves—I am this tree. Tree, cloud. Tomorrow, book or wind: the book I'll read, the wind I'll drink" (Pirandello, 227).

If this monologue marks what one might call the environmentalist level of the life mystique—the level that relates to the world as context— the protagonists in René Schickele's novel *Maria Capponi* repeatedly come up against its existentialist version. They encounter life and love as irresistible fate: "'You're so right, Maria,' I said. 'It's as if a ground-swell of life had suddenly flung us into each other, and we didn't know what to do.' Perhaps I'd expected her to cry out despairingly, 'I don't understand you!' Instead, she said: 'Claus, I know what you mean!' I stood there, overwhelmed. She hung on my neck. And although the little train rattled by, at that moment, she kissed me slowly, right on the mouth. Then she kissed me again and again, each time more feverishly. 'This!' she murmured fiercely between the kisses, 'This! This! Do you get it now? Is it clear to you? As clear as the sun? Or only as clear as the moon? Is this what we should do with each other? This and nothing but this!" (Schickele, 393). Even the setting for this scene of erotic excite-ment, a small town in southern France, is "abounding with life. And this life showed itself quite recklessly in the streets. The house doors stood open, and since only the narrow thresholds separated the streets from the rooms, we saw people working, sleeping, fighting, loving" (347). But unlike his Italian lover Maria, Claus, the narrator, cannot help associat-ing this ferment of Life with a glimpse of Death: "I was thinking about the 'sick spot' in myself, about the morbid weakness which now and then afflicted me and robbed me of all my strength to live. It made me long for sickness and care, for a deck chair at death's edge" (348). [see **Immanence = Transcendence (Death in Life)**]

The enthusiasm for Life's overwhelming strength that emerges from the collapse of the distinction between Authenticity and Artificiality is almost always accompanied by a certain disdain for—or sheer absence of—thought. This relation becomes obvious in the formula that Jorge Luis Borges uses to describe the reality of Buenos Aires: "Our life-reality is magnificent and our thought-reality is beggarly" (Borges, 13). The philosopher Martin Heidegger attempts to question the superiority of man's intellectual capacities over some nonintellectual existential reali-ties. This may be why, in the correspondence with his friend Elisabeth Blochmann, Heidegger frequently uses the notion of *Existenzfreudigkeit* ("existence-affirmation") as a toned-down version of all the more ec-static concepts of Life. *Existenzfreudigkeit* promotes acting and think-ing—but it is an inspiration that can only be gratefully received, never produced or initiated by the human will: "These days, I imagine that you're in the same mood that always comes over me at the beginning of the semester. It sets free the passion that is necessary for our work. Only new opportunities make possible the productivity through which we, as individuals, become what we are. Your feminine form of being . . . is exploring new venues—and this is not merely a consequence of your having a profession. It no doubt provides you with that *Existenzfreudigkeit* which, instead of resulting from success, is its primary inspiration" (October 7; Heidegger and Blochmann, 17).

Related Entries

Boxing, Bullfighting, Dancing, Gomina, Jazz, Revues, Roof Gardens, Authenticity vs. Artificiality, Immanence vs. Transcendence, Silence vs. Noise, Immanence = Transcendence (Death)

References

Roberto Arlt, *El juguete rabioso* (1926). Buenos Aires, 1980.
Antonin Artaud, "Théâtre Alfred Jarry" (1926). In Artaud, *Oeuvres complètes*, vol. 2. Paris, 1961.
Berliner Börsen-Zeitung.
Georges Bernanos, *Sous le soleil de Satan* (1926). Paris, 1973.
Jorge Luis Borges, *El tamaño de mi esperanza* (1926). Buenos Aires, 1993.
Sérgio Buarque de Holanda, "Marinetti novamente no Rio: As suas impressões do continente sul-americano relatadas durante uma visita a *O Jornal*" (1926). In Francisco de Assis Barbosa, ed., *Raízes de Sérgio Buarque de Holanda*. Rio de Janeiro, 1989.
André Coeuroy and André Schäffner, *Le Jazz*. Paris, 1926.
Kasimir Edschmid, *Basken, Stiere, Araber: Ein Buch über Spanien und Marokko* (1926). Berlin, 1927.
Ferdinand Fellmann, *Lebensphilosophie: Elemente einer Theorie der Selbsterfahrung*. Hamburg, 1993.
Yvan Goll, "Die Neger erobern Europa" (1926). In Anton Kaes, ed., *Weimarer Republik: Manifeste und Dokumente zur deutschen Literatur, 1918–1933*. Stuttgart, 1983.
Martin Heidegger and Elisabeth Blochmann, *Briefwechsel, 1918–1969*. Marbach, 1989.
D. H. Lawrence, *The Plumed Serpent*. London, 1926.
Thomas Mann, "Unordnung und frühes Leid" (1926). In Mann, *Sämtliche Erzählungen*. Frankfurt, 1963.
Luigi Pirandello, *Uno, nessuno e centomila* (1926). Milan, 1936.
René Schickele, *Maria Capponi*. Munich, 1926.

CENTER = PERIPHERY
(INFINITUDE)

....

The emergence of new political, economic, and cultural Centers outside Europe, beyond the traditionally unmarked Center in relation to which the rest of the world has been defined as Periphery [see **Center vs. Periphery**], transforms the parameters of spatial perception. The other source of dramatic change on this level of experience is the vast range of new devices in transportation and communication, which are bringing far-flung points on the globe closer together. [see **Airplanes, Automobiles, Elevators, Ocean Liners, Railroads, Telephones, Wireless Communication**] Martin Heidegger establishes an explicit relationship between the new technological possibilities for bridging distances and his own analysis, in *Sein und Zeit (Being and Time),* of space as a frame-condition for human existence (Heidegger, 102ff.). Through one of those hyphenations which are characteristic of his style as a philosopher and writer, Heidegger turns *Entfernung* ("distance") into its opposite, *Ent-fernung* ("undoing of farness"). This wordplay leads Heidegger to the thesis—analogous to and derived from the priority of *Zuhandenheit* ("ready to hand") over *Vorhandenheit* ("present at hand")—that, from an existential point of view, closeness (the result of an undoing of farness) has priority over distance. This thesis, however, obliges Heidegger to acknowledge—not without hesitation—that the new technologies of speed and transmission may well converge with the existential priority of eliminating distance: *"In Dasein there is an essential tendency toward closeness.* All the ways in which we speed things up, as we are more or less compelled to do today, push us on toward the conquest of remoteness [*Entferntheit*]. With the 'radio,' for example, *Dasein* has so expanded its everyday environment that it has accomplished a de-distancing [*Ent-fernung*] of the 'world'—a de-distancing whose implications for the meaning of *Dasein* cannot yet be visualized" (Heidegger, 105).

This theme of the collapse of distance is also apparent in a number of nonphilosophical discourses. Nobody generates more variants of it than the French writer Paul Morand:

Our fathers were sedentary. Our sons will be even more so, for they will have nowhere left to travel on the earth. To go and take the measure of the globe still holds some interest for us—but after us? . . . We're on our way toward the tour of the world on eighty francs. All that has been said about the poverty of man won't be truly borne out until the day that fare has been reached. To the long list of things that make existence unbearable, I add the fact that we are forced to live crowded together on a globe of which three-quarters is occupied, alas, by water (which could just as well have been found in the air or under the ground). We will succumb in the end; we will waste our lives in this locked compartment, sealed up in the economy class of this little sphere lost in space. For the earth is astonishingly small; only boats permit us to doubt this smallness, because they still move so slowly" (Morand, 10–11)

As devices belonging to a technology-dominated space, telephones and telegrams suggest that the old epistolary formula by which people promise to be "present in spirit" is being transformed into a palpable reality where absence comes close to presence. This is precisely what Benito Mussolini does when he sends greetings to a convocation of Futurists organized in honor of the poet Marinetti. He makes the transmissive medium of the telegram his message: "Consider me present at Futurist assembly synthesizing twenty years of great artistic political battles often consecrated with blood. Congress must be starting point not arrival point" (*Il Futurismo*, 2).

It is only a short step from such technologically grounded claims of presence to a new fascination with the possibilities of telepathy as spiritual interpenetration—a fascination to which Sigmund Freud feels compelled to react. [see **Wireless Communication**] But forms of existential closeness are certainly not the only—or most important—effects of the blurring of the distinction between Center and Periphery. Without this distinction, space can be neither measured nor mastered, because it may oscillate between infinite expansion and infinite contraction. Thus, the most outrageously ironic detail in Kafka's *Schloss* is the fact that K. is a surveyor (*Landvermesser*, literally "land-measurer"). For space seems constantly to be expanding and contracting around him. A case of such spatial instability is the passage that explains why K. never reaches the castle: "For the street he was on, the main street of the village, did not lead up to the castle hill. It only headed toward it and then, as if deliberately, turned aside; and though it did not lead away from the castle, it led no nearer to it either . . . He was also amazed at the size of the village, which seemed to have no end" (Kafka, 14). Sometimes, Kafka introduces images that make such distortions of space partly plausible, but he never returns to a Euclidean context. The parents of K.'s colleague Barnabas, for example, make strenuous efforts to come closer to K., despite mysterious spatial constraints: "The gouty old father . . . progressed more with the aid of his groping hands than by the slow movements of his stiff legs, and the mother, with her hands folded on her bosom, . . . was equally incapable of any but the smallest steps because of her stoutness. Both of them, father and mother, had been advancing from their corner toward K. ever since he had come in, and were still a long way off" (29). A space in which the distinction between Center and Periphery has collapsed, a space of Infinitude, is a space in which measuring distance and speed has become problematic (if not impossible). This difficulty corresponds to one that pilots frequently encounter when flying over desert landscapes: "You have no clear picture of the speed at which you're moving in an airplane . . . There are no indications by which you can measure the speed, because you're passing through nothing but air" (*Berliner Tageblatt*, April 8). [see **Airplanes**]

Incalculable spaces cannot be neutral frame-conditions for human actions and human behavior. Unlike the stable spaces that are based on the distinction between Center and Periphery, they sometimes exert magical influence. This is the implication of Siegfried Kracauer's description of a square in Marseilles: "See what is happening in the middle of the empty square: the power of the quadrangle pushes the prisoner toward the center. He is alone and not alone at the same time. He cannot see any observers, but their gaze penetrates the shutters and the wall. Groups of them cross the square and intersect in its center. Naked fear—to be exposed to them . . . In the middle of this condensation of images, nobody looks for the quadrangle. Upon thorough reflection, one would have to call its size moderate. But once the observers have taken their seats, it begins to expand and becomes a quadrangle without mercy, overwhelming the soft parts of the dreams" (Kracauer, 13). The association of magic with a collapsing Euclidean space recurs. Mountainous landscapes often inspire sexual desire, and sometimes are even expected to enhance fertility. [see **Mountaineering**] Conversely, the mortal fear of two shipwrecked sailors in the middle of the ocean transforms the seeming Infinitude of the space around them into an almost cozy environment: "The vast distances toward the horizon and the immensity of the sea shrank when the mist closed in on us. The sea became smaller with every passing minute, until we had the illusion that we were floating on an inland lake. As time went on, even this lake narrowed more and more. Now we felt as if we were drifting down a river. We had the sensation we could touch the banks with our hands" (Traven, 212–213). Spaces exert and react to supernatural influences—but no deity will ever represent such forces. [see **Immanence vs. Transcendence**] Although soldiers constantly get lost in the space of war, they always find a direction for their movement: "We are the only ones who have penetrated to this point, and it is true that what is going on here, despite the apparently boundless confusion, is clearly oriented" (Jünger, 130). Even after moments of blinding confusion, this orientation comes back like an instinct that is stronger than human calculation or rationality: "At first glance everything looks strange and chaotic, like a dream landscape whose details and improbabilities capture and dazzle the senses. For a moment, we are paralyzed and try to understand what is going on. Then we wake up—only to fall into confusion again amid this world of fire, whose innumerable layers are strangely connected and which the will of the blood can still penetrate as it pleases, with instinctive assurance" (136).

When the Periphery is no longer distinct from the Center, the peripheral border region is no longer peripheral—and may become a dwelling place. This transformation occurs on so many different levels that it assumes the form of an emblematic experience. Suburbs are beginning to appear in Argentinian literature as a central topic: "The outskirts, the suburbs, are spaces that actually exist in the real topography of the city, yet at the same time they can enter literature only when they are thought of as cultural spaces, when they are given a form based not only on

aesthetic but also on ideological qualities. One sees, then, a triple movement: the recognition of an urban reference, its linking to values, and its
construction as a literary reference. These operations make it possible to
conceive not only a 'realist' vision of the suburb, but also a perspective
from which to observe the suburban space" (Sarló, 180). At the same
time, the power Center of organized crime in the United States moves
from New York to Chicago—the former Periphery. This change in venue
is a result of the famous "Adonis Club Massacre" on Christmas Day,
1925, in New York, where Al Capone, on a visit from Chicago, single-
handedly decimated the Irish rivals of his former boss Frankie Yale.
Without ever trying to control New York, Capone manages to reduce
the traditional Center to peripheral status. And even in Chicago, the new
Center, Capone's power base lies primarily in the peripheral areas of the
city (Bergreen, 157ff.).

Similar transformations of the Periphery are occurring in the world of
international politics. Instead of simply facilitating separation, national
borders are now more and more defined as spaces of interaction: "The
world has shrunk since it was enveloped in electric wires and rails. It has
become too small to sustain zones of national economic influence . . .
and other such Walls of China. Today, the fates of all states and nations
are closely and inevitably interconnected" (Bittner, 516). Paul Morand
thinks that this development has begun far too early to foster true
understanding among nations: "The horrible beauty of our epoch is that
the races have mixed with one another without any mutual understanding, and without having had the time to get acquainted and learn
to tolerate one another. We have succeeded in constructing locomotives
that travel more quickly than our ideas" (Morand, 13). On the one hand,
living in border spaces means living without that feeling of "being inside" which is the ideal of geopolitics. [see **Center vs. Periphery**] On the
other hand, living in border spaces makes it impossible to see a country,
a culture, or any kind of system from outside. As an existential situation,
this experience dovetails with the standard job-description of architects
and engineers: they build systems of which they are an integral part, and
from which they therefore can never be dissociated or distanced. [see
Engineers] In the draft of one of his last poems, written between June 12
and 18, Rainer Maria Rilke celebrates the window as an emblem for the
centrality of the space-between-spaces and as an important new meta-

phor in poetry. Windows are part of the house, yet also part of the world around the house. They contain the promise, the ever-unfulfilled illusion, of a vista beyond themselves. Thus, within Rilke's poetic world, the observer can never overcome the threshold of the window:

> Long in place, far away from the living, set beneath the sun,
> Window that celebrates and is real;
> After harp and swan, last remaining
> Slowly canonized picture.
>
> We still need you, form cast lightly
> Into the houses,
> Promising an opening.
> Yet the most abandoned window on earth often
> strove for divine transfiguration.
>
> (Rilke, 265)

Borders become spaces—sometimes even central spaces—through the continual back-and-forth movements across the thresholds they mark. The rhythm of oscillation thus engenders a form. This perspective on the emergence of space as a form comes close to Einstein's new definition of space: "In the first place, we entirely shun the vague word 'space,' of which, we must honestly acknowledge, we cannot form the slightest conception, and we replace it by 'motion relative to a practically rigid body of reference'" (Einstein, 9). Einstein's favorite image for the "rigid body of reference" is the railway car. The railway is no longer conceived as bridging the distance between two points, but is seen as contributing to the emergence of space. In a phenomenological rather than scientific sense, this is also true for many athletic competitions. Of course, the distance covered by the participants in a six-day bicycle race is important (though not exclusively decisive) for victory and defeat. Seen from a different angle, however, the main function of the athletes' continuous movement around the infinite oval of the track is to constitute an intrinsically complex area for the public's amusement [see **Six-Day Races**]—a space to which neither athletes nor spectators can ever be peripheral.

For far longer than six days—in fact, for the entire year (December 1925 to February 1927)—several hundred soldiers of the Brazilian army under the leadership of Lieutenant Luís Carlos Prestes march through the provinces of their enormous country (Drummond, 47). [see **Individuality = Collectivity (Leader)**] What began as an attempt at a military coup soon turns into an action whose practical goals remain enigmatic: "The already superficial political action of the Prestes Column was weakened by its obsession with mobility—and it was finally defeated by general rejection on the part of the population" (Drummond, 64). If anything is clear in Prestes' own declarations, it is the absence of strategic objectives beyond the potentially infinite continuity of movement: "A war in Brazil will be a war of movement—in whichever province it may take place. For us, the revolutionaries, movement is victory" (6). There is no doubt, however, that such "victorious movement" reconstitutes—and thus reaffirms—the space of Brazil's national territory.

Related Entries

Airplanes, Automobiles, Elevators, Engineers, Mountaineering, Ocean Liners, Polarities, Railroads, Six-Day Races, Telephones, Wireless Communication, Center vs. Periphery, Immanence vs. Transcendence, Individuality = Collectivity (Leader)

References

Laurence Bergreen, *Capone: The Man and the Era.* New York, 1994.

Berliner Tageblatt.

Karl Gustav Bittner, "Werdet deutsche Menschen!" *Die Tat* 18, no. 1 (April–September 1926): 503–518.

José Augusto Drummond, *A Coluna Prestes: Rebeldes errantes.* São Paulo, 1991.

Albert Einstein, *Relativity: The Special and General Theory* (1916). New York, 1961.

Il Futurismo: Rivista Sintetica Illustrata 11 (11 January 1926).

Martin Heidegger, *Sein und Zeit* (written 1926, published 1927). Tübingen, 1984.

Ernst Jünger, *Feuer und Blut: Ein kleiner Ausschnitt aus einer grossen Schlacht* (1926). Hamburg, 1941.

Franz Kafka, *Das Schloss* (1926). Hamburg, 1968.

Siegfried Kracauer, "Zwei Flächen" (1926). In Kracauer, *Das Ornament der Masse.* Frankfurt, 1977.

Paul Morand, *Rien que la terre: Voyage.* Paris, 1926.
Rainer Maria Rilke, *Werke in drei Bänden,* vol. 2: *Gedichte und Übertragungen.*
  Frankfurt, 1966.
Beatriz Sarló, *Una modernidad periférica: Buenos Aires 1920 y 1930.* Buenos
  Aires, 1988.
B. Traven, *Das Totenschiff* (1926). Hamburg, 1954.

IMMANENCE = TRANSCENDENCE (DEATH)

The report on a steeplechase at the Grunewald racetrack published by the *Berliner-Volkszeitung* on May 14 contains a strangely philosophical paragraph. Under the title "Triumph of Death and Life," it presents the following description of the Alemanni Steeplechase, the most important competition of the day: "Bellac and Eulogist alternately took the lead, ahead of Rhineland and Hermes. Death and Life was coming in last. Death and Life galloped by the grandstand in fourth place. He remained in this position until they reached the stable area, when it seemed that Eulogist began to lose strength. In the final stretch, Death and Life pushed forward, jumped the last hurdle beside Rhineland, who had been leading until then, and came in first ahead of Pericles, who in the last few meters had passed Rhineland." While it is already quite remarkable to see Pericles compete with Eulogist, the name "Death and Life" ("Tod und Leben") is unusual enough in the context of horseracing to deserve special reflection. How can concepts like "Death" and "Life" become so popular, and so far from awe-inspiring, that they end up becoming a name for a racehorse? One possible answer to this question would point to an ongoing change in the relations between Immanence and Transcendence that occupies the minds even of those who never think about philosophy or theology. It could be described as the absorption of Transcendence into Immanence, and the simultaneous reemergence of Transcendence in the context of a new fascination with religion. But having been traditionally defined as a threshold between Immanence and Transcendence, Death also marks the one moment in which it is impossible to distinguish the world from what may lie beyond it. Thus, Death stands for a paradoxical simultaneity that may exist between Immanence and Transcendence; and the less Immanence is separated from Transcendence, the more people think and talk about Death. This intrinsically paradoxical concept of Death is frequently linked to a concept of life that itself represents the paradoxical unity of (and the impossibility of distinguishing between) Authenticity and Artificiality. Being a potential paradox itself, the formula "Death and Life" is thus a point of convergence for two of the most popular and most burning concerns of the moment. [see **Transcendence vs. Immanence, Authenticity vs. Artificiality (Life)**]

What remains difficult to explain is the particularly strong association between Death and life. In *La tentation de l'Occident* (*The Temptation of the West*), André Malraux attempts to solve this problem: "In order to destroy God, and after destroying him, the European spirit wiped out everything that could oppose itself to man. Having reached the culmination of its efforts, . . . it finds nothing but death" (Malraux, 203). The absorption of Transcendence into Immanence would be a side effect of the obsessive anthropocentrism that characterizes Western modernity. The only thing left to provide a contrast by which human existence can be defined—and given form—is Death. Moreover, the necessity of defining human existence seems only to grow in a world where their meanings are no longer guaranteed by a transcendentally grounded cosmology. Such a need to experience the limits, and through them the meaning, of human existence could well be the motive for the numerous rituals and competitions that enable people to watch others confronting Death—activities such as boxing, airplane flight, long-distance running, Channel swimming, bullfighting, and mountain climbing. [see **Airplanes, Boxing, Bullfighting, Endurance, Mountaineering**] Since efforts to scale the world's highest peak have already claimed the lives of thirteen people—without yielding definitive success—a rhetorical question by Sir Francis Younghusband, the first chairman of the Mount Everest Committee of the Royal Geographical Society and Alpine Club, is assuming a seriousness that he probably never intended: "Why not leave it at that? With the knowledge now obtained, the needs of science are satisfied. Should not further efforts be abandoned?" (Younghusband, 309). By way of an answer, he suggests that mountain climbing offers the opportunity to measure one's forces against the limits of Death: "Man means to *climb* Mount Everest—climb it on his own feet. That is the whole point. Only so does he get that pride in his prowess which is such a satisfaction to his soul. Life would be a poor affair if we relied always on the machine. We are too prone already to trust to science and mechanics instead of exerting our own bodies and our own spirit. And we thereby miss much of that enjoyment in life which exercising our faculties to the full brings with it" (18ff.).

If Death is the only and ultimate horizon with and against which to circumscribe human existence, and if there is no world "beyond" it, then Death, rather than being a threshold toward or an element of a transcendental sphere, becomes a part of human existence. In a poem on the corpse of a soldier killed in action, Fernando Pessoa focuses on this particular aspect of the vanishing distinction between Transcendence and Immanence:

> Bloodstains on his uniform.
> His arms open,
> White, blond, and lifeless,
> He is staring at the lost heaven
> With his tired, blind gaze.

Heaven has vanished for the young soldier precisely at the moment he expected it to become a home for his soul—that is, at the moment of his physical Death. The absence of a transcendental sphere leads Pessoa to an ironic comparison between the soldier's body and his cigarette case. The cigarette case can still serve a function—but there is absolutely no function left for the dead body:

> His cigarette case
> just fell from his pocket.
> His mother had given it to him.
> Ready to be used
> is the cigarette case.
> He is the one who is no longer
> ready to be used.
>
> (Pessoa, 31).

Rainer Maria Rilke's last draft for a poem, written only a few days before his Death on December 29, pushes this experience yet further. Even before the end of the body's life, Death is present in acute physical pain—and no existential future lies beyond this boundary:

> COME, o you final companion that I will recognize,
> Pain without relief in the fibers of my body:
> As I was burning in the spirit, look, I am burning
> In you. Long the wood resisted,
> Not responding to the flames with which you blaze.
> But now I feed you while I am burning in you.
> . . . . .
> Pure, without plans and free of a future,
> I climbed on the pyre of pain,
> Certain not to buy any time
> For this heart silent with exhaustion.
>
> (Rilke, 266).

There are two, precisely opposite reactions to the absence of Transcendence and the presence of Death in human life. The obvious (and obviously naive) reaction is an urge to escape Death—or to actively forget it. In Ramón del Valle-Inclán's novel *Tirano Banderas,* one of the characters embodies the latter attitude in all its triviality: "[To recognize] that a particular act is inevitable does not prepare us for its imminence. Death is inevitable, yet we construct our whole life in an effort to distance it from us" (Valle-Inclán, 250). The wish to escape Death, however, takes different forms depending on whether it focuses on the elementary angst one feels at the idea of life's coming to an end, or on the desire to be remembered by posterity. Among Spanish intellectuals, the Death of the great Catalan architect Antonio Gaudí inspires the second of these obsessions. On Thursday, June 10, as he is walking along his daily route from the construction site of the Sagrada Familia church to evening Mass in the same neighborhood, the seventy-four-year-old Gaudí is hit by a streetcar. He dies before any medical help arrives, because nobody recognizes him: the famous artist is an unremarkable-looking old man (Gumbrecht, 847–848). This scene resembles a nightmare that supposedly plays a crucial role in Miguel de Unamuno's literary and philosophical writings. Unamuno is obsessed with the fear that he will be forgotten after his Death, and feels a burning desire for immortality and eternity. [see **Present = Past (Eternity)**] The German critic Ernst Robert Curtius considers Unamuno one of the most important philosophers of his time—precisely because Unamuno keeps aloof from the ever-accelerating pace of historical time and change [see **Past vs. Present**]:

> The authentic, strong, impressive element in Unamuno's religiosity is his longing for eternity. If this eternal need of the soul has found new expression in an age fallen into "temporal relativity," we owe it to Unamuno. Many of us may not feel this need. But others will associate a feeling of liberation with Unamuno's voice, which, in our enlightened, skeptical, sophisticated Europe, remains unimpressed by the criticisms of common sense and the cautious gestures of erudition. Among European intellectuals, it is not considered tactful to talk about death and eternity. But isn't this repression the cause of many of our sufferings? In essence, Unamuno's . . . hunger for immortality is nothing but the instinct for survival. He does not want to die. (Curtius, 239–240)

The other reaction to the absence of Transcendence and the presence of Death in human existence is the decision to confront Death deliberately. This is the attitude that T. E. Lawrence learns to embrace during the war in Arabia: "Blood was always on our hands; we were licensed to it. Wounding and killing seemed ephemeral pains, so very brief and sore was life with us. With the sorrow of living so great, the sorrow of punishment has to be pitiless. We lived for the day and died for it . . . Bedouin ways were hard even for those brought up to them, and for strangers terrible: a death in life" (T. E. Lawrence, 31). There are less dramatic, middle-class ways of making Death a part of life. One might, for example, compose meticulous instructions for the disposal of one's corpse (Crane, 11–12). [see **Cremation**] Or one might found a discussion group devoted to Death, as do Jack Dempsey's friends Grantland Rice, Ring Lardner, and Gene Fowler: "The exclusive Morticians Club . . . met several times a week to discuss the intriguing aspects of death and its after-effects. Rice was the supreme fatalist; with Lardner and Fowler he would sit around poking fun at death. The high incidence of those dying slow and painful deaths from bad rotgut gave them overabundant food for thought while they sat and drank" (Dempsey and Dempsey, 185). The eagerness to confront Death—an obsession for wealthy Ameri-

IMMANENCE = TRANSCENDENCE (DEATH)

cans—launches Martin Heidegger into one of the most complex passages of *Sein und Zeit (Being and Time)*. Trying to argue that Death is indeed a part of human life, Heidegger goes so far as to claim that dying and human existence are coextensive from the perspective of their duration: "In actuality, *Dasein* is dying throughout its existence" (Heidegger, 251). This is the thought which should encourage confrontation with Death, anticipation of one's own Death in the imagination; it is also the thought which should encourage acceptance of the possibility of one's nonexistence, as well as acceptance of the facticity of one's Death. It is just such a complex existential leap into the future that Heidegger describes with the metaphor "Vorlaufen in den Tod," or "running ahead into death" (267).

Even more frequent than the complementary motifs of escaping and facing Death are the associations between Death (or the threat of Death) and sexual fulfillment. Mountainous landscapes appear to be the standard setting for such links. The hero and narrator in René Schickele's novel *Maria Capponi*, for example, has never known how passionate his wife can be—until the spring day on which a climbing accident traps them together in a crevasse. Here, nothing is left but the expectation of Death and the mutually warming presence of their bodies. [see **Mountaineering**] Leni Riefenstahl claims that she discouraged the sexual advances of both the male lead actor and the director of the film *The Holy Mountain* (and prevented them from killing themselves and each other out of frustration and jealousy)—but she certainly enjoys the eroticizing effect that the dangers of mountaineering have on the trio. In contrast, Bertolt Brecht's poem "Entdeckung an einer jungen Frau" ("Discovery on Behalf of a Young Woman") is a particularly serious variation on the same motif:

A sober goodbye in the morning, a woman
Standing without emotion on her threshold, seen without emotion.
Then I noticed a streak of gray in her hair,
And I couldn't make up my mind to leave.

Wordlessly I touched her breast, and when she asked
Why I, guest for one night, did not want
to leave the next morning (for this was the agreement),
I looked her straight in the face and said:

If it's just one more night, I'd like to stay.
But make good use of your time. The bad thing is
That you're standing here on the threshold.

Let's talk faster,
For we almost forgot that you're mortal.
And desire silenced my voice.

                                    (Brecht, 160ff.)

Perhaps the force of this poem—as well as that of bullfighting scenes by Hemingway, Montherlant, and Kracauer [see **Bullfighting**]—stems from the fact that the authors make no attempt to explain the connection between Death and sexual fulfillment. They merely describe, sometimes in meticulous detail, how the perception of Death's closeness triggers sexual desire. On the other hand, efforts to understand this phenomenon yield results that range from the unconvincing to the truly embarrassing. Theodor Lessing's claim that a general law links Death to erotic pleasure, for example, is hardly substantiated by the fact that bees die after losing their stinger—for the stinger does not have any reproductive (or "sexual") function: "Nature appears cruel to human eyes only because it binds together death and sexuality . . . Of ten thousand [male bees], only one is admitted into the heaven of love, and this happens only when he loses his stinger. At that moment, he experiences the well-known interconnectedness of love and death" (Lessing, "Biene und Wespe," 252, 255). Without any further explanation, D. H. Lawrence has the central female character in his novel *The Plumed Serpent* attribute the "finality of death" to a marriage that is based on the unchallenged sexual domination of the male partner: "Ah! and what a mystery of prone submission, on her part, this huge erection would imply! Submission absolute, like the earth under the sky. Beneath an over-arching absolute. Ah! what a marriage! How terrible! and how complete! With the finality of death, and yet more than death" (332–333). [see **Male vs. Female**] Walter Benjamin offers a particularly allusive thesis regarding the link between sexual gratification and Death: "Sexual fulfillment frees man from his secret, which consists not in sexuality but in its fulfillment—and which can perhaps be severed from him (never solved) only in this fulfillment. It can be compared to the fetters that keep him attached to life. The woman cuts through them, and the man becomes free to die, because he has lost his secret. This allows him to be reborn. And just as his mistress frees him from the spell of the mother, thus the woman literally frees him from Mother Earth. Woman is the midwife cutting the umbilical cord which the secret of nature has formed" (Benjamin, 140–145). Benjamin's reflection is as pretentious as it is unclear (Ritter). For what could be the secret from which men are freed through sexual fulfillment? Why would such newly achieved liberty set them free for their Death? And why would freedom for Death be a necessary condition for the birth of new life?

It is generally taken for granted that the proximity of Death enhances the intensity of life. Authors refer to this experience as a fact that requires no further explication: "Bullfighting—an object sometimes of scorn and sometimes of hyperbolic praise that calls it a national attribute, like an anthem or a flag—owes its reputation to emotion, because death is present in it" (*Blanco y Negro*, 80). In Ernst Jünger's epic of trench warfare, the same motif is rhetorically developed under the obvious influence of Nietzsche's discourse on Dionysian intoxication: "Everybody is drunk without wine, each living in a different, fabulous world. All of the usual laws appear to have been lifted [*aufgehoben*], and we find ourselves in a feverish dream of intensified reality—in another circle of the law, in another circle of humanity, which is itself in another circle of nature. Bundles of shadowy lines zoom through the air. The atmosphere, which has been shattered by the powerful air pressure of an explosion, makes the objects in our field of vision quiver and dance like images in a flickering film" (Jünger, 108). Adolf Hitler's description of the same Great War battlefields goes beyond the Dionysian. He encounters a situation in which the enhancement of life through Death becomes fear, and fear of Death in turn becomes a supreme state of Sobriety: "But the romance of battle had turned to horror. Enthusiasm gradually waned, and exuberant joy was smothered by the fear of death. The time came when everyone felt torn between the instinct for self-preservation and the voice of duty . . . This struggle had already been decided for me during the winter of 1915–1916. My will had finally become master. Whereas at the outset I had been able to join exuberantly and laughingly in the storm, now I was quiet and determined" (Hitler, 181). [see **Sobriety vs. Exuberance**]

Quiet determination may well be the ultimate level of enthusiasm. It emerges from the encounter between life and Death, but it also distances the self from life and Death: "Today our intoxicant will be wine; tomorrow it will be power. Tomorrow we will become stern judges over life and death. To hold life and death in one's hand makes a man feel proud" (Jünger, 49). [see **Male vs. Female**] In this passage, Jünger speaks of wielding power over the life and Death of other people; but determining one's own life and Death inspires the same respect and generates the same feeling of sober intensity. In Agatha Christie's *Murder of Roger Ackroyd,* the treacherous narrator attains the ultimate in contentment and self-respect when he decides to commit suicide so as to spare his sister Caroline the cruel disillusionment of learning that he is a murderer: "Well, she will never know the truth. There is . . . one way out . . . I should not like Caroline to know. She is fond of me, and then, too, she is proud . . . My death will be a grief to her, but grief passes" (Christie, 311–312). Hardly ever is a Communist politician as tolerant of a counterrevolutionary as Leon Trotsky is of Sergei Esenin, in an essay written shortly after Esenin's suicide: "The harshness of reality defeated him. On December 27, 1925, he admitted his inferiority, without provocation or reproach . . . Our age is a bitter one, perhaps the bitterest in the history of so-called civilized humanity. Born in this decade, the revolutionary is possessed by fanatical patriotism. Esenin was no revolutionary. The author of 'Pugachov' and 'The Ballad of 26' was the most intimate of lyric poets. And our age is not a lyrical age. This is the main reason Sergei Esenin, voluntarily and before his time, abandoned us and his age" (Toller, 163–164). Trying to discover analogies between human life and animal life, Theodor Lessing is eager to provide ethical legitimacy for suicide. Once again, however, the analogies turn out to be quite problematic: "'Qui potest mori, non potest cogi.' 'Invincible is he who knows how to die.' Self-destruction and suicide . . . exist in nature as well. The fox bites off its own limb to escape the iron trap. If necessary, the scorpion turns its poison stinger upon itself" (Lessing, 257).

By comparison, psychoanalysts seem little concerned with all these efforts to untangle the concepts of Immanence and Transcendence, Authenticity and Artificiality, Death and Life. Referring to an essay by Sigmund Freud entitled "Zeitgemässes über Krieg und Tod" ("Contemporary Reflections on War and Death"), the Dutch psychiatrist August Staerke explains how some religions, in trying to cope with the fear of Death, have claimed an identity between Death and life, just like some modern-day views: "Even civilized societies, in which the phenomenon of religion is far more complex, share some of the approaches of primitive societies in their handling of the fear of death. These approaches concern, above all, the physical fact of death. As a compensation, civilized societies establish and make plausible certain taboos of hygiene and cleanliness. Adherence to these prescriptions replaces the fear of death. An alternative approach lies in defining death as eternal—and therefore essential—life" (Staerke, 101). At Sigmund Freud's instigation, Staerke's essay, with its functional interpretation of the Death-and-life paradox, wins an award for psychoanalytic research and practice (*Almanach*, 93). This is quite astonishing because, simultaneously, Freud himself begins an essay on Death, life, and sexuality which—instead of taking a functional approach—is in fact a remythologization. Psychoanalysis, he claims, "derives all mental processes (apart from the reception of external stimuli) from the interplay of forces, which assist or inhibit one another, combine with one another, enter into compromises with one another, etc. All of these forces are originally in the nature of *instincts* . . . Theoretical speculation leads to the suspicion that there are two fundamental instincts which lie concealed behind the manifest ego-instincts and object-instincts: namely (a) Eros, the instinct which strives for ever closer union, and (b) the instinct of destruction, which leads toward the dissolution of what is living. In psychoanalysis the manifestation of the force of Eros is given the name 'libido'" (Freud, 265).

Related Entries

Airplanes, Boxing, Bullfighting, Cremation, Endurance, Mountaineering, Authenticity vs. Artificiality, Immanence vs. Transcendence, Male vs. Female, Present vs. Past, Sobriety vs. Exuberance, Authenticity = Artificiality (Life), Present = Past (Eternity)

References

Antología de Blanco y Negro, 1891–1936, vol. 9. Madrid, 1986.

Walter Benjamin, *Einbahnstraße* (1926). In Benjamin, *Gesammelte Schriften*, vol. 4, part 1. Frankfurt, 1972.

Berliner Volks-Zeitung.

Bertolt Brecht, "Entdeckung an einer jungen Frau." In Brecht, *Gesammelte Werke*, vol. 8. Frankfurt, 1967.

Agatha Christie, *The Murder of Roger Ackroyd.* London, 1926.

Hart Crane, *White Buildings.* New York, 1926.

Ernst Robert Curtius, "Unamuno" (1926). In Curtius, *Kritische Essays zur europäischen Literatur.* Bern, 1950.

Jack Dempsey and Barbara Piattelli Dempsey, *Dempsey.* New York, 1977.

Sigmund Freud, "Psycho-Analysis" (1926). In Freud, *Standard Edition of the Complete Psychological Works,* vol. 20. London, 1959.

Hans Ulrich Gumbrecht, *Eine Geschichte der spanischen Literatur.* Frankfurt, 1990.

Martin Heidegger, *Sein und Zeit* (written 1926, published 1927). Tübingen, 1984.

Adolf Hitler, *Mein Kampf* (1926). Munich, 1941.

Internationaler Psychoanalytischer Verlag, *Almanach für das Jahr 1926.* Vienna, 1926.

Ernst Jünger, *Feuer und Blut: Ein kleiner Ausschnitt aus einer grossen Schlacht* (1926). Hamburg, 1941.

D. H. Lawrence, *The Plumed Serpent* (1926). London, 1933.

T. E. Lawrence, *The Seven Pillars of Wisdom.* (1926). New York, 1936.

Theodor Lessing, "Spinne und Fliege" (1926), "Biene und Wespe oder Bürgerlich und Romantisch" (1926). In Lessing, *"Ich warf eine Flaschenpost ins Eismeer der Geschichte": Essays und Feuilletons, 1923–1933.* Neuwied, 1986.

Henry de Montherlant, *Les Bestiaires* (1926). Paris, 1929.

Fernando Pessoa, "O menino da sua mãe" (1926). In Pessoa, *Poesia.* Rio de Janeiro, 1959.

Rainer Maria Rilke, *Werke in drei Bänden,* vol. 2. Frankfurt, 1966.

Henning Ritter, "Thinking Incognito: On Walter Benjamin." *New Literary History* 27, no. 4 (Fall 1996): 595–604.

René Schickele, *Maria Capponi.* Munich, 1926.

August Staerke, "Geisteskrankheit und Gesellschaft." In Internationaler Psychoanalytischer Verlag, *Almanach für das Jahr 1926.* Vienna, 1926.

Ernst Toller, "Russische Reisebilder" (1926). In Toller, *Quer durch.* Heidelberg, 1978.

Ramón del Valle-Inclán, *Tirano Banderas* (1926). Madrid, 1978.

Francis Younghusband, *The Epic of Mount Everest.* London, 1926.

INDIVIDUALITY = COLLECTIVITY (LEADER)

Those who write about leadership often get entangled in paradoxes. Sometimes they even seem to take pleasure in it. According to general opinion, a true Leader must embody the Collectivity from which he emerges. He cannot be a Leader without such roots—but at the same time, he is more alone and more distant from the masses than any other individual. His solitude makes the Leader stand out, and this isolation is a condition for the charisma through which he attracts the attention and trust of a collective body. But ideally, the Leader also tries to follow the collective body he leads. Ideally, Individuality and Collectivity become inseparable in the body of the Leader. Ideally, the body of the Leader is a mystical body.

While the life of the Jewish philosopher Theodor Lessing is being threatened by hundreds of students who have turned their longing to find a Leader for the German race into a political program [see **Individuality vs. Collectivity**], he publishes an essay in which the body of the queen bee serves as a metaphor for leadership and in which a quotation from Bismarck lends a positive connotation to this role: "Like the rector of the University of Göttingen, the queen bee is newly selected every four years. During this time she must lay a million eggs, after experiencing the joy of love just once. She is definitely a prisoner of her people, and can say, as Bismarck does, 'I am their leader, but I must also follow them'" (Lessing, 256). In an interview with the newspaper *O Jornal do Brasil,* Filippo Marinetti describes the relation between Mussolini and the Italian nation from an only slightly different angle, while maintaining the paradox of mutual subordination. Instead of following those he leads, the Leader is driven by those he drives: "Mussolini is a man who is driven by the forces he drives, and I am sure that if one day he decided to stand still, Italy's young people would oblige him to march" (Buarque de Holanda, 77). But leadership is also part of the utopian aura that surrounds the concept of democracy. Speaking before a huge assembly of students on Tuesday, July 6, Gustav Stresemann, Germany's foreign secretary, begins by emphasizing this very implication: "You know that we often label the age in which we live 'the age of democracy.' In such an era, the problem of the leader and the masses is much more important than it is at other times" (Stresemann, 262). Leadership can be associated with hope for democracy only when preestablished hierarchical superiority is renounced. In the Soviet Union, teachers have no more rights over their students than the collective student body has over the teachers:

> The rules which the children have made for themselves forbid the wearing of hats in the building. In the lobby a teacher meets a child who has kept his hat on, and the teacher removes it with a peremptory gesture. The boy looks at him resolutely. "What are you doing? I am not your serf. You have offended me." He takes the case to a court which consists of the student council. Witnesses are heard, and the following ruling is handed down: The boy was in the wrong because he kept his hat on; he is reprimanded for it. But the teacher's behavior was also wrong: he didn't have the right to remove the hat from the boy's head without explanation. This example shows how schools are trying to foster the free development of individual and collective life." (Toller, 184–185)

Such unambiguous enthusiasm for the ideal of a paradoxical convergence of Individuality and Collectivity stands in sharp contrast to a pragmatic discourse that tries to assess, with ostentatious Sobriety, the achievements of several politicians who for a number of years have embodied the new principle of leadership. Referring to Benito Mussolini in Italy, Kemal Pasha in Turkey, Theodore Pangalos in Greece, and Miguel Primo de Rivera in Spain, an essay published by the *Berliner Tageblatt* on July 29 identifies a central problem in the everyday practice of such Leaders: if they wish to maintain their prestige, they must continue to impress their followers with outstanding achievements (Gum-brecht). "Those gentlemen who in a number of states have embraced the profession of dictator—with or without the pretext of parliamentary control—have to use the most complex strategies in order to secure the affection of their people. A dictator who does not constantly stand in the limelight, who does not give evidence on a daily basis of his superior force, who does not continually legitimize his status through outstanding achievements, is booed off the stage by the disappointed crowd." At any rate, the number of societies whose political systems are dominated by Leaders is rapidly growing. On January 8, Ibn Saud is proclaimed King of the Hijaz and Sultan of Nejd. In May, military revolts elevate General Pilsudski to the presidency in Poland and give General Gomes da Costa the equivalent role in Portugal. In July, when Gomes da Costa is exiled to the Azores and Stalin begins to contest the role of Trotsky, Zinoviev, Radek, and their followers in the Bolshevik Party, the parliament of Belgium confers dictatorial powers on its king to facilitate the resolution of a financial crisis. On December 17, Antanas Smetona arrests the members of the Lithuanian government, suspends the constitution, dissolves the parliament, and proclaims himself president (Langer, 986–1041). The widespread violence caused by these revolts does not seem to ruffle the relaxed, almost literary tone of the ongoing debate over the principles of leadership. Two days after Christmas, Walter Benjamin records, in loving detail, a reflection that his friend Asja Lacis makes during her stay at a Moscow sanatorium: "The hours which, during the past few days, she has spent lying outside on a deckchair have clearly improved her health. She is happy when she can hear the calls of the ravens in the open air. Moreover, she believes that the birds have established a well-functioning organization and that their leader tells them what they have to do. She thinks certain cries following a long silence are orders that they all obey" (Benjamin, 66). Heinrich Mann has not given up the dream of a world in which writers—instead of generals or ravens—would give the orders that everybody obeys: "The writer is always the leader of democracy, even in its defective forms. Without his influence, the public sphere would be at the mercy of particular interests. He is indispensable. The greater the degree of liberty a nation enjoys, the greater the prestige of the writer" (Mann, 298). In Valle-Inclán's novel *Tirano Banderas,* the conviction that leadership is essential and that Leaders are irreplaceable reappears as an ironic tautology: "Men of great foresight cannot be replaced except by men of great foresight!" (Valle-Inclán, 21).

The French writer Jules Romains offers yet another angle on the problem of leadership. His play *The Dictator,* which is first performed on Tuesday, October 5, at the Comédie des Champs-Elysées, presents the dilemma of a man who assumes dictatorial powers at a time of political crisis and thus claims to render a heroic service to his nation—but who is also obliged to destroy the political career of his best friend because this friend represents the radical wing of the parliamentary opposition. At no moment does Denis, Romains' benevolent dictator, enjoy or abuse his power. He maintains, with determined, superhuman effort, everyday order and through it individual and collective survival: "Acts of sabotage, overturned streetcars, brawls, deaths? Each moment a dispatch on my table, a packet of dispatches, a violent jolt of bad news, one conflict more, one breakdown more? Everything in ruins? Well! Here I am, trying as hard as I can to prevent everything from collapsing, to keep everything together, endeavoring yet again, and again, to make things last" (Romains, 29). Like a heroic pilot who is one with a plane that constantly threatens his life and who manages to keep it from crashing, this dictator endures all the attacks of a society he is determined to rescue. He engages in the impossible task of sustaining the crumbling structure he inhabits. [see **Airplanes, Endurance, Engineers**] No wonder the French press almost obsessively compares Romains' play to the classical tragedies of Corneille, for both focus less on the success of an action than on its form and beauty. [see **Action vs. Impotence**] Leadership is thus discussed from an existential perspective, rather than as a problem of political strategy. This is why vague allusions to the "failures" of parliamentarism, as in the following paragraph from a September 5 manifesto by the Spanish dictator Miguel Primo de Rivera, seem sufficient to legitimize dictatorship: "Now that the parliamentary system has failed in its present form and its inefficiency has finally been proven in the two countries most similar to our own, . . . no sane person would consider reestablishing it in Spain, where its three years of suspension have not dulled any decisive action on the international or economic fronts. On the contrary, this period has facilitated such action because it has silenced the bold, egoistic, or meddlesome voices which produced that system's discordant music" (García-Nieto, 148).

For Adolf Hitler, the political crisis is less a problem to be solved through leadership than an opportunity for the potential Leader to discover and prove his genius. In his description of how a Leader finds his way to power, he pays no attention to strategies: "Nearly always, such an impetus is needed in order to summon genius to action. Fate's hammer-stroke, which throws one person to the ground, suddenly finds steel in another, and although the shell of everyday life is broken, the nucleus lies open to the eyes of the astonished world. Society now resists and does not want to believe that the apparently 'identical' person is now suddenly supposed to be a 'different' being—a process that is repeated with every eminent individual" (Hitler, 321). The Leader's most important task is "to set the masses in motion" (118), and to this end he is ready to sacrifice all personal interests (167). But in contrast to the widely accepted notion of Leadership, in which the Leader is driven by the masses even as he inspires them, Hitler's concept denies this reciprocity. For him, politics is characterized by an almost hostile polarity between the Leader's genius and the inertia of the masses. Since he sees no need for collective approval of the Leader's decisions, he abhors the idea of a nonhierarchical relationship between the Leader and the populace: "Shouldn't the task of the leader lie in conceiving a creative idea or plan, rather than in making the ingeniousness of his plan understandable to a flock of sheep and blockheads for the purpose of begging for their gracious consent? . . . Has this crowd ever been able to grasp an idea before its greatness was proclaimed by its success? Is not every ingenious action in this world the visible protest of genius against the inertia of the masses?" (86).

Scarcely anyone ever raises the question of where a Leader will take his followers once he has set them in motion and once the original crisis that brought him to power is resolved. Does the concern with keeping things in motion replace the need to know the direction of the movement? Having emerged from a military revolt in Rio Grande do Sul, the southernmost state of Brazil, and having marched across the whole country, the Coluna Prestes (Prestes Column), a group of several hundred soldiers led by Captain Luis Carlos Prestes, arrives in the northern state of Maranhão in January. [see **Center = Periphery (Infinitude)**] By the end of the year, Prestes and his men have covered almost fifteen thousand miles and are planning to seek political asylum in Bolivia (Drummond,

26–47; Werneck Sodré, 29ff.). The march of the Coluna Prestes began as a derailed strategic maneuver during a civil war. Now it has become a symbol of political resistance, and even a mission to educate the Brazilian people (Drummond, 57). The only evidence of this function during the year is the movement of these soldiers, zigzagging and circling across the map of Brazil, almost like a dance or a six-day race. But so long as Prestes keeps his followers in motion, they do not ask where he is leading them.

Related Entries

Airplanes, Dancing, Endurance, Engineers, Six-Day Races, Individuality vs. Collectivity, Action vs. Impotence, Center = Periphery (Infinitude)

References

Walter Benjamin, *Moskauer Tagebuch* (1926). Frankfurt, 1980.
Berliner Tageblatt.
Sérgio Buarque de Holanda, "Marinetti, homen político" (1926). In Francisco de Assis Barbosa, ed., *Raízes de Sérgio Buarque de Holanda*. Rio de Janeiro, 1989.
José Augusto Drummond, *A Coluna Prestes: Rebeldes errantes*. São Paulo, 1991.
María Carmen García-Nieto, Javier M. Donézar, and Luis López Puértola, eds., *La dictadura, 1923–1930: Bases documentales de la España contemporánea*, vol. 7. Madrid, 1973.
Hans Ulrich Gumbrecht, "'I redentori della vittoria': Über den Ort Fiumes in der Genealogie des Faschismus." In Hans Ulrich Gumbrecht, Friedrich Kittler, and Bernhard Siegert, eds., *Der Dichter als Kommandant: D'Annunzio erobert Fiume*. Munich, 1996.
Adolf Hitler, *Mein Kampf* (1926). Munich, 1941.
William L. Langer, *An Encyclopedia of World History*. Boston, 1980.
Theodor Lessing, "Biene und Wespe oder Bürgerlich und Romantisch" (1926). In Lessing, *"Ich warf eine Flaschenpost ins Eismeer der Geschichte"*: *Essays und Feuilletons, 1923–1933*. Neuwied, 1986.
Heinrich Mann, "1926." In Mann, *Sieben Jahre: Chronik der Gedanken und Vorgänge*. Berlin, 1929.
Jules Romains, *Le Dictateur: Pièce en quatre actes*. In *La petite illustration: Revue hebdomadaire*, 23 October 1926.

Gustav Stresemann, "Student und Staat: Rede vor dem Verein Deutscher Studenten" (Berlin, 6 July 1926). In Stresemann, *Reden und Schriften: Politik, Geschichte, Literatur, 1897–1926,* vol. 2. Dresden, 1926.

Ernst Toller, "Russische Reisebilder" (1926). In Toller, *Quer durch: Reisebilder und Reden.* Munich, 1978.

Ramón del Valle-Inclán, *Tirano Banderas* (1926). Madrid, 1978.

Nelson Werneck Sodré, *A Coluna Prestes: Análise e depoimentos.* São Paulo, 1975.

MALE = FEMALE
(GENDER TROUBLE)

The license to speak about sexual practices that diverge from the biological need for reproduction depends on a certain perspective from which
they appear as anomalies. As male homosexuality becomes an increasingly popular topic, the premise underlying the discussion holds that love
between men blurs the distinction between Male and Female, which is
viewed as natural. A favorite emblem for male forms of Gender Trouble
is the bullfighter, whose confrontation with the untamed forces of nature
paradoxically conjoins the traditionally male value of physical prowess
and the traditionally female attribute of physical inferiority. [see
Bullfighting, Male vs. Female] Despite the complexity of this emblem,
the popular imagination stereotypically—and obsessively—represents
homosexual men as effeminate. In Ramón del Valle-Inclán's novel *Tirano
Banderas*, a homosexual character—Spain's ambassador to a small Latin
American republic—is constructed via the simple logic of replacing supposedly male attributes with their female opposites: "The most excellent
Señor Don Mariano Isabel Cristino Queralt y Roca de Togores, Baron
of Benicarlés and Grand Master of Ronda, had the voice of a whore and
the gait of a ballerina. Eye-catching, big, unusual, highly skilled at whispering and gossip, he was naturally mellifluous. He spoke through his
nose like a Frenchman, and beneath his fleshy eyelids there was a touch
of perverse literature. He was a useless and pompous figure, a literary
snob, a dilettante in decadent literary circles, celebrating the rituals and
glories of French meter" (Valle-Inclán, 29). [see **Dancing, Authenticity**

vs. Artificiality, Silence vs. Noise] The same binary logic of substitution is apparent in the description of the ambassador's lover (a young bullfighter, of course), who is characterized through a number of items that police agents find in his home: "A packet of letters. Two photoportraits with dedications. A walking stick with a gold handle and monogram. A cigarette case with a monogram and a coronet. A necklace, two bracelets. A wig with blond ringlets, otherwise dark. A makeup case. Some silk underwear, with bows" (69). Another feature of the discussion on homosexuality is the narrative restriction according to which only one member of a couple can appear as "truly" homosexual, while the other is seen as pursuing a nonsexual interest through their relationship. Not only is the "originally" heterosexual partner assumed to derive considerable economic advantage from his consent; he also regularly uses homosexuality's illegality and social disrepute to blackmail his lover. When the young bullfighter tells the Spanish ambassador about the police raid on his house which produced evidence of their relationship, the diplomat immediately assumes that his lover wishes to extort more money from him: "My dear Francis, you're a scoundrel! All this is a trick of yours to get money out of me—you're tormenting me." "Little Isabel, do you see this crucifix? I swear by all that is most sacred: I'm telling the truth." The baron, filled with fear and distrust, repeats, "You're a scoundrel!" (219).

Novelists and legal systems alike base their accounts of male homosexuality on the premise that multiple asymmetries exist between partners. In the trial of the mass murderer Friedrich Haarmann, the judges simply cannot imagine that Haarmann freely gave the clothes of his victims to his friend Hans Grans, and that Grans in no way pressured him with direct or indirect threats. [see **Murder**] In Bertolt Brecht's *Lebenslauf des Boxers Samson-Körner* (*Life of the Boxer Samson Körner*), the homosexual cook Jeremiah Brown forces a stowaway on an ocean liner to pay for silence and complicity with daily sexual favors. [see **Ocean Liners**] Even in those rare cases where homosexual relationships appear as (at least temporarily) based on mutual affection, there is always a dramatic turning point when one of the partners discovers—or admits—his "true" heterosexual orientation. In Egon Erwin Kisch's play *Die Hetzjagd* (*The Hunt*), Alfred Redl, the director of the Austro-Hungarian intelligence service, leaves town for an extended period, during which his lover Stefan Hromadka forms the project of marrying a young teacher named Franzi Mittringer. Although Kisch describes Stefan and Franzi as surprisingly sympathetic to Redl's feelings, the "legitimate" couple quite naturally—and quite cruelly—suggest that Redl pay the legal fees for their wedding. The plot subsequently confirms the generally accepted image of homosexual love, even if Kisch ends up presenting Redl as a tragic hero. Promising Stefan lavish gifts and unheard-of military promotions, Redl manages to buy back his lover's affection for a brief time. [see **Automobiles**] Meanwhile, however, it has become apparent that the Russian secret service, aware of Redl's homosexuality, has forced him to assume the role of double agent. When the Austrian police confront him with evidence of his treason, Redl commits suicide, leaving the way clear for Franzi and Stefan's marriage.

No treatment of male homosexuality ever questions the assumption that it is an "anomaly" which, in one way or another, must be repressed for the good of society. Having hit bottom in the social hierarchy of Buenos Aires, Silvio Astier, the sixteen-year-old protagonist of Roberto Arlt's novel *El juguete rabioso (The Furious Toy)*, shares a room in an asylum with a filthy man of uncertain age who confesses he is tormented by the desire to become a woman. By way of self-apology, he explains that he comes from a rich family but was "perverted" to homosexual practice by a private teacher. The novelist's double message is unambiguous: homosexuals are effeminate, and nobody is born homosexual. Once Silvio Astier has established a hierarchical relation with his new acquaintance by proving his superior physical force, he can afford to take a less aggressive tone in their conversation: "Why don't you go to some doctor, . . . some specialist in nervous disorders?" (Arlt, 93). Such condescending recommendations for medical or psychological treatment are the most "tolerant" reactions that homosexuals can expect from the more enlightened strata of society. In its *Almanach* for the year 1926— along with essays by Sigmund Freud, Thomas Mann, Hermann Hesse, Stefan Zweig, and others—the Internationaler Psychoanalytischer Verlag publishes an article by Dr. Oskar Fischer, a pastor from Zurich, who offers detailed instructions for sexual education from a perspective that is surprisingly similar to that of Silvio Astier in Arlt's novel: "Many parents have no clear picture of how much unhappiness sexual deviance produces. If they only knew about the sufferings of so many homosexuals, sadists, masochists, fetishists, and other sexual perverts, and if they understood how closely pathological sexual desire and the inability to love an appropriate partner are related to severe psychic and so-called nervous diseases, they would be shocked by their own lack of interest in this enormously important field. The development of a sexuality that accords, on the one hand, with the highest ethical standards and, on the other, with the biological functions of humankind must be among the highest goals of our education" (Fischer, 105–106).

In its confident certitude, this affirmation of "normality" relates biological reproduction and sexual "normality" to individual well-being, to moral and intellectual excellence, and, mediated through the love of God, even to a religiously grounded cosmology. But portrayals of homosexual love that seem to come from an inside perspective (portrayals that are always indirect) are in general accompanied by a suspension of cognitive assurance and by complicated episodes of introspection. In Thomas Mann's story "Unordnung und frühes Leid" ("Disorder and Early Sorrow"), Dr. Cornelius, a professor of history, feels an almost Oedipal affection for his five-year-old daughter, Lorchen: "She is undeniably his. She consciously basks in the profound tenderness with which he embraces her little body (a tenderness that, like all deep feelings, conceals a certain sadness) and in the love that shines from his eyes as he kisses her fairylike hand or her dear forehead, with its intricate pattern of fine blue veins" (Mann, 496). Somewhat vaguely, however, Cornelius knows that this love for his child undermines his intellectual rigor as a historian. For if history registers the constant changes that constitute human life in all its complexity, the professor's unconditional love for Lorchen is a feeling that remains unaffected by such ongoing transformations: "In this love for his young daughter, his conservative nature, his sense of the everlasting, has found a refuge from the hurtful modern age. A father's love, a baby at its mother's breast—aren't these timeless, and therefore supremely sacred and beautiful? Yet Cornelius, thinking matters over in the darkness, glimpses something in his love which is not quite right. From a theoretical point of view, for the sake of science, he silently admits this. There is a motive underlying his love, inherent in its very nature. The motive is animosity: toward the history of the present moment, which is still taking shape, hence not history at all; and on behalf of true history, which has already occurred—that is to say, death" (498). [see **Present = Past (Eternity)**] Mann never lets Cornelius' reflections exceed the limits of this highly academic interior monologue. But is there more behind the professor's fatherly affection than a resistance to historical change? The narrative suggests that Cornelius has an interest in good-looking young men, particularly in his servant Xaver Kleinsgütl—described as "hatless in all types of weather, wearing a long shirt jauntily adorned with a leather belt" (491) [see **Stars**]—and in an engineering student named Max Hergesell, whom the professor's teenaged children have invited to a dance party: "A young man sporting a good deal of white shirt-front and a little black string-tie . . . Pretty as a picture, with his dark hair and rosy cheeks—shaved, naturally, but showing a hint of whiskers" (p. 505). [see **Engineers, Gramophones**] While the professor takes a walk, to escape the noisy house and plan his next lecture, Hergesell, trying to please his hosts, dances with little Lorchen. By the time Cornelius returns, she has become so wrought up with childish love for the young man that, although it is long past her bedtime, she cannot fall asleep; she is sobbing into her pillow, with two nurses standing by helplessly. Only Kleinsgütl understands this situation. He asks Hergesell to come to the nursery, and the narrator remarks that the father is almost as impressed by the young man's appearance as his daughter is: "Max Hergesell draws near Lorchen's crib, wearing his evening jacket, with his hint of whiskers and his charming dark eyes, obviously happy to be playing the role of swan knight and fairy-tale prince, as if saying: 'Here I am! Now all desires are fulfilled and all tears will cease!' Cornelius is moved nearly as much as Lorchen herself" (520). Without knowing it, he is doubly jealous and doubly pleased: jealous of Lorchen's childish infatuation with Hergesell and of Hergesell's friendly gesture toward Lorchen; pleased with Hergesell's impressive appearance and with his calming influence on the suffering child. The professor is filled, briefly, with a strange ambivalence: "Young Hergesell leans over the bars of the crib and chatters away, more for the father's ear than the child's, but Lorchen does not know this—and the father's feelings toward him are an extraordinary mixture of gratitude, embarrassment, and hatred" (521). Moments later, the world returns to its fragile state of order. Cornelius has persuaded himself that the distance which Lorchen, in her sleep, is taking from Hergesell is comparable to his own distance from the young man: "What a good thing," he says to himself, "that she sinks deeper into forgetfulness with every breath! That for children the night that separates one day from the next is like an abyss! Surely, by tomorrow young Hergesell will be a mere dream, unable to cast gloom over her little heart" (522).

This convergence of implicit homosexual attraction with the theme of loss and recuperation of precarious intellectual certainty is by no means exclusive to Mann's story. Having spent the previous summer with Salvador Dalí and feeling increasing physical desire for him, Federico García Lorca publishes a long, complex ode to his friend in the April issue of the *Revista de Occidente* (Etherington-Smith, 62ff.). It contains no overt reference to the poet's homosexual longings, but from the outset it is filled with images of geometry, measurement, and transparent order: "A rose in the high garden that you desire. / A circle in the pure syntax of steel" (García Lorca, 618). Gradually the reader becomes aware that this motif points to something which has been lost and is urgently needed:

> A desire for forms and limits defeats us.
> Here comes the man who sees with the yellow straightedge.
> Venus is a white still-life
> And the butterfly collectors flee.
>
> (García Lorca, 619)

Lorca's admiration for Dalí the painter—and for Dalí the beloved who fails to respond to his love, yet does not reject it—is manifested as praise of an artist who, rather than pretending that he has found certainty, never gives up his search for guideposts and limits, and who continues in full awareness of the endlessness of this quest:

> O, Salvador Dalí, of the olive voice!
> I do not praise your imperfect adolescent paintbrush,
> Or your palette, which haunts the color of your time,
> But I praise the yearning of your imperfection.
> . . . . .
> I sing your beautiful striving for Catalan light,
> Your love of what cannot possibly be explained.
> I sing of your astronomical and tender heart.
>
> (García Lorca, 619, 621)

From a thematic viewpoint, no text could be more different from Mann's "Unordnung und frühes Leid" and García Lorca's "Oda a Salvador Dalí" than T. E. Lawrence's *Seven Pillars of Wisdom,* a voluminous account of the effect of the Great War on Arabia. Nevertheless, the theme of forbidden sexual desire accompanied by a crisis of cognitive certainty provides an interpretive frame for this text—a frame that goes beyond the scope of its dense historical reference. [see **Uncertainty vs. Reality**] The book is dedicated to a loved one for whom Lawrence wanted to win liberty, and who has died:

> I loved you, so I drew these tides of men into my hands
> and wrote my will across the sky in stars
> to earn you Freedom, the seven pillared worthy house,
> that your eyes might be shining for me
> when we came.
> . . . . .
> Love, the way-weary, groped to your body, our brief wage
> ours for the moment
> before earth's soft hand explored your shape, and the blind
> worms grew fat upon
> your substance.
>
> (Lawrence, 5)

This allusion is never completely clarified in the hundreds of pages of Lawrence's narrative. Only the first paragraph of the brief epilogue may close the open bracket: "Damascus had not seemed a sheath for my sword, when I landed in Arabia; but its capture disclosed the exhaustion of my main springs of action. The strongest motive throughout had been a personal one, not mentioned here, but present to me, I think, every hour of these two years. Active pains and joys might fling up, like towers, among my days; but, refluent as air, this hidden urge re-formed, to be the persisting element of life, till near the end. It was dead, before we reached Damascus" (661).

On a less intimate level, Lawrence writes explicitly about homosexual practices. He does so, however, under the license of the conventional understanding that, in the specific situation of warfare, such practices are an unavoidable substitute for heterosexual contacts:

> The body was too coarse to feel the utmost of our sorrows and of our joys. Therefore, we abandoned it as rubbish: we left it below us to march forward, a breathing simulacrum, on its own unaided level, subject to influences from which in normal times our instincts would have shrunk. The men were young and sturdy; and hot flesh and blood

unconsciously claimed a right in them and tormented their bellies with strange longings. Our privations and dangers fanned this virile heat, in a climate as racking as can be conceived. We had no shut places to be alone in, no thick clothes to hide our nature. Man in all things lives candidly with man . . . Later, some . . . swore that friends quivering together in the yielding sand with intimate hot limbs in supreme embrace, found there hidden in the darkness a sensual co-efficient of the mental passion which was welding our souls and spirits in one flaming effort." (30)

In addition to what is overtly expressed in these sentences, it is the narrator's effort to distance himself from their content which gives the text a strong sexual tension. This distance finds its complement and confirmation in his inability to engage in what he sees as the "absolutism" and "superficiality" of bodily contacts (an inability that does not characterize male bodies): "To put my hand on a living thing was defilement; and it made me tremble if they touched me or took too quick an interest in me. This was an atomic repulsion, like the intact course of a snowflake. The opposite would have been my choice if my head had not been tyrannous. I had a longing for the absolutism of women and animals, and lamented myself most when I saw a soldier with a girl, or a man fondling a dog, because my wish was to be as superficial, as perfected" (563). Whatever the cause of this inhibition, it generates a longing for certainty and security: "There was my craving to be liked— so strong and nervous that never could I open myself friendly to another. The terror of failure in an effort so important made me shrink from trying; besides, there was the standard; for intimacy indeed seemed shameful unless the other could make the perfect reply, in the same language, after the same method, for the same reason" (563). All that remains is an overly sophisticated passion that intensifies, rather than satisfies, desire: it is the pleasure which the narrator takes in seeing himself reflected in another mind whose curiosity has not yet been awakened. "There was a special attraction in beginnings, which drove me into everlasting endeavour to free my personality from accretions and project it on a fresh medium, that my curiosity to see its naked shadow might be fed. The invisible self appeared to be reflected clearest in the still water of another man's yet incurious mind" (566).

In contrast to such psychological and discursive complexities, female homosexuality has the lightness of a phenomenon that is allowed to exist as long as it does not require explicit acknowledgment, and that can even be acknowledged as long as it presents itself as transitory or episodic. For example, the male admirers of Josephine Baker are not really shocked to see her closely embraced by beautiful woman in a tuxedo (Kessler, 456). Anyone can obtain detailed information regarding the location of lesbian bars and lesbian meeting places in cities like Berlin or Paris (von Soden and Schmidt, 160ff.). The pictorial elements of their newspaper advertisements are completely unambiguous [see **Bars**], and progressive pedagogical treatises recommend tolerance toward sexual relationships among young women—as long as these relationships are merely side paths on the "natural" way toward heterosexuality: "We should speak openly about the kind of friendship which is so important among girls of that age. And we should not pretend that it is nothing but the exchange of harmless secrets. These girls know only too well what is going on; they just don't know what it means. It is our duty to explain to them that it is neither a horrible crime nor an interesting vice. It is nothing but a detour" (Kaus, 361).

Related Entries

Automobiles, Bullfighting, Dancing, Engineers, Gramophones, Murder, Stars, Authenticity vs. Artificiality, Male vs. Female, Silence vs. Noise, Sobriety vs. Exuberance, Uncertainty vs. Reality, Present = Past (Eternity)

References

Roberto Arlt, *El juguete rabioso* (1926). Buenos Aires, 1980.

Bertolt Brecht, *Der Lebenslauf des Boxers Samson-Körner* (1926). In Brecht, *Gesammelte Werke*, vol. 2. Frankfurt, 1967.

Judith Butler, *Gender Trouble: Feminism and the Subversion of Identity.* New York, 1990.

Meredith Etherington-Smith, *The Persistence of Memory: A Biography of Dalí.* New York, 1992.

Oskar Fischer, "Elternfehler in der Erziehung der Sexualität und Liebe." In Internationaler Psychoanalytischer Verlag, *Almanach für das Jahr 1926.* Vienna, 1926.

Federico García Lorca, "Oda a Salvador Dalí" (1926): In García Lorca, *Obras completas.* Madrid, 1971.

Gina Kaus, "Wie ein Mädchenbuch aussehen sollte" (1926). In Anton Kaes, ed., *Weimarer Republik: Manifeste und Dokumente zur deutschen Literatur, 1918–1933.* Stuttgart, 1983.

Harry Graf Kessler, *Tagebücher, 1918–1937.* Frankfurt, 1961.

Egon Erwin Kisch, *Die Hetzjagd: Eine Tragikomödie in fünf Akten des K.u.K. Generalstabs.* In Kisch, *Hetzjagd durch die Zeit.* Berlin, 1926.

T. E. Lawrence, *The Seven Pillars of Wisdom.* (1926). Garden City, N.Y., 1936.

Thomas Mann, "Unordnung und frühes Leid" (1926). In Mann, *Sämtliche Erzählungen.* Frankfurt, 1963.

Ramón del Valle-Inclán, *Tirano Banderas* (1926). Madrid, 1978.

Kristine von Soden and Maruta Schmidt, eds., *Neue Frauen: Die zwanziger Jahre.* Berlin, 1988.

PRESENT = PAST
(ETERNITY)

....

The future often becomes absorbed in a Present that seems to be ahead of itself. But this is not the only shift taking place in everyday time-structures. [see **Present vs. Past**] Likewise, the distinction between Past and Present risks disappearing because the process in which each Past is replaced by a new Present seems to have quickened so dramatically that individual ways of thinking and collective modes of life can no longer adapt: "Man's prospects are not at present so rosy that he can neglect any means of improving them. He has recently made a number of changes in his customs and ways of life, partly with intention, partly by accident. These changes are involving such widespread further changes that the fairly near future is likely to see an almost complete reorganization of our lives, in their intimate aspects as much as in their public. Man himself is changing, together with his circumstances; he has changed in the past, it is true, but never perhaps so swiftly. His circumstances are not known to have ever changed so much or so suddenly before, with psychological as well as with economic, social and political dangers. This suddenness threatens us" (Richards, 15). Such rapid change causes pain, and it sometimes leads to situations in which the Past, instead of being left behind, haunts the Present. People refer to the swiftness and depth of the transformation with words that are normally reserved for important events. But the historical change remains a quasi-event because, paradoxically, its accelerated rhythm precludes its being conceptualized and interpreted—at least with traditional formulas and artistic genres: "It will take thirty or more years before this overwhelming transformation of our intellectual and moral values is turned into the small coin of everyday interactions" (Blei, 402).

There are only a handful of types of behavior and professional roles that are synchronized with this new rhythm: reporters, who replace interpretation by sheer surface-perception; brokers, who never possess the object of their mediation; the rapid and perpetual movement from one tavern or bar to the next—a movement that, when sustained, prevents stagnation and alcohol addiction. All these activities, working in concert, seem to push life to the level of a colorful surface. [see **Bars, Reporters, Authenticity vs. Artificiality**] Only at this level, if at all, can one hope to keep pace with relentless, widespread change. But even if it is possible (though by no means easy) to maintain a minimum of orientation, the rapid pace inevitably affects the ways in which time is experienced. Such secondary change—that which results from an acceleration of change—leaves seismic traces in the texts of the poet Johannes Becher. As a Marxist, Becher has certain expectations about the ways in which Past, Present, and future should relate. This may be why he registers so precisely a process in which these three temporal divisions increasingly overlap and which ultimately makes it impossible to keep them apart (let alone to deduce "laws of change"). Becher's favorite word for this collapse is *Ineinander-Geschehen* ("event-merging"):

> To sink, sinking worlds
> like hammer-blows a leaden thunder surrounds
> the mouth of a dream-singer, sounding of the
> lips, lips connecting themselves
> to the lips . . . Beams—
> whispering. O, event-merging of all worlds!
>   (Becher, 46–47; also 57ff.)

An alternative repertoire of images stages the same crisis from the opposite angle. Instead of emphasizing the blurring of the boundary between Past and Present, these images present the border as a sometimes dangerous gap. For Becher, such metaphors of discontinuity have the virtue of offering an associative link with the Communist notion of revolution:

Wave the blood-red flags, and
howling victory your squadrons cut through the night
like rifts of flames. A light
burst scarlet-large.
Shooting sparks strangle
the world-horror dancing.

(Becher, 116)

Precariousness leading to an ultimate loss of temporal structure: this is the key experience associated with the impression of accelerated change. Unstructured time, however—time as matter (or substance of time), as one may say—seems to offer itself as a medium ready to be inscribed, structured, and manipulated (Luhmann, 45–69). This situation facilitates images of the expansion or contraction of time through new ways of organizing labor. Although these different images all point to the same kind of process—namely, to a gain in the efficiency with which labor is performed—it appears as an extension of time from the perspective of productivity, and as a reduction of time from the perspective of the workers' schedule. [see **Assembly Lines, Strikes, Timepieces**] A similar oscillation accounts for the public's fascination with athletic performance. An athlete who breaks the record of a predecessor can be seen either as covering a longer distance in the same amount of time, or as taking less time to cover the same distance. [see **Six-Day Races, Endurance**] Slow-motion and time-lapse photography emphasize the impression that time can be retarded or accelerated according to different economic, technical, or scientific needs. This impression forms the basis for a popular concept of relativity which, although it is different from Einstein's theory, is used for didactic purposes even by such eminent scholars as the astronomer A. S. Eddington: "The motions of the electrons are as harmonious as those of the stars but in a different scale of space and time, and the music of the spheres is being played on a keyboard fifty octaves higher. To discover this elegance we must slow down the action, or alternatively accelerate our own wits, just as the slow-motion film resolves the lusty blows of the prize-fighter into movements of extreme grace and insipidity" (Eddington, 20). Since such analogies confirm the belief that it is possible to gain, lose, spend, or save time, they generate a discourse in which time appears as a commodity. While the slogan "Time is money" merely conceptualizes this perspective, more sophisticated reflections try to—ironically or seriously—assess the market value of time: "Everybody in the world, bureaucrat or boss, takes it for granted that our sort of people have ages of time to waste. It's different with those who have money. They can arrange everything with money, and so they never have to wait. We who cannot pay with cold cash have to pay with our time" (Traven, 41).

Time is a commodity, and this presupposes that time is experienced as an agent of change. The historical specificity of the Present lies in the vanishing of goals toward which change is supposed to lead. Devoid of internal structures and goals, however, time suggests nothing but continuous movement, without any rest or fulfillment: "What our age has discovered is that in the moment in which one is changing, in which one is moving, one feels better. It's impossible to go so far away that we find the desire to return home. I realize here, at the moment of landing, that I do not like traveling—that I like only movement. It is the sole truth, the sole beauty. I will not be ashamed of my life so long as it is mobile. The only fixed point: the idea of change" (Morand, 31–32). Continuous movement is but one of the concepts that emerge from a chronotope without structure, a chronotope in which Present, Past, and future can no longer be kept apart. Another is Eternity. For time without structure is eternal change, change without beginning or end. Indeed, so obvious and frequent is the chain of associations between the experience of accelerated change, the loss of time-structures, and the concept of Eternity, that different versions of Eternity can be distinguished.

In the first version, Eternity simply follows from the absence of immanent time-structures: "There is no progress or regress. There is no beginning or end. There are no eras, and there is no history." Starting with this radical statement, the philosopher Theodor Lessing tries to explain the prevailing impression that temporal structures exist only as projections of human consciousness. This leads him to the conclusion that "man circles through eternity in a train named 'consciousness'" (Lessing, 384–385). Discussing the notion of "historical evolution," the historian Kurt Riezler postulates that the interplay between "fate" and "freedom" cannot be reduced to recurrent and therefore predictable patterns of change. If, however, infinite modalities of this interplay generate a number of historically different phenomena, the sheer fact of the interplay between fate and freedom is eternal: "The interplay between freedom and fatality is immutable—despite all the mutability in form and degree.

Every freedom contains fatality, and even the blindest form of fatality contains some freedom" (Riezler, 225).

The second version of the concept of Eternity has an existential, even heroic aspect. It serves as a consolation for the feeling of insecurity and homelessness arising from the impression that historical change is occurring ever more rapidly. The *Berliner Börsen-Zeitung* offers the heroic concept of Eternity to readers of its New Year's issue: "What we need above all, in a time like ours, is a firm heart. But only a heart in which the thought of eternity dwells can be firm . . . Remember what you are, how long you will be what you are—and what you will someday become! Then your sorrows will seem trivial, your daily struggles and sufferings will appear unimportant, and all of them will ultimately disappear in the vast, deep ocean of eternity." With obvious irony, Thomas Mann, in his story "Unordnung und frühes Leid," attributes a similar thought to the historian Professor Cornelius, who lives in a society that is rife with tensions between Past and Present: "As he takes his usual stroll along the river before dinner, the professor is sunk in thought. The nature of timelessness and eternity, he says to himself, is akin to that of the past. And it is much more compatible with the nervous system of a history professor than are the excesses of the present. The past is immortalized, meaning that it is dead. And death is the source of all godliness and enduring meaning" (Mann, 498). [see **Immanence = Transcendence (Death)**]

The third version is linked to mythology, and attracts mainly intellectuals who live in areas of the cultural periphery that are associated with the future. [see **Authenticity vs. Artificiality, Center vs. Periphery**] This concept of Eternity expresses resistance to change, which becomes the basis of a quasi-transcendental dignity. The desire for such dignity must be why the student yearbook of Stanford University contains, along with essays on the universities of Oxford, Paris, and Tokyo, a description of the University of Cairo. This institution inspires respect precisely because it deprives its students of all the elements of modern life that Stanford students enjoy: "The Mohammedan parent desires for his son an education which will secure him an honored place among the learned of his own community, rather than one which will command success in the modern professions or in official life. The Mohammedan scholar's lack of scientific interest has greatly retarded the economic progress of his people. The same wooden plow and the same primitive level which are found pictured in the tombs of the Egyptian kings are seen today in the hands of the workmen in Cairo. Nevertheless, [the university] has a great socializing influence" (*1926 Quad*, 98). If, with reference to an institution, Eternity is a form of continuity that is grounded in an immemorial Past, the concept is often projected onto an even broader time-span when it refers to landscape and nature. This is the case with Hart Crane's mythologizing portrait of North Labrador:

> A land of leaning ice
> Hugged by plaster-grey arches of sky,
> Flings itself silently
> Into eternity . . .
> Cold-hushed, there is only the shifting of moments
> That journey toward no Spring—
> No birth, no death, no time nor sun
> In answer.
>
> (Crane, 21)

At first glance, Jorge Luis Borges seems much less serious than Crane when, in one of his poems, he writes about the "mythical founding of Buenos Aires." Beginning with the opening stanzas, the scenes from the Past that he evokes are full of commonplaces obviously drawn from history books and historical maps:

> And was it by this river of drowsiness and mud
> That the ships arrived to found my homeland?
> Would the little painted boats be wrecked
> between the seaweed and the treacherous current?
>
> Thinking it over carefully, we must suppose that the river
> was bluish then, as if it had come from the sky,
> with a little red star to mark the place
> where Juan Díaz fasted and the Indians ate.
>
> (Borges, 95)

But the more Borges develops this bookish mythology, the clearer it becomes that he is unwilling to separate the Past of the moment of founding from the Present of Buenos Aires and from the modern topography of the city, including the names of its neighborhoods and streets, politicians and musicians:

> They set up a few rickety huts on the coast,
> and slept at a distance. They say that in Riachuelo,
> though, plots were hatched at the rivermouth.
> That was an entire block in my neighborhood: in Palermo.

> But an entire block in the middle of a field
> exposed to the dawns, the rains, and the winds.
> The block seems to be still in my neighborhood:
> Guatemala, Serrano, Paraguay, Gurruchaga.

> . . . . .
> The neighborhoods already opted for "Yrigoyen."
> Some piano flung out the tangos of Saborido.
>
> (Borges, 95–96)

And in the final six verses, this overlapping of the city's Past and Present, this loss of temporal structure, makes Buenos Aires as eternal as nature.

> A cigar case perfumed the desert
> like a rose. The evening had sunk back into yesterdays.
> The men shared an illusory past.
> Only one thing was missing: the sidewalk opposite.

> I think it is an illusion that Buenos Aires had a beginning.
> I find it as eternal as the water and the air.

Related Entries

Assembly Lines, Bars, Endurance, Reporters, Six-Day Races, Strikes, Timepieces, Authenticity vs. Artificiality, Center vs. Periphery, Present vs. Past, Immanence = Transcendence (Death)

References

Associated Students of Stanford University, *The 1926 Quad.*
Johannes R. Becher, *Maschinenrhythmen.* Berlin, 1926.
Berliner Börsen-Zeitung.
Franz Blei, "Bemerkungen zum Theater" (1926). In Anton Kaes, ed., *Weimarer*

Republik: Manifeste und Dokumente zur deutschen Literatur, 1928–1933. Stuttgart, 1983.

Jorge Luis Borges, "Fundación mítica de Buenos Aires" (1926). In Borges, *Obra poética, 1923–1977.* Buenos Aires, 1977.

Hart Crane, *White Buildings.* New York, 1926.

A. S. Eddington, *The Internal Constitution of the Stars.* Cambridge, 1926.

Fritz Heider, "Ding und Medium." *Symposion* 1 (1926): 109–157.

Theodor Lessing, "Es ist nur ein Übergang" (1926). In Lessing, *"Ich warf eine Flaschenpost ins Eismeer der Geschichte": Essays und Feuilletons, 1923–1933.* Neuwied, 1986.

Niklas Luhmann, "Zeichen als Form." In Dirk Baecker, ed., *Probleme der Form.* Frankfurt, 1993.

Thomas Mann, "Unordnung und frühes Leid" (1926). In Mann, *Sämtliche Erzählungen.* Frankfurt, 1963.

Paul Morand, *Rien que la terre: Voyage.* Paris, 1926.

I. A. Richards, "Science and Poetry" (1926). In Richards, *Poetries and Science.* New York, 1970.

Kurt Riezler, "Der Begriff der historischen Entwicklung." *Deutsche Vierteljahrsschrift für Literaturwissenschaft und Geistesgeschichte* 4 (1926): 193–225.

B. Traven, *Das Totenschiff* (1926). Hamburg, 1954.

FRAMES

AFTER LEARNING FROM HISTORY

It's about time, at least for professional historians, to respond seriously to a situation in which the claim that "one can learn from history" has lost its persuasive power. A *serious* response—beyond merely repeating apologetic discourses and gestures—would certainly have to address the paradox that books about the past continue to attract a growing number of readers, and that history as a subject and as a discipline remains unchallenged in most Western systems of education, whereas professors, academic administrators, and those who pay tuition all somehow feel that the legitimizing discourses about the functions of history have degenerated into ossified rituals. Perhaps we would miss their decorative pathos if they disappeared from history books and in commencement-day speeches; perhaps we would be sad if the past ceased to be a topic in quiz shows and a point of reference in the rhetoric of some politicians. But nobody relies on historical knowledge in practical situations anymore. In the closing years of the twentieth century, people no longer consider history to be a solid ground for everyday decisions about financial investments or environmental crisis management, about sexual mores or preferences in fashion. To respond *seriously* to this change would mean that professional historians (of politics, culture, literature, and so on) would have to begin thinking about its consequences—without being apologetic, and without feeling obliged to prove wrong those who, never expecting to learn from history, have no use for all the knowledge about the past that we preserve, publish, and teach. It is true, however, that sometimes those contemporaries enjoy reading what we write. Could "learning" and "using" just be the wrong words, and could admitting this perhaps enable historians to enjoy a gain in intellectual freedom and imagination, rather than suffer a loss of income?

At any event, there is a long Western genealogy of increasingly complex reactions to the fear (or the hope) that one cannot learn from history even through ever more complicated intellectual techniques. What we retrospectively call "learning from examples" was the conviction that there existed a stable correlation between certain actions and their positive or negative outcomes. Identifying such correlations, transposing them to different contexts, and applying them like recipes in everyday situations were the primary ways in which medieval societies used knowledge about the past.[1] The practice of learning from examples survived unquestioned for many centuries because the belief that time is a natural and inevitable agent of change in the everyday world was not institutionalized until the early modern era. This very belief became the central element in a construction of time that we now term "historical consciousness," and that we tend to misinterpret as an immutable condition of human life. After 1500, the conception of time as a necessary agent of change began to undermine the validity of historical "examples" whose reputed applicability had depended on the (largely unstated) premise that the implications, structures, and functions of human behavior and actions were influenced only slightly, if at all, by their specific contexts.[2]

The Quarrel of the Ancients and the Moderns, which spanned the late seventeenth and early eighteenth centuries, has been canonized as the intellectual event that ultimately invalidated the (to our mind "unhistorical") medieval construction of history.[3] For the first time, different periods and different cultures were seen as incommensurable, and people began asking whether it was possible to learn anything at all from history. The answer to this question—the way out of the early modern crisis of historical learning—was what we still refer to as the "philosophy of history." It transformed the structures of knowledge about the past from a collection of isolated histories (or "examples") into the totalizing image of history as a movement which would continuously transform the frame-conditions of human action. Learning from history could therefore no longer be based on the sameness of these frame-conditions, and could no longer consist in the transposition of patterns of behavior from the past to the present. On the contrary, historical knowledge began to define itself as the possibility of predicting the directions that history as an ongoing, all-inclusive movement of change would take in the future. In other words, the "philosophy of history" claimed to narrow the horizon of otherness by which the future was expected to become different from the past. If this growing complexity in the techniques of learning from history generated an acute sense of the inevitable otherness of each future and each past—an otherness that especially characterized the intellectual scene in Europe during the nineteenth century (as "historical consciousness" and "historical culture")—it is equally true that, despite a flourishing rhetoric which hailed the importance of historical knowledge, the impact of such knowledge on concrete forms of everyday practice had already begun to diminish.

Until recently, this depragmatization of historical knowledge was obscured by the fact that no other invention of Western intellectual history had obtained a greater chance of proving its validity than the "philosophy of history," specifically within the Communist world. At least on an official level of self-reference, the everyday life of more than half the world's population became dependent on the claim that it was possible to extrapolate "laws" of future change from the systematic observation of past change—and that, in the long run, social systems based on this type of extrapolation would necessarily prevail over those in which the "philosophy of history" was confined to a specific style of academic thought. When European Communism collapsed after 1989, this experiment—which had long been unique by virtue of its sheer size—again demonstrated its uniqueness by becoming the most costly failure of all intellectual experiments ever undertaken.[4] One may certainly argue that the fall of the Communist states did not—and will never—invalidate the explicit ethical goals and standards of Marxism. But the apparently deliberate blindness with which many European and American intellectuals refuse to accept the consequences of Communism's breakdown for the status and practical value of historical knowledge can be explained only by their fear of jeopardizing their traditional social role as those "who know better" about the future than politicians, economists, or scientists (a highly compensatory role, since they are generally less well paid). At the same time, contemporary societies are characterized by a need to predict the future—a need that is perhaps more imperative now than ever before. But this need goes along with a practice, especially in politics and economics, whereby efforts to describe the future through

"historical" induction from the past and present are increasingly replaced by the calculation of risk—which takes as its first principle the
unpredictability of the future.[5]

Those who find this picture too dramatic or too pessimistic (but why
should it be seen as exclusively pessimistic?) may find comfort in more
conciliatory readings of our situation. My provocative stance thus far is
meant to fulfill a heuristic function: only if we literally cut ourselves off
from the possibility of returning to the old and worn-out patterns of
"learning from history" will we be obliged to think *seriously* about
different ways of using our historical knowledge. Indeed, long before the
political events of 1989, and independently from the decreasing impact
of historical knowledge on practical life, there were clear symptoms of
an intellectual discontent with the premises and implications of that style
of thinking which (justifiably or not) has become associated with the
name of Hegel. In the 1930s, Alexandre Kojève arrived at the conclusion
that humanity, having fulfilled all of its material needs, had reached the
end of history.[6] After the end of history as continuous change, however,
the need to predict the future could be expected to vanish—and with it
the "philosophico-historical" application of our knowledge about the
past. In the 1960s, Michel Foucault began using Nietzsche's notion of
"genealogy" to underscore the claim that his own reconstructions of past
discursive systems and their transformations did not presuppose the
existence of "laws" governing such change and therefore did not pretend
to have any prognostic function[7] (although many of Foucault's followers
seem to have fallen back into the role of philosophers of history). When
Hayden White and others began to problematize the traditional distinction between fictional texts (especially novels) and historiography,[8] they
did so on the basis of the observation that historians' writing was oriented not merely (and perhaps not even mainly) by real-world structures,
but to a large extent by intrinsic problems of discursive, stylistic, and
poetic organization and composition. To the "ontological" doubt about
whether the movements of history were still governed—if they ever had
been—by identifiable "laws," such reflections added the question (typical for an intellectual culture in which constructivism had become a
powerful philosophical option) of whether texts were at all capable of
representing historical "reality." Yet without the certainty of real-world
reference as a cognitive possibility and a basis for argument, most of the
claims concerning the practical functions of historiography and histori-

cal knowledge are untenable. Some scholars—and probably a majority of undergraduate students—have therefore abandoned the past as a serious intellectual field (though mostly without recognizing that a concentration on the contemporary world does not by any means eliminate the problems of discursive reference).[9] Those who are enamored of the past react either with stoic contempt for such lack of "historical consciousness" or with a desperate insistence on the inherited repertoire of arguments in favor of its didactic value. However aggressive such apologetic attitudes may be, modern historians, in comparison to their nineteenth-century predecessors, feel defeated.

✂

American "New Historicism" has managed to transform some of these apparent losses into postmodern virtues. It is true that, even more clearly than in the case of other academic fashions (and there's nothing wrong with fashions), New Historicism cannot be defined through a coherent set of philosophical options and discursive rules.[10] Rather, it is a stylistic gesture (in the broadest meaning of this concept) that brings together in a loose and, to be sure, often very impressive aggregate different currents from the present intellectual climate. New Historicism's main ingredient is a strong (if not violent) reading of Michel Foucault's historiographic practice according to which reality is constituted by discourses. The concept of "discourse" is seldom defined, and therefore remains comfortably couched between what literary historians used to call "textual genres" and what some sociologists refer to as "social knowledge." More important, however, it is still an open question whether one can and should assume the existence of a "reality beyond" the phenomenal level of discourse. With or without such a metadiscursive "reality" in mind, New Historians restrict the field of their research, and the field of what can possibly be known about the past, to the world of discourses. This self-limitation overlaps with a second philosophical option (referred to above as "constructivist") which claims that what we normally speak of as "realities" are nothing but discourses or structures of social knowledge—and that therefore such realities have to be understood as "social constructions."[11] It is probably the view of realities as socially constructed which has launched the (strange but now familiar) neohistorical habit of referring to cultural phenomena or institutions as "inventions," and of reconstructing their transformations and confluences as "negotiations." If neohistorians use such metaphors to characterize their view of their subject, they never forget to insist that this view converges with the "inventiveness" of their own historiographic writing. This notion could not be more different from the traditional conviction that writing history is nothing but representing (in the sense of depicting) historical realities. New Historians claim a freedom similar to that of fiction writers: they are eager to tell "good stories," and enjoy discussing the "poetics" of historiography. Sometimes (especially among those "reflexive anthropologists" who share the writerly gestures of the neohistorians), such laudable intentions generate frame-narratives about how an author came to write a certain "story"—narratives that end up being longer than the historiographic or anthropological texts themselves.

Only a few decades ago, all of this would have caused a scandal in the field of history, and, luckily for the New Historians' public success, it still succeeds in scandalizing some contemporary "mainstream historians." The potential for making waves within the profession is of course no argument against New Historicism—and even less so in a situation where the classic modes of writing history seem to be exhausted. What bothers me about New Historical practice is, rather, the impression that it has fallen prey to the metaphors emerging from its constructivist strain, and that these metaphors have led to a situation in which the old paradigm of history writing as a precondition for "learning from history" has been replaced by the supremely pretentious implication that history writing means "making history." On a first (and comparatively harmless) level, phrases such as "the invention of class-based society" or "the negotiation of class interests" seem to have encouraged the belief that such realities are indeed products of human intentionality and human actions. What makes things worse, however, is the frequent (and again implicit) conflation of the monumental subject-position presupposed by this language and the "poetic" subjectivity which neohistoricists claim for themselves as writers of historiography. Wherever this conflation occurs, it generates the illusion expressed in the following equations: writing history = inventing historical reality; inventing historical reality = making historical reality. This seems to be why discussions about the "politics" of certain academic discourses are often conducted with a passion and seriousness which would make a neutral observer think that the fate of entire nations and social classes is at stake, and that the question is indeed no longer how one can learn from history but how historians can make (real!) history.

Whenever New Historicism displays such self-importance, it fails to offer persuasive answers to questions concerning what historians should do "after learning from history." Rather, it appears as a new form of compensation engendered by intellectuals' age-old feeling that they are far more remote from any position of political influence than they deserve. But while the claim to occupy a place of influence in the political system has no truly negative consequences as long as the (both frustrating and healthy) distance between the academic world and the world of politics is maintained, the confusion between historians' unavoidable subjectivity and the "inventedness" of historical reality remains troubling. Not, of course, because the "transformation of historiography into literature" may motivate some historians to become more ambitious about their writing. The *serious* problems begin when the insistence on historians' subjectivity leads to the elimination of the premise that there is a reality beyond such subjectivity—and to the elimination of the desire (as impossible to fulfill as any other desire) to reach this reality. As soon as New Historicism deprives itself of this desire, it no longer differs from fiction and thus can never become a substitute for traditional historiographic discourse, which was based on a claim of real-world reference. But, then, even Stephen Greenblatt, the most eminent New Historian, confesses that his work is driven by the desire to reach past realities, by "the desire to speak with the dead."[12]

Since the philosophico-historical paradigm has lost much of its credibility in the contemporary situation, and since New Historicism—which, at least briefly in the United States, seemed capable of taking its place—has yielded to the temptations of such poetico-heroic subjectivity, there remains the question of what we can and should do with our knowledge about the past. In the ongoing search for an answer, one might well begin by bracketing the normative and pedagogical side of this question ("What should we do?"), and simply concentrate on the fact that this knowledge exerts an abiding fascination. In other words, I propose to focus (from the point of view of both concrete historical research and a theory of history) on the basic "desire for historical reality" that seems to underlie all the changing rationalizations and legitimations of historiography and of history as a discipline. Such a move will give us distance from worn-out discussions and discourses—a distance that may permit the emergence of new conceptions about the uses of historical knowledge. At least for the intermediary reflections below, the *serious* question is therefore not what we can do with our historical knowledge but, rather, what drives us toward past Realities—independent of possible practical aims.

In order to find an answer, I will return to an argument that dates from a time when it was much less problematic to speak about the practical functions of historical knowledge—an argument whose philosophical precariousness I make no attempt to deny.[13] It is based on a sociological interpretation of Husserl's transcendental concept of *Lebenswelt* ("life-world"),[14] which must be distinguished from the prevailing use of this word with reference to historically and culturally specific milieus. So as to mark this distinction, I will call such milieus "everyday-worlds."[15] In its classic transcendental meaning, the term "life-world" comprehends the totality of possible forms of behavior that we—or, more precisely, the traditions of Western culture—attribute to human beings. Each particular culture, each everyday-world, can then be seen as a specific concretization and selection of possibilities contained in the life-world. Somewhat paradoxically, however, the life-world includes the human capacity to imagine actions and forms of behavior which it explicitly excludes from the range of human possibilities. These imaginings can be illustrated by the attributes that different cultures have invented for their gods—such as "eternity," "omnipresence," "omniscience," or "almightiness." Since such capacities can be imagined (although the life-world concept excludes them from the reality of human life), they inevitably turn into objects of desire. It is therefore possible to argue that many of the actions performed and many of the artifacts produced within the boundaries of the life-world receive their initial impulse from—and remain energized by—the desire to reach what human imagination projects beyond such boundaries. This reflection leads to the assumption that, for example, many of the more recent advances in communications technology are driven by a desire for omnipresence; that the enormous memory capacities of computers (which generally far exceed the needs of their buyers) emerge out of a desire for omniscience; and that, finally, the wish to overcome the limits that birth and death impose on experience has to do with humans' desire for eternity. It is this desire for eternity which grounds historical and utopian discourses.

But such "irrational" desires are almost regularly concealed by explicit functions and motivations adapted to the various intrinsic rationalities of specific everyday-worlds. In our own social and economic environment, there are indeed good enough reasons for the existence of computers, fax machines, and prognostic methods—beyond their possible grounding in a desire for omnipresence. Yet we lack similarly convincing rationalizations for our knowledge about the past. This lack makes it easy to see that what specifically drives us toward the past is the desire to penetrate the boundary that separates our lives from the time span prior to our birth. We want to know the worlds that existed before we were born, and experience them directly. "Direct experience of the past" would include the possibility of touching, smelling, and tasting those worlds in the objects that constituted them.[16] The concept emphasizes a long-underestimated (if not repressed) sensual side of historical experience—without necessarily being a problematic "aestheticization of the past." For a past touched, smelled, and tasted does not necessarily become beautiful or sublime. Some practices and media in our contemporary historical culture seem to have reacted to this desire for sensual experience. It would be difficult, for example, to explain the new enthusiasm for archival research by adducing the mere need to accumulate more and more historical documents. Rather, touching the original manuscript of a text whose exact words would be more easily accessible in a critical edition seems to make a difference for many scholars. Philological editions on hypercard reinsert the reader into the simultaneity of long-forgotten discursive environments. At the same time, filmmakers pay more attention than ever to the meticulous reconstruction of historical detail on every possible level—so that in movies such as *The Name of the Rose, Amadeus,* or *Mephisto* it has become more important to provide spectators with the illusion of living in a medieval monastery, in late eighteenth-century Vienna, or in Berlin around 1935 than to engage them in specific plots or arguments. Nowhere is this shift in the style of historical culture more obvious than in museums. They long ago abandoned the taxonomic principle which traditionally structured their exhibits, and now tend to organize them as a reconfiguration of historical environments—ranging from prehistoric landscapes to medieval market-places to 1950s drugstores—in which visitors can literally become immersed.[17]

✍

There is an interesting convergence between these practices of a new historical culture and some current philosophical debates. While films and museums have come to focus on environments rather than narratives, our conception of historical time as a sequence has been historicized. Based on the concept of time as a necessary agent of change, the classic notion of historical time had assumed an asymmetry between the past as a circumscribed space of experience and the future as an open horizon of expectations.[18] Between a circumscribed past and an open future, the present appeared as the—sometimes imperceptibly brief[19]—transitional moment in which human actions took place as selections among different possible scenarios for the future. In other words, the present was experienced as constantly moving away from the past and entering the future.[20] Since the 1970s, however, what we perceive as "the present" has been considerably extended—transforming itself into a space of simultaneity.[21] The origin of such a "broader present" lies in a growing reluctance to cross the boundary between the present and the future (or, alternatively, the impression that this boundary has become an ever-receding line).[22] For since the optimism over the concept of progress has faded, the future has become threatening again: it is now inhabited by images of nuclear catastrophe and the pollution of our natural environment, of overpopulation and the spread of epidemic diseases. And even those who resist such pessimism have difficulty coming up with any positive (let alone utopian) scenario. On the other side of our broadening present, new methods of reproducing past worlds (from sound recording to historical cuisine to facsimile editions) deluge us with their products. These transformations of our future and our past have brought forth a present in which images of the future and reminiscences of the past overlap in increasing degrees of—mostly unstructured—complexity.

As a symptom of the general incompatibility between simultaneity and subjectivity, we can observe a temporal coincidence between, on the one hand, the emergence of such a complex present, and, on the other, multiple philosophical problematizations of the figure of subjectivity.[23]

Niklas Luhmann has tried to explain this correlation. He describes "historical time" as a space of operation which emerged as fitting the subject and its actions. If "action," at least within the sociological tradition inaugurated by Max Weber, can be defined as present behavior that is oriented by the imagining of a future situation to whose materialization a subject wishes to contribute on the basis of experience from the past, then it is indeed the subject's action that links past, present, and future as a temporal sequence. Retrospectively, the action in the (past) present and the previous experience in which it is grounded appear as the "causes" for the (now present) future—and this retrospective view unites subject, action, and historical time in an image of humankind as "creator of worlds." This means that outside the sequentiality of historical time, situations or artifacts cannot appear as created by human action. Conversely, in the absence of a subject and its actions, the sequentiality of historical time becomes a space of simultaneity that does not allow for any relations of cause and effect. A world of simultaneity is a world that cannot present itself as an effected world because it does not provide a position of temporal priority; hence the resistance of the historico-philosophical paradigm to situations and models of simultaneity, including the urge to dissolve ("merely chronological") simultaneity into ("philosophical" or "typological") nonsimultaneity.[24] Luhmann underscores the need to develop such a concept of simultaneity as a "theory of the present." The recent interest in paradox—that is, in the simultaneity of two incompatible positions or concepts—can be seen as a first step in this direction.[25] In contrast, Hegel's "philosophy of history" is based on the principle that one can undo paradoxes by transforming the simultaneity of thesis and antithesis into a narrative.

The desire for immediate experience of the past has emerged within the broad new dimension of the present. This new present is a frame for the experience of simultaneity, and simultaneity can be associated with a crisis in the category of "the subject." Likewise, the crisis in this category implies a problematization of the notion of "understanding." Understanding and interpreting have always been (more or less explicitly) related to a topology in which a "surface" had to be penetrated in order to reach a "depth"—which was expected to be an aspect of Truth.[26] This model was linked to the assumption that whatever could become the object of an interpretation was the expression of a subject whose intentions or inner thoughts resulted from an act of understanding. What turned interpretation into a sort of moral obligation was the complementary implication that either the subject could try to conceal this inner sphere or that, despite the subject's best intentions, the inner sphere could never find adequate articulation on any textual surface. On its most pretentious level, interpretation (and "hermeneutics" as the theory of interpretation) claimed that its power to reveal was superior to the subject's self-perception.

In contrast to interpretation and hermeneutics, the desire for direct experience of past worlds is aimed at the sensual qualities of surfaces, rather than at spiritual depth. Developing a motif from Derrida's earlier books and playing against the hermeneutic tradition, David Wellbery discusses the fact that we can see a written page as pure "exteriority" (that is, as exteriority without any "depth") as soon as we suppress the urge to associate it with a subject.[27] The notion of "exteriority" marks three different forms of distance vis-à-vis the hermeneutic topology: we no longer search for a depth concealed by a surface; we no longer see the signs (or rather the traces) on a page as a sequence, but learn to perceive them as a simultaneity; we cease to suppose that such sequences are governed by a causality grounded in subjectivity and action, and adopt a premise of randomness. But how can we account for the survival of the impression that we "interpret" and that we "understand the other" if we opt for a theory of discourse that refuses to offer a space for the subject and for the constitutive distinction between a surface level and a depth level? A systemic critique of hermeneutics would have to start with a rephrasing of the human psyche ("psychic systems") and of human societies ("social systems") as "autopoetic systems."[28] Autopoetic systems maintain themselves by intrinsically producing and reproducing all of their constitutive elements, and they do so in a permanently unstable balance with their environments. Autopoetic systems react intrinsically to "perturbations" coming from these environments, but they do not "see" them—and they therefore cannot gain insight into the inner sphere of any other system in their environment. According to systems theory, our impression that such insight into another person's psyche is possible comes from an intrinsically produced distinction between the observing system's self-reference and its external reference. This distinction can be refined by further differentiating the (intrinsically produced) external reference into a self-reference and an external reference. In other words, we imagine the psyche of the people whom we think we observe.

The external reference's self-reference is what the observing Self confuses with the Other's self-reflexivity, and the external reference's external reference contains what the Self takes for the Other's image of the Self. What we call "understanding" or "interpretation" is, according to this formulation, a system's oscillation between its own internal reference and the internal reference it attributes to a system that is part of its external reference. If understanding, then, appears as a system-intrinsic process—and no longer as an "(inter)penetration" or "bridging" between subjects, one loses the possibility of evaluating such understanding on the basis of its "adequacy." What we only imagine does not have the status of an external reality against which we could hold any perceptions. Given that historical interest can spring from a desire to "directly experience" past worlds, Luhmann's critique of the concept of "understanding" has two consequences. The first of these two consequences takes us back to a somewhat uncomfortable proximity with constructivism: there is no way in which we—as "psychic systems"—can bypass the need to create those past worlds which we want to experience as otherness. The second consequence yields a new formula for a possible function (even a rationalization) of our desire for history—and thus goes further than we wish to go with this argument and in this entire book. Understanding, as an intrinsic component of Otherness within an observing system, adds to the complexity of this system—and therefore to the degree of flexibility with which it can react to perturbations from its environment.

Pursuing these relations between the desire for unmediated experience of the past and contemporary transformations of concepts such as "simultaneity," "subjectivity," and "understanding" has not led us far enough (it's taken us only back to constructivism), but it has also led us too far (to a hypothesis concerning possible functions of historical culture). Both too far and not far enough because our discussion has postponed a comment that was due since the words "reality" and "direct experience" first appeared in this text without being immediately crossed out. How can one use these words without naiveté or embarrassment in a philosophical climate whose dominant self-descriptions are based on supplementarity and absence? Instead of providing an—inevitably apologetic—answer, one might perhaps do better to respond with another question. What could be the point of so much insistence on supplementarity and absence (epistemological conditions that Western thought has confronted for more than a century) if this insistence were not the symptom of an irrepressible desire for presence? And what could be the point of so much insistence on the unbridgeable distance that separates us from past worlds if it were not the desire to re-present—to make present again—those past worlds? Historical culture cannot avoid living between its endeavor to fulfill such desire for presence and an awareness that this is an impossible self-assignment. Therefore, historical culture—if it wishes to preserve its identity as a form of experience different from the experience of fiction—must try to "conjure" the reality of past worlds, without indulging in naive analogies with magic but acknowledging the inevitable subjectiveness of every such construction of historical otherness. Yet as soon as historical culture openly opts for this desire for re-presentation (which is not a given), it cannot help being ironic, for it then re-presents the past as a "reality" though it knows that all re-presentations are simulacra.[29]

Or is it too much of a concession to the spirit of supplementarity to label this situation "ironic"? After all, we *can* touch (and smell!) old newspapers, visit medieval cathedrals, and look into the faces of mummies. These objects are part of the world that we sensually experience; they are spatially nearby and "ready-to-hand"[30] to gratify our desire for historical immediacy. Rather than looking exclusively for the conditions that make immediacy possible, we also have to let it happen. After an initial experience of immediacy, a more scholarly attitude will take over and will remind us of the time span that separates our present from those objects. Scholarship suggests that the past has to become "present-at-hand," that it can be seen "objectively" only if we purify our relation to it by eliminating our desire for immediacy. This effort to establish cognitive distance as a condition for "objective" historical experience can make us blind to our desire for direct experience of the past—which is best served when we do not seek such distance.

While writing this book, I was continually going through old newspapers and dusty books that nobody had read for decades. I never drove my car without listening to jazz recorded in 1926, and I repeatedly watched silent movies made in that year. The main challenge for my writing was therefore to prevent this indulgence in historical immediacy, this ready-to-hand, from turning into the present-at-hand of historical distance and "objectivity." How far can a book go in providing, or rather in maintaining, (the illusion of) such direct experience of the past? How far can a book go in fulfilling a desire to which other media have quite successfully responded in recent years? What happens if, in writing history, one simply follows this desire instead of burdening it with myriad philosophical constraints and pedagogical tasks? It is precisely the interest in exploring this potential of historical writing and of the medium we call the "book" which persuaded me that I should not include photographs and other visual documents here. For they produce an effect of immediacy which easily overwhelms any that can be provided by a text. My hope is that, in the absence of pictures, the words from the past which I abundantly quote will provide a similar—but phenomenologically and psychologically different—effect.

⤝⤞

As an "essay on historical simultaneity," my book is a practical answer to the question of how far a text can go in providing the illusion of direct experience of the past. I make no effort to transform this answer into a "method," for I have always been convinced that claiming the rigor of a "method" is a trope by which humanists seek an easy escape from their traditional inferiority complex vis-à-vis scientists. All I can provide by way of self-commentary is a retrospective highlighting of the most important decisions and lines of orientation that emerged during the composition process. Rather than dignifying this commentary with the epistemological status of a "method," I present it simply as *six rules of thumb for history writing, after learning from history.* These rules overlap, since they point to the (impossible) possibility of a certain historiographic practice, which my own writing, I hope, sometimes approximates.

1

If we distance ourselves from the desire to "learn from history" and to "understand" the past, then *we free ourselves from the obligation to begin historiographic texts by legitimizing the specific relevance of the past moments we choose to write about.* What the German tradition used to call "threshold years," for example, do not exist within a discourse emphasizing historical simultaneity, because this discourse aims at isolating and making present a past[31] instead of establishing a continuity between the past and the present. In the intellectual neighborhood of hermeneutics and subject-philosophy, threshold years were regarded as moments of transition (often marked by "events" of great symbolic significance) between different institutional frames for human action. The interpretation of threshold years was expected to yield particularly important insights into the "laws" of historical change. But if it is true that this Hegelian frame of assumptions has begun to recede, we may no longer be obliged to subordinate archives and narratives to the economy of such historico-philosophical legitimation. As soon as we admit that the choice among possible topics for our research need not follow those criteria of relevance, the old intellectual obsession with "going against the grain" becomes equally obsolete—meaning that historians are no longer obliged, among other things, to promote "hitherto underestimated" years and events. In exchange, the fluctuating public interest in certain segments of the past can then be accepted as a good enough orientation to follow. For instance, the widespread attention that in past decades has been so frequently generated by "commemorative years" certainly stimulates the desire of countless potential readers to directly experience worlds like those of 1789 or 1492—even if such years were first chosen as commemorative years on the basis of their reputation as historical thresholds.

Regarding the year 1926, I wish to emphasize that it neither fulfills the classic requirement of being a threshold year nor anticipates any forthcoming public anniversary. I first chose it as an emblem of randomness[32] because it seems to be one of the very few years in the twentieth century to which no historian has ever attributed specific hermeneutic relevance. Later on, I noticed that my selection had probably been preconsciously oriented by a construction of family history. I believed that two of my grandparents had died in 1926: Theresa Bender in Dortmund-Hörde, from septicemia following a premature delivery, and Vinzenz Schraut, in Würzburg, from the consequences of an injury sustained as a soldier during the First World War.[33] The impossible wish to hear the voices of my grandparents (for it is true that voices are particularly strong in creating an illusion of presence), to know what had occupied their minds, and to see their worlds with their eyes was responsible for my fascination with documents from the years of their adult lives.[34]

Should I then draw the more general conclusion that, while the year selected must antedate my own birth (in 1948), it also must be recent enough to provide an association with persons whom I can identify as my relatives? Could I have chosen the year 926, instead of 1926?[35] Disregarding all the problems that have to do with the availability and precise dating of sources from the Middle Ages, I tend to think that one could indeed write a similar book about the year 926. For although only an initial feeling of closeness will trigger the desire for direct experience of the past, such closeness need not be the closeness of family history. I am writing these lines during a stay in Charlottesville, Virginia—and quite naturally my proximity to so many buildings planned and designed by Thomas Jefferson motivates my wish to know more about—"to get closer to"—the history of American independence.[36] Likewise, for all my academic education as a "Romanist," I did not even begin to become interested in the history of Argentinian culture until I first visited Buenos Aires—not to speak of the impact that vestiges of medieval buildings in my hometown must have had on my choice of a dissertation topic.[37] But while I thus cheerfully admit that no general relevance can be postulated for the year 1926, I hope and believe that the deliberate subjectiveness of the choice need not prevent this book from being useful to readers who study the 1920s from different (and probably "more relevant") angles. This is why, in the concluding chapter, I try to show the more general fruitfulness of my approach through a paradigmatic analysis of Martin Heidegger's book *Sein und Zeit (Being and Time)*, which was written in 1926—an analysis based on the synchronic reconstruction of that year's everyday-worlds.

2

The perspective of historical simultaneity does not depend on the choice of a one-year span—this goes without saying. Any arguable decision about the time span to be treated hinges first of all on the proportion between the available sources and the projected length of the book (or, for that matter, the projected dimensions of the exhibit). Whereas it would be technically difficult to carry out a similar project on a single year from, say, the seventh century B.C., one could easily fill hundreds of pages with references to every month, every week, and probably even every day of the year 1926. A strategic advantage of the one-year span comes from the fact that years (and decades and centuries) often carry certain connotations for potential readers—connotations which may awaken and preorient their interest. In addition, years (not months or days) are used in standard classifications of printed materials (as well as of other artifacts and even of "events")—a circumstance that simply makes things easier for the historian of simultaneity.

Much more important than the time span chosen, however, is the decision to abstract (as far as possible) from the sequentiality and causality within the historiographic reconstruction of a chosen year (decade, month).[38] This decision does not bear directly on my primary goal of coming as close as possible to actual events and structures of experience which constituted the reality of the year 1926. Rather, the suspension of sequentiality arises from the choice of a specific angle of historical representation. In this case, it is the focus on a year as an environment, as a world within which people lived. Although one can of course retrospectively observe transformations and changes in everyday-worlds as environments within the course of a year, I think that, as a general rule, these changes are hardly ever experienced by the people who inhabit those worlds. The self-imposed imperative to suspend sequentiality obliges us to minimize recourse to the subject-centered concept of causality and to the genre of the historical narrative. Thus, we must ask what discourses and concepts we can elaborate in order to establish noncausal relations between the texts and artifacts to which we refer. An answer is all the more difficult to find as we have to expose ourselves to the unavoidable sequentiality of the text as medium. If we can come up with any solutions at all, they will be contributions to the above-mentioned "theory of the present," which we need but do not yet have.

3

Which texts and artifacts "belong" to the year 1926? According to our goal of coming as close as possible to the world of that time span, the range of pertinent materials potentially comprises the traces of all experiences that could be had in 1926. If one takes this formula seriously, it implies the obligation to deal with the almost infinite mass of such traces coming from periods and cultures prior to 1926—provided they were available in 1926. In order to narrow down this overwhelming complexity, I started by concentrating on books, objects, and events that attracted a certain level of public attention during the year in question. Among them, it makes no difference whether a text, say, was actually published for the first time in 1926, whether it was successfully reissued, or whether, even without a new edition, it simply became a topic of widespread discussion during that year. Once a first repertoire of materials is thus established, one may include objects that were produced in 1926 but entered the public sphere at a later date. Such inclusions have to rely on the impression that topics and concerns of particular public resonance during that year had an important impact on the objects to be analyzed. A certain amount of interpretive arbitrariness is of course the price that must be paid for working with hypotheses of this kind. Among the books that were written (not published) in 1926, I have therefore chosen only Heidegger's *Sein und Zeit*—a decision I was encouraged to make by some recently unearthed archival evidence that dates the actual writing process to April through December of 1926. In general, however, I resisted the temptation to use such evidence, because I was interested in exploring the challenges of chronological randomness. Sources without a clear 1926-inscription were simply considered as not available, even though in some cases they might have contributed to the refinement, illustration, and confirmation of some of my views.

But even that randomness is relative. Being used to enormous chronological breadth in the choice of sources for their narratives, many historians overlook the fact that what they reject as "chronological randomness" appears as random only in relation to a metaphysical claim according to which the past is structured by an underlying principle of causality. And there is yet another rule regarding the selection and status of sources: if the main criterion for the inclusion of texts is their status as traces of experience available in the year 1926, then the distinction between fictional and nonfictional texts becomes irrelevant. The only empirical difference I discovered between the value of nonfictional texts and that of fictional texts lies in the—rather unexpected—observation that, on average, fictional texts presented a much higher density of those concerns and perspectives which I came to identify as specific to the year 1926.

4

I do not exactly remember the type of documents I started with, but I do know that, at a very early stage, I abandoned all nonchronological criteria of selection. Any sources, artifacts, or events dating back to 1926 were potentially relevant. With this opening, I of course gave up the expectation of ever reaching a level of exhaustiveness. Though it was not particularly difficult to relinquish this aim, which was impossible anyway, I then faced the more practical question of *when I could consider my research on the available sources completed.* The obvious answer—obvious at least for any type of historical research pertaining to a recent historical period—points to a level of documentary density at which the analysis of further sources will yield no additional insights. There is a moment in every historical investigation where the recurrence of certain types of materials and conclusions becomes empty—or (to use a contrasting metaphor) a moment where our picture of the past reaches a level of saturation. While of course one cannot theorize about the question of when, exactly, the search for sources and materials from the past comes to such a "natural" end, it is obvious that any given historiographic text can carry (and use) only a limited amount of documentary evidence. Seen from this perspective, my style of work was thoroughly inductive. I was eager to let my reading and writing be guided by what became visible as predominant structures of 1926 (instead of following the New Historical pattern of "inventing" such structures), and I have tried to minimize interpretative commentary in the presentation of my results. Of course I know that a historian cannot help "inventing" past worlds—but I still hope that my "construction" comes as close as possible to world views *from within 1926.* Thus, the critical question to which I am ready to respond is not whether there are events, works of art, or books that I have "forgotten" in my reconstruction of 1926, but rather whether their inclusion would have changed in any important way my description and simulation of those past world views.

The empirical observation of recurrence—in contrast to totalization—served in yet another important way as a working principle for my project. It was geared toward identifying multiple topics and concerns that had captured attention in 1926. This meant, first of all, that I could forgo any speculation about levels of preconscious "depth" underlying the cultural manifestations with which I worked. But the decision to focus on surface phenomena and to resist in-depth interpretation also motivated my endeavor to describe them as succinctly and impersonally as possible, the prevailing use of the present tense being a further trace of this ambition. One might say—if one can bracket, at least for a moment, all the philosophical problems that come with this formula from the poetics of literary modernism—that the surface phenomena which I describe "mean" what they "are." Using a conceptual distinction belonging to the phenomenological tradition, one could also say that they refer to the level of "lived experience" *(Erleben)* and not to that of "experience" *(Erfahrung),* because *Erfahrung* always presupposes that an interpretive perspective has already been applied to *Erleben.* Rather than using the term "historemes" (as Wlad Godzich proposed to me in conversation), I would refer to the surface phenomena which I describe as "configurations." For the word "configurations" (or, as Norbert Elias would probably have said, "figurations") emphasizes an aspect of form and perception, whereas the neologism "historemes" resonates with "narremes," a concept that used to be applied when treating the "depth level" of narrative texts.[39]

5

What kind of "historical reality" emerges from a reconstruction that— against all odds—attempts to fulfill the desire for direct experience of the past? I sometimes arrived at the illusion (and, taking into account the historical materials I was working with, one may claim that it was not only an illusion) of being surrounded by the everyday-worlds of 1926. Such memories of the most exciting moments during the years I worked on this project eventually suggested the book's title, *In 1926,* which, grounded in the pleasure of having the historical materials ready-to-hand, cannot deny an at least metonymic proximity to Heidegger's notion of "being-in-the-world." Wanting to be-in-the-world of 1926 through writing a book had quite a number of practical consequences. The world that one must find and reconstruct is an everyday-world, a world of normality (Heidegger says that his existential analysis required focusing on "average everydayness" and "facticity"). Corresponding to the desire of being-*in*-1926, such an everyday-world has to be an environment, an imagined realm, that brings together different phenomena and configurations in a space of simultaneity (hence my insistence on this perspective in section 2, above). But in calling the everyday-world of 1926 a "space of simultaneity," I wish to do more than point to its temporal dimension. With the nonmetaphorical meaning of the word "space," I also allude to the desire to bring phenomena and configurations into an (illusory or not-so-illusory) position of spatial closeness. Only such proximity would indeed enable us to touch, smell, and hear the past.[40] As an aspect of time, however, simultaneity allows for paradoxical relations among the phenomena re-presented. For if what we call a paradox is the simultaneous presence of two contradictory terms, it follows logically that a historiographic perspective of simultaneity engenders multiple paradoxes.

Choosing simultaneity as a frame-condition for this book not only required a tolerance toward paradoxes. It also excluded, independent of any philosophical preferences, the possibility of treating subjects as agents, because actions can be credited with agency only in a narrative, and narratives require sequentiality. The world of 1926 therefore appears here as a stage without actors. This of course does not mean that I am "not interested in people," but is a consequence of the form I chose for the re-presentation of a past year. In renouncing the sequentiality of a narrative plot, I also forgo the most "natural" criterion for selecting among the historical materials. What are the limits of my research, and of the re-presentations based on this research, if I do not pursue or construct a story line? Certainly not the boundaries of any "national culture"—and not even (at least not by way of any logical deduction or induction) the limits of Western culture. The only reason my pictures of the world in 1926 are de facto confined to Western culture lies in the (highly contingent and deplorable) fact that all the materials accessible to my linguistic and semiotic competence come from the West. Whether the various pictures I present really coalesce into a larger panorama of Western culture is another empirical question. The materials seem to point to a fairly coherent network of everyday phenomena, with national idiosyncrasies as well as suggestions of openings toward non-Western worlds. Somewhat paradoxically, the various totalizing world-pictures that emerged within this framework belong to the more idiosyncratic elements. They constitute a second level of reference for the concept of "world," a level occupied by multiple and normally well-circumscribed ideas—as opposed to what I call "the world of 1926," which constitutes this book's ultimately unattainable object of re-presentation. Inside each national or regional culture, the totalizing world-pictures are generally not experienced as "specific" in any sense (neither "black," nor "Western," nor "middle-class," nor "Italian"). But it is easy to delineate their individual profiles by focusing on the inclusions and exclusions through which they are defined. What we could call "Central European culture of 1926," for example, is obsessed with establishing a contrast between the Soviet Union and the United States; it includes an image of Asia but excludes, even as a geographic entity, most of Africa. At the same time, Central European culture eagerly discovers and admires African-American forms of expression. What this world-picture clearly renounces, though (except perhaps in the case of France), is the existence of a transcendental horizon (the concept of "world" is about to become a purely immanent one). From a Latin-American perspective, in contrast, the world-picture includes the United States and Europe but does not seem to share the focus on the Soviet Union. Within such contiguities, overlappings, and differences between multiple everyday-worlds, my reconstruction does not—at least not intentionally—privilege any single perspective or observer position. If many of the individual configurations that I describe seem to center on references to the metropolitan cultures of Berlin, New York, and Buenos Aires (rather than, say, the culture of Paris), such a focus reflects, I hope, the effect of condensation and of the mutual feedback between predominant structures of relevance in 1926. This book tries to situate itself by identifying those places "where the action was."

Finally, how can one find a substitute for the notion of "event" in the context of an "essay on historical simultaneity"? Such a substitution is unavoidable, because the traditional use of this concept presupposes a plot structure (within which the "event" marks a turning point). At the same time, however, events point to the interference of contingency, to whatever resists total integration into the internal logic of a plot. In order to find an equivalent for the concept of "event" within a reconstruction of simultaneity, we have to focus on this second semantic component. An "event" would then be whatever threatens the structures of existing everyday-worlds without being accessible for formulation and interpretation within them. In this sense, we could speculate about the uncontrollable impact of technology (or of technology as it interacts with the natural environments of everyday-worlds) as a potential stimulus for events. Events could arise from the accumulated effects of different cultural codes as they converge or diverge. Events could be a result of external couplings by which everyday-worlds join with other everyday-

worlds in their environments (think, for example, of the coupling between modern theoretical physics and the military—two everyday-
worlds sharing an environment).

On the level of history writing—which, as I have said, turned out to
be a level of empirical experience for my work—the most frequently
observed phenomena and configurations in the year 1926 seemed to fall
into three categories. There are certain artifacts, roles, and activities (for
example, Airplanes, Engineers, Dancing) which require human bodies to
enter into specific spatial and functional relations to the everyday-worlds
they inhabit. Borrowing a word first used within the context of historical
research by Michel Foucault,[41] I call such relations—the ways in which
artifacts, roles, and activities influence bodies—*dispositifs,* or *arrays.*
Coexisting and overlapping in a space of simultaneity, clusters of arrays
are often zones of confusing convergence, and they therefore tend to
generate discourses which transform such confusion into the—deparadoxifying—form of alternative options (say, Center vs. Periphery, or
Individuality vs. Collectivity, or Authenticity vs. Artificiality). Since identifying the *binary codes* in which such discourses are grounded turns out
to be surprisingly easy, and since they provide principles of order within
the unstructured simultaneity of everyday-worlds, one might reserve the
concept of "culture" for the ensemble of such codes.[42] This would be an
alternative to a recent tendency to use the notion of "culture" as coextensive with "everyday-worlds"—a usage in which the concept becomes
too large to allow for any distinctions.

There is reason to assume, however, that individual codes are not
integrated into overall systems, and that the codes sometimes do not even
succeed in maintaining their deparadoxifying function (in 1926 this
seems to be the case, for example, with the binary gender distinction or
with the contrast between Transcendence and Immanence). Such *collapsed codes* are particularly visible because, as areas of malfunction and
entropy, they attract specific discursive attention and, often, specific
emotional energy. From a theoretical point of view, collapsed codes have
to be located on the boundary between the internal sphere of everyday-
worlds and that zone "beyond" everyday-worlds which we noted as a
possible substitute for the concept of "event." Collapsed codes belong
to everyday-worlds, inasmuch as they are based on the binary codes that
provide order through deparadoxification. But as soon as the codes fail
to serve a deparadoxifying function, they move beyond what can be

expressed and conceptually controlled. This is why, in the sense of our definition of "event," the collapse of codes implies a potential for change, and why it would be wrong to see this collapse exclusively from the perspective of loss and malfunction.

6

Arrays, codes, and breakdowns of codes are the three levels on which I present the different objects and configurations that appeared central within the everyday-worlds of 1926. *But is it possible to integrate these various objects and configurations into a historiographic discourse?* Although I have developed some elementary hypotheses about the relations that connect the three levels of phenomena, the nature of their interrelatedness is still not obvious enough to allow us to suggest a new form of historical writing. Similar reservations apply to the three individual levels. It is unlikely that different arrays and different codes (let alone collapsed codes) belonging to one and the same temporal moment ever enter into relations of a systemic character. And even if this were the case, we—in the position of immediate historical witnesses—definitely do not experience everyday-worlds as systems.

Likewise still unanswered is the question of what discursive form would most successfully enhance the illusion of being-in-a-past-world. I have opted for the encyclopedic structure of multiple entries, using the word "entry" to refer to the individual texts that constitute an encyclopedia or dictionary, but also using it as a way of stressing that everyday-worlds have neither symmetry nor center and can therefore be entered from many different directions.[43] Each entry leads toward an encounter with an element of concrete historical reality, and each of these elements is connected to other elements via myriad labyrinthine paths of contiguity, association, and implication. The arbitrariness of the alphabetical order in which the entries are presented and the encyclopedic device of cross-references mimic the nonsystematic character of our everyday experience and suggest that readers constitute the world of 1926 as an asymmetrical network,[44] as a rhizome rather than as a totality.[45]

Gustave Flaubert's *Dictionnaire des idées reçues (Dictionary of Received Ideas)*[46] is a—certainly unattainable—model for the re-presentation of past everyday-worlds through a network of entries. Being a mere notebook in which Flaubert collected the most frequently used common-places of contemporary French society, the *Dictionnaire* cannot be held up as a model of historiographic strategy, because he was not confronted with the task of making a past world present. But I don't know of any other text that provides latter-day readers with such a powerful illusion of experiencing a past everyday-world from inside. In addition to the decentering arbitrariness of the alphabetical order, two additional features greatly contribute to this effect. Flaubert treats his collected commonplaces as quotations, as fragments of a historical reality—and not as descriptions of this reality. They appear as quotes (although they are not enclosed in quotation marks) because there is no authorial voice or discourse to comment on them or put them into historical perspective. This absence, however, creates a prevailing irony. In reading Flaubert, we tend to attribute such irony to an author who destroys commonplaces by strictly limiting himself to their reiteration. The irony underlying my book, in contrast, could perhaps best be characterized as the irony of a project which tries to re-present the reality of a past world despite (or because of) its fundamental awareness that such a re-presentation is impossible. Knowing the impossibility of its own fulfillment, the desire for immediacy should not degenerate into the illusion of immediacy.

BEING-IN-THE-WORLDS OF 1926
Martin Heidegger,
Hans Friedrich Blunck,
Carl Van Vechten

....

✄

Not a Good Year

From a professional perspective, 1926 was not a good year for the philosopher Martin Heidegger. In 1923, he had left the University of Freiburg and his beloved retreat at Todtnauberg in the Black Forest (where his wife had built a cabin for the family the previous year)[1] to accept a long-awaited offer from the University of Marburg. But his new position was only an *Extraordinariat*, which, like an associate professorship in the American academic world, left at least one further step to climb on the career ladder. This was probably why—although the new appointment gave him and his family financial stability in the hard times of postwar Germany, and although his relatively short list of publications made him academically vulnerable—Heidegger would never be satisfied with his employment at Marburg. Even in his acceptance letter to the dean of the Faculty of Philosophy (June 18, 1923), he seemed to be using delaying tactics with his new university, by not giving the titles and topics of the courses he was expected to teach:

To Your *Spektabilität:*[2]
I humbly confirm that today I received an offer from your university concerning an *Extraordinariat* in philosophy, with the rights and status of an *Ordentlicher Professor.* I shall accept this offer. At the same time, I humbly ask Your *Spektabilität* the favor of transmitting to the vener-

able faculty my most profound gratitude for the trust invested in me. I
shall permit myself to mail the descriptions of my future courses immediately after receiving such request from my colleagues in the Department of Philosophy. With the expression of my most sincere respect,
and remaining at Your *Spektabilität*'s disposition,

Dr. Martin Heidegger

In the ensuing years, Heidegger's lack of enthusiasm for Marburg grew
into a general feeling of alienation from what he provocatively began to
call "academic philosophy." He advertised to colleagues and students
that he spent virtually every vacation day far away from them in the
Black Forest cabin. Having enjoyed, during his Freiburg years, a unique
reputation as a charismatic and promising teacher of philosophy,[3]
Heidegger soon become so frustrated at Marburg that he considered
accepting an offer to spend three years as a highly paid research fellow
in Japan—although he thoroughly hated traveling.[4]

In 1925, Heidegger was nominated by his Marburg colleagues for a
full professorship *(Ordinariat)* at the age of thirty-six[5]—which was not
unusual, even by average academic standards. But although his mentor,
Edmund Husserl, who was widely respected throughout the German
academic community, praised him in his letter of recommendation as a
"philosopher in the grand style" and (ironically) as a potential "leader
(Führer) amid the confusions and weaknesses of the present,"[6] the Ministry of Science, Art, and National Education in Berlin was reluctant to
follow such suggestions—undoubtedly because the candidate had not yet
produced a substantial monograph. In their correspondence with the
ministry, Heidegger's colleagues therefore repeatedly alluded to an unpublished work on Aristotle (which would never appear) and, at a later
stage, to a manuscript which was eventually published in the spring of
1927 as the first part of *Sein und Zeit*—and which, despite its epoch-
making importance, would forever remain without a sequel. Although
Heidegger, from his early Marburg years to the end of his life, fostered
the impression that this manuscript had long been finished and kept
secret,[7] the actual writing of *Sein und Zeit* must have taken place between February and December 1926.[8]

In a letter of January 27, 1926, the ministry had informed the search
committee for the *Ordinariat* in philosophy that, "for all the recognition
of Professor Heidegger's teaching success, it nevertheless [seems] inad-

missible . . . to grant him a permanent full professorship of the historical stature of [the Marburg] chair in philosophy."[9] This unequivocally negative response must have spurred Heidegger's colleagues to ask him directly for that book-length manuscript which nobody had yet seen. These are the words from the minutes of a committee meeting on February 25, signed by the dean, Max Deutschbein, a professor of English: "The committee decided unanimously to urge Heidegger to have some copies of his handwritten text of *Sein und Zeit* typed and delivered to the dean. The committee further declared that it would be desirable to have the text also in galleys. The committee would then send the copies for evaluation to a number of scholars, still to be named."[10] The undated remark with which Dean Deutschbein supplemented these minutes makes it clear beyond any doubt that the manuscript in question was nonexistent, or at least very far from completion: "Heidegger declares that he is prepared to get the aforementioned manuscript to the printer by April 1, and to keep the dean apprised of the progress of the typesetting."[11] In the first weeks of 1926, Heidegger most likely had only two projects on his desk: the unfinished revision of a seventy-five-page manuscript on the topic of time which, in 1924, had been rejected by the *Deutsche Vierteljahrsschrift für Literaturwissenschaft und Geistesgeschichte* (*German Quarterly for Literary Studies and Intellectual History*, then the most innovative journal of the humanities in Germany); and a typescript prepared by his student Simon Moser of a course entitled "Geschichte des Zeitbegriffs" ("History of the Concept of Time"), which Heidegger had taught during the summer semester of 1925.[12] Virtually the entire first half of the book must therefore have been written between February 26 (the last day of the winter semester) and April 1, 1926, when Heidegger mailed the first 175 pages of *Sein und Zeit* (up to paragraph 38) to Max Niemeyer Verlag. On April 2—in very general terms, and without mentioning that the manuscript was far from being complete—Heidegger informed Deutschbein of his progress with the work. What he offered "as a sheaf of paper decorated with flowers"[13] to Edmund Husserl for his sixty-seventh birthday on April 8 therefore cannot have been the "almost completed text," as Heidegger would later remember.

Husserl and a number of other, mostly younger philosophers helped Heidegger correct the galleys, which he began to receive on April 14.[14] When Deutschbein mailed the first 175 pages of *Sein und Zeit* to Berlin on June 18, again urging Heidegger's appointment, he adopted the candidate's own strategy of simply not mentioning the fragmentary status of the text: "The faculty believes itself justified in making this request, since Heidegger has in the interim committed his work on 'being and time' to print."[15] The truth was, however, that after returning another fifty-five pages of corrections to the typesetter in early June, Heidegger had suspended work on *Sein und Zeit* due to his current occupations at the university, as he wrote in a letter to his friend Karl Jaspers on July 31 (the last day of the summer semester). It would be some time before he could give better news—as usual, from his cabin in the Black Forest. This news didn't come until October, when, in letters to Jaspers and to the Marburg theologian Rudolf Bultmann, Heidegger announced that the "pause in revising and typesetting" had yielded positive results, enabling him to finish a clean copy of the book's second section by November 1. But he had lost the race to meet the demands of the Berlin bureaucracy. On November 25, Dean Deutschbein received the second— and now definitive—rejection of the faculty's nomination: "I wish to communicate that the minister, upon reexamining all the represented points of view, cannot follow the recommendation to grant Professor Dr. Heidegger the tenured full professorship."[16]

Understandably, Heidegger in the following weeks sought consolation and support through correspondence with his philosophical friends. Nobody offered stronger words of solidarity and appreciation than Edmund Husserl: "[I am happy to see] that you are committed to the work through which you will become who you are, and with which (as you well know) you have already begun fulfilling your own being as a philosopher . . . Nobody believes more firmly in you than I, and I am also convinced that, in the end, no resentment you might feel will be able to throw you off the track. Nothing can divert you from the importance of doing what you alone can do."[17] Husserl's passionate words were designed to persuade Heidegger that, although he had failed to reach the concrete professional goal of an *Ordinariat,* there was still great philosophical, even existential significance to finishing *Sein und Zeit.* Since Heidegger was indeed no longer under any time pressure, he seems to have entertained, at least for a few weeks, the idea of completing the entire book as it is outlined at the end of the introductory chapter. But the published text represents only about two-thirds of the first part.[18]

More than ever—and more understandably than ever—Heidegger was now inclined to distance himself from the academic world of Marburg and to idealize the solitude of his cabin. In a letter of December 22 to Elisabeth Blochmann, a family friend, he plays out this contrast and its meaning for what he still considered an unfinished manuscript:

> It would be appropriate for this letter to come from the cabin; it should be written when the beech-logs are crackling on the fire and a thick cap of snow lies on the roof, and the quiet solitude of the mountains is intensified by the snow-covered landscape. Instead, here I sit [in Marburg] working on the transitional chapter. The usual obligations during the semester deprived me of the necessary concentration. The vacation will bring the project to a close before the end of the year . . . On January first, I will go to Heidelberg, where I will stay with Jaspers until the tenth. I'm looking forward to philosophizing, not only in soliloquy and in contact with history, but face-to-face with him.[19]

It is not perfectly clear which part of the manuscript Heidegger was referring to as the "transition chapter."[20] The final paragraph of the published version had already gone to the printer in early November. He was probably working on an introduction to a passage entitled "Time and Being,"[21] which he envisioned as the third section of the book's first part. That he would not immediately—or indeed ever—continue beyond the second section was the result of the discussions with Jaspers, which Heidegger mentions in his Christmas letter to Elisabeth Blochmann.[22] These discussions were overshadowed by a sad event that occurred in late 1926: "The decision to discontinue publication took shape on the day we received news of Rilke's death."[23] *Sein und Zeit* finally appeared in April 1927—and indeed turned out to be the immediate and overwhelming success that Heidegger's Marburg colleagues and, even more so, Edmund Husserl had always predicted. The year 1927 was thus a good one for Heidegger, bringing him belated but important rewards. In October, he was appointed to a full professorship at Marburg, but this promotion to the rank of *Ordinarius* did not change his prejudice against the town and its university. The damage had been done. He had soured on the place. Less than twelve months later he was offered an appointment at Freiburg as Husserl's successor, and by the winter semester of 1928–1929 he was teaching at his alma mater again.

The Year in the Book

There can thus be no doubt that the complete published text of *Sein und Zeit* dates back to the year 1926. Theodore Kisiel has shown that Heidegger even invented some of the book's central concepts, such as "thrownness," "existential" *(Existential)*, "lighting," and "repetition," during the difficult final months of the writing process.[24] Of course, these recently established historical facts neither diminish nor increase the philosophical importance of *Sein und Zeit*. But they justify my using Heidegger's book in my effort to make present the worlds of 1926. Although the evocation of such historical presence has been the explicit goal of my experiment, one may of course legitimately ask whether the results of this experiment can be used in a way that relates to the standards of history as a discipline. This concluding chapter is therefore devoted to seeking a historical understanding of *Sein und Zeit* on the basis of my re-presentation of the year 1926 and in comparison with two contemporary novels, one by Hans Friedrich Blunck and the other by Carl Van Vechten.

"Understanding," in this context, does not primarily mean trying to reconstruct Heidegger's subjective intentions and views as he wrote his manuscript.[25] And since I have no certified competence in the field, I cannot claim that the following reading of *Sein und Zeit*, against the backdrop of so many brilliant interpretations of Heidegger's most famous work, will yield any new philosophical insights. Rather, I wish to show that some of the principal philosophical concerns in his book, some decisive elements in the structure of its argument, and perhaps Heidegger's entire contribution to Western philosophy[26] can be read as originating in a reaction to the emotional, intellectual, and political environments of 1926.[27] This aspect of *Sein und Zeit* becomes visible when one rereads the book from the perspective of historical simultaneity. To be more specific, it is my impression that the cultural codes which I have described as typical of 1926, specifically those threatened by possible collapse, were the driving elements behind Heidegger's thought. Occasionally, even some of the much more concrete "arrays" that occupy the primary level in my historical reconstruction of 1926 can appear as elements of discontinuity within the highly abstract philosophical discourse of *Sein und Zeit*. My most ambitious claim, however, is that

Heidegger—in employing some of his arguments in the book without any further explication (that is, without explicitly eliminating potential alternatives)—followed the orientation of a specific set of prevailing cultural codes. This constellation of codes has everything to do with the intellectual phenomenon that Hugo von Hofmannsthal, in 1927, termed the *konservative Revolution*.[28] Both this contextualization and the comparisons that I shall make between Heidegger's text and the novels by Blunck and Van Vechten are well within the bounds of my experiment in historical simultaneity. Still, we cannot—and should not—avoid the classic question (with its diachronic dimension) of whether Heidegger's position in 1926 predestined him to assume a specific role during the first year of the Nazi regime. My reading will, at least indirectly, confirm what has become general knowledge since the debate provoked by Victor Farías' book:[29] Heidegger's attempt, in 1933 and 1934, to influence the Nazis' cultural and educational politics, together with his grotesque endeavor to become "ein Führer des Führers" ("a leader of leaders"),[30] was grounded in certain motifs that his philosophy shared with the ideology of the National Socialist Party. Although I agree in principle with those scholars who state that this contamination does not tarnish the philosophical importance of Heidegger's thought (because the structure in which Heidegger brings the motifs together is more complex than—and intrinsically different from—that of the Nazi ideology),[31] I cannot help being troubled, to say the least, by such a contiguity.

These mixed feelings may well come from a lack of experience in dealing with perspectives of simultaneity as it is endemic to our ways of viewing and using history. *Sein und Zeit* cannot of course be identified with Nazi ideology—though it shares multiple motifs and concerns with a 1926 novel by Hans Friedrich Blunck, who in 1933 was to be appointed president of the Reichsschrifttumskammer (National Commission on Writing). On the other hand, Heidegger's central argument shows a much more surprising but equally clear affinity with a narrative as culturally remote as *Nigger Heaven,* one of the most sympathetic and popular literary depictions of the Harlem Renaissance. The problem that intrigues me here is therefore not so much one of observing and identifying phenomena which, at least in Western culture, attest to homogeneity in the year 1926. Rather, the challenge lies in seeing what conclusions I can draw from the abundance of such observations.

....

Epistemological Losses and Ontological Compensations

Heidegger's main concern in writing *Sein und Zeit* was, I believe, to preserve those functions which the classic subject-object distinction had fulfilled in Western philosophy—and to achieve this in full awareness of an epistemological environment that excluded the possibility of seriously opting for the subject-object paradigm. [see **Uncertainty vs. Reality**] The key element of this paradigm, an element that we normally take for granted in our everyday behavior, is the conviction that if a subject occupies an external, distanced, "eccentric" position, this will enhance the validity of all of the subject's observations and judgments concerning the world of objects. It used to be the function of this presupposition (and hence the function of the subject-object paradigm) to dignify certain observations as "definitive," "substantive," or "objective" so that they could become unquestionable ground for decisions, actions, and attributions of value.

As one of several departures from the subject-object paradigm that have occurred in European philosophy since the late nineteenth century, Husserl's phenomenology began by problematizing the "natural attitude of the mind" *(natürliche Geisteshaltung)* inherent in the subject-object paradigm—by which Husserl meant the mutually eccentric position attributed in the epistemological tradition to "outside objects" and to "human consciousness" as they interrelate.[32] Having engaged, from 1918 on, in an intense exchange of ideas with Husserl and having even taught introductory courses in phenomenological philosophy on a regular basis,[33] Heidegger had played, both intellectually and institutionally, an active (though limited) role in the breaking away from the subject-object paradigm. At least until the publication of *Sein und Zeit,* it was mainly this role which determined his identity as a philosopher in the academic world.[34] But the loss of an eccentric—or transcendental—position guaranteeing the "objectivity" of any observation was not limited to philosophy. The plot structures of successful novels such as Agatha Christie's *Murder of Roger Ackroyd* or Arthur Schnitzler's *Traumnovelle (Dream Story),* and of Alfred Hitchcock's film *The Lodger,* were all based on the impression that there no longer existed any outside position from which reality could be objectively observed, judged, and mastered. [see **Uncertainty vs. Reality**] This change triggered a series of conceptual and epistemological substitutions; furthermore, it intensified a collective desire for objectivity and for values that could not be relativized. Often detached from any understanding of the theory to which it refers, the word "relativity" became an object of fascination and fear in this environment. Indeed, it may have contributed to the emergence of that very longing for a stable cognitive ground which became the focus of the Conservative Revolution. Motivated by a feeling that the world had lost orientation, morality, and existential meaning, this desire did more than merely confirm the widespread disillusionment with liberal politics and ideology; the climate of the Conservative Revolution also affected those intellectuals who knew how impossible it was to return to a more stable epistemology and unambiguous values. Part of the uncanny brilliance that impresses us in the works of some Conservative Revolutionaries is precisely a result of the tension between avant-garde thinking and a simultaneous—but primarily extraphilosophical—desire for existential stability.[35]

Ontological Compensations and Conceptual Negotiations

Through Heidegger's concern with the concepts and values of "substance" and "substantiality," *Sein und Zeit* offers an almost unmediated reflection of this desire for existential stability. It appears almost unmediated because his commitment to substance, rather than being a constitutive part of his line of argument, seems to fulfill its function by producing a general feeling of assurance in the early chapters of the book. [see **Immanence vs. Transcendence**] In a paragraph devoted to defining world-experience as "a context of assignments" *(Verweisungszusammenhang)*, for example, Heidegger insists that this definition does not imply the dissolution of any experience of substance into pure functionality:

> This "system of relations," as something constitutive for worldhood, is so far from volatilizing the Being of the ready-to-hand within-the-world, that the worldhood of the world provides the basis on which such entities can for the first time be discovered as they are "substantially" "in themselves." And only if entities within-the-world can be encountered at all is it possible, in the field of such entities, to make accessible what is just present-at-hand and no more. By reason of their

Being-just-present-at-hand-and-no-more, these latter entities can have their "properties" defined mathematically in "functional concepts." Ontologically, such concepts are possible only in relation to entities whose Being has the character of pure substantiality. Functional concepts are never possible except as formalized substantial concepts.[36]

While he thus underlines the substantiality of what used to be the object side within the traditional cognitive paradigm, Heidegger challenges the classic subject concept with words that seem to echo Husserl's early work: "The problem [arises] of how this knowing subject comes out of its inner 'sphere' into one which is 'other and external,' of how knowing can have any object at all, and of how one must think of the object itself so that eventually the subject knows it without needing to venture a leap into another sphere."[37] In a later passage, Heidegger distances himself explicitly from Kant's concern, in the *Critique of Pure Reason,* to prove the existence of a "real world" outside the subject's mind—a proof that Heidegger deems unnecessary.[38] By exclusively underscoring this resubstantialization of "reality," however, some interpretations of *Sein und Zeit*[39] miss the other side of a continuous "oscillation" in which Heidegger rejects the subject-object paradigm and simultaneously claims to preserve the very cognitive certainty which it had provided.[40] His approach condenses the contradiction of an intellectual culture that no longer provides an outside perspective for its descriptions and self-descriptions while it longs, more than ever, for its scientific insights to be impartial and for its technological innovations to be nonarbitrary. [see **Sobriety vs. Exuberance**]

As a consequence of this ambiguity, it is not clear how one should understand Heidegger's programmatic definition of "phenomenology" in the introductory chapter of *Sein und Zeit:* "Thus, the term 'phenomenology' expresses a maxim which can be formulated as 'To the things themselves!' It is opposed to all free-floating constructions and accidental findings; it is opposed to taking over any conceptions which only seem to have been demonstrated; it is opposed to those pseudo-questions which parade themselves as 'problems,' often for generations at a time."[41] If there is anything consistently unequivocal in the various interpretations of these words, it is the impression that, from a rhetorical perspective, they function like a spell (hence the exclamation mark) against any epistemological considerations—and perhaps even against any practical fears—of uncertainty. But could Heidegger seriously have wanted to neglect all the arguments which, in the decades preceding *Sein und Zeit,* philosophers had accumulated to prevent any unproblematic return "to the things themselves"? Or did he mean to suggest that Husserl's emerging conception of the world as constituted by the transcendental subject was the new sense of the old desire to reach "the things themselves"? Heidegger's answer to this question does neither.

On several levels, *Sein und Zeit* refers to and then rephrases basic concepts and claims of the epistemology that Heidegger wished to supersede. Although it has been correctly remarked that the concepts yielded by his analysis of *Dasein* ("human existence") are implicitly transhistorical,[42] he carefully avoids those abstract and explicitly generalizing statements which had become characteristic of the philosophy of subjecthood and which appealed to a desire for cognitive certainty among so many of his contemporaries. By insisting, instead, on the "average everydayness"[43] of the phenomena in question, Heidegger produces an impression of concreteness and substantiality for the reference level of his own discourse, yet continues to claim that he is dealing with generalizable conditions of *Dasein.*[44] The most important element in his renegotiation of the subject-object paradigm, however, is the complex notion of "being-in-the-world." He introduces it as a description of *Dasein*'s basic condition:

> The entity to which Being . . . belongs is one which we have characterized as that entity which in each case I myself am *(bin).* The expression *bin* is connected with *bei,* and so *ich bin* ("I am") means in its turn "I reside" or "dwell alongside" the world, as that which is familiar to me in such and such a way. "Being" *(Sein)* as the infinitive of *ich bin* (that is to say, when it is understood as an *existentiale*), signifies "to reside alongside," "to be familiar with." *"Being-in" is thus the formal existential expression for the Being of Dasein, which has Being-in-the-world as its essential state.*[45]

Setting aside, in the context of our reading, Heidegger's always problematic etymological speculations (but he never pretended to be a linguist!), we once again encounter here the strategy of conceptual compromise. By letting the world surround *Dasein*—and subsequently by assigning a position of centrality to *Dasein*—Heidegger inverts the relation of eccentricity and distance that had formerly defined the subject's position vis-à-vis the world. But while this move seems at first glance to imply a radical reduction of the distance between *Dasein* and the world, the metaphor of "dwelling" maintains the suggestion of a residual gap between them.

Against such a reading, one could argue that Heidegger problematizes (though not without some counter-relativization) the understanding of being-in-the-world as a straightforwardly spatial situation: "The term 'Being-in' [does not] mean a spatial 'in-one-another-ness' of things present-at-hand, any more than the word 'in' primordially signifies a spatial relationship of this kind."[46] Still, is it really possible to imagine a situation of "familiarity" between *Dasein* and world, as Heidegger evokes it, without *Dasein* and the world being related—and separated—by some kind of spatial configuration? Ultimately, the idea of a certain distance, however minimal, between *Dasein* and the world is not eliminated. On a different level of argument, it is interesting to note that Heidegger's general tendency to reduce the importance of the spatial dimension[47] may not depend on the denial of a spatial relation between world and *Dasein*. Rather, it could be one of those motifs in *Sein und Zeit* which show the direct impact of contemporary culture on Heidegger's thinking. We have seen how, in 1926, people's various reactions to new technologies of transportation and communication converged in the impression of implosion and loss of space, and how this experience triggered an active rethinking of temporal structures on different levels. [see **Center vs. Periphery, Present vs. Past, Center = Periphery**] Heidegger's effort to play down the spatial connotations of his metaphors and concepts may therefore just be the obverse of that particular experience which, in the second part of *Sein und Zeit,* led him to highlight "time" as the meaning of *Dasein.*

After substituting everydayness for abstractness, and "being-in-the-world" for distanced observation, Heidegger—in the third stage of his revision of the subject-object paradigm—tackles the concept of "action," which, for contemporary philosophy and the nascent discipline of sociology, was the standard reference in discussing the correspondence between the subject and its environments. *Sein und Zeit* replaces action with the concept of "care" *(Sorge).*[48] Heidegger's notion of care is similar in two respects to Max Weber's then influential concept of action. First, the notion of care is oriented toward the future; second, it is based on a concept of self (as the functional equivalent of what sociology calls the *Handlungs-Subjekt*).⁴⁹ The question is then why, despite these overlappings, Heidegger avoids the concept of action—and this question leads to a double answer. Action would attribute to *Dasein* the implications of independence and agency—would maintain the strong version of the subject—which Heidegger tries to exclude from the rephrasing of the subject-object relation. This desire to scale down the subject certainly corresponds with the widespread contemporary skepticism about the effectiveness of the subject's actions. [see **Action = Impotence (Tragedy)**] But there is also an aesthetic (or stylistic) preference that may have played a role in this substitution. In contrast to the word "care," which, at least in contemporary English, has strongly feminine connotations, the German word *Sorge* and its Latin equivalent, *cura*, could have evoked an archaic ("preontological")⁵⁰ understanding of existence for Heidegger and his first-generation readers. [see **Authenticity vs. Artificiality**]

Despite these subtle conceptual negotiations, it is obvious that everydayness, being-in-the-world, and *Sorge* cannot satisfy that desire for cognitive certainty which had been fulfilled by the subject-object paradigm prior to its crisis. But readers of *Sein und Zeit* do not have to worry about this question because Heidegger, by means of two definitions, makes guaranteeing such certainty the point of departure for his book. He distinguishes *Sein* ("Being")—the most fundamental category, the ground and plenitude of reality—from *Seiendes* ("being," "entities"), meaning *Sein*'s appearance, pure surface, the primary dimension of human experience. On this basis, *Dasein* (human existence) is described as the one form of being *(des Seienden)* that has the potential of becoming aware of its Being *(sein Sein)*:

> Dasein is an entity which does not just occur among other entities. Rather, it is ontically distinguished by the fact that, in its very Being, Being is an *issue* for it. But in that case, this is a constitutive state of *Dasein*'s Being, and this implies that Dasein, in its Being, has a relationship toward that Being—a relationship which itself is one of Being. And this means further that there is some way in which *Dasein* understands itself in its Being, and that to some degree it does so explicitly. It is peculiar to this entity that with and through its Being, this Being is disclosed to it. *Understanding of Being is itself a definitive characteristic of* Dasein's Being. Dasein is ontically distinctive in that it *is* ontological.⁵¹

Heidegger provides no arguments for this point, which is decisive for his book inasmuch as it implies the two components that are indispensable for an ontological analysis of human existence. The reader has to accept that there is Being, and that *Dasein*—and only *Dasein*—is privileged to understand it. Heidegger could safely assume that his readers' longing for ontological certainty was strong enough to accept any complex suggestion of this kind. *Sein und Zeit* begins with a quote from Plato's *Sophist* that points to the difficulty of understanding the meaning of the word "being" *(seiend)*. Heidegger continues by asserting that the meanings of the words "being" *(seiend)* and "Being" *(Sein)* are lost, and that moreover all questions concerning these meanings have been dismissed. Thus, by presupposing Being's "forgottenness" *(Seinsvergessenheit)*, he replaces possible arguments with his assumption that Being exists.

Instead of Truth

Heidegger's definitions of *Sein* and *Dasein* do not yet contain or prefigure his answer to the question concerning the meaning *(Sinn)* of *Dasein*. Not until the second part of *Sein und Zeit* does he develop a new concept of time, which constitutes the meaning of *Dasein* (and thus explains the title of the book). Large passages of the book's first part,[52] in contrast, are dedicated to problems of conceptual readjustment that directly or indirectly stem from the introductory definitions of *Dasein* and *Sein*. If we can say, for example, that *Dasein*'s understanding of Being, in Heidegger's philosophy, takes over the place which the notion of "truth" had traditionally occupied, how can we then think the relation between Being and truth? Heidegger argues that truth is a condition of *Dasein*, that *Dasein* is always "being in the truth."[53] At the same time, "being in the truth" is a condition for the possibility of "untruth,"[54] which can only mean that *Dasein* implies a potential—not a promise—of reaching truth. But this does not explain how truth would be different from Being. Heidegger provides no definitive answer to this question. What becomes obvious, however, is his (perhaps unintended) tendency to relativize the value of the notion of "truth"—which historically belongs to the conceptual repertoire of the subject-object paradigm. Having stated that "Being and truth 'are' equiprimordially" in their relation to *Dasein*, he postpones any further clarification of how Being and truth relate to each other, planning to return to the topic in his discussion of the meaning of Being.[55] The book, however, does not come back to this problem. It ends with Heidegger's answer to the question concerning the meaning of *Dasein;* the meaning of Being remains unresolved.

As a consequence of his rephrasing of the truth-concept and of the notions of action and subject, Heidegger cannot present the "uncovering" of Being as an act of the subject. Such an attribution would contradict his complex strategy of going beyond the subject-object paradigm. The heroic standard role of the modern subject as one who discovers truth is therefore superseded by Being's capacity to uncover itself:

> What is to be demonstrated is solely the Being-uncovered . . . of the entity itself—*that entity* in the "how" of its uncoveredness. This uncoveredness is confirmed when that which is put forward in the assertion (namely, the entity itself) shows itself *as that very same thing.* "Confirmation" signifies *the entity's showing itself in its selfsameness.* The confirmation is accomplished on the basis of the entity's showing itself. This is possible only in such a way that the knowing which asserts and which gets confirmed is, in its ontological meaning, itself a *Being toward* Real entities, and a Being that *uncovers.*[56]

Within the topology of the subject-object paradigm which Heidegger is so eager to replace, this would mean that the activity in the process of cognition shifts from the subject pole to the object pole. Within the conceptual construction of *Sein und Zeit,* the motif of the self-uncovering of Being has the important consequence that truth (the appearance of Being) cannot be produced or willed. It can only be awaited, and all that *Dasein* will be able to contribute is its openness.

Once again it becomes evident how a structurally important element of Heidegger's discourse mirrors extraphilosophical attitudes, in particular the longing of the Conservative Revolution for a prophetic discourse. [see **Immanence vs. Transcendence**] Since Heidegger's tone is quiet, sometimes almost academically dispassionate, it is all the more striking to find sentences of blatant aggressivity where he argues in favor of what he later dubs "the piety of thinking" *(die Frömmigkeit des Denkens),* and against skepticism. Although from the outset the philosophical gesture of *Sein und Zeit* is absolutely incompatible with any skeptical attitude, this cannot fully explain the hatred with which Heidegger con-

ducts the self-immunization of his position: "A skeptic can no more be
refuted than the Being of truth can be 'proved.' And if any skeptic of the
kind who denies the truth factically *is,* he does *not* even *need* to be
refuted. Insofar as he *is* and has understood himself in this Being, he has
obliterated *Dasein* in the desperation of suicide; and in doing so, he has
also obliterated truth."[57] The association between renouncing a position
of transcendence and choosing suicide is becoming frequent in 1926. [see
Immanence = Transcendence (Death)] What is unique—and sometimes
hard to accept—in Heidegger's philosophical position is the (potentially
paradoxical) simultaneity between the absence of a religiously grounded
transcendence and a cognitive certainty whose gesture invariably reminds us of religiously grounded world views.

Opting for Authenticity

One of the more complex problems in Heidegger's revision of the subject-object paradigm derives from a double determination of being-in-
the-truth as a condition of *Dasein.* On the one hand, it means that truth
is but a possibility of *Dasein.* On the other hand, however, it implies that
Dasein will not always willingly seize this potential. Consequently, while
Heidegger does not provide any answer to the question of how *Dasein*
could be ultimately persuaded or obliged to choose its possibility of
existential plenitude,[58] he paints a particularly colorful philosophical
picture of the contrast between *Dasein*'s "authenticity" *(Eigentlichkeit)*
and its "inauthenticity." [see **Authenticity vs. Artificiality**]. More than
any other motif in *Sein und Zeit,* it is this contrast which attracts and
brings together codes, values, and metaphors from a range of contemporary discourses.[59] The most essential value-associations in this context
are those between "authenticity" and (Heidegger's concept for) individuality *(Jemeinigkeit),* and between "inauthenticity" and (a number of
negative concepts related to) the public sphere. [see **Individuality vs.
Collectivity**]

> And because Dasein is in each case essentially its own possibility, it *can,*
> in its very Being, "choose" itself and win itself; it can also lose itself
> and never win itself; or it can only "seem" to do so. But only insofar
> as it is essentially something which can be *authentic*—that is, something

of its own—can it have lost itself and not yet won itself. As modes of Being, *authenticity* and *inauthenticity* (these expressions have been chosen terminologically in a strict sense) are both grounded in the fact that any *Dasein* whatsoever is characterized by mineness. But the inauthenticity of *Dasein* does not signify any "less" Being or any "lower" degree of Being. Rather, it is the case that even in its fullest concretion *Dasein* can be characterized by its inauthenticity—when busy, when excited, when interested, when ready for enjoyment.[60]

In the mode of inauthenticity, *Dasein* "falls to" *(verfällt)* "the publicness of the 'they'" *(der Öffentlichkeit des Man)* and becomes an unidentifiable part of it.[61] Bertolt Brecht's pun on the word *man* in the title of his 1926 play *Mann ist Mann* refers to a plot which tells of a specific case of such "falling to the publicness of the 'they'"—more precisely, the loss of a man's individuality in the process of his integration into the anonymous collectivity of military action. What gives a specifically conservative connotation to Heidegger's use of these concepts, especially in comparison with Brecht, is the fusion of the "they" with the public sphere as expressed in the phrase "the publicness of the 'they.'" If any further evidence were needed to prove Heidegger's bias against the public sphere, it would lie in the superposition of a third code upon the cluster constituted by authenticity/inauthenticity and individuality/collectivity. Inauthenticity and collectivity, the negative values, are associated with "idle talk" *(Gerede)*, whereas authenticity and individuality are linked to silence. [see **Silence vs. Noise**] By explicitly including certain modes of reading and writing in the concept of "idle talk," Heidegger transforms it into a key element of his notoriously anti-intellectual and anti-academic position.

> And indeed this idle talk is not confined to vocal gossip, but even spreads to what we write, where it takes the form of "scribbling" . . . In the latter case, the gossip is not based so much upon hearsay. It feeds upon superficial reading . . . The average understanding of the reader will *never be able* to decide how much has been drawn from primordial sources with a struggle and how much is just gossip. The average understanding, moreover, will not want any such distinction, and does not need it, because of course it understands everything. The groundlessness of idle talk is no obstacle to its becoming public; instead it encourages this.[62]

More demanding than the description of inauthenticity through concepts like "the 'they'" or "idle talk" is, at least for Heidegger, the characterization of authenticity—for he wants authenticity to be the absence of any superfluous forms of behavior. [see **Sobriety vs. Exuberance**] The simple difficulty of not having any salient points of reference in order to describe authenticity may have persuaded Heidegger to focus mainly on silence in the passages concerning this topic. But since silence could be confused with muteness, he had to insist that only those who have something to say can "keep silent." Under this condition, silence appears as an authentic—and paradoxical—"mode of discoursing" *(Modus des Redens),* and, even more important, as "genuine potentiality-for-hearing" *(das echte Hörenkönnen).*[63] The following random evocation of things that one might hear before shifting to the existentially deeper attitude of "hearkening" *(horchen)* constitutes one of the more remarkable irruptions of contemporary everydayness into the philosophical discourse of *Sein und Zeit.* Without introducing any systematic distinctions, Heidegger alludes to two different registers of things to be heard, one of them produced by technology, and the other (so to speak) heavily authentic: "What we 'first' hear is never noises or complexes of sounds, but the creaking wagon, the motorcycle. We hear the regiment on the march, the north wind, the woodpecker tapping, the fire crackling."[64]

But the culminating mode of authenticity, the attitude which silence and hearkening facilitate, the position, finally, that constitutes "mineness" and can redeem *Dasein* from its "fallenness to the 'they,'" is resoluteness *(Entschlossenheit).*[65] Resoluteness is the disposition to project oneself onto the world, a disposition to act (although, as we have seen, Heidegger carefully avoids the word *handeln)*—a disposition, however, that is permeated by a complete awareness *Dasein's* nullity *(Nichtigkeit)* and of its primordial guilt *(Schuld).* Resoluteness seems to be the willingness to act in situations which one would normally characterize as situations of undecidability; it is the willingness to accept the nullity and tragedy of human existence—and to act in spite of them. The pathos with which Heidegger invests the notion of resoluteness reminds one of the aesthetic halo with which the Conservative Revolution surrounded the concept of *Tat.* [see **Action vs. Impotence, Action = Impotence (Tragedy)**] For readers in the 1920s, further associations with the different conceptual connections and extensions of Heidegger's authen-

ticity/inauthenticity binarism must have abounded. In addition, the philosopher himself spared no effort to make his own life seem like an
illustration of his notion of *Eigentlichkeit*. During the Marburg years, he
pretended that "silent walks through the surrounding forests" with his
famous colleague Paul Natorp were the only form of social contact he
cared about.[66] If the silent promenades of these thinkers could be perceived as elitist, "elite" definitely did not mean "intellectuals" or "academics" for Heidegger. Rather, he seized every opportunity to express
his admiration for workers and Black Forest peasants.[67] In his professional life, therefore, Heidegger's goal to become an *Ordinarius* (and
thus part of the established academic elite) was not always easy to
reconcile with his resentful ambition to be—and to appear—different.
With more amusement than protest, the wife of his colleague Ernst
Cassirer (whom Heidegger must have seen as the incarnation of that
worldliness he decried) observed his effort to stand out as "authentic"
amid people whom he no doubt judged to be the elite of scribblers and
idle talkers, assembled on the occasion of an academic dinner party:

> All the guests had arrived, the women in evening gowns, the men in
> dinner suits. At a point when the dinner had been interrupted for some
> time with seemingly endless speeches, the door opened, and an incon-
> spicuous little man came into the room, looking as awkward as a
> peasant who had stumbled into a royal court. He had black hair and
> dark piercing eyes, rather like some workman from southern Italy or
> Bavaria; an impression which was soon confirmed by his regional ac-
> cent. He was wearing an old-fashioned black suit . . . For me, what
> seemed the most worrying thing was his deadly seriousness and his total
> lack of a sense of humor.[68]

Carefully thought through as they were, the forms of Heidegger's self-
presentation probably fed back into his philosophical discourse. This
could be how "being-at-home," as a concretization of being-in-the-
world, became an important systematic concept for Heidegger, who
wanted nothing so much as to stay at home. Since this would never be
his lot, however, being-at-home seems part of the inauthenticity of the
"they" and a reason for "tranquillized self-assurance."[69] Authentic
Dasein, in contrast, exposes itself to the "uncanniness" of the world, to

its *Un-heim-lichkeit*—not unlike the obsessive nationalism which was
then flourishing in remote colonial spaces. [see **Center vs. Periphery**]
Uncanniness and the quest for authenticity finally come together in what
constitutes the most immediate social dimension of Heidegger's work—
namely, his language. This language is based on an enthusiasm for (often
purely invented) historical meanings and on a passion for etymological
speculations that make even newly created words look archaic. There is
of course no linguistic reason to believe that elements selected from
ancient strata of a national language offer more insights or more terminological precision than their younger equivalents. Heidegger's style as a
writer simply endows the past and the unfamiliar with authenticity. [see
Present vs. Past, Authenticity vs. Artificiality]

But for all the massive rhetorical investment through which *Sein und
Zeit* refines and illustrates the contrast between authenticity and inauthenticity, Heidegger does not offer a solution to the question of how
Dasein can be motivated to opt for authenticity. There is reason to
speculate[70] that Heidegger was not even interested in opening his philosophy to this type of problem, because then he would have had to
discuss an ethical dimension. On the other hand, authenticity was so
high a value in Heidegger's work—and in contemporary culture—that
he could not completely leave its choice to individual discretion. This is
where the traditionally religious topology of the "call of conscience"
(Gewissensruf)[71] comes in; it is a motivation that bypasses the social
sphere as the dimension for ethical decisions, and activates the hermeneutic capacity of hearkening to Being. But Heidegger's existentially
recycled call of conscience does not provide any specific orientation for
Dasein. The call of conscience only reminds *Dasein* that "it owes something"—reminds *Dasein* of its *Schuld*:

> *Wanting to have conscience is . . . the most primordial existential pre-*
> *supposition for the possibility of factically coming to owe something.*
> *In understanding the call,* Dasein *lets its ownmost Self take action in*
> *itself . . .* in terms of that potentiality-for-Being which it has chosen.
> Only so can it *be* answerable . . . Factically, however, any taking-action
> is necessarily "conscienceless," not only because it may fail to avoid
> some factical moral indebtedness, but because, on the null basis of its
> null projection, it has, in Being with Others, already become guilty

toward them. Thus, one's wanting-to-have-a-conscience becomes the taking-over of that essential consciencelessness within which alone the existential possibility of *being* "good" subsists.[72]

It is no coincidence that the word *Schuld,* which plays such an important role in this part of Heidegger's book, is translated variously as "owing," "indebtedness," and "guilt." Only the last of these meanings, however, helps us understand Heidegger's provocative—(un)ethical—paradox according to which "consciencelessness" is the only means of "'being' good." If, when we use the word "conscience," we normally mean a type of behavior that tends to avoid any unnecessary detriment to the other, and if, in the absence of a transcendental dimension, the nullity of human existence does not offer any secure basis on which we could ever hope to avoid becoming detrimental to others, then "consciencelessness" (and being guilty of it) becomes an inevitable condition of acting (or should we say "caring"?)—and therefore a necessary component of any situation in which one at least stands a chance of being "good." [see **Immanence = Transcendence (Death)**] In contrast, if we define *Schuld* as "indebtedness" or "owing" (an "owing," it is true, without any explicit reference to an addressee), then Heidegger's discourse—perhaps despite the author's intention—gives the impression that opting for authenticity is a tribute to an unnamed transcendental authority. [see **Immanence vs. Transcendence**]

✄

For many of Heidegger's readers in the late 1920s, the question of whether (and why) authenticity was owed may have been much less important than it appears to us. For them, the concept of authenticity—and its illustrations: individualism and resoluteness, silence and sobriety—were so heavily value-laden that they outshone by their sheer aesthetic appeal whatever was evoked as inauthentic. In addition, opting for authenticity seems to have been one of the few forms of behavior that Heidegger associated with gender—perhaps the only important cultural code of 1926 to which *Sein und Zeit* makes no explicit reference. The convergence of the gender code with the authenticity code is marked by the concept "affirmation of existence" *(Existenzfreudigkeit),* which Heidegger uses in his correspondence with Elisabeth Blochmann, a professor of pedagogy. A friend of Elfride Heidegger's, Blochmann had spent several days during the summer of 1926 at the Heideggers' cabin at Todtnauberg. In a letter of October 7, the philosopher recalls the visit with pleasure:

> That I am allowed to share Elfride's friendship with you is both an enrichment and an obligation for me. During our brief sojourn together on the sunny hillside before your descent into the valley, I came to understand that you are holding your existence firmly in your hands. On your first visit to the cabin, you gave as much as you received. These days, I imagine that you're in the same mood that always overcomes me at the beginning of the semester. It sets free the passion that is necessary for our work. Only new opportunities make possible the productivity through which we, as individuals, become what we are. Your feminine form of being, whose meaning Elfride has acquainted me with in recent years, is exploring new venues—and this is not merely a consequence of your having a profession. It no doubt provides you with that *Existenzfreudigkeit* which, instead of resulting from success, is its primary inspiration.[73]

Clearly trying to show respect for Blochmann's self-image as a modern "professional" woman, Heidegger nevertheless departs from the widespread view that a professional life neutralizes gender difference. [see **Male = Female (Gender Trouble)**] Rather, he encourages Blochmann to understand her "form of being" and her success as consequences of her femininity. As the reference to Elfride shows, Heidegger is convinced that the value of such femininity is not neutralized by a professional life and is even independent of it. For him, accepting and affirming what he perceives as a primary gender difference is a way of affirming (and, as the most common meaning of the German word *Existenzfreudigkeit* suggests, of enjoying) one's authentic existence. [see **Male vs. Female**] Given the various associations that surround the value of authenticity in Heidegger's thought, it is not surprising that, only a month later, in yet another letter to Blochmann, he sets *Existenzfreudigkeit* against the inauthenticity of the metropolitan world of Berlin, where she has just been appointed to a new position: "How are things going for you? The welter and strangeness will depress you only temporarily—in the end, they will make your mind freer. The big city, whose riddles you have already sensed, will not alter your *Existenzfreudigkeit.*"[74] If the affirmation of existence, in the environment of the big city, can no longer limit itself to affirmation of the authentic, it still can prevail as an affirmation of life in general. [see **Authenticity = Artificiality (Life)**]

Why Time?

Whereas the first part of *Sein und Zeit* ("Preparatory Fundamental Analysis of *Dasein*") offers an ontological analysis of *Dasein*, the second part ("*Dasein* and Temporality") explores the meaning of human existence. "Meaning" *(Sinn)* is defined as "that wherein the understandability . . . of something is maintained—even of something which is not visible explicitly and thematically."[75] Heidegger's treatment of this question has become so famous that today it is difficult not to assume automatically that *Dasein* means "time." But why, for example, doesn't he point to being-in-truth instead of time? Why wouldn't it be convincing to define *Dasein* by referring to the privilege of having its Being uncovered? Again, Heidegger does not discuss (or eliminate) alternative answers to a key question of his book; and again this lack of alternatives leads us to speculate about the unconscious effect that contemporary culture may have had on his thought.

We know that, as early as the fall of 1922, Heidegger conceived the idea of a book on Aristotle which would discuss the viability of an ontology under the epistemological conditions of his own historical moment.[76] [see **Uncertainty vs. Reality**] His interest in time as a philosophical issue arose later and, probably not by coincidence, in connection with two public lectures and a publication project for a recently founded and particularly successful academic journal, the *Deutsche Vierteljahrsschrift für Literaturwissenschaft und Geistesgeschichte.*[77] Time was a ubiquitous philosophical topic, both in the academic world and among the intellectually interested public, because it had only recently surfaced in the history of Western thought as a condition of human life which, instead of being a given, had to be constituted. The discussion of time had bifurcated: one branch was concerned with individual time-perception and its morphology, and the other—in which a new relationship between present, past, and future was at stake—with

the philosophy of history. [see **Present = Past (Eternity), Present vs. Past**]
Heidegger's lecture of July 25, 1924, to the Marburg Theologians' Society (a lecture that Gadamer has called the earliest version of *Sein und
Zeit*) seems to have focused mainly on the importance of time for individual existence. In contrast, the "semipopularizing series of ten lectures
at Kassel, given in pairs over five evenings," between April 16 and April
21, 1925, treated issues in relation to the philosophy of history, as
indicated by their title: "Wilhelm Dilthey's Research Work and the Present Struggle for a Historical Worldview."[78] Despite this thematic emphasis, it was in the Kassel lectures, before an audience of nonspecialists,
that Heidegger first brought together the individual and collective levels
of the time phenomenon, as well as the question, now identified as
ontological, of the meaning of *Dasein*. According to Heidegger, the key
challenge that made it necessary to discuss *Dasein* in relation to time as
an ontological problem lay in the most recent epistemological "crises"
and "revolutions" in the sciences.

However plausible this coupling of an ontology of *Dasein* with the
topic of time may have appeared within the cultural environment of
1926, Heidegger could not avoid identifying and elaborating a concept
that could serve as a common denominator for the two parts of his book.
This structurally important place in *Sein und Zeit* is occupied by the
notion of *Sorge* ("care"). By asking, "What makes possible the totality
of the articulated structural whole of *Sorge,* in the unity of its articulation as we have developed it?"[79] Heidegger gains the opportunity to
present this central component of his "fundamental analysis of *Dasein*"
as intrinsically constituted by the dimensions of time. If, as we have
already seen, the concept of *Sorge* evokes particularly intense discussion
of action and time among contemporary philosophers and sociologists,
the contribution that *Sein und Zeit* makes to this discussion is certainly
not the most convincing or elegant part of the book. Associating three
different concepts from the analysis of *Dasein* with the classic three
divisions of time,[80] Heidegger obviously wishes to portray as homogeneous what is perhaps the most arbitrary—or most daring—element of his
book. The future is paired with "understanding," the present with "fallenness," and the past with "state of mind" or "mood" *(Befindlichkeit,
Stimmung)*. Heidegger devotes little effort to explaining these links. But
the passage on moods presents a distinction between "fear" and "anxiety" *(Furcht* and *Angst)*,[81] which is crucial to the book's second part.

Fascinating Death

The contrast between fear and anxiety is parallel to that between "being-at-home" and "the uncanny." Fear takes its "orientation from what we encounter in the immanence of the within-the-world."[82] Because of such dependence on encounters within-the-world, fear makes *Dasein* "forget and back away in the face of a factical potentiality-for-Being."[83] But what fear actually forgets becomes clear only through its contrast with "anxiety," which Heidegger labels as the more "basic state-of-mind."[84]

> Anxiety discloses an insignificance of the world; and this insignificance reveals the nullity of that with which one can concern oneself—in other words, the impossibility of projecting oneself upon a potentiality-for-Being which belongs to existence and which is founded primarily upon one's objects of concern. The revealing of this impossibility, however, signifies that one is allowing the possibility of an authentic potentiality-for-Being to be illuminated. What is the temporal meaning of this revealing? Anxiety is anxious about naked *Dasein* as something that has been thrown into uncanniness.[85]

The uncanniness of *Dasein*, which both being-at-home and fear would like to forget, has the same cause as the "impossibility of projecting oneself upon a potentiality-for-Being which belongs to existence." This cause is death, the unavoidable horizon that limits *Dasein* in all its projects and attempts at being meaningful. But it is also the horizon of *Dasein*, which, according to Heidegger, contributes more than anything else to the beauty of authenticity and resoluteness, and of actions carried out in that spirit.[86] [see **Action vs. Impotence, Authenticity vs. Artificiality**] "Anxiety arises out of Being-in-the-world as thrown . . . But anxiety can mount authentically only in a Dasein which is resolute. He who is resolute knows no fear; but he understands the possibility of anxiety as the possibility of the very mood which neither inhibits nor bewilders him. Anxiety liberates him *from* possibilities which 'count for nothing' . . ., and lets him become free *for* those which are authentic."[87] Despite the (generally acknowledged) influence of Kierkegaard's philosophy on these passages, it is obvious that Heidegger's fascination with anxiety and death mirrors numerous variations on the same topic in the literature of 1926 (from Hemingway's *The Sun Also Rises,* via Schickele's *Maria Capponi* and D. H. Lawrence's *The Plumed Serpent,* to Montherlant's *Les Bestiaires*), new leisure activities and new interests in the exotic [see **Bars, Gramophones, Mummies**], and myriad innovative—and dangerous—athletic pursuits and spectacles. [see **Boxing, Bullfighting, Endurance, Hunger Artists, Mountaineering, Six-Day Races**] All of these phenomena constitute a complex reaction to the vanishing of a sphere of transcendence that had generally been accepted as "real" [see **Cremation, Transcendence = Immanence (Death)**]—and *Sein und Zeit* participates in this reaction. Eliminating the question (not the possibility) of a "life after death,"[88] and expecting that his readers will still see death as opposed to life (or, at least, that they will maintain the idea of death's being a transition to a different form of existence), Heidegger himself makes every effort to define death as part of being-in-the-world: "*Dasein* does not, proximally and for the most part, have any explicit or even theoretical knowledge of the fact that it has been delivered over to its death, and that death thus belongs to Being-in-the-world. Thrownness into death reveals itself to *Dasein* in a more primordial and impressive manner in the state-of-mind which we have called 'anxiety.'"[89] At the same time, death is seen as based on "mineness"[90]—that is, as an exclusively and purely individual dimension of experience. Heidegger explains this mineness, as well as the proposed association between death and resoluteness, through the fact that death confronts individual *Dasein* with nullity, with the possibility of its own impossibility.[91] It is the confrontation with its own impossibility which, according to Heidegger, may persuade *Dasein* to opt for resoluteness—that is, for the possibility of its authentic Being.

Emerging in the Present

While the conceptualization of anxiety occurs in a chapter entitled "Temporality and Everydayness," the second part of *Sein und Zeit* culminates in the unfolding of a new philosophical concept for the relation between temporality and "historicality" *(Geschichtlichkeit).* Heidegger's double approach to the phenomenon of time thus reflects both the genesis of his book and, more important, the two different perspectives from which the phenomenon of time had become problematic for his contemporaries. Reacting to challenges arising mainly from the institutionalization of new technologies, philosophers were concerned with inventing new patterns of time-coordination in the everyday sphere, but they were also struggling to find a new philosophical coordination between past, present, and future. [see **Present = Past (Infinitude), Present vs. Past**]

Heidegger's idea to invert the classic relationship between historical time and existential time, by deriving historicality from the essentially temporal character of *Dasein* (instead of subordinating existential time to historical time), has become one of the most influential motifs of his book: "In analyzing the historicality of *Dasein* we shall try to show not that this entity is 'temporal' because it 'stands in history,' but that, on the contrary, it exists historically and can so exist only because it is temporal in the very basis of its Being."[92] How exactly historicality is supposed to emerge from the temporality of *Dasein* is described in a dense passage which brings together a number of the previously developed key-concepts and which, at the same time, resonates with many of the nonphilosophical discourses of 1926. In its first part, this passage focuses on the future and the past:

> If *Dasein*, by anticipation, lets death become powerful in itself, then, as free for death, *Dasein* understands itself in its own *superior power,* the power of its finite freedom, so that in this freedom, which "is" only in its having chosen to make such a choice, it can take over the *powerlessness* of abandonment to its having done so, and can thus come to have a clear vision for the accidents of the Situation that has been disclosed. But if fateful *Dasein*, as Being-in-the-world, exists essentially in Being-with-others, its historicizing is a cohistoricizing and is determinative for it as *destiny.* This is how we designate the historicizing of the community, of a people. Destiny is not something that puts itself together out of individual fates, any more than Being-with-one-another can be conceived as the occurring together of several Subjects.[93]

Instead of associating the future with understanding and the past with different states-of-mind, as he had suggested in the context of his structural analysis of *Sorge*, Heidegger's vision of historicality assigns death (the most individual experience) to the future, whereas fate, as materialized in the collectivity of a people *(Volk)* is linked with the past. [see **Individuality vs. Collectivity**] In their interplay, the newly defined future and past deconstruct the teleological directionality that characterizes the classic version of historical time. Death, as a possibility lying in the future, is the primary experience of *Dasein*. Undercutting all projects and projections of human activity, it leads back to the past as the inescapable collective determination of individual *Dasein*. After going through future and past, *Dasein* finds itself in a present whose status is no longer that of a transitional moment.

> Only an entity which, in its Being, is essentially *futural,* so that it is free for its death and can let itself be thrown back upon its factical "there" by shattering itself against death—that is to say, only an entity which, as futural, is equiprimordially in the process of *having been*—can, by handing down to itself the possibility it has inherited, take over its own thrownness and be *in the moment of vision* for "its time." Only authentic temporality, which is at the same time finite, makes possible something like fate—that is to say, authentic historicality.[94]

This concentration on the present, which pervades the last stage in the argument of *Sein und Zeit,* converges with the impression—so prevalent in the cultural environment of 1926—that, given the number of urgent challenges coming from the present, one cannot afford to devote a great deal of attention to either the past or the future. [see **Present vs. Past**] Emphasis on the present fosters an aesthetic view of action, as we have already seen with regard to Heidegger's notion of resoluteness and certain popular concepts of action.[95] [see **Action vs. Impotence**] What distinguishes Heidegger's reflections on time from contemporary social knowledge is the way in which he connects individuality and collectivity with the three divisions of time. Formerly, collectivity was seen as a central promise (or threat) of the future; individuality appeared as a value and a mode of life related to the past. [see **Individuality vs. Collectivity**] In contrast, Heidegger's historicality, which is derived from existential time, presents the past as fate, as a heritage that comes with belonging to a people. For him, the future holds nothing but the individual experience of *Dasein*'s nullity. Yet despite this difference between Heidegger's concept and the vague form of time in contemporary social knowledge, it remains true that, in both cases, the present is the chronotope where collectivity and individuality converge—and where the ap-

pearance of a leader can therefore be expected.[96] [see **Individuality =
Collectivity (Leader)**]

A Different Option for the Same

Compared to Heidegger, Hans Friedrich Blunck had no reason to complain about 1926. Having worked for some time as a legal counsel in the
finance department of the city of Hamburg, he was now promoted to the
highly visible and influential position of *Syndikus* (provost) at the University of Hamburg. Before assuming his new duties, Blunck took a
vacation. He and his wife traveled, as nonpaying guests of the Hamburg–
South America Line, from Hamburg to Rio de Janeiro in the recently
inaugurated tourist class.[97] [see **Ocean Liners**] Thus, for two members of
the same generation, the same nationality, and comparable levels of
education, Heidegger and Blunck could not have experienced 1926 more
differently. Yet the concepts and values they applied to their own lives
and to human existence in general were strikingly similar. Whenever
Blunck thought about his future duties and projects as head administra-
tor of the University of Hamburg, his favorite concept was *Sorge*.[98] Like
Heidegger, he pretended to resent any superfluous use of words—and he
thus developed a prejudice against parliamentary forms of politics: "Despite my strong social concerns, I do not fit into the parties of the Left.
Perhaps this is because I am too much of a northern German not to see
that loud Internationalism—like the noise of some groups which have
been sticking to our parties for the past seven years—is a tactical mistake."[99] Given this suspiciously distanced way of viewing the world of
politics, it is not surprising that Blunck expressed as much distaste as
Heidegger for modern urban life, especially that of Berlin: "I've learned
to despise Berlin . . . I hate the freedom of the bog. The things one sees
here! Advertisements for every kind of perversion, journals for sadists,
images of the most repellent sexuality—and all in the name of freedom!"[100]

Though it is likely that Blunck and Heidegger had heard of each other,
there is no reason to assume any mutual influence. Still, their lives have
so many events and aspects in common that Blunck's biography resembles a north German version of Heidegger's.[101] Blunck was born in
Hamburg-Altona on September 3, 1888, one year and twenty-three days

before Heidegger. He mentions excursions in the north German landscape with his family and with the *Wandervogel* organization (a national
hiking group with a right-wing orientation) as decisive experiences of his
childhood and adolescence. Blunck studied law in Heidelberg and in
Kiel, earning a doctorate in 1910 (three years earlier than Heidegger).
Atypically for the prewar era (but like Heidegger), Blunck never partici-
pated wholeheartedly in the student movements that were then a particularly dynamic force within German nationalism. Also like Heidegger,
he served mainly in bureaucratic functions during the Great War and
therefore did not see any military action that could have become the
topic of heroic retrospectives. Shortly after the war, Blunck became a
legal counsel for the State. Without any particular problems or, it seems,
any impressive achievements, he climbed the standard career ladder,
which culminated in his appointment as *Syndikus* at the University of
Hamburg in 1926. Two years later, when Heidegger, after achieving the
rank of *Ordinarius,* could finally afford to distance himself from academic philosophy, Blunck decided to quit his career as a civil servant in
order to dedicate himself exclusively to his literary work, which had
begun during the prewar years. He became a full-time novelist, story-
teller, and poet, occasionally publishing journalistic essays on cultural
politics.

In 1919, three years before the Heidegger family began to spend their
vacations in the cabin at Todtnauberg, Blunck had acquired a farmhouse
in the northernmost part of Germany, where, despite his professional
obligations in Hamburg, he and his wife tried to lead a part-time existence as amateur peasants. Later on, they would allow young enthusiasts
of Blunck's work to share this life with them, motivated by pedagogical
concerns similar to those that inspired the "academic camps" *(Wissen-
schaftslager)* which Heidegger organized in 1933.[102] Less than half a year
after the National Socialist Party's "seizure of power," Blunck was appointed to the Academy of Poetry in the Prussian Academy of the Arts.[103]
In the same year, on November 15, Joseph Göbbels appointed Hans
Friedrich Blunck the first president of the newly founded Reichsschrifttumskammer. While it is difficult to ascertain the precise reasons for this
promotion, there can be no doubt that Blunck's (semi)political star had
already begun to fall as early as the spring of 1934, about the time that
Heidegger resigned as head of the University of Freiburg after only one
year in the office. On October 3, 1935, in a ceremony described by the

press as "sober and modest, but warm and personal,"[104] the party hardliner Hanns Johst became Blunck's successor. This did not come as a surprise.[105] Blunck had probably underestimated the power of the party hierarchy over what he tried to bring into play—namely, individual artistic and ideological merit.[106] Like Heidegger, Blunck never fell into disgrace with the Nazi party. He was awarded the Goethe Medal in 1938, and in the same year the government entrusted him with a modest cultural mission following the annexation of Austria.[107]

In 1926, with some public acclaim but seemingly without any financial reward,[108] Blunck had published his novel *Kampf der Gestirne (Battle of the Stars)*. It would be the second part of a trilogy entitled *Die Urväter-Saga (Saga of the Forefathers)*, in which he aimed at "a world view based on the history of the German people, going beyond the vision of the State and the divisions between the social classes."[109] Despite its prose form, *Kampf der Gestirne* uses elements of the heroic poem: the tone, the archaic vocabulary, the formulaic expressions, and the technique of thematic contrast. Like Heidegger, Blunck seems to associate such (artificially produced) discursive archaisms with authenticity and with a particular truth-value. But it is even more interesting to observe that Blunck structures his novel like an allegory of the contrast between authenticity and inauthenticity (*Eigentlichkeit* and *Uneigentlichkeit*) as it is developed, with much greater complexity, in *Sein und Zeit*. This contrast is central to *Kampf der Gestirne* because Blunck's late Stone Age protagonists (his fictional ancestors of the German *Volk*) are divided into two realms, the Empire of the Day/Sun ("authenticity") and the Empire of the Night/Moon ("inauthenticity"). Although there is no logical reason that readers should opt for the Empire of the Sun, Blunck's value attributions leave as little doubt about the choice he advocates as Heidegger's parallel arguments do.

The most striking lexical convergence between *Kampf der Gestirne* and *Sein und Zeit* lies in the dominant role that both books assign to the binarism *Sorge* versus *Furcht* ("care" versus "fear"). It first appears on the third page of Blunck's novel, in the characterization of Lärmer ("he who makes noise"), a conqueror who belongs to the Empire of the Moon. Lärmer wants to win the trust of conquered peoples by reinstituting the magic rituals which his defeated predecessor Elk, the "innovator,"[110] had abandoned. In doing so, Lärmer gives in to the fear *(Furcht)* that he and his partisans feel at night. Within Blunck's impeccable binary logic, this makes him neglectful of planning and carrying out his actions *(Sorge)* during the day. "For Lärmer gave in to the dream-fear of humans; he reestablished the ancient rituals and dances devoted to the stars of the dark. His fear [*Furcht*] during the night was stronger than his care [*Sorge*] during the day."[111] Like Heidegger, Blunck gives the noun *Sorge* connotations different from the conventional ones ("sorrow," "grief," "distress"). Only in this way can *Sorge* come to mean the opposite of *Furcht*. *Sorge* includes any kind of future-oriented action aimed at superseding the old world of magic and witchcraft. Unlike Heidegger, however, Blunck uses the words *Furcht* and *Angst* synonymously; for the plot of *Kampf der Gestirne,* the distinctions already existing in everyday language are sufficient.

The only other way in which Blunck's construction of the contrast between authenticity and inauthenticity differs from Heidegger's has to do with gender. Whereas fear and anxiety pervade the entire Empire of the Night like a spell, in the Empire of the Day only women are plagued by these emotions. Blunck thus presents authenticity as a predominantly male mode of life, a temptation that Heidegger (as we saw in his correspondence with Elisabeth Blochmann) manages to resist. Indirectly, however, the women's *Angst* often produces positive effects because, at least in the Empire of the Day, it causes men to intensify their *Sorge:*

> The boats leaked, and the girls and daughters of Birres were terribly frightened [*hatten Angst*] by the dark flood which entered the hulls. For the first time, the heroes had to take care [*hatten Sorge*] of their captives. But they had so recently fallen in love that they were willing to bear it all without muttering. Still, when they carried the boats across the land, they first tied their free hands to the girls' hands, because they thought it dangerous to leave such young folk alone in the dark.[112]

But *Furcht* and *Angst* evoke more than "night" and "femininity." They also connote what Heidegger calls "idle talk." This is why a character whose name is Lärmer must belong to the Empire of the Moon. The heroes of the Empire of the Sun, in contrast, act and react in silence—as if they were peasants from Heidegger's Black Forest. Even the most life-threatening events only make them more pensive: "'Shall I ask the sun, or will you seek Lady Flode's advice?' Ull remains silent, but circumstances will not leave him in peace. Once again, this will be the ground of his thinking."[113] Such imposing male attitudes force the weaker protagonists—particularly the women—to withdraw, and sometimes even to repress their idle talk: "Huge and powerful, the old man takes his stand before the entrance to the king's court, and immediately the chattering women disappear into their rooms."[114]

Despite such unmistakable semantic contrasts, it is not always easy for the protagonists to make the right choice. Even Ull, the strongest and most taciturn of the warriors serving under the Empire of the Sun, needs occasional exhortations to adhere to authenticity. Like *Dasein* in *Sein und Zeit,* Ull's existence is often marked by the calling of voices *(Rufe),* whose origin seems to oscillate between immanence and transcendence:

> Hor calls in his sleep. Ull gets up, but he must first look into the flame's red brain—searching the core around which its dress is flickering. And while he gazes straight into the red pit, a log bends and bursts. A flame flares high and burns his eyelashes. "My office," says Bra and holds his hand between the king and the fire. The calls of warning come again, but they are different from Hor's voice. Ull awakes from his thoughts; the wind is beating and drumming against the ground. His dog jumps up and listens. Then the sound ceases. Did someone call? Ull is again alone with Bra's quiet words and lets him speak about Hilboe, about her brother Hill in the east and about her sister Flode in the west. And the king tells about the day when the sun wanted to leap off the rock right in front of him, and he asks him to interpret this.[115]

Even the boldest of Blunck's heroes find something uncanny *(unheimlich)* in such moments, when they are defenseless against the powers of the night and the magic of those powers.[116] But for Blunck, as for Heidegger, the uncanny bears exclusively positive connotations. Those who are capable of enduring anxiety and the uncanny without falling prey to the spell of the night, those in whose lives death is constantly present, will (in silence, of course) achieve the greatest deeds.

Ull has to kill his beloved wife, Solmund, because she yielded to the spell of the moon and the stars. To avenge her death, Solmund's brother, the sorcerer Borr, challenges Ull:

> "Hear me, Ull," shouted Borr, crying with rage, "Where is my sister, whom you stole from me? Where is she whom I cherished as the apple of my eye? Where is she whom you found and took away?"

But the king remained silent.

"Hear me, drunkard! Why did you come here? Oh, why, miserable man, have you talked to humans about the sun, though you were nothing but my dear one's spouse? Why did you steal the child who protected my nights, and why did you think she was of the light? Why did you not know that I was raising a simple girl for myself?

While he thus spoke, and moreover spoke untrue words, the king's steps became faster, and foam stood on his lips.[117]

Ull is not stronger than Borr. His superiority in battle derives, like the resoluteness described by Heidegger, both from the courage with which Ull faces his own death and from his willingness to stand for a people's collective fate: "Only the king's faith was greater . . ., and his pity for his people, who did not have a leader, was stronger than the force which Borr drew from the moonlit night."[118] Silently opting for what Blunck presents as the authenticity of existence, standing between collective fate and the individual facticity of death, Ull becomes the much-needed leader of the people when he destroys his enemy in the early dawn: "Ull seized Borr by the neck, threw him high into the air, and let him fall under his own body. And he strangled him when the first light of day showed red in the east."[119]

Life Means Not to Opt

For all of Blunck's fascination with authenticity, African culture, which had become the standard symbol of this value in the modernist canon, was not to his taste. On his voyage to Rio de Janeiro, Blunck was shocked to see a black customs officer examine the personal belongings which he and his wife carried in their suitcases: "My wife's heart stood still as the soot-black customs officer turned up our white laundry with his fingers. But it was touching to see how he put it all back in order."[120] Riding through the city in a streetcar, the German travelers receive some comfort from the fact that, even in neighborhoods with a predominantly black population, Rio de Janeiro still offers spectacular vistas: "We seemed in mortal danger riding on that streetcar, whose track runs through suburban gardens and negro neighborhoods—but always with lovely views of the city below."[121] It is safe to assume that Emmes and

Hans Friedrich Blunck (and, for that matter, Elfride and Martin Heidegger) would scarcely have enjoyed the ebullient African-American culture of contemporary Harlem, as it was so well described by the white writer Carl Van Vechten in his popular novel *Nigger Heaven*, which Alfred A. Knopf published in August 1926.[122] For life in Harlem was the true model, the original of everything that made conservative German intellectuals such as Heidegger and Blunck so intensely hate its copy, Berlin. Harlem, to them, meant music halls and revues, jazz and the Charleston, booze and cocaine, prostitution, transgressive sexuality, and (diametrically opposed to silence) an exuberant urban culture of continual verbalization. European philosophers and poets who dreamed of dwelling in mountain cabins or in a farmhouses near the sea dreaded New York—especially Harlem—as synonymous with that very artificiality and superficiality into which the future threatened to dissolve their values of profound authenticity. [see **Authenticity vs. Artificiality**]

This outside view of metropolitan life would not be worth mentioning if, from an inside perspective (which, surprisingly perhaps, Van Vechten was capable of offering), the culture of Harlem had not been a much more ambiguous and therefore much more complex phenomenon. Mary Love, the main character in *Nigger Heaven,* is a young black woman whose parents have brought her up to be proud of her race and who is thus free to appreciate both the classic and the contemporary canons of white culture. In her profession as a librarian and in her private life, Mary Love cultivates the modern taste for sobriety, and the preference for this mode of living makes her different from her good friend Olive Hamilton, with whom she shares a modest apartment. [see **Sobriety vs. Exuberance**]

> The walls were brightened by framed reproductions of paintings by Bellini and Carpaccio which Mary had collected during a journey through Italy. Olive's personal taste inclined to the luxurious. Her dressing-table was hung in lace over pink satin, and her bed was covered with a spread of the same materials. On the dressing-table was laid out a toilet-set of carved ivory, an extravagance which had cost her a great deal of economy in other directions. A bottle of Narcisse Noir stood near the toilet-set. Framed, on a table and on the walls, were many photographs of friends. A French worsted doll lay dejected in the corner. Mary's taste was more sober. There was only one picture in her

room, a reproduction of the Mona Lisa. Her bed-cover was plain white; her dressing table austere and generally devoid of articles, save for an inexpensive brush, comb, and mirror.[123]

Being an intellectual value rather than a sensual perception, this sobriety, together with Mary Love's taste for the art of the past, makes it plausible that she would opt for authenticity instead of artificiality and sensuality, even regarding her own African-American culture. Without much encouragement from friends or professional superiors, Mary is organizing an exhibit of "primitive" African sculpture and handicrafts. What she finds in this ancient culture is not only a collective legacy but also an approximation of the truth inherent in elementary forms.

> She had principally been occupied in borrowing from several private collections specimens of primitive African sculpture, and she had been astonishingly successful—lucky, she called it—in unearthing worthy examples, representing the creative skill of a variety of tribes from different localities in Africa. Moreover, early dates were more or less reasonably ascribed to some of them. One strangely beautiful head was said to have been executed in the tenth century, or even earlier, while a box, exquisite in proportion and design, was said to have been created in the fourteenth century. Mary was beginning to recognize the feel of the older work, the soft, smooth texture, like that of the best Chinese porcelains, of the wood, so different from that of the coarser, later pieces. She knew something, too, now, about the more primitive design, lovelier in its conception, because it was more honest, than the more elaborate later traceries, created under Portuguese influence."[124]

The configuration of values and choices that make Mary Love, a fictional character, organize an exhibit on archaic African art is similar to the motivation that makes Hans Friedrich Blunck, a lawyer and poet, write novels on the life of prehistoric Germanic tribes. Yet two things distinguish them. First, Mary's preference for authenticity is eccentric among black people, whereas Blunck's is typical of the German intellectual mainstream. Second, African culture occupies an eccentric position within the current cultural mapping of the West, which is dominated by the European culture of which Blunck's book is a part. Still, the fictional Mary Love and the real Hans Friedrich Blunck both choose authenticity, which, according to Heidegger, is decisive for any form of *Dasein*. They seem to do so because they—more or less vaguely—see authenticity as being related to a promise that essence will be revealed. This, however, means that, in spite of all evident contrasts, opting for the authentic, as it constitutes the center of Heidegger and Blunck's world, is also available as an existential option in the world of Carl Van Vechten's Harlem.

In contrast to Heidegger, Blunck, and possibly even Van Vechten, do not seem to have opted for authenticity—or for those artificial sounds and shiny surfaces which, especially in the first part of *Nigger Heaven,* clearly occupy the foreground of the imagined world. Another black protagonist, Mary's lover Byron Kasson, a talented young writer, fails in his professional aspirations and loses Mary's love precisely because he yields to the temptation of the senses. The plot of *Nigger Heaven* culminates in a nightclub with the (all-too allegorical) name *Black Venus,* where Byron is wrongly arrested on suspicion of murder:

> It all became a jumble in Byron's mind, a jumble of meaningless phrases accompanied by the hard, insistent, regular beating of the drum, the groaning of the saxophone, the shrill squealing of the clarinet, the laughter of the customers and occasionally the echo of the refrain, "Baby, won't you come home today?" A meaningless jumble. Like life. Like Negro life. Kicked down from above. Pulled down from below. No cheer but dance and drink and happy dust . . . and golden-browns. Wine, women, and song, and happy dust. Gin, shebas, Blues, and snow. However you looked at it . . . Whatever you called it.[125]

This surface liveliness of "negro life," Van Vechten suggests, is but an illusion of true vitality. In contrast, Mary Love's opting for authenticity makes her appear strangely inhibited—so inhibited that she, as much as Byron, fails to find a viable frame for their love. What makes things even worse for Mary is her acute awareness of this lack—a lack which she is unable to overcome. Mary knows that she herself will never feel the intensity which she observes in the relationship between Olive and Howard, Olive's future husband: "She saw that Howard was Olive's man and that she was his woman. It was more than a marriage; it was a primitive consecration. She saw that each would fight—kill if need be—to retain the other's love. This realization made her feel her own lack more keenly than ever. How had she, during the centuries, lost this vital instinct?"[126] In contrast to Byron, Howard and Olive manage to participate in the vibrant superficiality of "negro life" without falling victim to it. And in contrast to Mary Love, Olive and Howard feel no need to devote themselves to the profound values of authenticity, though they are quite capable of appreciating them. What Van Vechten seems to advocate (and what he refers to with the term "vital instinct") is a mode of life that avoids the choice between authenticity and the artifice of surface worlds. This mode of life keeps the authentic and the artificial simultaneously present. A worthwhile life, at least according to Van Vechten's understanding, is achieved by opting not to opt between the two values. [see **Authenticity** = **Artificiality (Life)**] We can assume that many contemporary American intellectuals shared this attitude, especially those whose quest for "true" authenticity had been frustrated by their travels in Europe. There, "opting not to opt" between authenticity and artificiality was probably a much less popular attitude. Occasionally, however, in texts written by European authors, non-opting is an attitude that emerges under specific circumstances: as an unattainable ideal in Schickele's *Maria Capponi,* for example, and as a strategy for survival under the imposed-upon life conditions of the big city, in the concept of *Existenzfreudigkeit* which Martin Heidegger recommends to his friend Elisabeth Blochmann.

Making Present a Field

The texts and the worlds of Martin Heidegger, Hans Friedrich Blunck, and Carl Van Vechten have brought us back, perhaps surprisingly, to a classic concern in the writing of history. They have brought us back to the questions of historical totality and historiographic totalization. In my analysis of *Sein und Zeit,* I tried (both willingly and with the fear of violating the premises underlying this book) to show that Heidegger had combined and woven into a complex structure a strikingly broad range of cultural codes from the worlds of 1926—so broad a range, indeed, that it ended up including all the individual codes that I had identified in my historical research. To underscore this experience is of course not to say that the object-side of what I describe as the year 1926 constitutes a unity or a totality independent of any particular perspective or position. It does imply, however, that it was possible, from within the year, to see the worlds of 1926 as a totality. By trying to show, subsequently, that texts as different in their complexity, status, and origin as *Sein und Zeit, Kampf der Gestirne,* and *Nigger Heaven* share certain key motifs and perspectives, I ultimately dealt not only with totality as a phenomenon intrinsic to my historical field of reference, but found myself confronted—on a practical (or rhetorical) rather than on a philosophical level—with the temptation to attempt a historiographic totalization. I was indeed trying to invent aspects and forms of representation that would provide a view of the different worlds of 1926 as a unity.

Yet it is true that totality and totalization became issues only because I exposed my project (of making present a year of the past) to the question of whether it was capable of yielding some results that would be regarded as useful—even from a less eccentric viewpoint. I wish to emphasize, therefore, that the possibility (or impossibility) of a historical totality and the problems of historiographic totalization have nothing to do with the primary, and perhaps crude, desire behind this book—the desire, that is, of coming as close as possible to making present a moment of the past, and of making it "present" in the fullest possible sense of the word. Such effects of presence, I assume, are more likely to come through reference to concrete historical detail than through abstract, "totalizing" overviews. At any rate, it is enough to say that effects of presence do not systematically depend on totality or totalization. For myself, the experiment detailed in this book came to a successful and early fulfillment during the few—but real—moments in the composition process when I managed (or rather happened) to forget that I was *not* living in 1926. And I suppose that, on the reader's side, there will be no other way of assessing the failure or success of what, in the introduction to this book, I offered as my intellectual wager.

Regarding the relationship between (the classic value of) historical totality and the (more recent?) desire for a past made present, one can perhaps go even a step further. Not only are effects of presence independent of totality and totalization, but one can indeed claim (as I have already done, though from a different angle, in the preceding chapter) that the vanishing of our belief in historical totality and a waning interest in historiographic totalization are important—if not necessary—preconditions for the latest changes in our fascination with the past. At this point, we could again take up the question of why these ideals have become so attenuated in recent years. The answer would lead us to the (in)famous crisis of subjecthood and agency, and to the way in which subjecthood and agency relate to what Western culture has called, since the late eighteenth century, "historical time." But I will cut short what threatens to become an infinite (and obsessive) regression. The point is that even those who, like me, no longer believe in learning from history or in historical agency (and who therefore are reluctant to continue writing narratives of history) still need specific textual forms whenever they want to write and speak about the past. What we need, more precisely, are genres capable of becoming forms of *Anschauung*. Perhaps such genres cannot avoid producing effects of totalization—but we have recently come to understand that they at least need not take the shape of narratives.

This distance vis-à-vis the form of the historical narrative has opened the way for two basic types of experiments. One might attempt, as Ferdinand Braudel did in his book on the Mediterranean world, to write the history of a space. In such a discourse, the possibility of attributing all points of reference to a certain space allows one to perceive unity amid the diversifying effects of time. Or one might try, as I have done in this book (an experiment that seems to have more literary than historiographic predecessors—think of *Ulysses*), to write the history of a short span of time, a history in which the possibility of attributing all points of reference to this span of time allows one to perceive unity amid the diversifying effects of spatial distance. The Mediterranean world is considered a unity, although we know that the Mediterranean of the twelfth century was not the same as the Mediterranean of the sixteenth century. The year 1926 is considered a unity, although we know that 1926 in Berlin was not the same as 1926 in Paris. The *Anschauungsform* which emerges from the latter experiment—in particular, from the discussion of authenticity in Heidegger's *Sein und Zeit,* Blunck's *Kampf der Gestirne,* and Van Vechten's *Nigger Heaven*—can perhaps best be characterized as a "field" (and I of course mean "field" in its disciplinary rather than agricultural sense). A field is, first of all, a space comprising a number of possibilities that are available everywhere within its limits. This corresponds to my claim that all the arrays, cultural codes, and code breakdowns that I have described (and others besides) were available as a potential throughout the Western cultural world in 1926. Second, positionality is crucial within any field—despite the general availability of a number of options, which gives it homogeneity. For instance, we have seen that it was quite likely for German writers, in 1926, to opt for authenticity, whereas opting for the simultaneity between authenticity and artificiality (that is, "life") was a choice preferred by and associated with American intellectuals. Positionality produces position-specific expectations and (more important, and despite these expectations) the possibility of mutual understanding, because, within a field, one can always at least imagine those options which, due to one's specific positionality, one is not likely to choose. Positionality within a field, then, has to do with probabilities of choice and attribution; it never imposes itself as an absolute constraint. Thus, Heidegger could develop and cultivate, as a vision of horror, his ideas about life in the big city, whereas Carl Van Vechten would probably not have been astonished to learn that some philosophers in Germany preached an almost religious belief in the authenticity of peasant ways of life. Third, and as a consequence of positionality's being a matter of probability, the boundaries of historical fields are vague. For example, even if one excluded Shanghai from the Western culture of 1926, there were strong cultural and communications links between Shanghai and the world of New York. Paris, in contrast, was the center of the prevailing mental map of the West—but its culture was, if one may say so, "less central" and more limited in options than that of New York or Berlin.

Finally, I wish to emphasize one more time that, although positionality generates profiles of likely choice and creates vague boundaries, the complete set of options that define a field is potentially available at every point within this field. For the people living in 1926, these options were, as Heidegger says, "ready-to-hand," meaning that they were always already in use—and only rarely the objects of reflection. For example, some people would have considered authenticity the highest value of human existence, while others would have hated authenticity—but scarcely anyone would have spoken about authenticity and artificiality as a binary opposition or a cultural code. The ability to notice and conceptualize such oppositions and codes comes with distance: it belongs to that being-in-the-world which Heidegger calls the "present-at-hand." I have tried, in this book, to make arrays, codes, and code breakdowns from 1926 present-at-hand again, so that these elements, especially by evoking the idea or even the desire for the ready-to-hand, could suggest the illusion of living in 1926. Yet the present-at-hand excludes the possibility of ever really using what is made intellectually available. Thus, while I certainly cannot prevent readers from wishing to opt for authenticity, like Heidegger and Blunck, or from wishing to reject, for example, Van Vechten's concept of life (which is based on the simultaneity of the authentic and the artificial), my book of course does not advocate any particular attitude toward authenticity—or toward any other value.

It is with this measure of self-clarification that I wish to conclude my essay on historical simultaneity. The work has evoked, at least for me, pleasant and sometimes uncanny effects of presence. Yet these effects inevitably belong to the present-at-hand, and thus do not create the illusion that one ever could or should live through 1926 again.

NOTES

ACKNOWLEDGMENTS

INDEX

NOTES

....

After Learning from History

1. See Hans Ulrich Gumbrecht, Ursula Link-Heer, and Peter-Michael Spangenberg, "Zwischen neuen Einsichten und neuen Fragen: Zur Gestalt der romanischen Historiographie des Mittelalters," in Gumbrecht, Link-Heer, and Spangenberg, eds., *La littérature historiographique des origines à 1500*, in *Grundriss der romanischen Literaturen des Mittelalters*, vol. 11, part 1 (Heidelberg, 1986), pp. 1133–1152.

2. See the brilliant interpretation of Montaigne in Karlheinz Stierle, "Geschichte als Exemplum—Exemplum als Geschichte: Zur Pragmatik und Poetik narrativer Texte," in Stierle, *Text als Handlung* (Munich, 1975), pp. 14–48, esp. pp. 37ff.; and Reinhart Koselleck's classic essay, "Historia Magistra Vitae: Über die Auflösung des Topos im Horizont neuzeitlich bewegter Geschichte," in Koselleck, *Vergangene Zukunft: Zur Semantik geschichtlicher Zeiten* (Frankfurt, 1979), pp. 38–66.

3. Regarding the Quarrel, the standard reference is Hans Robert Jauss, "Aesthetische Normen und geschichtliche Reflexion in der 'Querelle des Anciens et des Modernes,'" introduction to Charles Perrault, *Parallèle des Anciens et des Modernes en ce qui regarde les Arts et les Sciences* (Munich, 1964), pp. 8–64. For the impact of the *Querelle* on the historiographic discourses of the European Enlightenment, see Hans Ulrich Gumbrecht, "Modern, Moderne, Modernismus," in Otto Brunner, Werner Conze, and Reinhart Koselleck, eds., *Geschichtliche Grundbegriffe: Historisches Lexikon zur politisch-sozialen Sprache in Deutschland*, vol. 4 (Stuttgart, 1978), pp. 93–131, esp. pp. 99ff. An English translation can be found in Gumbrecht, *Making Sense in Life and Literature* (Minneapolis, 1992), pp. 79–110.

4. For a reaction to this situation from an epistemological perspective, see the essays in Niklas Luhmann, *Beobachtungen der Moderne* (Opladen, 1992).

5. Niklas Luhmann, "Die Beschreibung der Zukunft," ibid., pp. 129–148.

6. Kojève's lectures on Hegel's *Phenomenology of Spirit* appear in English in Raymond Queneau, Allan Bloom, and James H. Nichols, Jr., eds., *Introduction to the Reading of Hegel: Lectures on "The Phenomenology of Spirit"* (Ithaca, 1980).

7. Michel Foucault, "Nietzsche, la généalogie, l'histoire," in Suzanne Bachelard et al., eds., *Hommage à Jean Hyppolite* (Paris, 1971), pp. 145–172. Regarding Foucault's reflections on the "uses of history," some of his most varied positions come up in interviews; see, for example, Paul Rabinow, ed., *The Foucault Reader* (New York, 1984), pp. 373ff.

8. See Hayden White, *Metahistory: The Historical Imagination in Nineteenth-Century Europe* (Baltimore, 1973); and Reinhart Koselleck, H. Lutz, and Jörn Rüsen, eds., *Formen der Geschichtsschreibung: Theorie der Geschichte*, vol. 4 (Munich, 1982).

9. Indeed, Luhmann argues that, when one concentrates on the present, these problems become more acute. See *Beobachtungen der Moderne*, pp. 11–50, 129–148.

10. See H. Aram Veeser, "Introduction," in Veeser, ed., *The New Historicism* (New York, 1989), pp. ixff.

11. This phrase became popular through Peter L. Berger and Thomas Luckmann, *The Social Construction of Reality* (Garden City, N.Y., 1966).

12. Stephen Greenblatt, *Shakespearean Negotiations: The Circulation of Social Energy in Renaissance England* (Berkeley, 1988), p. 1.

13. For a more detailed discussion of this approach, see Gumbrecht, *Making Sense in Life and Literature*, pp. 33–75.

14. See Alfred Schütz and Thomas Luckmann, *Strukturen der Lebenswelt* (Neuwied, 1975).

15. On the historical background for this terminological decision, see Hans Ulrich Gumbrecht, "'Everyday-World' and 'Life-World' as Philosophical Concepts: A Genealogical Approach," *New Literary History* 24 (1993–1994): 745–761.

16. I was first encouraged to discuss this unacademic desire in an academic context by certain passages and phrases in Nietzsche's *Jenseits von Gut und Böse*. See Hans Ulrich Gumbrecht, "Wie sinnlich kann Geschmack (in der Literatur) sein? Über den historischen Ort von Marcel Prousts *Recherche*," in Volker Kapp, ed., *Marcel Proust: Geschmack und Neigung* (Tübingen, 1989), pp. 107–126, esp. pp. 155ff. A much more sophisticated (and daring) discussion of what I see as the same problem is Michael Taussig, *Mimesis and Alterity: A Particular History of the Senses* (New York, 1993).

17. For the prehistory of this "style," see Timothy Lenoir and Cheryl Lynn Ross, "The Naturalized History Museum," unpublished manuscript, Stanford, 1993. Years ago I used to visit, on an almost weekly basis, the Ruhrland

Museum (Essen) specifically for its display on the social and cultural history of industrialization in Germany. There, museumgoers could use sports equipment (such as dumbbells) from the early twentieth century, and, while sitting in a 1920s pub, could listen to a recording of one of the first soccer broadcasts ever aired in Europe.

18. See Reinhart Koselleck, "'Erfahrungsraum' und 'Erwartungshorizont': Zwei historische Kategorien," in Koselleck, *Vergangene Zukunft,* pp. 349–375.

19. This way of experiencing the present informs Baudelaire's famous definition, in *Peintre de la vie moderne,* of modernity as "le transitoire, le fugitif, le contingent."

20. Some of the central concepts in Edmund Husserl's phenomenology of time (such as *Bewusstseinsstrom, Protention,* and *Retention*) try to describe this experience. See Husserl, "Zur Phänomenologie des inneren Zeitbewusstseins (1893–1917)," *Husserliana,* vol. 10 (The Hague, 1966).

21. One can illustrate this change by pointing to the fact that a definition of "the present" which is frequently taken for granted by academics of my generation (i.e., the time-span between the "students' revolution" of the late 1960s and the current 1990s) has meanwhile come to include more years than the period between the end of World War I and the end of World War II.

22. The metaphor of the "receding line" is a leitmotif in the introductory chapter of Jacques Derrida, *De la grammatologie* (Paris, 1967). For an application of this idea to the "present" epistemological situation, see Hans Ulrich Gumbrecht, "Ende des Theorie-Jenseits?" in Rudolf Maresch, ed., *Zukunft oder Ende: Standpunkte, Analysen, Entwürfe* (Munich, 1993), pp. 40–46.

23. See Niklas Luhmann, "Gleichzeitigkeit und Synchronisation," in Luhmann, *Soziologische Aufklärung,* vol. 5: *Konstruktivistische Perspektiven* (Opladen, 1990), pp. 95–130.

24. "Ungleichzeitigkeit des Gleichzeitigen" is another central concept of Reinhart Koselleck's thought. See, in particular, "'Neuzeit': Zur Semantik moderner Bewegungsbegriffe," in Koselleck, *Vergangene Zukunft,* pp. 300–348.

25. A (not so) randomly chosen example is Hans Ulrich Gumbrecht and K. Ludwig Pfeiffer, eds., *Paradoxien, Dissonanzen, Zusammenbrüche: Situationen offener Epistemologie* (Frankfurt, 1991).

26. The history of this topology (i.e., the topology of the "hermeneutic field") is retraced in Hans Ulrich Gumbrecht, *The Non-Hermeneutic* (Stanford, 1998).

27. David Wellbery, "The Exteriority of Writing," *Stanford Literature Review* (1991–1992): 11–24.

28. For this (re)construction of a systemic notion of "understanding," see Hans Ulrich Gumbrecht, "'Interpretation' vs. 'Understanding Systems,'" *Cardozo Law Review,* special issue (1992): 283–300.

29. Significantly, I would not have perceived this "irony" in my own project

and text without the comments of Richard Roberts in several discussions at the Stanford Humanities Center during the 1993–1994 academic year.

30. I of course refer to the formulation of this concept in Heidegger's *Sein und Zeit,* although I do not see (or claim) any connection between my own project and the theory of history which Heidegger develops in that book. For an "application" of Heidegger's thought to present-day discussions among historians, see Reinhart Koselleck, *Hermeneutik und Historik: Sitzungsberichte der Heidelberger Akademie der Wissenschaften (Philosophisch-historische Klasse),* Report 1 for 1987 (Heidelberg, 1987). My own—epistemologically oriented— use of Heidegger's concepts "ready-to-hand" and "present-at-hand" goes back to a discussion with Francisco Varela during a colloquium entitled "Beyond Dualism: Epistemological Convergences between the Sciences and the Humanities?" Stanford University, March 1994.

31. I allude to Benjamin's famous metaphor of the "panther's leap into history"—which I try to use without the (ambitious) political connotations inherent in its original version.

32. "The Year 1926" was the topic of a seminar that I taught with Ursula Link-Heer at the University of Siegen (Germany) during the winter semester of 1987–1988.

33. In the course of my work, I discovered that neither of these two grandparents had actually died in 1926. But my error made the choice of the year 1926 only "more random"—meaning more fitting for my experiment.

34. Regarding this aspect of our relation to the past, see my essay "Narrating the Past as If It Were Your Own Time," in Gumbrecht, *Making Sense in Life and Literature,* pp. 60ff.

35. Bliss Carnochan first confronted me with this question.

36. A particularly impressive example of historical re-presentation is Jay Fliegelman, *Declaring Independence: Jefferson, National Language, and the Culture of Performance* (Stanford, 1993).

37. Hans Ulrich Gumbrecht, *Funktionswandel und Rezeption: Studien zur Hyperbolik in literarischen Texten des romanischen Mittelalters,* Diss., University of Konstanz, 1971 (Munich, 1972).

38. With this "abstraction from sequentiality," my book departs from other essays in historical simultaneity—for example, Jean Starobinski, *1789: Les emblèmes de la raison* (Paris, 1979); or Jürgen Kuczynski, *1903: Ein normales Jahr im imperialistischen Deutschland* (Berlin, 1988).

39. "Figuration" was a key concept in Norbert Elias' historiographic practice. See Peter R. Gleichmann, Johan Goudsblom, and Hermann Korte, eds., *Human Figurations: Essays for Norbert Elias* (Amsterdam, 1977).

40. Again in reference to Nietzsche. See note 16, above.

41. See, for example, Michel Foucault, *Dispositive der Macht: Über Sexualität, Wissen und Wahrheit* (Berlin, 1978), pp. 119ff.

42. I borrow from Niklas Luhmann the idea that different social systems are based on different binary codes. See, among other essays by Luhmann, "Ist Kunst codierbar?" in Luhmann, *Soziologische Aufklärung*, vol. 3 (Opladen, 1981), pp. 245–266. See also Hans Ulrich Gumbrecht, "Pathologies in the System of Literature, " in Gumbrecht, *Making Sense in Life and Literature*, pp. 247–271. Furthermore, it was Luhmann who first suggested associating the concept of "culture" with the deparadoxifying function of "binary codes" ("Ökologie des Nichtwissens," in Luhmann, *Beobachtungen der Moderne*, p. 201).

43. In this sense, the sequence of short texts that constitute Starobinski's *1789: Les emblèmes de la Raison* can be read as a similarly "decentering" structure of "entries"—although it is not presented in alphabetical order.

44. Interestingly, the "network" metaphor was used only in the English title *(Discourse Networks)* of Friedrich Kittler's doubly synchronic analysis, *Aufschreibesysteme 1800/1900* (Munich, 1985).

45. See Gilles Deleuze and Félix Guattari, *Rhizom* (Berlin, 1977).

46. Flaubert's notes, which were found in a folder labeled "Dictionnaire des idées reçues," were not published until 1961. Closer to the year 1926, two pathbreaking novels, James Joyce's *Ulysses* (1922) and Alfred Döblin's *Berlin Alexanderplatz* (1929), observed the same principle of constituting (semi-) fictional worlds on the basis of commonplaces and everyday perspectives.

Being-in-the-Worlds of 1926

1. See Martin Heidegger and Elisabeth Blochmann, *Briefwechsel, 1918–1969*, ed. Joachim W. Storck (Marbach, 1989), p. 138. Storck's note reads: "*Todtnauberg:* village in the southern part of the Black Forest. It was here that Elfride Heidegger built the solitary cabin [*Hütte*] for Martin Heidegger which henceforth became the thinker's favorite vacation site."

2. *Spektabilität* is the traditional German title for a university dean. The letter (Hessisches Staatsarchiv Marburg, Best. 307d, Acc. 1966/10) reads: "Eurer Spektabilität teile ich ergebenst mit, dass ich heute einen Ruf für das dortige Extraordinariat für Philosophie mit Rechten und Stellung eines ordentlichen Professors erhalten habe. Ich werde den Ruf annehmen. Zugleich bitte ich Eure Spektabilität ergebenst, einer hohen philosophischen Fakultät meinen aufrichtigsten Dank für das in mich gesetzte Vertrauen übermitteln zu wollen. Die Ankündigung der Vorlesungen und Übungen erlaube ich mir, sofort nach Rükfrage bei den Herrn Fachvertretern einzusenden. Mit dem Ausdruck au-

frichtigster Hochachtung bin ich Eurer Spektabilität sehr ergebener Dr. Martin Heidegger."

3. Hans Georg Gadamer, one of his earliest students, testifies to this. See Gadamer, *Philosophische Lehrjahre: Eine Rückschau* (Frankfurt, 1977), pp. 28–45, 210–221; and idem, "Hermeneutik im Rückblick," in Gadamer, *Gesammelte Werke,* vol. 10 (Tübingen, 1995), pp. 3–13.

4. I take this detail from Hugo Ott's well-researched book *Martin Heidegger: Unterwegs zu seiner Biographie* (Frankfurt, 1988), pp. 123ff.

5. In a letter of August 5, 1925, to the Ministry of Science, Art, and National Education in Berlin (the decision to go ahead with this proposal was made at a committee meeting on June 24). See Theodore Kisiel, *The Genesis of Heidegger's "Being and Time"* (Berkeley, 1993), p. 479.

6. See Ott, *Martin Heidegger,* p. 125.

7. See Heidegger, *Zur Sache des Denkens* (Tübingen, 1969), pp. 80–81 (quoted after Kisiel, *Genesis,* p. 481): "'Professor Heidegger, you must publish something now. Do you have a presentable manuscript?' With these words, the dean of the Philosophy Faculty at Marburg came into my office one day during the winter semester of 1925–1926. 'Certainly,' I answered, and the dean replied: 'But it must be printed quickly' . . . Thus, it became necessary to submit to the public work that I had long kept to myself. Through Husserl's mediation, the publishing house of Max Niemeyer agreed to print the first fifteen galleys of the work immediately." ("'Herr Kollege Heidegger: Jetzt müssen Sie etwas veröffentlichen. Haben Sie ein geeignetes Manuskript?' Mit diesen Worten betrat der Dekan der Marburger Philosophischen Fakultät eines Tages im WS 1925/26 mein Studierzimmer. 'Gewiss,' antwortete ich. Worauf der Dekan entgegnete: 'Aber es muss rasch gedruckt werden' . . . Nun galt es, lang gehütete Arbeit der Öffentlichkeit zu übergeben. Der Max Niemeyer Verlag war durch Husserls Vermittlung bereit, sofort die ersten 15 Bogen der Arbeit zu drucken.")

8. The following reconstruction of the writing process which led to the 1927 version of *Sein und Zeit* is based on Kisiel, *Genesis,* pp. 477–489, as well as on my own research at the Hessische Staatsarchiv.

9. "Bei aller Anerkennung der Lehrerfolge des Professors Heidegger erscheint es mir doch nicht angängig, ihm eine etatmässige ordentliche Professur von der historischen Bedeutung des dortigen Lehrstuhls für Philosophie zu übertragen."

10. "Die Kommission beschließt einstimmig, Herrn Heidegger nahezulegen, die von ihm in Ms. niedergelegte Schrift über *Sein und Zeit* in einer gewissen Anzahl von Masch. Ex. herstellen zu lassen und dem Dekan zu überreichen. Weiterhin erklärt die Kom. es für dringend erachtenswert, außerdem die Schrift in Druckfahnen zu erhalten. Die Kommission wird dann die Ex. einer Anzahl

noch zu bestimmender Gelehrten zur Begutachtung vorlegen." (This texts departs slightly from Kisiel's transcription of the same document.)

11. "Herr Heidegger erklärt sich bereit, das fragliche Ms. ab 1. April in Druck zu geben, fernerhin den Dekan über den Stand des Druckes zu orientieren."

12. See Kisiel, *Genesis*, pp. 478, 488–489.

13. Oral reminiscence by Malvine Husserl; see Kisiel, *Genesis*, pp. 483, 563. See the reproduction of Heidegger's handwritten dedication to Husserl in Hans Rainer Sepp, ed., *Edmund Husserl und die phänomenologische Bewegung: Zeugnisse in Text und Bild* (Freiburg, 1988), p. 334.

14. An undated and unfinished entry by Deutschmann in Heidegger's file (not mentioned by Kisiel) must have been written during those weeks: "Heidegger has presented the galleys . . . to the Ministry."

15. "Die Fakultät glaubt sich zu dieser Bitte berechtigt, da Herr Heidegger in der Zwischenzeit seine Arbeit über 'Sein und Zeit' in den Druck gebracht hat."

16. "[Teile] ich mit, dass der Herr Minister dem Vorschlag, dem Professor Dr. *Heidegger* die planmäßige ordentliche Professur zu übertragen, auf Grund erneuter Überprüfung aller nur dargelegten Gesichtspunkte nicht zu folgen vermag."

17. ". . . das grosse Glück, dass Sie im Druck des Werkes stehen, an dem Sie zu dem erwachsen, der Sie sind und mit dem Sie, wie Sie wohl wissen, Ihr[em] eigene[n] Sein als Philosoph eine erste Verwirklichung gegeben haben . . . Niemand hat einen größeren Glauben an Sie als ich, und auch den, dass schließlich nichts an Ressentiment Sie verwirren und Sie von dem ablenken wird, was reine Auswirkung des Ihnen Anvertrauten . . . ist" (quoted after Ott, *Martin Heidegger*, p. 126).

18. *Sein und Zeit*, 15th ed. (Tübingen, 1984), pp. 39–40.

19. Heidegger and Blochmann, *Briefwechsel*, pp. 18–19. "Eigentlich müßte der Brief von der Hütte kommen; geschrieben sein, wenn die Buchenklötze knistern u. die Hütte eine ganz dicke Schneehaube hat, u. die Stille und Einsamkeit der Berge in der verschneiten Landschaft noch unmittelbarer da ist. Statt dessen sitze ich hier—am Übergangskapitel. Die Semesterarbeit nahm mir die rechte Konzentration. Die Ferientage sollen im alten Jahr den Abschluss bringen . . . Am 1. Januar fahre ich bis zum 10. nach Heidelberg zu Jaspers. Ich freue mich darauf, nicht nur im Selbstgespräch und im Verkehr mit der Geschichte, sondern in der gegenwärtigen Kommunikation philosophieren zu dürfen."

20. See Kisiel, *Genesis*, pp. 485, 564.

21. See *Sein und Zeit*, p. 39.

22. See Kisiel, *Genesis*, pp. 485–486.

23. Heidegger, quoted in Kisiel, p. 486. "Der Entschluß zum Abbruch der Veröffentlichung wurde gefasst an dem Tage, als uns die Nachricht vom Tode R. M. Rilkes traf."

24. See Kisiel's "Genealogical Glossary of Heidegger's Basic Terms, 1915–1927," in Kisiel, *Genesis,* pp. 490–511.

25. According to Jürgen Habermas, it was the distance Heidegger tried to take from the concrete details of his historical and social environment which made his work so open to its "unfiltered" influences: "Such abstraction from the complexities of social life accounts for Heidegger's unfiltered use of popular trends in the interpretation of that historical moment. The more real history disappeared behind 'historicity,' the more Heidegger was prone to engage in pretentious and naive reference to such diagnoses." See "Martin Heidegger: Werk und Weltanschauung," in Habermas, *Texte und Kontexte* (Frankfurt, 1991), p. 52.

26. Such a generalizing evaluation of the status of *Sein und Zeit*—and, subsequently, of the contribution that a historical reading could make—of course depends on how seriously one takes the *Kehre* ("turn") which, according to Heidegger, changed the trajectory of his thinking from the mid-1930s on. For a synopsis of different positions concerning the *Kehre,* see Ernst Behler, *Confrontations: Derrida, Heidegger, Nietzsche* (Stanford, 1991), pp. 40ff.

27. A similar program has been carried out, quite successfully, by Pierre Bourdieu in *The Political Ontology of Martin Heidegger* (Stanford, 1991). In contrast to him, I will limit my demonstration to those motifs which can be specifically associated with the year 1926. And whereas Bourdieu identified only individual elements of *Sein und Zeit* as being rooted in its historical environment, I shall focus, rather, on the structure of the book's argument.

28. See Bourdieu, *Political Ontology,* p. 115. For the (pre)history of this concept, see Ferdinand Fellmann, *Gelebte Philosophie in Deutschland: Denkformen der Lebensweltphänomenologie und der kritischen Theorie* (Freiburg, 1983), pp. 98–109.

29. The original French version of *Heidegger et le nazisme* was published by Editions Verdier (Lagrasse, 1987).

30. See Habermas, "Martin Heidegger," pp. 67ff.

31. See ibid., p. 53; Behler, pp. 40ff.; and the essays by Hans Georg Gadamer, Philippe Lacoue-Labarthe, and Jacques Derrida in *Critical Inquiry* (Winter 1989). In contrast, Jean-François Lyotard, in *Heidegger et "les juifs"* (Paris, 1988), p. 109, is more reluctant to establish such a relationship between Heidegger's work und his later political activities: "Je répète que toute déduction, même très médiatisée, du 'nazisme' heideggerien à partir du texte de *Sein und Zeit* est impossible" ("I insist that any deduction, however 'mediated,' of Heidegger's 'Nazism' on the basis of *Sein und Zeit* is impossible"). Nevertheless, Lyotard is

much more serious than other commentators in his condemnation of Heidegger's silence on the topic of the Holocaust after 1945.

32. See, for example, Edmund Husserl, *Die Idee der Phänomenologie: Fünf Vorlesungen,* ed. Walter Biemel, 2nd ed. (The Hague, 1973), p. 17.

33. See Ott, *Martin Heidegger,* pp. 102, 114.

34. Thus, when Heidegger, as noted above, dedicated a manuscript containing the opening chapters of his first major book to his mentor on the latter's sixty-seventh birthday ("To Edmund Husserl, in veneration and friendship"), he was not—or at least not primarily—being opportunistic. On Husserl's growing philosophical alienation from Heidegger following the latter's return to Freiburg in 1928, and on Heidegger's hostility toward his Jewish senior colleague after 1933 (including the elimination of the dedication in the fifth edition of *Sein und Zeit,* published in 1941), see Ott, *Martin Heidegger,* pp. 167ff.

35. This was true even for the later stages in Husserl's work, although he cannot be counted among the intellectuals of the Conservative Revolution. See Ferdinand Fellmann, *Gelebte Philosophie,* pp. 80–98.

36. Quoted from *Being and Time,* trans. John Macquarrie and Edward Robinson (San Francisco, 1962), p. 122. The German version is on p. 88 of *Sein und Zeit,* 15th ed. (Tübingen, 1984). "Dieses 'Relationssystem' als Konstitutivum der Weltlichkeit verflüchtigt das Sein des innerweltlich Zuhandenen so wenig, daß auf dem Grunde von Weltlichkeit der Welt dieses Seiende in seinem 'substantiellen' 'An-sich' allererst entdeckbar ist. Und erst wenn innerweltliches Seiendes überhaupt begegnen kann, besteht die Möglichkeit, im Felde dieses Seienden das nur noch Vorhandene zugänglich zu machen. Diese Seiende kann auf Grund seines Nur-noch-Vorhandenseins hinsichtlich seiner 'Eigenschaften' mathematisch in 'Funktionsbegriffen' bestimmt werden. Funktionsbegriffe dieser Art sind ontologisch überhaupt nur möglich mit Bezug auf Seiendes, dessen Sein den Charakter reiner Substanzialität hat. Funktionsbegriffe sind immer nur als formalisierte Substanzbegriffe möglich." Heidegger makes a similar statement regarding "substantiality" in his critique of Descartes' *Cogito.* See *Sein und Zeit,* pp. 92–93.

37. *Being and Time,* p. 87; *Sein und Zeit,* p. 60. "Wie kommt dieses erkennende Subjekt aus seiner inneren 'Sphäre' hinaus in eine 'andere und äußere,' wie kann das Erkennen überhaupt einen Gegenstand haben, wie muss der Gegenstand selbst gedacht werden, damit am Ende das Subjekt ihn erkennt, ohne daß es den Sprung in eine andere Sphäre zu wagen braucht?"

38. *Sein und Zeit,* pp. 202–208.

39. See, for example, Walter Biemel, *Martin Heidegger: Mit Selbstzeugnissen und Bilddokumenten* (Hamburg, 1973), pp. 46, 64.

40. See Ralph Kray and Thomas Studer, "Kognitives Oszillieren: Philosophische Adiaphora in der Daseins-Analyse Martin Heideggers," in Hans Ulrich

Gumbrecht and K. Ludwig Pfeiffer, eds., *Paradoxien, Dissonanzen, Zusammen-brüche: Situationen offener Epistemologie* (Frankfurt, 1991), pp. 143–158. See also Behler, *Confrontations*, p. 32.

41. *Being and Time*, p. 50; *Sein und Zeit*, pp. 27–28. "Der Titel 'Phäno-menologie' drückt eine Maxime aus, die also formuliert werden kann: 'zu den Sachen selbst!'—entgegen allen freischwebenden Konstruktionen, zufälligen Funden, entgegen der Übernahme von nur scheinbar ausgewiesenen Begriffen, entgegen den Scheinfragen, die sich oft Generationen hindurch als 'Probleme' breitmachen." See Husserl's rather skeptical handwritten comments in his pri-vate copy of *Sein und Zeit*, regarding Heidegger's use of the concept "phenome-nology," in Sepp, ed., *Edmund Husserl*, p. 335. According to recently published working notes by Heidegger (*Heidegger Studien* 11 [1995]), his reservations regarding Husserl's understanding of this maxim referred to the role of priority given to consciousness in the latter's thinking.

42. See Habermas, "Martin Heidegger," p. 61.

43. "Durchschnittliche Alltäglichkeit"; see *Sein und Zeit*, pp. 16–17, 43. For the history of the concept of "everydayness," which played a crucial role in the epistemological changes that took place around 1900, see Hans Ulrich Gum-brecht, "'Everyday-World' and 'Life-World' as Philosophical Concepts: A Ge-nealogical Approach," *New Literary History* 24 (1993–1994): 745–761.

44. In addition to being a substitute for abstractness, the notion of every-dayness contributes to the anti-intellectual tone in Heidegger's rhetoric. See Bourdieu, *Political Ontology*, pp. 13, 50–51.

45. *Being and Time*, p. 80; *Sein und Zeit*, p. 54. "Dieses Seiende, dem das In-sein in dieser Bedeutung zugehört, kennzeichneten wir als das Seiende, das ich je selbst bin. Der Ausdruck 'bin' hängt zusammen mit 'bei'; 'ich bin' besagt wiederum: ich wohne, halte mich auf bei . . . der Welt, als dem so und so Vertrauten. Sein als als Infinitiv des 'ich bin,' d.h. als Existential verstanden, bedeutet wohnen bei . . . vertraut sein mit. . . . *In-Sein ist demnach der formale existenziale Ausdruck des Seins des Daseins, das die wesenhafte Verfassung des In-der-Welt-seins hat.*"

46. "Das In-Sein meint so wenig ein räumliches 'Ineinander' Vorhandener, als 'in' ursprünglich gar nicht eine räumliche Beziehung der genannten Art bedeutet."

47. See, in particular, *Sein und Zeit*, pp. 110ff.

48. That *Sorge* is indeed meant to replace *Handlung* becomes explicit only in the second part of *Sein und Zeit* (see pp. 300–301).

49. See *Sein und Zeit*, pp. 191–200.

50. *Sein und Zeit*, p. 197 (see, in particular, footnote 1). Hans Blumenberg gives a reading of Heidegger's reading of an "ancient Latin fable" concerning

cura; see Blumenberg, *Die Sorge geht über den Fluß* (Frankfurt, 1987), pp. 197–200.

51. *Being and Time,* p. 32; *Sein und Zeit,* p. 12. "Das Dasein ist ein Seiendes, das nicht nur unter anderem Seienden vorkommt. Es ist vielmehr dadurch ontisch ausgezeichnet, daß es diesem Seienden in seinem Sein *um* dieses Sein selbst geht. Zu dieser Seinsverfassung des Daseins gehört aber dann, dass es in seinem Sein zu diesem Sein ein Seinsverhältnis hat. Und dies wiederum besagt: Dasein versteht sich in irgendeiner Weise und Ausdrücklichkeit in seinem Sein. Diesem Seienden eignet, dass mit und durch sein Sein dieses ihm selbst erschlossen ist. *Seinsverständnis ist selbst eine Seinsbestimmtheit des Daseins.* Die ontische Auszeichnung des Daseins liegt darin, daß es ontologisch *ist.*"

52. Here and on the following pages, I of course refer to the published version of *Sein und Zeit*—not Heidegger's (uncompleted) outline of the entire project.

53. *Sein und Zeit,* p. 227.

54. Ibid., p. 222.

55. Ibid., p. 230.

56. *Being and Time,* p. 261; *Sein und Zeit,* p. 218. "Zur Ausweisung steht einzig das Entdeckt-sein des Seienden selbst, *es* im Wie seiner Entdecktheit. Diese bewährt sich darin, daß sich das Ausgesagte, das ist das Seiende selbst, als *dasselbe* zeigt. *Bewährung* bedeutet: *sich zeigen des Seienden in Selbigkeit.* Die Bewährung vollzieht sich auf dem Grunde eines Sichzeigens des Seienden. Das ist nur so möglich, daß das aussagende und sich bewährende Erkennen seinem ontologischen Sinne nach ein *entdeckendes Sein* zum realen Seienden selbst ist."

57. *Sein und Zeit,* p. 229. "Ein Skeptiker kann nicht widerlegt werden, so wenig wie das Sein der Wahrheit 'bewiesen' werden kann. Der Skeptiker, wenn er faktisch *ist,* in der Weise der Negation der Wahrheit, *braucht* auch *nicht* widerlegt zu werden. Sofern er *ist* und sich in diesem Sein verstanden hat, hat er in der Verzweiflung des Selbstmords das Dasein und damit die Wahrheit ausgelöscht."

58. See Lyotard, *Heidegger et "les juifs,"* p. 109.

59. Bourdieu, *Political Ontology,* esp. pp. 79ff., makes the same observation.

60. *Being and Time,* p. 68; *Sein und Zeit,* p. 42–43. "Und weil Dasein wesenhaft je seine Möglichkeit ist, *kann* dieses Seiende in seinem Sein sich selbst 'wählen,' gewinnen, es kann sich verlieren, bzw. nie und nur 'scheinbar' gewinnen. Verloren haben kann es sich nur und noch nicht gewonnen haben kann es nur, sofern es seinem Wesen nach mögliches *Eigentliches,* das heißt sich zueigen ist. Die beiden Seinsmodi der *Eigentlichkeit* und *Uneigentlichkeit*—diese Ausdrücke sind im strengen Wortsinne terminologisch gewählt—gründen darin, daß Dasein überhaupt durch Jemeinigkeit bestimmt ist. Die Uneigentlichkeit des

Daseins bedeutet aber nicht etwa ein 'weniger' Sein oder einen 'niedrigeren' Seinsgrad. Die Uneigentlichkeit kann vielmehr das Dasein nach seiner vollsten Konkretion bestimmen in seiner Geschäftigkeit, Angeregtheit, Interessiertheit, Genußfähigkeit."

61. *Sein und Zeit,* p. 175. For the "they" *(Man),* see also p. 268.

62. *Being and Time,* pp. 212-213; *Sein und Zeit,* pp. 168-169. "Und zwar bleibt dieses [Gerede] nicht eingeschränkt auf das lautliche Nachreden, sondern breitet sich aus im Geschriebenen als das 'Geschreibe.' Das Nachreden gründet hier nicht so sehr in einem Hörensagen. Es speist sich aus dem Angelesenen. Das durchschnittliche Verständnis des Lesers wird *nie* entscheiden *können,* was ursprünglich geschöpft und errungen und was nachgeredet ist. Noch mehr, durchschnittliches Verständnis wird ein solches Unterscheiden gar nicht wollen, seiner nicht bedürfen, weil es ja alles versteht. Die Bodenlosigkeit des Geredes versperrt ihm nicht den Eingang in die Öffentlichkeit, sondern begünstigt ihn."

63. *Sein und Zeit,* p. 165.

64. *Being and Time,* p. 207; *Sein und Zeit,* p. 163. "Zunächst hören wir nie und nimmer Geräusche und Lautkomplexe, sondern den knarrenden Wagen, das Motorrad. Man hört die Kolonne auf dem Marsch, den Nordwind, den klopfenden Specht, das knisternde Feuer."

65. See *Sein und Zeit,* esp. pp. 297-301.

66. Biemel, *Martin Heidegger,* p. 33. See also Bourdieu, *Political Ontology,* pp. 19-20.

67. In the spring of 1930, for example, when Heidegger, having acquired a nationwide reputation after the publication of *Sein und Zeit,* rejected an offer from the University of Berlin, he claimed that this decision had been suggested by "his friend, the seventy-five-year-old Black Forest peasant." Seeing his conversation-partner as a metonym for authentic *Dasein,* Heidegger emphasized that the peasant had not even needed to speak in order to convince him. The anecdote is recounted in Bourdieu, p. 51. Concerning the details of the Berlin offer, see Victor Farías, *Heidegger und der Nationalsozialismus* (Frankfurt, 1989), pp. 124ff.

68. Quoted from Bourdieu, p. 48. As always, this portrait reveals as much about its author as about the person described. Heidegger's regional accent was Swabian, and would therefore remind only a northern German, such as Frau Cassirer, of Bavaria. It is also striking that she compares her own milieu with that of a "royal court." Finally, Heidegger's suit was far from being simply "old-fashioned." It was tailored according to the theories of the neo-Romantic painter Otto Ubelohde, who advocated a return to folk costume. See P. Hühnerfeld, *In Sachen Heidegger: Versuch über ein deutsches Genie* (Munich, 1961), p. 55.

69. *Sein und Zeit,* p. 188. For *Unheimlichkeit,* see p. 189.

70. An example is Heidegger's reluctance to make (or difficulty in making?) "being-in," his concept for wordliness, compatible with otherness and the sphere of the social; see *Sein und Zeit*, pp. 117ff. See also his concept of "guilt" (footnote 72).

71. And the then still-exciting technological topology of the telephone—if one trusts Avital Ronell, *The Telephone Book: Technology, Schizophrenia, Electric Speech* (Lincoln, 1989).

72. *Being and Time*, p. 334; *Sein und Zeit*, p. 288. Probably because of its similarity to a traditional discourse of morality, this is one of the very few passages in *Sein und Zeit* that contain the verb *handeln*. "*Das Gewissen-haben-wollen ist . . . die ursprünglichste existentielle Voraussetzung für die Möglichkeit des faktischen Schuldigwerdens. Rufverstehend läßt das Dasein das eigenste Selbst aus seinem gewählten Seinkönnen* in sich handeln. *Nur so kann es verantwortlich* sein. *Jedes Handeln aber ist faktisch notwendig 'gewissenlos,' nicht nur weil es faktische moralische Verschuldung nicht vermeidet, sondern weil es auf dem nichtigen Grunde seines nichtigen Entwerfens je schon im Mitsein mit Anderen an ihnen schuldig geworden ist. So wird das Gewissen-haben-wollen zur Übernahme der wesenhaften Gewissenlosigkeit, innerhalb der allein die existentielle Möglichkeit besteht, 'gut' zu* sein.'"

73. Heidegger and Blochmann, *Briefwechsel*, p. 17. "Daß ich an Elfridens Freundschaft teilnehmen darf, ist mir Beglückung und Verpflichtung zugleich. Die kurze Rast am sonnigen Hang vor Ihrer Fahrt ins Tal, sagte mir, daß Sie Ihre Existenz fest im Griff haben. Ihr erster Hüttenaufenthalt aber hat nicht weniger geschenkt als er empfangen. Jetzt denke ich Sie mir in der Stimmung, die mich zu Semesterbeginn überkommt u. die rechte Leidenschaft der Arbeit löst: neue Möglichkeiten des Wirkens schaffen erst die Produktivität, durch die der Einzelne erst wird, was er ist. Ihr frauliches Wirken, dessen Sinn mir Elfride seit Jahren mehr u. mehr erschließt, geht auf neuen Wegen u. ist keine bloße Auswirkung eines Berufs. Das muß Ihnen eine eigene 'Existenzfreudigkeit' geben, die nicht nachträglich aus faktischen Erfolgen einem zufällt, die sie vielmehr allererst wirkt."

74. Ibid., p. 18 (letter from November 10, 1926). "Wie es Ihnen wohl gehen mag? Das Fremde und Vielerlei wird Sie nur zeitweilig bedrücken, um Sie freier zu machen. Und die grosse Stadt, deren Rätsel Sie wohl schon gespürt haben, wird Ihrer 'Existenzfreudigkeit' gleichwohl nichts anhaben können."

75. *Being and Time*, pp. 370–371; *Sein und Zeit*, p. 324. "Sinn [ist] das, worin sich die Verstehbarkeit von etwas hält, ohne daß es selbst ausdrücklich und thematisch in den Blick kommt."

76. See Kisiel, *Genesis*, p. 311.

77. Ibid., pp. 477–479.

78. Ibid., pp. 315, 357–358. See also Hans-Georg Gadamer, "Heidegger und

die Marburger Theologie," in Gadamer, *Kleine Schriften*, vol. 1 (Tübingen, 1967), pp. 82–92.

79. *Being and Time*, p. 371; *Sein und Zeit*, p. 324. "*Was ermöglicht die Ganzheit des gegliederten Strukturganzen der Sorge in der Einheit ihrer ausgefalteten Gliederung?*"

80. See *Sein und Zeit*, pp. 336–349.

81. Ibid., pp. 341ff. See also the "preparatory analyses," pp. 140ff., 237ff.; and Heidegger's use of the concept of *Stimmung* (with reference to the Black Forest and to Christmas) in his letters to Elisabeth Blochmann of November 10, 1926, and December 22, 1926.

82. *Being and Time*, p. 392; *Sein und Zeit*, p. 342. "Orientierung auf das innerweltlich Begegnende."

83. Ibid. "Vergessende[s] Ausrücken vor einem faktischen, entschlossenen Seinkönnen."

84. Ibid. "Grundbefindlichkeit."

85. *Being and Time*, pp. 393–394; *Sein und Zeit*, p. 343. "Die in der Angst erschlossene Unbedeutsamkeit der Welt enthüllt die Nichtigkeit des Besorgbaren, das heißt die Unmöglichkeit des Sichentwerfens auf ein primär im Besorgten fundiertes Seinkönnen der Existenz. Das Enthüllen dieser Unmöglichkeit bedeutet aber ein Aufleuchten-lassen der Möglichkeit eines eigentlichen Seinkönnens. Welchen zeitlichen Sinn hat dieses Enthüllen? Die Angst ängstet sich um das nackte Dasein als in die Unheimlichkeit Geworfenes."

86. That the awareness of death intensifies the experience of life was a central motif in the rhetoric of Fascist rituals during the 1920s and 1930s. See, for example, Hans Ulrich Gumbrecht, *Eine Geschichte der spanischen Literatur* (Frankfurt, 1990), pp. 862–865 (episode concerning Miguel de Unamuno).

87. *Being and Time*, p. 395; *Sein und Zeit*, p. 344. "Die Angst erhebt sich aus dem In-der-Welt-sein als geworfenem Sein zum Tode . . . Eigentlich aber kann die Angst nur aufsteigen in einem entschlossenen Dasein. Der Entschlossene kennt keine Furcht, versteht aber gerade die Möglichkeit der Angst als *der* Stimmung, die ihn nicht hemmt und verwirrt. Sie befreit *von* 'nichtigen' Möglichkeiten und läßt freiwerden *für* eigentliche."

88. *Sein und Zeit*, p. 248.

89. *Being and Time*, p. 295; *Sein und Zeit*, p. 251. "Daß es seinem Tod überantwortet ist und dieser somit zum In-der-Welt-sein gehört, davon hat das Dasein zunächst und zumeist kein ausdrückliches oder gar theoretisches Wissen. Die Geworfenheit in den Tod enthüllt sich ihm ursprünglicher und eindringlicher in der Befindlichkeit der Angst."

90. See *Sein und Zeit*, p. 240.

91. *Sein und Zeit*, p. 262.

92. *Being and Time*, p. 428; *Sein und Zeit*, p. 376. "Die Analyse der Geschichtlichkeit des Daseins versucht zu zeigen, daß dieses Seiende nicht

'zeitlich' ist, weil es 'in der Geschichte steht,' sondern dass es umgekehrt geschichtlich nur existiert und existieren kann, weil es im Grunde seines Seins zeitlich ist."

93. *Being and Time*, p. 436; *Sein und Zeit*, p. 384. "Wenn das Dasein vorlaufend den Tod in sich mächtig werden läßt, versteht es sich, frei für ihn, in der eigenen *Übermacht* seiner endlichen Freiheit, um in dieser, die je nur 'ist' im Gewählthaben der Wahl, die *Ohnmacht* der Überlassenheit an es selbst zu übernehmen und für die Zufälle der erschlossenen Situation hellsichtig zu werden. Wenn aber das schicksalhafte Dasein als In-der-Welt-sein wesenhaft im Mitsein mit Anderen existiert, ist sein Geschehen ein Mitgeschehen und bestimmt als *Geschick*. Damit bezeichnen wir das Geschehen der Gemeinschaft, des Volkes. Das Geschick setzt sich nicht aus einzelnen Schicksalen zusammen, sowenig als das Miteinandersein als ein Zusammenvorkommen mehrerer Subjekte begriffen werden kann."

94. *Being and Time*, p. 437; *Sein und Zeit*, p. 385. "*Nur Seiendes, das wesenhaft in seinem Sein* zukünftig *ist, so daß es frei für seinen Tod an ihm zerschellend auf sein faktisches Da sich zurückwerfen lassen kann, das heißt nur Seiendes, das als zukünftiges gleichursprünglich* gewesend *ist, kann, sich selbst die ererbte Möglichkeit überliefernd, die eigene Geworfenheit übernehmen und* augenblicklich sein für 'seine Zeit.' *Nur eigentliche Zeitlichkeit, die zugleich endlich ist, macht so etwas wie Schicksal, das heißt eigentliche Geschichtlichkeit möglich.*" Macquarrie and Robinson translate *augenblicklich sein* as "being in the moment of vision," a rendering that does not have the connotations of speed and immediacy that characterize the German adverb *augenblicklich*.

95. See *Sein und Zeit*, p. 410.

96. On Heidegger's efforts to assume a role of leadership (and not only in the intellectual sphere), see Ott, *Martin Heidegger*, pp. 148, 220.

97. See Hans Friedrich Blunck, *Licht auf den Zügeln*, vol. 1 of *Lebensbericht* (Mannheim, 1953), pp. 391, 406–408.

98. Ibid., pp. 408, 457. "Other than that, we had to take good care of the university. Public relations materials, books, and reports were necessary. The new support committee, too, . . . received additional money and new assignments, which implied a great deal of responsibility." ("Daneben die gute Sorge um die Universität. Druckschriften, Bücher und Berichte waren notwendig. Auch der schon bestehende Wohlfahrtsausschuß, . . . erhielt neue Mittel und Aufgaben, die eine grosse Verantwortung bedeuteten.")

99. Ibid., p. 479. "Ich paße aber auch, obwohl stark sozial veranlagt, nicht in die Linksparteien, schon deshalb nicht, weil ich viel zu stark Niederdeutscher bin, um einen lärmenden Internationalismus nicht für taktisch verkehrt zu halten—Lärm bestimmter Gruppen, sie haften indes den Parteien seit sieben Jahren an."

100. Ibid., p. 467. Blunck has a French member of the Pen Club pronounce

these words, which clearly reflect his own judgment. "Ich habe gelernt, Berlin zu verabscheuen . . . Ich haße die Freiheit des Pfuhls. Was ich hier beobachte, die Reklame für das Pervertierte, die Zeitschriften des Sadismus, Bilder der widrigsten Sexualität—und alles in Namen der Freiheit!"

101. I take the following details from Christian Jenssen's overly enthusiastic and politically tendentious book, *Hans Friedrich Blunck: Leben und Werk* (Berlin, 1935), which he seems to have written in close collaboration with Blunck himself.

102. See Ott, *Martin Heidegger,* pp. 214–223.

103. See the documents in Joseph Wulf, ed., *Literatur und Dichtung im Dritten Reich: Eine Dokumentation* (Munich, 1966), pp. 36ff.

104. Ibid., p. 197.

105. See Jenssen, *Hans Friedrich Blunck,* p. 22—a comment written before the official end of Blunck's tenure as president of the Reichschrifttumskammer. "The appointment of Hans Friedrich Blunck to lead German literature [is] an appointment which, due to the writer's other obligation—namely, his obligation to his work—will doubtless be only temporary." ("Die Berufung Hans Fr. Blunck's zur Führung des deutschen Schrifttums, [ist] eine Berufung, die mit Rücksicht auf die andere Verpflichtung des Dichters—nämlich die zu seinem Werk—wohl nur eine zeitweilige sein kann.")

106. Wilhelm Baur (member of the National Socialist party since November 1920) officially complained about Blunck's half-hearted support in Baur's conflict with Heinz Wismann (party member since 1932). See Wulf, *Literatur und Dichtung,* pp. 317—318.

107. See the documents in Wulf, pp. 221–222, 305.

108. See Blunck, *Licht auf den Zügeln,* pp. 446–447.

109. Jenssen, *Hans Friedrich Blunck,* p. 112. In his autobiographical retrospective of 1953 (*Licht auf den Zügeln,* pp. 409–410), Blunck tries to present the trilogy as a plea for a supranational view of European prehistory.

110. See Blunck, *Kampf der Gestirne* (Jena, 1926), p. 2. "Elk belonged to the innovators in the country." ("Elk gehörte zu den Neuerern im Land.")

111. Ibid., p. 3. "Denn Lärmer gab der Traumfurcht der Menschen nach, er stellte die alten Gebräuche und die Tänze vor den Gestirnen des Dunkels wieder her, seine Furcht in der Nacht war stärker als die Sorge am Tag."

112. Ibid., p. 85. "Die Boote nahmen Wasser und die Mägde und Töchter Birres hatten eine entsetzliche Angst vor der dunklen Flut, die in die Kähne schlug. Die Helden hatten die erste Sorge mit der Beute. Sie waren indeß noch zu jung verliebt, um das nicht willig und ohne Murren zu ertragen. Aber wenn sie die Boote über Land schleppten, banden sie erst die freie Hand an ihre Mädchen, es schien ihnen doch nicht ohne Gefahr, solch junges Volk allein im Dunkeln zu lassen."

113. Ibid., p. 79. "'Soll ich die Sonne fragen oder willst du zu Frau Flode

fahren, um Rat zu holen?' Ull schweigt, aber die Dinge lassen ihn nicht. Es wird ihm zum andernmal der Grund seines Denkens."

114. Ibid., p. 209. "Gross, gewaltig tritt der Greis vor des Königshofs Tor, undim gleichen Augenblick verschwinden die schwatzenden Weiber in ihren Hütten." See also p. 179: "The assembled messengers of the nations are drinking, and they talk and praise his might—some, however, remain silently in awe" ("Der Völker Boten sind versammelt und trinken und schwatzen schon und loben seine Kraft, oder schweigen zum Lobe").

115. Ibid., p. 78. "Hor ruft im Schlaf, Ull erhebt sich, aber er muß der Flamme noch einmal in das rote Hirn sehen, sucht den Kern, den irgendwo ihr Kleid umspann. Wie er jedoch steil in den roten Kübel starrt, krümmt sich ein Holz und zerspringt. Eine Stichflamme springt auf und sengt die Wimpern. "Mein Amt," sagt Bra und hält die hand zwischen den König und das feuer. Es ruft wieder warnend, aber anders als Hors Stimme. Ull fährt aus seinen gedanken hoch, der Wind klopft und trommelt gegen die dumpfe Erde. Sein Hund springt auf und spitzt die Ohren, dann geht es vörüber. Rief jemand? Ull ist wieder mit Bras leisen Worten allein und läßt sich von Hilboe, von ihrem Bruder Hill im Osten und ihrer Schwester Flode im Westen berichten. Und der König erzählt, wie einst die Sonne vor ihm aus dem felsen springen wollte und läßt sich's deuten."

116. See, for example, ibid., p. 51. "Borr seemed uncanny to them. They called him 'the Borr gazer' because he had the evil eye." ("Unheimlich war ihnen Borr, den sie Borrglotzer nannten, weil er den bösen Blick an sich hatte.")

117. Ibid., pp. 188—189. "'Hör Ull,' schrie Borr da und heulte vor Zorn, 'wo ist meine Schwester, die du mir raubtest? Wo ist, was mir lieb war wie mein Augapfel, das du fandest und nahmst?' Aber der König schwieg. 'Höre, du Trunkener, wozu bist du ausgezogen? Ach, was hast du Erbärmlicher die Menschen von der Sonne beschwatzt und warst doch nur meiner Liebsten Gemahl? Was raubtest du mir das Kindlein, das meine Nächte schirmte, und meintest, vom Licht zu nehmen und wußtest nicht, daß ich mir ein einfältig Dirnlein zog?' Wie er so sprach und auch unwahr sprach, schritt der König schneller, und der Schaum stand ihm vor dem Lippen."

118. Ibid., p. 190. "Nur der Glaube war grösser bei . . . dem König, und das Mitleid mit seinen führerlosen Völkern war stärker als Borrs Kraft aus der mondhellen Nacht."

119. Ibid. "Da packte Ull ihn am Nacken, schleuderte ihn hoch und warfihn unter sich. Und er erwürgte ihn, als das erste Frührot im Osten stand."

120. Blunck, *Licht auf den Zügeln*, p. 415. "Als der russchwarze Zollbeamte mit seinen Fingern die weisse Wäsche unserer Koffer durchwühlte—[stand] meiner Frau das Herz still, aber er ordnete und strich alles mit rührender Vorsicht wieder glatt."

121. Ibid. "Eine . . . lebensgefährlich anmutende Strassenbahn, die . . . durch

Gartenvororte und Negerquartiere, aber immer mit schönen Aussichten auf die in der Tiefe ruhende Stadt . . . niedereilt."

122. I quote from the fourteenth printing, January 1928. On the origins of *Nigger Heaven* and its reception, especially among black intellectuals, see Bruce Kellner, *Carl Van Vechten and the Irreverent Decades* (Norman, Okla., 1968), esp. pp. 195–223. None of the book's critics seems to have questioned Van Vechten's expertise regarding life in Harlem. But a number of influential black writers, above all W. E. B. Du Bois, took offense at the title of the novel. Van Vechten intended this title to be part of the black discourse which he tried to imitate (in general, with remarkable success).

123. *Nigger Heaven,* pp. 41–42.

124. Ibid., pp. 55–56.

125. Ibid., p. 278.

126. Ibid., pp. 91–92. See also pp. 89–90: "She cherished an almost fanatic faith in her race, a love for her people in themselves, and a fervent belief in their possibilities. She admired all Negro characteristics and desired earnestly to possess them. Somehow, so many of them, through no fault of her own, eluded her. Was it because she was destined to become an old maid . . .? Savages! Savages at heart! And she had lost her birthright, this primitive birthright which was so valuable and important an asset, a birthright that all the civilized races were struggling to get back to—this fact explained the art of Picasso or Stravinsky. To be sure, she, too, felt this African beat—it completely aroused her emotionally—but she was conscious of feeling it. This love of drums, of exciting rhythms, this naive delight in glowing color—the color that exists only in cloudless, tropical climes—this warm, sexual emotion, all these were hers only through a mental understanding. With Olive these qualities were instinctive."

ACKNOWLEDGMENTS

···

THANKS to Ulla Link-Heer for co-teaching that poorly prepared seminar in the cold Siegen winter of 1987–1988 (and for liking what she saw coming out of it); to Maria Ascher for more generosity than I deserved, and for intellectual taste; to Friedrich Balke for offering to translate; to Kerstin Behnke for many more quotes than anybody could use; to John Bender for inventing the title; to Günter Blamberger for wasting his summer vacations on a book that wasn't his; to Karl Heinz Bohrer for treating me as an American author; to Steven Brown for being a Heideggerian; to Judith Butler for much-needed teachings; to Bliss Carnochan for not buying the bit about grandparents; to Regina Casper for sharing a favorite text; to Patricia de Castries for fabulous memories; to João Cezar de Castro Rocha for more than a scent of *cachaça*; to Christopher for loving the corpses in every museum; to Wanda Corn for an insight about tragedy; to Luiz Costa Lima for twenty-six years of friendship and intellectual challenge; to Bill Egginton for not being too tough on my writing; to Josh Feinstein for laughing at Kaleidoskop Weimar; to Wlad Godzich for seeing things that I could not see; to Melissa Goldman for liking the other entries; to Carlo Ginzburg for wanting photographs; to Stephen Greenblatt for smiling at so many numbers; to Max Grosse for reminding me of literature; to Hanni for speaking about his coffin; to Robert Harrison for proving me wrong; to Thomas Harrison for a beautiful alternative; to Fritz Hochrein for letting me speak at his birthday; to Yasushi Ishii for the jazz tapes; to Charlie Junkerman for a sunny year; to Alice Kaplan for being around during the following year; to Friedrich Kittler for what his brain has accomplished and for being a Freund; to Reinhart Koselleck for teaching me history; to Laura for liking the old days; to Tim Lenoir for trying to teach me Einstein; to Pericles Lewis for unbeatable translations; to Henry Lowood for buying old newspapers that he didn't have to buy; to Niklas Luhmann for quoting this book before it was written; to Jean-François Lyotard for telling me to take the necessary time, and for inventing the "reading dossier" ("User's Manual"; to Marco for asking me how one could work so long on somebody who looked so much like Hitler; to Karl Maurer for telling me that the "Murder" entry did not work; to Eric Méchoulan for the honor of speaking at Kings College; to Winfried Menninghaus for a sober (but not sobering) reading; to María Menocal for liking the alphabetical order; to Walter Moser for being skeptical; to Brad Prager for having me rewrite translations from German; to Christopher Prendergast for exerting time-pressure; to Richard Roberts for being duly scandalized; to Henning Ritter for not wanting Blunck; to Kathrin Rosenfield for Prestes; to Paul Rottmann for being born in 1926; to Jörn Rüsen for love-hating this project; to Sara for joining me fifty-six years later; to Frank Schirrmacher for wanting to teach 1926; to Jeffrey Schnapp for helping me be a fake Italianist; to Ulrich Schulz-Buschhaus for his generous reading; to Marielou Smitten for support beyond the conventions of collegiality; to Donna Soave for being so organized; to Susan Stephens for thinking that I needed a sabbatical; to Helen Tartar for getting mad (for a day or so); to Bernhard Teuber for linking me up with the Vatican: to Thea for avoiding cemeteries; to Margaret Tompkins for bearing with me; to Johanne Villeneuve for being authentic; to Benno Wagner for not giving up on me; to Lindsay Waters for productive resistance; to David Wellbery for inviting me to a job talk; to Brett Wells for mastering the paradox of a sympathetic reading of proofs; to Hayden White for imagining Vienna during that year; to Paul Zumthor for much-needed encouragement; *above all, to Ricky for enjoying the manuscript (and, I hope, the author): nothing would be the same without her, and this is why the book is hers.*

INDEX

....

LaVergne, TN USA
09 January 2011
211664LV00001B/4/P